AQA Science

Exclusively endorsed and approved by AQA

Teacher's Book

GCSE Physics

Nelson Thornes

...iness

Published in 2006 by:
Nelson Thornes Ltd
Delta Place
27 Bath Road
CHELTENHAM
GL53 7TH
United Kingdom

06 07 08 09 10 / 10 9 8 7 6 5 4 3

A catalogue record for this book is available from the British Library

ISBN 0 7487 9648 7

Cover photographs: wave by Corel 391 (NT); static electricity by
Photodisc 29 (NT); astronaut by Photodisc 34 (NT)

Cover bubble illustration by Andy Parker
Illustrations by Bede Illustration

Page make-up by Wearset Ltd

Printed in Croatia by Zrinski

The following people have made an invaluable contribution to this
book:

Pauline Anning, Jim Breithaupt, Nigel English, Ann Fullick, Patrick
Fullick, Richard Gott, Keith Hirst, Paul Lister, Niva Miles, John
Scottow, Glenn Toole.

GCSE Physics   Contents

Welcome to AQA Physics

Teaching suggestions

Ideas on how to use features in the Student Book, suggestions for Gifted and Talented, Special Needs, ICT activities and different learning styles are all covered here, and more.

Practical support

For every practical in the Student Book you will find this corresponding feature which gives a list of equipment needed, safety references and further guidance to carry out the practical. A worksheet is provided on the e-Science CD ROM for each practical.

Activity notes

Each activity in the Student Book has background information notes on how to organise it effectively.

Icons

⚡ appears in the text where opportunities for investigational aspects of 'How Science Works' are signposted in the AQA specification.

❓ appears in the text where AQA have signposted opportunities to cover societal aspects of 'How Science Works' in the specification.

e-Science CD ROM

This contains a wide range of resources – animations, simulations, photopluses, Powerpoints, activity sheets, practical skill sheets, homework sheets – which are linked to Student Book pages and help deliver the activities suggested in the Teacher Book.

AQA Science for GCSE is the only series to be endorsed by AQA. The *GCSE Physics* Teacher Book is written by experienced science teachers and is designed to make planning the delivery of the specification easy – everything you need is right here! Information is placed around a reduced facsimile of the Student Book page, allowing you quick reference to features and content that will be used in the lesson.

How science works

This is covered in the section at the beginning of the Student Book, in the main content, in the end of chapter spreads, and in the exam-style questions and 'How Science Works' questions. The corresponding teacher's notes give you detailed guidance on how to integrate 'How Science Works' fully into your lessons and activities.

Exam-Style Questions

There are multiple-choice questions for Physics A and structured questions for Physics B. They are ranked in order of difficulty. All questions are useful to complete, no matter which specification is being taken, as they cover the same content. 'How Science Works' is integrated into some exam-style questions and there are separate 'How Science Works' questions to give additional practice in this area.

Lesson structure

This feature provides ideas for the experienced teacher, support for the newly qualified teacher and structure for cover lessons. Available for every double page lesson spread, it contains a variety of suggestions for how the spread could be taught, including starters and plenaries of varying lengths, as well as suggestions for the main part of the lesson.

Answers to questions

They're all here! All the questions in the Student Book are answered in the Teacher Book. Each answer is located in the corresponding feature in the Teacher Book. For example, answers to yellow in-text questions in the Student Book can be found in the yellow feature in the Teacher Book.

Key Stage 3 curriculum links:

This expands the 'What you already know' unit opener of the Student Book and gives QCA Scheme of Work references for relevant knowledge that may need revisiting before starting on the unit.

ACTIVITIES & EXTENSIONS

This highlights opportunities to extend a lesson or add activities, providing notes and tips on how to carry them out.

SPECIFICATION LINK-UP

This gives clear references to the AQA specification for the lesson, with additional notes and guidance where appropriate.

KEY POINTS

This feature gives ideas on how to consolidate the key points given in the Student Book, and how to use the key points as a basis for homework, revision or extension work.

Key Stage 3 Link-up

Sc1 Scientific enquiry

How Science Works does not relate directly to the individual statements in the Key Stage 3 Programme of Study. However, it builds on all of the knowledge, understanding and skills inherent in Sc1.

It is expected that students will be familiar with:

- the need to work safely
- making a prediction
- controls
- the need for repetition of some results
- tabulating and analysing results
- making appropriate conclusions
- suggesting how they might improve methods.

RECAP ANSWERS

1 Helen predicted, 'The more wire there was, the more the magnet would pick up.'

2 The number of coils.

3 The mass of iron picked up.

4 E.g. The battery (voltage)/the iron bar.

5 E.g. The current/type of wire/thickness of wire.

6

Number of coils	Mass iron picked up (grams)
6	1.2
8	1.5
12	2.1
15	3.0

7 A suitable graph, with number of coils on X axis and mass of iron on Y axis. Points plotted correctly, axes labelled (including units) and line of best fit drawn.

8 E.g. as the number of coils increased, the mass of iron picked up increased/an increased number of coils wrapped around an iron bar increases the strength of the magnet.

9 E.g. Helen could have repeated her results.

Teaching suggestions

Finding out what they know

Students should begin to appreciate the 'thinking behind the doing' developed during KS3. It would be useful to illustrate this by a simple demonstration (e.g. solar cells) and posing questions that build into a flow diagram of the steps involved in a whole investigation. This could lead into the recap questions to ascertain each individual student's progress. Emphasis should be placed on an understanding of the following terms: prediction, independent, dependent and control variables and reliability.

The recap questions should identify each individual student's gaps in understanding. Therefore it is best carried out as an assessment. It might be appropriate to do questions 7, 8 and 9 for homework.

Revealing to the students that they are using scientific thinking to solve problems during their everyday life can make their work in science more relevant. Other situations could illustrate this and should be discussed in groups or as a class.

Activity notes

Will the 2012 Olympics be about athletics or physics? Students could investigate web sites that illustrate how physics is used by the modern athlete to improve performance. The physics of pole vaulting is a good example, where the maximum height gain due to the energy of the running athlete is about 5 metres. Heights over this are achieved by the athlete causing the pole to bend and hence depend on the physical properties of the pole.

KEY POINTS

- Students should appreciate the need for safety in the laboratory.
- Students should be aware of the processes involved in the design of an investigation.
- Students should have notes that bring out the meaning of key words related to the design of an investigation.
- Students should be aware of the importance of observation to starting an investigation.
- Students should be aware of the small steps that science makes towards more certain theories.

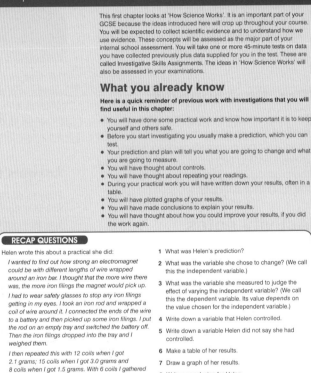

H1 | How science works

This first chapter looks at 'How Science Works'. It is an important part of your GCSE because the ideas introduced here will crop up throughout your course. You will be expected to collect scientific evidence and to understand how we use evidence. These concepts will be assessed as the major part of your internal school assessment. You will take one or more 45-minute tests on data you have collected previously plus data supplied for you in the test. These are called Investigative Skills Assignments. The ideas in 'How Science Works' will also be assessed in your examinations.

What you already know

Here is a quick reminder of previous work with investigations that you will find useful in this chapter:

- You will have done some practical work and know how important it is to keep yourself and others safe.
- Before you start investigating you usually make a prediction, which you can test.
- Your prediction and plan will tell you what you are going to change and what you are going to measure.
- You will have thought about controls.
- You will have thought about repeating your readings.
- During your practical work you will have written down your results, often in a table.
- You will have plotted graphs of your results.
- You will have made conclusions to explain your results.
- You will have thought about how you could improve your results, if you did the work again.

RECAP QUESTIONS

Helen wrote this about a practical she did:

I wanted to find out how strong an electromagnet could be with different lengths of wire wrapped around an iron bar. I thought that the more wire there was, the more iron filings the magnet would pick up.

I had to wear safety glasses to stop any iron filings getting in my eyes. I took an iron rod and wrapped a coil of wire around it. I connected the ends of the wire to a battery and then picked up some iron filings. I put the rod on an empty tray and switched the battery off. Then the iron filings dropped into the tray and I weighed them.

I then repeated this with 12 coils when I got 2.1 grams; 15 coils when I got 3.0 grams and 8 coils when I got 1.5 grams. With 6 coils I gathered 1.2 grams. I used the same battery throughout.

It was difficult because I couldn't scrape off all of the iron filings.

1 What was Helen's prediction?

2 What was the variable she chose to change? (We call this the independent variable.)

3 What was the variable she measured to judge the effect of varying the independent variable? (We call this the dependent variable. Its value *depends* on the value chosen for the independent variable.)

4 Write down a variable that Helen controlled.

5 Write down a variable Helen did not say she had controlled.

6 Make a table of her results.

7 Draw a graph of her results.

8 Write a conclusion for Helen.

9 How do you think Helen could have improved her results?

2

For example:

'How did you learn to use gears on a bike'? You noticed that people changed gear when they were going up or down hills (observation). You had been told that you should use a high gear when going down hill and a low gear for going up hills (knowledge).

You use your observations and your knowledge to make a prediction that switching down a gear will help you when going up hill. You then test your prediction and see what the results are. You stop pedalling and change gear. The chain comes off! You check again on the next hill, whilst continuing to pedal, to see if you get

SPECIFICATION LINK-UP

Section 10.1

This opening chapter covers the complete specification for 'How science works – the procedural content'.

'How science works' is treated here as a separate chapter. It offers the opportunity to teach the 'thinking behind the doing' as a discrete set of procedural skills. However, it is of course an integral part of the way students will learn about science and those skills should be nurtured throughout the course.

It is anticipated that sections of this chapter will be taught as the opportunity presents itself during the teaching programme. The chapter should also be referred back to at appropriate times when these skills are required and in preparation for the internally assessed ISAs.

The thinking behind the doing

Science attempts to explain the world in which we live. It provides technologies that have had a great impact on our society and the environment. Scientists try to explain phenomena and solve problems using evidence. The data to be used as evidence must be reliable and valid, as only then can appropriate conclusions be made.

A scientifically literate citizen should, amongst other things, be equipped to question, and engage in debate on, the evidence used in decision-making.

The reliability of evidence refers to how much we trust the data. The validity of evidence depends on the reliability of the data as well as whether the research answers the question. If the data is not reliable, the research cannot be valid.

To ensure reliability and validity in evidence, scientists consider a range of ideas which relate to:

- *how we observe the world;*
- *designing investigations so that patterns and relationships between variables may be identified;*
- *making measurements by selecting and using instruments effectively;*
- *presenting and representing data;*
- *identifying patterns, relationships and making suitable conclusions.*

These ideas inform decisions and are central to science education. They constitute the 'thinking behind the doing' that is a necessary complement to the subject content of biology, chemistry and physics.

How science works for us

Science works for us all day, every day. You do not need to know how a mobile phone works to enjoy sending text messages. But, think about how you started to use your mobile phone or your television remote control. Did you work through pages of instructions? Probably not!

You knew that pressing the buttons would change something on the screen (*knowledge*). You played around with the buttons, to see what would happen (*observation*). You had a guess at what you thought might be happening (*prediction*) and then tested your idea (*experiment*).

If your prediction was correct you remembered that as a *fact*. If you could repeat the operation and get the same result again then you were very pleased with yourself. You had shown that your results were *reliable*.

Working as a scientist you will have knowledge of the world around you and particularly about the subject you are working with. You will observe the world around you. An enquiring mind will then lead you to start asking questions about what you have observed.

Science moves forward by slow steady steps. When a genius such as Einstein comes along then it takes a giant leap. Those small steps build on knowledge and experience that we already have.

Each small step is important in its own way. It builds on the body of knowledge that we have. Galileo was able to demonstrate how an object accelerates and he called the acceleration 'g'. Sir Isaac Newton was able to show how 'g' could be calculated from his laws of motion and gravitation. Many years later, Henry Cavendish proved Newton's law of gravitation by experiment and used it to make the first scientific measurement of the mass of the Earth.

DID YOU KNOW?

The Greeks were arguably the first true scientists. They challenged traditional myths about life. They set forward ideas that they knew would be challenged. They were keen to argue the point and come to a reasoned conclusion.

Other cultures relied on long established myths and argument was seen as heresy.

Thinking scientifically

Figure 1 Playing basketball

ACTIVITY

No matter how good a player you are, if the ball is not properly inflated then you cannot play well. As the balls get used during the game it is possible that some of them will get soft. They should all bounce the same.

How high the ball bounces will depend on lots of variables. It will depend on:

- what the ball is made of,
- how much air has been pumped in,
- what the temperature of the air is,
- what the floor surface is made of, and
- how hard you throw it.

It is impossible to test all of these during a match.

The simple way is to drop a ball from a certain height and see how high it bounces. Can you work out a way to see how changing the height from which a ball is dropped can test how high it bounces? This could then be used as a simple test during the match to see if the balls are good enough.

You can use the following headings to discuss your ideas. One person should be writing your thoughts down, so that you can discuss them with the rest of your class.

- What prediction can you make about the height the ball is dropped from and the height it will bounce to?
- What would be your independent variable?
- What would be your dependent variable?
- What would you have to control?
- Write a plan for your investigation.
- How could you make sure your results were reliable?

3

Checking for misconceptions

Some common misconceptions that can be dealt with here and throughout the course are:

- The purpose of controls – some students believe that it is about making accurate measurements of the independent variable.
- The purpose of preliminary work – some believe that it is the first set of results.
- That the table of results is constructed after the practical work – students should be encouraged to produce the table before carrying out their work and complete it during their work.
- That precision is the number of places of decimals they can write down.
- That anomalies are identified after the analysis – they should preferably be identified during the practical work or, at the latest, before any calculation of a mean.
- They automatically extrapolate the graph to its origin.
- Lines of best fit must be straight lines.
- Some will think you repeat readings to make sure your investigation is a fair test.

Special needs

Cloze statements can be used for essential notes.

Gifted and talented

Discussion could range into the importance of chance in scientific discoveries. Louis Pasteur called it 'chance favouring the prepared mind'. George de Mestral whilst out walking was intrigued by some fruits with hooks on them, because they stuck to his trousers. He went on to invent Velcro. During the Second World War, Stanley Hey, a Physics teacher, was working on a radar system and in particular some interference that kept occurring. He noticed that it occurred in the East in the morning and in the West at night and found by chance that the Sun produced radio waves. This eventually led to the development of radio astronomy and the discovery of galaxies.

Learning styles

Kinaesthetic: Constructing a table and graph of results.
Visual: Observing the demonstration.
Auditory: Listening to ideas of others on scientific opinions.
Interpersonal: Discussing the bouncing basketball problem.
Intrapersonal: Reviewing personal knowledge from KS3.

---

the same results. This time it works, so you try again on the next hill to see if it works again (reliability). Perhaps you have twelve gears. Does it help to switch to the other gear ratio? Does it help if you stand up? This could lead to a discussion of the need for controls. Scientists work in exactly the same way – this is 'How science works'.

Collect newspaper articles and news items from the television to illustrate good and poor uses of science. There are some excellent television programmes illustrating good and poor science. Have a competition for who can bring in the poorest example of science used to sell products – shampoo adverts are a very good starter!

Fundamental ideas about how science works

LEARNING OBJECTIVES

Students should learn:

- The different types of variable.
- That evidence needs to be valid and reliable.
- That variables can be linked causally, by association or by chance.
- To distinguish between opinion based on scientific evidence and non-scientific ideas.

LEARNING OUTCOMES

Students should be able to:

- Recognise different types of variable.
- Suggest how an investigation might demonstrate its reliability and validity.
- State that variables can be linked causally, by association or by chance.
- Identify when an opinion does not have the support of valid and reliable science.

DID YOU KNOW?

Benjamin Thompson measured the time it took to boil a fixed volume of water while boring the cannon with a specially blunted borer. He showed that there was heat generated but that the cannon had not lost any of its thermal properties thus disproving the caloric theory. He also invented the 'Baked Alaska' during his work on thermal conduction.

SPECIFICATION LINK-UP How Science Works

Section 10.2
Fundamental ideas

Evidence must be approached with a critical eye. It is necessary to look closely at how measurements have been made and what links have been established. Scientific evidence provides a powerful means of forming opinions. These ideas pervade all of 'How science works'.

Students should know and understand

- *It is necessary to distinguish between opinion based on valid and reliable evidence and opinion based on non-scientific ideas (prejudice, whim or hearsay).*
- *Continuous variables (any numerical values), where used, give more information than ordered variables, which are more informative than categoric variables. A variable may also be discrete, that is, restricted to whole numbers.*
- *Scientific investigations often seek to identify links between two or more variables. These links may be:*
  - *causal, in that a change in one variable causes a change in another*
  - *due to association – changes in one variable and a second variable are linked by a third variable*
  - *due to chance occurrence.*

Lesson structure

STARTER

Crazy science – Show a video clip of one of the science shows that are aimed at entertainment rather than education or an advert that proclaims a scientific opinion. This should lead into a discussion of how important it is to form opinions based on sound scientific evidence. (5–10 minutes)

MAIN

- From a light-hearted look at entertainment science, bring the thalidomide example into contrast (if appropriate with video clips) and discuss how tragic situations can be created by forming opinions that are not supported by valid science.
- Show how some metals conduct electricity better than others. Review some of the terminology from KS3. Discuss, in small groups, the different ways in which the independent and the dependent variables could be measured, identifying these in terms of continuous, ordered and categoric measurements.
- Discuss the usefulness in terms of forming opinions of each of the proposed measurements.
- Consider that this might be a commercial proposition and the students might be advising an investor in a company on which metal to use in a product.
- Discuss how they could organise the investigation to demonstrate its validity and reliability to a potential investor.
- Discuss whether the relationship shows a causal link, a chance link or a link by association.

PLENARIES

Evidence for opinions – Bring together the main features of scientific evidence that would allow sound scientific opinions to be formed from an investigation. (5 minutes)

Analyse conclusions – Use an example of a poorly structured investigation and allow the students to critically analyse any conclusions drawn, e.g. data from an investigation into different forms of insulation, using calorimeters and cooling curves. (10 minutes)

Teaching suggestions

- **Special needs.** Lists of possible variables could be made from which to select the most appropriate. Cloze statements can be used for essential notes.

- **Gifted and talented.** Discussion could range into the context in which scientific progress is made. Students could discuss the situation in which Galileo was put on a charge of heresy, by the Catholic Church, for challenging the Earth-centred view of the universe. This could be related to the Church's ready acceptance of the Big Bang theory in more recent years.

- **Learning styles**

  Visual: Observing resistance in different wires.

  Auditory: Listening to the ideas of others on scientific opinions.

  Interpersonal: Discussing the variables associated with testing the wires.

  Intrapersonal: Considering the ethics of the thalidomide case and possibly the use of animals for testing human drugs.

Practical support

Equipment and materials required

Different wires set up in a circuit to illustrate their resistances.

HOW SCIENCE WORKS

H2 — Fundamental ideas about how science works

LEARNING OBJECTIVES

1 How do you spot when a person has an opinion that is not based on good science?
2 What is the importance of continuous, ordered and categoric variables?
3 What is meant by reliable evidence and valid evidence?
4 How can two sets of data be linked?

NEXT TIME YOU...

... read a newspaper article or watch the news on TV ask yourself if that research is valid and reliable. (See page 5.) Ask yourself if you can trust the opinion of that person.

Science is too important for us to get it wrong

Sometimes it is easy to spot when people try to use science poorly. Sometimes it can be funny. You might have seen adverts claiming to give your hair 'body' or sprays that give your feet 'lift'!

On the other hand, poor scientific practice can cost lives.

Some years ago a company sold the drug thalidomide to people as a sleeping pill. Research was carried out on animals to see if it was safe. The research did not include work on pregnant animals. The opinion of the people in charge was that the animal research showed the drug could be used safely with humans.

Then the drug was also found to help ease morning sickness in pregnant women. Unfortunately, doctors prescribed it to many women, resulting in thousands of babies being born with deformed limbs. It was far from safe.

These are very difficult decisions to make. You need to be absolutely certain of what the science is telling you.

a) Why was the opinion of the people in charge of developing thalidomide based on poor science?

Deciding on what to measure

You know that you have an independent and a dependent variable in an investigation. These variables can be one of four different types:

- A **categoric** variable is one that is best described by a label (usually a word). For a magnet, its type is a categoric variable, e.g. horseshoe magnet or bar magnet.
- A **discrete** variable is one that you describe in whole numbers. The number of coils on an electromagnet is a discrete variable.
- An **ordered** variable is one where you can put the data into order, but not give it an actual number. The strength of different magnets compared to each other is an ordered variable, e.g. one bar magnet is stronger than another bar magnet.
- A **continuous** variable is one that we measure, so its value could be any number. Distance (as measured by a ruler, tape or distance sensor) is a continuous variable, e.g. 37 cm, 43 cm, 54 cm, 76 cm.

When designing your investigation you should always try to measure continuous data whenever you can. This is not always possible, so you should then try to use ordered data. If there is no other way to measure your variable then you have to use a label (categoric variable).

Figure 1 Student recording a range of temperatures – an example of a continuous variable

b) Imagine you were testing a solar cell, what would be better:
   i) putting a light bulb into the circuit to see how bright it was, or
   ii) using a voltmeter to measure the potential difference?

Making your investigation reliable and valid

When you are designing an investigation you must make sure that others can get the same results as you – this makes it reliable.

You must also make sure that you are measuring the actual thing you want to measure. If you don't, your data can't be used to answer your original question. This seems very obvious but it is not always quite so easy. You need to make sure that you have controlled as many other variables as you can, so that no-one can say that your investigation is not valid. A valid investigation should be reliable and answer the original question.

Figure 2 Road sign which uses solar cells

c) State one way in which you can show that your results are valid.

How might an independent variable be linked to a dependent variable?

Variables can be linked together for one of three reasons:

- It could be because one variable has caused a change in the other, e.g. the longer the heater is on the more energy is transferred. This is a *causal link*.
- It could be because a third variable has caused changes in the two variables you have investigated, e.g. there is a relationship between the time of year and the energy produced by wind turbines. This is because there is an *association* between the two variables. Both of the variables are caused by the increased amount of wind at certain times of the year.
- It could be due simply to chance, e.g. increased use of mobile phones and increased rates of diabetes.

d) Describe a causal link that you have seen in physics.

Figure 3 Different room heaters

DID YOU KNOW?

In the 18th century Benjamin Thompson investigated heat. He is supposed to have used a lathe to make the barrel of a cannon – under water! He did this to find out how much heat was made by the friction of the cutting tool. I wonder how he controlled his variables!!

SUMMARY QUESTIONS

1 Name each of the following types of variables described in a), b) and c).

   a) People were asked how efficient each of five different heaters was: 'cheap and hot', 'cheap, but not much heat', 'it was fine', 'great, kept me warm' were some of the answers.
   b) These people were asked which ones they would buy. They put the five heaters into order.
   c) The five heaters were tested by measuring their energy input and output.

2 Research on the possible harmful effects of mobile phones states that 'Little research ... has been published in the peer-reviewed literature'. What does this statement mean?

KEY POINTS

1 Be on the lookout for non-scientific opinions.
2 Continuous data is more powerful than other types of data.
3 Check that evidence is reliable and valid.
4 Be aware that just because two variables are related it does not mean that there is a causal link between them.

4 | 5

SUMMARY ANSWERS

1 a) categoric
  b) ordered
  c) continuous

2 The investigation can be shown to be reliable if other scientists can repeat their investigations and get the same findings. Because it is reliable, opinions formed from it are more useful.

Answers to in-text questions

a) The original animal investigation did not include pregnant animals/was not carried out on human tissue, and so was not valid, when the opinion was formed that it could be given to pregnant women.

b) Using a voltmeter. Continuous measurements (variables) are more powerful.

c) Control all (or as many as possible) of the other variables.

d) A simple causal relationship described.

KEY POINTS

- Students should appreciate the need for sound science before opinions can be valued. They could challenge others in their group by presenting deliberately unfair tests and ask the others to spot the mistakes.

- Students should have notes that bring out the meaning of the key words, including 'continuous, discrete, categoric, ordered, valid and reliable'.

H3 Starting an investigation

LEARNING OBJECTIVES

Students should learn:

- How scientific knowledge can be used to observe the world around them.
- How good observations can be used to make hypotheses.
- How hypotheses can generate predictions that can be tested.
- That investigations must produce valid results.

LEARNING OUTCOMES

Students should be able to:

- State that observation can be the starting point for an investigation.
- State that observation can generate hypotheses.
- Recall that hypotheses can generate predictions and investigations.
- Show that the design of an investigation must allow results to be valid.

Teaching suggestions

- **Learning styles**

  Kinaesthetic: Practical activities.

  Visual: Observations made.

  Auditory: Listening to group discussions.

  Interpersonal: Discussing hypotheses and predictions.

  Intrapersonal: Answering question c).

- **Teaching assistant.** The teaching assistant could be primed to ask appropriate questions and to prompt thought processes in line with the theme of the lesson.

Answers to in-text questions

a) Yes/No depending on response and how much detail of physics you want to go into at this stage!

b) The second driver was tired.
   The second car was driving too fast.
   The second car was travelling too close.
   The first car had no brake lights.
   Any three of the above would be appropriate.

c) e.g. Observation: bridge is twisting.
   Hypothesis: high wind velocity caused it to twist.

d) He did not use a blackout, light was coming from other sources. The results are not valid.

SPECIFICATION LINK-UP   How Science Works

Section 10.3

Observation as a stimulus to investigation

Observation is the link between the real world and scientific ideas. When we observe objects, organisms or events we do so using existing knowledge. Observations may suggest hypotheses and lead to predictions that can be tested.

Students should know and understand

- *Observing phenomena can lead to the start of an investigation, experiment or survey. Existing theories and models can be used creatively to suggest explanations for phenomena (hypotheses). Careful observation is necessary before deciding which are the most important variables. Hypotheses can then be used to make predictions that can be tested.*

- *Data from testing a prediction can support or refute the hypothesis or lead to a new hypothesis.*

- *If the theories and models we have available to us do not completely match our data or observations, then we need to check the validity of our observations or data, or amend the theories or models.*

Lesson structure

STARTER

Linking observation to knowledge – Discuss with students any unusual events they saw on the way to school. If possible take them into the school grounds to look and listen to events. Try to link their observations to their scientific knowledge. They are more likely to notice events that they can offer some scientific explanation for. This may well need prompting with some directed questions. Once students have got used to making observations, get them to start to ask questions about those observations. (10 minutes)

Demo observation – Begin the lesson with a demonstration – as simple as lighting a match or more involved such as a bell ringing in a bell jar, with air gradually being withdrawn. Students should, in silence and without further prompting, be asked to write down their observations. These should be collated and questions be derived from those observations. (10 minutes)

MAIN

- Work through the first section and allow time for students to discuss question a.

- If in the lab, allow students to participate in a 'scientific happening' of your choice, e.g. dropping paper cups with different masses in. Preferably something that they have not met before, but which they will have some knowledge of. As an alternative, if possible take students onto the school field where there will be many opportunities to observe the roof structure of buildings, or size of wires on electricity pylons compared to telephone wires, or siting of phone masts.

- If students need some help at this point, they should try question b).

- In groups they should discuss possible explanations for one agreed observation. Encourage a degree of lateral thinking.

- Ask the group to select which of their explanations is the most likely, based on their own knowledge of science.

- Work these explanations into a hypothesis.

- Individually each student should try question c). Gather in ideas and hypotheses. Use a hypothesis that suggests that the bridge started to oscillate at a certain wind speed.

- Students, working in groups, can now turn this into a prediction.

- They could suggest ways in which their prediction could be tested using a model and wind tunnel. Identify independent, dependent and control variables and the need to make sure that they are measuring what they intend to measure.

- Go over question c) as a class.

PLENARIES

Poster – Students to design a poster that links 'Observation + knowledge – hypothesis – prediction – investigation'. (10 minutes)

Discussion on ideas of the past – Development of the knowledge that the planets revolve around the Sun – it could be useful here to illustrate how scientists struggled with these ideas in the past. The story could be used at many points in this chapter but is particularly useful here. Briefly – Aristarchus (third-century BC) proclaimed that the Earth revolved around the Sun. This idea was largely disregarded, as it didn't seem to fit the available evidence, e.g. we do not appear to be moving, the Sun and stars do; all objects fall towards Earth. In the sixteenth-century AD, Copernicus reasserted the idea, but whilst he could refute some of the objections, his data was poor and didn't adequately predict planetary positions, i.e. his predictions were not fully supported because of inaccurate data. His hypothesis was correct.

Later that century, Tycho Brahe was given immense sums of money to investigate these theories. He was able to set up four lots of measuring devices (no lenses available, therefore no telescopes). He therefore was able to repeat readings at the same time to improve accuracy. He was accurate to 1/30°. Unfortunately whilst Tycho was a brilliant observer he was a poor theoretician and thought his measurements fitted the hypothesis that the planets revolved around the Sun, but that the Sun revolved around the Earth. It took his assistant Johannes Kepler, (who suffered from multiple vision and myopia) to put his brilliant theoretical brain to the task. He was able to deduce from Tycho's brilliant measurements that the planets revolved around the Sun and that they had elliptical rather than circular orbits. This theory was perfectly matched by the data. It was now possible to predict the position of planets, with greater precision than ever before.

It is thought that these ideas about the Earth revolving around the Sun gave rise to the modern use of the term 'revolutionary'.

Practical support

Equipment and materials required
Paper cups or baking cases and small masses plus timing device.

DID YOU KNOW?
Charles Wilson was awarded the Nobel prize for physics in 1927. His chamber led to important discoveries about the properties of sub-atomic particles and even the discovery of antimatter.

KEY POINTS
• Students should have notes relating observations to knowledge to hypothesis to prediction and to investigation. They should also have some notes on what it means to design validity into an investigation.

HOW SCIENCE WORKS

H3   Starting an investigation

LEARNING OBJECTIVES
1 How can you use your scientific knowledge to observe the world around you?
2 How can you use your observations to make a hypothesis?
3 How can you make predictions and start to design an investigation?

Observation

As humans we are sensitive to the world around us. We can use our many senses to detect what is happening. As scientists we use observations to ask questions. We can only ask useful questions if we know something about the observed event. We will not have all of the answers, but we know enough to start asking the correct questions.

If we observe that the weather has been hot today, we would not ask if it was due to global warming. If the weather was hotter than normal for several years then we could ask that question. We know that global warming takes many years to show its effect.

When you are designing an investigation you have to observe carefully which variables are likely to have an effect.

a) Would it be reasonable to ask if the wind turbine in Figure 1 generates less electricity in the rain? Explain your answer.

Amjid was waiting to cross at a zebra crossing. A car stopped to let him cross while a second car drove into the first car, without braking. Being a scientist, Amjid tried to work out why this had happened . . . while the two drivers argued! He came up with the following ideas:
• The second driver was tired.
• The second car had faulty brakes.
• The first car stopped too quickly.
• The second car was driving too fast.
• The second car was travelling too close.
• The second car had worn tyres.
• The first car had no brake lights.

b) Discuss each of these ideas and use your knowledge of science to decide which three ideas are the most likely to have caused the crash.

Observations, backed up by really creative thinking and good scientific knowledge can lead to a hypothesis.

What is a hypothesis?

A hypothesis is a 'great idea'. Why is it so great? – well because it is a great observation that has some really good science to try to explain it.

For example, you observe that small, thinly sliced chips cook faster than large, fat chips. Your hypothesis could be that the small chips cook faster because the heat from the oil has a shorter distance to travel before it gets to the potato in the centre of the chips.

Figure 1 A wind turbine

DID YOU KNOW?
Charles Wilson used to climb mountains to study cloud formations. He devised a cloud chamber in the laboratory to study cloud formation in more detail. He passed alpha particles through the cloud and unexpectedly observed a visible trail. This provided first-hand evidence of the existence of subatomic particles.

c) Check out the photograph in Figure 2 and spot anything that you find interesting. Use your knowledge and some creative thought to suggest a hypothesis based on your observations.

When making hypotheses you can be very imaginative with your ideas. However, you should have some scientific reasoning behind those ideas so that they are not totally bizarre.

Remember, your explanation might not be correct, but you think it is. The only way you can check out your hypothesis is to make it into a prediction and then test it by carrying out an investigation.

$$\text{Observation} + \text{knowledge} \longrightarrow \text{hypothesis} \longrightarrow \text{prediction} \longrightarrow \text{investigation}$$

Starting to design a valid investigation

An investigation starts with a prediction. You, as the scientist, predict that there is a relationship between two variables.
• An independent variable is one that is changed or selected by you, the investigator.
• A dependent variable is measured for each change in your independent variable.
• All other variables become control variables, kept constant so that your investigation is a fair test.

If your measurements are going to be accepted by other people then they must be valid. Part of this is making sure that you are really measuring the effect of changing your chosen variable. For example, if other variables aren't controlled properly, they might be affecting the data collected.

d) Look at Figure 3. Darren was investigating the light given out by a 12V bulb. He used a light meter in the laboratory that was set at 10cm from the bulb. What might be wrong here?

Figure 2 The Tacoma Narrows bridge in the USA twisting just before it collapsed!

Figure 3 Testing a light bulb

SUMMARY QUESTIONS
1 Copy and complete using the words below:

controlled	dependent	hypothesis	independent
	knowledge	prediction	

Observations when supported by scientific ...... can be used to make a .... This can be the basis for a .... A prediction links an ...... variable to a ...... variable. Other variables need to be ....

2 Explain the difference between a hypothesis and a prediction.

KEY POINTS
1 Observation is often the starting point for an investigation.
2 Hypotheses can lead to predictions and investigations.
3 You must design investigations that produce valid results if you are to be believed.

6   7

SUMMARY ANSWERS

1 Observations when supported by scientific *knowledge* can be used to make a *hypothesis*. This can be the basis for a *prediction*. A prediction links an *independent* variable to a *dependent* variable. Other variables need to be *controlled*.

2 A hypothesis seeks to explain an observation – it is a good idea. A prediction tests the hypothesis in an investigation.

H4

Building an investigation

LEARNING OBJECTIVES

Students should learn:

- How to design a fair test.
- The purpose of a trial run.
- How to ensure accuracy and precision.

LEARNING OUTCOMES

Students should be able to:

- Design a fair test and understand the use of control groups.
- Manage fieldwork investigations.
- Use trial runs to design valid investigations.
- Design accuracy into an investigation.
- Design precision into an investigation.

Teaching Suggestions

- **Learning styles**

  Kinaesthetic: Carrying out experiment.

  Visual: Reading instruments.

  Auditory: Listening to the outcomes of experiments from different groups.

  Interpersonal: Discussing the quality of results.

  Intrapersonal: Considering fair tests in relation to athletics.

- **Teaching assistant.** The teaching assistant could support pupils who have physical or coordination difficulties with practical work. The purpose of the experiment will need reinforcing for lower abilities.

Practical support

Equipment and materials required

Supply the classic test circuit with variable resistor for each group. Some groups have analogue and some digital meters.

The resistance experiment can be expanded to investigate length with the idea that producing a line graph can give a better estimate of the true resistance of the wire.

ACTIVITY & EXTENSION

SPECIFICATION LINK-UP   How Science Works

Section 10.4

Designing an investigation

An investigation is an attempt to determine whether or not there is a relationship between variables. Therefore it is necessary to identify and understand the variables in an investigation. The design of an investigation should be scrutinised when evaluating the validity of the evidence it has produced.

Students should know and understand

- *An independent variable is one that is changed or selected by the investigator. The dependent variable is measured for each change in the independent variable.*
- *Any measurement must be valid in that it measures only the appropriate variable.*

Fair test

- *It is important to isolate the effects of the independent variable on the dependent variable. This may be achieved more easily in a laboratory environment than in the field where it is harder to control all variables.*
- *A fair test is one in which only the independent variable affects the dependent variable, as all other variables are kept the same.*
- *In field investigations it is necessary to ensure that variables that change their value do so in the same way for all measurements of the dependent variable.*
- *When using large-scale survey results, it is necessary to select data from conditions that are similar.*
- *Control groups are often used in biological and medical research to ensure that observed effects are due to changes in the independent variable alone.*

Choosing values of a variable

- *Care is needed in selecting values of variables to be recorded in an investigation. A trial run will help to identify appropriate values to be recorded, such as the number of repeated readings needed and their range and interval.*

Accuracy and precision

- *Readings might be repeated to improve the reliability of the data. An accurate measurement is one that is close to the true value.*
- *The design of an investigation must provide data with sufficient accuracy.*
- *The design of an investigation must provide data with sufficient precision to form a valid conclusion.*

Lesson structure

STARTER

Head start – Start, for example, with a video clip of a 100 m race. This has to be a fair test. How is this achieved? Then show the mass start of the London marathon and ask if this is a fair test. Then move on to ask why there is no official world record for a marathon. Instead they have world best times. This could lead discussion into how difficult it is to control all of the variables in the field. You could go back to suggest that athletes can break the 100 m world record and for this not to be recognised because of a helping wind. (10 minutes)

That's not fair! – Challenge students with a test you set up in an 'unfair' way. You can differentiate by making some errors obvious and some more subtle. Students can observe then generate lists of mistakes in small groups. Ask each group to give one error from their list and record what should have been done to ensure fair testing until all suggestions have been considered. (10 minutes)

MAIN

- Move into group discussion of in-text question a). Other examples of field testing might include setting up wind farms or testing controls of a new aeroplane.

- Group discussions on how and why we need to produce survey data. Use a topical issue here. It might be appropriate to see how it should *not* be done by using a vox pop clip from a news programme.

- Students should work in groups to discuss question b). One person in each group should have the responsibility of reporting their answers to the class in a brief plenary.

- It is important that students appreciate the difference between accuracy and precision. They could be given a circuit to test the resistance of a specific length of wire. Each group will be given the same instructions and the same apparatus, except that some groups will have analogue meters and others digital. To increase accuracy they should be told to repeat their readings. They should be told that the most accurate readings will be taken by those that use their equipment most carefully.

- On completion each group submits its best attempt at an accurate result. The teacher has calculated the theoretical resistance for the wire. The nearest is declared the winner.

- Try finding the average of the whole class and see if this is more accurate.

- See how accurate the analogue meters were compared to the digital.

- Use the data gathered to award a prize to the group showing the greatest accuracy.

- Repeat the class competition but this time consider the range of their repeat measurements, i.e. judge their precision.

- Find the maximum range for the whole class – who got the highest reading/who got the lowest? Can we explain why? Gather suggestions.

PLENARIES

Prize giving! – The winning group should explain why they think they got the most accurate results. The winning group should explain why they think they got the most precision. (5 minutes)

Precision and accuracy – Discuss precision and accuracy in small groups then gather feedback. (10 minutes)

SUMMARY ANSWERS

1 Trial runs give you a good idea of whether you have the correct *conditions*; whether you have chosen the correct *range*; whether you have enough *readings*; if you need to do *repeat* readings.

2 Any example that demonstrates understanding of the two terms, e.g. I measured the resistance of the wire as 3.5 Ohms, 4.8 Ohms, 2.2 Ohms, 3.8 Ohms, 3.2 Ohms . The average of my results is 3.5 Ohms and the manufacturer's results are 3.5 Ohms. My results were accurate but not precise.

3 Control all the variables that might affect the dependent variable, apart from the independent variable whose values you select.

KEY POINTS

- The students must be able to appreciate the difference between accuracy and precision. Ask students for their own definitions without the use of the textbook.
- They sometimes confuse accuracy with the sensitivity of an instrument. Also, in calculations, some students will write irrelevant places of decimals. Ask students to comment on an example.

HOW SCIENCE WORKS

H4   Building an investigation

LEARNING OBJECTIVES

1 How do you design a fair test?
2 How do you make sure that you choose the best values for your variables?
3 How do you ensure accuracy and precision?

Figure 1 Racing car travelling at speed

Fair testing

A fair test is one in which only the independent variable affects the dependent variable. All other variables are controlled, keeping them constant if possible.

This is easy to set up in the laboratory, but almost impossible in fieldwork. Imagine you are studying the acceleration of different racing cars. You would choose the same race track and try them at the same time. This means that all of the many variables (e.g. weather) change in much the same way, except for the one you are investigating.

a) How would you set up an investigation to see how the wing setting on the rear of the car affected its top speed down the straight?

If you are investigating two variables in a large population then you will need to do a survey. Again it is impossible to control all of the variables. Imagine you were investigating how much electricity different sized families used. You would have to choose families from the same sized house, with the same level of insulation to test. The larger the sample size you test, the more reliable your results will be.

Control groups are used in investigations to try to make sure that you are measuring the variable that you intend to measure. When investigating the effects of using a mobile phone, the control group would be a similar group of people who did not use a mobile phone.

Choosing values of a variable

Trial runs will tell you a lot about how your early thoughts are going to work out.

Do you have the correct conditions?
Suppose you have a small water heater to test. You want to find out the best voltage to use. You test different voltages but only very small changes in temperature were recorded. This might be because:

- the heater was not left on long enough.
- too much water was being heated.
- the heater was not powerful enough.

Have you chosen a sensible range?
If there is a big temperature change, but the results all look about the same:

- you might not have chosen a wide enough range of voltages.

Have you got enough readings that are close together?
If the results are very different from each other:

- you might not see a pattern if you have large gaps between readings over the important part of the range.

DID YOU KNOW?

William Herschel was interested in finding which wavelengths of light could cause an increase in temperature. He set up a prism that shone sunlight on to a thermometer. As the Sun passed it cast different colours on to the thermometer. Once the spectrum of visible light had passed, his attention passed to the thermometer. He was amazed to observe after lunch that even though the thermometer had no visible light shining on it, the thermometer reading had risen. He had discovered infra-red radiation.

Accuracy

Accurate results are very close to the *true value*.

Your investigation should provide data that is accurate enough to answer your original question.

However, it is not always possible to know what that true value is.

How do you get accurate data?
- You can repeat your results and your mean is more likely to be accurate.
- Try repeating your measurements with a different instrument and see if you get the same readings.
- Use high quality instruments that measure accurately.
- The more carefully you use the measuring instruments, the more accuracy you will get.

Precision and reliability

If your repeated results are closely grouped together then you have precision and you have improved the reliability of your data.

Your investigation must provide data with sufficient precision. It's no use measuring a person's reaction time using the seconds hand on a clock! If there are big differences within sets of repeat readings, you will not be able to make a valid conclusion. You won't be able to trust your data!

How do you get precise and reliable data?
- You have to repeat your tests as often as necessary.
- You have to repeat your tests in exactly the same way each time.

A word of caution!

Be careful though – just because your results show precision does not mean your results are accurate. Look at the box opposite.

b) Draw a thermometer scale showing 4 results that are both accurate and precise.

The difference between accurate and precise results

Imagine measuring the temperature after a set time when an immersion is used to heat a fixed volume of water. Two students repeated this experiment, four times each. Their results are marked on the thermometer scales below:

- Precise results are grouped closely together.
- Accurate results will have a mean (average) close to the true value.

SUMMARY QUESTIONS

1 Copy and complete using the following terms:

   range   repeat   conditions   readings

Trial runs give you a good idea of whether you have the correct ......; whether you have chosen the correct ......; whether you have enough ......; if you need to do ...... readings.

2 Use an example to explain how results can be accurate, but not precise.

3 Briefly describe how you would go about setting up a fair test in a laboratory investigation. Give your answer as general advice.

KEY POINTS

1 Care must be taken to ensure fair testing – as far as is possible.
2 You can use a trial run to make sure that you choose the best values for your variables.
3 Careful use of the correct equipment can improve accuracy.
4 If you repeat your results carefully they are likely to become more reliable.

Answers to in-text questions

a) Any variables associated with the weather, the track surface, fuel used, driver, must vary in the same way for each test.

b) Diagram of thermometer showing the true value with 4 readings tightly grouped around it.

H5 Making measurements

LEARNING OBJECTIVES

Students should learn:

- That they can expect results to vary.
- That instruments vary in their accuracy.
- That instruments vary in their sensitivity.
- That human error can affect results.
- What to do with anomalies.

LEARNING OUTCOMES

Students should be able to:

- Differentiate between results that vary and anomalies.
- Explain why it is important to use equipment properly.
- Explain that instruments vary in their accuracy and sensitivity.
- State the difference between random and systematic errors.

Teaching suggestions

- **Special needs.** Students will need support when interpreting data on trolleys and identifying evidence for random and systematic error.

- **Gifted and talented.** Demonstrate a different experiment in which there is a built-in systematic error, e.g. measuring the resistance of a wire that is heating up.

- **Learning styles**
  Kinaesthetic: Taking measurements.
  Visual: Observing systematic error.
  Auditory: Listening to explanations of differences between random and systematic errors.
  Interpersonal: Group discussions to determine how to accurately measure a person's height.
  Intrapersonal: Answering questions d) and e).

- **ICT link-up.** Using data logging to exemplify minor changes in dependent variables provides a good opportunity to include ICT in the lesson.

Practical support

A laser/sonic measure and the instructions to illustrate its usage and sensitivity. It would be a good idea to have these printed for the students. Also tape, metre rule and 30 cm rule.

Other equipment is dependent on the type of demonstration used to show systematic error.

SPECIFICATION LINK-UP   How Science Works

Section 10.5

Making measurements

When making measurements we must consider such issues as inherent variation due to variables that have not been controlled, human error and the characteristics of the instruments used. Evidence should be evaluated with the reliability and validity of the measurements that have been made in mind.

A single measurement
- *There will always be some variation in the actual value of a variable no matter how hard we try to repeat an event.*
- *When selecting an instrument, it is necessary to consider the accuracy inherent in the instrument and the way it has to be used.*
- *The sensitivity of an instrument refers to the smallest change in a value that can be detected.*
- *Even when an instrument is used correctly, human error may occur which could produce random differences in repeated readings or a systematic shift from the true value which could, for instance, occur due to incorrect use or poor calibration.*
- *Random error can result from inconsistent application of a technique. Systematic error can result from consistent misapplication of a technique.*
- *Any anomalous values should be examined to try to identify the cause and, if a product of a poor measurement, ignored.*

Lesson structure

STARTER

Demonstration – Demonstrate different ways of measuring the width of the lab. Use a 30 cm rule, a metre rule, a tape and a laser/sonic measure. Discuss the relative merits of using each of these devices for different purposes. Discuss the details of the measuring instrument – its percentage accuracy, its useful range and its sensitivity. (10 minutes)

MAIN

- In small groups, devise the most accurate way to measure a person's height. They can have any equipment they need. Students will need to think about what a person's height includes, e.g. hair flat or not, shoes off or not. They might suggest a board placed horizontally on the head, using a spirit level, removing the person being measured and then using the laser/sonic measure placed on the ground. Take care to follow manufacturer's instructions when using the laser.

- Choose a person to try out this technique. Stress that we do not have a true answer. We do not know the person's true height. We trust the instrument and the technique that is most likely to give us the most accurate result – the one nearest the true value.

- In groups, answer question a).

- Individually answer questions b) and c).

- Demonstrate an experiment in which there is a built-in systematic error, e.g. using an analogue meter that doesn't return to zero or measuring radioactivity without taking background radiation into account.

- Point out the difference between this type of systematic error and random errors. Also, how you might tell from results which type of error it is. You can still have a high degree of precision with systematic errors.

- Complete questions d) and e) individually.

- Encourage students to identify anomalies whilst carrying out the investigation so that they have an opportunity to check and replace them.

PLENARIES

Check list – Draw up a check list for an investigation so that every possible source of error is considered. (10–15 minutes)

Human vs computer – Class discussion of data logging compared to humans when collecting data. Stress the importance of data logging in gathering data over extended or very short periods of time. (See 'Activity & extension ideas' box.)

KEY POINTS

- The students need to demonstrate an appreciation that accuracy and precision of measurement is a key feature in a successful investigation.

HOW SCIENCE WORKS

H5 Making measurements

LEARNING OBJECTIVES

1 Why do results always vary?
2 How do you choose instruments that will give you accurate results?
3 What do we mean by the sensitivity of an instrument?
4 How does human error affect results and what do you do with anomalies?

Figure 1 Mark testing how fast a trolley goes down a ramp

DID YOU KNOW?

The Big Bang that created the universe, probably lasted about 10^{-30} second – now I wonder who measured that!

Using instruments

Do not panic! You cannot expect perfect results.

Try timing one swing of a pendulum using a stop watch that measures to 0.01 s. Do you always get the same time? Probably not. So can we say that any measurement is absolutely correct?

In any experiment there will be doubts about actual measurements.

a) Look at Figure 1. Suppose, like this student, you tested the time it takes for one type of trolley to run down the track. It is unlikely that you would get two readings exactly the same. Discuss all the possible reasons why.

When you choose an instrument you need to know that it will give you the accuracy that you want. That is, it will give you a true reading.

Perhaps you have used a simple force meter in school for measuring force. How confident were you that you had measured the true force? You could use a very expensive force meter to calibrate yours. The expensive force meter is more likely to show the true reading that is accurate – but are you really sure?

You also need to be able to use an instrument properly.

b) In Figure 1 the student is measuring the time it takes for the car to reach the finish line. Why is he unlikely to get a true measurement?

When you choose an instrument you need to decide how accurate you need it to be. Instruments that measure the same quantity can have different sensitivities. The instrument with the greatest sensitivity is the one that can detect the smallest change in the quantity being measured.

Choosing the wrong scale can cause you to miss important data or make silly conclusions, for example 'The amount of gold was the same in the two rings – they both weighed 5 grams.'

c) Match the following timers to their best use:

Used to measure	Sensitivity of timer
Time taken to sail around the world	0.1 seconds
Timing a car rolling down a slope	1.0 seconds
Timing ten oscillations of a pendulum	1 minute
Timing a pizza to cook	1 hour

Errors

Even when an instrument is used correctly, the results can still show differences.

Results might differ due to a random error. This is most likely to be due to a poor measurement being made. It could be due to not carrying out the method consistently.

The error might be systematic. This means that the method was carried out consistently but an error was being repeated.

Check out these two sets of data that were taken from the investigation that Mark did. He tested five different trolleys. The third line is the time expected from calculations:

Type of trolley used	a	b	c	d	e
Time taken for trolley to run down ramp (seconds)	12.6	23.1	24.8	31.3	38.2
	12.1	15.2	24.3	32.1	37.6
Calculated time (seconds)	10.1	13.1	22.1	30.1	35.3

d) Discuss whether there is any evidence for random error in these results.
e) Discuss whether there is any evidence for systematic error in these results.

Anomalies

Anomalous results are clearly out of line. They are not those that are due to the natural variation you get from any measurement. These should be looked at carefully. There might be a very interesting reason why they are so different. If they are simply due to a random error, then they should be discarded (rejected).

If anomalies can be identified while you are doing an investigation, then it is best to repeat that part of the investigation.

If you find anomalies after you have finished collecting data for an investigation, then they must be discarded.

SUMMARY QUESTIONS

1 Copy and complete using the words below:

    accurate   discarded   random   sensitivity   systematic
                        use   variation

There will always be some ...... in results. You should always choose the best instruments that you can to get the most ...... results. You must know how to ...... the instrument properly. The ...... of an instrument refers to the smallest change that can be detected. There are two types of error – ...... and .... Anomalies due to random error should be ....

2 Which of the following will lead to a systematic error and which to a random error?
   a) Using a weighing machine, which has something stuck to the pan on the top.
   b) Forgetting to re-zero the weighing machine.

KEY POINTS

1 Results will nearly always vary.
2 Better instruments give more accurate results.
3 Sensitivity of an instrument refers to the smallest change that it can detect.
4 Human error can produce random and systematic errors.
5 We examine anomalies; they might give us some interesting ideas. If they are due to a random error, we repeat the measurements. If there is no time to repeat them, we discard them.

10   11

SUMMARY ANSWERS

1 There will always be some *variation* in results. You should always choose the best instruments that you can to get the most *accurate* results. You must know how to *use* the instrument properly. The *sensitivity* of an instrument refers to the smallest change that can be detected. There are two types of error, *random* and *systematic*. Anomalies should be *discarded*.

2 **a)** systematic, **b)** random.

Answers to in-text questions

a) Generally a failure to control variables, e.g. trolley not taking the same route; not taking the time as it crosses the line.
Student might not react as quickly when stopping watch.

b) Student is standing too far away and at the wrong angle to see when the trolley reaches the line.

c)

Used to measure	Sensitivity of times
Time taken to sail around the world	1 hour
Timing a car rolling down a slope	0.1 seconds
Timing ten oscillations of a pendulum	1.0 seconds
Timing a pizza to cook	1 minute

d) First attempt for b is the random error.

e) Average results are close to individual results, which are consistently different to the calculated time.

H6 Presenting data

LEARNING OBJECTIVES

Students should learn:

- What is meant by the range and the mean of a set of data.
- How to use tables of data.
- How to display data.

LEARNING OUTCOMES

Students should be able to:

- Express accurately the range and mean of a set of data.
- Distinguish between the uses of bar charts and line graphs.
- Draw line graphs accurately.

Teaching Suggestions

- **Gifted and talented.** These students could be handling two dependent variables in the table and graph, e.g. cooling and weight loss of a beaker of water with time, with repeat readings included.

- **Learning styles**

  Kinaesthetic: Practical activities.

  Visual: Making observations and presenting data.

  Auditory: Listening to group discussions.

  Interpersonal: Participating in group discussions on the choice of suitable tables/graphs.

  Intrapersonal: Produce own table and graph.

- **ICT link-up.** Students could use a set of data with, e.g., Excel to present the data in different ways, such as pie charts, line graphs, bar charts, etc. Allow them to decide on the most appropriate form. Care needs to be given to 'smoothing' which does not always produce a line of best fit.

SPECIFICATION LINK-UP   How Science Works

Section 10.6

Presenting data

To explain the relationship between two or more variables, data may be presented in such a way as to make the patterns more evident. There is a link between the type of graph used and the variable they represent. The choice of graphical representation depends upon the type of variable they represent.

Students should know and understand

- *The range of the data refers to the maximum and minimum values.*
- *The mean (or average) of the data refers to the sum of all the measurements divided by the number of measurements taken.*
- *Tables are an effective means of displaying data but are limited in how they portray the design of an investigation.*
- *Bar charts can be used to display data in which the independent variable is categoric and the dependent variable continuous.*
- *Line graphs can be used to display data in which both the independent and dependent variables are continuous.*

Lesson structure

STARTER

Excel – Prepare some data from a typical investigation that the students may have recently completed. Use all of the many ways of presenting the data in Excel to display it. Allow students to discuss and reach conclusions as to which is the best method. (10 minutes)

Newspapers – Choose data from the press – particularly useful are market trends where they do not use 0,0. This exaggerates changes. This could relate to the use of data logging which can exaggerate normal variation into major trends. (5 minutes)

MAIN

- Choose an appropriate topic to either demonstrate or allow small groups to gather data. E.g. cooling of water against time; force applied and degree of bending in rules; investigate the period of a pendulum. Any topic that will allow rapid gathering of data. Be aware that some data will lead to a bar chart, this might be more appropriate to groups struggling to draw line graphs.

- Students should be told what their task is and therefore know how to construct an appropriate table. This should be done individually prior to collecting the data. Refer to the first paragraph under 'Table'.

- Group discussion on best form of table.

- Carry out data gathering, putting data directly into table. Refer to the second paragraph under 'Table'.

- Individuals produce their own graphs. Refer to the 'Next time you . . .' box.

- Graphs could be exchanged and marked by others in the group, using the criteria in the paragraph mentioned above.

PLENARIES

Which type of graph? – Give students different headings from a variety of tables and ask them how best to show the results graphically. This could be done as a whole class with individuals showing answers as the teacher reveals each table heading. Each student can draw a large letter 'L' (for line graph) on one side of a sheet of paper and 'B' (for bar chart) on the other, ready to show their answers. (5 minutes)

Key words – Students should be given key words to prepare posters for the lab. Key words should be taken from the summary questions in the first six sections. (10 minutes)

Crossword – The students should complete a crossword based on the previous five lessons. (15 minutes)

ACTIVITY & EXTENSION IDEAS

Lower-attaining students should start with bar charts and move on to line graphs. Higher-attaining students ought to be practising the skills learned earlier whilst gathering their data. They could also be given more difficult contexts that are more likely to produce anomalies. They could, for example, be given a context that produces both random and systematic errors.

H6 Presenting data

LEARNING OBJECTIVES

1 What do we mean by the 'range' and the 'mean' of the data?
2 How do you use tables of results?
3 How do you display your data?

Figure 1 Student using an LDR with a light bulb

For this section you will be working with data from this investigation:

Mel shone a lamp onto a light dependent resistor (LDR). She measured how quickly energy was transferred to the lamp and the resistance of the LDR.

The room was kept as dark as possible while she made the readings.

Tables

Tables are really good for getting your results down quickly and clearly. You should design your table **before** you start your investigation.

Your table should be constructed to fit in all the data to be collected. It should be fully labelled, including units.

In some investigations, particularly fieldwork, it is useful to have an extra column for any notes you might want to make as you work.

While filling in your table of results you should be constantly looking for anomalies.

● Check to see if a repeat is sufficiently close to the first reading.
● Check to see if the pattern you are getting as you change the independent variable is what you expected.

Remember a result that looks anomalous should be checked out to see if it really is a poor reading or if it might suggest a different hypothesis.

Planning your table

Mel knew the values for her independent variable. We always put these in the first column of a table. The dependent variable goes in the second column. Mel will find its values as she carries out the investigation.

So she could plan a table like this:

Rate of energy transferred to the lamp (W)	Resistance of LDR (Ω)
0.5	
1.4	
2.6	
4.8	
8.4	

Or like this:

Rate of energy transferred to the lamp (W)	0.5	1.4	2.6	4.8	8.4
Resistance of LDR (Ω)					

All she had to do in the investigation was to write the correct numbers in the second column to complete the top table.

Mel's results are shown in the alternative format in the table below:

Rate of energy transferred to the lamp (W)	0.5	1.4	2.6	4.8	8.4
Resistance of LDR (Ω)	4000	3000	1000	350	150

The range of the data

Pick out the maximum and the minimum values and you have the range. You should always quote these two numbers when asked for a range. For example, the range is between .... (the lowest value) and .... (the highest value) – and don't forget to include the units!

a) What is the range for the dependent variable in Mel's set of data?

The mean of the data

Often you have to find the mean of each repeated set of measurements. You add up the measurements in the set and divide by how many there are. Miss out any anomalies you find.

The repeat values and mean can be recorded as shown below:

Rate of energy transferred to the lamp (W)	Resistance of LDR (Ω)			
	1st test	2nd test	3rd test	Mean

Displaying your results

Bar charts

If you have a categoric or an ordered independent variable and a continuous dependent variable then you should use a bar chart.

Line graphs

If you have a continuous independent and a continuous dependent variable then a line graph should be used.

Scatter graphs or scattergrams

Scatter graphs are used in much the same way as line graphs, but you might not expect to be able to draw such a clear line of best fit. For example, if you wanted to see if lung capacity was related to how long you could hold your breath, you would draw a scatter graph with your results.

SUMMARY QUESTIONS

1 Copy and complete using the words below:

categoric   continuous   mean   range

The maximum and minimum values show the ...... of the data. The sum of all the values divided by the total number of the values gives the .... Bar charts are used when you have a ...... independent and a continuous dependent variable. Line graphs are used when you have ...... independent and dependent variables.

2 Draw a graph of Mel's results from the bottom of page 12.

NEXT TIME YOU...

... make a table for your results remember to include:
● headings,
● units,
● a title.

... draw a line graph remember to include:
● the independent variable on the x-axis,
● the dependent variable on the y-axis,
● a line of best fit,
● labels, units and a title.

GET IT RIGHT!

Marks are often dropped in the exam by candidates plotting points incorrectly. Also use a line of best fit where appropriate – don't just join the points 'dot-to-dot'!

KEY POINTS

1 The range states the maximum and the minimum values.
2 The mean is the sum of the values divided by how many values there are.
3 Tables are best used during an investigation to record results.
4 Bar charts are used when you have a categoric or an ordered independent variable and a continuous dependent variable.
5 Line graphs are used to display data that are continuous.

12

13

SUMMARY ANSWERS

1 The maximum and minimum values show the *range* of the data. The sum of all the values divided by the total number of the values gives the *mean*. Bar charts are used when you have a *categoric or ordered* independent and a *continuous* dependent variable. Line graphs are used when you have *continuous* independent and dependent variables.

2 Appropriate line graph drawn.

Answers to in-text question

a) Dependent variable – 150 Ω to 4000 Ω

KEY POINTS

● The students should be able to produce their own correctly labelled table and graph.

H7 | Using data to draw conclusions

LEARNING OBJECTIVES

Students should learn:

- How to use charts and graphs to identify patterns.
- How to draw accurate conclusions from relationships.
- How to improve the reliability of an investigation.

LEARNING OUTCOMES

Students should be able to:

- Identify patterns using charts and graphs.
- Develop patterns and relationships into conclusions.
- Evaluate the reliability of an investigation.

Teaching Suggestions

- **Special needs.** Provide a flow diagram so that students can see the process as they are going through it.

- **Gifted and talented.** Students could take the original investigation then design out some of the flaws, producing an investigation with improved validity and reliability.
  Summary question 2 could be examined in some detail and the work researched on the web.

- **Learning styles**
  Kinaesthetic: Drawing graphs.
  Visual: Observing tests.
  Auditory: Discussing the concepts of reliability and validity of whole investigations.
  Interpersonal: Generating a flow diagram together.
  Intrapersonal: Evaluating the reliability and validity of their own tests.

- **ICT link-up/activity.** Students could use a set of data with, e.g., Excel to produce a range of presentations. They could decide on the most appropriate form. Care should be given to 'smoothing' which does not always produce a line of best fit.

SPECIFICATION LINK-UP   How Science Works

Section 10.7

Using data to draw conclusions

The patterns and relationships observed in data represent the behaviour of the variables in an investigation. However, it is necessary to look at patterns and relationships between variables with the limitations of the data in mind.

Students should know and understand

- *Patterns in tables and graphs can be used to identify anomalous data that require further consideration.*

- *A line of best fit can be used to illustrate the underlying relationship between variables.*

- *The relationships that exist between variables can be linear (positive or negative), directly proportional, predictable curves, complex curves and relationships not easily represented by a mathematical relationship.*

Evaluation

- *In evaluating a whole investigation the reliability and validity of the data obtained must be considered. Reliability and validity of an investigation can be increased by looking at data obtained from secondary sources, through using an alternative method as a check and by requiring that the results are reproducible by others.*

- *Conclusions must be limited by the data available and not go beyond them.*

Lesson structure

STARTER

Starter graphs – Prepare a series of graphs that illustrate the various types of relationships in the specification. Each graph should have fully labelled axes. Students should, in groups, agree statements that describe the patterns in the graphs. Gather feedback from groups and discuss. (10 minutes)

MAIN

- Using the graphs from the previous lesson, students should be taught how to produce lines of best fit. Students could work individually with help from the first section of H7.

- They should identify the pattern in their graph.

- They now need to consider the reliability and validity of their results. They may need their understanding of reliability and validity reinforced. How this is achieved will depend on the investigation chosen in H6 'Presenting data'. Questions can be posed to reinforce their understanding of both terms. If the investigation was not carefully controlled, then it is likely to be unreliable and invalid, thus posing many opportunities for discussion. There is also an opportunity to reinforce other ideas such as random and systematic errors.

- If the previous activity is unlikely to yield these opportunities, then a brief demonstration of a test, e.g. homemade helicopters falling, could be used. Students should observe the teacher and make notes as the tests are carried out. They should be as critical as they can be, and in small groups discuss their individual findings. One or two students could be recording the results and two more plotting the graph as the teacher does the tests. These could be processed immediately onto the screen.

- Return to the original prediction. Look at the graph of the results. Ask how much confidence the group has in the results.

- Review the links that are possible between two sets of data. Ask them to decide which one their tests might support.

- Now the word 'conclusion' should be introduced and a conclusion made . . . if possible! It is sometimes useful to make a conclusion that is 'subject to . . . e.g. the reliability being demonstrated'.

PLENARIES

Flow diagram – When pulling the lesson together it will be important to emphasise the process involved – graph – line of best fit – pattern – question the reliability and validity – consider the links that are possible – make a conclusion – summarise evaluation. This could be illustrated with a flow diagram generated by a directed class discussion.
(5 minutes)

Key words – Students should be given key words to complete the posters for the lab.
(10 minutes)

ACTIVITY & EXTENSION IDEAS

Students should be able to transfer these skills to examine the work of scientists and to become critical of the work of others. Collecting scientific findings from the press and subjecting them to the same critical appraisal is an important exercise. They could be encouraged to collect these or be given photocopies of topical issues suitable for such appraisal.

How science works

HOW SCIENCE WORKS

H7 Using data to draw conclusions

LEARNING OBJECTIVES

1 How do we best use charts and graphs to identify patterns?
2 What are the possible relationships we can identify from charts and graphs?
3 How do we draw conclusions from relationships?
4 How can we improve the reliability of our investigation?

Identifying patterns and relationships

Now that you have a bar chart or a graph of your results you can begin to look for patterns. You must have an open mind at this point.

Firstly, there could still be some anomalous results. You might not have picked these out earlier. How do you spot an anomaly? It must be a significant distance away from the pattern, not just within normal variation.

A line of best fit will help to identify any anomalies at this stage. Ask yourself – do the anomalies represent something important or were they just a mistake?

Secondly, remember a line of best fit can be a straight line or it can be a curve – you have to decide from your results.

The line of best fit will also lead you into thinking what the relationship is between your two variables. You need to consider whether your graph shows a linear relationship. This simply means can you be confident about drawing a straight line of best fit on your graph? If the answer is yes – then is this line positive or negative?

a) Say whether graphs (i) and (ii) in Figure 1 show a positive or a negative linear relationship.

Look at the graph in Figure 2. It shows a positive linear relationship. It also goes through the origin (0,0). We call this a **directly proportional** relationship.

Your results might also show a curved line of best fit. These can be predictable, complex or very complex! Look at Figure 3 below.

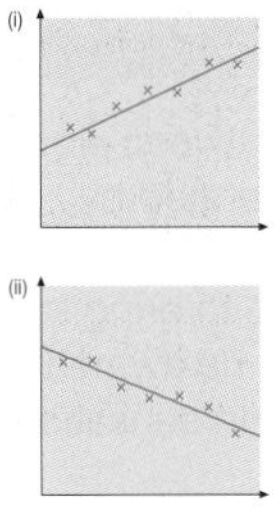

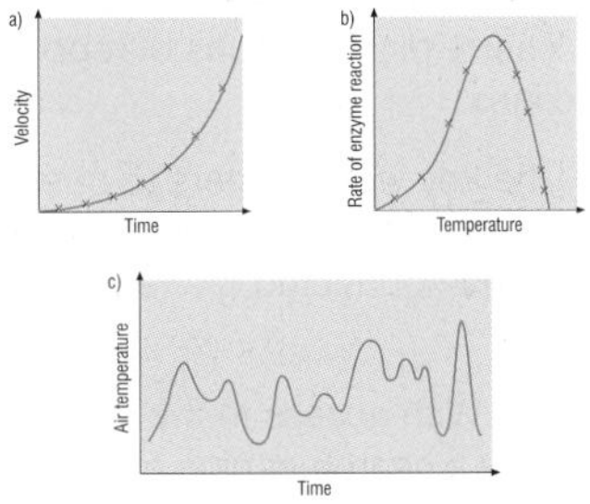

Figure 1 Graphs showing linear relationships

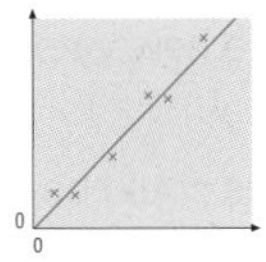

Figure 2 Graph showing a directly proportional relationship

Figure 3 a) Graph showing predictable results. b) Graph showing complex results. c) Graph showing very complex results.

Drawing conclusions

Your graphs are designed to show the relationship between your two chosen variables. You need to consider what that relationship means for your conclusion.

There are three possible links between variables. (See page 5.) They can be:

● causal,
● due to association, or
● due to chance.

You must decide which is the most likely. Remember a positive relationship does not always mean a causal link between the two variables.

Poor science can often happen if a wrong decision is made here. Newspapers have said that living near electricity sub-stations can cause cancer. All that scientists would say is that there is possibly an association. Getting the correct conclusion is very important.

You will have made a prediction. This could be supported by your results. It might not be supported or it could be partly supported. Your results might suggest some other hypothesis to you.

Your conclusion must go no further than the evidence that you have. For example, tests that show an electricity sub-station produces a magnetic field that can be detected up to 5 metres away cannot be used to say the magnetic field is present further away.

Evaluation

If you are still uncertain about a conclusion, it might be down to the reliability and the validity of the results. You could check these by:

● looking for other similar work on the Internet or from others in your class,
● getting somebody else to re-do your investigation, or
● trying an alternative method to see if you get the same results.

SUMMARY QUESTIONS

1 Copy and complete using the words below:

anomalous   complex   directly   negative   positive

Lines of best fit can be used to identify ...... results. Linear relationships can be ...... or .... If a graph goes through the origin then the relationship could be ...... proportional. Often a line of best fit is a curve which can be predictable or ....

2 Nasma knew about the possible link between cancer and living near to electricity sub-stations. She found a quote from a National Grid Company survey of sub-stations:

'Measurements of the magnetic field were taken at 0.5 metre above ground level within 1 metre of fences and revealed 1.9 microteslas. After 5 metres this dropped to the normal levels measured in any house.'

Discuss the type of experiment and the data you would expect to see to support a conclusion that it is safe to build houses over 5 metres from an electricity sub-station.

NEXT TIME YOU...

... read scientific claims, think carefully about the evidence that should be there to back up the claim.

DID YOU KNOW?

Pythagoras of Samos declared that 'Everything is number'. He believed that everything in the Universe can be explained by simple mathematical relationships. He went on to discover the relationship between the length of a string and the sound it produces when it vibrates.

He developed this idea into a theory that the Sun, the Moon and the planets produced a sort of music that kept them in their orbits!

KEY POINTS

1 Drawing lines of best fit help us to study the relationship between variables.
2 The possible relationships are linear, positive and negative; directly proportional; predictable and complex curves.
3 Conclusions must go no further than the data available.
4 The reliability and validity of data can be checked by looking at other similar work done by others, perhaps on the Internet. It can also be checked by using a different method or by others checking your method.

14

15

SUMMARY ANSWERS

1 Lines of best fit can be used to identify *anomalous* results. Linear relationships can be *positive* or *negative*. If a graph goes through the origin then the relationship could be *directly* proportional. Often a line of best fit is a curve which can be predictable or *complex*.

2 Survey of substations – measure voltage drop – measure 'microteslas' – at different distances from substation – also in houses well away from substations – repeat all readings several times – fieldwork – check accuracy of measuring instruments.

KEY POINTS

● The students should appreciate the process involved from the production of a graph to the conclusion and evaluation.

Answers to in-text question

a) i) Positive linear relationship.

   ii) Negative linear relationship.

H8 Scientific evidence and society

LEARNING OBJECTIVES

Students should learn:

- That science must be presented in a way that takes into account the reliability and the validity of the evidence.
- That science should be presented without bias from the experimenter.
- That evidence must be checked to appreciate whether there is any political influence.
- That the status of the experimenter can influence the weight attached to a scientific report.

LEARNING OUTCOMES

Students should be able to:

- Make judgements about the reliability and the validity of scientific evidence.
- Identify when scientific evidence might have been influenced by bias or political influence.
- Judge scientific evidence on its merits, taking into account the weight given to it by the status of the experimenter.

Teaching suggestions

- **Special needs.** Provide a diagram with the key points in order of discussion so that students can see the process as they are going through it.
- **Gifted and talented.** Students might be able to attend a local public enquiry or even the local town council as it discusses local issues with a scientific context or consider the report of a local issue.
- **Learning styles**
  Kinaesthetic: Role play.
  Visual: Researching data.
  Auditory: Class and small group discussion on possible bias in newspaper reporting of scientific issues.
  Interpersonal: Class and small group discussion on siting of nuclear power station.
  Intrapersonal: Considering the influences on research to personal life.
- **ICT link-up/activity.** The Internet exercise on researching the issue of mobile phone masts in the main part of the lesson is a good ICT activity. This could considerably increase the volume and improve the presentation of data for discussion. Some students may require support for downloading data from the Internet.

SPECIFICATION LINK-UP   How Science Works

Section 10.8

Societal aspects of scientific evidence

A judgement or decision relating to social-scientific issues may not be based on evidence alone, as other societal factors may be relevant.

Students should know and understand

- *The credibility of the evidence is increased if a balanced account of the data is used rather than a selection from it which supports a particular pre-determined stance.*
- *Evidence must be scrutinised for any potential bias of the experimenter, such as funding sources or allegiances.*
- *Evidence can be accorded undue weight, or dismissed too lightly, simply because of its political significance. If the consequences of the evidence might provoke public or political disquiet, the evidence may be downplayed.*
- *The status of the experimenter may influence the weight placed on evidence; for instance, academic or professional status, experience and authority. It is more likely that the advice of an eminent scientist will be sought to help provide a solution to a problem than a scientist with less experience.*

Lesson structure

STARTER

Ask a scientist – It is necessary at this point to make a seamless join between work which has mostly been derived from student investigations to work generated by scientists. Students must be able to use their critical skills derived in familiar contexts and apply them to second-hand data. One way to achieve this would be to bring in newspaper cuttings on a topic of current scientific interest. They should be aware that some newspaper reporters will 'cherry-pick' sections of reports to support sensational claims that will make good headlines.

Students could be prompted by the key word posters to question some of the assumptions being made. This could be presented as a 'wish-list' of questions they would like to put to the scientists who conducted the research and to the newspaper reporter. (10 minutes)

Researching scientific evidence – With access to the Internet, students could be given a topic to research. They should use a search engine and identify the sources of information from, say, the first six web pages. They could then discuss the relative merits of these sources in terms of potential for bias.

MAIN

- The following points are best made using topics that are of immediate importance to your students. The examples used are only illustrative. Some forward planning is required to ensure that there is a plentiful supply of newspaper articles, both local and national, to support the lesson. These could be displayed and/or retained in a portfolio for reference.
- Working in pairs, students should answer question a. They should write a few sentences about the headline and what it means to them. Follow this with a class discussion, building up many more questions that need to be answered.
- It might be possible to follow this article on the Internet to find out what is unsafe about X-rays. It should lead to a balanced discussion of the possible benefits and hazards of having an X-ray.
- Use the next section to illustrate the possibility of bias in reporting science. Again use small group discussions followed by whole class plenary.

- If you have access to the Internet for the whole class, then it is worth pursuing the issue of mobile phone masts in relation to their political significance. Pose the question: 'What would happen to the economy of this country if it was discovered that mobile phone masts were dangerous?' Would different people come together to suppress that information? Should they be allowed to suppress scientific evidence? Stress that there is no such evidence, yet people have that fear. Why do they have that fear? Should scientists have the task of reducing that fear to proper proportions? There is much to discuss.

- Small groups can imagine that they are preparing a case against the siting of a nuclear power station close to their village. They could be given data that relates to pollution levels from similar power stations. Up-to-date data can be obtained from many websites. Students could be given the data as if it were information provided at a public enquiry for the nuclear power station. They should be asked to prepare a case that questions, e.g., the reliability and the validity of the data.

ACTIVITY & EXTENSION

Students could role play a public enquiry. They could be given roles and asked to prepare a case for homework. The data should be available to them so that they all know the arguments before preparing their case. Possible link here with the English department. This activity could be allocated as a homework exercise

PLENARIES

Group report – Groups should report their findings on the nuclear power station case to the class. (10 minutes)

Scientific data posters – Groups could prepare posters that use scientific data to present their case for or against any of the developments discussed. (10–15 minutes)

KEY POINTS

- The students should show in discussions that they can apply the skills developed in their own investigative work to scientific evidence generated by professional scientists.

HOW SCIENCE WORKS

H8 — Scientific evidence and society

LEARNING OBJECTIVES

1 How can science encourage people to have faith in its research?
2 How might bias affect people's judgement of science?
3 Can politics influence judgements about science?
4 Do you have to be a professor to be believed?

Now you have reached a conclusion about a piece of scientific research. So what is next? If it is pure research then your fellow scientists will want to look at it very carefully. If it affects the lives of ordinary people then society will also want to examine it closely.

You can help your cause by giving a balanced account of what you have found out. It is much the same as any argument you might have. If you make ridiculous claims then nobody will believe anything you have to say.

Be open and honest. If you only tell part of the story then someone will want to know why! Equally, if somebody is only telling you part of the truth, you cannot be confident with anything they say.

a) 'X-rays are safe, but should be limited' is the headline in an American newspaper. What information is missing? Is it important?

You must be on the lookout for people who might be biased when representing scientific evidence. Some scientists are paid by companies to do research. When you are told that a certain product is harmless, just check out who is telling you.

b) Suppose you wanted to know about safe levels of noise at work. Would you ask the scientist who helped to develop the machinery or a scientist working in the local university? What questions would you ask, so that you could make a valid judgement?

MOBILE PHONE TUMOUR RISK?

Swedish researchers found that the risk of developing an ear tumour increased if you used a mobile phone. The study was of 750 people. This type of tumour affects one in 100,000 people and the risk increased four times if you used the phone for more than 10 years.

We also have to be very careful in reaching judgements according to who is presenting scientific evidence to us. For example, if the evidence might provoke public or political problems, then it might be played down.

Equally others might want to exaggerate the findings. They might make more of the results than the evidence suggests. Take as an example the siting of mobile phone masts. Local people may well present the same data in a totally different way from those with a wider view of the need for mobile phones.

c) Check out some web sites on mobile phone masts. Get the opinions of people who think they are dangerous and those who believe they are safe. Try to identify any political bias there might be in their opinions.

The status of the experimenter may place more weight on evidence. Suppose an electricity company wants to convince an inquiry that it is perfectly reasonable to site a wind turbine in remote moorland in the UK. The company will choose the most eminent scientist in that field who is likely to support them. The small local community might not be able to afford an eminent scientist. The inquiry needs to be carried out very carefully to make a balanced judgement.

VILLAGERS PROTEST AGAINST WIND FARM

There was considerable local opposition from local villagers to building a wind farm near the A14 road in Cambridgeshire. Planners turned down the application after seven months of protests by local residents. Some described it as being like 16 football pitches rotating in the sky. Others were concerned at the effect on the value of their houses. Friends of the Earth were, in principle, in favour. The wind farm company said that it would provide energy for 20,000 homes.

SUMMARY QUESTIONS

1 Copy and complete using the words below:

    status   balanced   bias   political

Evidence from scientific investigations should be given in a ...... way. It must be checked for any ...... from the experimenter.
Evidence can be given too little or too much weight if it is of ...... significance.
The ...... of the experimenter is likely to influence people in their judgement of the evidence.

2 Collect some newspaper articles to show how scientific evidence is used. Discuss in groups whether these articles are honest and fair representations of the science. Consider whether they carry any bias.

3 Extract from BBC web site about Sizewell nuclear power station:

'A radioactive leak can have devastating results but one small pill could protect you. "Inside out" reveals how for the first time these life-saving pills will be available to families living close to the Sizewell nuclear power station.'

Suppose you were living near Sizewell power station. Who would you trust to tell you whether these pills would protect you from radiation? Who wouldn't you trust?

How science works

DID YOU KNOW?

A scientist who rejected the idea of a causal link between smoking and lung cancer was later found to be being paid by a tobacco company.

KEY POINTS

1 Scientific evidence must be presented in a balanced way that points out clearly how reliable and valid the evidence is.
2 The evidence must not contain any bias from the experimenter.
3 The evidence must be checked to appreciate whether there has been any political influence.
4 The status of the experimenter can influence the weight placed on the evidence.

16   17

SUMMARY ANSWERS

1 Evidence from scientific investigations should be given in a *balanced* way. It must be checked for any *bias* from the experimenter. Evidence can be given too little or too much weight if it is of *political* significance. The *status* of the experimenter is likely to influence people in their judgement of the evidence.

2 Identification of any bias in reports.

3 Should be independent. Should have the necessary skills as a scientist. Should not be capable of being influenced politically.

Answers to in-text questions

a) E.g. what level of X-rays are safe?; if they are safe why should they be limited?; what evidence is there?; what is meant by limited?; who did the research?

b) Scientist in the local university; e.g. did she repeat her tests?; did she get someone else to repeat them?; what instruments were used?; what was the sensitivity of the instruments?; how were the readings of noise level taken?

c) Identification of any political bias, this could be from companies and individuals as well as governments.

H9

How is science used for everybody's benefit?

Note that if there are particular difficulties with teaching this context of science then equivalent work can be located in the Chemistry and Biology books.

ACTIVITY & EXTENSION

You could visit a local museum to see how local industry might have used science for its technologies. Check with your trips coordinator and LEA for guidance.

SPECIFICATION LINK-UP   How Science Works

Section 10.8 continued

- *Scientific knowledge gained through investigations can be the basis for technological developments.*
- *Scientific and technological developments offer different opportunities for exploitation to different groups of people.*
- *The uses of science and technology developments can raise ethical, social, economic and environmental issues.*
- *Decisions are made by individuals and by society on issues relating to science and technology.*

Section 10.9

Limitations of scientific evidence

Science can help us in many ways but it cannot supply all the answers.

We are still finding out about things and developing our scientific knowledge. There are some questions that we cannot answer, maybe because we do not have enough reliable and valid evidence.

And there are some questions that science cannot answer at all. These tend to be questions where beliefs and opinions are important or where we cannot collect reliable and valid scientific evidence.

Lesson structure

STARTER

Technological development Part 1 – Choose a technological development where students can appreciate the science that underpins its operation. Your choice will be largely based on the students' level of scientific knowledge. Examples might include: a light bulb, a pendulum clock, a thermometer, digital thermometer, resistor, antacid tablets and a pair of scissors. Provide a variety of appropriate pieces of technology to be available, enough for one per small group

Asking students to offer any scientific knowledge that they have related to that technological development can generate discussions. The knowledge can then be evaluated in terms of its importance to the technological development. (10 minutes)

Science as a basis for technological development – Choose a topic that the students have studied from the substantive content or KS3. Or demonstrate a simple phenomenon such as passing a current through a wire to generate heat. Allow the students to generate their own ideas as to how this scientific knowledge could be used to develop a range of technologies. (10 minutes)

MAIN

- Divide the students into small groups and give each group a different technological development. They should be asked to discuss the different uses to which they have been put. They could offer other ideas for which they might not have been used. They do not have to stay with that actual example but can drift into other developments.
- A plenary session in which one of the group reports their findings to the others. Discussions could then include whether these uses were of general benefit or not.
- If any groups come up with novel ideas as to how to make better use of some of the technology, then you could spin the idea of economic development.
- Do any of the ideas raise environmental issues?
- Do any of the ideas raise ethical issues?
- Do any of the ideas raise social issues?

- At this point it might be appropriate to cut to the example of nuclear power stations and radioactive waste in the student book. Students could read through this on their own or it could be read and explained as a class or in small groups with support. It might be appropriate to intervene at points to make sure the relevance of each of the learning objectives is appreciated.

- How the discussion is handled will depend on how the reading was organised. It would be useful to allow small group discussion for questions 3 and 4.

PLENARIES

Technological development Part 2 – Take another technological development, such as a mobile telephone and use it as an example to help the group discuss all of the issues raised by the lesson. (5 minutes)

HOW SCIENCE WORKS

H9

How is science used for everybody's benefit?

LEARNING OBJECTIVES

1 How does science link to technology?
2 How is science used and abused?
3 How are decisions made about science?
4 What are the limitations of science?

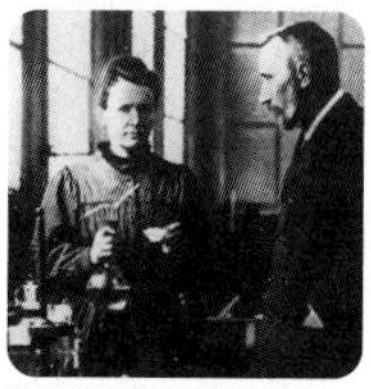

Figure 1 Marie Curie and her husband Pierre Curie

Figure 2 Stamp honouring Ernest Rutherford

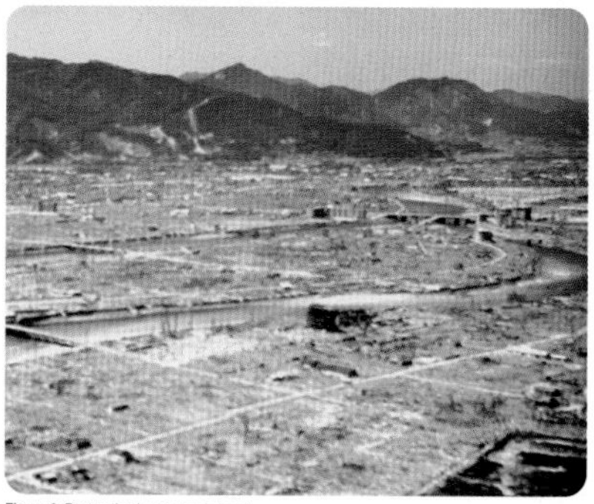

ANTIGUA & BARBUDA $6

In 1896, Henri Becquerel worked in a laboratory in Paris. He noticed that a packet of uranium salts had left a mark on a photographic plate, even though the plate was wrapped in paper. It looked as though light had got in – but that wasn't possible.

He told a young student, Marie Curie, to investigate. She called the effect 'radioactivity'. Becquerel, Marie and her husband Pierre were awarded the 1903 Nobel Prize for Physics for the work they did on radioactivity.

Ernest Rutherford worked on these radioactive materials and discovered that immense amounts of energy could be released from very small amounts of matter. He also noticed that it always took the same amount of time for a particular substance to lose half of its radioactivity. He realised that they could be used to date materials. He investigated radioactivity and demonstrated the principles that led to the development of radioactive tracers and devices such as the modern smoke detector.

Marie Curie continued with her investigations. Because of the reputation of radioactivity, it was used to enhance toothpaste and people would bathe in radioactive springs. Marie Curie eventually died of leukaemia.

Rutherford discovered the atomic nucleus by using his knowledge to fire alpha particles at gold foil and deducing that an atom was nearly all empty space with a small dense nucleus. For his discovery of the nucleus, he was awarded the 1909 Nobel Prize (for Chemistry!)

Figure 3 Destruction by an atomic bomb

Once the structure of the nucleus had been determined, the scientific knowledge was there for many technologies to be developed. By 1940 scientists could begin development of the atomic bomb which was exploded over Japan in 1945.

Some people argue that by using these bombs it shortened the Second World War and fewer people were killed. Others argue that using science in such a destructive way is ethically wrong.

Nuclear power stations now deliver 11% of the world's energy needs. They do not produce carbon dioxide, but they do produce radioactive waste. This waste is likely to be potentially dangerous for many thousands of years.

Radioactive materials are used extensively in hospitals for diagnosis of illness and for curing diseases such as cancer.

There is still a great deal to learn about the atom and radioactivity. There are cosmic sources of gamma rays in space which are being explored by satellites. They were first discovered in the Cold War by US satellites. They thought the enemy were testing nuclear bombs in space. More observations led to the conclusion that the sources are massive explosions in distant galaxies. Who knows what will be found?

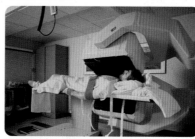

Figure 4 Radioactive tracers emit gamma rays which can be detected by special cameras

SUMMARY QUESTIONS

Use the account of the development of radioactivity technology to answer these questions.

1 What early scientific work enabled the smoke detector to be developed?

2 Describe some of the many different ways in which radioactive materials have been used.

3 a) Identify some of these issues raised by the use of radioactive materials: i) ethical, ii) social, iii) economic, iv) environmental.
   b) Which of these issues are decided by individuals and which by society?

DID YOU KNOW?

If you could release all of the energy you have in the atoms that make up your body, you could explode with the force of thirty atom bombs! Don't ever claim that you do not have enough energy.

KEY POINTS

1 Scientific knowledge can be used to develop technologies.
2 People can exploit scientific and technological developments to suit their own purposes.
3 The uses of science and technology can raise ethical, social, economic and environmental issues.
4 These issues are decided upon by individuals and by society.
5 There are many questions left for science to answer. But science cannot answer questions that start with 'Should we .... ?'

18   19

Teaching suggestions

- **Special needs.** Small groups will need sympathetic support to work their way through these ideas. It might be more appropriate to separate the lesson in two, dealing with the science behind the technologies separately from the issues raised.

- **Gifted and talented.** Students could research their own scientific story and respond to the same issues, e.g. the story of the atom bomb.
  The scientific research that led to an understanding of the uses of electricity led to the technological development of the light bulb. This could be contrasted with the invention of the candle by Egyptians, without prior scientific work. Definitions of science as opposed to technology could be explored. The Egyptians also had weighing scales, cosmetics, inks, locks and, at the time, were well ahead of the Greeks in terms of these technological developments.

- **Learning styles**
  Kinaesthetic: Examining the technology.
  Visual: Observing equipment.
  Auditory: Class and small group discussion on uses of science and technological developments.
  Interpersonal: Class and small group discussion.
  Intrapersonal: Reflecting on the issues related to the use of atomic weapons.

SUMMARY ANSWERS

1 a) Could be some differences which would be fine, e.g. prediction; design; safety; controls; method; repeat; table; results; repeat; graph; conclusion; improve.

2 a) Scientific opinion is based on reliable and valid evidence, an opinion might not be.

b) Continuous variable because it is more powerful than an ordered or a categoric variable.

c) A causal link is where only one independent variable has an effect on one dependent variable, an association has a third variable involved.

3 a) A hypothesis is an idea that fits an observation and the scientific knowledge that is available.

b) As the diameter of the wire increases, the resistance decreases
or as the diameter of the wire increases the resistance increases.

c) A prediction can be tested.

d) The hypothesis could be supported or refuted or it might cause you to change your hypothesis.

e) The theory on which you based the hypothesis might have to be changed.

4 a) When all variables but the one being used are kept constant.

b) Do you have the correct conditions?; have you chosen a sensible range?; have you got enough readings that are close together?; will you need to repeat the readings?

c) If repeat results are close enough together.

d) See how close the actual results are to the predicted results.

5 E.g. was the electromagnet wiped clean after each test?; was the current/voltage kept constant?; was the weighing machine tared?

6 a) Take the highest and the lowest.

b) The sum of all the readings divided by the number of readings.

c) When you have an ordered or categoric independent variable and a continuous dependent variable.

d) When you have a continuous independent variable and a continuous dependent variable.

7 a) Examine to see if it is an error, if so, repeat it. If identified from the graph, it should be ignored.

b) Identify a pattern.

c) That it does not go further than the data, the reliability and the validity allow.

d) By repeating results, by getting others to repeat your result by checking other equivalent data.

8 a) The science is more likely to be accepted.

b) They might be biased due to who is funding the research or because they are employed by a biased organisation. There might be political influences, the public might be too alarmed by the conclusions.

9 a) For many scientific developments there is a practical outcome which can be used – a technological development. Many technological developments allow further progress in science.

b) Society.

SUMMARY QUESTIONS

1 a) Fit these words into order. They should be in the order that you might use them in an investigation.

design; prediction; conclusion; method; repeat; controls; graph; results; table; improve; safety

2 a) How would you tell the difference between an opinion that was scientific and a prejudiced opinion?

b) Suppose you were investigating the loss of heat from a beaker of hot water. Would you choose to investigate a categoric, continuous or ordered variable? Explain why.

c) Explain the difference between a causal link between two variables and one which is due to association.

3 a) You might have noticed that different items of electrical equipment in the house use different diameters of wire. You ask the question why? You use some accepted theory to try to answer the question.

Explain what you understand by a hypothesis.

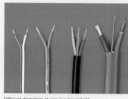

Different diameters of wire in a household

b) The diameter of the wire can affect the resistance of the wire. This is a hypothesis. Develop this into a prediction.

c) Explain why a prediction is more useful than a hypothesis.

d) Suppose you have tested your prediction and have some data. What might this do for your hypothesis?

e) Suppose the data does not support the hypothesis. What should you do to the theory that gave you the hypothesis?

4 a) What do you understand by a fair test?

b) Suppose you were carrying out an investigation into how changing the current in an electromagnet affects the magnetic field. You would need to carry out a trial. Describe what a trial would tell you about how to plan your method.

c) How could you decide if your results showed precision?

d) It is possible to calculate the theoretical magnetic field around a coil. How could you use this to check on the accuracy of your results?

5 Suppose you were watching a friend carry out an investigation using the equipment shown opposite. You have to mark your friend on how accurately he is making his measurements. Make a list of points that you would be looking for.

Student using an electromagnet to pick up iron filings

6 a) How do you decide on the range of a set of data?

b) How do you calculate the mean?

c) When should you use a bar chart?

d) When should you use a line graph?

7 a) What should happen to anomalous results?

b) What does a line of best fit allow you to do?

c) When making a conclusion, what must you take into consideration?

d) How can you check on the reliability of your results?

---

10 a) Increasing the height of the turbine blades would increase the power output.

b) Height of the turbine blades.

c) Power output.

d) 32–85 m

e) Use the same turbine in the same location or the same weather condition.

f) Ensured that the weather conditions did not alter as the investigation continued or bring several test rigs and use them all at the same time.

g) 139 kW is significantly lower than 162 kW and so could be considered an anomaly produced by a random error.

h) Yes there is a difference between all of the readings that is greater than the difference in the repeat readings (anomaly excepted).

i) Correct labelling; correct units; correct plotting; reasonable axes; height on X axis, power output on Y axis.

j) Line of best fit that ignores the anomaly.

k) Positive linear relationship between the height of the wind turbine and the power generated. (Note if they think it is a curve they have probably plotted the 85 m reading as 90 m.)

l) Increasing height has increased the power output. However this was only in the weather conditions at that time and there was some doubt over the 32 m reading, which should have been repeated.

m) E.g. the actual power output is small compared to the visual amenity lost. That the electricity company will want to build them as tall as they possibly can. That the increase in power output is greatest at 32 m so they could be smaller.

n) Independent expert.

8 a) Why is it important when reporting science to 'tell the truth, the whole truth and nothing but the truth'?

b) Why might some people be tempted not to be completely fair when reporting their opinions on scientific data?

9 a) 'Science can advance technology and technology can advance science.' What do you think is meant by this statement?

b) Who answers the questions that start with 'Should we ...'?

10 Wind turbines are an increasingly popular way of generating electricity. It is very important that they are sited in the best place to maximise energy output. Clearly they need to be where there is plenty of wind. Energy companies have to be confident that they get value for money. Therefore they must consider the most economic height to build them. Put them too high and they might not get enough extra energy to justify the extra cost of the turbine. Before deciding finally on a site they will carry out an investigation to decide the best height.
The prediction is that increasing the height will increase the power output of the wind turbine.
A test platform was erected and the turbine placed on it. The lowest height that would allow the turbines to move was 32 metres. The correct weather conditions were waited for and the turbine began turning and the power output was measured in kilowatts.

The results are in the table.

Height of turbine (m)	Power output 1 (kW)	Power output 2 (kW)
32	162	139
40	192	195
50	223	219
60	248	245
70	278	270
80	302	304
85	315	312

a) What was the prediction for this test?

b) What was the independent variable?

c) What was the dependent variable?

d) What is the range of the heights for the turbine?

e) Suggest a control variable that should have been used.

f) This is a fieldwork investigation. Is it possible to control all of the variables? If not, say what you think the scientist should have done to produce more accurate results.

g) Is there any evidence for a random error in this investigation?

h) Was the sensitivity of the power output measurement satisfactory? Provide some evidence for your answer from the data in the table.

i) Draw a graph of the results for the second test.

j) Draw a line of best fit.

k) Describe the pattern in these results.

l) What conclusion can you make?

m) How might this data be of use to people who might want to stop a wind farm being built?

n) Who should carry out these tests for those who might object?

How science works teaching suggestions

- **Literacy guidance.** The externally-set test for every ISA has a question in which the scoring of marks is in part dependent on skills such as presenting information, developing an argument and drawing a conclusion.

- Where students are asked for an explanation, they have the opportunity to write answers in continuous prose and practise their literary skills. Look for good grammar, clear expression and the correct spelling of scientific terms. Question 5, for example, would encourage the development of an argument. Question 6 – how to present data and question 7c) – drawing a conclusion. Questions relating to terms used in How Science Works should allow students to express their understanding of those terms, e.g. question 3a).

- **Higher- and lower-level answers.** Clear understanding is needed for the answer to question 3a) and higher-attaining students would be expected to include reference to the hypothesis matching observations to accepted theory. Lower-attaining candidates should be able to say that a hypothesis is a 'good idea'. The most demanding question is question 9.

- **Special needs.** Students may be able to cope with question 1 if provided with the words on flash cards and asked to assemble them in the best order and with question 4a). Lower-ability students would be generally better served by considering these questions in class where they can have access to support, texts and group discussion. Some of the questions could be altered and put into a context taken from the text.

- **How and when to use these questions**
  - The questions are page referenced and most could be used as summary questions for homework or for discussion and plenary sessions in the lesson.
  - Question 1 is a summary of the design of an investigation and, together with a clear diagram, would make an excellent Revision card.
  - Questions 2, 3, 5 and 8 could be used for class discussion.
  - Question 10 should be prepared for homework and discussed in small groups. It brings together many of the skills that have/will have been learned throughout the course.

Key Stage 3 curriculum links

The following link to '**What you already know**':

- About the variety of energy resources, including oil, gas, coal, biomass, food, wind, waves and batteries, and the distinction between renewable and non-renewable resources.

- About the Sun as the ultimate source of most of the Earth's energy resources and to relate this to how coal, oil and gas are formed.

- That electricity is generated by means of a variety of energy resources.

- The distinction between temperature and heat, and that differences in temperature can lead to transfer of energy.

- Ways in which energy can be usefully transferred and stored.

- How energy is transferred by the movement of particles in conduction, convection and evaporation, and that energy is transferred directly by radiation.

- That, although energy is always conserved, it may be dissipated, reducing its availability as a resource.

QCA Scheme of work
7I Energy
7J Electrical circuits
8I Heating and cooling
9I Energy and electricity

RECAP ANSWERS

1 a) Coal, natural gas, oil.

   b) Solar power, wind power.

2 a) Tidal power.

   b) Solar heating; solar heating uses panels to heat water. They can be heated by the Sun even on cloudy days to provide hot water.

3 a) Conduction.

   b) Convection, radiation.

   c) Radiation.

4 a) When it burns, it releases energy and reacts with oxygen to form other substances. It cannot therefore be re-used again.

   b) It would need to be stored in a large tank, which would take up too much space and be too heavy.

   c) It can be switched on and off easily. A storage tank at home isn't needed because it flows through pipes into the home.

PHYSICS

P1a | Energy and energy resources

What you already know

Figure 1 North sea oil – our reserves of fossil fuels are running out

Here is a quick reminder of previous work that you will find useful in this unit:

- Fuels store energy from the Sun.
  Coal, oil and natural gas are examples of fossil fuels. These fuels were formed over millions of years from dead plants and marine animals.

- We generate most of our electricity in power stations that burn fossil fuels. The Earth's reserves of fossil fuels will run out sooner or later.

- We can use renewable energy sources, such as wind, waves and running water, to generate electricity. Renewable energy sources never run out because they do not burn fuel.

Heat energy is transferred from high to low temperatures. Heat transfer takes place in three different ways:

1 Conduction happens in solids, liquids and gases.
   - Metals are good conductors of heat.
   - Gases and most other non-metals are poor conductors.
   - Poor conductors, such as glass, are called thermal insulators.

2 Convection only happens in liquids and gases.
   - The flow of the liquid or gas due to convection is called a convection current.
   - Convection is more important than conduction in liquids and gases.

3 *Radiation* is energy carried by waves.
   - The Sun radiates energy into space.
   - The Earth absorbs only a tiny fraction of the energy radiated by the Sun.
   - Plants need sunlight for photosynthesis.

Sunlight

Apples

Runner

Figure 2 Renewable energy?

RECAP QUESTIONS

1 a) Which fuels listed below are fossil fuels?

   coal   natural gas   hay   oil   wood

   b) List two renewable sources of energy that do not need water.

2 a) Which one of the following renewable energy resources does not depend on energy from the Sun?

   solar heating   tidal power
   wind power   wave power

   b) Which of the above renewable energy resources is most reliable? Explain your answer.

3 Complete the sentences below.

   a) Heat transfer in a solid is due to ....
   b) Heat transfer in a liquid is due to ...... and ....
   c) Heat transfer through a vacuum is due to ....

4 a) Why is natural gas not a renewable source of energy?
   b) Why is natural gas not suitable as a source of energy for road vehicles?
   c) Give two reasons why natural gas is a very suitable fuel for cooking?

22

Activity notes

Try recording the radio shows on audio or video tape (or with a web camera) for later viewing. The students will put in more effort if they feel that a record of their work is being kept. The tapes can form part of the discussions for later in this chapter, providing a useful opportunity for peer/self assessment. At that point, the students may like to rewrite their scripts in the light of their new knowledge and understanding gained.

SPECIFICATION LINK-UP

Unit Physics 1a

Energy and Electricity

How is heat (thermal energy) transferred and what factors affect the rate at which heat is transferred?

Sometimes we want to transfer heat effectively from one place to another. At other times we want to reduce the rate of heat loss as much as we can. To be able to do either of these things we need to know how heat is transferred and which methods of heat transfer are most important in particular cases.

What is meant by the efficient use of energy?

Many devices take in input energy in one form and transform (change) it to output energy in another form. They never transform all of the input energy to the output form we want, or transfer (move) it all to the place we want. We need to know how efficient devices are so that we can choose between them and try to improve them.

Why are electrical devices so useful?

We often use electrical devices because they transform electrical energy to whatever form of energy we need at the flick of a switch.

How should we generate the electricity we need?

Various energy sources can be used to generate the electricity we need. We must carefully consider the advantages and disadvantages of using each energy source before deciding which energy source(s) it would be best to use in any particular situation.

How long will the resources last?

The students will be aware of the limits of fossil fuel resources, but perhaps not in the uncertainty of the figures which have remained roughly the same for the last 30 years. Ask them to find out about recent discoveries of new oil reserves and how these affect the predictions. They could debate the political and social problems caused by these new found resources.

Checking for misconceptions

The students will already have strong ideas about energy, some of which could be quite wrong. Some common misconceptions that can be dealt with here and throughout the unit are:

- 'Temperature and thermal energy are the same thing'; it can be very difficult to get the difference across. You could discuss or show that a small object at high temperature only has a small amount of thermal energy and that it can only raise the temperature of a larger object slightly. Try placing a very hot metal rod into a cold bucket of water. The temperature will not rise by a measurable amount.

- 'When things are burnt, energy is used up.' The conservation of energy is a fundamental concept in physics, the students need to be encouraged to think about how the energy becomes dissipated (spread out) but is never 'used up'.

- 'Global warming is caused by damage to the ozone layer.' The students need to know that these are two entirely separate problems.

- 'The smoke from cooling towers is pollution.' Lead them to a discussion about the tall chimney where the polluting gases really escape.

- 'Nuclear fuel is renewable.' Because the fuel is reprocessed some students have the idea that it can be used again. They should be told that only a small proportion of the fuel is used before the waste has to be removed and then the *remaining* fuel can be used in new fuel rods.

Teaching suggestions

Finding out what they know

- A good way to check on the students' prior knowledge would be to have them draw a mind map centred on the word 'energy'. Provide them with a template to give them some prompts with main branches labelled 'resources', 'forms', 'heat transfer' and 'measuring'.

- The students could draw out a simple flow chart about how fossil fuels are formed to check their knowledge. There is an Animation, P1a 'Oil formation' available on the GCSE Physics CD ROM.

O Chapters in this unit

- O **Heat transfer**
- O **Using energy**
- O **Electrical energy**
- O **Generating electricity**

P1a 1.1

Thermal radiation

Students should learn:

- The nature of thermal radiation.
- That the amount of thermal radiation emitted increases with the temperature of the object.

Most students should also be able to:

- State that there is radiation, similar to light but invisible, that is emitted by all objects.
- Explain that the hotter an object is the more infra-red radiation it emits.
- Describe thermal radiation as electromagnetic waves.

Teaching suggestions

- **Special needs.** Incomplete diagrams explaining the greenhouse effect should be provided for the students to finish.
- **Gifted and talented.** Infra-red satellite imagery is used in weather forecasting and analysis of land use. These students could investigate how IR satellites are used to monitor the weather and to analyse how land is used in different countries. They could find out how different types of vegetation or habitation show up in infra-red imagery or even other parts of the electromagnetic spectrum. There are many excellent images available to explore on the Internet; they could start with the various 'landsat' or weather forecasting web sites.
- **Learning styles**

    Kinaesthetic: Placing objects in temperature order.

    Visual: Observing IR images and the solar oven demonstration.

    Auditory: Listening to ideas of others on uses of IR cameras and sunlight.

    Interpersonal: Discussing the way heat reaches the Earth.

    Intrapersonal: Making deductions about the amount of energy emitted by an object.

SPECIFICATION LINK-UP   UNIT P1a.11.1

- *Thermal (infra-red) radiation is the transfer of energy by electromagnetic waves.*
- *All bodies emit and absorb thermal radiation.*
- *The hotter a body is the more energy it radiates.*

Lesson structure

STARTER

Seeing at night – Search the web for infra-red images, show them and see if the students can identify the objects. Can the students tell the hot parts from the cold? (5–10 minutes)

Hand warming – Ask students to draw a diagram explaining why holding your hands *in front* of a fire warms them up. (5 minutes)

How can you tell that something is hot? – What ways are there for identifying if an object is hot without touching it? (5 minutes)

MAIN

- Discuss how being in sunlight makes you feel warm while the shade can feel cool. Why is this?
- Discuss infra-red images and how all objects are giving off invisible infra-red radiation due to the thermal energy in them. Link the temperature of the object to the amount of energy emitted.
- Demonstrating the rise in temperature mentioned in the text requires a bright white light source. A sensitive thermometer or sensor should also be used.
- Discuss the meaning of the words 'radiate' (to spread out from a source) and 'radiation' (the energy that is spread) to make sure the students have a full understanding.
- Emphasise that there is empty space (a vacuum) between the Earth and the Sun and that infra-red radiation passes through this vacuum easily, otherwise we would receive no heat energy from the Sun.
- Check that the students can understand or draw a ray diagram showing this information.
- You can use a diagram to show how all of the energy is focused in a solar oven, pointing out that the rays travel in straight lines; just like visible light.
- As a simple alternative, a magnifying glass can be used to ignite a piece of paper to show how high temperatures can be reached.
- A discussion of the greenhouse effect is best presented using a diagram to point out what you mean by wavelength. Two diagrams can be used to link the greenhouse effect with a real greenhouse.
- Check that students do not link the greenhouse effect with ozone; this is a common misconception.

PLENARIES

Temperature order – Show a list of objects or materials (e.g. Sun's surface, boiling water, etc.) and get the students to put them in temperature order. (5 minutes)

Using thermal cameras – Get the students to describe the situations where a thermal camera would come in useful. (10 minutes)

True/false – Show some statements about infra-red radiation and ask the students to hold up cards indicating if they are true or false. (5 minutes)

Practical support

Demonstrating infra-red radiation

You may want to do this as a demonstration if you don't want to coat a lot of thermometers with paint.

Equipment and materials required

For each group: bright white light source (power supply and ray box), sensitive thermometer (to 0.5°C) with bulb painted matt black, clean prism.

Details

Shine the light through the prism and produce the spectrum (this could be projected on the wall if you are just demonstrating). Position the thermometer just beyond the red part of the spectrum and the temperature reading will rise.

Demonstrating a solar oven

Small solar ovens are available and can be used to boil small quantities of water. As an alternative, an old parabolic car headlight can be used. If a match is mounted at the focus of the parabola (this takes some practice) and the headlight is pointed towards a bright light source (such as the Sun or another headlight) the match will ignite.

Answers to in-text questions

a) The water is cooler than the rhino, so there is less radiation from it.

b) The radiation from the rhino reflects at the water surface so the water surface acts like a mirror.

ACTIVITY & EXTENSION IDEAS

Measuring IR radiation
- The amount of radiation produced by a hot object can be measured with an IR probe and a data logger.

Equipment and materials required
Data logging systems with IR probes, 12V bulbs and variable power supplies (or variable resistors) to produce varying currents.

Details
The students could investigate the amount of IR energy produced by a bulb with different currents and so different temperatures. By changing the current through the bulb, the temperature increases and so should the amount of IR radiation emitted.

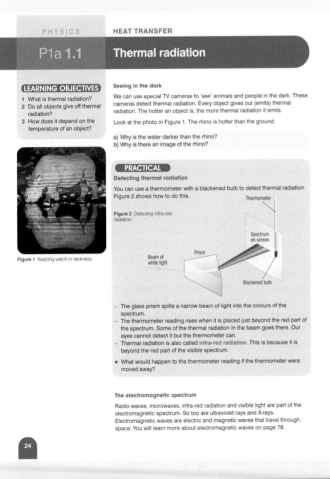

PHYSICS   HEAT TRANSFER

P1a 1.1 Thermal radiation

LEARNING OBJECTIVES
1 What is thermal radiation?
2 Do all objects give off thermal radiation?
3 How does it depend on the temperature of an object?

Seeing in the dark

We can use special TV cameras to 'see' animals and people in the dark. These cameras detect thermal radiation. Every object gives out (emits) thermal radiation. The hotter an object is, the more thermal radiation it emits.

Look at the photo in Figure 1. The rhino is hotter than the ground.

a) Why is the water darker than the rhino?
b) Why is there an image of the rhino?

Figure 1 Keeping watch in darkness

PRACTICAL
Detecting thermal radiation

You can use a thermometer with a blackened bulb to detect thermal radiation. Figure 2 shows how to do this.

Figure 2 Detecting infra-red radiation

- The glass prism splits a narrow beam of light into the colours of the spectrum.
- The thermometer reading rises when it is placed just beyond the red part of the spectrum. Some of the thermal radiation in the beam goes there. Our eyes cannot detect it but the thermometer can.
- Thermal radiation is also called infra-red radiation. This is because it is beyond the red part of the visible spectrum.
- What would happen to the thermometer reading if the thermometer were moved away?

The electromagnetic spectrum

Radio waves, microwaves, infra-red radiation and visible light are part of the electromagnetic spectrum. So too are ultraviolet rays and X-rays. Electromagnetic waves are electric and magnetic waves that travel through space. You will learn more about electromagnetic waves on page 78.

Energy from the Sun

The Sun emits radiation in all parts of the electromagnetic spectrum. Fortunately for us, the Earth's atmosphere blocks most of the radiation, such as ultraviolet rays, that would harm us. But it doesn't block thermal radiation from the Sun.

Figure 3 shows a solar furnace. This is a giant reflector that focuses sunlight.

The temperature at the focus can reach thousands of degrees. That's almost as hot as the surface of the Sun, which is at 5500°C.

The greenhouse effect

The Earth's atmosphere acts like a greenhouse made of glass. In a greenhouse, shorter wavelength radiation from the Sun can pass through the glass. However, longer wavelength thermal radiation is trapped inside by the glass. So the greenhouse stays warm.

Gases in the atmosphere, such as water vapour, methane and carbon dioxide, act like the glass. They trap the thermal radiation given off from the Earth. These gases make the Earth warmer than it would be if it had no atmosphere.

But the Earth is becoming too warm. If the polar ice caps melt, it will cause sea levels to rise. Cutting back our use of fossil fuels will help to reduce 'greenhouse gases'.

SUMMARY QUESTIONS

1 Complete the table to show if the object emits infra-red radiation or light or both.

Object	Infra-red	Light
A hot iron		
A light bulb		
A TV screen		
The Sun		

2 How can you tell if an electric iron is hot without touching it?

3 a) Explain why penguins huddle together to keep warm.
   b) Design an investigation to model the effect of penguins huddling together. You could use beakers of hot water to represent the penguins.

Figure 3 A solar furnace in the Eastern Pyrenees, France

FOUL FACTS
If we don't combat global warming, sea levels will rise. London's sewage system wouldn't be able to cope with this – there would be rats, disease and nasty smells everywhere!

DID YOU KNOW?
Solar heating panels heat water by absorbing solar energy directly. Solar cells turn solar energy directly into electricity. Lots of solar panels on roof tops would reduce our use of fossil fuels. (See pages 66 and 67 for more about solar panels.)
- Why do solar panels in Britain always face south?

KEY POINTS
1 Thermal radiation is energy transfer by electromagnetic waves.
2 All objects emit thermal radiation.
3 The hotter an object is, the more thermal radiation it emits.

24

25

SUMMARY ANSWERS

1

Object	Infra-red	Light
A hot iron	✓	✗
A light bulb	✓	✓
A TV screen	✗	✓
The Sun	✓	✓

2 Put your hand near it and see if it gets warm due to radiation from the iron.

3 a) They lose less heat through radiation when they huddle together because they radiate heat to each other.

  b) Student plan – look for design of a fair test.

KEY POINTS

- Ask students to explain how thermal radiation passes from the Sun to the Earth using a diagram.

- Students should write a sentence linking the amount of thermal radiation emitted to the temperature of an object.

P1a 1.2

Surfaces and radiation

LEARNING OBJECTIVES

Students should learn that:

- Matt black surfaces are the best emitters and absorbers of thermal radiation.

- Silver surfaces are the worst emitters and absorbers of thermal radiation.

LEARNING OUTCOMES

Most students should be able to:

- Describe which surfaces are the best emitters of thermal radiation.

- Describe which surfaces are the best absorbers of radiation.

Some students should also be able to:

- Explain how the choice of a surface colour can affect the rate of temperature change of an object.

Teaching suggestions

- **Learning styles**

  Visual: Looking at the heating and cooling results displayed graphically.

  Auditory: Discussing why objects are painted different colours and the experiment's results.

  Interpersonal: Giving feedback about results.

  Intrapersonal: Evaluating outcome of experiment.

  Kinaesthetic: Doing practical activities.

- **Teaching assistant.** The teaching assistant could manage the queue to test out the Leslie's cube while you move on.

- **ICT link-up.** Use data loggers and temperature sensors for the practical work when possible. These are easy to operate and produce far more detailed evidence of heating and cooling. The students can spend much more time on analysing the evidence instead of plotting graphs for every experiment.

KEY POINTS

The students should be able to write a short paragraph comparing silver and matt black surfaces containing the correct use of the terms 'absorb, emit and reflect'.

SPECIFICATION LINK-UP   P1a.11.1

- Dark, matt surfaces are good absorbers and good emitters of radiation.

- Light, shiny surfaces are poor absorbers and poor emitters of radiation.

Lesson structure

STARTER

Out in the sun – Discuss with students how it feels to go out in a black tee shirt on a sunny day or, alternatively, what it is like getting into a black car on a sunny day. Ask them to explain why they think they feel hotter. (5 minutes)

Definitions – Show the students the key words for this spread (absorb, reflect, emit) and ask them to write down their own definitions. (5–10 minutes)

Polar bears – Ask the students what colour polar bears are and list reasons for this. (5 minutes)

MAIN

- Most students will understand that the inside of a black car feels very hot on a sunny day, so start with these ideas about heating.

- A Leslie's cube is ideal to demonstrate that two surfaces at the same temperature can give off different amounts of thermal radiation. An infra-red sensor can be used to detect levels of IR radiation from the cube.

- The difference is easily felt by placing the back of the hand a few centimetres from the surfaces, but care must be taken that the students do not actually touch the surface.

- Watch out for misunderstanding of the word 'absorb'; many students have the impression that it means that the surface somehow 'sucks in' the energy from its surroundings.

- This spread presents an early opportunity for assessing the students' practical skills. They need to know that these skills are being monitored and will form part of their final grade. Have a poster on the wall to remind students of the criteria.

- You can also introduce some of the concepts covered in 'How Science Works' in this lesson, e.g. the nature of different types of variable, how to present results and evaluating the design of investigations.

- If time is available, and you plan to try both practical activities, then the students should be able to use the same equipment for both. If time is short, then half the students can do one of the practical tasks while the other half does the second. They can share results and ideas at the end.

- After the emission practical, check that the students actually achieved the results you expected; the difference in temperature can be small and it is not unusual to reach the wrong conclusion.

- Discuss how to improve the practical to make it more fair or accurate.

- The second practical works best on very sunny days, you may need to start it early on dull days and leave it running for a while.

- Check understanding of both the absorption and emission practicals and, in particular, correct use of the key words.

PLENARIES

Choosing the right colour – Give the students a series of simple scenarios, such as 'What colour cup should you use to keep orange juice cold on a hot day?' and ask them to give reasons. (5 minutes)

Without words – Ask the students to draw illustrations showing that black surfaces are better emitters and absorbers, without using any words. (5 minutes)

Quick quiz – Try a quick verbal quiz to check understanding of key ideas. (5 minutes)

ACTIVITY & EXTENSION IDEAS

The cooling experiment can be expanded into a more detailed investigation allowing assessment of the students' skills.

A coffee conundrum

A cup of coffee is left for 10 minutes to cool down. Would the coffee end up cooler if the milk was poured in immediately after it was made, or after 5 minutes? (This makes an ideal data logging investigation.)

Equipment and materials required

Two identical cups, coffee powder, milk, kettle and data loggers.

Leslie's cube

The Leslie's cube was devised by Sir John Leslie to demonstrate the importance of surface colour on the radiation of energy. With data-logging equipment, the experiment can be expanded to show that the dull black surface always radiates more energy than the silver one and that the amount of energy radiated depends on the temperature of the water in the cube.

Equipment and materials required

Leslie's cube, data-logging equipment (including two IR sensors and a temperature probe), kettle.

Details

Set up the cube with two IR sensors one 5 cm from the matt black surface and another 5 cm from the silver one. Place a temperature probe into the container and add boiling water (take care!). Record the cooling of the container and the amount of energy radiated from the surfaces over a period of up to half an hour. The students can then analyse the results and reach conclusions about the relationships. If only one IR probe is available, the students can describe the relationship between the temperature and the amount of energy radiated by each surface separately; to save time record some data in advance for comparison.

Practical support

✎ Testing different surfaces

Equipment and materials required

Kettles or another way of heating water. For each group: two beakers, two thermometers (to 0.5°C), aluminium foil and black card, elastic bands (to hold the card on), stopclock, a measuring cylinder.

Details

It's possible to use painted beakers or boiling tubes as in the absorption tests activity below. It is essential to use lids on the containers to reduce evaporation; aluminium foil works well and the thermometers can be poked through it to get a good seal. Higher starting temperatures give greater temperature drops in reasonable times but the students will need to be extra careful with hot water.

✎ Absorption tests

Equipment and materials required

For each group: two coloured beakers, two thermometers (to 0.5°C), heat-resistant mat.

Details

The beakers should be painted in advance; aerosol car paint works very well and is available in matt black, chrome silver and other colours. Two coats of paint seem to work better than one and it is possible to get decent results by substituting boiling tubes for the beakers.

PHYSICS   HEAT TRANSFER

P1a 1.2   Surfaces and radiation

LEARNING OBJECTIVES

1 Which surfaces are the best emitters of radiation?
2 Which surfaces are the best absorbers?

Which surfaces are the best emitters of radiation?

Rescue teams use thermal blankets to keep accident survivors warm. A thermal blanket has a light, shiny outer surface. This emits much less radiation than a dark, matt surface. The colour and smoothness of a surface affects how much radiation it emits.

Dark, matt surfaces emit more radiation than light, shiny surfaces.

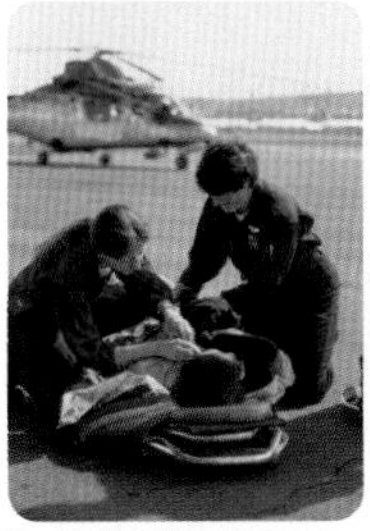

Figure 1 A thermal blanket in use

PRACTICAL

Testing different surfaces

To compare the radiation from two different surfaces, you can measure how fast two beakers (or cans) of hot water cool. One beaker needs to be wrapped with shiny metal foil and the other with matt black paper. Figure 2 shows the idea. At the start, the volume and temperature of the water in each beaker need to be the same.

● Why should the volume and temperature of the water be the same at the start?
● Which one will cool faster?

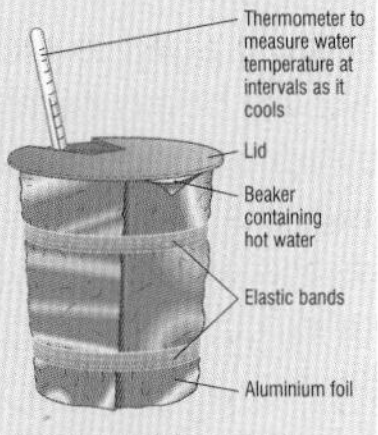

Thermometer to measure water temperature at intervals as it cools

Lid

Beaker containing hot water

Elastic bands

Aluminium foil

Figure 2 Testing different surfaces

Which surfaces are the best absorbers of radiation?

When you use a photocopier, why are the copies warm? This is because thermal radiation from a lamp dries the ink on the paper. Otherwise, the copies will be smudged. The black ink absorbs thermal radiation more easily than the white paper.

● A dark surface absorbs radiation better than a light surface.
● A matt surface absorbs radiation better than a shiny surface because it has lots of cavities. Look at Figure 3. It shows why these cavities trap and absorb the radiation.

Dark, matt surfaces absorb radiation better than light, shiny surfaces.

a) Why does ice on a road melt faster in sunshine if sand is sprinkled on it?
b) Why are solar panels painted matt black?

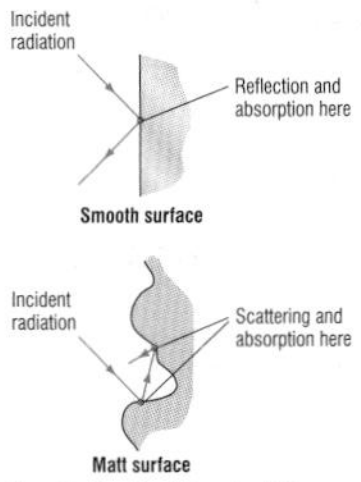

Incident radiation — Reflection and absorption here

Smooth surface

Incident radiation — Scattering and absorption here

Matt surface

Figure 3 Absorbing infra-red radiation

26

PRACTICAL

Absorption tests

To compare absorption by different surfaces, you can use identical beakers with cold water in. The beakers need to be coated with paint of different colours and different textures.

– The volume and the starting (initial) temperature of the water in each beaker must be the same.
– Place the beakers in a sunlit room in the sunlight.
– Use a thermometer to see which beaker warms up fastest.

● Why is it important to use the same volume of water in each beaker?
● Which beaker in Figure 4 do you think would warm up fastest? Give a reason for your answer.

Figure 4 Testing absorbers

SUMMARY QUESTIONS

1 Explain the following:
   a) Houses in hot countries are usually painted white.
   b) Solar heating panels are painted black.

2 A metal cube filled with hot water was used to compare the heat radiated from its four vertical faces, A, B, C and D.

An infra-red sensor was placed opposite each face at the same distance, as shown in Figure 5. The sensors were connected to a computer. The results of the test are shown in the graph below.

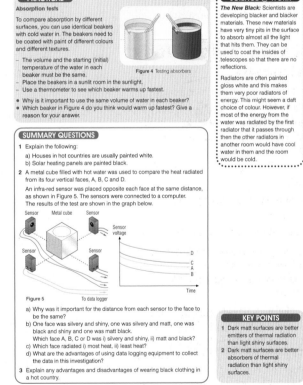

Sensor   Metal cube   Sensor

Sensor voltage

Sensor   Sensor

D
C
A
B

Time

Figure 5   To data logger

   a) Why was it important for the distance from each sensor to the face to be the same?
   b) One face was silvery and shiny, one was silvery and matt, one was black and shiny and one was matt black.
      Which face was i) silvery and shiny, ii) matt and black?
   c) Which face radiated i) most heat, ii) least heat?
   d) What are the advantages of using data logging equipment to collect the data in this investigation?

3 Explain any advantages and disadvantages of wearing black clothing in a hot country.

SCIENCE @ WORK

The New Black: Scientists are developing blacker and blacker materials. These new materials have very tiny pits in the surface to absorb almost all the light that hits them. They can be used to coat the insides of telescopes so that there are no reflections.

Radiators are often painted gloss white and this makes them very poor radiators of energy. This might seem a daft choice of colour. However, if most of the energy from the water was radiated by the first radiator that it passes through then the other radiators in another room would have cool water in them and the room would be cold.

KEY POINTS

1 Dark matt surfaces are better emitters of thermal radiation than light shiny surfaces.
2 Dark matt surfaces are better absorbers of thermal radiation than light shiny surfaces.

27

SUMMARY ANSWERS

1 a) White buildings stay cooler than dark buildings, are better reflectors than dark buildings and they absorb less solar radiation.
  b) A black surface absorbs solar radiation better than a light surface.
2 a) To ensure a fair test.   b) i) D   ii) B   c) i) B   ii) D
  d) Greater accuracy, collects multiple sets of data at whatever time intervals you choose.
3 In direct sunlight black will absorb heat readily, but in shade black will emit heat more readily.

Answers to in-text questions

a) A sandy surface is rough, not smooth, so it absorbs solar radiation more than a smooth icy surface. The sand grains become warm and melt the ice.

b) They absorb solar radiation better than any other type of surface.

P1a 1.3

Conduction

SPECIFICATION LINK-UP   P1a.11.1

- *The transfer of energy by conduction . . . involves particles and how this transfer takes place.*

- *Under similar conditions different materials transfer heat at different rates.*

LEARNING OBJECTIVES

Students should learn that:

- Metals are good thermal conductors because they have free electrons that carry energy.

- Non-metals solids are generally poor conductors because they rely on atomic vibrations to carry energy.

LEARNING OUTCOMES

Most students should be able to:

- State that metals are good conductors of thermal energy.

- List poor conductors or insulators.

Some students should also be able to:

- Explain why metals are good conductors of thermal energy in terms of electron behaviour.

Teaching suggestions

- **Learning styles**

  Kinaesthetic: Carrying out a range of experiments.

  Visual: Obtaining precise results.

  Auditory: Explaining and listening to the outcomes of experiments from different groups.

  Interpersonal: Evaluating the quality of results.

  Intrapersonal: Making a conduction model analogy.

- **Teaching assistant.** The teaching assistant could support students who have physical or coordination difficulties with practical work. It is especially important to keep the containers dry.

- **Homework.** List the materials used for insulation in your own home and where they are found. Why are these materials chosen?

Answers to in-text questions

a) Plastic and wood are poor thermal conductors, so the handle doesn't get hot.

b) The material the rods are made from is the independent variable. The dependent variable is the time taken for the wax to melt.

c) Felt.

d) The starting temperature.

Lesson structure

STARTER

The wooden spoon – Ask the students to come up with an explanation of why it is alright to leave a wooden spoon in a pan of soup when heating it, but not a metal spoon. (5 minutes)

Electrons in the spotlight – Electrons are very important particles used to explain many of the properties of metals. Ask the students to list all the facts that they know about electrons and the properties of metals, to see if they can link them. (10 minutes)

A heat-proof mat – Is a heat-proof mat *really* heat-proof? The students design an experiment to find out just how heat-resistant the material is. (10 minutes)

MAIN

- Carry out the testing rods activity. Adding drawing pins attached to the end of the rods with petroleum jelly, so that they fall off when the jelly melts, gives a touch of drama.

- If you tried the heat-proof mat starter, you could show how slowly the mat conducts by heating a cube of ice with a Bunsen through a mat sitting on a tripod.

- The conduction/insulation practical is a fairly simple concept but is quite fiddly to do successfully. Give the students adequate time to set it up carefully and then get readings (5–10 minutes of cooling).

- The students should be encouraged to make accurate and precise readings during the experiment and this would be an excellent time to introduce data logging as an alternative to watching a thermometer for a long time.

- After the practical, the students should be able to tell you which material was the best conductor and which was the worst.

- This lesson gives another opportunity to cover aspects of 'How Science Works', e.g. the reliability of data collected, the nature of variables and experimental design.

- The poor conductivity of air can be shown by holding an ice cube (in tongs) alongside a Bunsen flame, where it melts only slowly, and then a few centimetres above the top of the flame.

- The concept of free electrons will be unfamiliar to many students. A visual approach with animation is ideal for introducing this concept

- An analogy, such as students staying in their place (representing ions in a metal) and throwing objects to each other (representing electrons carrying thermal energy), can be used with the *right* kind of group.

- After explaining this, the students should be able to tell you what the electrons do to get energy from one end to the other.

- Conduction by lattice vibration again requires clear diagrams to picture this idea. An ionic lattice model (e.g. sodium chloride) can help a lot here.

PLENARIES

A model for conduction – Challenge the students to come up with an analogy for lattice vibration, to give them a visual idea of what is going on. They could come up with holding each other at arm's length and passing a shake along a line. (5–10 minutes)

An electron story – Students describe their experience as an electron in a metal rod being heated at one end. (5–10 minutes)

Acrostic conduction – Can the students come up with an acrostic explaining 'conduction'? (This is quite a challenge.) (5–10 minutes)

Practical support

Conducting rods
Equipment and materials required
As a demonstration: set of metal rods with wax/petroleum jelly on one end (aluminium, copper, steel, brass and possibly glass), drawing pins, Bunsen burner, tripod, heat-resistant mat, eye protection.

Details
- Specialised conduction demonstration apparatus works better than simple rods. Some metal strips have liquid crystal strips mounted on them and can be placed in hot water; this gives a much more visual demonstration and the students can see the temperature gradient through the metals.

- Aluminium's melting point is lower than the temperature of a blue Bunsen flame, so be careful not to melt the aluminium rod. A glass rod can be heated strongly until the glass is red hot and yet the other end is still cool demonstrating just how poor a conductor it is.

Testing sheets of material
Equipment and materials required
Kettles or another way of heating water. For each group: two containers (beakers or metal cans), two thermometers (to 0.5°C), sample materials (cotton wool, felt, paper, foam, etc.), two elastic bands, stop clock and a 100 cm³ measuring cylinder.

Details
It can be difficult to control this experiment because the materials are different thicknesses, and if the materials get wet a lot of energy is lost through the process of evaporation. Make sure that the students take care in lagging the containers and that they are on an insulated base, otherwise much of the energy is conducted into the bench. When carrying out practicals using cans of water, it is essential to use covers as heat loss by evaporation is significant and will affect the results. The experiment works best with hotter water, but this increases the hazards.

Safety: Take care as some objects remain hot for a considerable time.

ACTIVITY & EXTENSION IDEAS
- The insulation experiment can be expanded to investigate the effectiveness of different thicknesses of materials, e.g. are two layers of felt twice as good as one? (Varying the 'number of layers' is an example of an investigation in which the independent variable is a discrete variable – see 'How Science Works'.)

- Why do blocks of cold metal feel colder than blocks of cold wood? Give the students some blocks straight from the freezer and ask them to explain the difference.

PHYSICS   HEAT TRANSFER

P1a 1.3   Conduction

LEARNING OBJECTIVES
1 What materials make the best conductors and insulators?
2 Why are metals good conductors?
3 Why are non-metals poor conductors?

Conductors and insulators
When you have a barbecue, you need to know which materials are good thermal conductors and which are good insulators. If you can't remember, you are likely to burn your fingers!

Testing rods of different materials as conductors
The rods need to be the same width and length for a fair test. Each rod is coated with a thin layer of wax near one end. The uncoated ends are then heated together.

Look at Figure 2.

The wax melts fastest on the rod that conducts heat best.

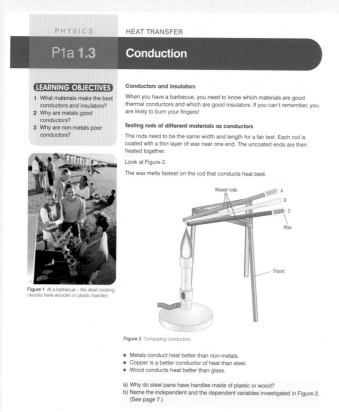

Figure 1 At a barbecue – the steel cooking utensils have wooden or plastic handles

Figure 2 Comparing conductors

- Metals conduct heat better than non-metals.
- Copper is a better conductor of heat than steel.
- Wood conducts heat better than glass.

a) Why do steel pans have handles made of plastic or wood?
b) Name the independent and the dependent variables investigated in Figure 2. (See page 7.)

PRACTICAL
Testing sheets of materials as insulators
Use different materials to insulate identical cans (or beakers) of hot water. The volume of water and its temperature at the start should be the same. Use a thermometer to measure the water temperature after the same time. The results should tell you which insulator was best.

The table gives the results of comparing two different materials using the method above.

c) Which material, felt or paper, was the best thermal insulator?
d) Which variable shown in the table was controlled to make this a fair test?

Material	Starting temperature (°C)	Temperature after 300 s (°C)
paper	40	32
felt	40	36

Conduction in metals
Metals contain lots of free electrons. These electrons move about at random inside the metal and hold the positive ions together. They collide with each other and with the positive ions. (Ions are charged particles.)

Ion Electron Atom

Figure 4 Energy transfer a) in a metal, b) in a non-metal

When a metal rod is heated at one end, the free electrons at the hot end gain kinetic energy and move faster.

- These electrons diffuse (i.e. spread out) and collide with other free electrons and ions in the cooler parts of the metal.
- As a result, they transfer kinetic energy to these electrons and ions.

So energy is transferred from the hot end of the rod to the colder end.

In a non-metallic solid, all the electrons are held in the atoms. Energy transfer only takes place because the atoms vibrate and shake each other. This is much less effective than energy transfer by free electrons. This is why metals are much better conductors than non-metals.

SUMMARY QUESTIONS
1 Choose the best insulator or conductor from the list for a), b) and c).
    fibreglass   plastic   steel   wood
  a) …… is used to insulate a house loft.
  b) The handle of a frying pan is made of …… or …….
  c) A radiator in a central heating system is made from …….
2 a) Choose a material you would use to line a pair of winter boots? Explain your choice of material.
  b) How could you carry out a test on 3 different lining materials?
3 Explain why metals are good conductors of heat.

DID YOU KNOW?
Materials like wool and fibreglass are good thermal insulators. This is because they contain air trapped between the fibres. Trapped air is a good insulator. We use insulators like fibreglass for loft insulation and for lagging water pipes.

Figure 3 Insulating a loft. The air trapped between fibres make fibreglass a good thermal insulator

KEY POINTS
1 Conduction in a metal is due mainly to free electrons transferring energy inside the metal.
2 Non-metals are poor conductors because they do not contain free electrons.
3 Materials such as fibreglass are good insulators because they contain pockets of trapped air.

28   29

SUMMARY ANSWERS

1 a) Fibreglass.   b) Wood, plastic.   c) Steel.

2 a) Felt or synthetic fur could be used, because they are good insulators.

  b) Student plan. Look for design of a fair test.

3 The free electrons that gain kinetic energy diffuse through the metal quickly, passing on energy to other electrons and ions in the metal.

KEY POINTS

- The students should be able to draw a diagram comparing conduction in a metal and a non-metal.

- They should be able to explain why 'fluffy' materials are good insulators.

P1a 1.4   Convection

SPECIFICATION LINK-UP   P1a.11.1

- *The transfer of energy by . . . convection involves particles and how this transfer takes place.*
- *Under similar conditions different materials transfer heat at different rates.*

LEARNING OBJECTIVES

Students should learn:

- How convection current carry thermal energy in fluids.
- How expansion and changes in density cause convection currents.

LEARNING OUTCOMES

Most students should be able to:

- Give examples of where convection currents occur.
- Describe the process of convection in terms of particle movement in liquids and gases, and explain why convection cannot happen in solids.

Some students should also be able to:

- Give a detailed description of convection in terms of particle movement, expansion and density changes.

Teaching suggestions

- **Special needs.** Students could use worksheets with the processes in a convention current mixed up. They can cut these up and stick them in their books in the correct sequence.

- **Learning styles**

  Kinaesthetic: Making convection mobiles.

  Visual: Observing convection currents and visualising particle behaviour.

  Auditory: Explaining the sea breeze.

  Interpersonal: Reporting on the cause of coastal breezes.

  Intrapersonal: Making deductions about particle behaviour.

- **Homework.** Convection currents are very important in the oceans and dramatically affect the weather of the British Isles. Compare London's winter to Moscow's. The students could research the effect of the Gulf Stream and what the weather would be like without it. As an alternative, they could find out about El Niño.

- **ICT link-up.** Use animations to show the behaviours of solids, liquids and gases as they are heated and expand.

Lesson structure

STARTER

Density demonstration – Demonstrate the expansion of a material when heated (mercury in a thermometer, a ball and chain, etc.) and ask the students to explain what is happening in terms of particle behaviour. (10 minutes)

Heat haze – Search a web image bank for photographs of heat haze above a road and ask students to describe what they think is happening. Link this back to the black road absorbing a lot of infra-red radiation and becoming very hot. (5 minutes)

What is a fluid? – The students list the properties of solids, liquids and gases to check their understanding of the particle model. (10 minutes)

MAIN

- Emphasise the fact that a fluid is a substance where the *particles* can move past each other so both gases and liquids are fluid. Because gases have completely separated particles, these can flow faster than liquids.

- Demonstrating the chimney effect with the apparatus shown in the diagram is very helpful. Brown corrugated card produces a lot of fine smoke when it is stubbed out, and the students can see the flow of smoke down the first chimney and up the second.

- If you have convection heaters, you can demonstrate (or let the students have a go at making) spirals of paper hung on string. These move due to the current above the heater. Don't leave big ones up because they can set off motion sensitive alarms in the middle of the night!

- Convection currents in water can be shown using a small potassium permanganate crystal placed carefully in the bottom of a large beaker, and heating gently using a Bunsen burner directly beneath it; the larger the beaker, the better the effect. A glass convection loop is much better than a beaker if one is available. See 'Practical support'.

- The students need to go through the stages that cause a convection current with emphasis on the use of the correct words at each stage. They could label a diagram or draw a flow chart.

- Make sure that they are using the terms 'expand' and 'contract' correctly before the plenary.

PLENARIES

The sea by night – Using the ideas from this lesson, the students can draw a diagram and give an explanation about why there is a breeze from the land to the sea in the evening at the coast. (5 minutes)

Convection loops – Test understanding of convection, conduction and radiation with a question loop game. (5 minutes)

Heat transfer diagram – Let the students draw a mind map linking their ideas about conduction, convection and radiation. (10–15 minutes)

Practical support

Chimney effect

The chimney apparatus is fairly standard, but can be improvised if necessary. The container must have a glass or Perspex front, so that air cannot enter from this route. Point out to students that using a fire with a chimney is the cause of some drafts in houses.

Demonstrating convection in liquids

- The potassium manganate(VII) can be placed at the bottom of the beaker by the following method so that it does not dissolve as it falls:
  Fill the beaker with water. Place your thumb over the end of a glass tube and push it into the beaker so that it touches the bottom and doesn't let any water in. Take your thumb off and, hopefully, the tube will remain empty. Finally drop the crystal down the tube using forceps and remove the tube. Then you should get a perfectly placed crystal.
- With a glass convection loop, the crystal should be placed at the top and the tube heated at the bottom. Don't try to get it in the bottom corner.

Safety: Potassium manganate(VII) is harmful. Its crystals will stain hands and clothing. Handle crystals with tweezers.

Answers to in-text question

a) The water from the taps would be cold.

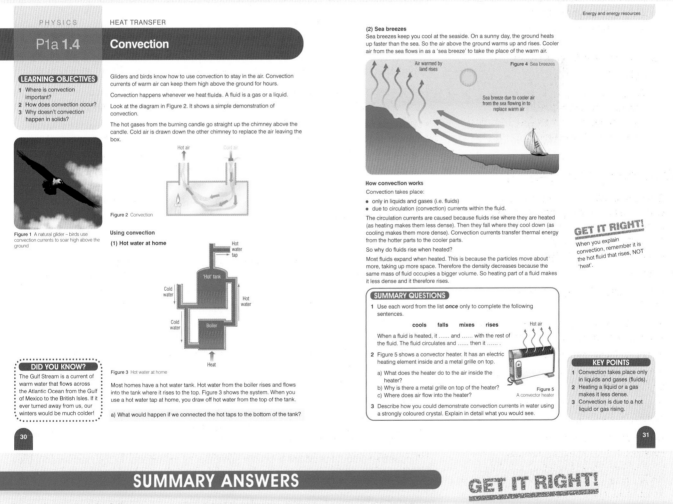

SUMMARY ANSWERS

1 Rises, mixes, cools, falls.

2 **a)** It heats it and makes it rise.

  b) The hot air passes through the grille into the room.

  c) Cold air flows in at the bottom.

3 Drop the crystal into a beaker of water through a tube. Heat gently under one corner. The colour rises above point of heating travels across the top and falls at opposite side of beaker (where density of cooler water is greater). The colour then travels across the bottom of the beaker to replace lower density warmer water that rises above the Bunsen flame.

GET IT RIGHT!

Hot **substances** rise when they expand – don't say 'Heat rises'.

KEY POINTS

The students should be able to label a diagram showing a convection current or draw a flowchart describing what is happening at each stage.

P1a 1.5

Heat transfer by design

LEARNING OBJECTIVES

Students should learn:

- The factors that affect the rate of thermal energy transfer.
- That understanding thermal energy transfer allows us to design ways of controlling the flow of thermal energy.
- How this understanding can be used to reduce or increase thermal energy transfer in a variety of situations.

LEARNING OUTCOMES

Most students should be able to:

- Investigate factors that affect the rate of thermal energy transfer.
- Describe how thermal energy transfer is reduced in houses to keep them warm.

Some students should also be able to:

- Explain, in detail, how the design of a vacuum flask reduces thermal energy transfer.

Teaching suggestions

- **Gifted and talented.** These students should be calculating the volume to surface area ratio of the containers.
- **Learning styles**

  Kinaesthetic: Doing practical activities.

  Visual: Making observations and presenting data.

  Auditory: Explaining the operation of a vacuum flask.

  Interpersonal: Discussing how objects cool down.

  Intrapersonal: Evaluating and giving feedback about experiments.
- **ICT link-up.** Use temperature sensors and data logging software to capture more detail and save time plotting the graphs in the experiments.

SPECIFICATION LINK-UP   P1a.11.1

- *Under similar conditions different materials transfer heat at different rates.*
- *The shape and dimensions of a body affect the rate at which it transfers heat.*
- *The bigger the temperature difference between a body and its surroundings, the faster the rate at which heat is transferred.*

Students should use their skills, knowledge and understanding of 'How Science Works':

- *to evaluate ways in which heat is transferred in and out of bodies, and ways in which the rates of these transfers can be reduced.*

Lesson structure

STARTER

Keeping warm – How could you keep a cup of tea warm? The students should come up with some ideas. (10 minutes)

Cooling down – How can a substance be cooled quickly? (10 minutes)

Famous five – Get the students to name five famous scientists that have physical units named after them. [Newton, Joule, Watt, Kelvin, Hertz, Ampere, Ohm] (5 minutes)

MAIN

- With the students watching, fill a glass beaker and a vacuum flask with the same volume of boiling water at the start of the lesson for later.
- If a radiator from a small refrigerator is available, this makes an excellent prop to discuss how to design an object to give out thermal energy quickly. Emphasise the way the surface area is maximised to allow air to flow and carry away thermal energy.
- You can discuss how a cup of tea can be cooled by blowing over it, although this also involves evaporation.
- Students can investigate the difference in cooling for objects with a large surface area and those with a small surface area, as described in 'Practical support'. You can leave this running while moving on to the vacuum flask demonstration. Others can look at different initial temperatures. All investigative aspects of 'How Science Works' can be covered here.
- Some students will struggle in understanding that the larger beaker has a smaller surface area to volume ratio. Cubic containers may help the students, if some are available.
- Vacuum flasks in various states of construction (without the silvering) can be shown to explain their features. It is important to emphasise that there is no air between the glass walls; show them the point where the air has been sucked out before sealing.
- Show the students the difference in temperature of the water in the cup and the flask to illustrate how good the flask is at keeping water hot. Check that the students can describe what each feature of the flask does to prevent heat loss.
- The students should have little difficulty explaining how heat loss can be reduced in houses and could produce a simple summary of the effects. In the next lesson, they will prioritise which methods to use first based on pay back time.

PLENARIES

Warming up the lab – The students can list or design improvements to prevent heat loss from the laboratory. (5 minutes)

Crossword – The students should complete a crossword based on the previous five lessons. (15 minutes)

How does the flask know? – A vacuum flask also keeps cold contents cold. Ask the students to explain how. (10 minutes)

Practical support

Demonstrating the effectiveness of a vacuum flask

Equipment and materials required
Vacuum flask, kettle, similarly sized beaker, two thermometers.

Details
Fill the flask and beaker with the same volume of boiling water. Put the lid on the flask and allow the containers to cool for as long as possible during the lesson. The flask will keep the water very hot, usually above 80°C, while the beaker will be quite cool. For an even greater difference leave the beaker on a conductive surface.

Investigating the rate of heat transfer

Equipment and materials required
Large (500 cm³) and small (250 cm³) glass beakers, data loggers, temperature sensors, thermometers, Bunsen burners, mats and tripods, aluminium foil for lids, eye protection.

Details
Fill the beakers with hot water and then boil the water with the Bunsen to make sure that they both start at the same temperature. Turn off the Bunsen burners, carefully add a foil lid and monitor the cooling for 10 minutes. The smaller beaker should cool substantially more than the larger one. These ideas can lead to a more complete investigation of the relationship between surface area and cooling.

Students can then investigate if the temperature difference between the water and its surroundings affects its rate of cooling.

ACTIVITY & EXTENSION IDEAS

- Computer components become exceptionally hot and this thermal energy needs to be removed. The microprocessor will have a cooling system and the case will be designed to allow energy to be convected out. You could open up the case of a PC and explain how the cooling systems work in terms of conduction, convection and radiation.
  Safety: Ensure PC cannot be plugged into the mains.

- Sir James Dewar invented the vacuum flask (or Dewar Jar). The students could research the history of this and his other important chemical discoveries.

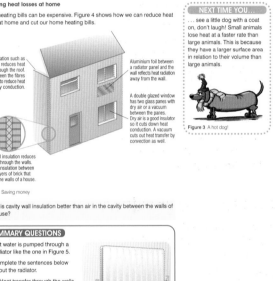

PHYSICS — HEAT TRANSFER

P1a 1.5 — Heat transfer by design

LEARNING OBJECTIVES
1 What factors affect the rate of heat transfer from a hot object?
2 What can we do to keep things hot?
3 What can we do to cut down heat losses from a house?

Figure 1 A car radiator helps to transfer heat from the engine

Cooling by design
Lots of things can go wrong if we don't control heat transfer. For example, a car engine that overheats can go up in flames.

The cooling system of a car engine transfers thermal energy from the engine to a radiator. The radiator is flat so it has a large surface area. This increases heat loss through convection in the air and through radiation.

Most cars also have a cooling fan that switches on when the engine is too hot. This increases the flow of air over the surface of the radiator.

a) Why are car radiators painted black?
b) What happens to the rate of heat transfer when the cooling fan switches on?

The vacuum flask
If you are outdoors in cold weather, a hot drink from a vacuum flask keeps you warm. In the summer the same vacuum flask is great for keeping your drinks cold.

The liquid is in the double-walled glass container.

- The vacuum between the two walls of the container cuts out heat transfer by conduction and convection between the walls.
- Glass is a poor conductor so there is little heat conduction through the glass.
- The glass surfaces are silvery to reduce radiation from the outer wall.

c) List the other parts of the flask that are good insulators. What would happen if they weren't good insulators?

PRACTICAL

Investigating heat transfer

Carry out investigations to find out:
- how the starting temperature of a hot object affects its rate of cooling
- how the size of a hot object affects how quickly it cools.
- Name the independent variable in each investigation. (See page 7.)
- What are your conclusions in each case?

Figure 2 A vacuum flask

Labels on Figure 2:
- Plastic cap
- Double-walled plastic container
- Plastic protective cover
- Hot or cold liquid
- Sponge pad (for protection)
- Inside surfaces silvered to stop radiation
- Vacuum prevents conduction and convection
- Plastic spring for support

Reducing heat losses at home
Home heating bills can be expensive. Figure 4 shows how we can reduce heat losses at home and cut our home heating bills.

Loft insulation such as fibreglass reduces heat loss through the roof. Air between the fibres also helps to reduce heat loss by conduction.

Aluminium foil behind a radiator panel and the wall reflects heat radiation away from the wall.

A double glazed window has two glass panes with dry air or a vacuum between the panes. Dry air is a good insulator so it cuts down heat conduction. A vacuum cuts out heat transfer by convection as well.

Cavity wall insulation reduces heat loss through the walls. We place insulation between the two layers of brick that make up the walls of a house.

Figure 4 Saving money

d) Why is cavity wall insulation better than air in the cavity between the walls of a house?

SUMMARY QUESTIONS

1 Hot water is pumped through a radiator like the one in Figure 5.

Complete the sentences below about the radiator.
a) Heat transfer through the walls of the radiator is due to ....
b) Hot air in contact with the radiator causes heat transfer to the room by ....
c) Heat transfer to the room takes place due to ....

Figure 5 A central heating radiator

2 Some double-glazed windows have a plastic frame and a vacuum between the panes.
a) Why is a plastic frame better than a metal frame?
b) Why is a vacuum between the panes better than air?
c) Design a test to show that double glazing is more effective at preventing heat loss than single glazing?

3 Describe, in detail, how the design of a vacuum flask reduces the rate of thermal energy transfer.

NEXT TIME YOU...
... see a little dog with a coat on, don't laugh! Small animals lose heat at a faster rate than large animals. This is because they have a larger surface area in relation to their volume than large animals.

Figure 3 A hot dog!

KEY POINTS
1 A radiator has a large surface area so it can lose heat easily.
2 Small objects lose heat more easily than large objects.
3 Heat loss from a building can be reduced using:
- aluminium foil behind radiators.
- cavity wall insulation.
- double glazing.
- loft insulation.

32

33

SUMMARY ANSWERS

1 a) Conduction. b) Convection. c) Radiation.

2 a) A metal frame conducts heat to the outside; plastic is a poor thermal conductor so it does not.

  b) A vacuum would not transfer heat by convection, but air would.

  c) Student plan. Look for design of a fair test.

3 Student explanation to include the role played by the plastic cap, double-walled plastic container, silvered inside surfaces, vacuum layer.

Answers to in-text questions

a) To increase heat loss by radiation.

b) It increases.

c) The plastic case, the screw cap lid, the plastic support spring, the sponge pads. They would conduct heat away from the glass container.

d) Cavity wall insulation does not transfer heat by convection, because it is a solid but air would.

KEY POINTS

The students should be able to list the ways that energy loss from a house and vacuum flask can be reduced and explain how the methods work. They could match together cards showing the parts with the effect.

P1a 1.6   Hot issues

P1a.11.1

Substantive content that can be
re-visited in this spread:

- All bodies emit and absorb thermal
  radiation.

- The hotter a body is the more energy
  it radiates.

Students should use their skills,
knowledge and understanding of 'How
Science Works':

- to evaluate ways in which heat is
  transferred in and out of bodies and
  ways in which the rates of these
  transfers can be reduced.

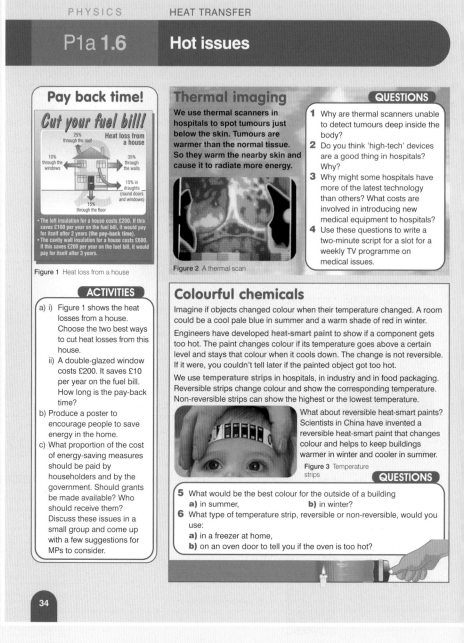

PHYSICS   HEAT TRANSFER

P1a 1.6   Hot issues

Pay back time!

Cut your fuel bill!

25% Heat loss from
through the roof   a house

10%
through the
windows

35%
through
the walls

15% in
draughts
(round doors
and windows)

15%
through the floor

- The loft insulation for a house costs £200. If this
  saves £100 per year on the fuel bill, it would pay
  for itself after 2 years (**the pay-back time**).
- The cavity wall insulation for a house costs £600.
  If this saves £200 per year on the fuel bill, it would
  pay for itself after 3 years.

Figure 1 Heat loss from a house

ACTIVITIES

a) i) Figure 1 shows the heat
      losses from a house.
      Choose the two best ways
      to cut heat losses from this
      house.
   ii) A double-glazed window
       costs £200. It saves £10
       per year on the fuel bill.
       How long is the pay-back
       time?
b) Produce a poster to
   encourage people to save
   energy in the home.
c) What proportion of the cost
   of energy-saving measures
   should be paid by
   householders and by the
   government. Should grants
   be made available? Who
   should receive them?
   Discuss these issues in a
   small group and come up
   with a few suggestions for
   MPs to consider.

Thermal imaging

We use thermal scanners in
hospitals to spot tumours just
below the skin. Tumours are
warmer than the normal tissue.
So they warm the nearby skin and
cause it to radiate more energy.

Figure 2 A thermal scan

QUESTIONS

1 Why are thermal scanners unable
  to detect tumours deep inside the
  body?
2 Do you think 'high-tech' devices
  are a good thing in hospitals?
  Why?
3 Why might some hospitals have
  more of the latest technology
  than others? What costs are
  involved in introducing new
  medical equipment to hospitals?
4 Use these questions to write a
  two-minute script for a slot for a
  weekly TV programme on
  medical issues.

Colourful chemicals

Imagine if objects changed colour when their temperature changed. A room
could be a cool pale blue in summer and a warm shade of red in winter.

Engineers have developed **heat-smart paint** to show if a component gets
too hot. The paint changes colour if its temperature goes above a certain
level and stays that colour when it cools down. The change is not reversible.
If it were, you couldn't tell later if the painted object got too hot.

We use **temperature strips** in hospitals, in industry and in food packaging.
Reversible strips change colour and show the corresponding temperature.
Non-reversible strips can show the highest or the lowest temperature.

What about reversible heat-smart paints?
Scientists in China have invented a
reversible heat-smart paint that changes
colour and helps to keep buildings
warmer in winter and cooler in summer.

Figure 3 Temperature
strips

QUESTIONS

5 What would be the best colour for the outside of a building
  a) in summer,   **b)** in winter?
6 What type of temperature strip, reversible or non-reversible, would you
  use:
  a) in a freezer at home,
  b) on an oven door to tell you if the oven is too hot?

Teaching suggestions

Activities

Pay back time – Have the students investigate the energy efficiency
of the school. They could find out the cost of heating the school and
come up with ways of saving money. The school may even try to
make some changes.

A life-saving invention – It is possible to demonstrate the idea
behind the Davy lamp with a Bunsen burner and a *fine* metal gauze.
Place the gauze above the Bunsen before lighting it beneath the
gauze. After lighting the flame should stop at the gauze; the gas
above does not ignite. You should also be able to light the flame
above the gauze with another match to show that there is gas there.

Colourful chemicals – Heat-smart paints are used in some cooking
pans to show that the pan is hot enough to cook in. If one is
available then demonstrate it to the class.

Extension or homework

Measuring temperature – Temperature sensitive strips are
commonly available and it is easy to use these to measure the
temperature of your forehead.

Research on the safety lamp – Contrary to popular belief, the first
safety lamp was not invented by Davy and he never pretended to be
the inventor. The students could find out more details about the
evolution of such lamps, including the design by Dr William Reid
Clanny.

Summary

The students can make a summary of the methods of energy
transfer and how these can be increased or reduced.

Who am I?

A life-saving invention

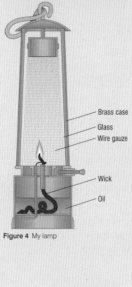

I was already a famous scientist when I invented my lamp in 1813. My invention saved the lives of countless coal miners. Before my lamp, coal miners used candles to see underground. The candle flames often caused fatal accidents. They ignited pockets of methane gas, causing explosions in the mine.

As professor of chemistry at the Royal Institution in London, I made important discoveries about gases. I investigated flames and discovered that wire gauze could stop a flame spreading. The wire conducted heat away from the flame and lowered its temperature so the flame couldn't go through it.

QUESTIONS

7 a) What would happen if the gauze had a hole in it?

b) Why was it important to inspect a lamp before it was taken down a mine?

c) What replaced this lamp?

8 Do some research to find out more about the life of the above scientist. Present the main events as a series of bullet-pointed statements. Colour code those connected to his personal life and those connected to his work in science.

Sir Humphry Davy

- Brass case
- Glass
- Wire gauze
- Wick
- Oil

Figure 4 My lamp

Science and safety

TRAGEDY ON CAMPUS!

Two students were found dead in their flat yesterday. Police said they had been overcome by fumes from a poorly ventilated gas fire. A spokesman for the gas supplier warned anyone with a gas fire at home to make sure that the room is well-ventilated and that the gas fire is serviced regularly.

Gas heaters and boilers need good ventilation. Figure 5 shows how a gas heater works. Hot air and gases produced by the flames rise and escape to the outside through a ventilation duct. Colder air is drawn in at the bottom.

If the ventilation is poor, carbon monoxide gas is produced. As this is lethal to inhale, people can die as a result of poor ventilation. Gas heaters and boilers need servicing regularly.

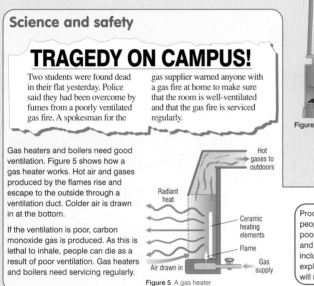

- Hot gases to outdoors
- Radiant heat
- Ceramic heating elements
- Flame
- Air drawn in
- Gas supply

Figure 5 A gas heater

ACTIVITY

Produce a leaflet to make people aware of the dangers of poorly-ventilated gas heaters and boilers. Make sure you include scientific information, explained so that most people will understand.

35

ANSWERS TO QUESTIONS

Activities

a) i) Add cavity-wall insulation to reduce heat loss through the walls and loft insulation to reduce heat loss through the roof.

ii) 20 years.

b) Poster.

c) Discussion.

Questions

1 Thermal energy from a deep tumour would be conducted to the surrounding parts and would not reach the surface of the body.

2 The students should appreciate that the devices can assist with a range of treatments but they come at a cost. Is this money better spent on other things?

3 The hospitals may be part of a research programme, they could be sponsored by manufacturer to test the technology or they could be given extra money by a private benefactor or they could even be charging for its use.

4 TV script.

5 a) White. **b)** Black.

6 a) Non-reversible. **b)** Reversible.

7 a) The heat from the flame could escape, raising the temperature of the methane so that it ignites.

b) To make sure that the gauze was not damaged.

c) A modern flame safety-lamp and electronic methanometers.

8 Student research.

Special needs

Provide a partly completed mind map or spider diagram template for the summary task on the previous page. The template should have the main branches already on and some of the sub-branches too. Make sure that the students understand that they can use pictures on the map.

Gifted and talented

Can a perfect absorber of radiation ever be made? The students could research a 'black body emitter' and find out how a simple box with a hole can be used to absorb all energy that passes into it. They could find out about other objects that absorb all of the radiation that falls on them.

Learning styles

Kinaesthetic: Researching the history of safety lamps.

Visual: Creating a mind map of summary information.

Auditory: Reading aloud information.

Interpersonal: Discussing the costs of medical treatment.

Intrapersonal: Considering how heat-sensitive material can be used.

ICT link-up/activity

It is preferable to measure the cooling and heating of substances with a data logger. This way a complete record is kept and the students have more time to discuss the processes of energy transfer.

There are plenty of opportunities to use the Internet for research purposes. Students should have a clear goal to this research; perhaps a 3 minute talk or presentation on the topic.

1 a) It absorbs solar radiation more easily than a smooth shiny surface does.

b) A smooth shiny surface is better because it would not get as hot in sunlight.

c) It absorbs solar radiation better and the water gets hotter than with any other surface.

d) A matt black surface is a better emitter of radiation than any other surface.

2 a) Electrons, collide.

b) Ions, vibrate.

3 a) By conduction through the plate.

b) The larger the surface area, the greater the heat loss due to radiation and convection from the plate. This stops the metal plate and the component becoming too hot.

4 a) Convection. **b)** Radiation.
c) Conduction. **d)** Radiation.

Summary teaching suggestions

- Use these questions to get an overview of thermal energy transfer. The students should have a sound grasp of the mechanisms of conduction, convection and radiation and which is important in any particular medium.

- For question 1, the students should be using the terms 'absorption' and 'emission' correctly.

- The answers to question 3 should allow you to go back over the idea that increasing the surface area increases the rate of heat loss. Discuss the design of radiators in general. These are designed to maximise surface area and so increase the rate of thermal energy transfer.

- Question 4 should allow you to check that the students realise that there can be more than one mechanism working at once; some will think that water cannot conduct thermal energy and this misconception should be corrected.

1 a) Why does a matt surface in sunshine get hotter than a shiny surface?

b) What type of surface is better for a flat roof – a matt dark surface or a smooth shiny surface? Explain your answer.

c) A solar heating panel is used to heat water. Why is its top surface painted matt black?

d) Why is a car radiator painted matt black?

2 Choose the correct word from the list for each of the four spaces in the sentences below.

collide   electrons   ions   vibrate

a) Heat transfer in a metal is due to particles called ...... moving about freely inside the metal. They transfer energy when they ...... with each other.

b) Heat transfer in a non-metallic solid is due to particles called ...... inside the non-metal. They transfer energy because they ....

3 A heat sink is a metal plate or clip fixed to an electronic component to stop it overheating.

a) When the component becomes hot, how does heat transfer from where it is in contact with the plate to the rest of the plate?

b) Why does the plate have a large surface area?

4 Complete each of the sentences using words from the list below.

conduction   convection   radiation

a) ...... cannot happen in a solid or through a vacuum.

b) Heat transfer from the Sun is due to ....

c) When a metal rod is heated at one end, heat transfer due to ...... takes place in the rod.

d) ...... is energy transfer by electromagnetic waves.

1 The transfer of thermal energy through space from the Sun to the Earth is by
A Conduction
B Convection
C Condensation
D Radiation (1)

2 Infra-red radiation is absorbed, reflected and emitted to different extents by different surfaces. Which of the following statements best applies to **dark, matt** surfaces?
A They are good emitters of infra-red radiation.
B They are good reflectors of infra-red radiation.
C They are poor absorbers of infra-red radiation.
D They are poor emitters of infra-red radiation. (1)

3 The diagram shows water being heated in a saucepan on a hotplate.
Match words from the list with the numbers **1** to **4** in the sentences.
A conduction
B convection
C radiation
D insulator

Heat energy is transferred through the base of the saucepan by ......**1**......
Heat energy is transferred through the water in the saucepan by ......**2**......
Some energy is transferred from the hotplate to the air by ......**3**......
The handle of the saucepan is made from wood because wood is a good ......**4**....... (4)

4 The diagram shows some ways of reducing energy loss from a house.

EXAM-STYLE ANSWERS

1 D *(1 mark)*

2 A *(1 mark)*

3 1 Conduction
2 Convection
3 Radiation
4 Insulator *(1 mark each)*

4 a) C
b) A
c) D
d) A *(1 mark each)*

5 a) Its surface area (size). *(1 mark)*
Its temperature (how hot it is). *(1 mark)*

b) Shiny surfaces are poor radiators (emitters). *(1 mark)*
So the potatoes cool more slowly (stay hot for longer). *(1 mark)*

c) The potatoes would cool more quickly *(1 mark)* (their temperature falls faster) because black surfaces are good radiators (emitters). *(1 mark)*

d) i) Heat energy is transferred from the outside of the potato to the inside by conduction. *(1 mark)*
The potato is mainly water and water is a poor thermal conductor. *(1 mark)*
ii) The metal skewer is a good thermal conductor and conducts heat into the centre of the potato *(1 mark)* so it cooks more quickly. *(1 mark)*

The table shows the cost of fitting, and the annual savings on energy bills, for different methods of reducing energy loss from a house.

Method of reducing energy loss	Cost of fitting	Annual saving
Cavity wall insulation	£800	£100
Double glazing	£4000	£80
Draught proofing	£60	£60
Loft insulation	£300	£60

(a) Which method pays for itself in the shortest time?

    A cavity wall insulation   B double glazing

    C draught proofing   D loft insulation   (1)

(b) Which method reduces energy loss by the greatest amount?

    A cavity wall insulation   B double glazing

    C draught proofing   D loft insulation   (1)

(c) The time it takes for the saving on energy bills to equal the cost of installing the insulation is called the pay-back time. What is the pay-back time for loft insulation?

    A 1 year   B 2 years

    C 3 years   D 5 years   (1)

(d) Fitting double glazing reduces energy loss by . . .

    A conduction   B convection

    C evaporation   D radiation   (1)

5 A cook at a barbecue has baked some potatoes. He takes them off the barbecue.

(a) The hot potatoes radiate thermal energy. The amount of thermal energy radiated by a potato depends upon the nature of its surface. Name two other variables that affect the amount of thermal energy radiated by a potato.   (2)

(b) The cook wraps the hot potatoes in clean, shiny foil. Explain why.   (2)

(c) Explain what the difference would be if the cook wrapped the potatoes in black, dull foil.   (2)

(d) Suggest why:

    (i) the outside of the potatoes cooks before the inside.   (2)

    (ii) some cooks put metal skewers through the potatoes before they put them on the barbecue.   (2)

HOW SCIENCE WORKS QUESTIONS

Tamsin was asked to investigate how quickly different metals conducted heat. She was given four metal rods. They were made of brass, steel, iron and copper. She was told to stick pins to the metal rods, using a jelly that easily melted. She thought carefully about how to do the investigation. She decided to stick the pins to the metal rods and then heat the rods with a Bunsen burner. She would time how long it took for the pins to fall off.

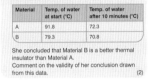

Tamsin is going to need some help getting reliable and valid results.

a) How should she arrange these pins on the metal rods? Explain your ideas.   (2)

b) How should the pins be attached to the metal rods?   (1)

c) How should she heat the metal rods? She only has one Bunsen burner.   (1)

d) How could she make the results more accurate? Explain your ideas.   (2)

e) Tamsin will need a table to record her results. Produce a table for Tamsin.   (3)

f) What type of graph should Tamsin use to present her results?   (1)

g) Once Tamsin has had a go at the investigation, she suggests that you try it to see if you get the same results. How might this show the reliability of Tamsin's results?   (1)

h) In another lesson Tamsin investigated which of two materials was the better thermal insulator. She wrapped a copper beaker in each material, A and B, then filled the beaker with hot water. Here are her results:

Material	Temp. of water at start (°C)	Temp. of water after 10 minutes (°C)
A	91.8	72.3
B	79.3	70.8

She concluded that Material B is a better thermal insulator than Material A.
Comment on the validity of her conclusion drawn from this data.   (2)

Exam teaching suggestions

- When considering surfaces that are good absorbers and emitters, students may be misled by the fact that central heating radiators are usually painted in light colours with a gloss finish. It is important to point out that radiators are painted to fit the décor of the room they are in and not to be efficient radiators of heat.

- Question 4 provides pupils with practice in extracting information from a table. After students have attempted this question it is worthwhile having a class discussion of what information is required for each part, and how it is used.

- Question 4 contains several phrases that require interpretation. Students need to know what 'pay-back time' is and how it is calculated.

- Question 5 will differentiate between weaker and stronger students. All students should be able to answer part a) however parts b) and c) are more demanding and require a more thorough understanding of heat radiation. Expect weaker students to score around half of the marks available.

HOW SCIENCE WORKS ANSWERS

a) Minimum should be that pins on the different rods are all the same distance along the rod. Better candidates might suggest that they place pins at intervals along the rods.

b) E.g. Using the same amount of Vaseline each time.

c) The metal rods should be heated in the same way each time by the Bunsen, i.e. they should be in the same part of the Bunsen flame. Better candidates might consider that they should protect the pins from radiant energy direct from the Bunsen burner, as this would make the results invalid.

d) The procedure should be repeated to increase the accuracy. Close agreement between repeated readings will improve reliability, but can't guarantee accuracy! There might be other ideas, depending on how much detail they have in the first answers.

e) This will depend on how many pins and whether they have repeats, but look for accurately labelled tables and simple layout.

f) Bar chart – categoric independent variable (and continuous dependent variable).

g) Having a second person repeat your investigation and get the same results indicates reliability.

h) Although the results appear to support her conclusion as the water cooled down more slowly with material B, the test was not valid because the initial temperatures were not the same.

How science works teaching suggestions

- **Literacy guidance**
  - Key terms that should be clearly understood are: reliability, validity and accuracy.
  - Questions expecting a longer answer, where students can practise their literacy skills are: a) and c).

- **Higher- and lower-level questions.** a) and c) are higher-level and answers for these questions have been provided at this level. Lower-level questions are a), c) and d) and the answers are also at this level.

- **Gifted and talented.** Able students could consider improving accuracy by, e.g. better positioning of the heater perhaps using a coil. They might consider ambient temperature as an important control.

- **How and when to use these questions.** When wishing to develop sound design of methods. Group discussions could be profitable.

- **Special needs.** The equipment could be put out for discussion.

P1a 2.1

Forms of energy

SPECIFICATION LINK-UP   P1a.11.2
• Energy *can only be transformed from one form to another form.*

LEARNING OBJECTIVES

Students should learn:

- The words commonly used to describe energy in a range of situations.
- To describe how energy is transfered in common situations.
- That gravitational potential energy and kinetic energy are often transferred.

LEARNING OUTCOMES

Most students should be able to:

- Describe in what form of energy is stored in fuels, hot objects and stretched objects.
- Draw simple energy transfer diagrams showing changes in energy.

Some students should also be able to:

- Describe, in detail, energy transfers involving gravitational, kinetic and thermal energy.

Teaching suggestions

- **Special needs.** Provide a list of the forms of energy with examples. The students should add their own later.
- **Gifted and talented.** Are sound and thermal energy just forms of kinetic energy? Get the students to research and explain the links, then decide if we really need to use the terms 'sound energy' and 'thermal energy'.
- **Learning styles**

  Kinaesthetic: Manipulating objects in energy circus.

  Visual: Making observations.

  Auditory: Explaining energy transfers in devices.

  Interpersonal: Debating ways of describing energy.

  Intrapersonal: Making deductions about energy transfers in energy circus.
- **Teaching assistant.** The teaching assistant can work with groups in the energy circus or follow a group that needs particular assistance.
- **Homework.** The students should make a list of the energy transfers that take place in devices at home.

Lesson structure

STARTER

What is energy? – Ask students to express their ideas about what the word 'energy' means. (5–10 minutes)

How can we describe energy? – Get the students to produce a list of the words that they have used in Key Stage 3 to describe energy and give an example of how to use each word. (5 minutes)

Off like a rocket – Show the students a video of a firework rocket (search for 'fireworks' at www.video.google.com). Ask them to draw an energy transfer diagram of what they see happening. (5 minutes)

MAIN

- Fuels are a familiar form of chemical energy and sample fuels should be made available for the students to look at.
- Most students will already be aware of many of the words used to describe energy. Ask them to write out a complete list of these words with an example showing each one. The 'correct' list should be: 'thermal (heat), light, sound, electrical, kinetic (movement), chemical, gravitational potential, elastic/strain, nuclear'.
- Some students tend to think of 'potential' as a form of energy all on its own and not just a way of describing stored energy, e.g. 'strain' and 'chemical' are both potential energy. This misconception should be corrected at this point.
- An apple (or board duster) is a handy prop for discussing gravitational potential energy. They have around 1 J of gravitational potential energy when held 1 m off the floor.
- Dropping something large to ensure it makes a loud noise shows the energy transfer from gravitational potential to sound and thermal.
- Energy transfer diagrams (or Sankey diagrams) are very common and the students should draw a number of them. It is important that they label these only with the correct terms.
- After discussing the forms of energy, allow the students to explore simple energy transfers in an energy circus as described in 'Practical support'.
- Make sure that the students have described the correct energy transfer for each of the devices.
- It is always worth demonstrating the heating effect of a current in a wire. Use a thin constantan or Nichrome wire, and let it ignite a piece of paper on a heat-proof mat. Don't forget to discuss the energy changes in the burning paper.

PLENARIES

Energy links – Get the students to draw a large circle with all of the forms of energy listed around the outside. They must then link the forms together with a sentence form each containing a device that can transfer the first form to the second. (10 minutes)

What's the transfer? – Ask the students to describe simple energy transfers going on around the room, e.g. the ticking of a clock, the growth of a plant or the ringing of the bell marking the end of the lesson. (5 minutes)

One big energy transfer – Ask the students to draw a complete energy transfer diagram showing the transfers that have happened to produce the sound of them clapping hands, starting from the Sun: [Nuclear → light → chemical (in plants) → chemical (in humans) → kinetic → sound → thermal]. (5 minutes)

Practical support

Demonstrating energy transfers

Throughout this unit, the students will see a range of energy transfers. You should challenge them to describe the transfers in each of them using only the recognised terms, avoiding common misconceptions like 'steam energy'. Using many small demonstrations continually reminds the students that all transfers can be described fairly simply.

Energy circus

The students can carry out a range of simple experiments and describe the energy transfers involved. Some suggested objects/transfers are:

- A yo-yo.
- A portable radio.
- A kettle.
- Dropping a steel ball bearing onto a wooden block.

- A dynamo.
- A hairdryer.
- An MP3 player.
- Burning a candle or fuel burner.

More difficult ones are:

- Citric acid solution and sodium hydrogencarbonate. This is an unusual endothermic reaction: can the students explain what is happening? [thermal → chemical]
- A remote-control car: what energy is reaching the car? [radio waves]

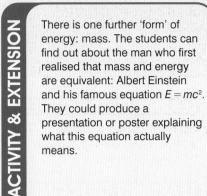

There is one further 'form' of energy: mass. The students can find out about the man who first realised that mass and energy are equivalent: Albert Einstein and his famous equation $E = mc^2$. They could produce a presentation or poster explaining what this equation actually means.

Answers to in-text questions

a) Electrical energy.
b) High speed train (*Train de grand vitesse*).
c) It is lost to the surroundings through heat transfer.

PHYSICS USING ENERGY

P1a 2.1 Forms of energy

LEARNING OBJECTIVES
1 What forms of energy are there?
2 How can we describe energy changes?

On the move

Cars, buses, planes and ships all use energy from fuel. They carry their own fuel. Electric trains use energy from fuel in power stations. Electricity transfers energy from the power station to the train.

Torch

Skier

Microwave oven

Figure 2 Energy changes

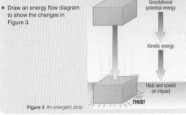

Figure 1 The French TGV (Train à grande vitesse) electric train can reach speeds of more than 500 km/hour

We describe energy stored or transferred in different ways as *forms of energy*.

Here are some examples of forms of energy:

- *Chemical energy* is energy stored in fuel (including food). This energy is released when chemical reactions take place.
- *Kinetic energy* is the energy of a moving object.
- *Gravitational potential energy* is the energy of an object due to its position.
- *Elastic (or strain) energy* is the energy stored in a springy object when we stretch or squash it.
- *Electrical energy* is energy transferred by an electric current.
- *Thermal (heat) energy* of an object is energy due to its temperature. This is partly because of the random kinetic energy of the particles of the object.

a) What form of energy is supplied to the train in Figure 1?
b) What does TGV mean?

We say that energy is *transformed* when it changes from one form into another.

38

In the torch in Figure 2, the torch's battery pushes a current through the bulb. This makes the torch bulb emit light and it also gets hot. We can show the energy changes using a flow diagram.

Look at the example below:

chemical energy in the battery → electrical energy → light energy + thermal energy

c) What happens to the thermal energy of the torch bulb?

PRACTICAL

Energy changes

When an object starts to fall freely, it gains kinetic energy because it speeds up as it falls. So its gravitational potential energy changes to kinetic energy as it falls.

Look at Figure 3. It shows a box that hits the floor with a thud. All of its kinetic energy changes to heat and sound energy at the point of impact. The proportion of kinetic energy transformed to sound is much smaller than that changed to heat.

- Draw an energy flow diagram to show the changes in Figure 3.

Gravitational potential energy

Kinetic energy

Heat and sound on impact

THUD!

Figure 3 An energetic drop

SUMMARY QUESTIONS

1 Copy and complete a) and b) using the words below:

electric   kinetic   gravitational potential   thermal

a) When a ball falls in air, it loses ...... energy and gains ...... energy.
b) When an electric heater is switched on, it changes ...... energy into ...... energy.

2 a) List two different objects you could use to light a room if you have a power cut. For each object, describe the energy changes that happen when it produces light.
   b) Which of the two objects in a) is:
      i) easier to obtain energy from,
      ii) easier to use?

3 Read the 'Science @ Work' box at the top of this page. Explain the energy changes involved in using a pile driver.

SCIENCE @ WORK

Tall buildings need firm foundations. Engineers make the foundations using a pile driver to hammer steel girders end-on into the ground. The pile driver lifts a heavy steel block above the top end of the girder. Then it lets the block crash down onto the girder. The engineers keep doing this until the bottom end of the girder reaches solid rock.

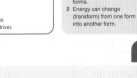

Figure 4 A pile driver in action

d) Where does the energy supplied to the hammer come from?

NEXT TIME YOU...

... ride a bike, think about what happens to the chemical energy stored in your body as you ride along. But make sure you watch where you're going!

KEY POINTS

1 Energy exists in different forms.
2 Energy can change (transform) from one form into another.

SUMMARY ANSWERS

1 a) Gravitational potential, kinetic. b) Electrical, thermal.

2 a) For example: a candle and a torch.
   A candle transfers chemical energy to light and heat. A torch transfers chemical to electrical and then light and heat.

   b) i) A torch is usually more convenient.
      ii) This is a matter of opinion.

3 Mechanical energy is transformed to gravitational potential energy as the pile driver lifts the heavy steel block. As the steel block falls, the gravitational potential energy is transformed into kinetic energy of the block. When the block hits the ground the kinetic energy is transformed into heat and sound energy.

KEY POINTS

The students should be able to draw a wide range of energy transfer diagrams. Give them some incomplete ones to fill in to check their understanding.

P1a 2.2

Conservation of energy

Teaching suggestions

- **Special needs.** Provide partly completed energy transfer diagrams to save time. The students still need to identify the missing energy forms or the device that performs the transfer.
- **Learning styles**
  Kinaesthetic: Manipulating the pendulum and 'bungee'.
  Visual: Imagining the flow of energy from object to object.
  Auditory: Discussing energy loss in transfers.
  Interpersonal: Discussing experimental observations.
  Intrapersonal: Appreciating that energy is not 'lost'.
- **ICT link-up.** Use video capture equipment to record the pendulum or 'bungee' for analysis. Some software can calculate speed and displacement.
- **Science @ work.** Roller coasters are so called because the cars just roll. They are lifted to a great height and then roll along the track without any external power; relying just on the transfer of gravitational energy to kinetic energy and back again. An exciting roller coaster takes a lot of scientific thought to design but not a lot to enjoy.

GET IT RIGHT!

Energy cannot be created or destroyed; only transferred.

KEY POINTS

Give the students a diagram of a simple rollercoaster and get them to label the points where there are energy transfers and where the kinetic and potential energy are greatest.

SPECIFICATION LINK-UP   P1a.11.2

- *Energy cannot be created or destroyed. It can only be transformed from one form to another form.*
- *When energy is transferred and/or transformed, only part of it may be usefully transferred or transformed.*

Lesson structure

STARTER

A plane journey – Ask the students to draw a cartoon of an aeroplane journey describing the changes in gravitational, kinetic and chemical energy. The aeroplane lands back at the same place it took off; ask them where the energy in the fuel has gone. (10 minutes)

Definition – What does the word 'conservation' mean? Ask the students to give examples of its use. (5 minutes)

Where does it all go? – Light a candle and ask the students to describe what happens to the chemical energy stored in the wax. (5–10 minutes)

MAIN

- The topic opens with a look at the transfer of gravitational potential energy to kinetic and back again. This is a common theme in examinations and time should be taken discussing the aspect with plenty of examples.
- Point out that energy is wasted during each transfer, so a roller coaster can never get as high as it first starts out.
- The law of conservation of energy is a very important one and must be emphasised strongly.
- The practical activities may take a bit of time to set up and are fiddly. The students should be thinking about how to improve the accuracy and reliability of the measurements (related to 'How Science Works') but it is unlikely they will think of using the shadow idea on their own.
- Use a webcam to record the pendulum swinging or you can record a video clip of the pendulum shadow in advance and show it during the lesson. If you project this onto a whiteboard, you can mark the heights of the swings as they happen.
- Watch and discuss a video of a bungee jump. Find one at www.video.google.com.
- An animation, P1a 2.2 'Conserving energy: the pendulum' is available on the GCSE Physics CD ROM.
- In most situations, where a system seems to be losing energy, this can be explained by frictional losses producing heat. This is true for both the pendulum and the bungee.
- Check that the students can explain what is causing loss of energy in these systems.
- You can demonstrate that the loss is caused by air resistance by attaching a piece of stiff card to the bob and increasing its drag. This reduces the swing rapidly.
- You can demonstrate the bungee example using a mass on a spring or, more excitingly, with a toy on a length of fishing elastic.
- You may be able to find designs for perpetual motion machines on the Internet along with descriptions of how these may work.

PLENARIES

Make up your own example – Get the students to make up their own example of conservation of energy listing where they think the energy goes. (10 minutes)

Conservation acrostic – Students write a short poem about energy based on the letters in the word 'conservation'. (5–10 minutes)

Measuring the energy in food – Ask the students to design a simple experiment to measure the energy in a food sample. They should minimise energy loss to the surroundings. (10 minutes)

Practical support

Pendulum swinging

Equipment and materials required

For each group: retort stand, string with bob (or 50 g mass tied to end), graph paper and some Blu-Tack to mount it, lamp.

Details

One way to measure the height of a pendulum swing is to shine a bright light onto it and measure the position of the shadow. Position the light so that the shadow falls on a piece of graph paper when the bob is swinging. The students mark where the shadow falls after a number of swings and then look at the pattern in height against time.

Bungee jumping

Equipment and materials required

For each group: retort stand, elastic with mass (or toy tied to end), graph paper and some Blu-Tack to mount it, lamp.

Details

A similar shadow technique to the above activity can be used to measure the height of the bounces.

ACTIVITY & EXTENSION

- Although perpetual motion devices are impossible to construct, a number of people have tried. The students could research these devices and may even come up with an explanation of why they did not work.

- Sometimes we want to get rid of kinetic energy quickly. Students could find out how we slow down planes on landing, or drag racers, and make a booklet or short presentation (this would be good for homework).

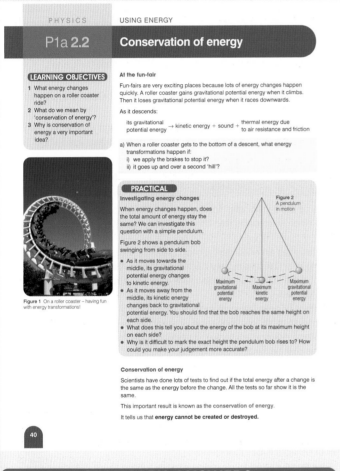

PHYSICS   USING ENERGY

P1a 2.2   Conservation of energy

LEARNING OBJECTIVES

1 What energy changes happen on a roller coaster ride?
2 What do we mean by 'conservation of energy'?
3 Why is conservation of energy a very important idea?

At the fun-fair

Fun-fairs are very exciting places because lots of energy changes happen quickly. A roller coaster gains gravitational potential energy when it climbs. Then it loses gravitational potential energy when it races downwards.

As it descends:

its gravitational potential energy → kinetic energy + sound + thermal energy due to air resistance and friction

a) When a roller coaster gets to the bottom of a descent, what energy transformations happen if:
   i) we apply the brakes to stop it?
   ii) it goes up and over a second 'hill'?

PRACTICAL

Investigating energy changes

When energy changes happen, does the total amount of energy stay the same? We can investigate this question with a simple pendulum.

Figure 2 shows a pendulum bob swinging from side to side.

- As it moves towards the middle, gravitational potential energy changes to kinetic energy.
- As it moves away from the middle, its kinetic energy changes back to gravitational potential energy. You should find that the bob reaches the same height on each side.
- What does this tell you about the energy of the bob at its maximum height on each side?
- Why is it difficult to mark the exact height the pendulum bob rises to? How could you make your judgement more accurate?

Figure 2 A pendulum in motion

Maximum gravitational potential energy — Maximum kinetic energy — Maximum gravitational potential energy

Figure 1 On a roller coaster – having fun with energy transformations!

Conservation of energy

Scientists have done lots of tests to find out if the total energy after a change is the same as the energy before the change. All the tests so far show it is the same.

This important result is known as the **conservation of energy**.

It tells us that **energy cannot be created or destroyed**.

Bungee jumping

What energy changes happen to a bungee jumper after jumping off the platform?

- Some of the gravitational potential energy of the bungee jumper changes to kinetic energy as the jumper falls with the rope slack.
- Once the slack in the rope has been used up, the rope slows the bungee jumper's fall. Most of the gravitational potential energy and kinetic energy of the jumper is changed into elastic (strain) energy.
- After reaching the bottom, the rope pulls the jumper back up. As the jumper rises, most of the elastic (strain) energy of the rope changes back to gravitational potential energy and kinetic energy of the jumper.

The bungee jumper doesn't return to the same height as at the start. This is because some of the initial gravitational potential energy has been changed to heat energy as the rope stretched then shortened again.

b) What happens to the gravitational potential energy lost by the bungee jumper?
c) Draw a flow diagram to show the energy changes.

Figure 3 Bungee jumping

PRACTICAL

Bungee jumping

You can try out the ideas about bungee jumping using the experiment shown in Figure 4.

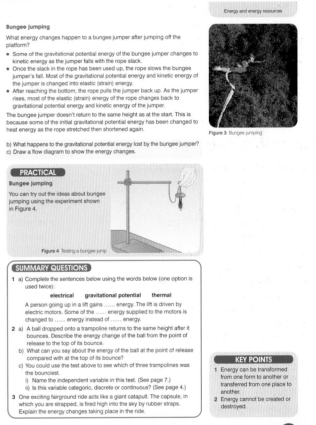

Figure 4 Testing a bungee jump

SUMMARY QUESTIONS

1 a) Complete the sentences below using the words below (one option is used twice):

   electrical   gravitational potential   thermal

   A person going up in a lift gains ...... energy. The lift is driven by electric motors. Some of the ...... energy supplied to the motors is changed to ...... energy instead of ...... energy.

2 a) A ball dropped onto a trampoline returns to the same height after it bounces. Describe the energy change of the ball from the point of release to the top of its bounce.
   b) What can you say about the energy of the ball at the point of release compared with at the top of its bounce?
   c) You could use the test above to see which of three trampolines was the bounciest.
      i) Name the independent variable in this test. (See page 7.)
      ii) Is this variable categoric, discrete or continuous? (See page 4.)

3 One exciting fairground ride acts like a giant catapult. The capsule, in which you are strapped, is fired high into the sky by rubber straps. Explain the energy changes taking place in the ride.

KEY POINTS

1 Energy can be transformed from one form to another or transferred from one place to another.
2 Energy cannot be created or destroyed.

40   41

SUMMARY ANSWERS

1 a) Gravitational potential, electrical, thermal, gravitational potential.

2 a) **On descent:** Gravitational potential energy → kinetic energy + thermal energy due to air resistance.
   On impact: Kinetic energy → elastic energy of trampoline + thermal energy due to impact + sound.
   On ascent: Elastic energy of trampoline → kinetic energy → gravitational potential energy + thermal energy due to air resistance.

   b) The ball has less energy at the top of its bounce than at the point of release.

   c) i) Type of trampoline.   ii) Categoric.

3 Elastic energy of the rubber straps is transformed into kinetic energy of the capsule. This kinetic energy is transformed into gravitational potential energy as the capsule rises to the top of its flight, etc. as in bungee jumper on page 41 in Student Book.

Answers to in-text questions

a) i) Kinetic energy changes to thermal energy in the brakes and thermal energy of the surroundings.

   ii) Kinetic energy changes to gravitational potential energy as it climbs the hill. The gravitational potential energy changes back to kinetic energy as it descends. Thermal energy of the surroundings due to air resistance and friction is produced throughout.

   Repeat several times (or use an electronic method of recording the highest position of the bob).

b) It is transformed by air resistance to thermal energy of the surroundings.

c)

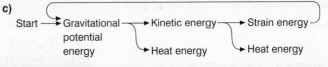

Start → Gravitational potential energy → Kinetic energy → Strain energy

Gravitational potential energy → Heat energy   Kinetic energy → Heat energy

P1a 2.3

Useful energy

LEARNING OBJECTIVES

Students should learn:

- That thermal energy is lost to the surroundings in energy transfers.
- That this 'wasted' thermal energy is no longer of use.

LEARNING OUTCOMES

Most students should be able to:

- Identify useful and wasted energy in transfers.
- Describe how friction is the cause of much wasted energy.
- Understand that energy that escapes to the surrounding as heat is not available for other energy transfers and so is useless.

Teaching suggestions

- **Gifted and talented.** What really causes frictional forces? Very smooth surfaces often produce larger frictional effects than rougher ones. Can the students come up with a detailed explanation of what is going on?

- **Learning styles**
  Kinaesthetic: Practical tasks.
  Visual: Observing frictional effects and recording experimental data.
  Auditory: Explaining the cause of friction.
  Interpersonal: Evaluating experimental technique.
  Intrapersonal: Evaluating experimental technique.

- **Homework**
  - The students can find details about surfaces. They should be able to find the most slippery surface in the world and possibly close-up pictures of different surfaces.
  - They could list other devices and decide on the useful and wasted energy.

SPECIFICATION LINK-UP   P1a.11.2

- *When energy is transferred and/or transformed only part of it may be usefully transferred/transformed.*
- *Energy which is not transferred/transformed in a useful way is 'wasted'.*
- *Both wasted energy and the energy which is usefully transferred/transformed are eventually transferred to their surroundings, which become warmer.*
- *Energy becomes increasingly spread out and becomes increasingly more difficult to use for further energy transformations.*

Lesson structure

STARTER

Useful or useless? – Show energy transfer diagrams and ask the students to identify the useful energy outputs and the useless ones in each case. Try some trick ones. (5–10 minutes)

Friction revision – Why do snooker balls stop rolling after being hit? Get the students to describe the ways that the initial kinetic energy is lost. (5 minutes)

Overheating – Ask students to explain why humans become hot when they work hard. How is this excess heat removed from the body? Why do we need to eat less in hot weather? (10 minutes)

MAIN

- In this unit avoid the use of the terms 'lost' for energy if possible; it implies that the energy disappears. The energy spreads into the surroundings and becomes useless or 'wasted'.
- A video clip of a car performing an emergency stop (search www.video.google.com or www.britishpathe.com) is an excellent way of getting the students to understand that the kinetic energy of a car has to go somewhere when it stops. A dramatic one with burning rubber works best.
- The technology department should have an electric drill and some scrap wood. With poor drilling technique (don't push into the wood; instead allow the bit to rub the sides) you should be able to get some smoke to show the heating effect. Sneakily putting a dab of oil on the drill bit seems to help too.
- Frictional effects are best explained using simple diagrams or animations. The surfaces rub or catch on each other and this rubbing causes heating. You can show the roughness of 'smooth' surfaces with micrographs or even electron micrographs.
- Rubbing two metal blocks across each other will show frictional heating. Adding oil should make the movement smoother.
- Check that the students understand that friction causes heating because of the forces between the surfaces of objects rubbing together.
- The students need to be encouraged to describe exactly where there is friction in a device. They should know about air resistance, drag in water, friction of surfaces in contact and around a pivot.
- If you have an exercise bicycle in the school, then this can be used to show the heating effect on the brake blocks. You could also put oil on the blocks to show that this reduces the friction and makes it harder to stop the wheel turning. An Animation, P1a 2.3 'Disk brakes on a car' is available on the GCSE Physics CD ROM.

PLENARIES

What's wrong? – Ask the students to correct this sentence 'When a car stops at traffic lights, the speed energy is destroyed by the brakes and is lost' [or similar]. (5 minutes)

Sticky problems – Get students to draw up a table of the ways friction can be reduced and give examples of exactly where this happens. (5 minutes)

Removing the heat – A car engine has many moving parts and produces a lot of heat. Get the students to describe how the friction is reduced and to think back and describe how that wasted energy is transferred to the surroundings. (10 minutes)

Practical support

Investigating friction

Many students will have looked into friction before, but you may wish to look in more detail here. The focus should be on improving the technique focusing on the accuracy and precision concepts of the specification (this relates to 'How Science Works').

Equipment and materials required

For each group: string, pulley, clamp, 10 × 50 g masses, 1 kg mass (with hoop), three different surfaces to test (desk surface, carpet tiles, rubber mat).

Details

The students place the 1 kg mass on the surfaces and attach it to a mass holder hanging over the desk via the pulley. The students then find out what mass is required to start the 1 kg sliding across the surface. To improve the accuracy of the measurements, encourage them to add smaller masses when they get near to the sliding point of the mass, so several runs will be required. The students may find out that their mats or carpet tiles start to move before the mass, so will need some tape or Blu-Tack to hold it in place. How does this work?

Safety: Protect floor from falling weights and keep feet clear.

ACTIVITY & EXTENSION IDEAS

It took scientists some time to come up with ideas about thermal energy, friction and work. The students could look into the concepts of 'phlogiston' and then 'caloric' to explain heating effects. These are fairly complex ideas; the students need to be careful that they don't confuse them with the more modern concept of thermal energy.

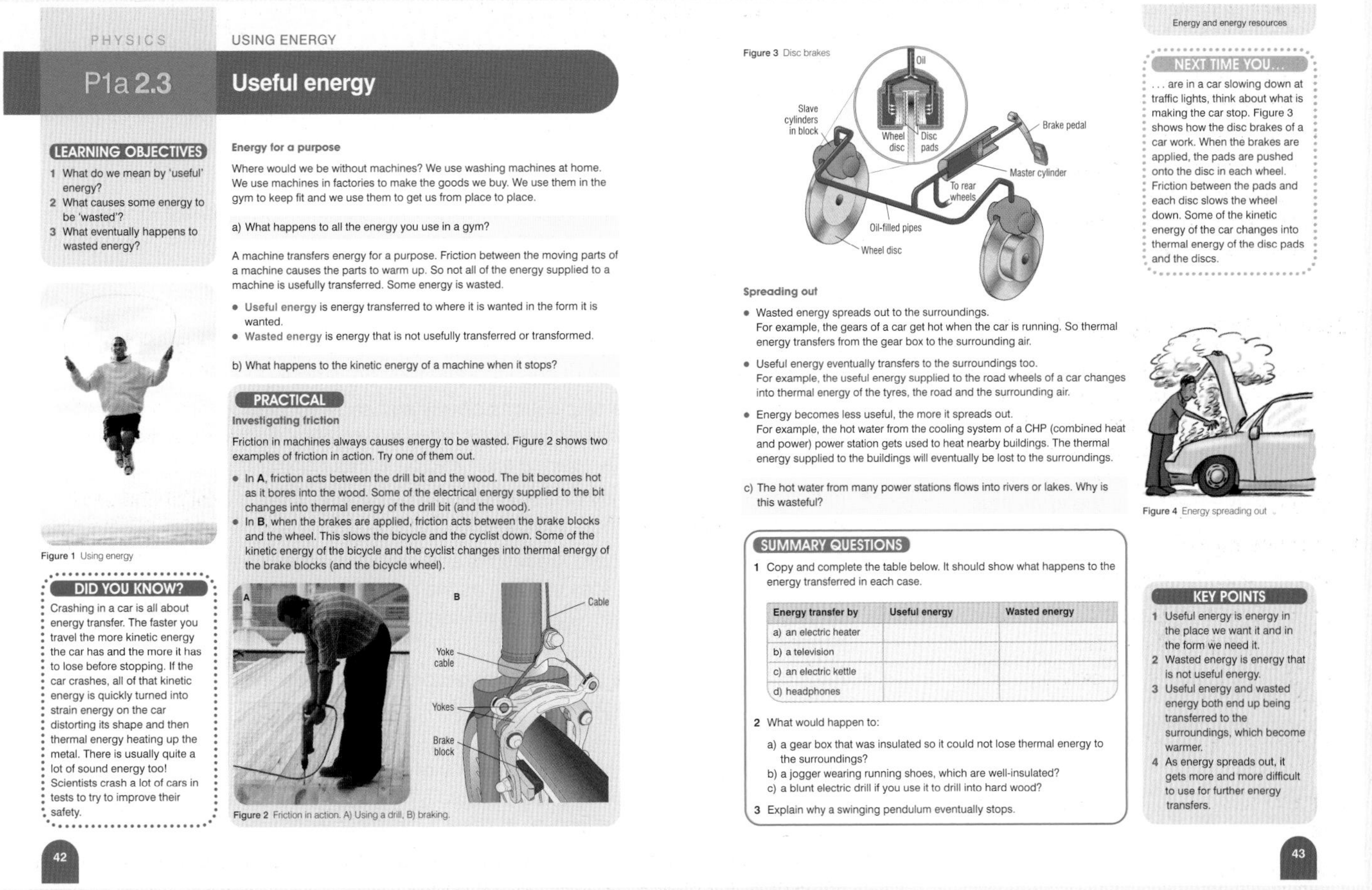

P1a 2.3   Useful energy

LEARNING OBJECTIVES

1 What do we mean by 'useful' energy?
2 What causes some energy to be 'wasted'?
3 What eventually happens to wasted energy?

Figure 1 Using energy

DID YOU KNOW?

Crashing in a car is all about energy transfer. The faster you travel the more kinetic energy the car has and the more it has to lose before stopping. If the car crashes, all of that kinetic energy is quickly turned into strain energy on the car distorting its shape and then thermal energy heating up the metal. There is usually quite a lot of sound energy too! Scientists crash a lot of cars in tests to try to improve their safety.

Energy for a purpose

Where would we be without machines? We use washing machines at home. We use machines in factories to make the goods we buy. We use them in the gym to keep fit and we use them to get us from place to place.

a) What happens to all the energy you use in a gym?

A machine transfers energy for a purpose. Friction between the moving parts of a machine causes the parts to warm up. So not all of the energy supplied to a machine is usefully transferred. Some energy is wasted.

- Useful energy is energy transferred to where it is wanted in the form it is wanted.
- Wasted energy is energy that is not usefully transferred or transformed.

b) What happens to the kinetic energy of a machine when it stops?

PRACTICAL

Investigating friction

Friction in machines always causes energy to be wasted. Figure 2 shows two examples of friction in action. Try one of them out.

- In **A**, friction acts between the drill bit and the wood. The bit becomes hot as it bores into the wood. Some of the electrical energy supplied to the bit changes into thermal energy of the drill bit (and the wood).
- In **B**, when the brakes are applied, friction acts between the brake blocks and the wheel. This slows the bicycle and the cyclist down. Some of the kinetic energy of the bicycle and the cyclist changes into thermal energy of the brake blocks (and the bicycle wheel).

Figure 2 Friction in action. A) Using a drill, B) braking.

Figure 3 Disc brakes

Spreading out

- Wasted energy spreads out to the surroundings.
  For example, the gears of a car get hot when the car is running. So thermal energy transfers from the gear box to the surrounding air.
- Useful energy eventually transfers to the surroundings too.
  For example, the useful energy supplied to the road wheels of a car changes into thermal energy of the tyres, the road and the surrounding air.
- Energy becomes less useful, the more it spreads out.
  For example, the hot water from the cooling system of a CHP (combined heat and power) power station gets used to heat nearby buildings. The thermal energy supplied to the buildings will eventually be lost to the surroundings.

c) The hot water from many power stations flows into rivers or lakes. Why is this wasteful?

SUMMARY QUESTIONS

1 Copy and complete the table below. It should show what happens to the energy transferred in each case.

Energy transfer by	Useful energy	Wasted energy
a) an electric heater		
b) a television		
c) an electric kettle		
d) headphones		

2 What would happen to:
   a) a gear box that was insulated so it could not lose thermal energy to the surroundings?
   b) a jogger wearing running shoes, which are well-insulated?
   c) a blunt electric drill if you use it to drill into hard wood?

3 Explain why a swinging pendulum eventually stops.

NEXT TIME YOU...

... are in a car slowing down at traffic lights, think about what is making the car stop. Figure 3 shows how the disc brakes of a car work. When the brakes are applied, the pads are pushed onto the disc in each wheel. Friction between the pads and each disc slows the wheel down. Some of the kinetic energy of the car changes into thermal energy of the disc pads and the discs.

Figure 4 Energy spreading out

KEY POINTS

1 Useful energy is energy in the place we want it and in the form we need it.
2 Wasted energy is energy that is not useful energy.
3 Useful energy and wasted energy both end up being transferred to the surroundings, which become warmer.
4 As energy spreads out, it gets more and more difficult to use it for further energy transfers.

SUMMARY ANSWERS

1

Energy transfer by	Useful energy	Wasted energy
a) an electric heater	thermal energy of the element	thermal energy of the case
b) a television	light energy, sound energy	thermal energy
c) an electric kettle	thermal energy of the water	thermal energy of steam and of the kettle itself
d) headphones	sound energy	thermal energy in the wire

2 a) It would heat up. The lubricating oil and the gears would get too hot.
  b) The feet would get too hot and sweaty.
  c) The drill would heat up and smoke if it burns the wood.

3 Air resistance causes friction as the pendulum swings. This produces heat and so the pendulum loses energy to the surroundings and stops.

Answers to in-text questions

a) It is gained by the surroundings as thermal energy.

b) It is transferred to the surroundings as thermal energy by friction between its moving parts and in the brakes, and by air resistance.

c) The hot water mixes with the cold water. Its thermal energy spreads out and can't be used again.

KEY POINTS

Can the students identify how energy is wasted in a variety of energy transfers?

P1a 2.4

Energy and efficiency

Teaching suggestions

- **Special needs.** Allow the students to use an experiment template with clear instructions and a results' table during the practical task.

- **Learning styles**

  Kinaesthetic: Setting up the apparatus.

  Visual: Obtaining accurate measurements.

  Auditory: Explaining the cause of friction.

  Interpersonal: Collaborating with others in practical work.

  Intrapersonal: Reviewing and evaluating results.

- **Homework.** A worksheet with additional calculations would be appropriate. You could provide data from the lifting experiment for the students to analyse if they did not try the task during the lesson.

- **Teaching assistant.** Have the teaching assistant help out with the practical and support those who have difficulty plotting graphs.

SPECIFICATION LINK-UP   P1a.11.2

- *The greater the percentage of the energy that is usefully transformed in a device, the more efficient the device is.*

Students should use their skills, knowledge and understanding of 'How Science Works':

- to calculate the efficiency of a device using:

$$\text{Efficiency} = \frac{\text{useful energy transferred}}{\text{by the device}} \div \frac{\text{total energy supplied}}{\text{to the device}}$$

- to evaluate the effectiveness and cost effectiveness of methods used to reduce energy consumption.

Lesson structure

STARTER

Efficiency – What is 'efficiency' and why do we want it? What are the advantages of an efficient device? (5 minutes)

Staying on – Ask the students to explain why some electrical devices last longer than others even though they use the same batteries. (5 minutes)

MAIN

- This may be the first time the students will have encountered an equation in the course; time should be spent ensuring that they get it right.

- They need to lay out the calculations clearly and show all of the stages of their working; emphasise that they will find it difficult to remember the correct technique and score full marks on a science examination without doing this.

- Investigating the efficiency of the winch may be difficult without a lot of equipment. A demonstration may be more practicable.

- Allow the students to record the results and produce a line graph. They should find that the motor becomes less efficient as the mass increases. This introduces concepts of 'How Science Works' involving presentation of data and relationships between variables.

- Ask them why they think the efficiency becomes less. [The main reason is that frictional forces in the motor increase but there is some extra air resistance that they may mention.]

- You may like to discuss how the efficiency of an elevator could be measured. Should the weight of the elevator itself be counted? This could lead onto a discussion of why it is not efficient (or cost effective) to drive a large car with only one person in it.

- Many students may own personal music players (MP3 players) or mobile phones, some of which have a much better battery life than others. These can form the basis of a discussion about the advantages of an efficient device.

- The calculations are not particularly challenging, but many students become confused about percentage or fractional efficiency.

- It is usually best to stick to the fractional efficiency, as this is commonly used in examinations and makes the equation easier to handle and rearrange.

- You should check through the answers with the students before the plenary.

PLENARIES

'The lads gave it 110%!' – Get the students to explain what's wrong with that statement. Can you put in more than 100% effort? (5 minutes)

Car efficiency – Give the students advertisements for cars and ask them to arrange them in order of energy efficiency, using the fuel consumption figures in the small print. Is a bus more energy efficient than a car? (5 minutes)

Energy efficiency poster – Students can draw a poster encouraging people to be more energy efficient in their home. (15–20 minutes)

Practical support

Investigating efficiency

This investigation can be used to develop and assess the students' investigative skills, in particular those related to measurement. If you do not have enough joule meters it is possible, but trickier, to use an ammeter, voltmeter and stopwatch combination using the equations below to calculate energy use.

Equipment and materials required

For each group: joule meter, variable power supply, small electric winch (motor), 5 × 100 g masses (each weighing 0.1 N), metre rule, clamps to secure the winches to benches.

Details

- The students will lift a range of masses a fixed height. A full metre is a good height, if the motor were 100% efficient it would require 0.1 J for each mass. In reality it will be much less efficient than this. If the winches are quite powerful, you may need to use larger masses to notice the reduction in efficiency.

- Some students may want to know how the joule meter measures energy. It calculates energy provided by measuring the current and potential difference across the motor. The energy used is then calculated using: energy = current × potential difference × time ($E=Pt$ and $P=IV$). The students will meet these equations later in the course.

Safety: Protect floor and keep feet clear from falling weights.

ACTIVITY & EXTENSION IDEAS

ACTIVITY & EXTENSION IDEAS

The students can research into car efficiency. A large amount of information is available about the performance of a car; the students can find this and produce a graph showing which is the most fuel efficient. Several groups could look into different classes of car to find the 'best in class' and share their findings.

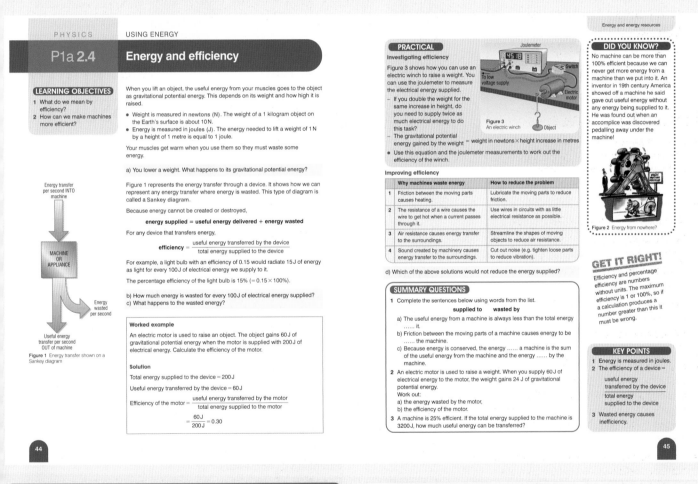

SUMMARY ANSWERS

1 a) Supplied to. b) Wasted by. c) Supplied to, wasted by.

2 a) 36 J b) 0.40 (or 40%)

3 800 J

GET IT RIGHT!

A more efficient machine is better at doing its job because it wastes less energy.

Answers to in-text questions

a) You use your muscles, so the gravitational potential energy is transformed in them to thermal energy.

b) 85 J

c) It is transformed to heat energy in the lamp holder and the surroundings.

d) 4

KEY POINTS

The students could calculate the useful energy output of a multistage transfer. For example a power station that has a boiler of efficiency 0.8, turbines with efficiency 0.7 and a generator of efficiency 0.9. What is the output for every 1000 J of input?

P1a 2.5   Energy and efficiency issues

PHYSICS   USING ENERGY

P1a 2.5   Energy and efficiency issues

Teaching suggestions

Activities

Ideas about energy – Provide each group with a large sheet of paper to express their ideas. As individuals, they could then produce an energy saving manifesto booklet, perhaps as homework.

The bouncy ball test – The students can investigate the bouncing of balls on hard surfaces. Squash and ping-pong balls are a good choice for most surfaces and golf balls work well on very hard floors. A ball from a computer mouse does not bounce well; see if the students can suggest why.

Equipment and materials required
For each group: metre rule, various balls.

A burning issue – As before, the students' reports can be recorded on video or with a digital camera or webcam. Alternatively, if you recorded some discussions from the start of the first chapter you might like to show them now as a starter to the debates.

Extension or homework

Research – Quite a lot of information is available about James Joule so the students could easily be set a homework task of researching his achievements. Did he really spend his honeymoon measuring the temperature of water beneath a waterfall or is this just a scientists' urban myth? An Animation, P1a 2.5 'Joule's experiment' is available on the GCSE Physics CD ROM.

Additional calculations – The students could complete several calculations from a worksheet on efficiency.

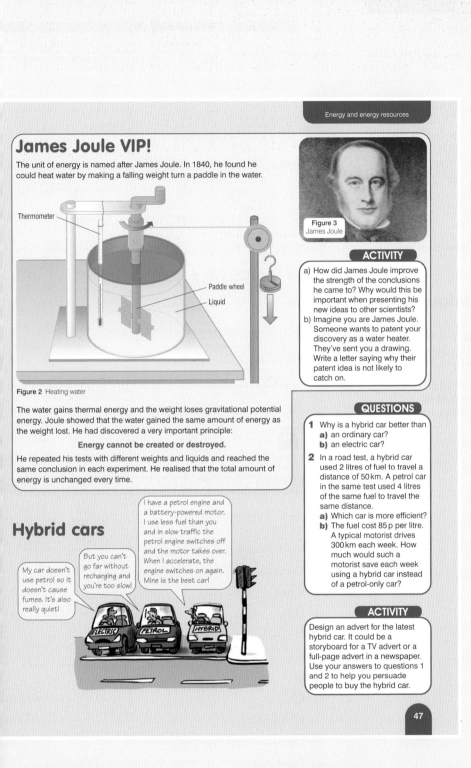

James Joule VIP!

The unit of energy is named after James Joule. In 1840, he found he could heat water by making a falling weight turn a paddle in the water.

Thermometer

Paddle wheel

Liquid

Figure 2 Heating water

Figure 3 James Joule

The water gains thermal energy and the weight loses gravitational potential energy. Joule showed that the water gained the same amount of energy as the weight lost. He had discovered a very important principle:

Energy cannot be created or destroyed.

He repeated his tests with different weights and liquids and reached the same conclusion in each experiment. He realised that the total amount of energy is unchanged every time.

ACTIVITY

a) How did James Joule improve the strength of the conclusions he came to? Why would this be important when presenting his new ideas to other scientists?

b) Imagine you are James Joule. Someone wants to patent your discovery as a water heater. They've sent you a drawing. Write a letter saying why their patent idea is not likely to catch on.

Hybrid cars

My car doesn't use petrol so it doesn't cause fumes. It's also really quiet!

But you can't go far without recharging and you're too slow!

I have a petrol engine and a battery-powered motor. I use less fuel than you and in slow traffic the petrol engine switches off and the motor takes over. When I accelerate, the engine switches on again. Mine is the best car!

ELECTRIC PETROL HYBRID

QUESTIONS

1 Why is a hybrid car better than
   a) an ordinary car?
   b) an electric car?

2 In a road test, a hybrid car used 2 litres of fuel to travel a distance of 50 km. A petrol car in the same test used 4 litres of the same fuel to travel the same distance.
   a) Which car is more efficient?
   b) The fuel cost 85p per litre. A typical motorist drives 300 km each week. How much would such a motorist save each week using a hybrid car instead of a petrol-only car?

ACTIVITY

Design an advert for the latest hybrid car. It could be a storyboard for a TV advert or a full-page advert in a newspaper. Use your answers to questions 1 and 2 to help you persuade people to buy the hybrid car.

47

ANSWERS TO QUESTIONS

The bouncy ball test

1 a) Rebound height will be lower than original height.

   b) Calculation using own results.

2 Use an electronic device/video recorder to measure peak of bounce.

3 Answer should refer to the spread of repeat measurements – the narrower the spread of repeat heights measured, the more precise the results.

4 For example, surface you drop the ball on (categoric), height you drop the ball from (continuous), type of ball/material it is made from (categoric).

5 We would need to repeat the tests over a range of drop heights to see if the relationship holds true for this particular ball dropped on to this particular surface. You could also investigate any of the variables mentioned in question 4 to find out the fraction of the initial gravitational potential energy lost in the impact in different circumstances – it is likely to differ i.e. we can't generalise across different types of ball and surface.

James Joule VIP!

a) He repeated his tests with different weights and liquids and reached the same conclusion each time. This made his theory a more powerful predictor, and it was easier to persuade his fellow scientists that the conservation of energy should be accepted as part of the body of scientific knowledge.

b) Letter backed up with quantitative explanation.

Hybrid cars

1 a) It uses less fuel per kilometre.

   b) Electric cars can't go very far without being recharged.

2 a) The hybrid car.

   b) £10.20

Learning styles

Kinaesthetic: Practical work with bouncy balls.

Visual: Watching video reports.

Auditory: Discussing efficiency issues.

Interpersonal: Debating the site of an incinerator.

Intrapersonal: Evaluating the usefulness of hybrid cars.

Special needs

Use a worksheet with partially completed calculations to teach the students how to lay out calculations.

Gifted and talented

These students could look into the topic of elastic and inelastic collisions using dynamics trolleys, perhaps using light gates to monitor the motion. They can find out which type of collision cause the greatest changes in energy.

Teaching assistant

Your teaching assistant can be very helpful in the recording of discussions or helping to generate ideas in group work.

ICT link-up

- Students can find information on the Internet about the latest hybrid car technology. See for example, www.hybridcars.com or try the various car brand name web sites.

SUMMARY ANSWERS

1 **1.** C **2.** D **3.** B **4.** A

2 Electrical, light, thermal, useful, wasted.

3 **a)** 0.15 (or 15 %) **b)** 8500 J

c)

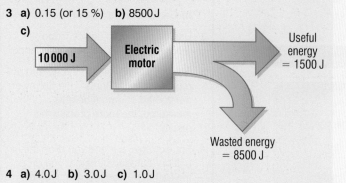

10 000 J → Electric motor → Useful energy = 1500 J

Wasted energy = 8500 J

4 **a)** 4.0 J **b)** 3.0 J **c)** 1.0 J

d) It was transformed to sound and thermal energy of the ball, the floor and the surroundings.

Summary teaching suggestions

- The first two questions are straightforward checks to see if the students can clearly identify the 'forms' of energy and spot the obvious use of each device. Question 3 should summarise the understanding of efficiency calculations.

- Question 4 checks another calculation, and should let you see that the students understand that the energy has to be accounted for; it is not lost in the impact but merely transferred to sound and heat.

SUMMARY QUESTIONS

1 The devices listed below transfer energy in different ways.

1. Car engine   2. Electric bell
3. Electric light bulb   4. Gas heater

The next list gives the useful form of energy the devices are designed to produce.

Match words A, B, C and D with the devices numbered 1 to 4.

A Heat (thermal energy)   B Light
C Movement (kinetic energy)   D Sound

2 Use words from the list to complete the sentences:

useful   wasted   thermal   light   electrical

When a light bulb is switched on, ... energy is changed into ...... energy and into ...... energy of the surroundings. The energy that radiates from the light bulb is ...... energy. The rest of the energy supplied to the light bulb is ...... energy.

3 You can use an electric motor to raise a load. In a test, you supply the winch with 10 000 J of electrical energy and the load gains 1500 J of gravitational potential energy.

a) Calculate its efficiency.
b) How much energy is wasted?
c) Copy and complete the energy transfer diagram below for the winch.

A → Electric motor → Useful energy = 1500 J → B

4 A ball gains 4.0 J of gravitational potential energy when it is raised to a height of 2.0 m above the ground. When it is released, it rebounds to a height of 1.5 m.

a) How much kinetic energy did it have just before it hit the ground? Assume air resistance is negligible.
b) How much gravitational potential energy did it have at the top of the rebound?
c) How much energy did it lose in the rebound?
d) What happened to the energy it lost on impact?

EXAM-STYLE QUESTIONS

1 On a building site a machine is used to lift a bag of sand from the ground to the top of a building.
What type of energy has the bag of sand gained?
A elastic potential energy
B gravitational potential energy
C kinetic energy
D thermal energy   (

2 What type of energy is stored in a stretched rubber band?
A chemical energy
B elastic strain energy
C gravitational potential energy
D kinetic energy   (

3 The picture shows a mobile that hangs over a baby's cot. The mobile plays a tune and rotates. It gets its energy from a battery. The electrical energy supplied by the battery is transformed into other forms of energy.

Match words from the list with the numbers 1 to 4 in the sentences.
A kinetic energy
B light
C sound
D thermal energy

A motor makes the mobile go round. The motor transforms electrical energy mainly into ......1....... When the mobile is switched on it becomes warm after a short while. This is because some of the electrical energy is transformed into ......2...... Speakers in the mobile transform electrical energy into ......3...... There is a 'power on' indicator on the mobile that transforms electrical energy into ......4...... .   (4

EXAM-STYLE ANSWERS

1 **B**   *(1 mark)*

2 **B**   *(1 mark)*

3 **1** Kinetic energy

2 Thermal energy

3 Sound

4 Light   *(1 mark each)*

4 a) **C**

b) **A**

c) **D**

d) **C**   *(1 mark each)*

5 a) Kinetic energy.   *(1 mark)*

b) Electrical energy to kinetic energy.   *(2 marks)*

c) There is friction between the moving parts of the motor.   *(1 mark)*

d) Efficiency = $\dfrac{\text{useful energy transferred by the device}}{\text{total energy supplied to the device}}$

Efficiency = $\dfrac{240\,000}{800\,000}$ *(1 mark)*

Efficiency = 0.3 (= 30%)   *(1 mark)*

4 An electric fan is used to move air around a room.

(a) The fan **usefully** transforms electrical energy into

  A elastic energy

  B heat energy

  C kinetic energy

  D sound   (1)

(b) Energy that is not usefully transformed by the fan is **wasted** as

  A heat energy and sound

  B heat energy only

  C kinetic energy and sound

  D sound energy only   (1)

(c) Which of the following statements about the energy wasted by the fan is **not** true?

  A It makes the surroundings warmer.

  B It can no longer be transformed in useful ways.

  C It becomes very thinly spread out.

  D It makes the surroundings cooler.   (1)

(d) A second design of fan transforms useful energy at the same rate but wastes less of the energy supplied to it. This means that the second fan

  A is 100% efficient.   B is less efficient.

  C is more efficient.   D has the same efficiency.

    (1)

5 A chair lift carries skiers to the top of a mountain.

(a) When the skiers get to the top of the mountain they have gained gravitational potential energy. As they ski back down the mountain what type of energy is this transformed into?   (1)

(b) The chair lift is powered by an electric motor. What useful energy transformation takes place in the motor?   (2)

(c) Some of the electrical energy supplied to the motor is wasted as heat. Why does this happen?   (1)

(d) The energy required to lift two skiers to the top of the mountain is 240 000 J. The energy supplied to the motor is 800 000 J. Calculate the efficiency of the motor.   (2)

HOW SCIENCE WORKS QUESTIONS

Whilst watching a tennis match I wondered why, when they asked for a new set of balls, they were fetched from a fridge. Could it be that they behave differently when they are hot? I decided to test this idea and set up a controlled investigation.

The tennis balls were heated to different temperatures and then dropped from the same height. I used a digital camera to photograph the bounce so that I could get an accurate reading of how high each ball bounced.

My prediction was that as the temperature increased the ball would bounce higher.

My results, and the manufacturer's results, are in this table.

Temperature (°C)	Height bounced (cm)	
	My results	Manufacturer's
3	11.0	14.0
10	37.3	40.5
19	53.9	57.1
29	64.1	67.0
40	70.2	73.4
51	74.5	77.5
60	74.3	79.3

a) Plot a graph of my results, including a line of best fit.   (3)

b) What is the sensitivity of the instrument used to measure the height of the bounce?   (1)

c) What is the pattern in the results?   (2)

d) What do these results suggest about my prediction?   (1)

e) Is there any evidence for a random error in my investigation? Explain your answer.   (2)

f) Is there any evidence for a systematic error in my investigation? Explain your answer.   (2)

g) What is the importance of these results to the professional tennis player?   (1)

49

HOW SCIENCE WORKS ANSWERS

a) Graph correctly labelled, with the temperature on the X axis and the height on the Y axis. The line of best fit should be a curve, with roughly the same number of points on each side. Check the points for accurate plotting.

b) The instrument is sensitive to 1 mm.

c) Rapid initial increase in bounce height. Increase is less as temperature is higher.

d) The prediction is correct within the range 3°C to 51°C. However it is not a simple increase. The prediction is not fully supported.

e) Yes, comment on the closeness of the points to the line of best fit or perhaps on the last two results at 51°C and 60°C.

f) The experimental results look to be consistently about 3 cm below those of the manufacturer. Except for the 60°C, which is 5 cm lower.

g) The bounce height of the ball will increase whilst the ball is warming up.

How science works teaching suggestions

- **Literacy guidance**
  - Key terms that should be clearly understood are: line of best fit, pattern, prediction, sensitivity, random error, systematic error.
  - Questions expecting a longer answer, where students can practise their literacy skills are: d) and f).

- **Higher- and lower-level answers.** Questions c) and d) are higher-level and answers for these questions have been provided at this level. Lower-level questions are b) and g) – the answers are also at this level.

- **Gifted and talented.** Able students could explore the importance of adequate testing of sports equipment from two points of view – safety and performance. E.g. sports shoes.

- **How and when to use these questions.** When wishing to develop graph-drawing skills and using the data to identify errors. To reinforce the idea of relevance of science to everyday occurrences.

- **Homework.** Compare the bounce of different balls or of the same ball on different surfaces.

- **Special needs.** The graph could be drawn to allow speedy access to the rest of the argument.

- **ICT link-up.** Opportunity to use ICT to review other sources of the same data and check its reliability.

Exam teaching suggestions

- Questions 1–3 could be used to test understanding of different forms of energy. For example, they could be used as part of a homework once pupils have discussed different energy transformations.

- When discussing energy transformations, encourage students to talk about 'wasted' energy rather than 'lost' energy.

- When describing energy transformations, weaker students often only state the final form(s) of energy. For example, in question 5b), in order to score both marks students must state that the energy transformation is from electrical energy to kinetic energy. If they fail to mention electrical energy they can only score one mark.

- There are three common sources of confusion associated with efficiency calculations such as the one in question 5d).

  1 Students confuse energy input and energy output with the result that they obtain efficiencies greater than one.

  2 Students may not have encountered calculations involving large numbers and consequently may find them off-putting.

  3 Students need to be reminded that efficiency is a ratio and consequently has no unit.

P1a 3.1   Electrical devices

Students should learn:

- That electrical devices are very useful.
- About a range of energy transformations that happen in electrical devices.

LEARNING OUTCOMES

Most students should be able to:

- Describe the energy transformations in a range of electrical devices.
- Choose a particular device for a particular purpose based on the energy transfer required.

Teaching suggestions

- **Gifted and talented.** These students could find out who first discovered how electricity could be used to produce movement. How and where was this first demonstrated? Was its importance realised?

- **Learning styles**

  Kinaesthetic: Cutting and pasting activity. (See plenaries.)

  Visual: Creating a mind map.

  Auditory: Discussing the right appliance for the right job.

  Interpersonal: Discussing the operation of electrical devices.

  Intrapersonal: Considering wasted energy in demonstrations.

- **Homework**
  - The students could find out where all the electrical effects demonstrated today are used in industry or around the school.
  - The 'no electricity' plenary could be used as the topic of a longer story that the students could write if not used during the lesson.

- **Science @ work.** The clockwork radio isn't the only device that can be used in locations without many resources. There are several clockwork torches that use the same principle. There is another design where you just shake the torch to charge it. This shaking makes a magnet move between coils of wire and generates a small electric current. It's handy if you are going to be trapped in a cave for a long time.

SPECIFICATION LINK-UP   P1a.11.3

- *Examples of energy transformations everyday electrical devices are designed to bring about.*
- *Examples of everyday electrical devices designed to bring about particular energy transformations.*

Students should use their skills, knowledge and understanding of 'How Science Works':

- *to compare and contrast the particular advantages and disadvantages of using different electrical devices for a particular application.*

Lesson structure

STARTER

Electricity everywhere – Ask the students to list all of the electrical devices that they use during the day. Include mains-powered and battery-operated. (5 minutes)

What is electricity? – The students should list or draw a mind map about what electricity is. (5–10 minutes)

Electricity dominoes – The students connect question/answer dominoes on basic electrical terms like current, voltage, cell etc. (5 minutes)

MAIN

- The core part of this topic is a discussion of why electricity is so useful in our society.
- The students will easily appreciate that electricity can be transformed into other forms of energy easily, so spend some time mentioning and showing the key devices that do the job.
- Show a wire heating when a current passes through it and ask students what this effect is used in.
- Use a heat-resistant mat and turn up the current until the wire becomes white hot (for a moment). Students need to be out of touching distance.
- Ask the students: 'What is this effect used in and how do we make sure that the wire does not melt?'
- Show an electric motor operating, pointing out the magnets, and ask how this effect is used. Also ask: 'What is the effect of increasing the current and providing more energy to the motor?'
- Demonstrate a simple electromagnet and again see if the students realise how this effect can be used in loudspeakers (have one handy with a signal generator).
- With each of the demonstrations, ask the students to consider how energy is being wasted to the surroundings.
- Once the students are aware of the range of possible transfers, they should discuss how to choose a particular device for a job.

PLENARIES

No electricity – The students should write a description of the problems they would have during the morning if there were no electricity. (10–15 minutes)

Electrical energy table – Give the students a cut-up table similar to the one in the textbook and ask them to assemble it to show the useful and wasted energy from more electrical devices. (5 minutes)

Making connections – Ask the students to complete the sentence 'Electrical energy is a very convenient form of energy because . . .' including these words: 'energy', 'transfer' and 'current'. (5 minutes)

Practical support

Demonstrating heating effect of electrical current

Materials and equipment needed

Low voltage power supply (variable), resistance wire, heat proof mat.

Demonstrating a motor

Ideally you should use a motor where the students can see the moving parts. This way you can describe the effect the current is having.

Demonstrating a loudspeaker

The loudspeaker should be a large one, and you should demonstrate that all it is doing is moving in and out by showing some low frequency vibrations.

FOUL FACTS

Electricity and life have been linked ever since scientists noticed that a battery could be used to make dead frogs' legs twitch like they were alive. Some thought that electricity might even be used to bring the dead back to life, and this was the idea that inspired the 17-year-old Mary Shelly to write her Frankenstein novel. Even today, scientists are accused of trying to produce 'Frankenstein foods' with genetic engineering.

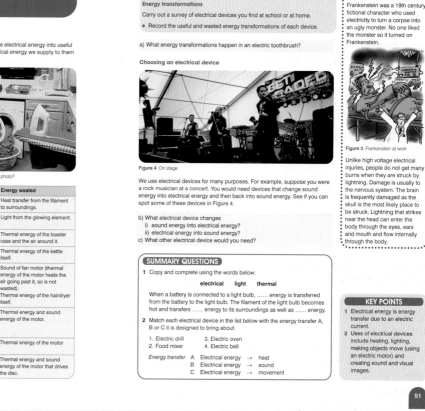

PHYSICS   ELECTRICAL ENERGY

P1a 3.1 Electrical devices

LEARNING OBJECTIVES

1 Why are electrical devices so useful?
2 What energy transformations take place in everyday electrical devices?
3 How do we choose an electrical device for a particular job?

DID YOU KNOW?

People without electricity supplies can now listen to radio programmes – thanks to the British inventor Trevor Bayliss. In 1999, he invented the clockwork radio and patented it. When you turn a handle on the radio, you wind up a clockwork spring in the radio. When the spring unwinds, it turns a small electric generator in the radio. It doesn't need batteries or mains electricity. Clockwork radios are now mass-produced and sold all over the world.

Figure 2 A clockwork radio

● What form of energy is stored in the spring of the clockwork radio when you wind it up?
● What happens to this energy when the spring unwinds?

Everyday electrical devices

We use electrical devices every day. They change electrical energy into useful energy at the flick of a switch. Some of the electrical energy we supply to them is wasted.

Figure 1 Electrical devices – how many can you see in this photo?

Device	Useful energy	Energy wasted
Light bulb	Light from the glowing filament.	Heat transfer from the filament to surroundings.
Electric heater	Thermal energy of the surroundings.	Light from the glowing element.
Electric toaster	Thermal energy of bread.	Thermal energy of the toaster case and the air around it.
Electric kettle	Thermal energy of water.	Thermal energy of the kettle itself.
Hairdryer	Kinetic energy of the air driven by the fan. Thermal energy of air flowing past the heater filament.	Sound of fan motor (thermal energy of the motor heats the air going past it, so is not wasted). Thermal energy of the hairdryer itself.
Electric motor	Kinetic energy of object driven by the motor. Potential energy of objects lifted by the motor.	Thermal energy and sound energy of the motor.
Personal stereo	Kinetic energy of the motor. Sound.	Thermal energy of the motor
Computer disc drive	Energy stored in magnetic dots on the disc.	Thermal energy and sound energy of the motor that drives the disc.

PRACTICAL

Energy transformations

Carry out a survey of electrical devices you find at school or at home.

● Record the useful and wasted energy transformations of each device.

a) What energy transformations happen in an electric toothbrush?

Choosing an electrical device

Figure 4 On stage

We use electrical devices for many purposes. For example, suppose you were a rock musician at a concert. You would need devices that change sound energy into electrical energy and then back into sound energy. See if you can spot some of these devices in Figure 4.

b) What electrical device changes
   i) sound energy into electrical energy?
   ii) electrical energy into sound energy?
c) What other electrical device would you need?

SUMMARY QUESTIONS

1 Copy and complete using the words below:

   electrical   light   thermal

   When a battery is connected to a light bulb, ... energy is transferred from the battery to the light bulb. The filament of the light bulb becomes hot and transfers ...... energy to its surroundings as well as ...... energy.

2 Match each electrical device in the list below with the energy transfer A, B or C it is designed to bring about.

   1. Electric drill   3. Electric oven
   2. Food mixer   4. Electric bell

   Energy transfer A   Electrical energy → heat
   B   Electrical energy → sound
   C   Electrical energy → movement

FOUL FACTS

Frankenstein was a 19th century fictional character who used electricity to turn a corpse into an ugly monster. No one liked the monster so it turned on Frankenstein.

Figure 3 Frankenstein at work

Unlike high voltage electrical injuries, people do not get many burns when they are struck by lightning. Damage is usually to the nervous system. The brain is frequently damaged as the skull is the most likely place to be struck. Lightning that strikes near the head can enter the body through the eyes, ears and mouth and flow internally through the body.

KEY POINTS

1 Electrical energy is energy transfer due to an electric current.
2 Uses of electrical devices include heating, lighting, making objects move (using an electric motor) and creating sound and visual images.

50   51

SUMMARY ANSWERS

1 Electrical, thermal, light.

2 1. C, 2. C, 3. A, 4. B.

DID YOU KNOW?

● Elastic energy.

● It transforms to electrical energy and thermal energy due to friction between the moving parts. The electrical energy transforms to sound energy and thermal energy due to resistance in the circuits.

Answers to in-text questions

a) Electrical energy transforms to kinetic energy of the brush, thermal energy due to friction between the moving parts and resistance, and sound.

b) i) A microphone.   ii) A loudspeaker.

c) An amplifier.

KEY POINTS

The students should be able to explain why electrical devices are so useful to us and what devices can perform these transfers.

P1a 3.2

Electrical power

- That the power rating of a device is a measure of how much energy it transfers each second.
- How to calculate the power of a device.

LEARNING OUTCOMES

Most students should be able to:

- State that the watt is the unit of power.
- Calculate the power output of devices using the equation Power = energy transformed ÷ time.

Some students should also be able to:

- Perform calculations involving the rearrangement of the equation.

Teaching suggestions

- **Special needs.** You may need to provide a layout template for the calculations for some students to develop the skills. These may contain partly completed equations.

- **Gifted and talented.** The power output of our Sun, a typical star, is much greater than the power needed for everybody on the Earth. How could we harness this power to meet our energy demands for the next billion years? The students could look into such exotic solutions, such as space mirrors, ring worlds and Dyson Spheres. The outcome could be a dramatic presentation of the far future.

- **Learning styles**

  Visual: Imagining the scale of the power output of the Sun.

  Auditory: Definitions of key words and units.

  Interpersonal: Discussing the meaning of 'power'.

- **Homework.** Further calculations may be useful. The students could look into the origin of the term 'horsepower' and find out how many watts one horsepower is.

SPECIFICATION LINK-UP   P1a.11.3

- *The amount of electrical energy a device transforms depends on how long the appliance is switched on and the rate at which the device transforms energy.*
- *The power of an appliance is measured in watts (W) or kilowatts (kW).*

Lesson structure

STARTER

Power – Ask the students to describe what they mean by the word 'power'. Ask: 'Who is the most powerful person in the world, what is the most powerful machine?' (5 minutes)

Big numbers – Give the students a set of SI prefixes and see if they can be placed in order of size. (5 minutes)

Using energy – Challenge the students to design an experiment to compare how much energy is stored in different batteries. (15 minutes)

MAIN

- Begin with a discussion of power and the clear scientific definition as 'the amount of energy transferred each second'.
- If you feel brave you may like to try a real physics joke, ask the students: 'Watt is the unit of power?' like a question. When they say that they don't know, then do it again!
- The unit 'watt' is exactly the same as 'a joule per second' and this is a common concept tested on examinations.
- Some students seem to struggle with the term 'per' and you may like to explain this as meaning 'each'.
- Emphasise that the prefix 'kilo' just means 'one thousand'. Check that the students can understand numbers like 2.4 kW and 0.5 kW, as some have difficulty; if they are struggling it is sometimes best to say the 'kilo' means 'multiply the number by one thousand'.
- Similarly, some students will need the prefix 'mega' explained to them carefully.
- Plenty of example calculations are required and the students need to develop a clear layout of these.
- A rigorous method should be stuck to, and you should check that the students are getting the correct answers with their method.
- Higher attaining students will need to rearrange the equation. Check with the mathematics department how this rearrangement is usually tackled to ensure consistency.
- Many students will be familiar with the rearrangement triangles but these often use symbols.
- The efficiency of weightlifters is not very good. Although the weightlifter may be producing a useful power output of 600 W, they may actually be using chemical energy at 1000 W. This is more than an electrical fire – so it's no wonder that they get hot!

PLENARIES

Matching the power – Give the students a set of pictures of household electrical devices and a set of power ratings. Ask them to match the ratings with the devices. (10 minutes)

Common units – Students match the units and the quantity they measure; include joule, kilowatt, kilowatt hour, second, joule per second, etc. (5 minutes)

Calculation loop – Similar to most loop games, but the students have calculation questions and numerical answers to match. (5 minutes)

ACTIVITY & EXTENSION IDEAS

The energy output of a battery can be measured using data logging techniques. Connect up two simple circuits containing a battery and a light bulb with a current sensor. In one circuit, use normal batteries and in the other use long-life batteries. Use the data logging software to record how the current changes over a long period of time, and present the graphs to the students during the next lesson for discussion. Do the long-life batteries last up to four times as long?

Practical support for extension idea
Equipment and materials needed
Batteries (two types), light bulbs, connecting leads, battery holders, current sensors, data loggers.

PHYSICS   ELECTRICAL ENERGY

P1a 3.2   Electrical power

LEARNING OBJECTIVES

1 What do we mean by power?
2 What are the units of power?
3 How can we calculate the power of a device?

Powerful machines

When you use a lift to go up, a powerful electric motor pulls you and the lift upwards. The lift motor transforms energy from electrical energy to gravitational potential energy when the lift is raised. We also get electrical energy transformed to wasted thermal energy and sound energy.

Figure 1 A lift motor

• The energy we supply per second to the motor is the power supplied to it.
• The more powerful the lift motor is, the faster it is able to move a particular load.

In general we can say that:

the more powerful a device, the faster the rate at which it transforms energy.

We measure the power of a device in watts (W) or kilowatts (kW).

For any device,

• its input power is the energy per second supplied to it.
• its output power is the useful energy per second transferred by it.

1 watt is a rate of transfer of energy of 1 joule per second (J/s).

1 kilowatt is equal to 1000 watts.

Power (in watts, W) = rate of transfer of energy

$$= \frac{\text{energy transferred (in joules, J)}}{\text{time taken (in seconds, s)}}$$

Worked example

A motor transfers 10 000 J of energy in 25 s. What is its power?

Solution

Power (in watts, W) = $\frac{\text{energy transferred (in joules, J)}}{\text{time taken (in seconds, s)}}$

Power = $\frac{10\,000\,\text{J}}{25\,\text{s}}$ = 400 W

NEXT TIME YOU...

... see the Sun set, think of all you could do with its almost unlimited power!

a) What is the power of a lift motor that transfers 50 000 J of energy from the electricity supply in 10 s?

Power ratings

Here are some typical values of power ratings for different energy transfer 'devices':

Device	Power rating
A torch	1 W
An electric light bulb	100 W
An electric cooker	10 000 W = 10 kW (where 1 kW = 1000 watts)
A railway engine	1 000 000 W = 1 megawatt (MW) = 1 million watts
A Saturn V rocket	100 MW
A very large power station	10 000 MW
World demand for power	10 000 000 MW
The Sun	100 000 000 000 000 000 000 MW

b) How many 100 W electric light bulbs would use the same amount of power as a 10 kW electric cooker?

Figure 2 Rocket power

Muscle power

How powerful is a weight lifter?

A 30 kg dumbell has a weight of 300 N. Raising it by 1 m would give it 300 J of gravitational potential energy. A weight lifter could lift it in about 0.5 seconds. The rate of energy transformation would be 600 J/s (= 300 J/0.5 s). So the weight lifter's power output would be about 600 W in total!

c) An inventor has designed an exercise machine that can also generate 100 W of electrical power. Do you think people would buy this machine in case of a power cut?

Figure 3 Muscle power

SUMMARY QUESTIONS

1 a) Which is more powerful?
   ii) A torch bulb or a mains filament lamp.
   iii) A 3 kW electric kettle or a 10 000 W electric cooker.
   b) There are about 20 million homes in Britain. If a 3 kW electric kettle was switched on in 1 in 10 homes at the same time, how much power would need to be supplied?

2 The input power of a lift motor is 5000 J. In a test, it transforms 12 000 J of electrical energy to gravitational potential energy in 20 seconds.
   a) How much electrical energy is supplied to the motor?
   b) What is its efficiency in the test?

3 Choose one of the energy transfer devices listed at the top of this page. Carry out some research and describe how it works.

4 A machine has a power rating of 100 kW. If the machine runs for 2 minutes, how much energy does it transfer?

KEY POINTS

1 The unit of power is the watt (W), equal to 1 J/s.
2 1 kilowatt (kW) = 1000 watts
3 Power (in watts) =
   $\frac{\text{energy transferred (in joules)}}{\text{time taken (in seconds)}}$

52   53

SUMMARY ANSWERS

1 a) i) A mains filament lamp.   ii) A 10 000 W electric cooker.
   b) 6 million kilowatts.

2 a) 100 000 J
   b) 0.12 (or 12%)

3 Student research activity.

4 12 000 J

Answers to in-text questions

a) 5000 W (5 kW)

b) 100

c) Probably not, as 100 W would keep one or two light bulbs on, but only when you pedal.

KEY POINTS

Can the students complete a table of calculations relating energy, power and time? The table should include values in kilowatts and hours.

P1a 3.3   Using electrical energy

LEARNING OBJECTIVES

Students should learn:

- How to calculate the energy transferred by mains supplied electrical devices.
- How to calculate the cost of operating electrical devices.

LEARNING OUTCOMES

Most students should be able to:

- Calculate the amount of energy used by a mains device (in kWh).
- Calculate the cost of the electricity used.

Some students should also be able to:

- Carry out rearrangement of the appropriate equations.

SPECIFICATION LINK-UP   P1a.11.3

- *The power of an appliance is measured in watts (W) or kilowatts (kW).*
- *Energy is normally measured in joules (J).*

Students should use their skills, knowledge and understanding of 'How Science Works':

- *to calculate the amount of energy transferred from the mains using:*

$$\underset{\text{(kilowatt-hour)}}{\text{energy transferred}} = \underset{\text{(kilowatt)}}{\text{power}} \times \underset{\text{(hour)}}{\text{time}}$$

- *to calculate the cost of energy transferred from the mains using:*

$$\text{Total cost} = \text{number of kilowatt-hours} \times \text{cost per kilowatt-hour}$$

Lesson structure

STARTER

Paying for electricity – The students should list the reasons that electricity should be paid for, e.g. the cost of materials, the workforce and the meter readers. How could these costs be reduced? (5–10 minutes)

How much? – Give the students a set of devices and the time they are used for (e.g. a TV for 4 hours). They must put them in operating cost order. (5 minutes)

Shopping – To check the students' ability to work out the cost of buying things, give them a shopping list (with multiples of some items) and ask them to work out the total. (5 minutes)

MAIN

- This is another quite mathematical concept with important calculations, but the most common difficulty is the name of the units.
- The students really need to understand that a 'kilowatt-hour' is a measure of an amount of energy, so spend some time going through this.
- Converting between kilowatt-hours and joules is quite common in examinations and this must form part of the discussion.
- The terms 'kilowatt hour' and 'unit' are often interchanged and the students need to be aware of both.
- Make sure that the students can work out how many units have been used when given two different meter readings.
- Some students struggle when talking about immaterial things like 'units', and you may need to give analogies like 'how many gobstoppers could you buy for £2 if they cost 7 p each' and so on.
- Having copies of some real electricity bills (with names and addresses removed) is handy and the students could check if the bills are correct. You will need to explain the standing charge to do this.
- Higher attaining students should work out how many units could be bought with a set amount of money.

PLENARIES

Big bill – Show the students a copy of the school electricity bill and ask them to think of ways they could reduce it. (10 minutes)

Choosing the best supplier – Give the students copies of two pricing structures: one with a standing charge, and one without a standing charge but with a higher price per unit. Ask the students to find out which company three different families should use. (10 minutes)

Calculation dominoes – Give groups a set of domino cards with questions and numerical answers. Let them play dominoes with them. (5–10 minutes)

Teaching suggestions

- **Special needs.** As before, a layout template for calculations will help a great deal.
- **Gifted and talented.** Can these students calculate the energy use from a 100 W bulb left running for a year, in joules?
- **Learning styles**

  Kinaesthetic: Playing a game of dominoes.

  Visual: Obtaining information from bills and meter readings.

  Auditory: Debating how to reduce electricity costs.

  Interpersonal: Discussing the benefits of saving energy.

  Intrapersonal: Interpreting information from an electricity bill.

- **Homework.** The students could check their own electricity bill and find out how much they are paying per unit. They could find out what each supply company is charging.
- **ICT link-up.** The students could use a simple spreadsheet to calculate the cost of the electricity used. They could then find out what would happen to the price if the cost per unit increased or decreased.

GET IT RIGHT!

We are charged for every kilowatt-hour (unit) of electrical energy we use.

NEXT TIME YOU . . .

In standby mode a large TV operates at 10 W. If it is left on standby for 12 hours it will use 0.12 kWh. That means it costs 0.84p per night or £3 per year.
Around the world machines in standby mode consume 4 TWh of energy in standby mode each year. (£280 million at UK prices.)

PHYSICS ELECTRICAL ENERGY

P1a 3.3 Using electrical energy

LEARNING OBJECTIVES

1 How can we work out the energy used by a mains device?
2 How is the cost of mains electricity worked out?

1650 – 1960 W
220 – 230 V ~
50 – 60 Hz

Figure 1 Mains power

GET IT RIGHT!

Remember that a kilowatt-hour (kWh) is a unit of energy.

How much electrical energy is transferred from the mains when you use an electric heater? You can work this out if you know its power and how long you use it for.

A 1 kW heater uses the same amount of electrical energy in 1 hour as a 2 kW heater would use in half-an-hour. For ease, we say that:

the energy supplied to a 1 kW device in 1 hour is 1 **kilowatt-hour (kWh)**.

We use the kilowatt-hour as the unit of energy supplied by mains electricity. You can work out the energy, in kilowatt-hours, used by a mains device in a certain time using this equation:

$$\text{Energy transferred} \atop \text{(kilowatt-hours, kW h)} = {\text{power of device} \atop \text{(kilowatts, kW)}} \times {\text{time in use} \atop \text{(hours, h)}}$$

For example,

- a 1 kW heater switched on for 1 hour uses 1 kW h of electrical energy (= 1 kW × 1 hour).
- a 1 kW heater switched on for 10 hours uses 10 kW h of electrical energy (= 10 kW × 1 hour).
- a 0.5 kW heater switched on for 6 hours uses 3 kW h of electrical energy (= 0.5 kW × 6 hours).

a) How many kW h are used by a 100 W lamp in 24 hours?

How many joules are there in 1 kilowatt-hour?

One kilowatt-hour is the amount of electrical energy supplied to a 1 kilowatt device in 1 hour. So 1 kilowatt-hour = 1000 joules/second × 60 × 60 s = 3 600 000 J.

NEXT TIME YOU...

... leave the TV on overnight, think about how much it is costing you. It's still using energy in standby mode.

Paying for electrical energy

The electricity meter in your home measures the amount of electrical energy your family uses. It records the total energy supplied, no matter how many devices you all use. It gives us a reading of the number of kilowatt-hours (kW h) of energy supplied by the mains.

NELEB

L. Jones
26 Homewood Road
Otwood M51 9YZ

Figure 3 Checking your bill

Meter readings present	previous	units	pence per unit	amount	VAT %
31534	30092	1442	5.79	83.49	Zero
Standing charge				07.30	
TOTAL NOW DUE				90.79	
PERIOD ENDED				31.3.06	

In most houses, somebody reads the meter every three months. Look at the electricity bill in Figure 3.

The difference between the two readings is the number of kilowatt-hours (or units) supplied since the last bill.

b) Check for yourself that 1442 kW h of electrical energy is supplied in the bill shown.

We use the kilowatt-hour to work out the cost of electricity. For example, a cost of 7p per kWh (or 7p per unit) means that each kilowatt-hour of electrical energy costs 7p. Therefore,

total cost = number of kWh used × cost per kW h

c) Work out the cost of 1442 kW h at 7p per kWh.

71787 7

kWh

150 rev/kWh CLASS 2

Figure 2 An electricity meter

SUMMARY QUESTIONS

1 Use words from the list to complete the sentences below.

  hour   kilowatt   kilowatt-hours

  a) The ...... is a unit of power.
  b) Electricity meters record the mains electrical energy transformed in units of ....
  c) One ...... is the energy transformed by a 1 ...... device in 1 ....

2 a) Work out the number of kW h transformed in each case below.
  i) A 3 kilowatt electric kettle is used 6 times for 5 minutes each time.
  ii) A 1000 watt microwave oven is used for 30 minutes.
  iii) A 100 watt electric light is used for 8 hours.
  b) Calculate the total cost of the electricity used in a) if the cost of electricity is 7.0p per kW h.

3 An electric heater is left on for 3 hours.
  During this time it uses 12 kWh of electrical energy. What is the power of the heater?

KEY POINTS

1 Energy transferred (kilowatt-hours, kWh) = power of device (kilowatts, kW) × time in use (hours, h)
2 Total cost = number of kWh used × cost per kWh

54

55

SUMMARY ANSWERS

1 a) Kilowatt.
  b) Kilowatt-hours.
  c) Kilowatt-hour, kilowatt, hour.

2 a) i) 1.5 kWh ii) 0.5 kWh iii) 0.8 kWh
  b) 19.6 p

3 4 kW

Answers to in-text questions

a) 2.4 kWh
b) Students to check answer.
c) £100.94

KEY POINTS

Give the students two meter readings and ask them to calculate the cost of the electricity used. Alternatively let them calculate the cost of running a range of devices for a typical day.

P1a 3.4

The National Grid

LEARNING OBJECTIVES

Students should learn:

- How the National Grid is used to transfer electricity around the country.

LEARNING OUTCOMES

Most students should be able to:

- Explain the advantages of providing electricity via a National Grid.
- Describe the role of pylons, cables and transformers in the national Grid.

Some students should also be able to:

- Explain why electricity is transferred at very high voltage.

Teaching suggestions

- **Gifted and talented.** These students could find out what a transformer is and how it operates. What is it made of and why does it have a *laminated* iron core?

- **Learning styles**

  Kinaesthetic: Researching effect of pylons on health.

  Visual: Viewing the structure of the National Grid.

  Auditory: Explaining the reasons for carrying electricity at high voltage.

  Interpersonal: Reporting on research.

  Intrapersonal: Considering the effect of pylons on the landscape.

- **Homework.** If the students did not redesign the 'danger of death' symbol, they could do this on a larger scale at home. They could produce a booklet warning of the hazards of messing with electricity pylons.

SPECIFICATION LINK-UP   P1a.11.3

- *Electricity is transferred from power station to consumers along the National Grid.*

Lesson structure

STARTER

Choosing wisely – Give the students samples of a range of materials and a list of their properties. Ask them to choose which materials would be suitable for particular jobs and to explain why. (5–10 minutes)

Where does electricity come from? – Ask the students to explain where the electricity to power the lights in your room actually comes from. Ask them what happens when the local power station is out of operation. (5 minutes)

Danger of death – Show the students a picture of the 'Danger of death' icon used on transformer sub-stations. Ask them what they think the danger is and what the icon is showing. You could also check the students' knowledge of other hazard symbols. (5 minutes)

MAIN

- Discussing the National Grid would be best with props. It may be possible to find a ceramic insulator or even a short length of pylon cable. Local electrical engineering companies may have off-cuts or broken parts.

- If you don't have a ceramic insulator, then you can discuss how the high voltages leads are insulated from the pylons by showing some pottery.

- An Interactive, P1a 3.4 'Power stations', is available on the GCSE Physics CD.

- Can the students identify their current location on the National Grid map? Are there any local power stations whose position can be found? (These often occur at the ends of lines or where they change direction.)

- If the students live close to a pylon they can describe how large they are and what they are made of.

- If a sample of aluminium cable is not available, then use sample blocks of aluminium and steel to compare the density of the two materials. The students will easily see the advantage of using aluminium.

- It also helps if the steel is a bit on the rusty side, so that you can show the aluminium is also easier to maintain.

- It is possible to demonstrate the saving in energy at higher voltages. See 'Practical support'; make sure you try it out in advance.

- The underground/over ground discussion could be expanded; see 'Activity and extension ideas' box.

PLENARIES

Danger of death 2 – This hazard icon is a personal favourite, but can the students produce an improved design? (10–15 minutes)

Pylon jeopardy – Students have to think up questions with answers that match components to the National Grid. (5 minutes)

Electrical flow – Give the students a set of cards describing the passage of electricity from the generator to the light bulb, and ask them to sort the cards into order. (5 minutes)

Practical support

Demonstrating high voltage energy transfer

To demonstrate that high voltages are more efficient at transferring electrical energy, the following method can be used. It is fiddly to get just right, so make sure that you have tested it first.

Equipment and materials needed

Two matched transformers with a step-up or step-down ratio of about five (e.g. 100 turns input and 500 turns output). Two 2 m lengths of thin wire with high resistivity (Nichrome or constantan work well), a 1.25 V lamp and a low voltage (1–1.5 V) a.c. power supply.

Details

- Connect the power supply directly to the lamp through the long wires. The lamp should light dimly at best. This is because most of the energy is being wasted in heating the wires. Don't leave this set up on for long or the wires could overheat.

- Next connect the wires to the step-up transformer at the power supply end and the step-down transformer at the lamp end. The voltage in the wires will increase by a factor of five and the current will be reduced by a similar amount. This will lead to a twenty-fifth of the heating effect and energy wastage so the lamp should be much brighter.

- To make the demonstration more like the National Grid, you could suspend the wires on retort stands.

Answers to in-text questions

a) Electrical energy would be wasted in the cables. Less electrical power would be supplied to the consumers.

b) Faults would be harder to find. The ground would need to be dug up to make the repair.

ACTIVITY & EXTENSION IDEAS

Do pylons affect our health? – Some groups believe that the electromagnetic fields produced by electrical cables seriously affect our health. The students can try to find out if there is any evidence supporting this position. It is important that the students understand the nature and quality of the evidence presented to them, so they can judge the validity of any conclusions drawn (this relates to 'How Science Works'). This can lead to a discussion about the nature of anecdotal evidence.

Choosing the right cables – There are a number of reasons for choosing which method and there is plenty of information available about how the decisions are made. The students could be given a scenario (or several) and choose which method to use to transfer electricity. The National Grid has its own web site which is a good place to start the research.

PHYSICS   ELECTRICAL ENERGY

P1a 3.4 The National Grid

LEARNING OBJECTIVES

1 Why is there a National Grid for electricity?
2 How does electricity from power stations reach our homes?

SCIENCE @ WORK

The cables of the National Grid system are well-insulated from each other and from the ground. The insulators used on electricity pylons need to be very effective as insulators – or else the electricity would short-circuit to the ground. In winter, ice on the cables can cause them to snap. Teams of electrical engineers are always on standby to deal with sudden emergencies.

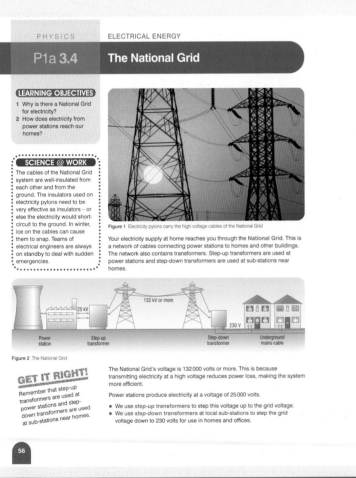

Figure 1 Electricity pylons carry the high voltage cables of the National Grid

Your electricity supply at home reaches you through the National Grid. This is a network of cables connecting power stations to homes and other buildings. The network also contains transformers. Step-up transformers are used at power stations and step-down transformers are used at sub-stations near homes.

Figure 2 The National Grid

GET IT RIGHT!

Remember that step-up transformers are used at power stations and step-down transformers are used at sub-stations near homes.

The National Grid's voltage is 132 000 volts or more. This is because transmitting electricity at a high voltage reduces power loss, making the system more efficient.

Power stations produce electricity at a voltage of 25 000 volts.

- We use *step-up* transformers to step this voltage up to the grid voltage.
- We use *step-down* transformers at local sub-stations to step the grid voltage down to 230 volts for use in homes and offices.

DEMONSTRATION

Watch a demonstration of the effect of a transformer using this apparatus.

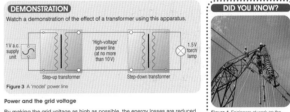

Figure 3 A 'model' power line

Power and the grid voltage

By making the grid voltage as high as possible, the energy losses are reduced to almost zero. This is because less current passes through the cables (for the same power delivered) so its heating effect is less.

a) What difference would it make if we didn't step up the grid voltage?

Underground or overground?

Lots of people object to electricity pylons. They say they spoil the landscape or they affect their health. Electric currents produce electric and magnetic fields that might affect people.

Why don't we bury all cables underground?

Underground cables would be:

- much more expensive,
- much more difficult to repair,
- difficult to bury where they cross canals, rivers and roads.

What's more, overhead cables are high above the ground. Underground cables could affect people more because the cables wouldn't be very deep.

b) Give two reasons why underground cables are more difficult to repair?

SUMMARY QUESTIONS

1 Complete the sentences below using words from the list.

bigger   down   smaller   up

a) Power stations are connected to the National Grid using step- ...... transformers. This type of transformer makes the voltage ....
b) Homes are connected to the National Grid using step- ...... transformers. This type of transformer makes the voltage ....

2 Would you buy a house next to an electricity sub-station? Find out why some people would be worried. What advice would you offer them?

3 a) Why is electrical energy transferred through the National Grid at a much higher voltage than it is generated in a power station?
b) Why are transformers needed to connect local sub-stations to the National Grid?

DID YOU KNOW?

Figure 4 Engineers at work on the Grid. They certainly need a head for heights!

The National Grid was set up in 1926. Before then, every town had its own power station. The voltages in nearby towns were often different. If there was a sudden demand for electricity in one town, nearby towns couldn't help because they had different voltages. The UK government decided electricity would be supplied to homes at 240 volts. This was lowered to 230 volts in 1994.

KEY POINTS

1 The National Grid is a network of cables and transformers.
2 We use step-up transformers to step up power stations' voltages to the grid voltage.
3 We use step-down transformers to step the grid voltage down for use in our homes.
4 A high grid voltage reduces energy loss and makes the system more efficient.

56   57

SUMMARY ANSWERS

1 a) Up, bigger.   b) Down, smaller.

2 Student research activity.

3 a) The higher the voltage, the smaller the current for the same power delivered. The power wasted due to heating of the cables is much less for a smaller current.

b) The grid voltage has to be stepped-down for use in homes. Step-down transformers are needed at the sub-stations.

KEY POINTS

Can the students explain why transformers are used to step-up and step-down the voltages in the National Grid?

P1a 3.5   Essential electricity issues

SPECIFICATION LINK-UP

P1a.11.3

Students should use their skills, knowledge and understanding of 'How Science Works':

- to calculate the cost of energy transferred from the mains using:

  Total cost = number of kilowatt-hours × cost per kilowatt-hour

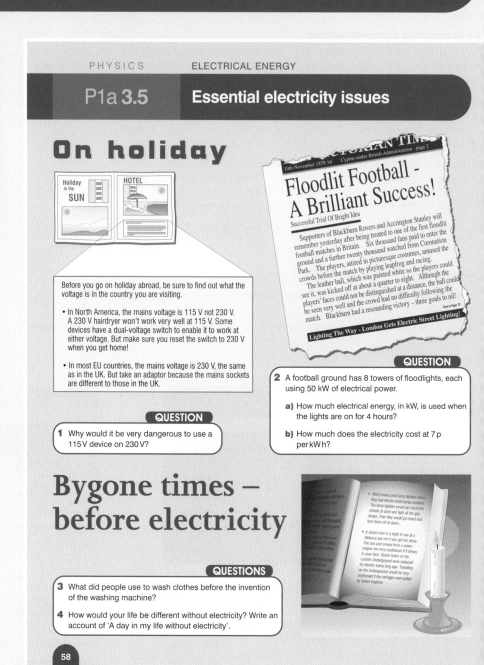

PHYSICS   ELECTRICAL ENERGY

P1a 3.5   Essential electricity issues

On holiday

Before you go on holiday abroad, be sure to find out what the voltage is in the country you are visiting.

- In North America, the mains voltage is 115 V not 230 V. A 230 V hairdryer won't work very well at 115 V. Some devices have a dual-voltage switch to enable it to work at either voltage. But make sure you reset the switch to 230 V when you get home!

- In most EU countries, the mains voltage is 230 V, the same as in the UK. But take an adaptor because the mains sockets are different to those in the UK.

QUESTION

1 Why would it be very dangerous to use a 115 V device on 230 V?

Floodlit Football – A Brilliant Success!

Successful Trial Of Bright Idea

Supporters of Blackburn Rovers and Accrington Stanley will remember yesterday after being treated to one of the first floodlit football matches in Britain. Six thousand fans paid to enter the ground and a further twenty thousand watched from Coronation Park. The players, attired in picturesque costumes, amused the crowds before the match by playing leapfrog and racing. The leather ball, which was painted white so the players could see it, was kicked off at about a quarter to eight. Although the players' faces could not be distinguished at a distance, the ball could be seen very well and the crowd had no difficulty following the match. Blackburn had a resounding victory – three goals to nil!

Lighting The Way - London Gets Electric Street Lighting!

QUESTION

2 A football ground has 8 towers of floodlights, each using 50 kW of electrical power.

   a) How much electrical energy, in kW, is used when the lights are on for 4 hours?

   b) How much does the electricity cost at 7 p per kWh?

Bygone times – before electricity

QUESTIONS

3 What did people use to wash clothes before the invention of the washing machine?

4 How would your life be different without electricity? Write an account of 'A day in my life without electricity'.

58

Teaching suggestions

Activities

Plugs – Why have different countries and different appliances got different plug designs? The students can research the designs for different countries and find out why some countries only have two pins. Why do some devices only need two wires instead of three?

Extension or homework

Even better plugs – Can the students design a better plug? They should design the shape and the materials, explaining these choices. Which parts should be conductors, which should be insulators? Why is the Earth pin slightly longer than the other two on a UK plug?

More about mains – The UK mains supply is 230 V alternating current. The students could find out why these decisions were taken. Ask: 'What does "alternating current" mean and what is it that causes it to change with a frequency of 50 Hz?' 'Why have the Americans got a system of 115 V at 60 Hz?'

Nikolai Tesla – Nikolai was a prolific inventor and excellent engineer. Although his broadcast power technology did not catch on, there are a large number of devices still in use that he invented. The students can find out what these devices are and how they affect their lives.

Lighting without electricity – Gas lamps and candle lamps are dim. Can the students find a way of making the flames brighter? Can they design a gas-lit torch where the light can be directed? This may involve a design that guides more oxygen to the flame or uses lenses to focus the beam.

Shop around?

You can get your electricity from any one of a number of different electricity companies. You can even get your gas and electricity from the same company. Companies offer different deals to attract new customers.

	Homepower	Power Co	PowerGreen
First 100 kW h of electricity	9p per kW h	10p per kW h	
Electricity above 100 kW h	7p per kW h	5p per kW h	8p per kW h

Go online now to find a better deal!

QUESTION

5 Look at the table opposite and work out which would be the best deal if

a) you use 100 kW h of electricity per month on average,

b) you use 300 kW h of electricity per month on average.

A not-so brilliant idea!

Nikolai Tesla was a brilliant electrical engineer. He made important inventions and discoveries about electric motors and generators. He even discovered how to supply electricity using radio waves. No cables were needed to supply the electricity. But no supply company would take his idea up. Why? – because anyone could tap into a radio power grid for free – just by putting an aerial up. The company wouldn't know who was using their electricity.

ACTIVITY

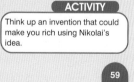

Think up an invention that could make you rich using Nikolai's idea.

59

ANSWERS TO QUESTIONS

1 Too much current would be pushed through it and it would burn out.

2 **a)** 1600 kWh **b)** £112

3 Tubs and wooden paddles.

4 Student's account.

5 **a)** PowerGreen. **b)** Power Co.

Science @ work

The idea of broadcast power has recently come to the fore again. Small (less than 1 cm^2) radio frequency identification tags (RFIDs) receive tiny amounts of energy from transmitters. They can then use the energy to send an ID signal back to a receiver. A whole shopping trolley full of items can be 'read' in seconds as it passes through a checkout. Not more checkout queues.

Learning styles

Kinaesthetic: Designing new plugs.

Visual: Thinking up a new invention.

Auditory: Reading information aloud.

Interpersonal: Discussing different mains systems.

Intrapersonal: Deducing problems.

Special needs

New football kits

How can football kits be redesigned to make them more visible to people with sight problems? Show some sample materials and discuss which would be the best for the teams to wear. Do some work under floodlights better than others? The students could design a test. Referees usually wear black, but should they change to white?

Gifted and talented

The problems with broadcast power

The fact that anybody can receive it is not the only problem with broadcast power systems. What other problems can the students think of? Are radio waves damaging to the body? What happens to the energy from the waves that are not received?

SUMMARY ANSWERS

1 a) i) A TV or visual display unit (VDU).   **ii)** An electric motor.

  b) i) Sound, thermal.   **ii)** Kinetic, thermal.

2 a) Joule, kilowatt-hour.

  b) C, B, A, D.

3 a) i) The higher one.   **ii)** 243   **iii)** £17.01

  b) i) 10   **ii)** 5 hours

4 a) 500 kWh   **b)** £35   **c)** £7

Summary teaching suggestions

- Question 1 is a simple check on the basics.

- Question 2 is more challenging, and you will probably find that some students still get confused when converting from watts to kilowatts and from minutes to hours. Check that the students understand that 10 minutes represents one-sixth of an hour, 100 W represents 0.1 kW and that they can perform calculations with these kinds of numbers.

- Questions 3 and 4 effectively summarise the important calculations and you should be encouraging the students to have a formal approach with several steps in order to lead to a clear answer; this approach will be needed for written examinations.

ELECTRICAL ENERGY: P1a 3.1 – P1a 3.5

SUMMARY QUESTIONS

1 a) Name a device that transforms electrical energy into:
  i) light and sound energy,
  ii) kinetic energy.

b) Complete the sentences below.
  i) In an electric bell, electrical energy is transformed into useful energy in the form of ...... energy and ...... energy.
  ii) In a washing machine, electrical energy is transformed into useful energy in the form of ...... energy and sometimes as ...... energy.

2 a) Which two units in the list below can be used to measure energy?

  joule   **kilowatt**   **kilowatt-hour**   **watt**

b) Rank the electrical devices below in terms of energy used from highest to lowest,
  A a 0.5 kW heater used for 4 hours,
  B a 100 W lamp left on for 24 hours,
  C a 3 kW electric kettle used 6 times for 10 minutes each time,
  D a 750 W microwave oven used for 10 minutes.

3 a) The readings of an electricity meter at the start and the end of a month are shown below.

0	9	3	7	2		0	9	6	1	5

  i) Which is the reading at the end of the month?
  ii) How many units of electricity were used during the month?
  iii) How much would this electricity cost at 7p per kWh?

b) A pay meter in a holiday home supplies electricity at a cost of 10p per kWh.
  i) How many kW h would be supplied for £1.00?
  ii) How long could a 2 kW heater be used for after £1 is put in the meter slot?

4 An escalator in a shopping centre is powered by a 50 kW electric motor. The escalator is in use for a total time of 10 hours every day.
  a) How much electrical energy in kW h is supplied to the motor each day?
  b) The electricity supplied to the motor costs 7p per kW h. What is the daily cost of the electricity supplied to the motor?
  c) How much would be saved each day if the motor was replaced by a more efficient 40 kW motor?

EXAM-STYLE QUESTIONS

1 The devices shown transform electrical energy into other forms of energy.

The list gives the useful form of energy the devices are designed to produce. Match the words in the list with the devices numbered **1** to **4**.

  A kinetic energy   **B** light
  C sound   **D** thermal energy

2 A 3 kW electric motor is switched on for 15 minutes. How much energy, in kilowatt hours, does it transfer during this time?
  A 0.0075 kWh   **B** 0.075 kWh
  C 0.75 kWh   **D** 7.50 kWh

3 Which of the following does **not** represent a unit of energy?
  A J   **B** kJ
  C kW   **D** kWh

4 The diagram shows the readings on a household electricity meter, in kWh, at the beginning and end of one week. Each kWh of electricity costs 8p.

1	8	2	4	2		1	8	5	1	1

At the beginning of the week   At the end of the week

(a) How many kWh of electricity were used during the week?
  A 242   **B** 269
  C 511   **D** 753

(b) On one day 30 kWh of electricity were used. How much would this electricity cost?
  A 24p   **B** 30p
  C £2.40   **D** £3.00

(c) During the week a 2 kW iron was used for 2.5 hours. How much energy was transformed by the iron?
  A 0.50 kWh   **B** 0.75 kWh
  C 5.00 kWh   **D** 7.50 kWh

EXAM-STYLE ANSWERS

1 **1** Kinetic energy

    2 Light

    3 Thermal energy

    4 Sound   *(1 mark each)*

2 **C**   *(1 mark)*

3 **C**   *(1 mark)*

4 a) **B**

    b) **C**

    c) **C**

    d) **C**   *(1 mark each)*

5 a) Electrical energy to heat energy.   *(1 mark)*

    b) Power is the rate at which the iron transforms energy. *(1 mark)*

    c) Energy transformed = 1.2 kW × 0.5 hour   *(1 mark)*
                          = 0.6 kW   *(1 mark)*
       Cost = 0.6 × 8p = 4.8p   *(1 mark)*

6 a) As the Grid joins all towns   *(1 mark)*
      any power station can supply any place.   *(1 mark)*

    b) i) Power losses in the cables are reduced at high p.d.s.
                                 (1 mark)
      ii) Supplied at 230 volts as the lower p.d. is safer. *(1 mark)*

    c) Transformer   *(1 mark)*
      Step-up   *(1 mark)*

    d) Underground cables would be:
      more difficult to lay   *(1 mark)*
      (difficult to bury under roads and rivers) more difficult to repair.   *(1 mark)*

(d) How much does it cost to use a 9 kW shower for half an hour?

A 3.6p   B 4.5p

C 36p   D 45p   (1)

A student uses an electric iron.

(a) What useful energy transformation takes place in the iron? (1)

(b) The iron has a power of 1.2 kW. What is meant by 'power'? (1)

(c) Electricity cost 8 p per kWh. How much does it cost the student to use the iron for 30 minutes? (3)

Each town in Britain used to have its own power station. Now electricity is supplied by a system called the National Grid.

(a) Why is the National Grid system better than each town having its own supply? (2)

(b) Electricity in power stations is generated at 25 000 volts. Explain why:
(i) it is transmitted across the National Grid system at 132 000 volts.
(ii) it is supplied to homes at 230 volts. (2)

(c) What is the name of the device used to change the potential difference of the mains supply from 25 000 volts to 132 000 volts before transmission across the National Grid? (2)

(d) Suggest why the cables of the National Grid are carried high above the ground rather than being buried underground. (2)

HOW SCIENCE WORKS QUESTIONS

Josh set up an investigation to measure the efficiency of a small electric motor. He set the motor up to lift different masses. By measuring the voltage and the current used, he could calculate the energy used by the motor to lift different masses to the same height.

Josh hypothesised that heavier masses would reduce the efficiency of a motor. His prediction was that, if he increased the mass lifted by the motor, it would use much more energy than the energy gained by the masses. He thought this would happen because the motor would require more energy and more heat would be lost. His results are in the table below.

Mass lifted (g)	Efficiency (%)
50	10
100	16
150	24
200	22
250	21
300	19
350	15

a) Plot a graph of these results. (3)

b) Describe the pattern shown by these results. (3)

c) Do these results wholly support, partly support or refute Josh's hypothesis? (1)

d) How could Josh improve the accuracy of these results? (1)

e) Why might these results not be reliable? (1)

f) How could Josh improve the reliability of these results? (1)

61

HOW SCIENCE WORKS ANSWERS

a) Graph correctly labelled, with mass lifted on the X axis and the efficiency on the Y axis. The line of best fit should be a curve, with roughly the same number of points on each side. Check the points for accurate plotting.

b) As the mass lifted increases, the efficiency increases, up to a point. After this the efficiency decreases as the mass increases.

c) The results partly support the hypothesis. Only with masses greater than 150 g does the efficiency decrease.

d) They should be repeated to increase accuracy.

e) The results have not been checked so might not be reliable.

f) To improve the reliability of these results, they could be checked by another person or by using data from other sources or by using a different method.

How science works teaching suggestions

- **Literacy guidance**
  - Key terms that should be clearly understood are: hypothesis, line of best fit, pattern, accuracy, reliability, efficiency.
  - Questions expecting a longer answer, where students can practise their literacy skills are: b) and f).

- **Higher- and lower-level answers.** Questions b), c), and d) are higher-level and the answers provided above are all at this level. Questions e) and f) are lower-level and the answers are also at this level.

- **Gifted and talented.** Able students could explore reasons for the changes in efficiency and produce new hypotheses to explain the different results.

- **How and when to use these questions.** When wishing to develop graph-drawing skills and using the data to identify patterns. The testing of a hypothesis through the production of a prediction that can be tested and the results used to develop that hypothesis. The first two questions could be completed for homework and the remainder discussed in small groups.

- **Homework.** Complete questions a) and b).

- **Special needs.** The graph could be drawn to allow speedy access to the rest of the argument.

Exam teaching suggestions

- The kilowatt hour should be introduced as a unit of energy. Its use should be explained as a sensible unit to measure energy used by domestic customers.

- Students should be reminded that when a unit is prefixed by 'kilo' the value is multiplied by 1000, as in kilogram and kilometre.

- Question 6 provides differentiation between weaker and stronger students. For example, in part a) weaker students are likely to state what the Grid does but perhaps not appreciate the implication in terms of versatility of power supply. Weaker students will find part d) difficult as it requires them to apply knowledge to an unfamiliar situation.

- Question 6 contains a number of technical terms, e.g. National Grid, supply, generate, system and transmit. You should be aware that this makes the language level quite demanding.

P1a 4.1   Fuel for electricity

LEARNING OBJECTIVES

Students should learn:

- How a fossil fuel based power station operates.

- The differences between using fossil fuels and nuclear fuels in electricity generation.

LEARNING OUTCOMES

Most students should be able to:

- Draw a flow chart showing the stages of electricity generation in a power station.

- Describe the similarities and differences between different power stations.

Some students should also be able to:

- Evaluate the advantages and disadvantages of nuclear power in comparison to fossil fuels.

Teaching suggestions

- **Special needs.** Students could be provided with a diagram of a power station and complete the labelling of the important components.

- **Gifted and talented.** If atoms are too small to see, how do we know what they are made of? The students should find out how the nuclear model of the atom was discovered.

- **Learning styles**
  Kinaesthetic: Researching information.
  Visual: Observing demonstrations.
  Auditory: Discussing nuclear power.
  Interpersonal: Reporting on waste disposal.
  Intrapersonal: Evaluating advantages and disadvantages of nuclear power in comparison to fossil fuels.

- **ICT link-up.** Many of the energy generating companies have web sites with information about power stations. Students can explore these to get a better idea of what is going on.

SPECIFICATION LINK-UP   P1a.11.4

- *In most power stations an energy source is used to heat water. The steam produced drives a turbine which is coupled to an electrical generator.*

- *Common energy sources include coal, oil and gas, which are burnt to produce heat and uranium/plutonium, in which nuclear fission produces heat.*

Students should use their skills, knowledge and understanding of 'How Science Works':

[?] • *to compare and contrast the particular advantages and disadvantages of using different energy sources to generate electricity.*

Lesson structure

STARTER

Burning? – What is burning? The students should draw a spider diagram or mind map covering what they know about combustion of fuels. (10 minutes)

Fossil fuels – Get the students to describe how coal, oil and natural gas have formed. This could be a flow chart or cartoon. (10 minutes)

Nuclear power – What do the students know about nuclear materials? Get them to list all their ideas and identify their misconceptions (e.g. radioactive things all glow in the dark). (5 minutes)

MAIN

- Start by demonstrating the combustion of some fuel. This could be a simple Bunsen flame or a spirit burner. Discuss energy being released during oxidation of carbon.

- You could put a conical flask of water above the flame and let it boil. Add a bung with a pipe to show steam generation.

- Link these ideas to electricity generation; an animation of the processes involved in a power station gets the stages across clearly. Emphasise the difference in scale and the high pressure and temperature of the steam in a power station.

- The students need to be able to state what each part of the power station does, so it is best to go through them thoroughly and check understanding at each stage.

- Demonstrate a turbine using the apparatus above or as outlined in 'Practical support'.

- When discussing the amount of energy produced by a kilogram of fuel use a
  [?] kilogram mass to give a visual clue. There is enough energy in a kilogram of coal to keep a bright (100 W) light bulb running for 1 thousand hours; that's over 41 days. There is enough energy released by 1 kg of uranium to keep the same bulb running for 10 million hours. That's over a thousand years.

- The students should be reasonably familiar with the parts of an atom and need to focus on the nucleus.

- You may be able to get the idea of fission across by showing a model nucleus made of small marbles of two colours (or similar) stuck together with Plasticine. (If students ask what the Plasticine represents, tell them it is a 'sea of gluons' and they shouldn't worry about it until they do their A-levels.)

PLENARIES

Anagrams – Ask students to decipher anagrams of important key words from this spread. (5–10 minutes)

Lightning (brain) storm – Some people suggest harnessing the electricity from lightning strikes for power. The students could brainstorm the advantages and disadvantages of this idea. (5–10 minutes)

Power station poem – The students could write an acrostic poem with the initial letters from 'power station'. (10 minutes)

ACTIVITY & EXTENSION IDEAS

? **Is nuclear power the future?** – Many countries are developing nuclear programmes to generate electricity, but is this the way forward? These are clear advantages and disadvantages between nuclear power and fossil fuels, so the students could produce a booklet allowing people to vote on which of the two methods should be developed further in the UK. The booklet should contain all of the facts from both sides of the argument and a detachable voting slip.

Waste – Ask students to come up with plans for the disposal of nuclear waste. They need to think up ideas to keep it safe, cool and easily identifiable for thousands of years. Perhaps they can research information about how it is stored now. Some might think that blasting it into space is a good idea, but they should be encouraged to think of the problems involved with this.

Answers to in-text questions

a) It goes into a cooling tower, where it condenses to water.

b) It is carried away by the hot water from the cooling tower escaping into the air.

Practical support

Demonstrating a turbine

It is possible to buy turbine demonstrating apparatus, but even if you haven't got any then the general principle is simple enough to show.

Equipment and materials required

Metal can with bung and glass pipe to let out steam, paper turbine or one of those fairground windmills on a stick, Bunsen, tripod and heat-proof mat.

Details

Half-fill the can with water and put the bung and glass tube in. Heat on a medium flame to get a decent flow of steam and then place the windmill in the flow and watch it turn. It is important to point out that the steam is invisible and can cause severe burns.

Tips: Keep the glass pipe short so that energy is not wasted and boil the water in a kettle beforehand to save a bit of time. You might get a faster flow of steam if you taper the end of the glass pipe, but sometimes this just causes the steam to condense so it is best to experiment to get the results you want.

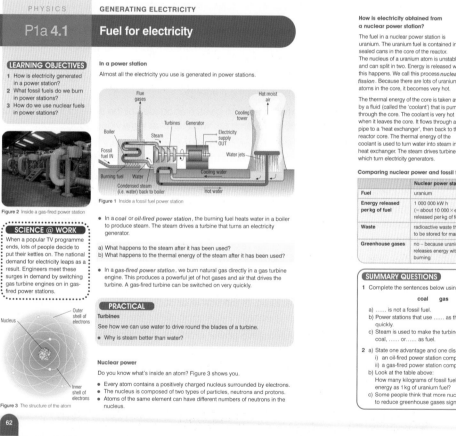

SUMMARY ANSWERS

1 a) Uranium. **b)** Gas. **c)** Oil, uranium.

2 a) i) Advantage of oil-fired power station: no radioactive waste; disadvantage: produces greenhouse gases.

ii) Advantage of gas-fired power station: can be started quicker; disadvantage – gas supplies will run out before coal supplies.

b) 10 000 kg

c) Student views. Look for arguments for and against in a balanced argument.

KEY POINTS

The students could draw a flow chart of the processes in a conventional and nuclear power station. As the processes are quite similar a single flow chart with two starting points would work well.

P1a 4.2   Energy from wind and water

LEARNING OBJECTIVES

Students should learn:

- How wind turbines can be used to generate electricity.
- How water can be used to generate electricity in a variety of ways.
- The advantages and disadvantages of the above methods of electricity generation.

LEARNING OUTCOMES

Most students should be able to:

- Describe how wind turbines generate electricity.
- Describe the different ways in which the flow of water can generate electricity.

Some students should also be able to:

- List some advantages and disadvantages of these methods of electricity generation.
- Evaluate the advantages and disadvantages of the methods of electricity generation.

Teaching suggestions

- **Gifted and talented.** Can the students design, and explain, a new form of wave power generator?
- **Learning styles**

  Kinaesthetic: Making a poster.

  Visual: Drawing an advertisement.

  Auditory: Explaining the benefits/ problems of renewable energy.

  Interpersonal: Debating the use of tidal barrages.

  Intrapersonal: Evaluating the impact on the environment.

- **Homework.** The students should be able to find out the location of the UK wind farms and find out why they were placed in these locations; can the students design a more attractive wind turbine?

SPECIFICATION LINK-UP   P1a.11.4

- *Energy from renewable energy sources can be used to drive turbines directly.*
- *Renewable energy sources used in this way include wind, the rise and fall of water due to waves and tides, and the falling of water in hydroelectric schemes.*

Students should use their skills, knowledge and understanding of 'How Science Works':

[?] • *to compare and contrast the particular advantages and disadvantages of using different energy sources to generate electricity.*

Lesson structure

STARTER

Water cycle recap – The students should draw a diagram explaining the water cycle. (10 minutes)

Tides and the Moon – Can the students explain how the Moon (and the Sun) cause tides? (10 minutes)

Wind and convection currents – Give the students a set of cards describing how wind is caused and ask them to put them in the correct order. (5 minutes)

MAIN

- You may want to show the students the ideas behind a turbine and generator. Although you won't be able to light up a bulb with wind power, you can demonstrate the principle with a hand-turned generator.
- If you have an exercise cycle with a dynamo, you can illustrate that turning the wheel more quickly produces more electrical energy.
- A video clip of a wind farm in operation gives a good idea of the scale of these structures and may also show the noise. Search for 'wind farm' at www.video.google.com.
- If you want to impress the noise problem on the students, play a sample in a continuous loop while they try to work through some of the summary questions.
- There are several alternative designs for wave-powered generators; you could ask the students how they think they work.
- The idea behind a hydroelectric scheme can be shown simply by letting water flow down a pipe from a raised reservoir. This can be directed onto a paddle wheel causing it to spin.
- You may need to show students accelerated video clips of a tide coming in or out, as they may not have seen the effect before.
- If you have access to the Internet, you may be able to find a web cam showing the current state of a major estuary. Is the tide in or out? Search the web for 'webcam estuary'.
- An Interactive, P1a 4.2 'Alternative power production' is available on the GCSE Physics CD ROM.
- [?] Compare and contrast advantages/disadvantages of the energy sources covered in this lesson as a class discussion.

PLENARIES

Wind farm advertisement – Design a poster to persuade a local community to allow a wind farm in the vicinity. Other students could design an 'anti' poster. (15–20 minutes)

Water everywhere – Most of the Earth's surface is covered with water. Ask the students to list all of the things we need water for and all of the problems we have with it. (10 minutes)

Designing a tidal barrier – The students should design a tidal barrier that generates electricity, allows traffic to cross the river, and lets boats through when necessary. (15 minutes)

Energy and energy resources

Practical support

Pumped storage

It is difficult to demonstrate this with improvised equipment, but with the correct kit it should be possible. You may wish to demonstrate it as two separate phases: pumping water uphill and then generating electricity as the water flows back.

Equipment and materials required
12 volt electric water pump, rubber tubing and two reservoirs (buckets).

Details
• Fill the lower reservoir with water and place one end of the tubing in it. Place the other in a second reservoir on a desk. You should be able to pump water to this height; if the second bucket is placed higher up you can also show the difficulty of pumping water 'uphill'.

• To drive a turbine is more difficult; you will need a specialised water turbine and generator connected to a lamp or similar. You will also need an upper reservoir with a hole to let water flow out and downhill to the generator.

ACTIVITY & EXTENSION IDEAS

Tidal barrages
Why not build a tidal barrage across the Severn or the Mersey? These rivers are ideal for generating lots of electrical energy, but what are the problems involved? Get the students to debate the issue and find out all of the potential problems.

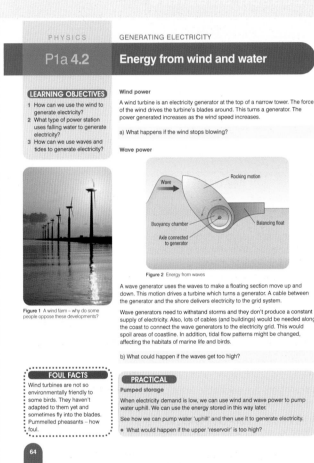

PHYSICS   GENERATING ELECTRICITY

P1a 4.2 — Energy from wind and water

LEARNING OBJECTIVES
1 How can we use the wind to generate electricity?
2 What type of power station uses falling water to generate electricity?
3 How can we use waves and tides to generate electricity?

Wind power
A wind turbine is an electricity generator at the top of a narrow tower. The force of the wind drives the turbine's blades around. This turns a generator. The power generated increases as the wind speed increases.

a) What happens if the wind stops blowing?

Wave power
A wave generator uses the waves to make a floating section move up and down. This motion drives a turbine which turns a generator. A cable between the generator and the shore delivers electricity to the grid system.

Wave generators need to withstand storms and they don't produce a constant supply of electricity. Also, lots of cables (and buildings) would be needed along the coast to connect the wave generators to the electricity grid. This would spoil areas of coastline. In addition, tidal flow patterns might be changed, affecting the habitats of marine life and birds.

b) What could happen if the waves get too high?

Figure 2 Energy from waves

Figure 1 A wind farm – why do some people oppose these developments?

FOUL FACTS
Wind turbines are not so environmentally friendly to some birds. They haven't adapted to them yet and sometimes fly into the blades. Pummelled pheasants – how foul.

PRACTICAL
Pumped storage
When electricity demand is low, we can use wind and wave power to pump water uphill. We can use the energy stored in this way later.
See how we can pump water 'uphill' and then use it to generate electricity.
● What would happen if the upper 'reservoir' is too high?

64

Hydroelectric power
We can generate hydroelectricity when rainwater collected in a reservoir (or water in a pumped storage scheme) flows downhill. The flowing water drives turbines that turn electricity generators at the foot of the hill.

c) Where does the energy for hydroelectricity come from?

Tidal power
Tidal power stations trap the water from each high tide behind a barrage. We can then release the high tide into the sea through turbines. The turbines drive generators in the barrage. One of the most promising sites in Britain is the Severn estuary. This is because the estuary becomes narrower as you move 'up-river' away from the open sea. So it 'funnels' the incoming tide and makes it higher than elsewhere.

Figure 4 A tidal power station

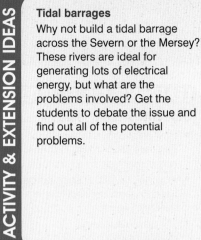
Figure 3 A hydroelectric scheme

d) Why is tidal power more reliable than wind power?

SUMMARY QUESTIONS
1 Complete the following sentences below using words from the list.

hydroelectric   tidal   wave   wind

a) ...... power does not need water.
b) ...... power does not need energy from the Sun.
c) ...... power is obtained from water running downhill.
d) ...... power is obtained from water moving up and down.

2 a) Use the table below for this question.
   i) How many wind turbines would give the same total output as a tidal power station?
   ii) How many kilometres of wave generators would give the same total output as a hydroelectric power station?
   b) Use the words below to fill in the location column in the table.

coastline   estuaries   hilly or coastal areas   mountain areas

	Output	Location
Hydroelectric power station	500 MW per station	
Tidal power station	2000 MW per station	
Wave power generators	20 MW per kilometre of coastline	
Wind turbines	2 MW per wind turbine	

c) Imagine you are a government adviser on alternative energy sources. Put the four methods in the table into an order to prioritise government spending. Explain your choices.

KEY POINTS
1 A wind turbine is an electricity generator on top of a tall tower.
2 A wave generator is a floating generator turned by the waves.
3 Hydroelectricity generators are turned by water running downhill.
4 A tidal power station traps each high tide and uses it to turn generators.

65

SUMMARY ANSWERS

1 a) Wind.
  b) Tidal.
  c) Hydroelectric.
  d) Wave.

2 a) i) 1000 ii) 25 km
  b) From top to bottom: hilly or coastal areas, estuaries, coastline, mountain areas.
  c) Student order of priority with reasoning.

Answers to in-text questions

a) No electricity is generated.
b) Too much electricity would be needed to pump the water 'uphill'.
c) From the gravitational potential energy of water in the reservoirs.
d) The tides are very predictable whereas the wind isn't.

KEY POINTS

The students could draw energy transfer diagrams for all of the devices in this spread. These should include 'wasted energy'.

65

P1a 4.3   Power from the Sun and the Earth

Teaching suggestions

- **Gifted and talented.** These students could find out how a solar cell actually works. This is quite a complex process but some may be up to it.

- **Learning styles**
  Kinaesthetic: Carrying out experiments.
  Visual: Observing the operation of solar cells and panels.
  Auditory: Discussing the effectiveness of solar cells.
  Interpersonal: Reporting on the location of geothermal power stations.
  Intrapersonal: Understanding how geothermal power stations work.

- **Homework.** As a research project, the students can find out where the best places to site geothermal power plants and solar power plants are. They should be reminded that the plants shouldn't be too far from civilisation.

- **Teaching assistant.** A teaching assistant will be of great help during the investigations or operating the solar heater.

Answers to in-text questions

a) A solar cell.   b) The motor stops.

c) The energy is from radioactive substances inside the Earth.

SPECIFICATION LINK-UP   P1a.11.4

- *Electricity can be produced directly from the Sun's radiation using solar cells.*
- *In some volcanic areas hot water and steam rise to the surface. The steam can be tapped and used to drive turbines. This is known as 'geothermal energy'.*

Students should use their skills, knowledge and understanding of 'How Science Works':
- *to compare and contrast the particular advantages and disadvantages of using different energy sources to generate electricity.*

Lesson structure

STARTER

Rock cycle recap – The students should draw a simple diagram showing the rock cycle and naming all of the rock types. (5–10 minutes)

Old faithful – Show a video clip of *Old Faithful* (search for 'Old Faithful' at www.video.google.com). Ask students if they have ever seen a geyser and if they know what causes them. (5 minutes)

Don't anger the volcano god! – Ancient civilisations believed that volcanic eruptions were caused when Gods became angered. What is the scientific explanation? (5 minutes)

MAIN

- Demonstrate a solar cell being used to turn a small fan; you may need a bright lamp to do this.
- If you have a data projector and are using this during the lesson, it is also a great light source for demonstrating solar cells on a dreary day. You can even show that some solar cells work better in different coloured light; just use coloured backgrounds to blank slides.
- You can show how inefficient the cells are by using a very bright light shining on a panel that is lighting up a small bulb.
- If students are not investigating how the amount of light falling on the cell affects the output, they can simply show this idea by moving the cell further from the lamp; the small bulb should grow visibly dimmer. Students can develop concepts of 'How Science Works' by considering how to gather quantitative data when investigating solar cells.
- Small solar-powered garden lights are available from garden centres quite cheaply. Charge one of these up during the day and then cover the light sensor during the lesson, to show that it has been charged by collecting energy from the Sun. Link this to the idea of using a battery to store the energy for night time's use which increases the expense.
- You may like to try to demonstrate the solar heating technique described in 'Practical support'.
- Show some images of solar cells used on satellites and discuss why they are an ideal solution for electricity generation in space.
- Demonstrating geothermal energy is not easy, so use video clips and diagrams to get the ideas across.
- The focus should be on understanding that the energy comes from radioactive materials.

PLENARIES

Solar car – Search the web for 'solar car video' to show the students a video clip of a solar car in action. Ask them to list the advantages and disadvantages of the design. (5–10 minutes)

Keep cool – Ask the students to come up with a design for a device that keeps you cooler the brighter the Sun is. They could produce an advertisement explaining how it works. (10–15 minutes)

Beware the wrath of the geyser gods! – Students make up their own myths about what causes geysers and you come up with flaws in the myth. (5–10 minutes)

Practical support

Solar cells
A solar cell can be demonstrated with a low-power electric motor.

Equipment and materials required
Solar cell, motor and lamp.

Details
A low-power motor will be required; complete kits containing a matched solar panel and motor are available. The students should be able to discover that the motor will turn faster the closer the lamp is to the cell. They might like to compare the speed of the motor in bright sunlight to that produced by a lamp.

Demonstrating solar heating
It is possible to show solar heating using sunlight or a bright lamp.

Equipment and materials required
Cold water tank and warmed water tank, two temperature sensors attached to a data logger, a pipe clamp, and a large metal plate sprayed matt black with a long thin tube mounted on it in a series of 's' shapes. The tube should also be black.

Details
The cold water tank can be a plastic beaker with a hole drilled in its side near the base so that a thin rubber tube can be attached. Clamp the tube at the top before starting. Connect the cold reservoir high up so that the water pressure will force water down through the long tube. Turn on the lamp to start heating the metal plate and then release a slow trickle of water. The water at the bottom should be warmer than that at the top.

Tips: Turn the lamp on a little in advance to allow the board to heat up a bit. You can also use ice cold water for the top reservoir; this causes the water to heat up due to the room temperature as it flows down the tube – it is cheating but works well.

Safety: Take care if using mains lamps – keep away from water.

Investigating solar panels
The students could investigate the energy output of solar panels. This provides an important opportunity to develop or assess investigative skills. There are two main variants:

- Investigating how the energy output is related to the area of the panel.
- Investigating how the energy output is related to the distance of the light source from the panel. These students can measure the output p.d. from the panel instead of the actual energy output.

Equipment required for each group: solar panel, bright lamp, sensitive ammeter and voltmeter, leads, metre rule or tape measure, black card to cover parts of panel.

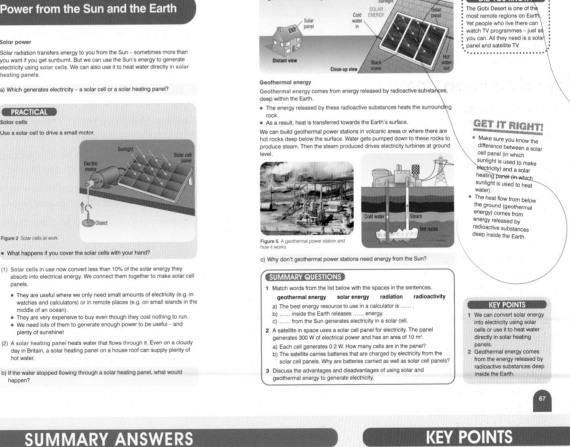

SUMMARY ANSWERS

1 a) Solar energy.
b) Radioactivity, geothermal energy.
c) Radiation.

2 a) 1500
b) To supply electricity when the solar panels are in darkness.

3 Student discussion on pros and cons of solar and geothermal energy.

KEY POINTS

- Can the students list the differences and similarities between a solar cell and a solar panel?
- They should be able to explain the origin of geothermal energy.

P1a 4.4

Energy and the environment

Students should learn:

- About how burning fossil fuels affects the environment.
- That there are severe potential hazards associated with the use of nuclear power and disposal of nuclear waste.

LEARNING OUTCOMES

Most students should be able to:

- Describe how burning fossil fuels affects the environment.
- Describe the ways in which using renewable energy resources affect the environment.

Some students should be able to:

- Explain the issues relating to nuclear fission.

Teaching suggestions

- **Learning styles**

  Kinaesthetic: Researching into decommissioning costs.

  Visual: Presenting research data.

  Auditory: Listening to news reports of disasters.

  Interpersonal: Debating the impact of nuclear disasters on the environment.

- **Homework.** Ask the students to work out how much money they could save each year if they replaced all of the light bulbs in their house with energy saving ones. They need to find the power rating of the bulbs to do this.

- **ICT link-up.** The students may like to research the details of the Chernobyl disaster. A lot of material is available on the Internet from a simple search, but they will have to be careful to find information at the correct level for them to understand.
  A PhotoPLUS, P1a 4.4 'Chernobyl', is available on the GCSE Physics CD ROM.

- **Teaching assistant.** The teaching assistant can support some of the debates and provide ideas to students. They will be invaluable on a field trip.

SPECIFICATION LINK-UP   P1a.11.4

- *Using different energy resources has different effects on the environment. These effects include the release of substances into the atmosphere, noise and visual pollution, and the destruction of wildlife habitats.*
- *The advantages and disadvantages of using fossil fuels, nuclear fuels and renewable energy sources to generate electricity. These include the cost of building power stations, the start-up time of power stations, the reliability of the energy source, the relative cost of energy generated and the location in which the energy is needed.*

Students should use their skills, knowledge and understanding of 'How Science Works':

[?] • *to compare and contrast the particular advantages and disadvantages of using different energy sources to generate electricity.*

Lesson structure

STARTER

Acid rain – Ask students to explain what acid rain is and what causes it. (5–10 minutes)

Renewable or not? – Give the students a list of energy resources and ask them to place them in either pile. (5 minutes)

Safe forever – The students should design the safest place on Earth. This is a location where materials could be locked away for thousands of years. (10–15 minutes)

MAIN

- This topic lends itself well to debate and students will wish to put their ideas forward.
- Many rule nuclear power out almost immediately without considering its benefits. You [?] may need to point out these benefits to the students to make sure that they put a bit of thought into the issue.
- It may be possible to find old news reports of the Chernobyl disaster to show.
- In this context, the term 'reliable' should be used to mean a resource that produces electricity in a predictable and fairly constant way.
- A tidal barrage is reliable, in that it will always be able to produce electricity in a well-understood pattern but the output varies from day to day.
- The damage to wildlife in the estuary, or to a habitat in flooded valleys, is the main environmental concern and is frequently tested in examinations.
- Students often confuse acid rain/global warming and the damaged ozone layer. Make sure that their ideas are clear.
- Check again that the students do not think that nuclear fuel is renewable. This is a common error.
- Have an energy saving bulb and a normal one available along with the pricing information. Ask the students which one they would buy. Can they work out how long it would take to get the extra money back? They might also notice that the energy efficient lamp takes some time to reach maximum brightness.

PLENARIES

What's the problem? – Hold up cards with environmental problems and ask the students to write down an energy resource that causes this problem. You could also use advantages cards. (5 minutes)

Greenhouse effect, ozone and acid rain – The students should write clear explanations of these three problems to make sure they do not get them confused. (5–10 minutes)

Energy resource crossword – Let the students complete a crossword of all of the key words from this chapter. (10 minutes)

Decommissioning – What is the real cost of building and decommissioning nuclear power stations? Ask the students to find out if any nuclear power stations have actually been fully dismantled and how much this has cost. Where has the waste from this decommissioning process been stored and how long will it be kept? What happens in countries that have nuclear power stations but are unable to afford to decommission them?

A field trip – It may be possible to arrange a field trip to visit a nearby fossil fuel power station or a nuclear one. This may be run in conjunction with another department, such as geography. If students go on such a trip make sure that they produce a suitable report: a few digital cameras or a video camera would help with this.

Safety: Follow local guidelines for out-of-school activities.

DID YOU KNOW?

After the Chernobyl disaster some radioactive caesium fell onto UK farmland and contaminated the grassland. Over 4 million sheep feeding off this grass became contaminated and dangerous for human consumption, so their slaughter was banned. Were the sheep lucky or unlucky? The final UK bans probably won't be lifted until 2026; that's 40 years after the accident.

PHYSICS   GENERATING ELECTRICITY

P1a 4.4   Energy and the environment

LEARNING OBJECTIVES
1 What do fossil fuels do to our environment?
2 Why are people concerned about nuclear power?
3 How do renewable energy resources affect our environment?

Can we get energy without creating any problems? Look at the chart in Figure 1.

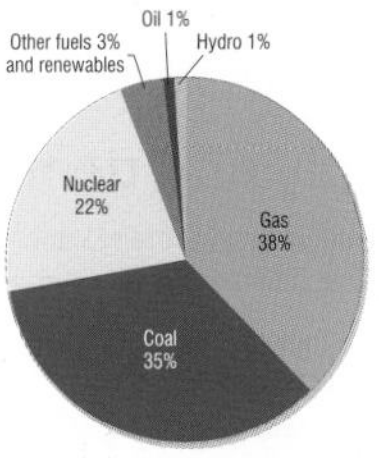

Figure 1 Energy sources for electricity

It shows the energy sources we use at present to generate electricity. What effect does each one have on our environment?

Fossil fuel problems

- When we burn coal, oil or gas, the chemical reaction makes 'greenhouse gases' such as carbon dioxide. These gases cause global warming. We only get a small percentage of our electricity from oil-fired power stations. We use much more oil to produce fuels for transport.
- Burning fossil fuels can also produce sulfur dioxide. This gas causes acid rain in the atmosphere. We can remove the sulfur from a fuel before burning it to stop acid rain. For example, natural gas has its sulfur impurities removed before we use it.
- Fossil fuels are not renewable. Sooner or later, we will have used up the Earth's reserves of fossil fuels. We will then have to find alternative sources of energy. But how soon? Oil and gas reserves could be used up within the next 50 years.

a) Which gas given off when we burn fossil fuels contributes towards:
   i) global warming?
   ii) acid rain?

FOUL FACTS
Farmers use methane gas from animal manure to generate electricity. The stronger the smell, the more electricity they get.

NEXT TIME YOU...
. . . get into a car, think about whether it would be better to walk instead.

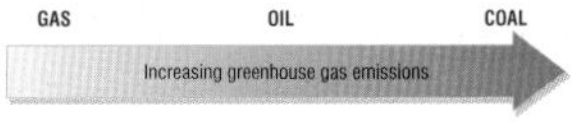

GAS   OIL   COAL

Increasing greenhouse gas emissions

Figure 2 Greenhouse gases from fossil fuels

Nuclear v renewable

We need to cut back on fossil fuels to stop global warming. Should we rely on nuclear power or on renewable energy in future?

(1) Nuclear power
Advantages
- No greenhouse gases (unlike fossil fuel).
- Much more energy from each kilogram of uranium fuel than from fossil fuel.

Disadvantages
- Used fuel rods contain radioactive waste, which has to be stored safely for centuries.
- Nuclear reactors are safe in normal operation. However, an explosion at one could release radioactive material over a wide area. This would affect these areas for many years.

b) Why is nuclear fuel non-renewable?

(2) Renewable energy sources and the environment
Advantages
Renewable energy resources
- never run out,
- do not produce greenhouse gases or acid rain,
- do not create radioactive waste products.

Disadvantages
- Wind turbines are unsightly and create a whining noise that can upset people nearby.
- Tidal barrages affect river estuaries and the habitats of creatures and plants there.
- Hydroelectric schemes need large reservoirs of water, which can affect nearby plant and animal life. Habitats are often flooded to create dams.
- Solar cells would need to cover large areas to generate large amounts of power.

c) Do wind turbines affect plant and animal life?

SUMMARY QUESTIONS
1 Choose words from the list to complete each of the sentences in a), b) and c).

acid rain   fossil fuels   greenhouse gas
plant and animal life   radioactive waste

a) Most of Britain's electricity is produced by power stations that burn ....
b) A gas-fired power station does not produce ...... or much ....
c) A tidal power station does not produce ...... like a nuclear power station does but it does affect ...... locally.

2 Match each energy source with a problem it causes.
Problem: A Acid rain, B Noise, C Radioactive waste, D Takes up land
Energy source: i) Coal, ii) Hydroelectricity, iii) Uranium, iv) Wind power

3 Make a leaflet for the general public explaining the issues involved in generating electricity using nuclear power.

DID YOU KNOW?
In 1986, some nuclear reactors at Chernobyl in Ukraine overheated and exploded. Radioactive substances were thrown high into the atmosphere. Chernobyl and the surrounding towns were evacuated. Many children from the area have since died from illnesses such as leukaemia. Radioactive material from Chernobyl was also deposited on parts of Britain.

Figure 3 Chernobyl, the site of the world's most serious accident at a nuclear power station

Figure 4 The effects of acid rain

KEY POINTS
1 Fossil fuels produce greenhouse gases.
2 Nuclear fuels produce radioactive waste.
3 Renewable energy resources can affect plant and animal life.

68

69

SUMMARY ANSWERS

1 a) Fossil fuels.
  b) Acid rain, greenhouse gas.
  c) Radioactive waste, plant and animal life.

2 i) A   ii) D   iii) C   iv) B

3 Student leaflet presenting a balanced argument for and against nuclear power.

Answers to in-text questions

a) i) Carbon dioxide.
   ii) Sulfur dioxide.

b) It turns into radioactive waste when it is used.

c) They affect birds and can upset humans.

KEY POINTS

Give the students beginnings and endings of sentences that they have to match up to make descriptions of the problems associated with electricity generation.

FOUL FACTS

Methane is actually an odourless gas: you can't smell it at all. The smell we get from natural gas used in cookers and Bunsens is actually the chemical 'mercaptan', which smells like rotten eggs. It is added to the natural gas so that we can detect leaks straight away and this reduces the risk of explosion. The smell from manure is a range of other 'aromatic' chemicals.

P1a 4.5   Big energy issues

SPECIFICATION LINK-UP

P1a.11.4

Students should use their skills, knowledge and understanding of 'How Science Works':

[?] • *to compare and contrast the particular advantages and disadvantages of using different energy sources to generate electricity.*

P1a 4.5   Big energy issues

Nuclear or not?

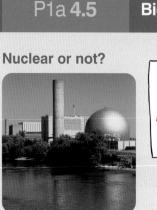

Figure 1 A nuclear power station

FOR –
About a quarter of Britain's electricity comes from nuclear power stations. Many of these stations are due to close by 2020. A new nuclear power station takes several years to build. So the Uk government must build new nuclear power stations.

AGAINST –
We don't want new nuclear power stations. We can get our electricity from renewable devices like wind turbines. We believe that renewable energy devices can provide enough electricity. We don't need new nuclear power stations.

ACTIVITY

Who is right? Find out what your friends think. Then read on before forming your opinion.

Supply and demand

The demand for electricity varies during each day. It is also higher in winter than in summer. Our electricity generators need to match these changes in demand.

Figure 2 Electricity demand

• Power stations can't just 'start up' instantly. The 'start up' time depends on the type of power station:

| natural gas | oil | coal | nuclear |

shortest start-up time ———→   ———→ longest start-up time

• Renewable energy resources are unreliable. The amount of electricity they generate depends on the conditions:

Hydroelectric	Upland reservoir could run dry.
Wind, waves	Wind and waves too weak on very calm days.
Tidal	Height of tide varies both on a monthly and yearly cycle.
Solar	No solar energy at night and variable during the day.

The variable demand for electricity is met by:

• using nuclear, coal and oil-fired power stations to provide a constant amount of electricity (the *base load* demand),
• using gas-fired power stations and pumped-storage schemes to meet daily variations in demand and extra demand in winter,
• using renewable energy sources when demand is high and renewables are in operation (e.g. use of wind turbines in winter when wind speeds are suitable),
• using renewable energy sources when demand is low to store energy in pumped storage schemes.

QUESTION

1 We need to cut back on fossil fuels to reduce greenhouse gases. What would happen if we went over completely to:

a) renewable energy?

b) nuclear power?

Teaching suggestions

Activities

[?] **The big energy debate** – The UK has signed up to a treaty to reduce carbon dioxide output; how can this best be done? Assign students (or small groups) a resource to research and present information about. After the presentations, the students vote on which resource should be used. A project like this will probably last at least a couple of hours, and it is best not to show all of the presentations; just choose the best one for each resource. As a slight alternative, the students could be provided with the information and take part in a debate with roles assigned to them by you. You could film this if resources are available, or if a media studies group want some practice.

Summing it all up – The students could draw a mind map linking all of the ideas from this chapter. This should be a big colourful poster-sized piece of work if possible. You can show or give them a template to start them off. The idea behind a mind map is that it should be drawn several times to set the ideas in the mind. The students should redraw their maps during the examination revision process.

Extension or homework

Nuclear waste storage – For homework, the students could find out about how and where nuclear waste is stored. What are the plans for dealing with it in the future? How is it transported from place to place?

Teaching assistant

The teaching assistant should join one of the groups with least confidence to help present their side of any debate.

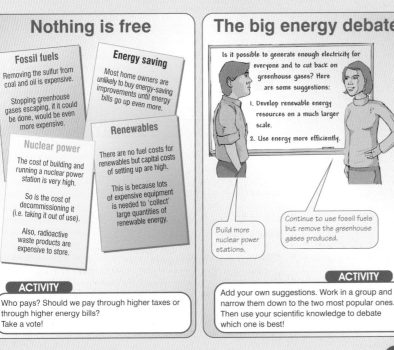

Fusion power

Energy from the Sun is produced by a process called **fusion**. Deep inside the Sun, the enormous pressure forces small nuclei to fuse together. These nuclei merge and form heavier nuclei. Energy is released in the process. Scientists have successfully built experimental fusion reactors that release energy – but not for long!

Research is continuing to find out how to turn small experimental reactors into a reactor that can supply large amounts of power. The benefits would be fantastic because we can get the fuel – hydrogen – from sea water. Even better, the reaction products, such as helium, are not radioactive!

Figure 3 Testing fusion

QUESTION

2 Explain why fusion reactors offer the promise of limitless fuel supplies and no pollution.

Nothing is free

Fossil fuels

Removing the sulfur from coal and oil is expensive.

Stopping greenhouse gases escaping, if it could be done, would be even more expensive.

Energy saving

Most home owners are unlikely to buy energy-saving improvements until energy bills go up even more.

Nuclear power

The cost of building and running a nuclear power station is very high.

So is the cost of decommissioning it (i.e. taking it out of use).

Also, radioactive waste products are expensive to store.

Renewables

There are no fuel costs for renewables but capital costs of setting up are high.

This is because lots of expensive equipment is needed to 'collect' large quantities of renewable energy.

ACTIVITY

Who pays? Should we pay through higher taxes or through higher energy bills?
Take a vote!

The big energy debate

Is it possible to generate enough electricity for everyone and to cut back on greenhouse gases? Here are some suggestions:

1. Develop renewable energy resources on a much larger scale.

2. Use energy more efficiently.

Build more nuclear power stations.

Continue to use fossil fuels but remove the greenhouse gases produced.

ACTIVITY

Add your own suggestions. Work in a group and narrow them down to the two most popular ones. Then use your scientific knowledge to debate which one is best!

71

ICT link-up/activity

Clearly this chapter lends itself to a research project in which the students find out about the costs and benefits of various resources. The students could be given a set of scenarios and produce a presentation showing possible solutions to the energy needs. For example, the needs of a large industrial city might best be met by a gas-fuelled power station, while an island community may opt for a tidal barrage or even wave power.

Learning styles

Kinaesthetic: Researching about nuclear waste.

Visual: Drawing a mind map.

Auditory: Discussing environmental problems.

Interpersonal: Debating issues.

Intrapersonal: Evaluating solutions to energy demand.

Gifted and talented

How close are we to getting nuclear fusion to work? Students could find out more detail about the progress that has been made and some of the problems that have been discovered:

- Nuclear fusion is a technology that may meet all of our energy needs one day, but even though the science is well understood it has proven very difficult to design and build a working reactor. How far off is one?

- Nuclear fusion is also not entirely clean. The reactor components may become radioactive after use, although not as dangerous as fission reactors. How does this happen?

SUMMARY ANSWERS

1 **a)** Coal, oil and natural gas.

b) Coal and oil.

c) Coal, oil, natural gas and wood.

d) Uranium.

e) Uranium.

2 **a)** **i)** Tidal. **ii)** Hydroelectric. **iii)** Wave. **iv)** Wind.

b) **i)** Wind. **ii)** Hydroelectricity. **iii)** Waves.

3 **a)** **i)** Geothermal. **ii)** Hydroelectric.

iii) Coal-fired. **iv)** Nuclear.

b) **i)** Non-renewable. **ii)** Non-fossil.

Summary teaching suggestions

- Students tend to find questions on power stations and the environment a little easier than the calculations in previous chapters, but there are a few common misconceptions to look out for. Some students will still think of uranium as very similar to fossil fuels and may think that it is burned; some will think that it is renewable; question 1 should reveal these problems.

- Questions 2 and 3 are straightforward, but watch out for those that think that wood is a fossil fuel (because 'all things that you burn are fossil fuels').

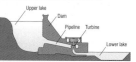

GENERATING ELECTRICITY: P1a 4.1 – P1a 4.5

SUMMARY QUESTIONS

1 Use the list of fuels below to answer a) to e).

coal   natural gas   oil   uranium   wood

a) Which fuels from the list below are fossil fuels?
b) Which fuels from the list cause acid rain?
c) Which fuels release chemical energy when they are used?
d) Which fuel releases the most energy per kilogram?
e) Which fuel produces radioactive waste?

2 a) Complete the following sentences using words from the list.

hydroelectric   tidal   wave   wind

i) ...... power stations trap sea water.
ii) ...... power stations trap rain water.
iii) ...... generators must be located along the coast line.
iv) ...... turbines can be located on hills or off-shore.

b) Which renewable energy resource transforms
i) the kinetic energy of moving air into electrical energy?
ii) the gravitational potential energy of water running downhill into electrical energy?
iii) the kinetic energy of water moving up and down into electrical energy?

3 a) Complete the sentences below using words from the list.

coal-fired   geothermal
hydroelectric   nuclear

i) A ...... power station does not produce greenhouse gases and uses energy which is from inside the Earth.
ii) A ...... power station uses running water and does not produce greenhouse gases.
iii) A ...... power station releases greenhouse gases.
iv) A ...... power station does not release greenhouse gases but does produce waste products that need to be stored for many years.

b) Wood can be used as a fuel. State whether it is
i) renewable or non-renewable,
ii) a fossil fuel or a non-fossil fuel.

EXAM-STYLE QUESTIONS

A hydroelectric power station uses two lakes.

Upper lake
Dam
Pipeline Turbine
Lower lake

1 As water flows from the top to the bottom lake it turns a turbine coupled to a generator that produces electricity. What is the energy transformation that takes place as the water flows?

A Electrical energy to kinetic energy.
B Gravitational potential energy to kinetic energy.
C Kinetic energy to gravitational potential energy.
D Kinetic energy to heat energy.

2 Where does geothermal energy come from?
A Radioactive processes in nuclear power stations.
B Radioactive processes within the Earth.
C The decay of organic material.
D The movement of the tides.

3 Renewable energy sources can be used to generate electricity. However these sources are not always available.
Match words from the list with the numbers **1** to **4** in the table.
A hydroelectric scheme
B solar cells
C tidal barrage
D wind farm

Renewable energy source	Source is available to generate electricity . . .
1	only during the daylight
2	only when the weather is suitable
3	only during certain periods of the day and night
4	usually whenever it is needed

72

EXAM-STYLE ANSWERS

1 **B** *(1 mark)*

2 **B** *(1 mark)*

3 **1** Solar cells

2 Wind farm

3 Tidal barrage

4 Hydroelectric scheme *(1 mark each)*

4 a) **B**

b) **B**

c) **D**

d) **C** *(1 mark each)*

5 a) By nuclear fission. *(1 mark)*

b) Water is heated and turned to steam. *(2 marks)*
The steam turns a turbine coupled to an electrical generator. *(2 marks)*

c) Advantages:
no CO_2 produced, so no greenhouse gases. *(1 mark)*
no SO_2 produced, so no acid rain. *(1 mark)*
Disadvantages:
produces nuclear waste that needs storing/disposal. *(1 mark)*
decomissioning is difficult. *(1 mark)*
risk of a large accident. *(1 mark)*

6 a) Coil, oil and gas. *(3 marks)*

b) i) CO_2 is a greenhouse gas *(1 mark)*
greenhouse gases trap energy from the Sun *(1 mark)*
causing global warming. *(1 mark)*
ii) SO_2 causes acid rain *(1 mark)*
killing trees and other plant life. *(1 mark)*

Wind energy, waves, tides, falling water and solar energy can all be used as energy sources to generate electricity.

(a) What do all these energy sources have in common?
- A They are available at any time of the day or night.
- B They are renewable energy sources.
- C They do not affect wildlife.
- D They do not cause any sort of pollution. (1)

(b) Which of these energy sources is most appropriate to generate electricity to run a well in a remote African village?
- A falling water
- B solar energy
- C tides
- D waves (1)

(c) Which of these energy sources is most likely to produce noise pollution when used to generate electricity?
- A solar energy
- B tides
- C waves
- D wind energy (1)

(d) Which of these energy sources is **least** likely to be associated with damaging wildlife or the habitat of wildlife when used to generate electricity?
- A falling water
- B tides
- C waves
- D wind energy (1)

In coal, gas and oil-fired power stations fuels are burnt to produce heat.

(a) How is heat produced in a nuclear power station? (1)

(b) How is the heat used to produce electricity? (4)

(c) Apart from the cost of the electricity what are the advantages and disadvantages of using a nuclear power station to produce electricity? (5)

In the UK there are three different fossil fuels burnt in power stations.

(a) Name the three fossil fuels. (3)

(b) During burning all fossil fuels release carbon dioxide into the atmosphere. Some also release sulfur dioxide.
- (i) Why does the release of carbon dioxide into the atmosphere produce a problem for the environment? (3)
- (ii) Why is the release of sulfur dioxide a problem for the environment? (2)

HOW SCIENCE WORKS QUESTIONS

Tamara was interested in solar cells. She had been given a solar cell panel in a physics kit and set out to find how surface area affected the voltage that the panel could produce. Her solar cell panel was 10 cm × 3 cm. She set up a circuit with a voltmeter and the solar cell panel.

Solar cell panel

She took the circuit into the garden and covered different parts of the panel with black paper. Her preliminary work showed that it did not matter which part of the solar cell panel was covered, just how much was covered.

a) What do you think Tamara did in her preliminary work? (2)
Her final results are in this table.

Part of panel covered	Test 1 (V)	Test 2 (V)	Average (V)
None	0.3	0.4	0.35
A bit	0.3	0.3	0.3
A bit more	0.2	0.3	0.25
Most	0.1	0.1	0.1
All	0.1	0.1	0.1

b) Tamara was pleased that her results showed what she had expected.
What do you think these results show? (1)

c) Farzana said that Tamara's independent variable was not good enough.
What did Farzana mean by this? (1)

d) How could Tamara have improved her independent variable? (1)

e) Farzana looked at the voltage readings and suggested to Tamara that they were not very useful.
Why do you think Farzana thought that the readings were not very useful? (1)

f) Farzana suggested that she used a better voltmeter.
What type of voltmeter do you think Farzana suggested? (1)

g) Is there any evidence of a zero error in Tamara's results? (1)

h) What could Tamara do about this? (1)

Exam teaching suggestions

- In question 3 students are required to match energy sources to their availability, which they may find difficult. The best way to answer questions like this is for students to read all of the statements first before they begin matching.

- Many students believe that renewable energy sources do not cause any sort of pollution and have no disadvantages connected with their use. Question 4 provides an opportunity to address this misconception.

- In answering question 5, part a), many students will think that nuclear fuels are 'burnt' and make no reference to nuclear fission.

- Question 5, part b) requires students to put the steps in the process of electricity generation into a sensible sequence. Many students will find this difficult.

- Explain to students that in order to gain all of the marks in question 5, part c), they must discuss both disadvantages and advantages associated with nuclear power. Many will simply talk about nuclear power stations being 'dangerous'. Those who do mention advantages may just say 'less pollution'. You should explain to students that in order to get all of the marks they must give specific details in their answers.

HOW SCIENCE WORKS ANSWERS

a) Tamara could have used a piece of card and placed it over different parts of the solar cell. All other variables would have been kept the same. Each time she would record the voltage. Each time the voltage would remain the same.

b) Results show that covering more of the solar cell reduces the voltage.

c) Tamara's independent variable was an ordered variable and so was not as powerful as a continuous variable.

d) To improve her independent variable, Tamara should have measured the area of the solar cell covered, this would have been a continuous variable. This would have allowed Tamara to produce a graph and her conclusion would have been more powerful.

e) The readings were only to 0.1 volts and this did not produce a difference between some of the readings for different exposures. The voltmeter was not sensitive enough.

f) Farzana probably suggested a digital voltmeter that read to 0.01 volts.

g) Yes, even when the solar cell is completely covered there is a reading of 0.1 volts.

h) She could start again! Realistically she should take 0.1 volts off each of the readings.

How science works teaching suggestions

- **Literacy guidance**
  - Key terms that should be clearly understood are: preliminary test, independent variable sensitivity, zero error.
  - Questions expecting a longer answer, where students can practise their literacy skills are: a) and e).

- **Higher- and lower-level answers.** Questions c), and d) are higher-level and the answers provided above are also at this level. Questions a) and b) are lower-level and the answers are also at this level.

- **Gifted and talented.** Able students could answer these questions without support.

- **How and when to use these questions.** Most students will need support to develop these ideas. Small group work or whole class discussion would be appropriate. The questions should develop an understanding of the need for careful choice of measuring instruments and the use of continuous independent variables.

- **Special needs.** Small groups will need to be led through the thought processes. They could have the equipment set up for them.

P1a   Examination-Style Questions

Examiner's comments

The end of unit spread should provide an opportunity to review the subject content of the whole unit. It is worthwhile having a revision lesson before students attempt the end of unit questions. This could be used as a means of testing understanding and identifying problem areas.

Students often confuse the terms fission and fusion.

Answers to Questions

Physics A

1	A			(1 mark)
2	C			(1 mark)
3	B			(1 mark)
4	1	D	solids	
	2	A	electrons	
	3	B	liquids	
	4	C	particles	(1 mark each)
5	1	B	power	
	2	C	joules	
	3	D	time	
	4	A	kilowatt-hours	(1 mark each)
6	B			(1 mark)

EXAMINATION-STYLE QUESTIONS

Physics A

1 In a nuclear power station the process that produces heat is called
   A   fission
   B   fusion
   C   radiation
   D   uranium   (1 mark)

See page 63

2 Which of these devices will transfer most energy?
   A   A 2 kW kettle used for 3 hours.
   B   A 3 kW heater used for 2 hours.
   C   A 4 kW motor used for 2 hours.
   D   A 7 kW shower used for 1 hour.   (1 mark)

See page 54

GET IT RIGH
The device with the bigg power rating may not transfer the most energ

3 Which of these statements about solar cells is correct?
   A   In a solar cell, water is heated which produces steam and drives a turbine.
   B   Solar cells can produce electricity directly from the Sun's radiation.
   C   Solar cells produce electricity even in the dark.
   D   Solar cells transform geothermal energy into electrical energy   (1 mark)

See pages 66–7

4 Thermal energy can be transferred in different ways.
   Match the words in the list with the numbers 1 to 4 in the sentences.
   A   electrons   B   liquids
   C   particles   D   solids
   Conduction occurs mainly in ......1...... All metals are good conductors because they have a lot of free ......2...... Convection occurs in gases and ......3......
   Radiation does not involve ......4......   (4 marks)

See pages 24–31

GET IT RIGH
Read through all of the sentences first and ma that they all make sens your choice of words you select your answe

5 Electrical devices transform energy from electrical energy to other forms.
   Match the words in the list with the numbers 1 to 4 in the sentences.
   A   kilowatt-hours   B   power
   C   joules   D   time
   The ......1...... of a device is the rate at which it transforms energy. Energy is normally measured in ......2...... The amount of electrical energy a device transforms depends on the rate at which the device transforms energy and the ......3...... for which it used. The amount of electrical energy transferred from the mains is measured in ......4......   (4 marks)

See pages 52–4

6 A student is doing an experiment on the rate of heat transfer from a beaker of hot water. Which of the following is true?
   A   The darker the colour of the beaker the slower the rate of heat transfer.
   B   The hotter the water the faster the rate of heat transfer.
   C   The shape of the beaker does not affect the rate of heat transfer.
   D   The temperature of the water does not affect the rate of heat transfer.   (1 mark)

See pages 26, 32–3

74

BUMP UP THE GRADE

Students should always set out calculations to show their working in order to gain credit for correct physics even if their final answer is wrong.

Many students fail to get all of the marks available in questions which ask for both advantages and disadvantages because they do not provide both.

Physics B

1 The chart shows the energy resources used to produce electricity in Britain.

See pages 62–9

Gas 34%
Nuclear 14%
Dual fuel 5%
Generated in France 4%
Hydroelectric (HEP and pumped storage) 3%
Oil 3%
Other 3%

(a) What percentage of the electricity is produced from coal? *(1 mark)*

(b) Give one advantage and one disadvantage, other than cost, of producing electricity from coal. *(2 marks)*

(c) In one power station, for every 1000 J of energy obtained from coal 300 J is wasted as heat. Use the following equation to work out the efficiency of the power station. Show clearly how you work out your answer.

$$\text{Efficiency} = \frac{\text{Useful energy transferred by the device}}{\text{Total energy transferred to the device}}$$ *(3 marks)*

See page 44

GET IT RIGHT!
When calculating efficiency make sure that you have correctly identified the useful energy transferred **by** the device and the total energy supplied **to** the device.

(d) In Britain 3% of the electricity is produced from *other* resources. One *other* resource is to use energy from the tides.
Discuss the advantages and disadvantages, other than cost, of producing electricity from tidal energy. *(3 marks)*

(e) Name one *other* resource, apart from the tides, not already given in the chart that is used to produce electricity. *(1 mark)*

2 A thermos flask is used to keep hot things hot and cold things cold. It does this by minimising heat transfer.
Explain how each of the following minimises heat transfer:

See page 32

(a) the tight fitting plastic stopper. *(2 marks)*

(b) the silver coating on the surfaces of the glass walls. *(2 marks)*

(c) the vacuum between the glass walls. *(2 marks)*

Physics B

1 (a) 34% *(1 mark)*

(b) Advantage: there are big reserves of coal in Britain. *(1 mark)*
Disadvantage: burning coal produces carbon dioxide and sulfur dioxide. *(1 mark)*

(c) Useful energy out = 1000 J *(1 mark)*
Useful energy in = 1000 + 300 = 13 000 J *(1 mark)*
$$\text{Efficiency} = \frac{1000}{1300} = 0.76$$ *(1 mark)*

(d) Disadvantages: dam has to be built across an estuary, destroying habitat of wildlife. *(1 mark)*
Only produces energy at certain times of the day. *(1 mark)*
Advantage: does not pollute the environment with greenhouse gases. *(1 mark)*

(e) Geothermal energy/wind energy/waves/solar energy. *(1 mark)*

2 (a) The plastic is a poor thermal conductor *(1 mark)*
tight fit prevents convection. *(1 mark)*

(b) Silver coating reduces radiation *(1 mark)*
because silver surfaces are poor absorbers and emitters. *(1 mark)*

(c) Vacuum reduces conduction *(1 mark)*
and convection between walls. *(1 mark)*

Key Stage 3 curriculum links

The following link to 'What you already know':

- That light travels in a straight line at a finite speed in a uniform medium.

- That non-luminous objects are seen because light scattered from them enters the eye.

- How light is reflected at plane surfaces.

- How light is refracted at the boundary between two different materials.

- That white light can be dispersed to give a range of colours.

- The effect of colour filters on white light and how coloured objects appear in white light and in other colours of light.

- How the movement of the Earth causes the apparent daily and annual movement of the Sun and other stars

- The relative positions of the Earth, Sun and planets in the Solar System.

- About the movements of planets around the Sun and to relate these to gravitational forces.

- That the Sun and other stars are light sources and that the planets and other bodies are seen by reflected light.

- About the use of artificial satellites and probes to observe the Earth and to explore the Solar System.

QCA Scheme of work
7L The Solar System and beyond
8K Light
9J Gravity and space

RECAP ANSWERS

1 **a)** The Moon, the Earth, the Sun.
   b) The Moon.

2 **a)** Star. **b)** Satellite. **c)** Planet. **d)** Sun.

3 Red, Orange, Yellow, Green, Blue, Indigo, Violet.

4 **a)** It reflects it.
   b) All colours of light are reflected the same by a mirror.
   c) An arrow pointing away from the source.

5 **a)** Gravity.
   b) The force of gravity between each planet and the Sun.
   c) The force of gravity between the rocket and the Earth.

Activity notes

GPS

GPS systems are now fairly cheap and your school may have one; check with your PE department if they go on walks and so on. It's quite good fun to hide a treasure in the school grounds and challenge a group to find it and return it to you. Position a small treasure and mark its position on the GPS system. Selected students could go out and see if they can find the treasure. A whole sport of 'geocaching' has grown up around this idea, with a large web site on the Internet.

Hubble trouble

The students should be able to find a great range of images taken from the Hubble Space Telescope, but the quality was not always this good. Some students could find out about the history of the telescope and how it was repaired a few years after launch in one of the most complicated space walks of all time. Other students could look into the ideas for replacing the Hubble.

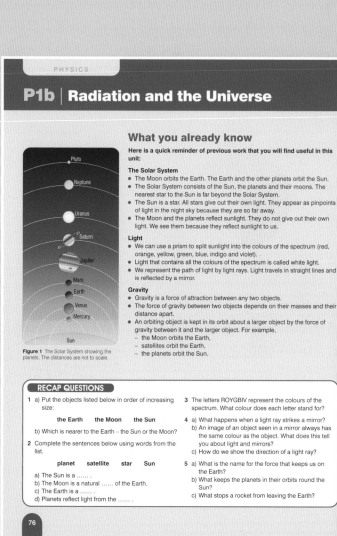

PHYSICS

P1b | Radiation and the Universe

What you already know

Here is a quick reminder of previous work that you will find useful in this unit:

The Solar System
- The Moon orbits the Earth. The Earth and the other planets orbit the Sun.
- The Solar System consists of the Sun, the planets and their moons. The nearest star to the Sun is far beyond the Solar System.
- The Sun is a star. All stars give out their own light. They appear as pinpoints of light in the night sky because they are so far away.
- The Moon and the planets reflect sunlight. They do not give out their own light. We see them because they reflect sunlight to us.

Light
- We can use a prism to split sunlight into the colours of the spectrum (red, orange, yellow, green, blue, indigo and violet).
- Light that contains all the colours of the spectrum is called white light.
- We represent the path of light by light rays. Light travels in straight lines and is reflected by a mirror.

Gravity
- Gravity is a force of attraction between any two objects.
- The force of gravity between two objects depends on their masses and their distance apart.
- An orbiting object is kept in its orbit about a larger object by the force of gravity between it and the larger object. For example,
  - the Moon orbits the Earth,
  - satellites orbit the Earth,
  - the planets orbit the Sun.

Figure 1 The Solar System showing the planets. The distances are not to scale.

Planets labelled: Pluto, Neptune, Uranus, Saturn, Jupiter, Mars, Earth, Venus, Mercury, Sun

RECAP QUESTIONS

1 a) Put the objects listed below in order of increasing size:

   the Earth   the Moon   the Sun

   b) Which is nearer to the Earth – the Sun or the Moon?

2 Complete the sentences below using words from the list.

   planet   satellite   star   Sun

   a) The Sun is a ....
   b) The Moon is a natural ...... of the Earth.
   c) The Earth is a ....
   d) Planets reflect light from the ....

3 The letters ROYGBIV represent the colours of the spectrum. What colour does each letter stand for?

4 a) What happens when a light ray strikes a mirror?
   b) An image of an object seen in a mirror always has the same colour as the object. What does this tell you about light and mirrors?
   c) How do we show the direction of a light ray?

5 a) What is the name for the force that keeps us on the Earth?
   b) What keeps the planets in their orbits round the Sun?
   c) What stops a rocket from leaving the Earth?

76

A mobile phone revolt!

You could show a map of the local town (the Geography department should have some) and place a transparent disc over it to signify the region affected by the mast. Shade one part of the disc to show the region most affected and another to indicate the range of the signal from the mast. Can the students find a suitable location for the mast in their own town? Discuss why the masts are placed on tall buildings and which buildings are used locally. Can you see any masts from your school? For higher attaining students, there is some data available about the effects of low-level microwave radiation on living organisms and the effect on schools. Try a search for terms like 'school phone mast' and you should find it on the Internet.

A Simulation, P1b 'Mobile phone masts', is also available on the GCSE Physics CD ROM.

SPECIFICATION LINK-UP

Unit Physics 1b

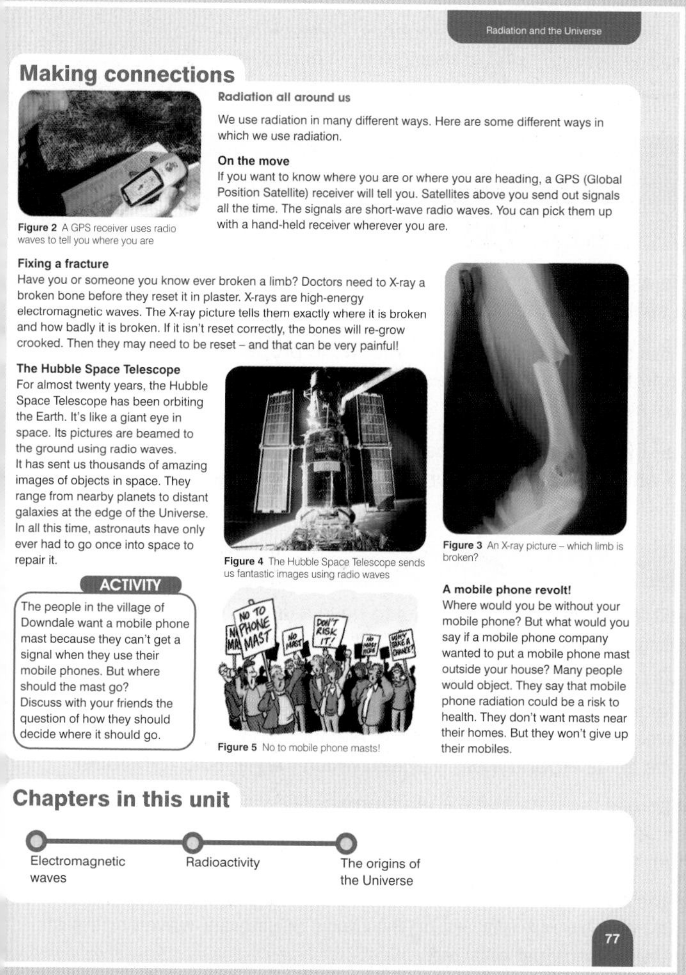

Radiation and the Universe

What are the uses and hazards of the waves that form the electromagnetic spectrum?

Electromagnetic radiations are disturbances in an electric field. They travel as waves and move energy from one place to another. They can all travel through a vacuum and do so at the same speed. The waves cover a continuous range of wavelengths called 'the electromagnetic spectrum'. The uses and hazards of the radiations in different parts of the electromagnetic spectrum depend on their wavelength and frequency.

What are the uses and dangers of emissions from radioactive substances?

Radioactive substances emit radiation from the nuclei of their atoms all the time. These nuclear radiations can be very useful, but may also be very dangerous. It is important to understand the properties of different types of nuclear radiation.

What do we know about the origins of the Universe and how it continues to change?

Current evidence suggests that the Universe is expanding and that matter and space expanded violently and rapidly from a very small initial point, i.e. the Universe began with a 'Big Bang'.

Making connections

Figure 2 A GPS receiver uses radio waves to tell you where you are

Radiation all around us

We use radiation in many different ways. Here are some different ways in which we use radiation.

On the move

If you want to know where you are or where you are heading, a GPS (Global Position Satellite) receiver will tell you. Satellites above you send out signals all the time. The signals are short-wave radio waves. You can pick them up with a hand-held receiver wherever you are.

Fixing a fracture

Have you or someone you know ever broken a limb? Doctors need to X-ray a broken bone before they reset it in plaster. X-rays are high-energy electromagnetic waves. The X-ray picture tells them exactly where it is broken and how badly it is broken. If it isn't reset correctly, the bones will re-grow crooked. Then they may need to be reset – and that can be very painful!

The Hubble Space Telescope

For almost twenty years, the Hubble Space Telescope has been orbiting the Earth. It's like a giant eye in space. Its pictures are beamed to the ground using radio waves. It has sent us thousands of amazing images of objects in space. They range from nearby planets to distant galaxies at the edge of the Universe. In all this time, astronauts have only ever had to go once into space to repair it.

Figure 4 The Hubble Space Telescope sends us fantastic images using radio waves

Figure 3 An X-ray picture – which limb is broken?

A mobile phone revolt!

Where would you be without your mobile phone? But what would you say if a mobile phone company wanted to put a mobile phone mast outside your house? Many people would object. They say that mobile phone radiation could be a risk to health. They don't want masts near their homes. But they won't give up their mobiles.

ACTIVITY

The people in the village of Downdale want a mobile phone mast because they can't get a signal when they use their mobile phones. But where should the mast go? Discuss with your friends the question of how they should decide where it should go.

Figure 5 No to mobile phone masts!

Chapters in this unit

- Electromagnetic waves
- Radioactivity
- The origins of the Universe

Space recap

Find out what the students already know by asking them to draw a diagram of the Solar System. The diagram should show all of the objects in the Solar System and how they are behaving. Check that the students know the order of the planets, have the Sun in the centre and can explain what is orbiting around what. Can they add numbers showing how long the Moon takes to orbit the Earth, etc?

Checking light

The students should be familiar with the colours of the spectrum and how white light is a mixture of these colours. Ask them to make a list of key words and definitions to do with light, including 'reflect', 'absorb' and 'spectrum' to check their knowledge. You might like to explain that there is not just one 'red' colour, but a continuous range of each of the colours that merge together. Show a range of colours to get this across. If you have a data projector, you can use a colour selector (available in most software) to show the range of colours. This will help when talking about the electromagnetic spectrum later.

Gravity

Understanding of gravity can be weak at the start of this unit, with only the higher attaining students being able to describe the relationships between the size of the force and the separation and masses. You might like to show a series of diagrams and ask them to decide if the force becomes larger or smaller as you make changes to the objects, e.g. what happens when you move the planets further apart or what happens when you reduce the mass of one of the planets?

Teaching suggestions

Common misconceptions

- It is still fairly common to find that students do not understand that the Sun is just a star like the billions of others; you might like to discuss the Sun as being a 'smallish, coolish' star that just happens to be a lot closer to us than any other star.

- Some students will be confused about colour mixing, this is especially important as they will have covered colour in art where they may talk about adding colour together to get new colours. This is subtractive colour mixing, as opposed to the mixing of coloured light. Demonstrating this early in the unit is quite important.

- There may still be some confusion about 'mass, weight and gravity'. Check that the students understand these words and that gravity is always an attractive force. With lower ability students it may be wise to check that they understand that 'down' is towards the centre of the Earth.

Chapters in this unit

- **Electromagnetic waves**
- **Radioactivity**
- **The origins of the Universe**

P1b 5.1

The electromagnetic spectrum

Students should learn:

- The names of the regions of the electromagnetic spectrum.
- What the term 'frequency' means in relation to a wave.
- That all electromagnetic waves travel at the same speed in a vacuum.
- How to calculate the wavelength of an electromagnetic wave.

Most students should be able to:

- State the parts of the electromagnetic spectrum in order of wavelength.
- Give definitions of the words frequency and wavelength.
- Describe the properties that all electromagnetic waves have in common.
- Use the wave speed equation to calculate wave speed.

Some students should also be able to:

- Rearrange and use the wave speed equation.

Teaching suggestions

- **Special needs**
  - Give the students a large diagram of the electromagnetic spectrum to annotate over the next few lessons. They can add uses and dangers to it as they go.
  - Provide templates to help the students perform the calculations.
- **Gifted and talented**
  Electromagnetic waves in other media
  The students have been told that electromagnetic waves all travel at the same speed in a vacuum, but is this true of other media? They can find out about how the speed depends on the wavelength and how this leads to dispersion in prisms and lenses.
- **Learning styles**
  Visual: Drawing wave models.

  Intrapersonal: Understanding the nature of electromagnetic radiation.
- **Homework.** The students can reinforce their understanding of the wave equation by trying some further calculations.

SPECIFICATION LINK-UP   P1b.11.5

- *Electromagnetic radiation travels as waves and moves energy from one place to another.*
- *All types of electromagnetic waves travel at the same speed through a vacuum (space).*
- *The electromagnetic spectrum is continuous, but the wavelengths within it can be grouped into types of increasing wavelength and decreasing frequency: gamma rays, X-rays, ultraviolet rays, visible light, infra-red rays, microwaves and radio waves.*
- *Electromagnetic waves obey the wave formula:*

  wave speed   = frequency × wavelength
  (metres/second, m/s)   *(hertz, Hz)*   *(metre, m)*

Lesson structure

STARTER

Rainbow – Get the students to list the colours of the spectrum in order. Then ask them to explain how they can split white light into these colours. (5–10 minutes)

What's a wave? – Give the students a set of cards with wave properties and non-wave properties. Can they separate them into two piles? Make sure you include one with 'needs a material to travel along'. (5 minutes)

Calculating speed – Can the students remember how to calculate the speed of something? Ask them to write down the equation and answer a couple of simple speed questions. (10 minutes)

MAIN

- Throughout these next few topics it will be useful to have a large diagram of the electromagnetic spectrum on the wall so that you can refer to it regularly.
- The students will have studied the electromagnetic spectrum at Key Stage 3, but many will be unfamiliar with the word 'electromagnetic'. You might like to simply explain that these waves are caused by changes in electric and magnetic fields. These are similar to the fields around a bar magnet, which they should remember.
- It is important to get across the idea that the electromagnetic waves travel best through empty space: a vacuum. When doing this, they all travel at the same speed (which is the maximum speed at which anything can travel).
- Also emphasise that the spectrum is continuous: there are ranges of each of the regions. This idea can be shown by discussing the range of different wavelengths of red pointing out that there is not just one 'red'.
- When discussing wave diagrams see 'Practical support'.
- You may wish to demonstrate some of the devices that use regions of the electromagnetic spectrum. While doing this, point out that most of them are producing or detecting energy that we cannot see.
- The main difficulty in the calculations will be the rather difficult numbers that electromagnetic waves present. You may find that some calculators cannot cope with them. Standard eight digit calculators cannot display 300 000 000; you may have to deal with velocities measured in kilometres per second instead.
- The students will have to take great care when performing the calculations and may find them easier if they 'cancel the zeros' in some of them, so that they end up with simple calculations like 3/9.
- With students that are more mathematically able, you may wish to use numbers in standard form, e.g. 3.0×10^8 m/s.

Practical support

Drawing and labelling waves

Wavelength is a reasonably simple concept, but many mistakes are made drawing and labelling waves in examinations. Point out that the wavelength can also be measured from trough to trough, or in fact any point in a wave to the next point that is doing *exactly* the same thing. Watch out for students who draw the wavelength incorrectly; this is usually from the point where the waves crosses zero displacement to the next zero, i.e. half a wavelength. A similar problem arises when labelling the amplitude on wave diagrams. This must be from the peak to the zero displacement position, i.e. half of the 'height' of the wave not the full 'height' as many students draw.

PLENARIES

Quick calculations – Show the students the wavelength of a few electromagnetic waves and ask them to quickly work out the wave speed and write it on their mini-whiteboard. (5–10 minutes)

More uses – Ask the students to describe one extra use for each of the regions of the electromagnetic spectrum. (10 minutes)

RMIVUXG? – The students may know an acronym to give the order of the visible light spectrum (ROYGBIV). Can they think up a method of remembering the regions of the electromagnetic spectrum? (5–10 minutes)

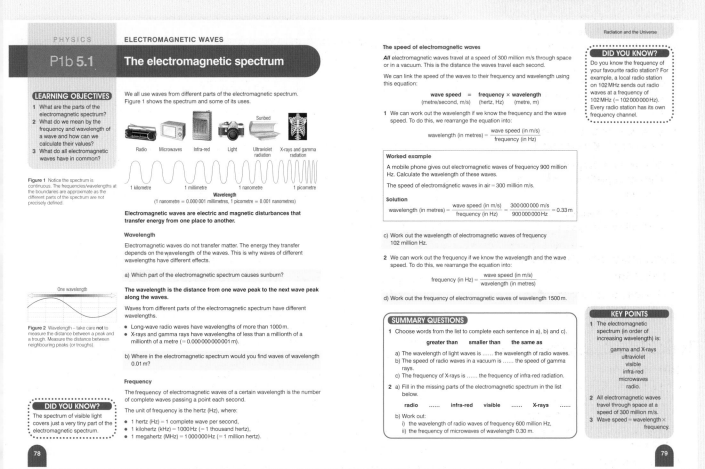

SUMMARY ANSWERS

1 a) Smaller than.

   b) The same as.

   c) Greater than.

2 a) Microwaves, ultraviolet, gamma rays.

   b) i) 0.5 m   ii) 1000 MHz

DID YOU KNOW?

National radio stations don't just send out signals on one frequency, they use several. This is because you may be in a region that receives signals from two transmitters, a situation that happens a lot when driving on motorways. If the station only broadcasts on one frequency, the two signals would interfere with each other and you would get very bad reception. Instead a good radio receiver should notice when the signal is getting weak, because you are moving too far away from one transmitter, and automatically retune to another frequency to pick up the same station from a nearer transmitter.

Answers to in-text questions

a) Ultraviolet.

b) Microwaves.

c) 2.94 m

d) 200 000 Hz

KEY POINTS

• The students should be able to draw a diagram of the electromagnetic spectrum and indicate which waves have the largest frequency and the longest wavelength.

• Can students use the wave speed equation for electromagnetic waves?

P1b 5.2 Gamma rays and X-rays

Practical support

X-rays

It may be possible to acquire an X-ray cassette from a local hospital or even dentist. They may also be able to provide help with obtaining X-ray images which are much better to handle than copies on paper. There may be confidentiality issues to deal with, but it is worth asking.

SPECIFICATION LINK-UP   P1b.11.5

- *Different wavelengths of electromagnetic radiation have different effects on living cells. Some radiations . . . . may cause cancerous changes and some may kill cells.*
- *The uses and hazards associated with the use of each type of radiation in the electromagnetic spectrum.*

Students should use their skills, knowledge and understanding of 'How Science Works':
- *to evaluate the possible hazards associated with the use of different types of electromagnetic radiation*
- *to evaluate methods to reduce exposure to different types of electromagnetic radiation.*

Lesson structure

STARTER

What's up Doc.? – Show the students a range of X-ray photographs and ask them to describe the problems they see. If you don't have originals, then you can find some obvious ones on the Internet. (5–10 minutes)

Definitions – Show the students the key words for this spread, 'absorb, reflect, emit', and ask them to write down their own definitions. (5–10 minutes)

X-ray vision – A certain alien superhero has the ability to see through objects by firing X-rays from his eyes. Ask the students to explain why this would not work and might not be too healthy for the people he is looking through. (5 minutes)

MAIN

- Start by discussing X-rays. The images are negative; the areas on the film image that are black have been exposed to X-rays while the white areas haven't. This shows that the X-rays have penetrated the soft tissues but have been absorbed by bones. An Animation is available on the GCSE Physics CD ROM to help explain this.
- This can lead to a discussion of why X-rays are harmful; the energy is absorbed in the body and damages cells, particularly cells in bones.
- You can also discuss the reason X-rays are absorbed by bone; it contains materials that are more dense, particularly calcium.
- This absorption by metals can be explained by using X-rays of fillings where the metal absorbs virtually all of the X-rays. X-rays of plates and screws in legs always fascinate.
- The difference between X-rays and gamma rays is basically how they are produced. X-rays are produced when high speed electrons are stopped by dense metals; the kinetic energy is converted into the X-rays. Gamma rays are produced by changes in the nuclei of atoms, these nuclear processes will be described in the next chapter.
- When talking about the safety precautions, you might like to ask the students what a dentist or doctor does when taking an X-ray.
- You may have a film badge to show the students, or you could mock one up from some plastic and aluminium. These badges offer no protection but they can be used to spot damage after the event.

PLENARIES

Radiation danger – Give the students the hazard symbol for ionising radiation and explain what it is supposed to represent. The students should add a list of safety precautions to the symbol; perhaps as icons below it. (5–10 minutes)

X-ray safety – Ask the students to draw illustrations showing how dentists or doctors reduce exposure to X-rays or gamma rays. (5–10 minutes)

The unknown – X-rays got their name because 'x' represents the unknown. Can the students think up a better name for them now that they understand their properties? (5 minutes)

Teaching suggestions

- **Special needs.** Present each student with a photocopy of an X-ray photograph so that they can label the areas where the X-rays pass through or are absorbed.
- **Learning styles**

  Kinaesthetic: Manipulating and examining X-ray images.

  Visual: Observing X-rays.

  Auditory: Explaining how X-rays are produced.

  Interpersonal: Discussing injuries.
- **ICT link-up.** If you have no other source of X-rays, then the Internet is a great source. To make them more realistic you could photocopy the images onto transparencies. Search on an image search engine for phrases like 'X-ray jaw' and 'X-ray chest' to find particular injuries. You could also find the analyses of the images so you know what is wrong.
- **Science @ work.** The cobalt-60 source used in these machines is very active. One such machine accidentally ended up being recycled in Mexico without the source being removed first. The resulting steel was sent around the world and only discovered when used in construction in the Los Alamos research centre in New Mexico, where it set off the radiation alarms. At least one person has died from exposure to the resulting radiation, possibly several more.

Answers to in-text questions

a) A crack is a gap that X-rays can pass through.

b) Yes.

c) To make sure it doesn't affect the surrounding normal tissue when it passes through the tumour.

d) To keep the light out without stopping the X-rays.

PHYSICS   ELECTROMAGNETIC WAVES

P1b 5.2   Gamma rays and X-rays

LEARNING OBJECTIVES

1 What do we use X-rays and gamma rays for?

2 Why are X-rays and gamma rays dangerous?

X-rays

Have you ever broken an arm or a leg? If you have, you will have gone to your local hospital for an X-ray photograph.

X-rays pass through soft tissue but they are absorbed by bones and thick metal plates. To make a radiograph or X-ray picture, X-rays from an X-ray tube are directed at the patient. A light-proof cassette containing a photographic film is placed on the other side of the patient.

Figure 1 a) Taking a chest X-ray. b) A chest X-ray.

- When the X-ray tube is switched on, X-rays from the tube pass through the patient's body. They leave a 'shadow' image on the film showing the bones.
- When the film is developed, the parts exposed to X-rays are darker than the other parts. So the bones appear lighter than the surrounding tissue which appears dark. The developed film shows a 'negative image' of the bones.

a) Why is a crack in a bone visible on a radiograph (X-ray image)?

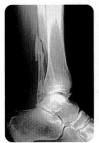

Figure 2 Spot the break

FOUL FACTS

We lose about 20% of the world's food through spoilage. One of the major causes is bacteria. The bacteria produce waste products that cause food poisoning. Exposing food to gamma radiation kills 99% of disease-carrying organisms, including *Salmonella* (found in poultry) and *Clostridium* (the cause of botulism).

Gamma radiation

Gamma radiation is electromagnetic radiation from radioactive substances. Gamma rays and X-rays have similar wavelengths so they have similar properties. For example, a lead plate will stop gamma radiation or X-rays if it is several centimetres thick.

Gamma radiation is used:

- to kill harmful bacteria in food,
- to sterilise surgical instruments,
- to kill cancer cells.

b) Will gamma radiation pass through thin plastic wrappers?

80

Radiation and the Universe

Using gamma radiation

Doctors and medical physicists use gamma therapy to destroy cancerous tumours. A narrow beam of gamma radiation is directed at the tumour. The beam is aimed at it from different directions in order to kill the tumour but not the surrounding tissue. The cobalt-60 source, which produces the gamma radiation, is in a thick lead container. When it is not in use, it is rotated away from the exit channel.

Figure 3 Gamma treatment

Rotation axis / Lead container / Cobalt–60 / Exit channel / Gamma beam

c) Why does the gamma beam need to be narrow?

Safety matters

Too much X-radiation or gamma radiation is dangerous and causes cancer. High doses kill living cells. Low doses cause cell mutation and cancerous growth. There is no evidence of a lower limit below which living cells would not be damaged.

Some people use equipment or substances that produce X-radiation or gamma radiation (or alpha or beta radiation) at work. (See page 97.) These workers must wear a film badge. If the badge is over-exposed to such radiation, its wearer is not allowed to continue working with the equipment.

d) Why does a film badge have a plastic case, and not a metal case?

Figure 4 A film badge tells you how much ionising radiation the wearer has received. Who might wear these?

SUMMARY QUESTIONS

1 Choose the correct words from the list to complete each sentence below.

        absorb   damage   penetrate

a) X-rays and gamma rays …… thin metal sheets.

b) Thick lead plates will …… X-rays and gamma rays.

c) X-rays and gamma rays …… living tissue.

2 When an X-ray photograph is taken, why is it necessary:

a) to place the patient between the X-ray tube and the film cassette?

b) to have the film in a light-proof cassette?

c) to shield those parts of the patient not under investigation from X-rays? Explain what would happen to healthy cells.

KEY POINTS

1 X-rays and gamma radiation are absorbed by dense materials such as bone and metal.

2 X-rays and gamma radiation damage living tissue when they pass through it.

3 X-rays are used in hospitals to take radiographs.

4 Gamma rays are used to kill harmful bacteria in food, to sterilise surgical equipment and to kill cancer cells.

81

SUMMARY ANSWERS

1 a) Penetrate.

  b) Absorb.

  c) Damage.

2 a) To make an image of the patient's bones on the film.

  b) To stop light from affecting the film.

  c) To prevent damage by the X-rays to the parts of the body not being X-rayed. High doses can kill living cells and low doses can cause cell mutation and cancerous growth.

KEY POINTS

The students could produce an information booklet aimed at patients about to have an X-ray or gamma ray treatment explaining what will happen to them.

P1b 5.3

Light and ultraviolet radiation

LEARNING OBJECTIVES

Students should learn that:

- Ultraviolet radiation has a higher frequency than visible light.

- UV light can be used to cause skin tanning and causes fluorescence.

- EM waves may be absorbed, reflected or transmitted by different media.

LEARNING OUTCOMES

Most students should be able to:

- Describe the uses and dangers associated with UV radiation.

- Draw diagrams illustrating the concepts of reflection, transmission and absorption.

Some students should also be able to:

- Explain what happens in reflection, transmission and absorption in terms of energy.

Teaching suggestions

- **Gifted and talented.** Why does the skin become tanned when exposed to sunlight? The students could find out what is happening to the skin and how changing colour helps protect the skin from further damage. They should make a brief report on the effects.

- **Learning styles**

  Kinaesthetic: Carrying out suncream experiments.

  Visual: Observing UV effects.

  Auditory: Explaining fluorescence.

  Interpersonal: Debating the healthiness of a tan.

  Intrapersonal: Evaluating the effectiveness of suncream.

- **ICT link-up.** Using a UV detector, you could monitor the UV levels throughout the day and the students could explore the results and discuss what times it is safer to go out in. How much longer could you stay out in the morning compared to mid-day, and still get the same dose of UV?

SPECIFICATION LINK-UP   P1b.11.5

- *Different wavelengths of electromagnetic radiation are reflected, absorbed or transmitted differently by different substances and types of surface.*

- *When radiation is absorbed, the energy it carries makes the substance which absorbs it hotter and may create an alternating current with the same frequency as the radiation itself.*

- *Different wavelengths of electromagnetic radiation have different effects on living cells. Some radiations mostly pass through soft tissue without being absorbed, some produce heat, some may cause cancerous changes and some may kill cells. These effects depend on the type of radiation and the size of the dose.*

Students should use their skills, knowledge and understanding of 'How Science Works':

- *to evaluate the possible hazards associated with the use of different types of electromagnetic radiation*

- *to evaluate methods to reduce exposure to different types of electromagnetic radiation.*

Lesson structure

STARTER

Filters – Shine a bright white light through a series of filters and ask the students to explain what is happening with a diagram. Use some combinations of filters. (5–10 minutes)

Tanning – Ask the students to describe how to get a suntan or how to avoid getting one. (10 minutes)

Fairground attractions – Can the students come up with explanations why some clothes glow on fairground rides and discos; ask then to explain where they think the energy comes from for this to happen. (5 minutes)

MAIN

- Using a data projector at the beginning of this lesson is very handy. You can use it as a bright light source to show dispersion through a prism producing a very bright spectrum. If the projector is ceiling mounted, then mount the prism on a stick.

- It is useful to demonstrate how ultraviolet can be used here, but great care must be taken with ultraviolet lamps and demonstrating fluorescence; see 'Practical support'. Many students will have seen the fluorescent effect at fairgrounds or discos.

- Check that the students understand that the ultraviolet light is being absorbed and the energy is then being reemitted as visible light; some think that the ink is giving out ultraviolet light.

- If you have a pair of sunbed 'goggles' and a ultraviolet photodiode or ultraviolet sensor, you may like to test them to demonstrate the importance of wearing them.

- During the discussion about the interaction of electromagnetic waves and materials, check understanding of the key words, especially 'transmitted'. Use the simple idea that glass transmits visible light. You might want to use an X-ray and link back to that.

- Try to get across the idea that the waves can carry a signal that can be picked up by a material when energy is absorbed by it.

PLENARIES

UV summary – The students produce a small table summarising the dangers and uses of UV light. (5–10 minutes)

UV and glass – A glass block absorbs UV light, but transmits visible light. The students must draw a diagram explaining this without *any* words. (5–10 minutes)

Cancer cover up – Students design a poster to warn about the dangers of UV radiation causing skin cancer. (15–20 minutes)

Practical support

Demonstrating fluorescence with UV light
Equipment and materials required
A UV lamp, a UV security marker, white cotton recently washed in biological washing powder; a room with blackout facilities.

Details
You must be cautious with the UV lamp in this demonstration. UV will damage the retina; the lamp must be used so that the students, and yourself, can *never* look into the bulb. This is especially important in a darkened room. Darken the room and let the lamp warm up for a few seconds before use. Shine it onto the washed cotton and it should glow noticeably (some washing powders seem to work better than others). Write on an object with the security markers and use the light to reveal the writing. During the demonstration some students will say that they can see the UV light; make sure you point out that this is merely violet light that is also produced by the bulb.

Safety: Purchase UV lamp from reputable, educational supplier and follow safety advice!

Answers to in-text questions
a) Shorter.

b) When ultraviolet radiation is directed at the ink, the ink absorbs it and emits light as a result.

c) Absorbed.

d) The ink is invisible until you shine UV light on it. Then the ink absorbs and emits it as light so objects can be marked with the security pen and ownership can be checked.

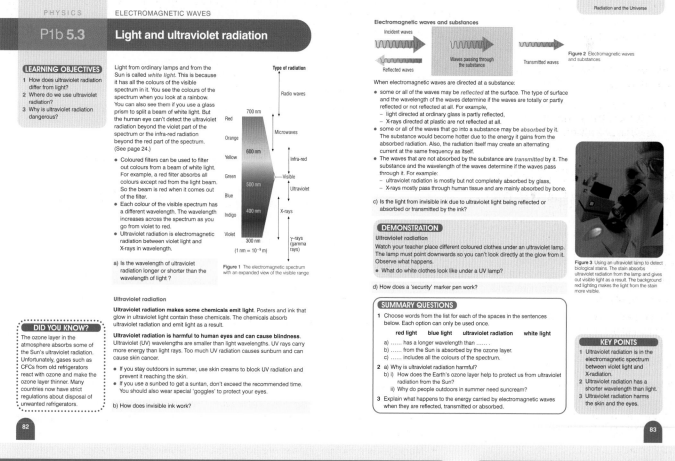

Figure 1 The electromagnetic spectrum with an expanded view of the visible range

SUMMARY ANSWERS

1 a) Red, blue. b) Ultraviolet radiation. c) White.

2 a) It harms the skin and can cause skin cancer. It damages the eyes and can cause blindness.

  b) i) It absorbs most of the ultraviolet radiation from the Sun.

   ii) Ultraviolet radiation causes sunburn. Suncreams stop UV radiation reaching the skin. Suncream absorbs the UV radiation that passes through the ozone layer.

3 Reflected – bounce off surface.
Transmitted – pass through substance.
Absorbed – substance gains energy from radiation and gets hotter. The radiation may cause an alternating current the same frequency as itself.

KEY POINTS
- Can the students describe the position of ultraviolet radiation in the electromagnetic spectrum?
- Can they describe the damage that ultraviolet radiation can cause to humans?

P1b 5.4

Infra-red, microwaves and radio waves

LEARNING OBJECTIVES

Students should learn:

- How microwaves heat material when they are absorbed by water molecules.
- The ways in which infra-red, microwaves and radio waves are used in communication systems.

LEARNING OUTCOMES

Most students should be able to:

- List the ways in which infra-red waves, microwaves and radio waves are used.
- Describe the relationship between the wavelength and frequency of these waves.

Some students should also be able to:

- Describe how alternating currents can be used to produce radio waves.
- Describe how radio waves induce alternating currents in aerials.

Teaching suggestions

- **Gifted and talented.** If you carry out the microwave experiment (and the transmitter is a polarised one; it usually is) you may like to challenge the students to find an explanation for polarisation. Point the transmitter and receiver directly at each other and switch on to show the maximum signal. Position a metal diffraction grille (a set of vertical wires) between the transmitter and receiver and rotate it. The signal should vary from maximum to zero just by rotating the plate.

- **Learning styles**

  Kinaesthetic: Investigating IR communications in the practical activity.

  Visual: Observing the transmission and blocking of signals.

  Auditory: Discussing development of phone communications.

  Interpersonal: Making deductions about what is happening to electromagnetic waves.

  Intrapersonal: Debating harm caused by microwave radiation.

SPECIFICATION LINK-UP   P1b.11.5

- *The uses and the hazards associated with the use of each type of radiation in the electromagnetic spectrum.*
- *When radiation is absorbed, the energy it carries makes the substance which absorbs it hotter and may create an alternating current with the same frequency as the radiation itself.*

Students should use their skills, knowledge and understanding of 'How Science Works':

- *to evaluate the possible hazards associated with the use of different types of electromagnetic radiation*
- *to evaluate methods to reduce exposure to different types of electromagnetic radiation.*

Lesson structure

STARTER

Infra-red recap – The students should produce a quick recap of what they know about IR already. A spider diagram would be ideal. (10 minutes)

Radio 'gaga' – Give the students a set of mixed-up sentences about radio waves and ask them to sort the words into the right order to produce correct sentences. (5–10 minutes)

Mb Fns – How does mobile phone texting work? Ask the students to explain how a text message gets from one phone to a phone in the same room. It's more complicated than most think. Can they write their answers in TXT? (5–10 minutes)

MAIN

- The first part of the lesson is basically a recap on the properties of infra-red radiation.
- The students should already be familiar with the heating effect of IR from a previous topic, but it is worth showing an IR heater again as reinforcement.
- Demonstrating an infra-red remote control should be fairly simple but the students may not be aware that the IR can be reflected, so try turning some equipment on by reflecting the signal off the whiteboard.
- Students may also be aware of IR transmitters on their mobile phones that can be used to transmit information short distances. You may like to investigate the maximum distance a message can be sent from.
- If you have a microwave oven available, you can use it to discuss shielding. The front door should contain a metal mesh used to absorb microwaves so that none leak out. These would be dangerous to people, as they would cause heating of the water in tissues. Simple microwave detectors are available.
- It is worth demonstrating a radio, especially one with a dial to adjust the frequency received. It is even better if you have a very old radio with the wavelength and frequency on the dial, so that you can discuss the connection between the two.
- You might be able to block the radio signal by placing an earthed aluminium foil shield around it so that you can explain that radio waves may be absorbed.
- If you have some walky-talkies you can test them out and see if the signal can be blocked by various materials.
- More modern mobile phones are equipped with Bluetooth technology. You can discuss this as superior communication systems to the IR mentioned above.

PLENARIES

EM wave summary – The students should produce a summary about all of the areas of the electromagnetic spectrum they have studied recently. (5 minutes)

Wave disasters – How can each type of electromagnetic wave be used to send an emergency or warning signal? Can the students think up ideas for all of them (e.g. visible light and lighthouse)? (5–10 minutes)

What's the frequency? – Give the students the frequency of some local radio stations and ask them to work out the wavelengths (and vice versa). (10–15 minutes)

Practical support

Testing infra-red signals

Infra-red signals are able to pass through several paper sheets as long at the batteries on the remote are in good order.

Equipment and materials required

Infra-red remote control and device. A TV is fine as is a data-projector.

Details

Simply place layers of paper over the transmitter one at a time to find out how many layers are needed to block the signal. You should find that larger transmitters, such as those for TVs, can send a signal through at least three sheets. Low-power transmitters, such as those operated by a button cell, struggle to get a signal through two sheets.

Demonstrating microwaves

If you have low-power microwave equipment, you may like to look at the laws of reflection for microwave radiation.

Equipment and materials required

Low-power microwave transmitter and receiver, aluminium screen, large protractor, A3 paper and ruler.

Details

Position the aluminium screen towards the back of the paper and mark its position. Draw a normal to the screen to measure angles from. Now position the transmitter so that it is off the normal and pointing to the centre of the screen. Move the receiver in an arc, always pointing to the centre of the screen, until a maximum reflected signal is found. Compare the angle of incidence and reflection for a few points to show that the law of reflection is obeyed. During the experiment discuss why aluminium is used as opposed to paper.

You may also like to investigate the penetrating power of the microwaves by seeing if they pass through various thicknesses of paper or card. Does making the paper wet make a difference? Why?

- The polished metal surface reflects the microwaves. The direction of the reflected waves is at the same angle to the metal plate as the direction of incident waves.

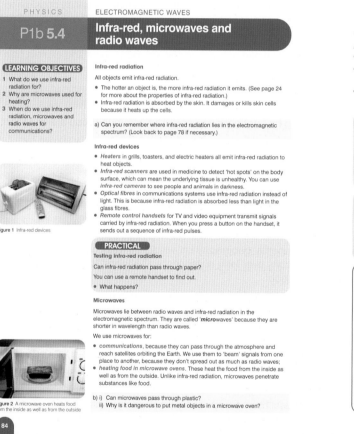

PHYSICS   ELECTROMAGNETIC WAVES

P1b 5.4

Infra-red, microwaves and radio waves

LEARNING OBJECTIVES

1 What do we use infra-red radiation for?
2 Why are microwaves used for heating?
3 When do we use infra-red radiation, microwaves and radio waves for communications?

Infra-red radiation

All objects emit infra-red radiation.

- The hotter an object is, the more infra-red radiation it emits. (See page 24 for more about the properties of infra-red radiation.)
- Infra-red radiation is absorbed by the skin. It damages or kills skin cells because it heats up the cells.

a) Can you remember where infra-red radiation lies in the electromagnetic spectrum? (Look back to page 78 if necessary.)

Infra-red devices

- *Heaters* in grills, toasters, and electric heaters all emit infra-red radiation to heat objects.
- *Infra-red scanners* are used in medicine to detect 'hot spots' on the body surface, which can mean the underlying tissue is unhealthy. You can use *infra-red cameras* to see people and animals in darkness.
- *Optical fibres* in communications systems use infra-red radiation instead of light. This is because infra-red radiation is absorbed less than light in the glass fibres.
- *Remote control handsets* for TV and video equipment transmit signals carried by infra-red radiation. When you press a button on the handset, it sends out a sequence of infra-red pulses.

Figure 1 Infra-red devices

PRACTICAL

Testing infra-red radiation

Can infra-red radiation pass through paper?

You can use a remote handset to find out.

- What happens?

Microwaves

Microwaves lie between radio waves and infra-red radiation in the electromagnetic spectrum. They are called '*micro*waves' because they are shorter in wavelength than radio waves.

We use microwaves for:

- *communications*, because they can pass through the atmosphere and reach satellites orbiting the Earth. We use them to 'beam' signals from one place to another, because they don't spread out as much as radio waves;
- *heating food in microwave ovens*. These heat the food from the inside as well as from the outside. Unlike infra-red radiation, microwaves penetrate substances like food.

b) i) Can microwaves pass through plastic?
   ii) Why is it dangerous to put metal objects in a microwave oven?

Figure 2 A microwave oven heats food from the inside as well as from the outside

84

Radio waves

Radio wave frequencies range from about 300 000 Hz to 3000 million Hz (where microwave frequencies start). Radio waves are longer in wavelength and lower in frequency than microwaves.

We use radio waves to carry radio, TV and mobile phone signals.

- Radio waves are emitted from an aerial when we apply an alternating voltage to the aerial. The frequency of the radio waves produced is the same as the frequency of the alternating voltage.
- When the radio waves pass across a receiver aerial, they cause a tiny alternating voltage in the aerial. The frequency of the alternating voltage is the same as the frequency of the radio waves received.

PRACTICAL

Testing microwaves

Look at the demonstration shown.

- What does this show?

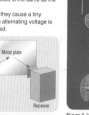

Metal plate

Figure 4 Testing microwaves   Transmitter   Receiver

Figure 3 A radio transmitter

KEY POINTS

	Frequency	Wavelength	Applications
Infra-red			heaters, communications (remote handsets, optical fibres)
Microwaves			microwave oven, communications
Radio waves			communications

SUMMARY QUESTIONS

1 Use words from the list to complete the sentences below:

infra-red radiation   light   microwaves   radio waves

a) In a TV set, the aerial detects ...... and the screen emits ....
b) In a microwave oven, food absorbs ......, heats up and emits ....

2 Complete the table below showing the type of electromagnetic radiation produced by each device a) to d).

Device	Infra-red	Microwave	Radio
a) Electric toaster			
b) Microwave oven			
c) TV broadcast transmitter			
d) Remote handset			

3 Describe how a radio transmitter produces radio waves and what happens to the radio waves at a receiver aerial.

DID YOU KNOW?

The sinking of the *Titanic* in 1912 claimed over 1500 lives. There weren't enough lifeboats for everyone. A few years earlier, two ships collided and everyone was saved – because an SOS radio message was sent out. Nearby ships got there in good time. Ship owners decided they didn't need lifeboats for everyone. After the *Titanic* disaster, they were made to put all the lifeboats back!

85

SUMMARY ANSWERS

1 a) Radio waves, light.

b) Microwaves, infra-red radiation.

2 a) Infra-red. b) Microwave. c) Radio. d) Infra-red.

3 An alternating voltage applied to an aerial produces radio waves which cause a small alternating voltage in the receiver aerial when they arrive there.

Answers to in-text questions

a) Between light and microwaves.

b) i) Yes.

ii) They cause the microwave oven to overheat, because metal objects absorb microwave radiation very easily.

KEY POINTS

The students could use a set of cards about the properties of the three groups of EM radiation to make up a table similar to the one in the Student Book.

P1b 5.5   Communications

Students should learn:

- That microwaves and radio waves are used in mobile phone networks.
- How the atmosphere, including the ionosphere, affects the range that different waves can travel.
- How optical fibres can be used to carry waves allowing them to be contained and travel around bends due to total internal reflection.

LEARNING OUTCOMES

Most students should be able to:

- Draw a simple diagram of the ways radio waves travel in the atmosphere.
- State that satellite TV signals are carried by microwaves.
- Draw a diagram explaining how light or infra-red waves travel along an optical fibre.

Some students should also be able to:

- Explain why microwaves can be used for satellite communications.

Teaching suggestions

- **Gifted and talented.** The students could investigate the relationship between wavelength, the size of gaps and the amount of diffraction that takes place.
- **Learning styles**

  Kinaesthetic: Investigating total internal reflection.

  Visual: Observing optical fibres.

  Auditory: Listening to a discussion of IT communications systems.

  Interpersonal: Collaborating in practical activity.

  Intrapersonal: Considering evidence from the practical activity.

- **ICT link-up**
  - One of your network technicians, or IT teachers, could present a brief talk about the school network, discussing all of the components (bridges, routers, modems etc.) and what they do.

SPECIFICATION LINK-UP   P1b.11.5

- *Radio waves, microwaves, infra-red and visible light can be used for communication.*
- *Microwaves can pass through the Earth's atmosphere and are used to send information to and from satellites and within mobile phone networks.*
- *Infra-red and visible light can be used to send signals along optical fibres and so travel in curved paths.*

Lesson structure

STARTER

Mix up in communications – Give the students a set of cards with communications technologies and electromagnetic waves and media that carry them and ask them to sort them out. (e.g. TV, radio waves, air). (10 minutes)

Get the message across – The students must think up as many ways as possible to communicate with each other and pass on a simple message, like 'I am hungry'. Speech is just one. (10 minutes)

Reflection – Can the students make a device to see around corners and explain how it works? They could just design it or perhaps even make it. (10–15 minutes)

MAIN

- The advantages of using higher frequency waves for communication are important.
- The concept of diffraction may not be well understood; it is typically shown by discussing waves passing and spreading out over hills.
- You can show the diffraction effect of waves with a ripple tank.
- Many students will not be aware that the atmosphere has many layers; you may wish to take a bit of time and show them a diagram of its structure from the Earth's surface to space.
- Using a globe to explain how the waves can reach places below the horizon is very helpful. You may find students' geography knowledge is weak when you are discussing communications over long distances, so it is good to show them the places you are talking about.
- If you are talking about satellite TV, you may wish to briefly mention the geostationary position of the satellites and the distances involved. With a typical globe (diameter 30 cm) the satellite would be nearly 1 m above the surface. This is part of the reason that satellite transmissions for communications show a 'time lag'.
- Demonstrate or allow the students to discover total internal reflection. See 'Practical support'.
- Demonstrate the optical fibre, see 'Practical support'.
- If you have a model optical fibre, a large curvy block designed to show multiple total internal reflections, you can show how the ray is contained within the glass; no energy leaves the glass.
- Optical fibres are used in endoscopes in medicine and also by spies and the military for seeing through walls or around corners. You may be able to find video clips of their use.

PLENARIES

Round the bend – Give the students a diagram of an optical fibre in a reasonably contorted path and ask them to draw the path of a ray that is shown entering the fibre. (5 minutes)

Sorry for the inconvenience – The students should design a leaflet from a TV or satellite TV company explaining why the television signal has been poor recently. (15–20 minutes)

Abbreviation dictionary – The students have encountered a lot of abbreviations over the past few lessons; they should make a list of these and their meanings. (10 minutes)

Practical support

Demonstrating an optical fibre

Optical fibres are easy to demonstrate in a lab even in fairly bright conditions.

Equipment and materials required

A length of optical fibre (anywhere between 2–10 m) a bright light source (preferably one that can be switched on and off quickly).

Details

Bend the fibre around several objects (perhaps the whole room). Don't bend it too much though, or the glass may crack; anything smaller than a 10 cm radius is dodgy. Allow one student to observe the distant end while you flash a torch into the near end. Even with the thinnest of fibres, the transmitted light should be obvious. The students can pass the fibre end along while the light is flashing.

Total internal reflection

The students may well be aware of this effect, but if they are not then it is simple to discover.

Equipment and materials required

For each group: ray box, power supply, single slit, blanking plates, rectangular glass or Perspex block (or semi-circular), protractor, ruler, pencil and A3 paper.

Details

The students position the block on the paper and draw around it to mark its position, in case it moves. They shine a ray of light at the front surface of the block at a small angle to the normal and mark the direction the ray enters and leaves the block. This is best done by marking the path of the ray with two small crosses, and then joining them with a straight line with the ruler. They then increase the angle and repeat the process. They should find that at a certain point, the ray is reflected by the back surface of the block; it is totally internally reflected.

PHYSICS | ELECTROMAGNETIC WAVES

P1b 5.5 Communications

LEARNING OBJECTIVES

1 Which waves do we use for mobile phones and satellite links?
2 Why can microwaves be used to carry satellite TV signals?
3 Why are optical fibres useful for communications?

Radio communications

The radio and microwave spectrum is divided into *frequency bands*. How we use each band depends on its frequency range. This is because the higher the frequency of the waves:

- the more information they can carry,
- the shorter their range (due to increasing absorption by the atmosphere),
- the less they spread out (because they diffract less).

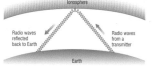

Figure 1 Using a car radio

Wavebands

Waveband	Frequency range	Uses
Microwaves	greater than 3000 MHz	Satellite links (e.g. phone and TV) Mobile phones
UHF (ultra-high frequency)	300–3000 MHz	Terrestrial TV Mobile phones
VHF (very high frequency)	30–300 MHz	Local radio (FM), Emergency services Digital radio
HF (high frequency)	3–30 MHz	Amateur radio, CB
MF (medium frequency – also called 'medium wave' or MW)	300 kHz – 3 MHz	National radio (analogue)
LF (low frequency – also called 'long wave' or LW)	less than 300 kHz	International radio (analogue)

(M = mega = million)

a) What is the difference between satellite TV and terrestrial TV?

DID YOU KNOW?

You can 'tune in' to distant LF radio stations at any time if your radio receiver is powerful enough. Long wave radio waves stay near the ground and follow the Earth's curvature.

Radio waves and the ionosphere

The ionosphere is a layer of gas in the upper atmosphere. It reflects radio waves that have frequencies less than about 30 MHz. So it reflects HF, MF and LF wavebands.

The ionosphere is stronger in summer than in winter. This is why you can listen to distant radio stations in summer but not in winter. Radio waves from these stations bounce back and forth between the ionosphere and the ground.

b) Why can't you listen to distant MF and HF radio stations in winter?

Figure 2 LF, MF and HF radio waves are reflected by the ionosphere. So they can be sent very long distances despite the curvature of the Earth.

c) Why can't you watch TV stations that are below the horizon?

Optical fibre communications

Optical fibres are very thin glass fibres. We use them to transmit signals carried by light or infra-red radiation. The light rays can't escape from the fibre. When they reach the surface of the fibre, they are reflected back into the fibre.

In comparison with radio waves and microwaves:

- optical fibres can carry much more information – this is because the frequency of light and infra-red radiation is much higher,
- optical fibres are more secure because the signals stay in the fibre.

d) Why can't we use optical fibres for satellite communications?

SUMMARY QUESTIONS

1 Choose the correct word from the list to fill in each of the spaces in the sentences below.

microwaves   radio waves

a) TV signals are carried by ....
b) Satellite TV signals are carried by ....
c) A beam of ...... can travel from the ground to a satellite but a beam of ...... waves cannot if its frequency is below 30 MHz.

2 a) Why is it not possible to tune your radio in to American local radio stations?
b) Why are signals in optical fibres more secure than radio signals?

3 Explain why we use microwaves for satellite communications.

Satellite TV

Satellite TV signals are carried by microwaves. We can detect them on the ground because they pass through the ionosphere. But you can't watch distant TV stations because the signals go straight through the ionosphere into space – they are not reflected back.

PRACTICAL

Optical fibres

Observe light shone into an optical fibre.

Figure 3 Optical fibres

- How are optical fibres used in hospitals?

KEY POINTS

1 The use we make of radio waves depends on the frequency of the waves.
2 Visible light and infra-red radiation are used to carry signals in optical fibres.

SUMMARY ANSWERS

1 a) Radio waves.
   b) Microwaves.
   c) Microwaves, radio waves.

2 a) Local radio stations transmit radio waves that are easily absorbed by the atmosphere so they can't travel far.
   b) The signals are carried by light or infra-red radiation, which can't be detected outside the fibre surface because it only enters or leaves at the ends.

3 Because microwaves are not reflected by the ionosphere. They pass straight through.

Answers to in-text questions

a) Satellite TV signals are from a transmitter on a satellite; terrestrial TV signals are from transmitters on the ground.

b) The signals pass into space because they do not reflect from the ionosphere.

c) The signals go straight through the atmosphere above you and into space.

d) Optical fibres are only suitable for fixed links.

KEY POINTS

The students should draw a diagram showing how different frequencies of waves are affected by the atmosphere.

P1b 5.6

Analogue and digital signals

SPECIFICATION LINK-UP   P1b.11.5
- *Communication signals may be analogue (continuously varying) or digital (discrete values only, generally on and off). Digital signals are less prone to interference than analogue and can be easily processed by computers.*

LEARNING OBJECTIVES

Students should learn:
- The differences between analogue (continually varying) and digital (binary) information.
- That digital signals are less prone to interference and noise effects and are simpler for computer systems to handle.

LEARNING OUTCOMES

Most students should be able to:
- Describe the differences between an analogue and digital signal.
- List the advantages that digital signal transmission has over analogue.

Some students should also be able to:
- Describe how an analogue signal can be converted to a digital one and vice-versa.

Teaching suggestions

- **Special needs.** Provide the students with an analogue signal graph already drawn and a table to fill in. They encode the graph and then try to redraw it from the numbers on another pre-prepared set of axes.
- **Gifted and talented.** Digital messages can become corrupted and distorted in a number of ways. The signal may spread as it passes along long fibres, or the noise level may be so high that bits are corrupted. Computer systems are designed to be able to correct for these errors automatically. The students can find out the basics of these problems and how they are detected and corrected.
- **Learning styles**
  Kinaesthetic: Modelling analogue and digital graphs.
  Visual: Drawing and observing analogue and digital information.
  Auditory: Listening to differences in signal quality.

Lesson structure

STARTER

Sound quality – Play the students a sound sample from a scratched record (or a real scratched record), ask them to explain what has happened to the sound to reduce the quality. You can also try this with a poor quality video cassette. (10 minutes)

Digital storage – How much information can various digital devices store? The students may be aware that a personal music player can hold 5 megabytes, but what does this mean in terms of songs and in terms of bits? (10 minutes)

Information overload – The students are given a set of cards with devices on them, and have to sort them into order by the amount of information one can hold. Examples include a CD, DVD, hard disk, digital video cassette and human brain. (5 minutes)

MAIN

- The difference between analogue information and digital information can be shown by showing a CD and a vinyl record. The CD contains a series of very small pits, representing a set of 0s and 1s, while the record has a groove that varies continually from side to side.
- You may be able to see this groove with a microscope (or better still a video microscope) but you may have to break the record.
- It is important to show some optical fibres to show that visible light can be transmitted along it. If you didn't do this on the last spread, then use the opportunity here.
- You should point out how thin the actual fibres are; most of the cable is actually protective wrapping to make it easier to handle.
- Try the analogue to digital conversion activity (see 'Practical support') to give an idea of how this conversion can be done. If time is short, you could provide the data to plot and the students can compare their results with your original.
- You might want to show how a letter can be encoded into binary bits in a byte. For example in ASCII, see 'ICT link-up'.
- It is simple to show the idea of a carrier wave to transmit a digital signal; just turn a torch on and off. The signal is the pattern of on and off, while the carrier is the electromagnetic wave.
- Modulation is a much more difficult concept to get across, especially frequency modulation. With visible light, amplitude modulation would result in changes of the brightness of the light, while frequency modulation would result in slight changes of colour. Try to discuss these ideas, but don't be too worried if there are difficulties.
- To show how easy it is to recognise a digital signal, show a diagram of a fairly badly corrupted one with noise spikes, and see if the students can translate it back into 0s and 1s.

PLENARIES

Analogue or digital – Give the students a set of cards and ask them if the information or communication method is analogue or digital. Include things like TV signals, MP3 players, tape recorders, phone signals, voices, etc. (5 minutes)

Communication crossword – The students should complete a crossword based on the electromagnetic spectrum and communications. (15 minutes)

Decoding – Give the students a binary message and a key to decode it, and see who can find the message first. You could use the ASCII code (see 'ICT link-up'). (5 minutes)

Teaching suggestions – continued

- **ICT link-up.** In ICT, characters are encoded into sequences of binary numbers. A simple system is called ASCII (American Standard Code for Information Interchange), where each character is represented by a pattern of seven bits plus an error check bit making a total of eight bits or a 'byte'. This allows for 128 possible characters, including the alphabet, numbers and punctuation symbols. For example 'a' is represented by the sequence 01100001 and 'b' by 01100010. More modern encoding systems are more complex allowing millions of characters.

Practical support

Converting analogue to digital and back

Equipment and materials required

Graph paper.

Details

Ask the students to draw a set of axes on the graph with 0–7 on the y-axis representing signal strength, and 0–15 on the x-axis representing time. They should then draw a random wave along the graph moving from left to right. Next they need to digitise this analogue wave. They should convert it into a table of numbers, but only integer numbers are allowed; so for every value of x they must write down the nearest whole number on the y-axis. Next they pass this table of data to another student, and ask them to plot a graph of the data and connect the points with a wave without seeing the original. After finishing, they can compare the two. Discuss how the copy can be made more accurate (greater resolution: 0–15 on the y-axis; faster sampling: 0–30 on the x-axis) and what advantages and problems this would have. This method leaves out the time consuming conversion to binary and back.

ACTIVITY & EXTENSION

Sending a message through a fibre

Can the students send a message through an optical fibre? You can set them this challenge for homework, or as a simple task during the lesson. For homework, they would have to come up with an encoding system of their own. Don't tell them what the message is going to be in advance.

DID YOU KNOW?

Optical fibres have more advantages too. A single fibre is a lot thinner than its metal equivalent, and so dozens can be bundled together in a thin package. Fibres are also not susceptible to 'cross talk' where a signal in one affects the signal in another (by induction). This is a big problem in long metal-wire bundles.

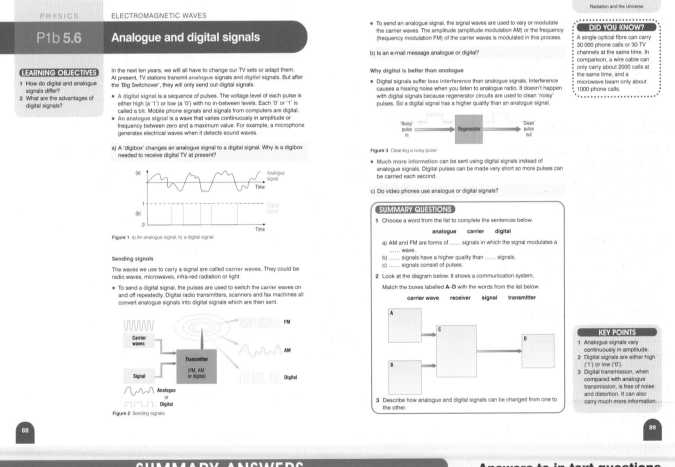

SUMMARY ANSWERS

1 a) Analogue, carrier.   b) Digital, analogue.   c) Digital.

2 A: carrier wave, B: signal, C: transmitter, D: receiver.

3 Analogue to digital: The voltage of the analogue waveform is 'sampled' (i.e. measured) automatically many times each second. Each voltage measurement is then turned electronically into a corresponding sequence of pulses. The digital signal consists of successive pulse sequences (i.e. a digital signal).
Digital to analogue: Each sequence of pulses of the digital signal is turned into a corresponding analogue voltage measurement. The analogue waveform consists of successive analogue voltage measurements.

Answers to in-text questions

a) To convert an analogue signal into a digital signal.

b) Digital.

c) Digital.

KEY POINTS

The students should make a table comparing analogue and digital signals.

P1b 5.7 Microwave issues

SPECIFICATION LINK-UP
P1b.11.5

Substantive content that can be revisited in this spread:

- *The electromagnetic spectrum is continuous but the wavelengths within it can be grouped into types of increasing wavelength and decreasing frequency: gamma rays, X-rays, ultraviolet rays, visible light, infra-red rays, microwaves and radio waves.*

- *The uses and the hazards associated with the use of each type of radiation in the electromagnetic spectrum.*

- *When radiation is absorbed, the energy it carries makes the substance which absorbs it hotter and may create an alternating current with the same frequency as the radiation itself.*

- *Different wavelengths of electromagnetic radiation have different effects on living cells. Some radiations mostly pass through soft tissue without being absorbed, some produce heat, some may cause cancerous changes and some may kill cells. These effects depend on the type of radiation and the size of the dose.*

Students should use their skills, knowledge and understanding of 'How Science Works':

- *to evaluate the possible hazards associated with the use of different types of electromagnetic radiation*

- *to evaluate methods to reduce exposure to different types of electromagnetic radiation.*

Teaching suggestions

Activities

Selling the radio spectrum – Mobile phone companies actually paid over £22 billion for their 3G UK licences, nearly making some of them bankrupt. The government used some of this to pay off debts from World War Two! Another large amount will be raised when the analogue TV bands are sold off. What do the students think should be done with this money?

The allocation of the spectrum is now controlled by Ofcom and their web site contains a complete breakdown of the uses of the radio spectrum. Search their site for the 'frequency allocation table'; it is a bit technical in parts, but it's interesting to see the varied uses of the frequencies.

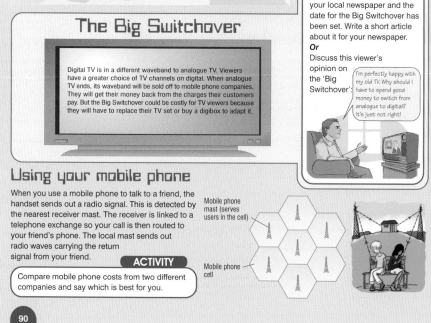

PHYSICS ELECTROMAGNETIC WAVES

P1b 5.7 Microwave issues

A key scientific invention

The Battle of the Atlantic was one of the most important battles in the Second World War. Enemy U-boat submarines almost stopped supplies from North America reaching Britain by sinking so many British cargo ships. But the submarine menace was defeated as a result of an invention in 1940 by the British scientists, John Randall and Henry Boot.

They invented the high-power magnetron. It was the first high-power microwave transmitter. It replaced the low-power microwave transmitters used until then in radar sets. The new high-power radar sets were fitted into aircraft and warships to find submarines when they surfaced.

Randall and Boot's invention was invaluable. Now we use it in microwave ovens as well as in radar systems.

QUESTION

1 A high-power radar set has a longer range than a low-power set. Why was this important in the Battle of the Atlantic?

The Big Switchover

Digital TV is in a different waveband to analogue TV. Viewers have a greater choice of TV channels on digital. When analogue TV ends, its waveband will be sold off to mobile phone companies. They will get their money back from the charges their customers pay. But the Big Switchover could be costly for TV viewers because they will have to replace their TV set or buy a digibox to adapt it.

ACTIVITY

Either
Imagine you are a journalist on your local newspaper and the date for the Big Switchover has been set. Write a short article about it for your newspaper.
Or
Discuss this viewer's opinion on the 'Big Switchover':

I'm perfectly happy with my old TV. Why should I have to spend good money to switch from analogue to digital? It's just not right!

Using your mobile phone

When you use a mobile phone to talk to a friend, the handset sends out a radio signal. This is detected by the nearest receiver mast. The receiver is linked to a telephone exchange so your call is then routed to your friend's phone. The local mast sends out radio waves carrying the return signal from your friend.

Mobile phone mast (serves users in the cell)

Mobile phone cell

ACTIVITY

Compare mobile phone costs from two different companies and say which is best for you.

90

A key scientific invention – By late in the war, radar had developed so much that a submarine could be detected at a range of several kilometres, even if it just popped up to replenish oxygen supplies or receive radio orders. The survival rates of U-boat crew were very low in the last couple of years of the war. The Germans tried to develop a U-boat that could stay under water for much longer, but the project was too late and the battle had already been lost. Once the convoy routes were secure, the build up to D-Day could begin.

You may like to look into 'stealth' technology developed to reduce the radar signature of planes and some ships. If you are discussing these ideas, then make sure that the students do not confuse radar with sonar.

The big switchover – Some areas of the UK have already switched entirely to digital transmissions, such as Llanstephan in Wales, as an experiment to see if it works well enough. There are still problems with digital television; not all of the country is covered by the signal, and reception is poor in a number of hilly areas. Should these people be provided with free satellite dishes? Should everybody else be given free 'digiboxes' when the switchover comes? This could cost hundreds of millions of pounds. The students can find a map of areas covered online or search by postcode; search for 'freeview coverage'.

Selling the radio spectrum

How can you sell radio waves? Mobile phone companies are only allowed to use a narrow band of frequencies in the UHF waveband. Mobile phone companies have to pay the Government to use these frequencies.

Who decides what each frequency band can be used for? Imagine the chaos if air traffic controllers and taxi drivers used the same frequency bands. Engineers advise the Government on the best use of each frequency band. Users are then required by law to keep to the band chosen for them.

ACTIVITY

Imagine a taxi firm uses an 'ambulance' radio channel by mistake. Write a short story about a 'mix-up' that happened when the taxi firm used the 'ambulance' radio channel.

Mobile phone hazards 12:00

Microwaves and short wave radio waves penetrate living tissues and heat the water inside living cells. This can damage or even kill the cells. Microwave ovens have safety switches that turn the microwaves off when the door is open. Also, the metal casing acts as a shield to stop microwaves from escaping.

Mobile phones send out radio waves when they are used. The waves are very low-power waves.

Is the radiation from a mobile phone hazardous? At the present time, there is no conclusive scientific evidence one way or the other. Some people believe that mobile phones can cause brain tumours. The government recommends caution, particularly for young people, until scientists and doctors can find out more.

Are mobile phones intrusive? People can get upset when mobile phone users share their views with everyone within hearing range. A videophone user who points the phone camera at someone else can be prosecuted. Mobile phone technology is here to stay but users should not upset other people or use mobile phones illegally.

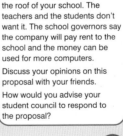

Menu   Contacts

QUESTION

2 **a)** Why might young people be more affected by mobile phone radiation than older people?

b) How would scientists see if there were a link (correlation) between the use of mobile phones and brain tumours?

c) How might scientists show that mobile phones cause brain tumours?

d) Mobile phones can be dangerous in other ways as well. Why is driving and talking on your mobile phone dangerous? You might step off the pavement at the wrong moment if you are talking to someone on your mobile at the same time. Design a poster to warn people about the dangers of using a mobile phone.

ACTIVITY

A mobile phone company wants to put a mobile phone mast on the roof of your school. The teachers and the students don't want it. The school governors say the company will pay rent to the school and the money can be used for more computers.

Discuss your opinions on this proposal with your friends.

How would you advise your student council to respond to the proposal?

91

---

1 The higher the power, the longer the range. Submarines could be detected further away using high-power radar.

2 **a)** Microwave radiation penetrates their skulls more than older skulls because their skulls are thinner. Also, smaller heads heat up more easily than bigger heads.

b) They could find out if people with brain tumours used mobile phones (e.g. average use per day per person) more than the average healthy person.

c) They could use a brain scanner to compare the brains of people who use mobile phones a lot with 'non-users'. They could conduct other tests as well, such as memory tests. They could also compare the brains of dead rats exposed to microwaves with those of unexposed rats.

d) The driver needs to concentrate on driving and is distracted by using a mobile phone at the same time.

Mobile phone hazards – You may have had a discussion about mobile phone hazards at the beginning of the chapter. If you have, you can briefly revisit the idea and see if any of the students have changed any of their opinions in light of their new knowledge. The debate here could be more focused on the social aspects of mobile phone use: where should they and where shouldn't they be allowed and the accidents that can happen when using them. There are many campaign sites available on the Internet, some with detailed information and others with vague assertions. This evidence must be evaluated before being used in any debate.

Extension or homework

The poster activities can be carried out at home, as can the research for the phone debate.

ICT link-up/activity

Information required for the debate on mobile phones and their masts is available on the Internet from a variety of sources. The students will need to evaluate the reliability of this information based on the agendas of those producing the sites; from phone companies, the government and campaign groups. This is useful for teaching about societal influences, required in the 'How Science Works' section of the specification.

Learning styles

Kinaesthetic: Role-play of mobile phone debate.

Visual: Obtaining information on phone maps.

Auditory: Discussing a range of issues.

Interpersonal: Discussing and debating.

Intrapersonal: Evaluating evidence from Internet research.

Gifted and talented

How does radar work? The students can make a booklet or presentation explaining how radio waves can be used to detect objects. They can even look into ways of avoiding being detected by radar, such as the common film tactic of 'flying in below the radar'.

1 a) D, A, B, C.

  b) i) Wave speed = wavelength × frequency

  ii) 300 million m/s

2 A: 2 **B:** 1 **C:** 3 **D:** 4

3 a) i) Ultraviolet radiation.

  ii) Light and infra-red radiation.

  iii) Gamma radiation.

  b) i) Gamma radiation.

  ii) Ultraviolet radiation.

  iii) Infra-red radiation.

4 a) i) Microwave, radio waves.

  ii) Mobile phone and TV.

  b) i) A digital signal has only two values. An analogue signal can have any value.

  ii) A digital signal is free of noise and distortion, unlike an analogue signal. A digital signal can carry more information than an analogue signal can. (See the next chapter for the explanations.)

Summary teaching suggestions

These questions mostly test the recall skills of the students and are straightforward. Some will have problems with the calculations however.

- For question 3 ii) lower ability students may not remember that filament lamps get hot, while for part iii) the higher attaining students may worry that strong infra-red radiation can damage the eyes.

- Question 4 b) should allow you to check students' understanding of the benefits of digital signals; a higher attaining student may well draw a diagram indicating the difference, and this approach should be encouraged.

1 a) Place the four different types of electromagnetic waves listed below in order of increasing wavelength.

  A Infra-red waves **B** Microwaves
  C Radio waves **D** Gamma rays

b) The radio waves from a local radio station have a wavelength of 3.3 metres in air and a frequency of 91 million hertz.
  i) Write down the equation that links frequency, wavelength and wave speed.
  ii) Calculate the speed of the radio waves in air.

2 At the top of page 282 you will find the typical wavelengths of electromagnetic waves.

Match each of **A**, **B**, **C** and **D** below with **1** to **4** in the second list.

  A 0.0005 mm **B** 1 millionth of 1 mm
  C 10 cm **D** 1000 m

  1 X-rays **2** light **3** microwaves **4** radio

3 a) Complete the following sentences using words from the list below.

  gamma radiation infra-red radiation
  light ultraviolet radiation

  i) The Earth's ozone layer absorbs ....
  ii) An ordinary lamp gives out ...... and ....
  iii) ...... passes through a metal object.
b) Which type of radiation listed above damages the following parts of the human body?
  i) the internal organs,
  ii) the eyes but not the internal organs,
  iii) the skin but not the eyes or the internal organs.

4 a) Complete each of the sentences below using words from the list.

  microwave mobile phone
  radio waves TV

  i) A ...... beam can travel from a ground transmitter to a satellite, but a beam of ...... cannot if its frequency is below 30 MHz.
  ii) ...... signals and ...... signals always come from a local transmitter.
b) i) Explain the difference between a digital signal and an analogue signal.
  ii) State and explain two advantages of digital transmission compared with analogue transmission.

EXAM-STYLE QUESTIONS

1 Electromagnetic waves can be grouped according to their wavelength and frequency.
Match the words in the list with the spaces 1 to 4 in the diagram.
  A gamma rays **B** microwaves
  C ultraviolet rays **D** visible light

  Increasing wavelength, decreasing frequency

  1 X-rays 2 3 Infra red rays 4 Radio waves

2 The number of waves passing a point each second is the ...
  A amplitude **B** frequency
  C speed **D** wavelength

3 Which of the following statements about the waves of the electromagnetic spectrum is true?
  A They all have the same frequency.
  B They all have the same wavelength.
  C They all travel at the same speed through space.
  D They cannot travel through a vacuum.

4 The uses of the radiations in different parts of the electromagnetic spectrum depend on their wavelength and frequency.

(a) Shadow pictures of the bones can be produced using ...
  A microwaves. **B** ultraviolet rays.
  C visible light. **D** X-rays.

(b) Which type of electromagnetic radiation is used to send signals from a TV remote control?
  A infra-red rays. **B** microwaves.
  C radio waves. **D** ultraviolet rays.

(c) Which type of electromagnetic radiation is used to sterilise surgical instruments?
  A gamma rays **B** microwaves
  C ultraviolet rays **D** visible light

(d) What is the equation that relates the speed, wavelength and frequency of the waves of the electromagnetic spectrum?
  A Speed = frequency × wavelength
  B Speed = frequency ÷ wavelength
  C Speed = wavelength ÷ frequency
  D Speed = wavelength + frequency

EXAM-STYLE ANSWERS

1 1 gamma rays

  2 ultraviolet rays

  3 visible light

  4 microwaves *(1 mark each)*

2 B *(1 mark)*

3 C *(1 mark)*

4 a) D

  b) A

  c) A

  d) A *(1 mark each)*

5 a) Visible light *(1 mark)*
  Infra red *(1 mark)*

  b) An analogue signal can have any value. *(1 mark)*
  A digital signal is a series of on and off (1 and 0) pulses. *(1 mark).*

  c) The signal picks up noise as it travels. *(1 mark)*
  The noise is also amplified. *(1 mark)*
  So amplified signal is different to the original. *(1 mark)*

6 a) May kill cells *(1 mark)*
  or cause cancer. *(1 mark)*

  b) Any three from:
  - causes tanning,
  - burning,
  - skin cancer,
  - damage to eyes. *(3 marks)*

  c) Cells are mostly water. *(1 mark)*
  Water is heated by microwaves causing damage/bursting. *(1 mark)*

5 (a) Information can be transmitted through optical fibres.
Name two types of electromagnetic wave used to carry information through an optical fibre. (2)

(b) Information can be sent as a digital signal or an analogue signal. What is the difference between a digital and an analogue signal? (2)

(c) A signal gets weaker as it travels and needs to be amplified. Explain why an amplified analogue signal will have deteriorated compared with the original signal. (3)

6 Astronauts in space wear special suits designed to prevent dangerous radiation from the Sun reaching their bodies.

Explain how each of these types of electromagnetic radiation can harm the body:

(a) gamma rays (2)

(b) ultraviolet rays (3)

(c) microwaves. (2)

HOW SCIENCE WORKS QUESTIONS

Your teacher has set up a demonstration of light radiation. She used a slide projector to shine light onto a prism. The prism split the light into the colours of the rainbow – a spectrum. Then a thermistor was placed into the spectrum of light.

Thermistors can be used to measure heat. When put into a circuit, the hotter the thermistor the greater the voltage, measured by a voltmeter.

You can get a better idea of what she did from this diagram.

The thermistor was gradually moved through the spectrum from the violet end to the red end and beyond. The voltage was taken every 10 seconds and the colour of light was also recorded.

Here are the results.

Time (seconds)	Voltage (mV)	Colour
0	745	none
10	750	violet
20	760	indigo
30	770	blue
40	780	green
50	790	yellow
60	800	orange
70	810	red
80	990	none

a) What is the pattern in these results? Complete the sentence:
The longer the wavelength of light ...... (1)

b) Which result could be an anomaly? (1)

c) What should be done with this anomaly? (2)

d) If you wanted to draw a graph showing how the voltage varied with time, explain what type of graph you would use. (2)

Exam teaching suggestions

- These questions should not be attempted until students have covered all of the work on the electromagnetic spectrum, including applications.

- Question 5 is about communications. A weaker student is likely to give only one example in part a).

- To gain both marks in question 5b), students must describe both digital and analogue signals. Weaker students will be able to describe a digital signal only.

- A common misconception is that students think noise consists of sound waves. Only the most able students are likely to score all three marks in question 5c). Weaker students will appreciate that the signal picks up noise but will not develop their answer beyond this.

HOW SCIENCE WORKS ANSWERS

a) The longer the wavelength of light the higher the voltage.

b) The reading after 80 seconds could be an anomaly.

c) The anomaly should be investigated further.

d) A line graph.
Because both the independent variable (time) and the dependent variable (voltage) are continuous variables.

How science works teaching suggestions

- **Literacy guidance**
  - Key terms that should be clearly understood are: anomaly pattern, thermistor.
  - Questions expecting a longer answer, where students can practise their literacy skills are: a) and c).

- **Higher- and lower-level questions.** Question c) is higher-level and the answer provided above is also at this level. Question a) is lower-level and the answer is also at this level.

- **Gifted and talented.** Able students could explore the reason for the increase in voltage as they moved through the spectrum. Also the reading when there is no light shining on the thermistor. Could this be a systematic error?

- **How and when to use these questions.** When wishing to develop the idea that anomalies should be considered for their cause and not simply dismissed. This could be a useful introduction to infra-red. It is a similar set up to the discovery of infra-red by William Herschel on September 11 in 1800. It is an example of the clever scientist who is prepared to accept that hypotheses can be wrong and errors can be turned to advantage.

- **Homework.** Collect examples of surfaces that feel hot if you do not touch them, but do not look hot.

- **Special needs.** The thermistor could be demonstrated.

P1b 6.1   Observing nuclear radiation

Students will learn:

- The basic structure of an atom.
- That unstable nuclei decay and emit invisible radiation when the structure of the nucleus changes to become more stable.
- That this radiation can be detected in a number of ways including by a GM tube.

LEARNING OUTCOMES

Most students should be able to:

- Draw a diagram illustrating the structure of an atom (nuclear model)
- State what we mean by a 'radioactive' substance.
- Describe ways in which radioactivity can be detected.

Some students should also be able to:

- Explain why some substances are radioactive.

Teaching suggestions

- **Learning styles**

  Kinaesthetic: Modelling the structure of an atom.

  Visual: Observing demonstrations/computer animations and simulations.

  Auditory: Listening to descriptions of nuclear processes.

  Interpersonal: Discussing the dangers of scientific research.

  Intrapersonal: Evaluating safety precautions.

- **ICT link-up**

  - The students cannot handle radioactive material, but the simulations on the GCSE Physics CD ROM allow them to explore ideas safely. These are an excellent way to visualise the behaviour of the particles and waves and to study absorption. They can also demonstrate the half-life of materials, a process that is too difficult to show with real substances in class. However, it is best to use these simulations alongside real apparatus if possible, to show that the models are linked to physical reality.

  - If you do not want the student to get too close to the sources, then you could connect a small video camera to a data projector to show the demonstrations more clearly.

SPECIFICATION LINK-UP   P1b.11.6

- *The basic structure of an atom is a small central nucleus composed of protons and neutrons surrounded by electrons.*
- *Some substances give out radiation from the nuclei of their atoms all the time, whatever is done to them. These substances are said to be radioactive.*

Lesson structure

STARTER

Seeing the invisible – How can we detect things that we cannot see? Ask students to come up with a list of things that we cannot see and how we can detect their presence, e.g. air, infra-red radiation. (5–10 minutes)

Atom – What does an atom look like? Ask the students to draw and label one before showing them our current (nuclear) model. Does an atom really *look* like this? (5–10 minutes)

Atom models – Give the students a set of cut-out protons, neutrons and electrons and ask them to make a model atom. (10 minutes)

MAIN

- Before carrying out any demonstrations involving radioactive material, make certain that you are familiar with local handling rules. (See 'Practical notes'.)
- Start by checking knowledge of atomic structure, protons, neutrons and electrons, as this is essential in discussing isotopes later.
- You can then discuss the history of the discovery of radioactivity. You should point out that although the initial discovery was accidental, the investigation into the cause was a thorough scientific one.
- Marie Curie died aged 67 partly because of her work. Similar things happened with early researchers into X-rays. This shows that even scientists under-estimate the hazards of their research.
- Show the presence of radiation due to the sources by using a GM tube or spark detector. (See 'Practical support'.)
- If you have a video camera and projector you may want to use it to show the detail of the experiment without getting the students too close.
- Use the Simulation P1b 6.2 'Alpha, beta and gamma radiation' on the GCSE Physics CD ROM to show the different types of radiation coming from the nucleus.
- Emphasise that nuclear radiation is caused by changes in the nucleus. You could link back to the difference between X-rays (caused by electrons) and gamma rays (caused by the nucleus).
- You might ask the students to draw the nucleus of a couple of isotopes to check that they understand the term. If you do this, it is worth reminding them that the nucleus is really spherical; not just a disc. Show a model made of marbles stuck together; if one falls off, then attribute it to nuclear decay.
- Some students may like to know why the nucleus decays. The reason for the nucleus changing is linked to energy. The nucleus changes so that it has less energy; the parts that make it up have become more tightly bound; this is yet another example of energy spreading out.

PLENARIES

Isotope analysis – The students are given a list of isotopes to draw the structure of, or diagrams of nuclei for them to describe. They could use a periodic table to help identify the element. (10 minutes)

Murder mystery – The body of a press photographer has been found in a sealed room, all of the film in her camera has gone black even though it hasn't been used. Write a letter to the police explaining what you think happened and how you know. (5–10 minutes)

It's elementary – Give the students a list of recently discovered elements and see if they can figure out what they are named after (Californium, Curium, Nobelium, etc). What would the students call an element that they discovered? What symbol would it have? (5 minutes)

Practical support

Demonstrating radioactive sources safely

Radioactive sources can be used to demonstrate important aspects of this chapter, but there are important safety considerations to take into account. Your school should have a set of local rules that apply to the storage and handling of radioactive sources, and these should inform you as to the ways to handle practical activities. You should make the students fully aware of the dangers associated with the sources, but also emphasise that you will be handling them with great care and they are in no danger as long as they too follow sensible procedures. You should discuss the reasons for the safety points below with the students:

- Do not handle radioactive sources until you have had a training session from the school Radiation Protection Supervisor.
- Under *no* circumstances allow the students to handle the sources.
- Always minimise exposure; keep the sources in the storage container whenever they are not being used and only demonstrate with the sources for the minimum time possible to get the concept across.
- Always handle the sources with tongs away from the trunk of your body to minimise exposure.
- Perform experiments in a large tray, so that if sources are dropped they do not roll and fall to the floor.
- Check all sources are returned to the storage container and storage facility before the end of the lesson.

Using a GM tube and ratemeter

The usual way of showing the presence of ionising radiation is by using a Geiger Müller tube and ratemeter. This has the advantage that the count rate is proportional to the activity, and some of the students will be familiar with the device from films and television.

Equipment and materials required

Geiger Müller tube, ratemeter (and possibly high voltage power supply), large plastic tray, tongs, radioactive sources, laboratory coat.

Details

The operating voltage of the GM tube is usually 400 V and this is usually provided by the ratemeter, but you may need an external supply for tubes that connect to computers. Check with the manual if you still have it. Position the detector in the tray and switch it on. Bring the sources close to the tube window and the ratemeter should count. If you can find a ratemeter that clicks, the demonstration is a lot more fun.

Using a spark detector

A spark detector can be used to show the presence of ionising radiation. Although they are now uncommon, they are a little more dramatic than the GM tube.

Equipment and materials required

Spark detector, high voltage power supply (possibly up to 4000 V), a large plastic tray, tongs, radioactive sources, laboratory coat.

Details

Ideally you should have the manual to find out what operating voltage is required, but you can test this out in advance. Position the detector in the tray and switch the power supply on. Bring the sources, one at a time, close to the wire on the detector. The radiation should ionise the air causing sparks between the grid and wire; the more active the source the more sparks. With this technique, you should be able to show the range of alpha and beta sources in air.

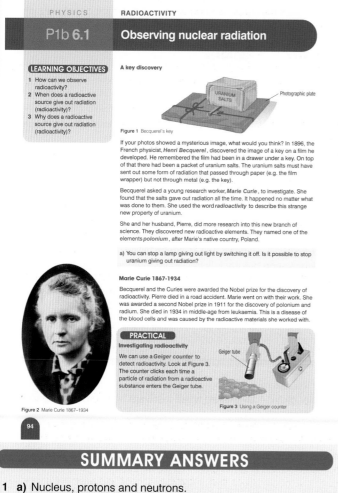

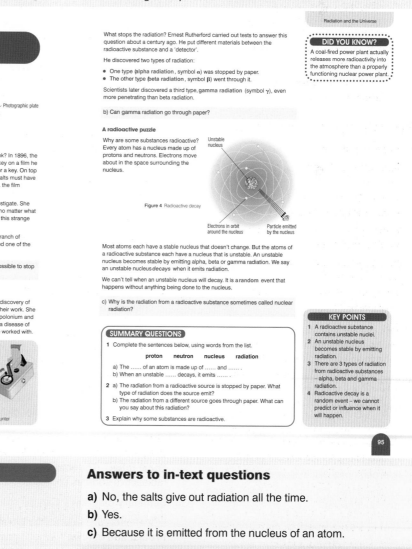

SUMMARY ANSWERS

1 a) Nucleus, protons and neutrons.

   b) Nucleus, radiation.

2 a) Alpha radiation.

   b) Beta or gamma radiation.

3 Because they have an unstable nucleus that can become more stable by emitting radiation.

Answers to in-text questions

a) No, the salts give out radiation all the time.

b) Yes.

c) Because it is emitted from the nucleus of an atom.

KEY POINTS

The students could make a glossary of the key words to make sure they understand them all.

P1b 6.2 Alpha, beta and gamma radiation

LEARNING OBJECTIVES

Students should learn that:

- The different radiations have different penetrating powers because they are absorbed by materials as they pass through.

- The range in air is different for each type of radiation and that they are affected differently by electric and magnetic fields.

- Nuclear radiation is ionising and this damages living cells causing cancer or cell death.

LEARNING OUTCOMES

Most students should be able to:

- Describe the penetrating powers of the three radiations.

- Describe the range in air of each type of radiation, their relative ionising power and how they are affected in a magnetic field.

- Evaluate which radiation is the most hazardous inside and outside of the human body.

- Describe ways of reducing the hazards presented when handling radioactive substances.

Some students should also be able to:

- Explain why radiation is dangerous.

Teaching suggestions

- **Gifted and talented.** Where do the beta particles come from? The beta particles are high-energy electrons that come from the nucleus, but there are no electrons in the nucleus! The students need to find an explanation of what is happening in the nucleus that is producing these electrons.

- **Learning styles**

  Kinaesthetic: Modelling with simulations.

  Visual: Observing demonstrations.

  Auditory: Explaining effects of radiation.

  Interpersonal: Discussion of radiation.

  Intrapersonal: Interpreting evidence from demonstrations.

SPECIFICATION LINK-UP P1b.11.6

- *The characteristics and properties of the three main types of nuclear radiation emitted by radioactive sources: alpha particles, beta particles and gamma rays.*

- *The uses of, and the dangers associated with, each type of nuclear radiation.*

Students should use their skills, knowledge and understanding of 'How Science Works':

- *to evaluate the possible hazards associated with the use of different types of nuclear radiation*

- *to evaluate measures that can be taken to reduce exposure to nuclear radiations.*

Lesson structure

STARTER

Magnetism – The students should be familiar with magnetic fields. Ask them to show their knowledge in a diagram/mind map/spider diagram. (10 minutes)

It's all Greek to me – Scientists use a lot of symbols in their work. Discuss the reasons that scientists use symbols for elements, equations, the names of things, etc. You might ask the students to list all of the symbols that they know the meaning of; they know more than they think. (5–10 minutes)

This isn't a Biology lesson! – Ask the students to draw and label the important parts of an animal cell. They should explain where the genetic information is stored. (5–10 minutes)

MAIN

- The Simulation P1b 6.2 'Alpha, beta and gamma radiation' on the GCSE Physics CD ROM shows the different types of radiation coming from the nucleus. A simulated experiment allows students to test what different types of radiation can penetrate.

- You may demonstrate the penetrating powers of radiations with the method set out in 'Practical support'.

- The difference between alpha and beta particles and the electromagnetic wave nature of gamma should be emphasised.

- Gamma radiation causes no change in the structure of the nucleus; it is really the nucleus dumping some excess energy it didn't lose in a previous decay.

- The lack of charge on the gamma rays accounts for their higher penetrating power; they interact with matter a lot less than alpha or beta.

- Depending on the structure of your course, the students will probably not have encountered the idea of ionisation before. It is important that they grasp the concept of the radioactive particle stripping away electrons from atoms and causing unwanted chemical reaction in cells.

- The main danger is that the cell will be damaged and reproduce out of control. Explain that this becomes more likely the larger the dose of radiation, but that it is possible for a single damaged cell to cause cancer so there is no minimum safe limit to radiation. We should therefore try to limit our exposure by keeping sources safely away from our bodies.

- The students will look at the natural background radiation later, but some may have noticed the Geiger counter clicking away even when there are no sources in the room.

PLENARIES

Local rules – The students should make a poster or booklet explaining how your radioactive sources should be stored and handled. (15–20 minutes)

Summary diagram – Can the students draw a single diagram that will summarise all of the information from today? (10 minutes)

Protect and survive – What if one of the radioactive sources was dropped and lost? How would it be found and what precautions would need to be taken during the search? (10 minutes)

Practical support

Penetrating power

The techniques used on the previous spread can be expanded to show the penetrating power of the three radiations. (Teacher demonstration only.)

Equipment and materials required

Geiger Müller tube, ratemeter (and possibly high voltage power supply), large plastic tray, tongs, radioactive sources, set of absorbers (paper, card, plastic, aluminium of various thicknesses and lead plates).

Details

Set the equipment up in the tray, as before, but add a mount to position a source in place. Between the source holder and detector position a holder to hold the absorbers. Make sure that the detector is less than 10 cm from the source holder or the alpha particles will not reach. Turn on the detector and then mount an alpha emitter in the holder and note the count rate. This function can be performed by most meters, but you may have to count for 20 seconds if not. Position a paper absorber between the source and detector and note the count rate. Test the beta source with paper, plastic and then aluminium plates. Test the gamma with aluminium and then various thicknesses of lead.

ACTIVITY & EXTENSION IDEAS

More detectors – There are other ways of detecting and analysing ionising radiation, including cloud and bubble chambers and photographic films. The students could find out about these devices and why they are used. Which of the devices reveals most about the radiation and in what circumstances are they used?

PHYSICS   RADIOACTIVITY

P1b 6.2   Alpha, beta and gamma radiation

LEARNING OBJECTIVES

1 How far can each type of radiation travel in air and what stops it?
2 What is alpha, beta and gamma radiation?
3 Why is alpha, beta and gamma radiation dangerous?

Penetrating power

Alpha radiation can't penetrate paper.

But what stops beta and gamma radiation? And how far can each type of radiation travel through air? We can use a Geiger counter to find out.

- To test different materials, we need to place each material between the tube and the radioactive source. Then we can add more layers of material until the radiation is stopped.
- To test the range in air, we need to move the tube away from the source. When the tube is beyond the range of the radiation, it can't detect it.

Look at the table below:

It shows the results of the two tests.

FOUL FACTS

Radium is an element. It is so radioactive that it glows with light on its own. Many years ago, the workers in a US factory used radium paint on clocks and aircraft dials. They often licked the brushes to make a fine point to paint very accurately on the dials. Many of them later died from cancer.

Type of radiation	Absorber materials	Range in air
alpha (α)	paper	about 10 cm
beta (β)	aluminium sheet (1 cm thick) lead sheet (2–3 mm thick)	about 1 m
gamma (γ)	thick lead sheet (several cm thick) concrete (more than 1 m thick)	unlimited

Gamma radiation spreads out in air without being absorbed. It does get weaker as it spreads out.

a) Why is a radioactive source stored in a lead-lined box?

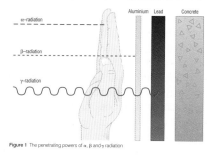

Figure 1 The penetrating powers of α, β and γ radiation

The nature of alpha, beta and gamma radiation

What are these mysterious radiations? They can be separated using a magnetic field. Look at Figure 2.

We use magnetic fields to deflect electron beams in a TV tube. The beams create the picture as they scan across the inside of the tube.

- β-radiation is easily deflected, in the same way as electrons. So it has a negative charge. In fact, a β-particle is a fast-moving electron. It is emitted by an unstable nucleus containing too many neutrons when it decays.
- α-radiation is deflected in the opposite direction to β-radiation because an α-particle has a positive charge. α-radiation is harder to deflect than β-radiation. This is because an α-particle is a lot heavier than a β-particle. It has a much greater mass. In fact, an alpha particle is two protons and two neutrons stuck together, the same as a helium nucleus.
- γ-radiation is not deflected by a magnetic field or an electric field. This is because gamma radiation is electromagnetic radiation so is uncharged.

Electric field between positive and negative metal plate

Beam of radiation

Figure 3 Radiation passing through an electric field

Note that α- and β-particles passing through an electric field are deflected in opposite directions.

b) How do we know that gamma radiation is not made up of charged particles?

Radioactivity dangers

The radiation from a radioactive substance can knock electrons out of atoms. The atoms become charged because they lose electrons. The process is called ionisation.

X-rays also cause ionisation. Ionisation in a living cell can damage or kill the cell. Damage to the genes in a cell can be passed on if the cell generates more cells. Strict rules must always be followed when radioactive substances are used.

Alpha radiation has a greater ionising effect than beta or gamma radiation. This makes it is more dangerous in the body than beta or gamma radiation. See page 81 for more information.

c) Why should long-handled tongs be used to move a radioactive source?

SUMMARY QUESTIONS

1 Choose words from the list to complete the sentences below:

   alpha   beta   gamma

   a) Electromagnetic radiation from a radioactive substance is called ...... radiation.
   b) A thick metal plate will stop ...... and ...... radiation but not ...... radiation.

2 Which type of radiation is: a) uncharged? b) positively charged? c) negatively charged?

3 Explain why ionising radiation is dangerous.

Radiation and the Universe

Beam of radiation enters a magnetic field

A magnetic field at right angles to the plane of the paper

α-radiation is deflected by the magnetic field

β-radiation is deflected in the opposite direction to α-radiation

γ-radiation and neutrons are undeflected by the magnetic field

Figure 2 Radiation in a magnetic field

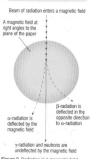

Figure 4 Radioactive warning

KEY POINTS

1 α-radiation is stopped by paper or a few centimetres of air.
2 β-radiation is stopped by thin metal or about a metre of air.
3 γ-radiation is stopped by thick lead and has an unlimited range in air.

96   97

SUMMARY ANSWERS

1 a) Gamma.
   b) Alpha and beta, gamma.

2 a) Gamma.
   b) Alpha.
   c) Beta.

3 Radiation can knock electrons from atoms. This ionisation damages the genes in a cell which can be passed on if the cell generates more cells.

FOUL FACTS

- Radium is still found in older clock faces, but there are very strict regulations about the repair and disposal of these. They are fairly harmless unless the material is ingested, because radium is an alpha emitter. The workers actually developed cancers of the bone, not cancers of the tongue, because the radium was absorbed into the bones instead of calcium

- Various non-radioactive phosphorus compounds are used in modem luminous clocks.

Answers to in-text questions

a) To stop the radiation, so it can't affect objects or people nearby.

b) It is not deflected by a magnetic or an electric field.

c) To keep the source out of range.

KEY POINTS

Get the students to correctly label a diagram showing the nature and penetrating power of the three radiations.

P1b 6.3   Half-life

LEARNING OBJECTIVES

Students should learn that:

- The activity of a radioactive source decreases with time because the number of unstable nuclei is decreasing.

- The half-life of a source is a measure of how long it takes for the activity of a source to reach half of its initial value.

LEARNING OUTCOMES

Most students should be able to:

- Define the term half-life in relation to the activity of a radioactive source.

- Determine the half-life of a source from a graph or table of data.

Teaching suggestions

- **Special needs.** Students should be provided with a results table with one set of results already filled in to help explain the idea.

- **Learning styles**

  Kinaesthetic: Practical dice activity.

  Visual: Observing and presenting evidence.

  Auditory: Explaining the evidence.

  Interpersonal: Evaluating quality of results.

  Intrapersonal: Interpreting evidence.

- **ICT link-up**

  - The half-life of most materials available to high schools is too long to measure in class. A simulation of decay is the best way to approach this topic.

  - Half-lives can be modelled in detail using a spreadsheet. The students could enter their results and plot the graph. For the more mathematically inclined, the spreadsheet can calculate a function of the decay curve which should be $y = y_0 e^{-(1/6)x}$ if results are ideal.

SPECIFICATION LINK-UP   P1b.11.6

- *The half-life of a radioactive substance is defined as 'the time it takes for the number of parent atoms in a sample of the substance to halve' or 'the time it takes for the count rate from a sample of the substance to fall to half its initial level'.*

Lesson structure

STARTER

An exponential decay puzzle – A farmer has a warehouse with two million corn cobs in it. Every day he sells exactly half of his remaining stock. How long before he has sold every last nugget of corn? (5–10 minutes)

An exponential growth puzzle – A philosopher places a grain of rice on the first square of a chess board, two on the next, four on the next and so on. How many go on the last (sixty-fourth) square? (5–10 minutes)

The big time – Give the students a set of events and time intervals, ask them to put them in order of duration. Examples include a second, a century, an epoch, the duration of a lesson and the time a match takes to burn. (10 minutes)

MAIN

- Begin by discussing the term 'isotope'. The students should be becoming familiar with the structure of the atoms and should quickly grasp that the number of neutrons may vary.

- 'Parent' and 'daughter' are important terms also. You could show a nuclear decay equation (or a simplified one) to get these terms across.

- The rolling dice decay model is an enjoyable experiment, but it can take a bit of time. To improve the average values the groups can share data and this will lead to a more precise half-life.

- At the end of the experiment, make sure that the students understand that the dice represented nuclei and removing them represented decay.

- They should have a reasonable understanding that the pattern is the same each time, even though we do not know exactly which of the dice decays each time.

- If you feel like being a bit 'all knowing', seal the answer in an envelope in advance and stick it to the board in plain sight. Then 'reveal' it at the end, which allows you to discuss the fact that we can accurately model random behaviour using mathematics.

- The experiment lends itself well to the ideas of repeating to improve reliability, but can also be used to explain that statistics work best on very large samples so the more dice the better the fit. (This relates to 'Ideas of reliability of data' in 'How Science Works'.)

- There is also opportunity to develop or assess graph plotting skills along with drawing lines of best fit. (This relates to 'Presenting data' in 'How Science Works'.)

- You can discuss what happens to the 'count rate' after each roll. The number of dice eliminated represents this and this rate should decrease as the number of surviving dice falls. This gives the students a decent understanding of why the count rate falls as time goes on.

PLENARIES

Careful! You can have your eye out with that! – An archaeologist claims to have found the arrow that killed King Harold in 1066. Can the students explain how a scientist would try to check this claim? (10 minutes)

Coin toss – If I have 120 coins and toss them all, removing all of the heads after each toss, how many tosses until I should only have 15 left? [3 tosses.] (5 minutes)

Activity and decay – Show the students a graph with three decay curves on them. Can they identify which has the longest half-life and which is the most active source? (5 minutes)

Practical support

Radioactive dice

This is a simple model of the randomness of radioactive decay and how to find the half-life.

Equipment and materials required

For each group: a set of 59 identical six-sided cubes and one cube of a different colour. The dice should have a dot on one face only. (You can use more or less dice depending on how many you have, but 60 works well.)

Details

The students roll the full set of dice, and after each roll they remove the dice that landed showing a spot. They record the number of dice 'surviving' and then roll only these dice, and so on. They continue this process of elimination for 20 rolls, or until no dice survives. During this, they should also note down when the special dice lands spot up causing it to be removed. If time permits, they repeat this process and calculate an average number of dice remaining after each roll. Plotting a graph of the number of dice remaining (y-axis) against roll number (x-axis) reveals that the dice behave like decaying atoms and a half-life can be calculated; this should be 4.16 rolls. The single dice should show that the process is random; it is impossible to predict when any individual dice will be eliminated. For some groups, it will be removed after the first roll and for others it will survive until the end.

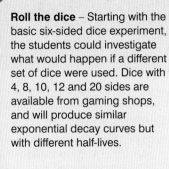

ACTIVITY & EXTENSION IDEAS

Roll the dice – Starting with the basic six-sided dice experiment, the students could investigate what would happen if a different set of dice were used. Dice with 4, 8, 10, 12 and 20 sides are available from gaming shops, and will produce similar exponential decay curves but with different half-lives.

P1b 6.3   Half-life

LEARNING OBJECTIVES

1 What happens to the activity of a radioactive isotope as it decays?
2 What do we mean by the 'half-life' of a radioactive source?

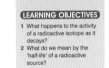

Example: the symbol for the uranium isotope with 92 protons and 146 neutrons is

$$^{238}_{92}U \text{ (or sometimes U-238)}$$

Figure 1 The symbol for an isotope

Every atom of an element always has the same number of protons in its nucleus. However, the number of neutrons in the nucleus can differ. Each type of atom is called an isotope. (So isotopes of an element contain the same number of protons but different numbers of neutrons.)

The activity of a radioactive substance is the number of atoms that decay per second. Each unstable atom (the 'parent' atom) forms an atom of a different isotope (the 'daughter' atom) when its nucleus decays. Because the number of parent atoms goes down, the activity of the sample decreases.

We can use a Geiger counter to monitor the activity of a radioactive sample. We need to measure the count rate due to the sample. This is the number of counts per second (or per minute). The graph below shows how the count rate of a sample decreases.

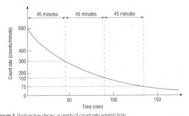

Figure 2 Radioactive decay: a graph of count rate against time

The graph shows that the count rate decreases with time. The count rate falls from:

- 600 counts per minute (c.p.m.) to 300 c.p.m. in the first 45 minutes,
- 300 counts per minute (c.p.m.) to 150 c.p.m. in the next 45 minutes.

The time taken for the count rate (and therefore the number of parent atoms) to fall by half is always the same. This time is called the half-life. The half-life shown on the graph is 45 minutes.

a) What will the count rate be after 135 minutes from the start?

The half-life of a radioactive isotope is the time it takes:

- for the number of nuclei of the isotope in a sample (and therefore the mass of parent atoms) to halve,
- for the count rate due to the isotope in a sample to fall to half its initial value.

The random nature of radioactive decay

We can't predict *when* an individual atom will suddenly decay. But we *can* predict how many atoms will decay in a certain time – because there are so many of them. This is a bit like throwing dice. You can't predict what number you will get with a single throw. But if you threw 1000 dice, you would expect one-sixth to come up with a particular number.

Suppose we start with 1000 unstable atoms. Look at the graph below:

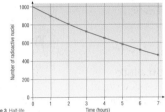

Figure 3 Half-life

If 10% disintegrate every hour,

100 atoms will decay in the first hour, leaving 900.
90 atoms (= 10% of 900) will decay in the second hour, leaving 810.

The table below shows what you get if you continue the calculations. The results are plotted as a graph in Figure 3.

Time from start (hours)	0	1	2	3	4	5	6	7
No. of unstable atoms present	1000	900	810	729	656	590	530	477
No. of unstable atoms that decay in the next hour	100	90	81	73	66	59	53	48

b) Use the graph in Figure 3 to work out the half-life of this radioactive isotope.

SUMMARY QUESTIONS

1 Complete the following sentences using words from the list below.

     half-life   stable   unstable

a) In a radioactive substance, ... atoms decay and become ....
b) The ...... of a radioactive isotope is the time taken for the number of ...... atoms to decrease to half.

2 A radioactive isotope has a half-life of 15 hours. A sealed tube contains 8 milligrams of the substance.

     What mass of the substance is in the tube:

a) 15 hours later?
b) 45 hours later?

NEXT TIME YOU...

...help someone choose numbers for the lottery, think about whether this is something you can predict. The balls come out of the machine at random; is there any way of predicting what they will be?

KEY POINTS

1 The half-life of a radioactive isotope is the time it takes for the number of nuclei of the isotope in a sample to halve.
2 The number of unstable atoms and the activity decreases to half in one half-life.

SUMMARY ANSWERS

1 a) Unstable, stable.
   b) Half-life, unstable.

2 a) 4 milligrams
   b) 1 milligram

Answers to in-text questions

a) 75 c.p.m.

b) 6.5 hours

NEXT TIME YOU ...

How random are lottery machines? Do all of the numbers have an equal chance of appearing? It is possible to find out these statistics to see just how fair the competition is. The national lottery has data about how often each ball has been picked on its web site.

KEY POINTS

The students should be given a decay curve graph showing several isotopes and use it to find the half-lives of them.

P1b 6.4

Radioactivity at work

Students should learn:

- That radioactive sources have a number of uses including thickness measurement, medical tracing and determining the age of materials.

Most students should be able to:

- Describe how a beta source can be used to measure the thickness of a material like aluminium foil.
- Describe how radioactive traces are used in medical analysis.
- Describe how radioactive isotopes can be used to determine the age of a rock or organic material.

Some students should also be able to:

- Evaluate the properties of a radioactive isotope to determine why it would make a good medical tracer.
- Find the age of an organic sample from date presented to them.

Teaching suggestions

- **Special needs.** Provide a partially completed flow chart for the operation of the foil press.
- **Gifted and talented.** Very large numbers of radioactive particles are produced in nuclear reactors. How are these particles contained and are there any that escape into the environment? The students may find out about neutrons and neutrinos.
- **Learning styles**

  Kinaesthetic: Researching into dating techniques.

  Visual: Observing absorption demonstration.

  Auditory: Reading aloud information.

  Interpersonal: Discussing uses of radioactivity.

  Intrapersonal: Understanding radiometric dating techniques.

- **ICT link-up.** A simulation of the absorption of beta particles by various resources is available. The students can find out for themselves how the particles are absorbed by different materials.

SPECIFICATION LINK-UP   P1b.11.6

- *The uses of, and the dangers associated with, each type of nuclear radiation.*

Students should use their skills, knowledge and understanding of 'How Science Works':
- *to evaluate the possible hazards associated with the use of different types of nuclear radiation*
- *to evaluate measures that can be taken to reduce exposure to nuclear radiations*
- *to evaluate the appropriateness of radioactive sources for particular uses, including as tracers, in terms of the type(s) of radiation emitted and their half-lives.*

Lesson structure

STARTER

Radiation misconceptions – The students will have seen a range of films in which radioactive materials have caused strange effects. Get them to list all of the things they think radioactivity can do, and then go through them deciding if they are true or false. (5–10 minutes)

Just how thick? – Ask the students to measure the thickness of a sheet of paper. Can they find out if all of the sheets are the same thickness? How? (5 minutes)

PhotoPLUS – View and discuss the PhotoPLUS on 'Radioactive issues', available on the GCSE Physics CD ROM. (10 minutes)

MAIN

- Using radioactivity to determine the thickness of a material is a fairly straightforward idea; you can link it to the idea of light being absorbed by paper. How many sheets of white paper will stop all light passing through it?
- The function of the foil press can best be shown as a flow chart with terms like: 'Is too much radiation getting through?' → 'Open up rollers a bit.'
- Demonstrate that the thicker a material is the less beta radiation passes through. This could be a quick demonstration as in 'Practical support', or you could look into it in more depth.
- When discussing radioactive tracers, you may be able to find a video clip of a tracer being used in the body to find a blood vessel blockage. (For example, search an image bank for 'radioactive tracer'.)
- The students should be made aware that the tracer must be picked for the job based on a range of factors, including the type of radiation it emits (gamma) and its biochemical properties, i.e. will it build up in the organ we want it to?
- There are isotopes suitable for a wide range of medical studies, some of which are artificially generated in nuclear reactors.
- You may want to talk about tracers used to find gas leaks and monitor the path of underground rivers. These too are carefully chosen.
- Carbon dating is only useful over a certain range of times and the materials must be organic. The limit is about 50 000 years, which is good enough for all recorded human history.
- It also needs to be calibrated against objects of known ages; ancient trees are handy for this. Ask the students how we know the age of these trees.
- Uranium dating is generally used to date rocks and is part of the evidence for the Earth being 4.5 billion years old.
- There are some assumptions that are made with dating processes and you may wish to discuss these with the students. Do the levels of carbon-14 remain constant in the atmosphere? Is there any other way of lead being produced in rocks?

Practical support

Demonstrating absorption

See local rules for handling radioactive sources.

It is possible to show how radioactivity can be used to measure the thickness of materials. (Teacher demonstration only.)

Equipment and materials required

GM tube and rate meter, set of aluminium absorbers, beta source, tongs.

Details

Mount the GM tube and absorber holder in line with the source holder. Position the source carefully and record the count rate (or take a count over 30 seconds). Test the aluminium absorbers one at a time, noting the decreasing count rate as the thickness of the aluminium increases.

You may wish to get the students to plot a graph of count rate against absorber thickness to determine how much aluminium is required to reduce the count to half of the original value. This half-value thickness is an important concept for absorption of gamma rays at Advanced level.

Answers to in-text questions

a) The detector reading increases and the pressure from the rollers is decreased.

b) Alpha radiation would be stopped by the foil. Gamma radiation would pass through it without any absorption.

c) B

d) It was formed recently (in geological terms).

PHYSICS RADIOACTIVITY

P1b 6.4 Radioactivity at work

LEARNING OBJECTIVES

1 How can we use radioactivity for monitoring?
2 What are radioactive tracers?
3 What is radioactive dating?

Figure 1 Thickness monitoring using a radioactive source

Uses of radioactivity

Radioactivity has many uses. For each use, we need a radioactive isotope that emits a certain type of radiation and has a suitable half life.

(1) Automatic thickness monitoring
This is used when making metal foil.

Look at Figure 1. The amount of radiation passing through the foil depends on the thickness of the foil. A detector on the other side of the metal foil measures the amount of radiation passing through it.

● If the thickness of the foil increases too much, the detector reading drops.
● The detector sends a signal to the rollers to increase the pressure on the metal sheet.

This makes the foil thinner again.

a) What happens if the thickness of the foil decreases too much?
b) Why is beta radiation, not alpha or gamma radiation, used here?

(2) Radioactive tracers
These are used to trace the flow of a substance through a system. For example, doctors use radioactive iodine to find out if a patient's kidney is blocked.

Figure 2 Using a tracer to monitor a patient's kidneys

Before the test, the patient drinks water containing a tiny amount of the radioactive substance. A detector is then placed against each kidney. Each detector is connected to a chart recorder.

● The radioactive substance flows in and out of a normal kidney. So the detector reading goes up then down.
● For a blocked kidney, the reading goes up and stays up. This is because the radioactive substance goes into the kidney but doesn't flow out again.

Radioactive iodine is used for this test because:

● its half life is 8 days, so it lasts long enough for the test to be done but decays almost completely after a few weeks,
● it emits gamma radiation, so it can be detected outside the body,
● it decays into a stable product.

c) In Figure 2, which kidney is blocked, A or B? How can you tell?

(3) Radioactive dating
This is used to find how old ancient material is, i.e. its age.

● *Carbon dating* is used to find the age of ancient wood.
Living wood contains a tiny proportion of radioactive carbon. This has a half-life of 5600 years. When a tree dies, it no longer absorbs any carbon. So the amount of radioactive carbon in it decreases.
To find the age of a sample, we need to measure the count rate from the wood. This is compared with the count rate from the same mass of living wood. For example, suppose the count rate in a sample of wood is half the count rate of an equal mass of living wood. Then the sample must be 5600 years old.

● *Uranium dating* is used to find the age of igneous rocks.
These rocks contain radioactive uranium, which has a half-life of 4500 million years. Each uranium atom decays into an atom of lead. We can work out the age of a sample by measuring the number of atoms of uranium and lead. For example, if a sample contains 1 atom of lead for every atom of the uranium, the age of the sample must be 4500 million years. This is because there must have **originally** been 2 atoms of uranium for each atom of uranium now present.

d) What could you say about an igneous rock with uranium but no lead in it?

SUMMARY QUESTIONS

1 Choose the correct word from the list to complete each of the following sentences:

alpha   beta   gamma

a) In the continuous production of thin metal sheets, a source of ...... radiation should be used to monitor the thickness of the sheets.
b) A radioactive tracer given to a hospital patient needs to emit ...... or ...... radiation.
c) The radioactive source used to trace a leak in an underground pipeline should be a source of ...... radiation.

2 a) What are the ideal properties of a radioactive isotope used as a medical tracer?
b) A sample of old wood was carbon dated and found to have 25% of the count rate measured in an equal mass of living wood. The half-life of the radioactive carbon is 5600 years. How old is the sample of wood?

DID YOU KNOW?

Smoke detectors save lives. A radioactive source inside the alarm sends out alpha particles into a gap in a circuit in the alarm. The alpha particles ionise the air so it conducts a current across the gap. In a fire, smoke absorbs the alpha particles so they don't reach the gap. The current across the gap drops and the alarm sounds. The battery in a smoke alarm needs to be checked regularly – to make sure it isn't dead. Otherwise you might be!

KEY POINTS

1 The use we can make of a radioactive substance depends on:
a) its half-life, and
b) the type of radiation it gives out.

100   101

Radiation and the Universe

PLENARIES

The dating game – Give the students a set of cards of historical events and a set of 'radioactive activities' that have been measured for artefacts from these events. Ask the students to match them up. (5 minutes)

The right isotope – Can the students match the isotope to the job it is used for? Give them a list of isotopes, the type of emitter they are and their half lives and see if the students can decide what they would be useful for. (10 minutes)

Radioactivity's great – Radioactivity has a fairly bad press; the students should produce a poster expounding the virtues of radioactive material. (15–20 minutes)

SUMMARY ANSWERS

1 a) Beta.
  b) Beta or gamma.
  c) Beta.

2 a) It needs to be detectable outside the body, non-toxic, have a short half-life (1–24 hours) and decay into a stable product.
  b) 11 200 years old.

KEY POINTS

The students could write a 'matching pair' question to link uses and description of radioactive sources. They can then swap questions and try answering them.

P1b 6.5 Radioactivity issues

PHYSICS   RADIOACTIVITY

P1b 6.5 Radioactivity issues

SPECIFICATION LINK-UP

P1b.11.6

Substantive content that can be revisited in this spread:

- *The uses of, and the dangers associated with, each type of nuclear radiation.*

Students should use their skills, knowledge and understanding of 'How Science Works':

- *to evaluate the possible hazards associated with the use of different types of nuclear radiation*
- *to evaluate measures that can be taken to reduce exposure to nuclear radiations*
- *to evaluate the appropriateness of radioactive sources for particular uses, including as tracers, in terms of the type of radiation emitted and their half-lives.*

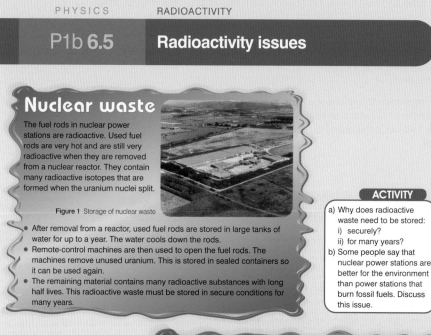

Nuclear waste

The fuel rods in nuclear power stations are radioactive. Used fuel rods are very hot and are still very radioactive when they are removed from a nuclear reactor. They contain many radioactive isotopes that are formed when the uranium nuclei split.

Figure 1 Storage of nuclear waste

- After removal from a reactor, used fuel rods are stored in large tanks of water for up to a year. The water cools down the rods.
- Remote-control machines are then used to open the fuel rods. The machines remove unused uranium. This is stored in sealed containers so it can be used again.
- The remaining material contains many radioactive substances with long half lives. This radioactive waste must be stored in secure conditions for many years.

ACTIVITY

a) Why does radioactive waste need to be stored:
   i) securely?
   ii) for many years?
b) Some people say that nuclear power stations are better for the environment than power stations that burn fossil fuels. Discuss this issue.

Chernobyl

When the nuclear reactors in Ukraine exploded in 1986, emergency workers and scientists struggled for days to contain the fire. More than 100 000 people were evacuated from Chernobyl and the surrounding area. Over thirty people died in the accident. Many more have developed leukaemia or cancer. It was, and remains (up to now), the world's worst nuclear accident.

Could it happen again?

- Most nuclear reactors are of a different design.
- The Chernobyl accident did not have a high-speed shutdown system like most reactors have.
- The operators at Chernobyl ignored safety instructions.

There are thousands of nuclear reactors in the world. They have been working for many years. Countries such as Sweden wanted to 'phase' them out after Chernobyl. Now they are planning new ones because they need electricity.

Figure 2 Chernobyl

ACTIVITY

Should the UK government replace our existing nuclear reactors with new ones? Debate this question with your friends and take a vote on it.

102

Teaching suggestions

Activities

Nuclear waste – Extensive details of the handling and storage of nuclear waste can be found from the Internet. A basic search for 'nuclear waste' will yield sites from BNFL, Greenpeace and a range of other pro and anti nuclear organisations.

Interestingly the device used to remotely handle dangerous materials is called a 'waldo'. These were thought up by the science fiction author Robert Heinlein, before they were actually turned into reality.

Chernobyl – You may have had a debate about Chernobyl and nuclear reactor safety during a previous section. If not, then the students are now better informed and a debate would be very useful. The debate should take into account the need to reduce global warming, the storage of waste produced and the safety record of nuclear power stations.

Radioactivity all around us – The students will most likely think of radioactivity being an unnatural phenomenon, and it is important to get across the idea that most of the dose that they receive is from natural sources. You can measure the amount of background radiation during the lesson. Radon gas is a major cause of lung cancer in the UK, with estimates of deaths at around 2500 per year. This compares to about 25 000 due to smoking. The gas is released from igneous rocks; (link back to geothermal energy) and the students may be interested in the areas that contain most of these rocks, such as Devon and Cornwall. Further information can be found from the Health Protection Agency (www.hpa.gov.uk) where radon detectors can be purchased. Shouldn't these be free?

Radioactivity on the move – This is an excellent opportunity to discuss the safety of radioactive material. Ask the students to list a list of safety precautions that they would impose when moving nuclear material by rail. Search the Internet for 'nuclear container test' to find video of a nuclear container being tested in a crash. They should also be able to find information about the ships that are used to transport material. How are these designed and protected?

Radioactivity all around us

When we use a Geiger counter, it clicks even without a radioactive source near it. This is due to **background radioactivity**. Radioactive substances are found naturally all around us.

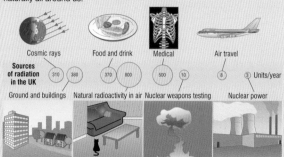

Figure 3 Sources of background radiation in the UK

Figure 3 shows the sources of background radioactivity. The numbers tell you how much radiation each person gets on average in a year from each source.

Radioactive risks

The effect on living cells of radiation from radioactive substances depends on:

- the type and the amount of radiation received (the dose), and
- whether the source of the radiation is inside or outside the body.

	Alpha radiation	Beta radiation	Gamma radiation
Source inside the body	**very dangerous!!!** – affects all the surrounding tissue	**dangerous!!** – reaches cells throughout the body	
Source outside the body	some **danger!** – absorbed by the skin; damages skin cells		

- The larger the dose of radiation someone gets, the greater the risk of cancer. High doses kill living cells.
- The smaller the dose, the less the risk – but the dose is never zero. So there is a very low level of risk to every one of us because of background radioactivity.

Radioactivity on the move

A nuclear power company needs to move radioactive waste from its nuclear power stations around the country to a specially designed storage site.

They intend to move the waste in strong metal containers which can withstand high-speed crashes. They plan to move the containers by train on main lines passing through towns and cities.

Lots of people are protesting about these plans. They want the waste moved by sea on ships. The company thinks that would be unsafe, as a ship might sink.

103

ACTIVITY

a) i) What is the biggest source of background radioactivity?
   ii) Which source contributes least to background radioactivity?
   iii) List the sources and say which ones could be avoided.
b) For a large part of the population, the biggest radiation hazard comes from radon gas, which gets into their homes. The dangers of radon gas can be minimised by building new houses that are slightly raised on brick pillars and modifying existing houses.
   Who should pay for alterations to houses, the government or the householder?
   Discuss this question.

QUESTIONS

1 Why is a source of alpha radiation very dangerous inside the body but not outside it?

2 Find out the hazard warning sign used on radioactive sources.

ACTIVITY

Imagine you and your friends are at a public inquiry into the company's plans. One of your group is to put forward the case for the company and someone else is to oppose it on behalf of other rail users. Other interested parties can also have their say. You need someone to 'chair' the meeting.
After you have heard all the evidence for and against the company's plans, take a vote on the plans.

ANSWERS TO ACTIVITY

a) i) Natural radioactivity in the air.
   ii) Nuclear power.
   iii) Air travel, nuclear testing; nuclear power could be avoided.

ANSWERS TO QUESTIONS

1 The alpha particles are very ionising and so cause a lot of damage to living cells. If they get into the lungs they will do a lot of harm. Our skin has a layer of dead cells that prevent the particle reaching living cells from the outside.

2 See image on page 301 in Student Book.

EXTENSION ACTIVITY

Radioactivity throughout the World
The students could extend their look at background radiation by finding out about radiation hot spots around the world.

Most will automatically think of power station accident sites but their are other natural hot spots in regions of India, China and Brazil.

ICT link-up

In the 'Radioactivity on the move' or 'Nuclear waste' activities, the groups can present their evidence as a slide show. This would allow them to use information and images from the Internet easily to support their case.

Learning styles

Kinaesthetic: Researching further information.

Visual: Obtaining and presenting information from the Internet.

Auditory: Explaining how radioactive material is kept safe.

Interpersonal: Reporting on background radiation.

Intrapersonal: Considering safety precautions used when handling materials.

SUMMARY ANSWERS

1 a) Gamma.

   b) Alpha.

   c) Beta.

   d) Beta.

   e) Alpha.

   f) Gamma.

2 1B, 2D, 3A, 4C.

3 a) Graph.

   b) 1 hour 40 minutes.

4 a) 2

   b) 11 200 years

Summary teaching suggestions

- Question 1 allows the students to summarise the properties of the three radiations; this should be straightforward as long as they have made some kind of summary table as they worked through the chapter.

- Question 4 tests understanding a little more deeply. Some students fail to understand the relationship between half-life and activity (a short half-life indicates greater activity).

- When the students plot the graph for question 3, watch out for those who insist on joining the points 'dot-to-dot'; this will lose them marks in the examination and give them an inaccurate half-life. Only higher attaining students seem to understand clearly that the count rate halves over *each* half-life, lower ability students may conclude that there have been four half lives because the activity is one-quarter of the original.

SUMMARY QUESTIONS

1 Which type of radiation, alpha, beta or gamma:
   a) can pass through lead?
   b) travels no further than about 10 cm in air?
   c) is stopped by an aluminium metal plate but not by paper?
   d) consists of electrons?
   e) consists of helium nuclei?
   f) is uncharged?

2 The table gives information about four radioactive isotopes **A**, **B**, **C** and **D**. Match each statement 1 to 4 with **A**, **B**, **C** or **D**.

   1 The isotope which gives off radiation with an unlimited range.
   2 The isotope which has the longest half-life.
   3 The isotope which decays the fastest.
   4 The isotope with the smallest mass.

Isotope	Type of radiation emitted	Half-life
A californium-241	alpha	4 minutes
B cobalt-60	gamma	5 years
C hydrogen-3	beta	12 years
D strontium-90	beta	28 years

3 The following measurements were made of the count rate due to a radioactive source.

Time (hours)	0	0.5	1.0	1.5	2.0	2.5
Count rate due to the source (counts per minute)	510	414	337	276	227	188

   a) Plot a graph of the count rate (on the vertical axis) against time.
   b) Use your graph to find the half-life of the source.

4 In a carbon dating experiment of ancient wood, a sample of the wood gave a count rate of 0.4 counts per minute. The same mass of living wood gave a count rate of 1.6 counts per minute.
   a) How many half-lives did the count rate take to decrease from 1.6 to 0.4 counts per minute?
   b) The half-life of the radioactive carbon in the wood is 5600 years. What is the age of the sample?

EXAM-STYLE QUESTIONS

1 Some people working in hospitals may be exposed to different types of nuclear radiation. Which of the following statements describes what they can do to reduce their exposure to nuclear radiation?
   A Wear a badge containing photographic film.
   B Wear a lead-lined apron.
   C Wear a sterile gown.
   D Wear rubber boots

2 The diagram shows an atom of carbon.
   Match the words in the list with the numbers **1** to **4** in the sentences.
   A Electrons   B Neutrons
   C Nucleus   D Positive

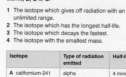

   Particles shown by the symbol × in the diagram are called ......**1**...... They orbit the ......**2**...... of an atom This is made up of protons and ......**3**...... Protons ha a ......**4**...... charge.

3 Which of the following statements about radioactive decay is true?
   A High pressures increase the rate of radioactive decay.
   B High temperatures increase the rate of radioactive decay.
   C Low temperatures increase the rate of radioactive decay.
   D Radioactive decay is unaffected by external conditions.

4 The three main types of nuclear radiation are alpha particles, beta particles and gamma radiation.
   (a) Which types of nuclear radiation will **not** go throu a sheet of paper?
       A Alpha particles only.
       B Beta particles only.
       C Both alpha particles and beta particles.
       D Both beta particles and gamma rays.
   (b) Which types of nuclear radiation can travel throu a sheet of aluminium several centimetres thick?
       A Alpha particles only.
       B Beta particles only.
       C Gamma rays only.
       D Both beta particles and gamma rays.

EXAM-STYLE ANSWERS

1 **B**   (1 mark)

2 1 **A** electrons   (1 mark)

   2 **C** nucleus   (1 mark)

   3 **B** neutrons   (1 mark)

   4 **D** positive   (1 mark)

3 **D**   (1 mark)

4 a) **A**   (1 mark)

   b) **C**   (1 mark)

   c) **D**   (1 mark)

   d) **B**   (1 mark)

5 a) (i) 60 seconds.   (2 marks)
           (between 55 and 65 seconds)   (1 mark)
       (ii) Half-life does not change/it is constant for any particular radioactive substance.   (1 mark)

   b) (i) Source B.   (1 mark)
       (ii) Beta radiation will be detected outside the body   (1 mark)
            short half-life so patient is not exposed for long.   (1 mark)

HOW SCIENCE WORKS QUESTIONS

(c) Smoke detectors used in houses often contain a source of alpha radiation. This radiation will not harm people in the house because . . .

A Alpha particles are not very ionising.

B Alpha particles are very ionising.

C Alpha particles do not damage human cells.

D Alpha particles travel only a few centimetres in air. (1)

(d) Alpha particles and beta particles are deflected by magnetic fields, but gamma rays are not. This is because gamma rays

A are too heavy.

B have no charge.

C move too quickly.

D move too slowly. (1)

5 The graph shows how the number of radioactive atoms in a sample of a radioactive gas changes with time.

(a) (i) Use the graph to find the half-life of the radioactive gas. (2)

(ii) Explain what will happen to the half-life as the sample of gas gets older. (1)

(b) A radioactive source is to be used as a medical tracer injected into the body. The table shows four sources that are available.

Radioactive source	Half-life	Radiation emitted
A	4 days	Alpha
B	6 hours	Gamma
C	10 years	Beta
D	10 years	Gamma

(i) Which source would be the most suitable to use? (1)

(ii) Explain your choice. (1)

How do you know who to believe?

'Low grade uranium dump is not a hazard' claim local officials

Press Release: Radioactive Waste

'Contractors have stated that low level radioactive waste, such as contaminated medical equipment, can be left for 10 to 15 years allowing most of the waste to decay.'

Environmental Protection Agency maintains that 'any exposure to radiation carries a risk, and the greater the exposure the greater the risk.'

'Australian authorities consider that a safe threshold level for radiation has not been decided scientifically. For safety at uranium mines they say that a level for the public is 1mSv per year and for the miners is an average of 20mSv per year over a three year period.

'The Food Standards Agency maintains that of the 175 samples of water tested, none broke the legal safety limits for radioactive pollution.

'World Health Organisation guidelines for drinking water recommend less that 0.1mSv per year in drinking water.

a) These press releases come from several different sources. Make a list of the sources and next to each source score them 1 to 5 as to whether you would trust them.
1 = no trust and 5 = total trust.
Explain your reasoning. (6)

b) What are the ethical, social, economic and environmental issues involved in making decisions about safe levels of radiation? You should use information from the press releases to help you in your answer. (4)

Exam teaching suggestions

- In question 1 some students will confuse monitoring exposure to nuclear radiation to reducing exposure and think that alternative A is the correct answer.

- Students learn about the factors that affect the rate of a chemical reaction and incorrectly assume that radioactive decay is affected in a similar way. It should be emphasised that radioactive decay is a totally random process which is unaffected by external conditions.

- Atomic structure may already have been covered in chemistry and therefore question 3 will be revision.

- Students will need to know the properties of alpha, beta and gamma radiations before attempting question 4.

- Question 5 provides students with practice of extracting information from a graph. In order to answer part b), students must demonstrate an ability to apply knowledge of the properties of different radiations in particular contexts.

HOW SCIENCE WORKS ANSWERS

a) Suggested table, but there could be many different ideas and this is really open to discussion.

Source	Score
Local official	1
Environmental Protection Agency	4
Food Standards Agency	4
World Health Organisation	5
Contractors	1
Australian authorities	2

Look for an understanding of bias/impartiality/vested interest etc. in reasoning given.

b) Ethical, e.g. should people make decisions about other citizens that could affect their health?
Social, e.g. protecting the environment is one thing, but what about the effects on the community in terms of lost jobs or poorer health services. Isn't it worth the risk?
Economic, e.g. are workers willing to take the increased risk so that they can earn more money? Are people willing to pay more money for their water to have it 100% safe?
Environmental, e.g. mining uranium increases radioactivity, but it is used for producing electricity in a way that does not cause global warming.

How science works teaching suggestions

- **Literacy guidance**
  - Key terms that should be clearly understood are: ethical, social, economic and environmental.
  - The question expecting a longer answer, where students can practise their literacy skills is b).

- **Higher- and lower-level questions.** Question b) is higher-level and the answer provided above is also at this level. Question a) is lower-level and the answer is also at this level.

- **Gifted and talented.** Able students could explore the importance of guidelines given in other areas of science, e.g. those for exposure to secondary smoking or for using X-rays in hospital or for exposure to chemicals in industry. Question a) could be developed into a survey of opinions.

- **How and when to use these questions.** When wishing to develop an awareness of the ethical, social, economic and environmental issues that compete with our safety. The discussions are best done in class, but it might be appropriate for some students to do question 1 at home and bring in the family's opinions for extra evidence.

- **Homework.** Question a) could be set as a homework activity.

- **Special needs.** Question b) might need rephrasing to tackle each issue separately. For example, 'Is it right that some people are exposed to more radiation than others?'

P1b 7.1   The expanding Universe

LEARNING OBJECTIVES

Students should learn that:

- The Universe is a vast collection of billions of galaxies each containing millions of stars.

- The velocity of distant galaxies can be measured by analysis of the red shifting of light from those galaxies.

- The evidence gained from red shift analysis proves that the Universe is expanding and is of finite age.

LEARNING OUTCOMES

Most students should be able to:

- State that the Universe contains a vast number of galaxies and stars.

- Explain that red shift evidence shows that the Universe is expanding.

Teaching suggestions

- **Learning styles**

  Kinaesthetic: Matching spectra cards.

  Visual: Imagining the expansion of the Universe.

  Auditory: Explaining the evidence for expansion.

  Interpersonal: Discussing and evaluating the evidence.

  Intrapersonal: Appreciating the model of the expanding Universe.

- **Gifted and talented**

  Emission spectra

  If you have a set of gas emission spectrum tubes, you can demonstrate the emission spectra of different hot gases. With a suitable diffraction grating and spectroscope, you can clearly see the distinct lines produced by different elements. If you don't have a spectroscope, you can still show the different colours from different elements. (You may also wish to link this idea to the flame tests for the applied science units.)

SPECIFICATION LINK-UP   P1b.11.7

- *There is a red shift in light observed from most distant galaxies. The further away galaxies are the bigger the red shift.*

- *How the observed red shift provides evidence that the Universe is expanding and supports the 'Big Bang' theory (that the Universe began from a very small initial point).*

Lesson structure

STARTER

How many stars? – Give the class estimates on the number of stars in a galaxy and the number of galaxies, and ask them to work out how many stars they could have each if they shared them out between the class. (5 minutes)

Our star – Get the students to list the reasons why the Sun is important to life on Earth. What does it provide the Earth with? (5–10 minutes)

Stars and planets – Give the students sets of cards describing the properties and behaviours of stars and planets, and ask them to sort them into two piles. (5–10 minutes)

MAIN

- Students are often enthusiastic about 'space' topics; time should be set aside to check their basic understanding and allow them to get into the topic before moving onto new ideas.

- You might like to ask the students why there are no photographs of the complete Milky Way galaxy; they should realise that we could never get a probe to sufficient distance.

- If you want to show a model galaxy, try using a blank CD with a small bulge of Plasticine in the centre. You can draw the spiral arms on the label. It's about the right proportions (according to NASA). We are on the western spiral arm about 1 cm from the rim.

- You can then show the separation of galaxies. Our neighbour Andromeda would be about 1 m away on this scale.

- A Doppler shift for sound (a similar effect to the red shift) can be demonstrated with a tube and a funnel. The students may be familiar with the effect when hearing sirens on cars passing by.

- It is useful to show the students simple samples of absorption spectra to show what these lines would look like. They can then show the effect of shifting the lines to the red part of the spectrum.

- The idea of an expanding universe that has no centre is a bit strange. The closest simple analogy is the surface of an expanding balloon. It is worth showing this: blow up a balloon with galaxies drawn on its surface and they all move further apart from one another and none of them are in the middle.

- The Universe is a bit like this; but it isn't expanding 'into' anything as it is expanding in three dimensions, not two like the surface of the balloon.

- Not quite everything in the Universe is moving apart. If time and student ability permits, you may like to talk about Andromeda and the 'blue shift' it shows. (See 'Activity and extension ideas'.)

PLENARIES

Space is big – Give the students a list of distances and ask them to put them in order (e.g. Earth to Moon, Earth to Sun . . . Milky Way to Andromeda). (5 minutes)

True or false – Give the students a set of 'facts' about galaxies and the Universe, and ask them to say if they are true or false. (5–10 minutes)

Corrections – Give the students a paragraph full of mistakes describing the expansion of the Universe. They must correct every mistake. (5–10 minutes)

ACTIVITY & EXTENSION IDEAS

Doppler and sound

A 1½ m length of hosepipe is ideal for this, but other tubes work reasonably. You need to stick a large funnel (firmly) in one end and then blow down the other, while swinging the tube above your head. The pitch (and so frequency and wavelength of the sound) changes as it swings towards and away from the students. When it is moving away, the wavelength is increased so the sound is lower pitched and vice versa.

Matching spectra

Can the students discover what elements are present in real stellar spectra? Give the students a card showing the absorption spectrum of the Sun and a set of spectra for different elements, some of which are present in the Sun; ask the students to work out which ones match. Make sure the cards are printed to the same scale though.

Andromeda ascendant

The Andromeda galaxy is one of our nearest galactic neighbours and it is getting nearer all the time. It's moving towards us at about half a million kilometres per hour and will eventually collide in three to four billion years' time. The students could look into the possible outcomes of this collision, and collisions on this scale generally. There are numerous excellent computer simulations, and Hubble Space Telescope images of real collisions, available on the Internet.

Answers to in-text questions

a) Because they are so far away.

b) It is is blue-shifted because its wavelength is reduced.

c) Galaxy Y.

SUMMARY ANSWERS

1 a) Orbiting.

b) Expanding.

c) Receding.

d) Approaching.

2 a) Earth, Sun, Andromeda galaxy, Universe.

b) i) Planet, star.

   ii) Red shift, galaxy.

THE ORIGINS OF THE UNIVERSE

P1b 7.1 — The expanding Universe

LEARNING OBJECTIVES

1 How big is the Universe and is its size changing?

2 What is a red shift?

We live on the third rock out from a middle-aged star on the outskirts of a big galaxy we call the Milky Way. The galaxy contains about 100 000 million stars. Its size is about 100 000 light years across. This means that light takes 100 000 years to travel across it. But it's just one of billions of galaxies in the Universe. The furthest galaxies are about 13 000 million light years away!

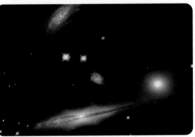

Figure 1 Galaxies

a) Why do stars appear as points of light?

NEXT TIME YOU…

… go out on a clear night, look up at the stars. Even on a very clear night, you can only see a few hundred nearby stars unless you use binoculars or a telescope.

Red shift

We can find out lots of things about stars and galaxies by studying the light from them. We can use a prism to split the light into a spectrum. The wavelength of light increases across the spectrum from blue to red. We can tell from the spectrum if a star or galaxy is moving towards us or away from us. This is because:

- the light waves are stretched out if the star or galaxy is moving away from us. We call this a red shift because the spectrum of light is shifted towards the red part of the spectrum.
- the light waves are squashed together if the star or galaxy is moving towards us. We call this a *blue shift* because the spectrum of light is shifted towards the blue part of the spectrum.

Also, the faster a star or galaxy is moving towards or away from us, the bigger the shift is.

Red shifts and blue shifts are examples of the Doppler effect. This is the change in the observed wavelengths (and frequency) of waves due to the motion of the source towards or away from the observer. Christian Doppler discovered the effect in 1842 using sound waves. He demonstrated it by sending an open railway carriage filled with trumpeters speeding past a line of trained listeners.

Laboratory source of light

Light from a receding galaxy

Figure 2 Red shift

b) What do you think happens to the light from a star that is moving towards us?

In 1929, Edwin Hubble discovered that the light from distant galaxies was 'red-shifted'. He found that the further a galaxy is from us, the bigger its red shift is. He concluded that:

- the distant galaxies are moving away from us (i.e. receding),
- the speed (of recession) of a distant galaxy is proportional to its distance from us.

Why should the distant galaxies be moving away from us? We have no special place in the Universe. So all the distant galaxies must be moving away from each other. In other words, **the whole Universe is expanding**.

c) Galaxy X is 2000 million light years away. Galaxy Y is 4000 million light years away. Which galaxy, X or Y, has the bigger red shift?

SUMMARY QUESTIONS

1 Complete the sentences below using words from the list.

   approaching   expanding   orbiting   receding

   a) The Earth is …… the Sun.
   b) The Universe is …… .
   c) The distant galaxies are …… .
   d) A blue shift in the light from a star would tell us it is …… .

2 a) Put these objects in order of increasing size:

   Andromeda galaxy   Earth   Sun   Universe

   b) Complete the sentences below using words from the list.

   galaxy   star   red shift   planet

   i) The Earth is a …… in orbit round a …… called the Sun.
   ii) There is a …… in the light from a distant …… .

DID YOU KNOW?

You can hear the Doppler effect when an ambulance with its siren on goes speeding past.

- When it approaches, the waves it sends out are squashed up so their frequency is higher (and the wavelength shorter) than when the siren is stationary.
- When it travels away from you, the waves it sends out are stretched out so their frequency is lower (and the wavelength longer) than when the siren is stationary.

KEY POINTS

1 Light from a distant galaxy is red-shifted to longer wavelengths.

2 The most distant galaxies are about 13 000 million light years away.

3 The Universe is expanding.

Teaching suggestions – continued

- **ICT link-up.** Why do scientists need more and more powerful computers? Simulations of galaxies smashing together may look nice, but it takes a lot of computing power to work out when a billion stars meet another billion stars. Many of the simulations on-line have been carried out by 'supercomputers' thousands of times more powerful than a simple PC. There is a PhotoPLUS, P1b 7.2 'Big bang', available on the GCSE Physics CD ROM. This could be used next lesson.

KEY POINTS

The students should draw a diagram showing what happens to light waves emitted from a galaxy moving *towards* us. They should use this to explain why the light would be shifted to the blue end of the spectrum.

P1b 7.2   The Big Bang

LEARNING OBJECTIVES

Students should learn that:

- The Universe is thought to have begun in a dramatic event called the Big Bang.

- The expansion of the Universe supports the Big Bang theory.

- The cosmic microwave background radiation is a primary piece of evidence leading to this conclusion.

LEARNING OUTCOMES

Most students should be able to:

- Describe the Big Bang as the event that generated the Universe.

- Describe the evidence for the expansion of the Universe and how it supports the Big Bang theory.

- State the evidence for this conclusion.

Some students should also be able to:

- Describe possible scenarios for the destiny of the Universe.

Teaching suggestions

- **Gifted and talented.** Just how small is 'small'? These students may wish to look into the concept of singularities: objects of zero volume and infinite density; it is from one of these that the Universe is thought to have originated. The ideas are closely linked to black holes, which the students will study later in the next topic; you may wish to leave this until then and link the two ideas together.

- **Learning styles**

  Kinaesthetic: Research into previous ideas about the Universe.

  Visual: Imagining the Big Bang.

  Auditory: Hearing the description of the end of the Universe.

  Interpersonal: Discussing the origin of the Universe.

  Intrapersonal: Considering the evidence for the Big Bang model.

- **ICT link-up.** There are several web sites explaining the Big Bang and theories about possible ends to the Universe. Some are a bit technical, but students may wish to find out more from them. Search at www.nasa.gov or www.bbc.co.uk.

SPECIFICATION LINK-UP   P1b.11.7

- *How the observed red shift provides evidence that the Universe is expanding and supports the 'Big Bang' theory (that the Universe began from a very small initial point).*

Lesson structure

STARTER

Bang! – Show a video clip of a large explosion and ask students to describe dramatically what is going on. (5 minutes)

Heat death – Remind students that all energy transfers lead to energy being wasted as heat. Ask them to describe what will happen when all of the energy the Universe started with is wasted. (5 minutes)

Your history – Give the students a list of historical events reaching back through human history, and then to the formation of the Earth. Ask them to put the events in order. (15 minutes)

MAIN

- This lesson is all about big ideas and how scientists have to provide evidence for them. (It is ideal for teaching aspects of 'How Science Works'.)

- Many students may ask what was before the Big Bang. The best approach is to talk about the meaning of 'before'. As scientists believe that time only started with the Big Bang there was no time before it, so it is meaningless to ask questions about what happened. A PhotoPLUS, P1b 7.2 'Big Bang', is available on the GCSE Physics CD ROM to help students explore the idea.

- Students may also be a bit confused by the term 'explosion'. The Big Bang is better described as a sudden expansion and the production of a lot of energy. As the Universe continues to expand, this energy gets more and more dissipated and so the Universe cools down.

- The main thrust of the lesson is to explain to the students that an idea like the Big Bang needs to have *evidence* before it is accepted by scientists. It is not enough to come up with the best sounding explanations. This links to the 'fundamental ideas' section of 'How Science Works'.

- Those that did not accept the theory were right to, until they were given evidence of the cosmic background radiation. They should then accept the new model, or come up with an alternative explanation that takes the new evidence into account.

- Changes to ideas like this are important to science; the students need to know that scientists will analyse new ideas and accept them if they explain the evidence better than the old ideas. This process ensures that scientific knowledge develops and becomes a better description of the Universe.

- You should also point out that recent discoveries, such as the possible speeding up of the expansion, will also have to be explained by scientists over the coming years; we do not have a complete description of the Universe and may never have.

- Conditions in the very early Universe were very different than they are now. The temperatures were so high that atoms could not exist, and even protons and neutrons could not form.

- The cosmic background is a result of this stretching of the wavelength; you can link this to the idea of red shift but the two processes are a bit different.

- The end of the Universe is still open to debate, and students should not worry too much about it. We have a few billion years to go before a 'Big Crunch' or a 'Big Yawn'.

PLENARIES

Better Big Bang – The term 'Big Bang' is not a very good one to describe the beginning of the Universe. Can the students come up with a better term for it? (5 minutes)

Can science answer everything? – Have a brief debate with the students about the limits of scientific understanding. Can all questions be answered by scientific research? (10 minutes)

ACTIVITY & EXTENSION IDEAS

A steady state

Some scientists heartily resisted the idea of a 'Big Bang' and expanding Universe. The students could find out who these where and what their objections were. Do all scientists agree on the Big Bang model now?

Improving evidence

Ever since the discovery of the cosmic microwave background radiation, scientists have been trying to find improved ways of measuring it so that they can find out the structure of the early Universe. The students can find out how satellites, including the COBE mentioned in the Student Book, have been used to map the radiations and find variations in it. There are several satellites that have been used, or are due for launch in the coming years, all with dedicated web sites.

DID YOU KNOW?

The microwave background radiation was discovered by accident in 1965 by Arno Allen Penzias and Robert Woodrow Wilson. They were trying to remove interference from microwave links in a communication system, but they couldn't find the source of this 'background noise even after replacing most of the electronic components. They then realised that the interference was actually coming from *everywhere* in the sky. Other scientists who had actually been searching for this predicted radiation had to watch when Penzias and Wilson were awarded the Nobel prize in 1978!

PHYSICS

THE ORIGINS OF THE UNIVERSE

P1b 7.2 The Big Bang

LEARNING OBJECTIVES

1 Why is the Universe expanding?
2 What is the Big Bang theory of the Universe?

The Universe is expanding, but what is making it expand? The **Big Bang theory** was put forward to explain the expansion. This states that:

- the Universe is expanding after exploding suddenly in a Big Bang from a very small initial point,
- space, time and matter were created in the Big Bang

Many scientists disagreed with the Big Bang theory. They put forward an alternative theory, the Steady State theory. The scientists said that the galaxies are being pushed apart. They thought that this is caused by matter entering the Universe through 'white holes' (the opposite of black holes).

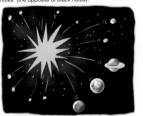

Figure 1 The Big Bang

Which theory is weirder – everything starting from a Big Bang or matter leaking into the Universe from outside? Until 1965, most people backed the Steady State theory.

It was in 1965 that scientists first detected microwaves coming from every direction in space. The existence of this **background microwave radiation** can only be explained by the Big Bang theory.

a) Scientists think the Big Bang happened about 13 000 million years ago. What was before the Big Bang?

Background microwave radiation

- It was created as high-energy gamma radiation just after the Big Bang.
- It has been travelling through space since then.
- As the Universe has expanded, it stretched out to longer and longer wavelengths and is now microwave radiation.
- It has been mapped out using microwave detectors on the ground and on satellites.

b) What will happen to background microwave radiation as the Universe expands?

DID YOU KNOW?

You can detect background microwave radiation very easily – just disconnect your TV aerial. The radiation causes lots of fuzzy spots on the screen.

108

Radiation and the Universe

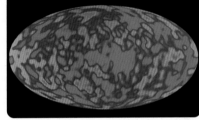

Figure 2 A microwave image of the Universe from COBE, the Cosmic Background Explorer satellite

The future of the Universe

Will the Universe expand forever? Or will the force of gravity between the distant galaxies stop them from moving away from each other? The answer to this question depends on their total mass and how much space they take up – in other words, the density of the Universe.

- If the density of the Universe is less than a certain amount, it will expand forever. The stars will die out. So will everything else as the Universe heads for a Big Yawn!
- If the density of the Universe is more than a certain amount, it will stop expanding and go into reverse. Everything will head for a Big Crunch!

Recent observations by astronomers suggest that the distant galaxies are accelerating away from each other. It looks like we're in for a Big Ride followed by a Big Yawn.

c) What could you say about the future of the Universe if the galaxies were slowing down?

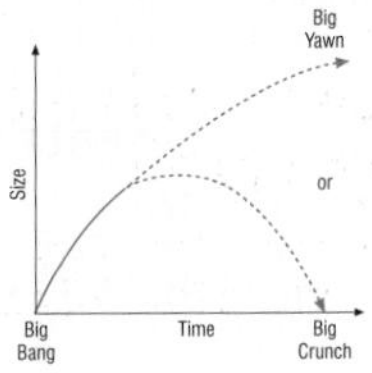

Figure 3 The future of the Universe

SUMMARY QUESTIONS

1 Complete the sentences below using words from the list.

created detected expanded stretched

a) The Universe was ...... in an explosion called the Big Bang.
b) The Universe ...... suddenly in and after the Big Bang.
c) Microwave radiation from space can be ...... in all directions.
d) Radiation created just after the Big Bang has been ...... by the expansion of the Universe and is now microwave radiation.

2 What will happen to the Universe:

a) if its density is less than a certain value?
b) if its density is greater than a certain value?

KEY POINTS

1 The Universe started with the Big Bang, a massive explosion from a very small point.
2 Background microwave radiation is radiation created just after the Big Bang.

109

SUMMARY ANSWERS

1 **a)** Created.
b) Expanded.
c) Detected.
d) Stretched.

2 **a)** The Universe will continue to expand.
b) The expansion will stop and reverse.

Answers to in-text questions

a) Nothing.

b) It will be stretched even more to longer wavelengths.

c) The expansion might reverse or it might just gradually stop.

KEY POINTS

The students should write a letter to a sceptical person trying to convince them of the evidence for the Big Bang theory and the expansion of the Universe.

P1b 7.3

Looking into space

Teaching suggestions

- **Gifted and talented.** What is a 'black hole'? The students can find out about how these are formed and how they behave. Will black holes eat up our entire galaxy one day in the distant future?

- **Learning styles**

  Kinaesthetic: Making and using telescopes.

  Visual: Observing astronomical images.

  Interpersonal: Discussing the advantages of space-based telescopes.

- **ICT link-up.** Students can view the PhotoPLUS, P1b 7.3 'Looking into space' from the GCSE Physics CD ROM in this lesson.

SPECIFICATION LINK-UP   P1b.11.7

- *Observations of the solar system and the galaxies in the Universe can be carried out on the Earth or from space.*

- *Observations are made with telescopes that may detect visible light or other electromagnetic radiations, such as radio waves or X-rays.*

Students should use their skills, knowledge and understanding of 'How Science Works':

- *to compare and contrast the particular advantages and disadvantages of using different types of telescope on Earth and in space to make observations on and deductions about the Universe.*

Lesson structure

STARTER

What's out there? – The students should list all of the different types of object that can be seen in space from the Earth's surface with the naked eye, and perhaps draw what they look like. (5–10 minutes)

Astronomical question loop – A chain of questions and answers about objects in the solar system. (5–10 minutes)

Shoddy solar system – Give the students a set of incorrect facts about the solar system and ask them to correct them. (5 minutes)

MAIN

- This is a fairly visual topic and benefits a lot from the use of images. Try to find some good slides of all of the objects mentioned in the spread to show the students when they come up. There are many good sources of amazing images and animations. (Search at www.nasa.gov or www.bbc.co.uk.

- The students should be aware of comets from Key Stage 3. It is interesting to show them some historical comet events: perhaps the Bayeux tapestry or the *Shoemaker Levy 9* and Jupiter collisions.

- There will probably be a discussion about what will happen if a comet or meteor hits the Earth about now. You can deal with this now or in the next spread later; have a look there for more information.

- If you are working in a large town or city, some students will not have been able to see the full detail of the Milky Way crossing the sky; it is well worth showing them just how many stars are out there.

- The school may have an astronomical telescope; the students can look through to see the magnification. They should notice, or you should point out, that the image is upside down (inverted). This doesn't bother astronomers; they get used to it.

- Try building the simple telescopes; the students may improve on the basic design.

- Link radio telescopes back to their understanding of the electromagnetic spectrum. Discuss that the telescopes have to be very large because radio waves carry a lot less energy than visible light.

- When discussing satellites, point out that the main benefit is that they are above the atmosphere. The atmosphere blocks quite a lot of the electromagnetic spectrum, so we would not be able to look at objects that emit in these regions from the Earth's surface.

PLENARIES

Jeopardy – Students have to think up questions about a list of astronomical objects and terms. (10 minutes)

Comet legends – Comets are often associated with bad luck or major events. Can the students come up with a comet legend about where they come from? (10 minutes)

It's life Jim – Is there life 'out there'? Discuss the sort of things we should be looking for to find evidence of alien life. (5–10 minutes)

Practical support

Making astronomical telescopes

Simple telescopes are easy to build, but fiddly to use.

Equipment and materials required

Metre rulers, 50 cm and 5 cm focal length converging lenses, some 75 cm lenses, Plasticine.

Details

Mount the 5 cm lens at one end of the ruler and the 50 cm lens 55 cm along the ruler using Plasticine. The students look through the fatter (5 cm) eyepiece lens and if they have aligned the lenses fairly straight, they should see an image. The image should be magnified by a factor of five, but will only show a small part of what the telescope is pointed at. The students should think about how they would be able to get a larger image and think up some ideas about improving magnification. Try the combination of 5 cm and 75 cm positioned 80 cm apart.

Improving telescopes

Once the students have explored basic telescopes, you could ask them to design improved models. Perhaps they could think of sturdier ways of mounting the lenses. Some students may try to think of ways of getting the image right way up; they could research 'terrestrial telescopes'.

Armageddon?

Should we be designing anti-comet and anti-asteroid measures? What can be done and would it work? The students could produce a report on the feasibility and usefulness of this idea. They would need to find out about the actual odds of an impact and how much damage it would cause.

KEY POINTS

The students should produce a table showing which types of EM radiation can penetrate the atmosphere and which cannot.

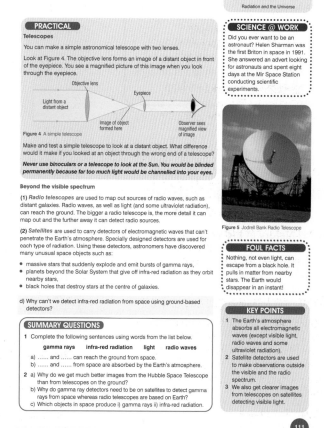

PHYSICS   THE ORIGINS OF THE UNIVERSE

P1b 7.3   Looking into space

LEARNING OBJECTIVES

1 What can we see in space?
2 What electromagnetic radiations, other than light, can we detect from space?
3 Why are observations from satellites better than those we make from the ground?

When we look at the night sky, we sometimes see unexpected objects in the sky, as well as planets and stars. Such objects include:

- shooting stars which are small objects from space that burn up when they enter the Earth's atmosphere,
- comets which are frozen rocks that orbit the Sun – we only see them when they get near the Sun because then they get so hot that they emit light,
- stars that explode (supernova) or flare up then fade (nova).

a) Which is nearer to us, a comet bright enough to see, or a shooting star?

We can see even more in the night sky with a telescope.

- A telescope makes stars appear much brighter. Because it is much wider than your eye, it collects much more light than your eye can. All the light it collects is channelled into your eye. So you can see stars too faint to see without a telescope.
- A telescope makes the Moon and the planets appear bigger. A telescope with magnification ×20 would make Venus appear 20 times wider. As well as that, you can see more detail. For example, you can see the Great Red Spot on the surface of Jupiter. This was first observed by Galileo almost 400 years ago.

b) Why can you see more stars by using a telescope?

The Earth's atmosphere affects telescopes on the ground. It scatters the light from space objects and makes their images fuzzy.

c) Why doesn't the Earth's atmosphere affect the Hubble Space Telescope?

Figure 1 A comet

Figure 2 Jupiter's Great Red Spot

Figure 3 Colliding galaxies – an image from Hubble Space Telescope. The Hubble Space Telescope (HST) is in orbit around the Earth. It gives us amazing images of objects in space. Compared with telescopes on the ground, HST enables us to see objects in much more detail. We can also see things that are much further away.

110

PRACTICAL

Telescopes

You can make a simple astronomical telescope with two lenses.

Look at Figure 4. The objective lens forms an image of a distant object in front of the eyepiece. You see a magnified picture of this image when you look through the eyepiece.

Figure 4 A simple telescope

Make and test a simple telescope to look at a distant object. What difference would it make if you looked at an object through the wrong end of a telescope?

Never use binoculars or a telescope to look at the Sun. You would be blinded permanently because far too much light would be channelled into your eyes.

Beyond the visible spectrum

(1) *Radio telescopes* are used to map out sources of radio waves, such as distant galaxies. Radio waves, as well as light (and some ultraviolet radiation), can reach the ground. The bigger a radio telescope is, the more detail it can map out and the further away it can detect radio sources.

(2) *Satellites* are used to carry detectors of electromagnetic waves that can't penetrate the Earth's atmosphere. Specially designed detectors are used for each type of radiation. Using these detectors, astronomers have discovered many unusual space objects such as:

- massive stars that suddenly explode and emit bursts of gamma rays,
- planets beyond the Solar System that give off infra-red radiation as they orbit nearby stars,
- black holes that destroy stars at the centre of galaxies.

d) Why can't we detect infra-red radiation from space using ground-based detectors?

SUMMARY QUESTIONS

1 Complete the following sentences using words from the list below.

     gamma rays   infra-red radiation   light   radio waves

a) …… and …… can reach the ground from space.
b) …… and …… from space are absorbed by the Earth's atmosphere.

2 a) Why do we get much better images from the Hubble Space Telescope than from telescopes on the ground?
b) Why do gamma ray detectors need to be on satellites to detect gamma rays from space whereas radio telescopes are based on Earth?
c) Which objects in space produce i) gamma rays ii) infra-red radiation.

SCIENCE @ WORK

Did you ever want to be an astronaut? Helen Sharman was the first Briton in space in 1991. She answered an advert looking for astronauts and spent eight days at the Mir Space Station conducting scientific experiments.

Figure 5 Jodrell Bank Radio Telescope

FOUL FACTS

Nothing, not even light, can escape from a black hole. It pulls in matter from nearby stars. The Earth would disappear in an instant!

KEY POINTS

1 The Earth's atmosphere absorbs all electromagnetic waves (except visible light, radio waves and some ultraviolet radiation).
2 Satellite detectors are used to make observations outside the visible and the radio spectrum.
3 We also get clearer images from telescopes on satellites detecting visible light.

111

SUMMARY ANSWERS

1 a) Light, radio waves.

   b) Gamma rays, infra-red radiation.

2 a) Light from objects in space has to pass through the Earth's atmosphere to reach ground-based telescopes. The Earth's atmosphere scatters the light slightly and 'smudges' the images out. HST is above the Earth's atmosphere, so its images aren't affected.

   b) Gamma rays can't pass through the atmosphere, so the detectors need to be above the atmosphere whereas radio waves can pass through the atmosphere.

   c) i) Massive exploding stars.

      ii) Planets beyond the Solar System.

Answers to in-text questions

a) A shooting star.

b) The telescope collects more light from a star than the unaided eye does. So stars too faint to be seen with the unaided eye can be seen with a telescope.

c) HST is in space above the atmosphere.

d) The infra-red radiation is absorbed by the molecules of the gases in the atmosphere.

P1b 7.4 Looking into the unknown

Candidates should know and understand:

- *Observations of the solar system and the galaxies in the Universe can be carried out on the Earth or from space.*

- *Observations are made with telescopes that may detect visible light or other electromagnetic radiations, such as radio waves or X-rays.*

Students should use their skills, knowledge and understanding of 'How Science Works':

- *to compare and contrast the particular advantages and disadvantages of using different types of telescope on Earth and in space, to make observations on and deductions about the Universe.*

Teaching suggestions

Activities

A short history of the Universe – The students should be able to find several web sites describing the early stages of the Universe. Many of these will be overly technical, but they should get the general idea that the Universe was very different than it is now: atoms did not exist and light could not travel. The students should extend their timeline into the current era, adding on information about the formation of our solar system and possibly even life on Earth. For what fraction of the life of the Universe has humans existed?

Galileo – There are many resources about Galileo Galilei and the students should prepare this information before the trial. You should be able to find transcripts from the trial, the charges, verdict and the recantation of the 'heretical' ideas by Galileo himself.

Mars Blog – The difficulties in getting to Mars in the first place should not be under-estimated. Ask the students to find out what resources would have to be taken for the trip and how long it would take with current technology. They should be able to find a lot of information about the surface of Mars, as several probes have visited recently.

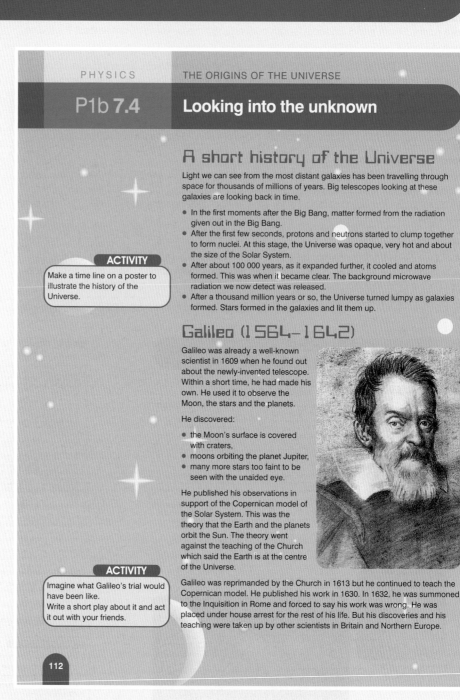

PHYSICS THE ORIGINS OF THE UNIVERSE

P1b 7.4 Looking into the unknown

A short history of the Universe

Light we can see from the most distant galaxies has been travelling through space for thousands of millions of years. Big telescopes looking at these galaxies are looking back in time.

- In the first moments after the Big Bang, matter formed from the radiation given out in the Big Bang.
- After the first few seconds, protons and neutrons started to clump together to form nuclei. At this stage, the Universe was opaque, very hot and about the size of the Solar System.
- After about 100 000 years, as it expanded further, it cooled and atoms formed. This was when it became clear. The background microwave radiation we now detect was released.
- After a thousand million years or so, the Universe turned lumpy as galaxies formed. Stars formed in the galaxies and lit them up.

ACTIVITY

Make a time line on a poster to illustrate the history of the Universe.

Galileo (1564–1642)

Galileo was already a well-known scientist in 1609 when he found out about the newly-invented telescope. Within a short time, he had made his own. He used it to observe the Moon, the stars and the planets.

He discovered:

- the Moon's surface is covered with craters,
- moons orbiting the planet Jupiter,
- many more stars too faint to be seen with the unaided eye.

He published his observations in support of the Copernican model of the Solar System. This was the theory that the Earth and the planets orbit the Sun. The theory went against the teaching of the Church which said the Earth is at the centre of the Universe.

ACTIVITY

Imagine what Galileo's trial would have been like.
Write a short play about it and act it out with your friends.

Galileo was reprimanded by the Church in 1613 but he continued to teach the Copernican model. He published his work in 1630. In 1632, he was summoned to the Inquisition in Rome and forced to say his work was wrong. He was placed under house arrest for the rest of his life. But his discoveries and his teaching were taken up by other scientists in Britain and Northern Europe.

112

Space invaders! – The odds of being killed in an event like an asteroid impact lie between 1 in 20 000 and 1 in 1 000 000 000 000 depending on the information source. This should reassure the students of their safety; although the dinosaurs may disagree. Even though an impact is unlikely, the damage would be tremendous – as the students will be aware of from a range of films and television programmes. Some sources claim that we are 'overdue' an impact: this is a misunderstanding of statistics that you may wish to correct. The fact that we have not had an impact in a long time does not increase the chance of one occurring next year or the year after. The chance is the same (very small) each year.

Some interesting impacts worth talking about are the Chicxulub 'Dinosaur killer' that hit the Yucatan peninsula 65 million years ago; the Barringer meteor crater in Arizona and the mysterious Tunguska impact. There are many web sites dedicated to meteor impacts. Search at www.nasa.gov or www.bbc.co.uk.

SETI – SETI has an interesting web site (www.seti.org) with a great deal of information about their activities. It also has detail of the 'Drake Equation' mentioned in the 'Gifted and talented'.

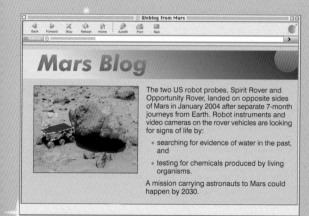

Mars Blog

The two US robot probes, Spirit Rover and Opportunity Rover, landed on opposite sides of Mars in January 2004 after separate 7-month journeys from Earth. Robot instruments and video cameras on the rover vehicles are looking for signs of life by:

- searching for evidence of water in the past, and
- testing for chemicals produced by living organisms.

A mission carrying astronauts to Mars could happen by 2030.

ACTIVITY

Imagine you're an astronaut on Mars. Write a weblog about a day in your life. Include some background music and photos.

Space invaders!

Asteroids are massive chunks of rock orbiting the Sun. They are found mostly between Mars and Jupiter. Sometimes, an asteroid gets pulled toward the Sun and crosses the Earth's orbit. In 1992, an asteroid narrowly missed the Earth. On a scale where the Sun is 1 metre away, it came within just 3 cm of the Earth! If it had hit the Earth, the impact could have killed millions of people.

ACTIVITY

Make a poster to convince people that the Government should pay for an asteroid 'early warning' system.

The search for extra-terrestrial intelligence (SETI)

The search for extra-terrestrial intelligence has gone on for more than 40 years. We can use radio telescopes to detect signals in a band of wavelengths. Such signals would indicate the existence of living beings. They would be at least as advanced as we are, perhaps on a planet in a distant solar system. Radio astronomers have searched without success for such radio signals. However, just one SETI signal would change our outlook for ever!

ACTIVITY

Imagine SETI signals have been detected from Andromeda. It is in all the newspapers, on radio and on TV. You do a survey of 100 people to see how people have reacted to this news. The results are in the table below.

Question	Yes	No
1. Have you heard about the discovery of signals from space aliens?	55	45
2. Should we send peaceful signals back?	70	30
3. Do you think the signals are from a more advanced civilisation than us?	30	70

a) Make a bar chart to display these findings.
b) Discuss with your friends what you would put into a 5-minute return signal. It could include video and audio, as well as text.

113

Extension or homework

The students can visit the SETI site at home and may like to become involved with the search by joining the SETI@home project. With this, they can get their home computer to analyse signals and perhaps discover alien life for themselves.

ICT link-up

Students can analyse the odds of discovering alien life in the Universe with online versions of the Drake equation. Search the Internet for 'Drake equation'. They can change the odds of each of the parameters and see how many intelligent species are predicted to be in our galaxy.

Teaching assistant

Your teaching assistant can be very helpful in the recording of discussions or helping to generate ideas in group work. They may also be of assistance with the construction of the telescopes.

Learning styles

Kinaesthetic: Constructing telescopes (if not done in previous lesson).

Visual: Imagining life on Mars.

Auditory: Explaining their ideas.

Interpersonal: Debating the treatment of Galileo.

Intrapersonal: Writing a report about asteroid impacts.

Gifted and talented

These students should discuss the chances of there being intelligent alien life in the Universe and our chances of contacting them. They should list all of the things that are needed by intelligent life, and then look into the Drake equation to find the chances of life being out there. The Drake equation is quite good to model using a spreadsheet.

SUMMARY ANSWERS

1 **a)** C, B, D, A.

b) i) Galaxy, wavelengths.   **ii)** Away, Universe.

2 **a)** An increase.

b) A red shift.

c) Away from us.

d) It would be shifted to smaller wavelengths.

3 **a) i)** Galaxy A.   **ii)** Galaxy C is further away than galaxy A.

b) i) It is expanding.   **ii)** We are not in any special place.

4 **a) i)** The Big Bang.   **ii)** Apart.   **iii)** Thousand million.

b) i) Radiation that has been travelling through space since just after the Big Bang.

ii) It proved the Big Bang theory of the Universe.

5 **a)** Telescope X.

b) It is above the Earth's atmosphere, so light reaching it is not affected by the atmosphere. Light reaching telescopes on the ground is scattered by the Earth's atmosphere so the images seen are blurred.

Summary teaching suggestions

- Question 1 is a bit of a simple starter and tests recall more than understanding. Most students should cope well even if they can't explain what they mean.

- The answers to questions 2 and 3 should show a real understanding of red shift, though some will have trouble putting it into words. In this case they could be encouraged to use a diagram.

- For question 5, some higher attaining students may wonder why a bigger telescope can see 'further'; you might like to discuss this in terms of being able to collect more photons (energy), so being able to detect *fainter* objects rather than more distant ones. Students should be using the term 'absorption' when talking about the atmosphere.

THE ORIGINS OF THE UNIVERSE: P1b 7.1 – P1b 7.4

SUMMARY QUESTIONS

1 a) Put the objects listed below in order of increasing size.

   A the Milky Way galaxy   B Jupiter
   C the Moon   D the Sun

b) Complete the following sentences.
  i) Light from a distant ...... is shifted to the red part of the spectrum. This is because it has been stretched to longer ....
  ii) The distant galaxies are moving ...... from each other because the ...... is expanding.

2 Light from a distant galaxy has a change of wavelength due to the motion of the galaxy.
a) Is this change of wavelength an increase or a decrease?
b) What is the name for this change of wavelength?
c) Which way is the galaxy moving?
d) What would happen to the light it gives out if it were moving in the opposite direction?

3 a) Galaxy A is further from us than galaxy B.
  i) Which galaxy, A or B, produces light with a greater red shift?
  ii) Galaxy C gives a bigger red shift than galaxy A. What can we say about the distance to galaxy C compared with galaxy A?
b) All the distant galaxies are moving away from each other.
  i) What does this tell us about the Universe?
  ii) What does it tell us about our place in the Universe?

4 a) Complete the following sentences.
  i) The Universe was created in a massive explosion called ....
  ii) The expansion of the Universe is making the distant galaxies move ....
  iii) The Universe was created about thirteen ...... years ago.
b) i) What is background microwave radiation?
  ii) What did the discovery of background microwave radiation prove?

5 a) An astronomical observatory has two big telescopes, X and Y. X is bigger than Y. Which one can see furthest into space?
b) The Hubble Space Telescope gives better images than any telescope on the ground. Why?

EXAM-STYLE QUESTIONS

1 Optical telescopes should never be used to look directly at the Sun because
A this would permanently damage the eyesight of the observer.
B this would make the telescope catch fire.
C there is nothing to see on the Sun.
D the image would always appear blurred. (1)

2 Astronomers believe that the Universe
A has always been the same size.
B is getting bigger.
C is getting smaller.
D was getting bigger but will now stay the same size. (1)

3 Astronomers study different bodies found in the Universe.
Match the words in the list with the numbers 1 to 4 in the table.

  Galaxies   Solar systems   Sun   Planets (4)

Body	Description
1	Main source of energy for the Earth
2	Give light that gives evidence about the origin of the Universe
3	Consist of a central star orbited by planets
4	Reflect light from the Sun

4 Observations of bodies in space are made with telescopes. Some telescopes are positioned on the ground and some are in orbit around the Earth.
(a) Which of these devices could **not** be used to make observations of the night sky?
  A Binoculars   B Camera
  C Cloud chamber   D Naked eye (1)
(b) Which of the following are **not** detected by telescopes?
  A Radio waves   B Sound waves
  C Visible light   D X-rays (1)
(c) One advantage of a telescope in orbit is that it produces clearer images.
This is because . . .
  A it is closer to the stars being observed.
  B it is warmer in space.
  C it is easier to move the telescope around.
  D light is not scattered by the atmosphere. (1)

EXAM-STYLE ANSWERS

1 **A** *(1 mark)*

2 **B** *(1 mark)*

3 **1** Sun

  2 galaxies

  3 solar systems

  4 planets *(1 mark each)*

4 a) **C**

b) **B**

c) **D**

d) **A** *(1 mark each)*

5 a) All matter was concentrated at a single point. *(1 mark)*
  A massive explosion sent all the matter outwards. *(1 mark)*

b) (i) Frequency of light from a moving source *(1 mark)*
  is moved towards red end of the spectrum. *(1 mark)*
  (ii) They are moving away from us. *(1 mark)*
  (iii) Space is expanding. *(1 mark)*
  So must have started from a single point. *(1 mark)*

6 a) (i) Venus and Mars are closest to Earth. *(1 mark)*
  (ii) Jupiter and Saturn are the biggest planets. *(1 mark)*

b) They are much further from the Earth than Mars. *(1 mark)*

c) It is much smaller than Uranus and Neptune *(1 mark)*
  and the furthest planet from the Earth. *(1 mark)*

(d) Which of the following statements is **not** true when applied to a large optical telescope in orbit?

   A It is easier to maintain than one on the ground.

   B The large mirrors are effectively weightless.

   C The mirrors do not suffer atmospheric corrosion.

   D Weather does not affect its performance. (1)

The Big Bang theory is one theory of the origin of the Universe.

(a) What are the main ideas of the Big Bang theory? (2)

(b) One piece of evidence for this theory is red-shift.

   (i) What is red-shift? (2)

   (ii) What does red-shift tell us about distant galaxies? (1)

   (iii) Explain how red-shift is evidence for the Big Bang theory. (2)

The following table gives some data about the planets in the Solar System.

Planet	Diameter (km)	Distance from the Sun (million km)
Mercury	4640	58
Venus	12230	108
Earth	12683	150
Mars	6720	228
Jupiter	141920	778
Saturn	120160	1431
Uranus	46880	2886
Neptune	49920	4529
Pluto	2284	5936

Use the information given in the table to help you answer the questions.

Some planets can be observed with the naked eye, but others can only be seen with a telescope. The ancient Greeks did not have telescopes.

(a) Suggest a reason why the ancient Greeks were able to observe:

   (i) Venus and Mars

   (ii) Jupiter and Saturn (2)

(b) Uranus and Neptune are much bigger than Mars but were unknown to the Greeks. Suggest why. (2)

(c) Why was Pluto discovered much later than Uranus and Neptune? (1)

HOW SCIENCE WORKS QUESTIONS

The Big Bang

Fred Hoyle, who studied physics at school in Yorkshire then at Cambridge University, first used the term the 'Big Bang', although he was a life-long opponent of the theory. Other opponents were the Soviet Union, who imprisoned scientists who supported the Big Bang theory. Pope Pius XII embraced the idea, but the church changed its mind later, before finally accepting it after the discovery of background microwave radiation in 1965.

One of the difficulties with the theory was that the universe seemed to be younger than the stars in it! So the theory produced a hypothesis that the universe must be much older than had been calculated. This produced a prediction that the distance to the galaxies must be greater than previously calculated.

Investigations were designed to find the true age of the universe, so that the theory could be supported . . . or not!

Technology was lacking to do these measurements. Bigger and better telescopes were built. Finally they gave the answer that the Big Bang supporters had wanted. The universe was at least twice as old as was previously measured and it fell to Fred Hoyle to record the discovery for the meeting of astronomers!

Fred Hoyle (1915–2001)

Use this account to give one example of each of the following:

a) a hypothesis (1)

b) a theory (1)

c) a prediction (1)

d) political influence (1)

e) the importance of technology to scientific progress. (1)

115

HOW SCIENCE WORKS ANSWERS

a) Hypothesis – the Universe is much older than present evidence suggests.

b) Theory – the Big Bang theory for the creation of the Universe.

c) Prediction – the distance to the galaxies must be greater than calculated.

d) Political influence – Soviet Union under Stalin, influenced the thinking of scientists.

e) Importance of technology – the building of a new, much larger and more powerful and accurate telescope.

How science works teaching suggestions

- **Literacy guidance**
  - Key terms that should be clearly understood are: hypothesis, theory, prediction, political influence, technology.
  - Students should be encouraged to keep their answers short and to the point.

- **Higher- and lower-level questions.** Questions a) and d) are higher-level and the answers provided above are also at this level. Questions b) and e) are lower-level and the answers are also at this level.

- **Gifted and talented.** Able students could explore the reasons for one of the churches at first supporting the Big Bang theory and then distancing itself.

- **How and when to use these questions.** When wishing to give an overview of scientific method. The question could be done as an exercise for individuals or as small group work.

- **Homework.** The whole question could be done for homework.

- **Special needs.** The story might need to be told to students and the questions asked as the story is told.

Exam teaching suggestions

- In order to answer these questions students need to be familiar with the following terms: Sun, Earth, galaxy, Universe and solar system.

- Many students will be under the impression that telescopes can only be used to detect visible light. In order to answer question 4 they should appreciate that telescopes can also be used to detect other electromagnetic radiations.

- Students should understand that telescopes in orbits around the Earth receive signals that have not been scattered by the atmosphere. Weaker students think these telescopes produce clearer pictures because they are closer to the stars.

- A lower-level answer to question 5 will say little more than 'the Universe started with a big explosion' and 'distant galaxies are moving away from us', thus gaining only two of the six marks available. More able students will be able to explain how the red shift supports the Big Bang theory.

P1b   Examination-Style Questions

Answers to Questions

Physics A

1	**C**		*(1 mark)*
2	**A**		*(1 mark)*
3	**1**	solar system	*(1 mark)*
	2	Universe	*(1 mark)*
	3	space	*(1 mark)*
	4	atmosphere	*(1 mark)*
4	**C**		*(1 mark)*

EXAMINATION-STYLE QUESTIONS

Physics A

1 The light coming to us from distant galaxies shows a change in wavelength. This change is called . . .   *(See pages 106–7)*

    A   Blue shift.

    B   Radio shift.

    C   Red shift.

    D   Star shift.   *(1 mark)*

2 What type of signal is shown on the diagram below?   *(See page 88)*

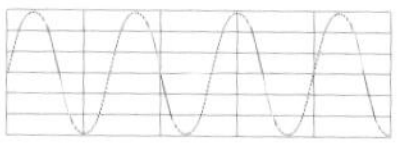

    A   Analogue

    B   Binary

    C   Digital

    D   Frequency   *(1 mark)*

3 Match the words in the list below with the numbers **1** to **4** in the sentences.   *(See page 110)*

    A   atmosphere

    B   solar system

    C   space

    D   universe

Observations of the ......**1**...... and the galaxies in the ......**2**...... can be carried out by telescopes on the Earth or in ......**3**...... Telescopes outside the Earth's ......**4**......are not affected by the weather.   *(4 marks)*

4 The half-life of the radioactive element americium is 500 years. A sample of americium contains 8 000 atoms. After how many years will the sample contain 1 000 atoms.   *(See page 101)*

    A   500 years

    B   1 000 years

    C   1 500 years

    D   2 000 years   *(1 mark)*

GET IT RIGH

Make sure you know wha meant by 'half-life' and h to use it in calculations.

116

GET IT RIGHT!

Some students may think that after two half-lives the whole of a sample of a radioactive isotope will have decayed. Students need to appreciate that after two half-lives, one-half of one-half, i.e. one-quarter of the original sample remains and thus the activity falls to one-quarter of the original.

The uses of the different types of electromagnetic radiation are often asked for in examination questions.

Students often lose marks in calculations by losing or gaining zeros. This is often the result of them not taking sufficient care in setting out their working. Many students will not, at this stage, be familiar with the use of standard form.

Physics B

Electromagnetic radiation can be used for many different purposes.

See pages 78–85

(a) Which electromagnetic radiation is used:

   (i) to take shadow pictures of bones?

   (ii) in sun beds?

   (iii) to sterilise surgical instruments? *(3 marks)*

(b) Electromagnetic radiation can be hazardous as well as useful.

   Explain why the skin should be protected from ultraviolet radiation. *(2 marks)*

(c) Microwaves can be used to cook food in a microwave oven.

   (i) Explain how microwaves cook food. *(2 marks)*

   (ii) Explain how the microwaves could harm you if they escaped from the oven. *(2 marks)*

(d) Some microwaves have a wavelength of 0.02 metres and a frequency of 15 000 million hertz.
Use the equation speed = frequency × wavelength to calculate the speed of these microwaves. *(2 marks)*

GET IT RIGHT!
Make sure you know at least one use of each type of electromagnetic radiation.

GET IT RIGHT!
This calculation involves a very large number. In setting out your working be careful not to lose or gain any zeros.

Some substances give out radiation from the nuclei of their atoms all the time. These substances are said to be radioactive.

See page 95
See pages 96–7

(a) Describe the basic structure of an atom. *(4 marks)*

(b) A teacher has two radioactive sources, one emits only alpha particles and the other emits only beta particles.
The sources are unlabelled. Describe a simple test he can do to determine which is which. *(3 marks)*

Physics B

1 (a) (i) X-rays *(1 mark)*

   (ii) Ultraviolet *(1 mark)*

   (iii) Gamma rays *(1 mark)*

(b) Ultraviolet radiation can damage/ionise skin cells. *(1 mark)*
This can cause changes in DNA/cause cancer. *(1 mark)*

(c) (i) Microwaves are absorbed by the water molecules in food. *(1 mark)*
This heats them up and so cooks the food. *(1 mark)*

   (ii) Human skin cells contain water, this absorbs microwaves. *(1 mark)*
The cells heat up and may be damaged. *(1 mark)*

(d) Speed = frequency × wavelength
Speed = 15 000 000 000 × 0.02 *(1 mark)*
Speed = 300 000 000 m/s *(1 mark)*

2 (a) Small central nucleus *(1 mark)*
containing protons and neutrons *(2 marks)*
surrounded by electrons. *(1 mark)*

(b) Place each source in turn a few centimetres from a detector. *(1 mark)*
Put a sheet of paper between the source and the detector. *(1 mark)*
The count rate will drop to almost zero for alpha source. *(1 mark)*

Key Stage 3 curriculum links

The following link to 'What you already know':

- How to determine the speed of a moving object and to use the quantitative relationship between speed, distance and time.

- That the weight of an object on Earth is the result of the gravitational attraction between its mass and that of the Earth.

- That unbalanced forces change the speed or direction of movement of objects and that balanced forces produce no change in the movement of an object.

- Ways in which frictional forces, including air resistance, affect motion [for example, streamlining cars, friction between tyre and road].

- How to design and construct series and parallel circuits, and how to measure current and voltage.

- That the current in a series circuit depends on the number of cells and the number and nature of other components and that current is not 'used up' by components.

- That energy is transferred from batteries and other sources to other components in electrical circuits.

Scheme of work
7J Electrical circuits
7K Forces and their effects
9I Energy and electricity
9K Speeding up

Making connections

Each of these vignettes provides you with an opportunity to discuss important scientific developments linked to exploration and would best be tackled as the story of our general urge to explore. Use the ideas to show the students why scientific developments are key in technological progress and that new ideas and discoveries will be needed if we are to reach further out into space. There are several space exploration missions active at one time; some more successful than others. You can provide the students with up-to-date information on the latest space probe. It is hard to predict the breakthroughs that could happen before 2099, but they might like to consider these possibilities:

- **Matter transmitters:** Could we 'beam' ourselves across the world?

- **Artificial intelligence:** Machines with the ability to think; they could potentially be smarter than humans.

- **Digitised humans:** One day we could leave our flesh bodies behind and our minds could run on smaller and more long-lasting hardware. This would be ideal for the long-time scale of space exploration.

- **Alien contact:** We might finally contact another intelligent species. Would it be friend or foe?

RECAP ANSWERS

1 a) Conductors: brass, copper; Insulators: air, plastic, wood.

   b) Two of: The battery might be 'flat'. The lamp might have 'blown'. A wire might have broken.

2 a) The force of gravity on you (i.e. your weight), the support force from the seat.

   b) i) The forces are balanced.

   ii) You would drop onto the floor.

3 a) Microwaves.

   b) X-radiation and γ radiation.

4 a) i) A charged atom.

   ii) X-radiation, α, β and γ radiation.

   b) i) α radiation.

   ii) The nucleus.

5 km for kilometres (distance), s for seconds (time).

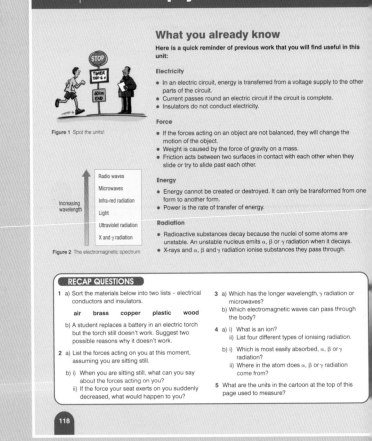

SPECIFICATION LINK-UP

Unit: Physics 2

How can we describe the way things move?

Even when things are moving in a straight line, describing their movement is not easy. They can move with different speeds and can also change their speed and/or direction (accelerate). Graphs can help us to describe the movement of the body. These may be distance–time graphs or velocity–time graphs.

How do we make things speed up or slow down?

To change the speed of a body an unbalanced force must act on it.

What happens to the movement energy when things speed up or slow down?

When a body speeds up or slows down, its kinetic energy increases or decreases. The forces that cause the change in speed do so by transferring energy to, or from, the body.

What is momentum?

The faster a body is moving the more kinetic energy it has. It also has momentum. When working out what happens to bodies as a result of explosions or collisions it is more useful to think in terms of momentum than in terms of energy.

What is static electricity, how can it be used and what is the connection between static electricity and electric currents?

Static electricity can be explained in terms of electrical charges. When electrical charges move we get an electric current.

What does the current through an electrical circuit depend on?

The size of the current in a circuit depends on how hard the supply tries to push charge through the circuit and how hard the circuit resists having charge pushed through it.

What is mains electricity and how can it be used safely?

Mains electricity is useful but can be very dangerous. It is important to know how to use it safely.

Why do we need to know the power of electrical appliances?

Electrical appliances transform energy. The power of an electrical appliance is the rate at which it transforms energy. Most appliances have their power and the potential difference of the supply they need printed on them. From this we calculate their current and the fuse they need.

What happens to radioactive substances when they decay?

To understand what happens to radioactive substances when they decay we need to understand the structure of the atoms from which they are made.

What are nuclear fission and nuclear fusion?

Nuclear fission is the splitting of atomic nuclei and is used in nuclear reactors as a source of heat energy that can be transformed to electrical energy. Nuclear fusion is the joining together of atomic nuclei and is the process by which energy is released in stars.

Making connections

Taking off!

To fly high, you need to take off first. The first powered flight was by the Wright brothers in 1903. Now planes can carry hundreds of people for thousands of miles in a few hours. We can send space probes far into space. Where will people have got to by the end of this century? Read on to find out where the physics in this unit can take you.

Jets and rockets

The first jet engine was invented by a British engineer, Frank Whittle. He worked out how to create a jet of hot gases by burning aviation fuel. He used his scientific knowledge of materials, energy and forces to design and test the first jet engine.

On the launch pad

Space is only a few miles above your head but gravity stops you going there – unless you are in a rocket. A rocket is a jet engine with its own oxygen supply. Jet planes don't need to carry oxygen to burn aviation fuel in their engines because they use oxygen in the atmosphere. But a single-stage rocket can't get far enough into space to escape from the Earth. The Russian physicist, Konstantin Tsiolovsky predicted in 1895 that space rockets would need to be multistage.

Keeping in touch

Space travel would be impossible without electronic circuits for control and communications. A radio signal from a space probe is weaker than the light from a torch lamp on the Moon. The communication circuits in a space probe detect and process very weak signals. On-board cameras and sensors collect and send information back to Earth. Control circuits operate on-board rockets to change the path of a space probe. The electronic circuits in a space probe need to be totally reliable.

Interstellar travel

Voyager 2 was launched in 1975. Now it is on its way out of the Solar System after sending back amazing pictures of the outer planets and their moons. Space probes and satellites need power supplies that last for many years.

Space travel by astronauts far from the Sun would need powerful electricity generators powered by nuclear reactors. Nuclear submarines carry small nuclear reactors for their electricity. New types of nuclear reactors such as fusion reactors would be better. The probes and the reactors would probably need to be built on the Moon, using local materials.

ACTIVITY

Discuss:

What things do you think people will be able to do in the year 2099 that we can't do today? What breakthroughs in science will these rely on?

Chapters in this unit

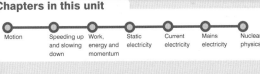

Motion | Speeding up and slowing down | Work, energy and momentum | Static electricity | Current electricity | Mains electricity | Nuclear physics

---

Teaching suggestions

Misconceptions

Motion of objects

- Many students will be used to describing speeds in miles per hour. It is hard to discourage them from this and no matter what you do, some will still be giving answers in m.p.h. on the final exam paper. Just try to minimise this number by not giving example of cars moving in miles per hour in the unit. Unfortunately you don't really have this option for the braking distance charts.

- Some will think that a force is required for an object to keep moving at a steady velocity. Because of friction and air resistance it is hard to demonstrate that the object will keep going unless a force is applied. Air tracks and lots of space-based examples may help.

- There are bound to be problems with the confusion between mass and weight. You may also find that students are confused about gravity and say things like 'the downward force on me is gravity' instead of 'the downward force is my weight'.

Electrical circuits

- Often students have the misconception that a battery produces electrons and then some of them are used up as they travel through components. It can be hard to discourage this idea; try to get across the picture of electrons as energy carriers; some computer animations are exceptionally helpful here.

- Incorrect positioning of voltmeters and ammeters is common; try to talk about the potential difference **across** a component and the current **through** it.

O Chapters in this unit

O **Motion**	O **Static electricity**
O **Speeding up and slowing down**	O **Current electricity**
O **Work, energy and momentum**	O **Mains electricity**
	O **Nuclear physics**

P2 1.1

Distance–time graphs

LEARNING OBJECTIVES

Students should learn:

- How to interpret the slope of a distance–time graph.
- How to calculate the speed of a body using the speed equation.
- How to use a distance–time graph to compare the speed of a body.

LEARNING OUTCOMES

Most students should be able to:

- State that the slope of a distance–time graph represents the speed.
- Use the speed equation to calculate the average speed of an object.

Some students should also be able to:

- Rearrange and use the speed equation.
- Compare the speed of an object using the slope of a distance–time graph.

Teaching suggestions

- **Gifted and talented.** Using the details from the train timetable (see 'Homework') the students can plot graphs to compare the speeds of local trains and expresses.

- **Learning styles**

  Kinaesthetic: Researching into speed records.

  Visual: Observing and presenting speed data.

  Auditory: Explaining ideas about motion.

  Interpersonal: Reporting changes in speed records.

  Intrapersonal: Interpreting data from graphs.

- **Homework**
  - Provide the students with a graph and ask them to describe the motion of the object. Higher attaining students should calculate the speed of the object during each stage of the motion.
  - Ask the students to get a bus or train timetable and a map. They should use the information in these to work out the average speed of the trains or buses between different locations.

SPECIFICATION LINK-UP   Unit: Physics 2.12.1

- *The slope of a distance–time graph represents speed.*

Students should use their skills, knowledge and understanding of 'How Science Works':

- *to construct distance–time graphs for a body moving in a straight line when the body is stationary or moving with a constant speed.*

Lesson structure

STARTER

Speedy start – Give the students a set of cards showing different moving objects and ask them to put them in order from fastest to slowest. (5 minutes)

Understanding graphs – Show the students slides of a range of graphs showing the relationship between two variables and ask them to describe what is happening. Alternatively, show Animation P2 1.1 'Distance–time graphs' from the GCSE Physics CD ROM. (5–10 minutes)

A quick quiz – Give the students a quick verbal quiz to check their understanding of the terms 'speed', 'distance' and 'time' and to find out if they remember how to calculate speed. (5 minutes)

MAIN

- Some students have difficulty understanding what you mean by the terms 'object' or 'body' and you will have to exemplify these ideas by talking about cars, trains or runners.
- Students can also have difficulty with the whole ideas of a 'time axis'. You might like to show time as moving on by revealing the graph from left to right, and discussing what is happening to the distance the object has moved over each second.
- There are quite a few that fail to understand that the flat (horizontal) portions of the graph show that the object is stationary. Emphasise that the distance isn't changing, even though time is; 'the object hasn't got any further away during this second so it must be still'.
- You should use additional simple graphs to discuss the motion of several objects until you are sure that the students can identify when the objects are moving fastest.
- The students should be familiar with the speed equation, but it may have been some time since they used it in Key Stage 3. A few practice questions should remind them of the basic idea.
- Be cautious of students using inappropriate units for speed such as 'm.p.h.' or even 'mps'(metres per second). If students find 'per' difficult, then just use 'each'.
- With higher attaining students, you can get them to read information off the graphs to calculate speed although this is covered in detail on page 126 in the Student Book at an appropriate level. They should be able to calculate the overall average speed and the speed during individual phases of the motion.
- With higher attaining students, you may like to discuss displacement instead of distance or you could leave this until you are discussing velocity in the next topic.
- The practical activity is a good way to round off the lesson, and it can be as brief as ten minutes long if bicycles are not involved.

PLENARIES

Interpreting a graph – Ask students to describe the motion represented in some graphs. Examples are found on page 121 links on the GCSE Physics CD ROM or on Animation P2 1.1 'Distance–time graphs'.

A driving story – Give the students a paragraph describing the motion of a car through a town, including moving at different speeds and stopping at traffic lights etc. Ask them to sketch a graph of the described motion. (10 minutes)

Oscillations – Show the students a pendulum swinging from side to side and ask them to sketch a distance–time graph of the motion. (5–10 minutes)

ACTIVITY & EXTENSION IDEAS

Detailed speed measurements

To make more detailed measurements of the speed of an object a distance sensor can be used.

Equipment and materials required

Distance sensor, data logger and a simple moving object.

Details

The distance sensor should be mounted in a fixed position and the object moves in front of it while the data logger records. You can use this to measure your distance in front of the meter while you walk back and forth at different speeds. The students can then analyse the graphs and see if they can describe the motion from them.

A need for speed

The students could find out about how the land speed record has changed over the past 150 years (from trains to rocket cars). They could plot a graph of the record speed against the year and see if they can extrapolate to find what the record will be in 50 years' time. A similar activity can be carried out for the air and water speed records.

DID YOU KNOW?

The fastest moving man-made object was the Helios 2 space probe. It travelled at about 67 km/s (67 000 m/s), which is Mach 203 (not that sound can travel in space). Space probes can travel so quickly, because there is no air resistance so they do not lose any of their kinetic energy. The probe Voyager 1 is travelling at 17.5 km/s and has been travelling for around 30 years. Ask: 'How far away is it?'

Practical support

Be a distance recorder!

Measuring speed is a simple activity and livens up what can be a fairly dry start to the motion unit.

Equipment and materials required

For each group: stopwatch, metre wheel. Clipboards and marker cones are also useful.

Details

The students should measure out distances first and then time each other walking, running, hopping or riding over these fixed distances. An outdoor netball court, or similar, can provide a set of straight and curved lines for the students to follow. You may like to see if the students travel faster along the straight edges or if they follow the curves on the court. If you intend to use bicycles, then a lot more space will be needed and the students must wear the appropriate safety gear. Check with the PE department to see if they have cones to mark out the distances and if they mind bicycles on their running tracks or shoes on their indoor courts!

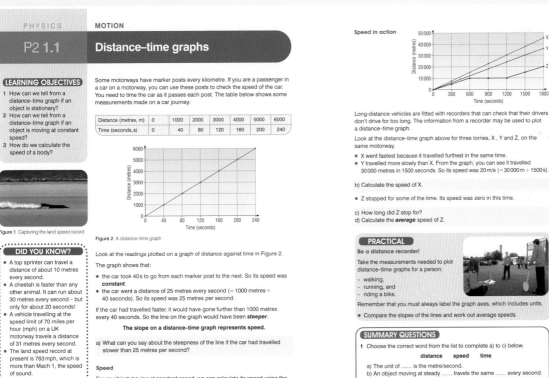

P2 1.1 Distance–time graphs

LEARNING OBJECTIVES

1 How can we tell from a distance–time graph if an object is stationary?
2 How can we tell from a distance–time graph if an object is moving at constant speed?
3 How do we calculate the speed of a body?

Figure 1 Capturing the land speed record

DID YOU KNOW?

- A top sprinter can travel a distance of about 10 metres every second.
- A cheetah is faster than any other animal. It can run about 30 metres every second – but only for about 20 seconds!
- A vehicle travelling at the speed limit of 70 miles per hour (mph) on a UK motorway travels a distance of 31 metres every second.
- The land speed record at present is 763 mph, which is more than Mach 1, the speed of sound.
- The air speed record was broken in November 2004 by X-43A, an experimental scram-jet plane. It reached 6600 mph or Mach 9.6! Whoosh . . .

Some motorways have marker posts every kilometre. If you are a passenger in a car on a motorway, you can use these posts to check the speed of the car. You need to time the car as it passes each post. The table below shows some measurements made on a car journey:

Distance (metres, m)	0	1000	2000	3000	4000	5000	6000
Time (seconds, s)	0	40	80	120	160	200	240

Figure 2 A distance–time graph

Look at the readings plotted on a graph of distance against time in Figure 2.

The graph shows that:

- the car took 40 s to go from each marker post to the next. So its speed was **constant**.
- the car went a distance of 25 metres every second (= 1000 metres ÷ 40 seconds). So its speed was 25 metres per second.

If the car had travelled faster, it would have gone further than 1000 metres every 40 seconds. So the line on the graph would have been **steeper**.

The slope on a distance–time graph represents speed.

a) What can you say about the steepness of the line if the car had travelled slower than 25 metres per second?

Speed

For an object moving at constant speed, we can calculate its speed using the equation:

$$\text{speed (metre/second, m/s)} = \frac{\text{distance travelled (metre, m)}}{\text{time taken (second, s)}}$$

The scientific unit of speed is the metre per second, usually written as metre/second or m/s.

Speed in action

Figure 3 Comparing distance–time graphs

Long-distance vehicles are fitted with recorders that can check that their drivers don't drive for too long. The information from a recorder may be used to plot a distance–time graph.

Look at the distance–time graph above for three lorries, X , Y and Z, on the same motorway.

- X went fastest because it travelled furthest in the same time.
- Y travelled more slowly than X. From the graph, you can see it travelled 30 000 metres in 1500 seconds. So its speed was 20 m/s (= 30 000 m ÷ 1500 s).

b) Calculate the speed of X.

- Z stopped for some of the time. Its speed was zero in this time.

c) How long did Z stop for?
d) Calculate the *average* speed of Z.

PRACTICAL

Be a distance recorder!

Take the measurements needed to plot distance–time graphs for a person:

– walking,
– running, and
– riding a bike.

Remember that you must always label the graph axes, which includes units.

- Compare the slopes of the lines and work out average speeds.

SUMMARY QUESTIONS

1 Choose the correct word from the list to complete a) to c) below.

distance   speed   time

a) The unit of ...... is the metre/second.
b) An object moving at steady ...... travels the same ...... every second.
c) The steeper the line on a distance–time graph of a moving object, the greater its ...... is.

2 A vehicle on a motorway travels 1800 m in 60 seconds. Calculate:
a) the speed of the vehicle in m/s.
b) how far it would travel at this speed in 300 seconds.

KEY POINTS

1 The steeper the line on a distance–time graph, the greater the speed it represents.
2 Speed (metre/second, m/s) = $\dfrac{\text{distance travelled (metre, m)}}{\text{time taken (second, s)}}$

SUMMARY ANSWERS

1 a) Speed.

  b) Speed, distance.

  c) Speed.

2 a) 30 m/s

  b) 9000 m

Answers to in-text questions

a) It would not have been as steep.

b) 25 m/s

c) 600 s

d) 11.1 m/s

KEY POINTS

The students can be given the opportunity to describe a journey in detail from a distance–time graph.

P2 1.2   Velocity and acceleration

Students should learn that:

- Velocity is the speed in a particular direction.
- Acceleration is the rate of change of velocity.

LEARNING OUTCOMES

Most students should be able to:

- Explain the difference between the velocity of an object and the speed.
- Calculate the acceleration of an object using the acceleration equation.

Some students should also be able to:

- Rearrange and use the acceleration equation.

Teaching suggestions

- **Gifted and talented.** These students may like to look into the details of the concepts of displacement and velocity. Ask: 'What is the average speed of a Formula One car over one whole lap? What is the average velocity for the complete lap?' The students could draw a diagram to explain the difference.

- **Learning styles**

  Visual: Observing and presenting graphical data.

  Auditory: Discussing and explaining experiences on fairground rides, etc.

  Interpersonal: Giving feedback about results.

  Intrapersonal: Evaluating outcome of experiment.

- **ICT link-up**

  - Distance sensors need to be used to measure velocity and changes in velocity accurately.
  - Motion can also be monitored with video equipment and frame by frame playback. (This relates to 'How Science Works': making measurements.)

SPECIFICATION LINK-UP   Unit: Physics 2.12.1

- *The velocity of a body is its speed in a given direction.*
- *The acceleration of a body is given by:*

$$\text{acceleration (metre second squared, m/s}^2) = \frac{\text{change in velocity (metre/second, m/s)}}{\text{time taken for change (second, s)}}$$

Students should use their skills, knowledge and understanding of 'How Science Works':

- *to construct velocity–time graphs for a body moving with a constant velocity or a constant acceleration.*

Lesson structure

STARTER

In the right direction – Give the students a map and ask them how to get from one location to another. They need to include distances and directions. (5 minutes)

Treasure island – Give the students a scaled map with hidden treasure, but at first only give them the times they have to walk for, then the speeds they must go at, and finally the matching directions. This shows how important direction is. (5 minutes)

Getting nowhere fast – A racing driver completes a full circuit of a 3 km racecourse in 90 seconds. Ask: 'What is his average speed? Why isn't he 3 km away from where he started?' (5 minutes)

MAIN

- Talking about fairground rides or roundabouts helps to get across the idea that you can be moving at a constant speed but be feeling a force. You can link this experience into the idea that unbalanced forces cause acceleration, see later topics.

- Some students will not see the difference between speed and velocity clearly and a few examples are needed. These can include simply walking around the room and describing your velocity.

- You might like to discuss a collision between two objects travelling at 30 and 31 km/h. If they collide while travelling in opposite directions the impact will be devastating, because the relative velocity is 61 km/h. If they collide when they are travelling in the same direction only a 'nudge' will be felt, because their relative velocity is only 1 km/h. Clearly the direction is very important.

- Check that all of the students can give an example of a velocity.

- Velocity–time graphs look similar enough to distance–time graphs to cause a great deal of confusion for students. Because they have just learned that the 'flat' region on a distance–time graph shows that the object is stationary, they will probably feel that this is true for the velocity–time graph too. Time should be taken to explain that the object is moving at a steady velocity.

- Many students are unclear of the units for acceleration (m/s²) and ask what the 'squared bit' is. If they are mathematically strong, you might like to show where the unit comes from using the equation but otherwise they should not worry about it.

- There may be some confusion with the terms 'acceleration', 'deceleration' and 'negative acceleration', especially if you consider objects that move backwards as well as forwards. For higher attaining students you should show a graph of the motion of an object moving forwards then backwards, and describe the acceleration in detail.

PLENARIES

One graph to another – Give the students a velocity–time graph, showing the movement of a car and asking them to sketch a matching distance–time graph. For higher attaining students you could use a challenging graph, where the car reverses for part of the movement. (5–10 minutes)

Comparing graphs – Ask the students to make a comparison of what a distance–time graph and a velocity–time graph show. (5–10 minutes)

Rolling, rolling, rolling – Three balls of the same size are rolled down the same slope. One is iron, one wood and one is a football. Ask: 'Which will reach the bottom first?' The students should explain their ideas. (5–10 minutes)

ACTIVITY & EXTENSION IDEAS

- **Acceleration, power and mass in vehicles** – The students could find out about what makes a vehicle good at accelerating. By finding out the power output (bhp or kW) and mass of some vehicles (include motorcycles), they could investigate if there is a relationship between mass, power and acceleration. They could explain how well the data fits any pattern.

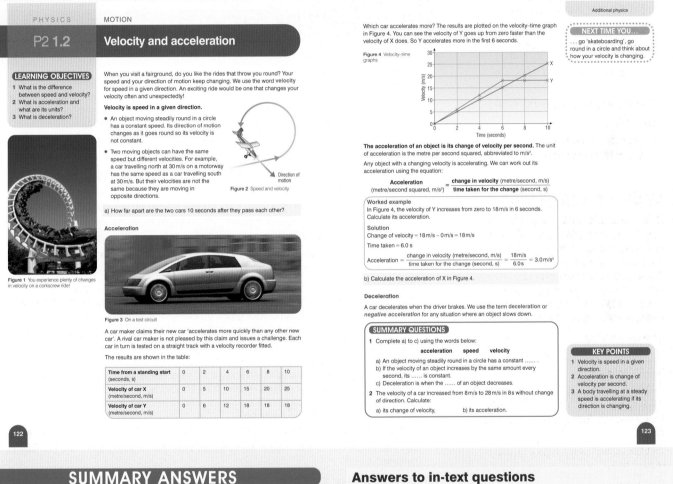

SUMMARY ANSWERS

1 a) Speed.

   b) Acceleration.

   c) Velocity.

2 a) 20 m/s   b) 2.5 m/s²

Answers to in-text questions

a) 600 m

b) 2.5 m/s²

KEY POINTS

The students could describe the movement of objects as represented by velocity–time graphs by labelling parts on an interactive whiteboard.

P2 1.3   More about velocity–time graphs

Teaching suggestions

- **Learning styles**

  Kinaesthetic: Carrying out a range of experiments.

  Visual: Obtaining precise results.

  Auditory: Explaining and listening to the outcomes of experiments from different groups.

  Interpersonal: Evaluating the quality of results as a group.

  Intrapersonal: Interpreting graphical information.

- **Homework.** The students could calculate the distance travelled by an object using a velocity–time graph.

- **ICT link-up.** Using route planner software, the students can find the distances between points on their journey to school or other locations. (see www.multimap.co.uk or maps.google.com.) They can time themselves travelling between these points and work out their average speed. Sharing this information will allow them to compare different modes of transport.

Answers to in-text questions

a) Less steep.

b) It would not be as steep.

c) Greater.

Lesson structure

STARTER

Comparing graphs – Ask the students to describe the differences in the movement of three cars as shown on the same velocity–time graph. You can also use distance–time graphs. (5–10 minutes)

Measuring speed – Ask: 'How many different ways can you think of to measure the speed of an object?' These could be techniques or devices like radar, sonar etc. (What about red shift?) (5 minutes)

Late again? – Give the students the distance from their last class to the laboratory and ask them to work out their speed on the journey to you, using the time it took them to arrive. Anybody travelling at less than 1 m/s clearly isn't keen enough! (5 minutes)

MAIN

- Demonstrate the results produced for test A in the Student Book. If you do not get a straight line, you might want to discuss air resistance as a force opposing the movement of the trolley.

- The investigation into the motion of an object is a good one if you have sufficient equipment. Alternatives using light gates do not give a simple comparison of the accelerations, but you may be able to demonstrate that the velocity has increased. (This relates to: 'How Science Works': types of variable; fair testing; relationship between variables.)

- As before, time should be taken to ensure that the students understand what the gradients of the different graphs mean. They should be encouraged to break the graph down and just look at one section at a time, in order to explain what is happening between these sections.

- There should be no difficulty explaining that braking will reduce the velocity of the car, but you might like to ask what braking would look like on the graph if the car was in reverse.

- When calculating the area under the graph, ensure that the students are not giving their answers as 'distance = 15 cm²' or similar. This can happen when they 'count boxes' or do their calculations based on the area being measured in centimetres. Make sure that they are reading the distances and times off the graph, not the actual dimensions of the shapes.

- Finally you could show what would happen if the deceleration took longer, by superimposing the new gradient over the old one and showing that the area is greater.

PLENARIES

Busy teacher – Wear a pedometer throughout the lesson, calculate your average step distance and then ask the students to work out how far you have moved and your average speed. (5 minutes)

Slow motion – If you have a movement sensor alarm in your lab, you could see if the students sit so still that the sensor light goes off. Can they move so slowly that the alarm does not trigger? (5 minutes)

Practical support

Movement and trolleys

Dynamics trolleys are an excellent way of studying motion, but class sets are very expensive. If none are available, then fairly large toy cars can be used for the basic experiments. Velocity sensors are also expensive and you may need to modify this experiment into a demonstration.

Equipment and materials required

Dynamics trolley, adjustable slope, protractor, and data-logging equipment including a velocity sensor.

Details

- Set up the equipment so that the angle of the ramp can be adjusted and easily measured. Make sure that the sensor is pointing along the path of the slope, otherwise the velocity will not be measured accurately. The students activate the sensor and then release the trolley.

- Repeating this for a range of slope angles should give the result that the steeper the slope the greater the acceleration.

Alternative equipment

Light gates

As an alternative to a velocity sensor, a set of light gates can be used in experiments. This involves mounting a card of known length on top of the trolley so that it interrupts the beam, and the sensor measures the time for this to take place. This data can be used to determine the velocity; some software will do this for you directly. To determine acceleration, you can use a slotted card that interrupts the beam twice. This allows you to determine acceleration by looking at the speed the trolley was travelling when it first interrupted the beam and the speed the second time. Several sets of light gates can be used to measure the velocity at different stages of the motion.

Distance sensors

These use ultrasound or infra-red to measure the distance to an object. Some software will convert these distance values into speed values and plot the required graphs.

ACTIVITY & EXTENSION IDEAS

Trolley aerodynamics

The ramp experiment can be expanded to look into the aerodynamic properties of the trolleys.

Equipment and materials required

Dynamics trolley, adjustable slope, protractor, stiff cardboard, scissors and data-logging equipment including a velocity sensor.

Details

Set up the equipment as in the earlier trolley experiment, but fix the ramp in one position. Mount various sized pieces of card on the back of the trolley for each run, and compare the accelerations. The trolley should accelerate less with larger pieces of card mounted on it. You may also find that the acceleration of the trolley gets less the faster it goes; shown by a curved velocity–time graph. This is due to the air resistance increasing at larger velocities; an important concept in car design.

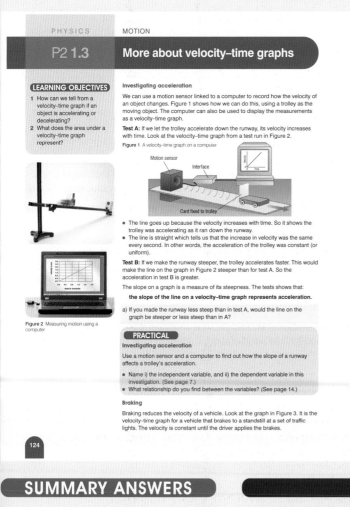

PHYSICS   MOTION

P2 1.3 More about velocity–time graphs

LEARNING OBJECTIVES

1 How can we tell from a velocity–time graph if an object is accelerating or decelerating?
2 What does the area under a velocity–time graph represent?

Investigating acceleration

We can use a motion sensor linked to a computer to record how the velocity of an object changes. Figure 1 shows how we can do this, using a trolley as the moving object. The computer can also be used to display the measurements as a velocity–time graph.

Test A: If we let the trolley accelerate down the runway, its velocity increases with time. Look at the velocity–time graph from a test run in Figure 2.

Figure 1 A velocity–time graph on a computer

- The line goes up because the velocity increases with time. So it shows the trolley was accelerating as it ran down the runway.
- The line is straight which tells us that the increase in velocity was the same every second. In other words, the acceleration of the trolley was constant (or uniform).

Test B: If we make the runway steeper, the trolley accelerates faster. This would make the line on the graph in Figure 2 steeper than for test A. So the acceleration in test B is greater.

The slope on a graph is a measure of its steepness. The tests shows that:

the slope of the line on a velocity–time graph represents acceleration.

a) If you made the runway less steep than in test A, would the line on the graph be steeper or less steep than in A?

Figure 2 Measuring motion using a computer

PRACTICAL

Investigating acceleration

Use a motion sensor and a computer to find out how the slope of a runway affects a trolley's acceleration.

- Name i) the independent variable, and ii) the dependent variable in this investigation. (See page 7.)
- What relationship do you find between the variables? (See page 14.)

Braking

Braking reduces the velocity of a vehicle. Look at the graph in Figure 3. It is the velocity–time graph for a vehicle that brakes to a standstill at a set of traffic lights. The velocity is constant until the driver applies the brakes.

Using the slope of the line:
- The section of the graph for constant velocity is flat. The line's slope is zero so the acceleration in this section is zero.
- When the brakes are applied, the velocity decreases to zero and the vehicle decelerates. The slope of the line is negative in this section.

Figure 3 Braking

b) How would the slope of the line differ if the deceleration had taken longer?

Look at the graph in Figure 3 again.

Using the area under the line:
- Before the brakes are applied, the vehicle moves at a velocity of 20 m/s for 10 s. It therefore travels 200 m in this time (= 20 m/s × 10 s). This distance is represented on the graph by the area under the line from 0 s to 10 s. This is the shaded rectangle on the graph.
- When the vehicle decelerates in Figure 3, its velocity drops from 20 m/s to zero in 5 s. We can work out the distance travelled in this time from the area of the purple triangle in Figure 3. This area is ½ × the height × the base of the triangle. So the vehicle must have travelled a distance of 50 m when it was decelerating.

The area under the line on a velocity–time graph represents distance travelled.

c) Would the total distance travelled be greater or smaller if the deceleration had taken longer?

SUMMARY QUESTIONS

1 Match each of the following descriptions to one of the lines, labelled A, B, C and D, on the velocity–time graph.
   1 Accelerated motion throughout
   2 Zero acceleration
   3 Accelerated motion, then decelerated motion
   4 Deceleration

2 Look at the graph in question 1. Which line represents the object that travelled:
   a) the furthest distance?   b) the least distance?

DID YOU KNOW?

A speed camera flashes when a vehicle travelling over the speed limit has gone past. Some speed cameras flash twice and measure the distance the car travels between flashes.

KEY POINTS

1 The slope of the line on a velocity–time graph represents acceleration.
2 The area under the line on a velocity–time graph represents distance travelled.

124   125

SUMMARY ANSWERS

1 1. B 2. A 3. D 4. C
2 a) A b) C

KEY POINTS

- Give the students a velocity–time graph and ask them to calculate the distance travelled.
- For higher attaining students this could include backwards motion.

P2 1.4   Using graphs

SPECIFICATION LINK-UP   Unit: Physics 2.13.1

Students should use their skills, knowledge and understanding of 'How Science Works':

- *to calculate the speed of a body from a distance–time graph. [HT only]*
- *to calculate the acceleration of a body from a velocity–time graph. [HT only]*
- *to calculate the distance travelled by a body from a velocity–time graph. [HT only]*

LEARNING OBJECTIVES

Students should learn:

- How to calculate the speed from a distance–time graph. [HT only]
- How to calculate the distance travelled from a velocity–time graph. [HT only]
- How to calculate the acceleration of an object from a velocity–time graph. [HT only]

LEARNING OUTCOMES

Most Higher Tier students should be able to:

- Calculate the slope of a distance–time graph and relate this to the speed of an object. [HT only]
- Calculate the slope of a velocity–time graph and hence the acceleration. [HT only]
- Find the area under a velocity–time graph for constant velocity and use this to calculate the distance travelled by an object. [HT only]
- Find the area under a velocity–time graph for constant acceleration and use this to calculate the distance travelled by an object. [HT only]

Teaching suggestions

- **Learning styles**

  Kinaesthetic: Making convection mobiles.

  Visual: Viewing and obtaining information from graphs.

  Auditory: Explaining what the graphs show about movement.

  Intrapersonal: Interpreting information.

- **Homework.** Follow-up work can be set on analysing or plotting a range of graphs of motion.

- **ICT link-up.** Simulation software can be used to investigate motion and to plot graphs of the behaviour. These can be either quite simple or rather complex, so you should be able to find something suitable for all ranges of ability. (See sunflowerlearning.com; www.fable.co.uk.

Lesson structure

STARTER

Finding areas – Get the students to calculate the total area of a shape made up of rectangles and triangles. (5–10 minutes)

Plot – Give the students a set of velocity–time data for a moving object, and ask them to plot a graph of displacement–time. (10 minutes)

Graph matching – The students have to match the description of the movement of objects with graphs of distance–time and velocity–time. (5–10 minutes)

MAIN

- This topic is for higher attaining students only, but you can use some ideas to reinforce the learning of middle abilities.

- Some students will prefer the term 'gradient' to 'slope'. As 'gradient' is the more correct term, it should be encouraged; but if the students are used to 'slope', then don't confuse them with two terms.

- With a bit of practice, they should have no difficulty determining slopes. Watch out for students reading off the total distance and total time instead of the change in distance and change in time.

- Get the students to describe what is happening to the speed of a range of objects. You might like to show graphs, followed by video clips, of objects doing what was shown in the graph, e.g. cars accelerating from 0–60 m.p.h. or balls bouncing, etc. (Search at video.google.com or altavista.com).

- When you move on to velocity–time graphs, yet again emphasise that these show something different. Hopefully the students will never get the two confused.

- The students should be reading the changes in velocity and time from the graphs, but some may make the same mistakes as mentioned previously.

PLENARIES

Pendulum bob – Show the students the oscillations of a pendulum and ask them to sketch a displacement–time graph and a matching velocity– time graph. A mass oscillating on a spring could be used instead. (10 minutes)

Dynamic definitions – The students should provide detailed definitions of speed, velocity, distance, displacement and acceleration, including how they are represented on graphs. (10 minutes)

It's all gone wrong – Give the students the work of an imaginary student who has made a number of mistakes when using the graphs. Ask them to correct all of the mistakes. (10–15 minutes)

The students should have found the distance travelled by an object from a velocity–time graph in the last topic, so challenge them with more difficult graphs of motion.

- You may want to see if they can find the distance travelled when the acceleration is not uniform. This would involve square counting techniques (see 'Counting Squares' below).

- For additional challenge, look into graphs showing the object moving back towards the origin. You could try some velocity–time graphs where the velocity becomes negative, and see if the students can calculate the distance the object ends up from the origin.

- **Counting squares** – One common technique for working out the area under a line on a graph is to count the squares on the graph paper. Anything less than half a square doesn't count and anything more than half a square counts as a complete square. This works reasonably well for simple graphs including those with straight gradients. You could discuss how to improve the accuracy of the method by using smaller and smaller squares on the graph paper. Make sure that the students know the distance each square of the graph paper represents.

Answers to in-text questions

a) 15 m/s

b) The speed decreased gradually and became constant.

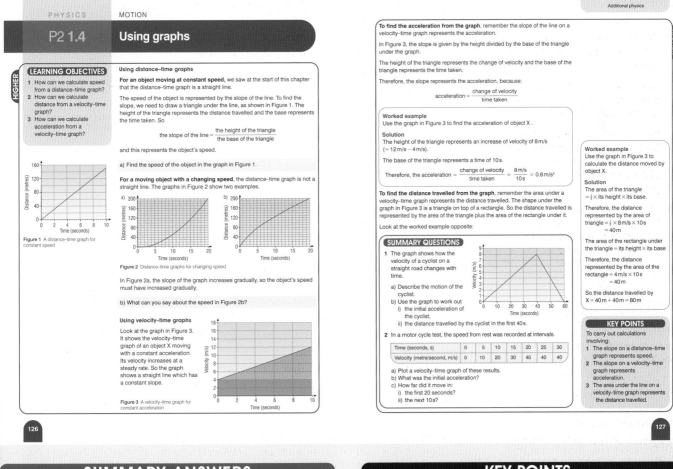

PHYSICS   MOTION

P2 1.4   Using graphs

LEARNING OBJECTIVES

1 How can we calculate speed from a distance–time graph?

2 How can we calculate distance from a velocity–time graph?

3 How can we calculate acceleration from a velocity–time graph?

Using distance–time graphs

For an object moving at constant speed, we saw at the start of this chapter that the distance–time graph is a straight line.

The speed of the object is represented by the slope of the line. To find the slope, we need to draw a triangle under the line, as shown in Figure 1. The height of the triangle represents the distance travelled and the base represents the time taken. So

$$\text{the slope of the line} = \frac{\text{the height of the triangle}}{\text{the base of the triangle}}$$

and this represents the object's speed.

a) Find the speed of the object in the graph in Figure 1.

For a moving object with a changing speed, the distance–time graph is not a straight line. The graphs in Figure 2 show two examples.

In Figure 2a, the slope of the graph increases gradually, so the object's speed must have increased gradually.

b) What can you say about the speed in Figure 2b?

Figure 1 A distance–time graph for constant speed

Figure 2 Distance–time graphs for changing speed

Using velocity–time graphs

Look at the graph in Figure 3. It shows the velocity–time graph of an object X moving with a constant acceleration. Its velocity increases at a steady rate. So the graph shows a straight line which has a constant slope.

Figure 3 A velocity–time graph for constant acceleration

To find the acceleration from the graph, remember the slope of the line on a velocity–time graph represents the acceleration.

In Figure 3, the slope is given by the height divided by the base of the triangle under the graph.

The height of the triangle represents the change of velocity and the base of the triangle represents the time taken.

Therefore, the slope represents the acceleration, because:

$$\text{acceleration} = \frac{\text{change of velocity}}{\text{time taken}}$$

Worked example

Use the graph in Figure 3 to find the acceleration of object X.

Solution

The height of the triangle represents an increase of velocity of 8 m/s (= 12 m/s − 4 m/s).

The base of the triangle represents a time of 10 s.

Therefore, the acceleration = $\frac{\text{change of velocity}}{\text{time taken}}$ = $\frac{8\,\text{m/s}}{10\,\text{s}}$ = 0.8 m/s²

To find the distance travelled from the graph, remember the area under a velocity–time graph represents the distance travelled. The shape under the graph in Figure 3 is a triangle on top of a rectangle. So the distance travelled is represented by the area of the triangle plus the area of the rectangle under it.

Look at the worked example opposite:

SUMMARY QUESTIONS

1 The graph shows how the velocity of a cyclist on a straight road changes with time.

a) Describe the motion of the cyclist.

b) Use the graph to work out
   i) the initial acceleration of the cyclist,
   ii) the distance travelled by the cyclist in the first 40 s.

2 In a motor cycle test, the speed from rest was recorded at intervals.

Time (seconds, s)	0	5	10	15	20	25	30
Velocity (metre/second, m/s)	0	10	20	30	40	40	40

a) Plot a velocity–time graph of these results.

b) What was the initial acceleration?

c) How far did it move in:
   i) the first 20 seconds?
   ii) the next 10 s?

Worked example

Use the graph in Figure 3 to calculate the distance moved by object X.

Solution

The area of the triangle = ½ × its height × its base.

Therefore, the distance represented by the area of triangle = ½ × 8 m/s × 10 s = 40 m

The area of the rectangle under the triangle = its height × its base

Therefore, the distance represented by the area of the rectangle = 4 m/s × 10 s = 40 m

So the distance travelled by X = 40 m + 40 m = 80 m

KEY POINTS

To carry out calculations involving:

1 The slope on a distance–time graph represents speed.

2 The slope on a velocity–time graph represents acceleration.

3 The area under the line on a velocity–time graph represents the distance travelled.

SUMMARY ANSWERS

1 **a)** The cyclist accelerates with a constant acceleration for 40 s, and then decelerates to a standstill in 20 s.

b) i) 0.2 m/s² **ii)** 160 m [**HT** only]

2 **a)** Graph. **b)** 2 m/s² **c) i)** 400 m **ii)** 400 m [**HT** only]

KEY POINTS

- The students should be able to analyse distance–time and velocity–time graphs in detail.

- They should be challenged by asking them to plot a complex graph and calculate both the distance travelled and acceleration of each phase of the motion.

P1a 1.5   Transport issues

SPECIFICATION LINK-UP

Unit: Physics 2.12.1

This spread can be used to revisit the following aspects covered in this chapter:

Students should use their skills, knowledge and understanding of 'How Science Works':

- to construct distance–time graphs for a body moving in a straight line when the body is stationary or moving with a constant speed.

- to construct velocity–time graphs for a body moving with a constant velocity or constant acceleration.

Teaching suggestions

Activities

- **The Big Fuel protest** –The debate is a good opportunity to develop the students' skills but they will need to find, or be provided with, evidence for their arguments. You could provide the students with details of the price of petrol and the amount of tax placed on it. Information is available on the Internet about the reasons people would reduce their car usage (search for 'petrol use statistics' and you should find information from DEFRA www.defra. gov.uk). The inefficiency of cars in cities can be linked with congestion as described below. If cities were less congested, there would be less stopping and starting and so less pollution.

- **Epic journeys** – Columbus's journey took 34 days and so his velocity was around 6.7 km/h. That isn't particularly fast, but he didn't go in a straight line. The Apollo 11 crew travelled at an average speed of nearly 4000 km/h. A conventional rocket would not have enough fuel to keep up the thrust for a year, but there are alternatives. A 'light sail' uses the thrust provided by photons from the Sun. The acceleration from a large sail would only be 0.5 mm/s^2, but this acceleration is constant and the probe could reach Pluto in less than 5 years. It's a bit more difficult to come back though.

- **Speed cameras** – For this activity, a template can be used to help the students work on their letter. A collection of letters for and against the issuing of cameras can make an effective display, along with photographs and maps of local camera installations.

The Big Fuel protest

In 2001, lorry drivers in Britain decided their fuel costs were too high so they blockaded fuel depots. They were angry at the government because most of the cost of the fuel is tax (which raises money for the government).

Garages ran out of petrol and drivers had to queue for hours to fill up. Car drivers were a lot more careful about using their precious fuel.

Car journeys in built-up areas use more fuel per kilometre than 'out of town' journeys at the same average speed. This is because cars slow down and speed up more often in built-up areas. More fuel is used by a car that keeps stopping and starting than one driven at constant speed.

On a motorway journey the faster the speed of a car, the more fuel it uses. Air resistance at high speed is much greater than at low speed, so more fuel is used.

QUESTION

The table shows some information about fuel usage by a petrol-engine car.

	Distance travelled per litre of fuel (km)	
	at 48 kilometres per hour (30 mph)	at 100 kilometres per hour (63 mph)
Driving in town	12	–
On the 'open road'	15	10

1 A driver on the 'open road' would use 6 litres of fuel to drive 60 kilometres at 100 km/h.
   a) How much fuel would the driver use to drive 60 km at 48 km/h:
      i) in town?   ii) on the open road?
   b) The driver pays 85 p per litre for petrol. How much would be saved on a motorway journey of 60 km by driving at 48 km/h instead of 100 km/h?

ACTIVITY

Discuss the issues below in a small group.

What are your views on the different ways that people might protest against the cost of fuel? Would you agree with the protesters? Think about the arguments that might be used by:

- An environmentalist
- A lorry driver
- An oil company
- A government official

Epic journeys

Journey 1: Christopher Columbus and his three ships left the Canary Islands on 8th September 1492. He reached the Bahama Islands on 12th October after a 5500 km journey across the Atlantic Ocean.

Journey 2: Neil Armstrong and Buzz Aldrin were the first astronauts to land on the Moon. They spent 22 hours on the Moon. The 380 000 km journey to the Moon took four days.

Journey 3: If a space rocket accelerated for a year at 2 m/s^2 (about the same as a car starting from rest), the rocket would reach a speed of 60 000 km/s – about a fifth of the speed of light.

QUESTION

2 Work out the speed, in kilometres per hour, of journeys 1 and 2.

128

- Students may be aware of devices used to detect speed cameras and they could discuss whether or not these devices should be made illegal. Some people think that a driver following the speed limits wouldn't need to know where the cameras are; others think that knowing where the cameras are helps you to be more aware of dangerous areas.

- **Congestion charges** – Congestion charges have been shown to reduce the number of cars entering the area and have also raised quite a lot of money. Congestion charges on motorways have also been suggested. Satellite technology could be used to track cars and charge people for using the motorways at peak times. Such a system would cost billions of pounds but could raise this money back quite quickly. Ask: 'Is it fair to charge people for using roads? Should they be charged per mile or per journey at peak times?'

- **Green travel** –You might like to provide a survey sheet for the students to use for this activity; it would make a good homework task. Surveys such as this are regularly carried out by local education authorities, in order for them to plan local transport needs; you may be able to get hold of this data. The idea of flexitime for schools is attractive to most students, but what happens if they have brothers or sisters in different year groups? Perhaps different schools could have different start and finish times to spread the rush hour out.

Speed cameras

Speed cameras are very effective in stopping motorists speeding. A speeding motorist caught by a speed camera is fined and can lose his or her driving licence. In some areas, residents are supplied with 'mobile' speed cameras to catch speeding motorists. Some motorists think this is going too far. Lots of motorists say speed cameras are being used by councils to increase their income.

A report from one police force said that where speed cameras had been introduced:

- average speeds fell by 17%,
- deaths and serious injuries had fallen by 55%.

Another police force reported that, in their area, as a result of installing more speed cameras in 2003:

- there were no child deaths in road accidents for the first time since 1927,
- 420 fewer children were involved in road accidents compared with the previous year.

ACTIVITY

Do you think congestion charges are a good solution to traffic problems in our cities? Discuss the issue with your friends and take a vote on the question.

Green travel

Travelling to and from school or work can take ages unless you live nearby. Everybody seems to want to travel at the same time. Traffic accidents and rail cancellations in the rush hour cause hours of chaos. Traffic fumes cause pollution and burning fuel produces greenhouse gases.

Green travel means changing the way we travel to improve the environment.

Here are some suggestions about a green travel plan for your school:

- School buses; use school buses instead of cars.
- Car sharing; encourage drivers to share their cars with other drivers.
- Flexitime; finish the school day at different times for each year group.
- Everybody should walk or cycle to school.

ACTIVITY

With the help of your friends, conduct a survey to find out

a) if people in your school and parents think a green travel plan is a good idea,

b) what they think of the suggestions above,

c) if they have any better suggestions.

Write a short report to tell your headteacher about your survey and your findings.

Was your sample large enough to draw any firm conclusions? Explain your answer.

ACTIVITY

Discuss with your friends:

a) Do the bullet-pointed statements opposite prove the argument that speed cameras save lives.

b) In what sort of areas do you think speed cameras should be used?

ACTIVITY

Should more residents be supplied with mobile speed cameras? Write a letter to your local newspaper to argue your case.

Congestion charges

Travelling across London by road was quicker a hundred years ago than it is today – even though modern cars can travel ten times faster than the horse-drawn carriages that were used then. Congestion charges were introduced in London in 2003 to improve traffic flow. If motorists enter the congestion zone without paying the daily charge, they are likely to be fined heavily.

People in Edinburgh in 2004 voted against proposals for congestion charges. But many people in other cities want to introduce them. However, lots of people who need to travel into cities think they are unfair.

129

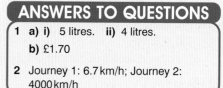

Special needs

Provide templates for all of the debates with important facts. The students must use this information in their discussions.

Gifted and talented

How would satellite tracking of cars work? The students can write a report on the proposed technology and discuss whether or not they think that this would be a good idea. Ask: 'Should the government be able to track the movement of every car in the country?'

Learning styles

Kinaesthetic: Researching about circumnavigation records.

Visual: Creating a mind map of summary information.

Auditory: Reading aloud information.

Interpersonal: Discussing the developments in pubic and private transport.

Intrapersonal: Considering how people can be discouraged from using their cars.

ICT link-up

Up-to-date information for most of these activities can be found on the Internet with a search. The easiest site to use to find out about human speed is www.olympic.org, which keeps Olympic and World records and is also a good history of how they have changed over the years.

Extension or homework

- **Economical cars** – Can the students find the fuel usage of their family's car? Diesel is a more expensive fuel, but many cars have diesel engines; ask: 'why is this?'

- **Around the world in 80 days** – Many people have circumnavigated the world in a variety of different ways. The students can find out the records for different methods (plane, boat, balloon, walking, motorbike, etc.) and calculate the average speeds.

- **Is transport getting better?** – Ask the students to find out the average speed of a car in London. Ask: 'Is this any faster than 30 years ago? What about the journey times from London to Edinburgh; has modern train design improved this significantly and, if not, why not?'

- **Measuring speeds** – The current world record for a 400 m freestyle swim is 220.08 seconds and the 400 m sprint is 43.18 seconds (as of July 2005). Ask: 'Can the speed of a swimmer or runner really be measured this accurately, is the swimming pool or running track built accurately enough to justify this level of precision in speed measurements? What about the 50 km walk record of 3:36.03?'

SUMMARY ANSWERS

1 a) 700 m

  b) 40 s

2 a) A to B

  b) i) 2000 m, 100 s

    ii) 20 m/s

3 a) i) 20 m/s

    ii) 2.5 m/s²

  b) −1.2 m/s² i.e. the declaration is 1.2 m/s²

4 a) 3.0 m/s²

  b) 2400 m

Summary teaching suggestions

- The questions here are mostly mathematical in nature and should show if the students are capable of the calculation required by the specification. Use them to check that the students have a solid grasp on the units for velocity and acceleration.

SUMMARY QUESTIONS

1 A train travels at a constant speed of 35 m/s. Calculate:
  a) how far it travels in 20 s,
  b) how long it takes to travel a distance of 1400 m.

2 The figure shows the distance–time graph for a car on a motorway.

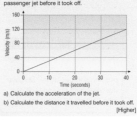

a) Which part of the journey was faster, A to B or B to C?
b) i) How far did the car travel from A to B and how long did it take?
  ii) Calculate the speed of the car between A and B?

3 a) A car took 8 s to increase its velocity from 8 m/s to 28 m/s. Calculate
  i) its change of velocity,
  ii) its acceleration.
b) A vehicle travelling at a velocity of 24 m/s slowed down and stopped in 20 s. Calculate its deceleration.

4 The figure shows the velocity–time graph of a passenger jet before it took off.

a) Calculate the acceleration of the jet.
b) Calculate the distance it travelled before it took off.
[Higher]

130

EXAM-STYLE QUESTIONS

1 The graph shows how far a marathon runner travels during a race.

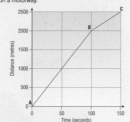

(a) What was the distance of the race? (1
(b) How long did it take the runner to complete the race? (1
(c) What distance did the runner travel during the first 2 hours of the race? (1
(d) For how long did the runner rest during the race? (1
(e) Ignoring the time for which the runner was resting, between which two points was the runner moving the slowest?
  Give a reason for your answer (2

2 The table gives values of distance and time for a cyclist travelling along a straight road.

Distance in metres	0	20	40	60	80	100
Time in seconds	0	2	4	6	8	10

(a) Draw a graph of distance against time. Two of the points have been plotted for you. (3

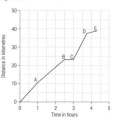

EXAM-STYLE ANSWERS

1 a) 38 km   *(1 mark)*

  b) 4.4 hours (4 hours 24 minutes)   *(1 mark)*

  c) 19 km   *(1 mark)*

  d) 30 minutes   *(1 mark)*

  e) Between D and E   *(1 mark)*
    Because the gradient is least between these points   *(1 mark)*

2 a) All points correctly plotted (lose 1 mark for each incorrect plot)
                                 (2 marks)
    Drawing line of best fit through the points   *(1 mark)*

  b) Distance travelled = 50 m   *(1 mark)*

  c) Time at 30 m = 3 seconds   *(1 mark)*

  d) Moving at a steady speed   *(1 mark)*

3 a) i) Speed   *(1 mark)*
    ii) Continuous   *(1 mark)*

  b) i) Bar chart   *(1 mark)*
    ii) Control variable   *(1 mark)*

  c) Acceleration = slope   *(1 mark)*
    Acceleration = 40/16   *(1 mark)*
    Acceleration = 2.5 m/s²   *(2 marks)*

  d) Distance = area under graph   *(1 mark)*
    Distance = $\frac{1}{2} \times (32 - 22) \times 40$ *(1 mark)*
    Distance = 200 m   *(1 mark)*

(b) Use your graph to find the distance travelled in 5 seconds. (1)

(c) Use your graph to find the time at which the distance is 30 metres. (1)

(d) Describe the motion of the cyclist. (1)

3 A van travels on a straight 'test-track' road. The graph shows how the speed of the van changes with time.

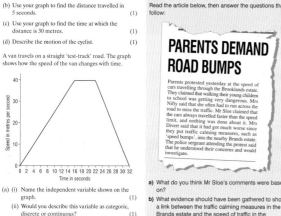

(a) (i) Name the independent variable shown on the graph. (1)

    (ii) Would you describe this variable as categoric, discrete or continuous? (1)

(b) (i) A manufacturer of vans makes four different types of van. How should they display the data so that potential buyers can best compare the top speed of the vans carrying the same load? (1)

    (ii) The data in (b) (i) is given for the same load each time. Would the load best be described as an independent, a dependent or a control variable? (1)

(c) Calculate the acceleration of the van during the first 16 seconds. Give a unit with your answer. (4)

(d) Calculate the distance travelled in metres between 22 and 32 seconds. (3)
[Higher]

HOW SCIENCE WORKS QUESTIONS

Read the article below, then answer the questions that follow:

PARENTS DEMAND ROAD BUMPS

Parents protested yesterday at the speed of cars travelling through the Brooklands estate. They claimed that walking their young children to school was getting very dangerous. Mrs Nifty said that she often had to run across the road to miss the traffic. Mr Sloe claimed that the cars always travelled faster than the speed limit, and nothing was done about it. Mrs Divert said that it had got much worse since they put traffic calming measures, such as 'speed bumps', into the nearby Brands estate. The police sergeant attending the protest said that he understood their concerns and would investigate.

a) What do you think Mr Sloe's comments were based on? (1)

b) What evidence should have been gathered to show a link between the traffic calming measures in the Brands estate and the speed of traffic in the Brooklands estate? (1)

On hearing about the protests a science teacher decided to carry out an investigation with his students. He decided to investigate the speed of the traffic outside Brooklands School.

c) Describe a method for measuring the speed of passing cars which includes using a stopwatch. (2)

d) What time of day should this survey be carried out? Why? (2)

e) Suggest how many cars should be surveyed. (1)

f) Should the drivers know they are being surveyed? Explain your answer. (2)

131

HOW SCIENCE WORKS ANSWERS

a) Mr Sloe's comments were based on non-scientific evidence. It could be hearsay or even prejudice. It is unlikely that all cars exceeded the speed limit.

b) It is very difficult to prove a causal relationship in this situation. Evidence from both streets before and after the road bumps would have helped to identify a link.

c) Students could measure a distance on the road and time how long it takes for any car to travel that distance. There are accuracy issues in this that could be discussed.

d) Survey should be carried out at sample times at regular intervals during the day, suggest 10 minutes every hour.

e) As many cars as possible should be surveyed, but at least ten for each sample. A preliminary test could be used to find out how many cars need to be sampled and how often.

f) No, drivers should not know they are being surveyed. It might cause them to behave differently. This is part of a control in such surveys.

How science works teaching suggestions

- **Literacy guidance**
  - Key terms that should be clearly understood: hearsay, prejudice, link, preliminary test.
  - Questions b) and c) expect longer answers, where students can practise their literacy skills.

- **Higher- and lower-level answers.** Question e) is a higher-level question and the answer provided above is also at this level. Question a) is lower level and the answer provided is also lower level.

- **Gifted and talented.** Able students could try to produce a survey technique that would control as many variables as possible and take account of others.

- **How and when to use these questions.** When wishing to develop ideas around non-scientific evidence and survey evidence.
  The questions would best be discussed in small groups.

- **Homework.** Students could gather data concerning people's views on the speed of traffic in their neighbourhood.

- **ICT link-up.** Students might like to develop their ideas in the lab by using light gates as a mock-up of the real situation. (See e.g. www.rogerfrost.com.)

Exam teaching suggestions

- Students often confuse distance–time and velocity–time graphs in examinations. They should practise using and drawing graphs and checking the quantities, units and scales.

- All students should understand that the slope of a distance–time graph represents speed, the slope of a velocity–time graph represents acceleration and the area under a velocity–time graph represents distance travelled.

- Higher-tier students need to know how to calculate speed, acceleration and distance travelled from the appropriate graphs.

- Many students think that they can work out the slopes of graphs by counting the squares on the graph paper, rather than by using the scales provided.

- Students can be assured that they can make marks on graphs provided on the examination paper if it helps their calculation. They should be encouraged to use large triangles when calculating slopes and show clearly where they have taken their readings from.

P2 2.1

Forces between objects

LEARNING OBJECTIVES

Students should learn that:

- Forces between objects are equal and opposite.
- Fiction is a contact force between surfaces.
- The unit of force is the newton (N).

LEARNING OUTCOMES

Most students should be able to:

- State that forces occur in equal and opposite pairs.
- Describe how frictional forces act between objects.

Some students should also be able to:

- Describe examples of equal and opposite forces acting when two objects interact.

Teaching suggestions

- **Gifted and talented.** Ask: 'What is the ideal launch angle of a projectile? Can you discover the ideal angle to fire a projectile and make it travel the furthest distance?' They need to design a launch system to make this investigation work.

- **Learning styles**

  Kinaesthetic: Skating to measure forces involved.

  Visual: Observing the action of forces on people.

  Auditory: Explaining how forces work in pairs.

  Interpersonal: Debating ways of describing energy.

  Intrapersonal: Making deductions about forces operating.

- **Homework.** Have the students describe how forces are used in various simple devices such as doors, tin openers, bicycles etc.

- **Teaching assistant.** Can your teaching assistant skate? Can you?

SPECIFICATION LINK-UP   Unit: Physics 2.12.2

- *Whenever two bodies interact the forces they exert on each other are equal and opposite.*

Lesson structure

STARTER

Picture the force – Show a set of diagrams of objects and ask the students to mark on all of the forces. Alternatively use Animation P2 2.1 'Pulling' from the GCSE Physics CD ROM. (5–10 minutes)

It's a drag – Show a video clip of a drag racer (search for drag racer at video.google.com) deploying parachutes to assist in braking. Ask the students to explain how the parachutes help to slow it down. (5 minutes)

Friction again – Demonstrate a trolley (or similar) rolling across the floor and ask the students to explain in detail why it stops. (5–10 minutes)

MAIN

- Some of the material here checks the students' understanding of basic forces; they need to be encouraged to draw clear diagrams of the forces acting on objects.

- It will help if the students have a clear understanding of what a one newton force feels like, so pass around a 100 g mass so they can get a feel for it. You could also give examples of very large forces (e.g. the force between the Sun and Earth) and very small forces (e.g. the force of attraction between adjacent students), to show the vast range of forces scientists deal with.

- The idea of equal and opposite forces needs to be reinforced with plenty of examples. Show a range of objects in equilibrium such as a boat, see saw, car rolling and identify the pairs of forces on diagrams. (Search for pictures at images.google.com.)

- The car stuck in mud situation is one where the forces do not appear to be equal and opposite. The force in the rope is clear (you can show this with a model) but this is not the only force at work. To analyse the situation more fully would require including the frictional forces and the forces exerted by the tractor on the Earth. As the car and tractor accelerate, the Earth is accelerated in the opposite direction by a tiny amount.

- You can demonstrate equal and opposite forces using skates (see 'Practical support') or by dragging objects along the floor with a string with newtonmeters at each end.

- It can be difficult to read moving newtonmeters, but the students will get the hang of it with practice. (This relates to 'How Science Works': making measurements and reliability.)

- When discussing the operation of wheels, you might like to go through some of the stages of the force being transferred to the wheel from the engine; especially with those interested in automotive engineering.

- To round off, you could show a car trying to accelerate too rapidly and skidding; this provides a visual answer to in-text question c). (Search for racing or skid at video.google.com.)

PLENARIES

The force is strong in which one? – Give the students a set of cards showing the size of the forces between objects (e.g force on a person due to the gravity of Earth, force produced by a tug of war team) and a description of the objects and ask them to match up the cards. (5–10 minutes)

Pulling power – Give the students cards describing ten (or more) players and ask them to assign them to two tug of war teams, so that the teams are balanced. There may be several solutions. (5 minutes)

Use the force loop – This is a simple loop card game, with questions about forces, friction and movement. (5 minutes)

Practical support

Action and reaction

This makes an interesting demonstration, but skateboards may be more in fashion.

Equipment and materials required

Two sets of roller skates or skateboards, full sets of safety equipment (helmet, pads etc.) a connecting rope, two newtonmeters.

Details

The students should firstly demonstrate the effect of pushing each other. If student A pushes student B forwards gently, then student A should move backwards. If the students are roughly the same size and the skates are similar, then you could show that they both move the same distance before friction stops them. One student can then try to pull the other with a rope; they should both move closer. Measuring the forces to show that they are identical in size is trickier; the rope becomes slack. You might want to pull a skater around instead and take force measurements at both ends of the rope.

PHYSICS SPEEDING UP AND SLOWING DOWN

P2 2.1 Forces between objects

LEARNING OBJECTIVES

1 When two objects interact, what can we say about the forces acting?
2 What is the unit of force?

Equal and opposite forces

Whenever two objects push or pull on each other, they exert equal and opposite forces on one another. The unit of force is the newton (abbreviated N).

- A boxer who punches an opponent with a force of 100 N experiences a reverse force of 100 N from his opponent.
- Two roller skaters pull on opposite ends of a rope. The skaters move towards each other. This is because they pull on each other with equal and opposite forces. Two newtonmeters could be used to show this.

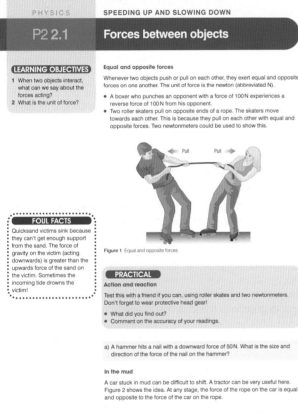

Figure 1 Equal and opposite forces

FOUL FACTS

Quicksand victims sink because they can't get enough support from the sand. The force of gravity on the victim (acting downwards) is greater than the upwards force of the sand on the victim. Sometimes the incoming tide drowns the victim!

PRACTICAL

Action and reaction

Test this with a friend if you can, using roller skates and two newtonmeters. Don't forget to wear protective head gear!

- What did you find out?
- Comment on the accuracy of your readings.

a) A hammer hits a nail with a downward force of 50 N. What is the size and direction of the force of the nail on the hammer?

In the mud

A car stuck in mud can be difficult to shift. A tractor can be very useful here. Figure 2 shows the idea. At any stage, the force of the rope on the car is equal and opposite to the force of the car on the rope.

To pull the car out of the mud, the force of the ground on the tractor needs to be greater than the force of the mud on the car. These two forces aren't necessarily equal to one another because the objects are not the same.

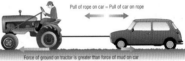
Pull of rope on car = Pull of car on rope

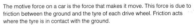
Force of ground on tractor is greater than force of mud on car

Figure 2 In the mud

b) A lorry tows a broken-down car. When the force of the lorry on the tow rope is 200 N, what is the force of the tow rope on the lorry?

Friction in action

The motive force on a car is the force that makes it move. This force is due to friction between the ground and the tyre of each drive wheel. Friction acts where the tyre is in contact with the ground.

Figure 3 Motive force

Direction of car

Force of tyre on road   Force of road on tyre

When the car moves forwards:

- the force of friction of the ground on the tyre is in the forward direction,
- the force of friction of the tyre on the ground is in the reverse direction.

The two forces are equal and opposite to one another.

c) What happens if there isn't enough friction between the tyre and the ground?

SUMMARY QUESTIONS

1 Complete the sentences below using words from the list.

| downwards | equal | opposite | upwards |

a) The force on a ladder resting against a wall is ...... and ...... to the force of the wall on the ladder.
b) A book is at rest on a table. The force of the book on the table is .... The force of the table on the book is ....

2 When a student is standing at rest on bathroom scales, the scales read 500 N.

a) What is the size and direction of the force of the student on the scales?
b) What is the size and direction of the force of the scales on the student?

KEY POINTS

1 When two objects interact, they always exert equal and opposite forces on each other.
2 The unit of force is the newton.

132   133

SUMMARY ANSWERS

1 a) Equal, opposite.
  b) Downwards, upwards.

2 a) 500 N downwards.
  b) 500 N upwards.

FOUL FACTS

Quicksand

On average, quicksand is actually more dense than the human body so it is difficult to sink in it further than your chest even if you panic. Survival guides suggest the following method of escape. Stay calm; if you don't struggle you *will* float. Slowly adjust your position so you are lying on your back and then wiggle your legs gently in a circular motion. You will crawl towards the edge. Don't get your friends to pull you out vertically; this apparently takes a very large force. It may be possible to investigate this with a cornflower based practical. (See activity and extension ideas.)

Answers to in-text questions

a) 50 N upwards.
b) 200 N
c) The wheels slip on the ground.

KEY POINTS

Ask the students to complete a range of diagrams demonstrating balanced forces.

P2 2.2

Resultant force

Students should learn:

- How to find the resultant force on an object.
- That a zero resultant force does not cause acceleration.
- That a non-zero resultant force causes acceleration.

Most students should be able to:

- Find the resultant force acting on an object when there are two forces acting in the same direction or in opposite directions.
- Describe how the resultant force will affect the movement of the object.
- Describe examples where an object acted on by two forces is at rest or in uniform motion.

Some students should be able to:

- Describe examples where the motion of an object acted on by two forces along the same line is changed by the action of the forces.

Teaching suggestions

- **Special needs.** Provide diagrams of objects so that the students can add force arrows and information about how the forces affect movement.
- **Gifted and talented**
  Forces at angles
  Some students may have studied vectors in mathematics and they could be challenged to find the resultant of two forces that are not in line. Start with a pair of perpendicular forces and see if the students can determine the magnitude and direction of the resultant using Pythagoras's theorem. Those talented in mathematics may be able to look into sets of forces that are not perpendicular.
- **Learning styles**
  Kinaesthetic: Making hovercraft and rockets.
  Visual: Observing the movement of objects with and without resultant forces acting on them.
  Auditory: Explaining the actions of forces on objects.
  Interpersonal: Discussing experimental observations.
  Intrapersonal: Evaluating their rocket design.
- **ICT link-up.** Use a distance sensor to monitor the movement of the air track glider.

SPECIFICATION LINK-UP   Unit: Physics 2.12.2

- *A number of forces acting on a body may be replaced by a single force that has the same effect on the body as the original forces all acting together. The force is called the 'resultant force'.*
- *If the resultant force acting on a stationary body is zero, the body will remain stationary.*
- *If the resultant force acting on a stationary body is not zero, the body will accelerate in the direction of the resultant force.*
- *If the resultant force acting on a moving body is zero, the body will continue to move at the same speed and in the same direction.*
- *If the resultant force acting on a moving body is not zero, the body will accelerate in the direction of the resultant force.*

Lesson structure

STARTER

Why do things stop? – Ask the students to explain why they think that a football kicked across a field eventually stops. (10 minutes)

Balanced forces – Show the students a toy boat floating on water and ask them to draw a diagram of all of the forces on the boat. Add small masses, one at a time, until the boat sinks. Ask them to draw a diagram showing the forces at the time when the boat was sinking. (5 minutes)

Mad maths – Give the students an addition sum that includes negative numbers to check their understanding. (5 minutes)

MAIN

- The calculation of resultant forces is generally easy when limited to one direction. The students must take care about the directions of the forces as some can get confused and simply add all of the numbers together.
- It is well worth making the hovercraft, but remember that the glue will take some time to cool so do this bit early.
- Demonstrating a linear air track is a good way of showing motion without friction, and it can help the students get to grips with the idea that objects only slow down because of the friction.
- If you have footage of a jet plane taking off, use it to discuss the forces involved. If it is of an aircraft carrier launch system, you can point out the extra force applied by the steam catapult and ask why this is necessary. (Search for 'jet plane' at video.google.com.)
- An aeroplane cruising is a good example of balanced forces. The students can draw a diagram and discuss the sensations they feel when they are in a plane like this. Because the forces are balanced, the students should feel no acceleration. If they close their eyes they would not be able to tell they were moving at all.
- Be careful that the students do not think that the force applied to the pedal is the actual braking force applied to the wheels. If this were the case, then a car would take a lot longer to stop.
- If the glue is set, then this is a good time to go back to the hovercraft. They should glide well on flat desks. Get the students to explain why they float; perhaps as a diagram.

PLENARIES

It's a tug o' war – Show the students a video of a tug of war (search for 'tug of war' at video.google.com); ask them to work out who will win by calculating the resultant forces. (10 minutes)

An uphill struggle – Ask: 'Why is it harder to push a car uphill rather than on a flat road? Is it easier to drag a piano up a ramp rather than up stairs? Why?' (10 minutes)

Hovercraft acrostic – Students write a short poem about how hovercrafts work based on the letters in the word 'hovercraft' and the ideas they have about forces. (5–10 minutes)

ACTIVITY & EXTENSION IDEAS

Water rockets

These are available as kits or can be improvised from plastic bottles.

Equipment and materials required

Foot pump, 1 litre plastic bottle (screw on top), launch rod, card for fins and possibly nose cone.

Details

- The bottles should be fitted with three equally spaced triangular stabilising fins made from stiff card. They also need a little loop so they can be placed upright from a pole stuck in the ground for launching. The trickiest part is fitting the pump to the cap so that pressure can be built up in the bottle before the connection pops off. You will have to experiment with this to get it just right.
- Fill the bottle about $\frac{1}{3}$ full of water and screw on the cap. Stand well back and pump up the pressure until the rocket launches spraying water everywhere. The rockets can reach heights of over 30 m so try to do this well away from roofs, as they seem to have a guidance system targeted on them. If time and several sets of equipment are available, you could let the students build their own (good homework) and have a competition as to which will fly the furthest. The students can change the launch angle (measured with a clinometer) and the amount of water in the rocket to find the optimum combination. This can be used to reinforce ideas from 'How Science Works', particularly the design of investigations.

Linear air track
Equipment and materials required

Linear air track, glider, elastic bands, light gates (optional).

Details

Set the track up so that it is horizontal and has an elastic buffer on both ends. If you are using light gates, set these up so that the glider has to pass through and cut the beam. Position a glider carefully in the middle of the track and turn the air on. If you have balanced the track it should stay still. Nudge it slightly to show that an unbalanced force accelerates it. The collisions with the buffers are nearly elastic and so the glider should stay at the same speed even after bouncing. This can be checked with the light gates or by simply timing the trolley between bumps.

Practical support

Investigating forces

Hovercraft are fun to make. There are various designs but this one uses an old CD.

Equipment and materials required

Balloons and balloon pump, old CD, thick paper, 'sports bottle' top and glue gun.

Details

Glue the sports bottle top onto the centre of the CD with the glue gun so that it covers the hole making sure that the seal around the edge is good. Let this cool for at least ten minutes. Blow up the balloon and carefully pull the end over the bottle top so that the air will be released through the base of the CD. The CD will act like a hovercraft. It is vastly improved by fixing a cylinder of paper around the top edge of the CD so that it holds the balloon vertically and stops it dragging on the desk. You should be able to blow up the balloon while it is still attached to the CD. Searching the Internet will yield a range of designs and pictures to help with this activity.

Answers to in-text questions

a) It stops because friction between the glider and the track is no longer zero.

b) The crate would slide across the floor after being given a brief push.

c) They are equal and opposite to each other.

d) It would have been greater.

SUMMARY ANSWERS

1 a) Less than. b) Greater than. c) Equal to.

2 a) It acts in the opposite direction to the direction in which the plane moves.
  b) It is zero.

P2 2.2 Resultant force

LEARNING OBJECTIVES

1 What is a resultant force?
2 What happens if the resultant force on an object is zero?
3 What happens if the resultant force on an object is not zero?

Most objects around you are acted on by more than one force. We can work out the effect of the forces on an object by replacing them with a single force, the **resultant force**. This is a single force that has the same effect as all the forces acting on the object.

When the resultant force on an object is zero, the object:
- remains stationary if it was at rest, or
- continues to move at the same speed and in the same direction if it was already moving.

PRACTICAL

Investigating forces

Make and test a model hovercraft floating on a cushion of air from a balloon, and/or
Use a glider on an air track to investigate the relationship between force and acceleration.

- What relationship do you find between force and acceleration? (See page 14.)

1 **A glider on a linear air track** floats on a cushion of air. Provided the track is level, the glider moves at constant velocity (i.e. with no change of speed or direction) along the track because friction is absent. The resultant force on the glider is zero.

Figure 1 The linear air track

a) What happens to the glider if the air track blower is switched off, and why?

2 **When a heavy crate is pushed across a rough floor**, the crate moves at constant velocity across the floor. The push force on the crate is equal and opposite to the force of friction of the floor on the crate. The resultant force on the crate is therefore zero.

b) What difference would it make if the floor were smooth?

Figure 2 Overcoming friction

When the resultant force on an object is not zero, the movement of the object depends on the size and direction of the resultant force.

1 **When a jet plane is taking off,** the thrust force of its engines is greater than the force of air resistance on it. The resultant force on it is the difference between the thrust force and the force of air resistance on it. The resultant force is therefore non-zero. The greater the resultant force, the quicker the take-off is.

Figure 3 A passenger jet on take-off

c) What can you say about the thrust force and the force of air resistance when the plane is moving at constant velocity at constant height?

2 **When a car driver applies the brakes,** the braking force is the resultant force on the car. It acts in the opposite direction to that in which the car is moving, so it slows the car down.

d) What can you say about the resultant force if the brakes had been applied harder?

KEY POINTS

	Object at the start	Resultant force	Effect on the object
1	at rest	zero	stays at rest
2	moving	zero	velocity stays the same
3	moving	non-zero in the same direction as the direction of motion of the object	accelerates
4	moving	non-zero in the opposite direction to the direction of motion of the object	decelerates

SUMMARY QUESTIONS

1 Complete the following sentences using words from the list.

greater than   less than   equal to

A car starts from rest and accelerates along a straight flat road.

a) The force of air resistance on it is ...... the motive force of its engine.
b) The resultant force is ...... zero.
c) The downward force of the car on the road is ...... the support force of the road on the car.

2 A jet plane lands on a runway and stops.

a) What can you say about the direction of the resultant force on the plane as it lands?
b) What can you say about the resultant force on the plane when it has stopped?

NEXT TIME YOU...

... are in a plane, think about the forces that are operating when you are taking off. What happens when a plane is taking off into a strong head wind?

Figure 4 Braking

GET IT RIGHT!

Remember that if a body is accelerating it can be speeding up, slowing down or changing direction. If a body is accelerating there must be a resultant force acting on it.

P2 2.3   Force and acceleration

Students should learn:

- The relationship between the resultant force on an object and its acceleration.

- How to use the equation $F = ma$ to determine the acceleration of an object.

LEARNING OUTCOMES

Most students should be able to:

- Calculate the force required to produce a given acceleration of an object of known mass.

- State that objects of larger mass require greater forces to cause large acceleration.

- Determine the direction of the acceleration on an object.

Some students should also be able to:

- Rearrange and use the equation: force = mass × acceleration.

Teaching suggestions

- **Gifted and talented**
  - See the more detailed acceleration investigation in the activity box.
  - Ask: 'Why doesn't the snooker table move when a ball hits the cushion?'

- **Learning styles**
  Kinaesthetic: Doing practical tasks.
  Visual: Recording experimental data.
  Auditory: Explaining the cause of friction.
  Interpersonal: Working together in small groups to generate data.
  Intrapersonal: Evaluating experimental technique.

- **ICT link-up.** A range of good simulations of force experiments are available. (See www.sunflowerlearning.com.)

SPECIFICATION LINK-UP   Unit: Physics 2.12.2

- *Force, mass and acceleration are related by the equation:*

$$\text{resultant force} = \text{mass} \times \text{acceleration}$$
$$\text{(newton, N)} \quad \text{(kilogram, kg)} \quad (\text{metre/second}^2, m/s^2)$$

- *If the resultant force acting on a moving body is zero, the body will continue to move at the same speed and in the same direction.*

- *If the resultant force acting on a moving body is not zero, the body will accelerate in the direction of the resultant force.*

Lesson structure

STARTER

Accelerator – Ask: 'What does the accelerator in a car do? How do you think it works?' (5–10 minutes)

Friction revision – Ask: 'Why do snooker balls stop rolling after being hit?' Ask the students to describe the ways that the initial kinetic energy is lost. (5 minutes)

Lift off – Show the students footage of a chemical rocket launch and ask them to describe as much of what is happening as possible using accurate scientific language. (10 minutes)

MAIN

- A DVD showing a snooker match is a very useful resource (a real table would be great!). You can use it to discuss what is happening to the balls during impact and their movement across the green baize. Remind the students that there are frictional forces at work.

- Pause the play and discuss the forces at work at each stage. With a data projector you can even draw force arrows over the action on your whiteboard. Show clips where the balls are moving in opposite directions and hit each other causing them to recoil. This can be used to illustrate forces in the opposite direction to motion, causing objects to decelerate or even accelerate in the other direction.

- The experiments can be simple or quite detailed depending on the time you have available. They produce quite a bit of data and can produce an excellent analysis task. The students should be encouraged to notice the limitations of the experiments and suggest improvements. As such, there are plenty of opportunities to cover 'How Science Works' concepts.

- As this is another fairly mathematically intensive topic, you will have to spend time on checking the students' ability to use the equation. As usual, encourage a rigorous layout to increase the chances of a correct answer.

- Finally watch out for students thinking that a moving object will always be moving in the direction of the resultant force. They need to understand that the object could be moving in the opposite direction, but slowing down.

PLENARIES

What's wrong? – Ask the students to correct this sentence: 'Objects always move in the direction of the resultant force.' (5 minutes)

I'm snookered – The students must draw a series of diagrams showing the forces involved in getting out of 'a snooker', where the object ball, the blue, is behind the pink. (10 minutes)

The tipping point – Show a diagram of a person trying to push a large box by shoving the top edge. Ask the students to explain why this would not work well and what should be done instead. (5 minutes)

ACTIVITY & EXTENSION IDEAS

More investigating force and acceleration
In this experiment, the students can discover the effect of different forces on acceleration or the effect of the objects mass.

Equipment and materials required
For each group: dynamics trolley (or similar), string, pulley, clamp, 10 × 20 g masses and mass holder, stopwatch and possibly motion sensor or light gates.

Details
- The students mount the pulley over the end of the desks. One end of the string is attached to the mass holder (which hangs down) and the other to the trolley. The mass is released and falls to the floor pulling the trolley with a constant force. With larger masses you will need to protect the floor and students' feet.
- The movement of the trolley can be monitored by a motion sensor, or the time it takes to move between two marked points can be recorded. The students can load the mass holder with different masses to increase the force on the trolley in order to investigate the effect of the size of the force on the acceleration. (This relates to: 'How Science Works': relationships between variables.) Some may even look into the effect of the mass of the trolley by loading it up with increasing mass and accelerating it with a fixed force. By analysing graphs and discovering that *a* is proportional to *F* and *a* is also inversely proportional to *m*, higher attaining students could link the concepts together to reach $F = ma$.

⬚ Practical support

Investigating force and acceleration
This is a simple experiment, except for keeping the force constant; the alternative (see activity box) is more accurate but needs more equipment.

Equipment and materials required
For each group: dynamics trolley, string, masses (similar to trolley mass), stopwatch and possibly motion sensor or light gates.

Details
The students pull the trolley along attempting to use a constant force by watching the newtonmeter. They should pull the trolley along a track of known distance so that they can compare the acceleration easily. If insufficient trolleys are available to double up, then just let the students add masses roughly equivalent to that of the trolley.

PHYSICS   SPEEDING UP AND SLOWING DOWN

P2 2.3 Force and acceleration

LEARNING OBJECTIVES
1 How does the acceleration of an object depend on the size of the resultant force?
2 What effect does the mass of the object have on its acceleration?

PRACTICAL

Investigating force and acceleration

Figure 1 Investigating the link between force and motion

We can use the apparatus above to accelerate a trolley with a constant force.

Use the newtonmeter to pull the trolley along with a constant force.

You can double or treble the total moving mass by using double-deck and triple-deck trolleys.

A motion sensor and a computer record the velocity of the trolley as it accelerates.
- What are the advantages of using a data logger and computer in this investigation?

You can display the results as a velocity–time graph on the computer screen.

Figure 2 shows velocity–time graphs for different masses. You can work out the acceleration from the gradient of the line, as explained on page 127.

Look at some typical results in the table below:

Resultant force (newtons)	0.5	1.0	1.5	2.0	4.0	6.0
Mass (kilograms)	1.0	1.0	1.0	2.0	2.0	2.0
Acceleration (m/s²)	0.5	1.0	1.5	1.0	2.0	3.0
Mass × acceleration (kg m/s²)	0.5	1.0	1.5	2.0	4.0	6.0

The results show that the resultant force, the mass and the acceleration are linked by the equation

resultant force = mass × acceleration
(newtons, N)   (kilograms) (metres/second²)

Worked example
Calculate the resultant force on an object of mass 6.0 kg when it has an acceleration of 3.0 m/s².

Solution
Resultant force = mass × acceleration = 6.0 kg × 3.0 m/s² = 18.0 N

a) Calculate the resultant force on a sprinter of mass 50 kg who accelerates at 8 m/s².

Figure 2 Velocity–time graph for different combinations of force and mass

| Force Mass (N) (kg) |
| 1.0 0.5 |
| 1.0 1.0 |
| 1.0 2.0 |

Maths notes
We can write the word equation on the previous page as:
Resultant force, $F = ma$,
where m = mass and a = acceleration.
Rearranging this equation gives $a = \dfrac{F}{m}$ or $m = \dfrac{F}{a}$

Worked example
Calculate the acceleration of an object of mass 5.0 kg acted on by a resultant force of 40 N.

Solution
Rearranging $F = ma$ gives $a = \dfrac{F}{m} = \dfrac{40\,N}{5.0\,kg} = 8.0\,m/s^2$

b) Calculate the acceleration of a car of mass 800 kg acted on by a resultant force of 3200 N.

Speeding up or slowing down
If the velocity of an object changes, it must be acted on by a resultant force. Its acceleration is always in the same direction as the resultant force.
- The velocity of the object increases if the resultant force is in the **same** direction as the velocity. We say its acceleration is positive because it is in the same direction as its velocity.
- The velocity of the object decreases (i.e. it decelerates) if the resultant force is **opposite** in direction. We say its acceleration is negative because it is opposite in direction to its velocity.

KEY POINT
$\dfrac{\text{Resultant force}}{\text{(newtons, N)}} = \dfrac{\text{mass}}{\text{(kilograms)}} \times \dfrac{\text{acceleration}}{\text{(metres/second}^2)}$

SUMMARY QUESTIONS
1 Complete a) to c) using the words below:
    acceleration   resultant force   mass   velocity
a) A moving object decelerates when a …… acts on it in the opposite direction to its …… .
b) The greater the …… of an object, the less its acceleration when a …… acts on it.
c) The …… of a moving object increases when a …… acts on it in the same direction as it is moving in.

2 Copy and complete the following table:

	a)	b)	c)	d)	e)
Force (newtons, N)	?	200	840	?	5000
Mass (kilograms, kg)	20	?	70	0.40	?
Acceleration (metre/second squared, m/s²)	0.80	5.0	?	6.0	0.20

FOUL FACTS
If you're in a car that suddenly brakes, your neck pulls on your head and slows it down. The equal and opposite force of your head on your neck can injure your neck.

Figure 3 A 'whiplash' injury

GET IT RIGHT!
If an object is accelerating there must be a resultant force acting on it.

136 / 137

SUMMARY ANSWERS

1 a) Resultant force, velocity.
  b) Mass, resultant force.
  c) Acceleration, resultant force.

2 a) 16 N
  b) 40 kg
  c) 12 m/s²
  d) 2.4 N
  e) 25 000 kg

Answers to in-text questions

a) 400 N
b) 4.0 m/s²

KEY POINTS

The students should complete a range of calculations using $F = ma$. This could be as a whole class or a loop game.

P2 2.4   On the road

LEARNING OBJECTIVES

Students should learn:

- That the resultant force on a vehicle travelling at constant velocity is zero.
- About the factors that affect the thinking distance of vehicles.
- About the factors that affect the braking distance of stopping vehicles.

LEARNING OUTCOMES

Most students should be able to:

- Use a chart to find the stopping distance, the braking distance and the thinking distance at a given speed.
- List and describe the factors that affect the stopping distance of a vehicle.
- Explain which are the most important factors for cars moving at a range of speeds.

Some students should also be able to:

- Differentiate between factors that affect the thinking distance, braking distance or both distances.

Teaching suggestions

- **Special needs.** Allow the students to use an experiment template with clear instructions and a results table during the practical task.

- **Learning styles**
  Kinaesthetic: Measuring reaction time.
  Visual: Obtaining accurate measurements.
  Auditory: Listening out for the key word.
  Interpersonal: Collaborating with others in practical work.
  Intrapersonal: Reviewing and evaluating results.

- **Homework.** The students could find out the facts about road deaths in the UK and their local area. Ask: 'What measures have been taken to reduce them?'

- **ICT link-up.** A fairly simple spreadsheet can be used to model stopping distances. This can incorporate speed, reaction times and surface conditions and will quantify how much effect each of these conditions has.

- **Teaching assistant.** Have the teaching assistant help out with the practical and also support those who have difficulty plotting graphs.

SPECIFICATION LINK-UP   Unit: Physics 2.12.2

- *When a vehicle travels at a steady speed the frictional forces balance the driving force.*
- *The greater the speed of a vehicle the greater the braking force needed to stop it in a certain distance.*
- *The stopping distance of a vehicle depends on the distance the vehicle travels during the driver's reaction time and the distance it travels under the braking force.*
- *A driver's reaction time can be affected by tiredness, drugs and alcohol.*
- *A vehicle's braking distance can be affected by adverse road and weather conditions and poor condition of the vehicle.*

Lesson structure

STARTER

Stop! – Ask the students to sort a set of cards about things which may or may not affect stopping distances for cars. (5 minutes)

Chances – Give the students a set of cards describing likely injuries and ask them to match them to car speeds in collisions. (5 minutes)

MAIN

- Video clips of vehicles braking and skidding make this topic more visually stimulating. (Search for video clips at video.google.com.)

- When discussing reaction times, you could try a simple experiment in concentration. At the beginning of the lesson give the students an unusual key word and ask them to put their hands up as quickly as possible whenever they hear it. Early in the lesson they will be quite quick but later, as their concentration flags, they will struggle.

- You could ask the students to evaluate the data used to produce the stopping distance chart. It is based on an alert driver, driving a medium-sized car, but it does not take into account the improved braking systems of modern cars and the increase in the size (mass) of the average car. This can lead to a discussion of whether large cars are safer or more dangerous to passengers and pedestrians.

- The students should understand the factors affecting overall stopping distance, but they need to be clear which affects the thinking distance and which affects the braking distance.

- The braking distance really depends on the kinetic energy of the car and the frictional force between the car and road. You can link these concepts with $F = ma$ from the previous topic and again with kinetic energy in lesson P2 3.2.

- Note that the speed of the car affects thinking and braking distance so it is the most important factor overall.

- Testing reaction time rounds the lesson off well, you can try the simple or advanced versions or even use driving simulation software. (This relates to 'How Science Works': reliability and validity of evidence.)

PLENARIES

I said stop! – Using the cards from the starter, students have to separate those that were correct into ones that affect thinking distance and ones that affect braking distance. Ask: 'Do some affect both?' Students could put them in order of importance for a car travelling at 30 m.p.h. (5–10 minutes)

Expect the unexpected – Use the unusual key word one more time as the students are packing away. (1 minute)

Additional physics

ACTIVITY & EXTENSION IDEAS

Advanced reaction times

It is possible to try out a more advanced version of the reaction times activity; one more like driving a car. It requires a bit more equipment but is more exciting.

Equipment and materials required

Stopwatch with electronic inputs to start and stop, comfy chair, two pedals, microphone.

Details

You need to make two pedals; the accelerator and the brake. These can be a couple of planks of wood connected with a hinge and then a strong spring to keep them apart. A switch, or micro switch is positioned so that pressing the planks together closes it. You may need to put a block of wood between the planks to ensure that the switch does not get crushed by over-enthusiastic students. The start input of the stopwatch should be connected to a microphone so that the clock starts when you shout. The brake should have a switch that stops the clock when pressed. The 'driver' sits in the comfy chair with his/her foot resting on the accelerator pedal. Stand behind the driver; let them relax for a while and then shout 'boo'. The driver needs to press the stop pedal as fast as possible and the stopwatch should show the reaction time. The switch on the accelerator can be connected to a light to ensure that no cheating goes on. You can also test to see if reactions improve with practice or are better with sound (bangs) than light (flashing bulbs).

Practical support

Testing reaction times

This is a fairly simple activity only requiring a stopwatch with separate start and lap-time buttons.

Equipment and materials required

Stopwatches.

Details

The students can try the simple activity and see the wide range of response times. They should appreciate that the times improve with practice and when they are fully concentrating on the clock. In a real car situation, the driver would not be able to focus on one simple task so the times would be significantly greater. For a more advanced suggestion, see the activity box.

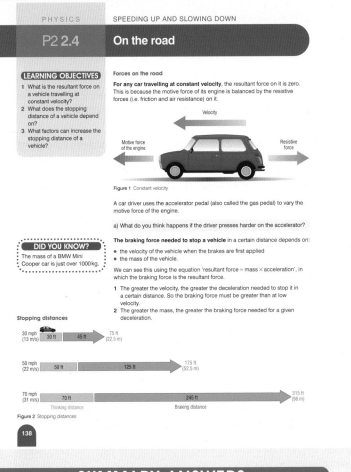

PHYSICS   SPEEDING UP AND SLOWING DOWN

P2 2.4   On the road

LEARNING OBJECTIVES

1 What is the resultant force on a vehicle travelling at constant velocity?
2 What does the stopping distance of a vehicle depend on?
3 What factors can increase the stopping distance of a vehicle?

Forces on the road

For any car travelling at constant velocity, the resultant force on it is zero. This is because the motive force of its engine is balanced by the resistive forces (i.e. friction and air resistance) on it.

Velocity

Motive force of the engine   Resistive force

Figure 1 Constant velocity

A car driver uses the accelerator pedal (also called the gas pedal) to vary the motive force of the engine.

a) What do you think happens if the driver presses harder on the accelerator?

DID YOU KNOW?

The mass of a BMW Mini Cooper car is just over 1000 kg.

The braking force needed to stop a vehicle in a certain distance depends on:

• the velocity of the vehicle when the brakes are first applied
• the mass of the vehicle.

We can see this using the equation 'resultant force = mass × acceleration', in which the braking force is the resultant force.

1 The greater the velocity, the greater the deceleration needed to stop it in a certain distance. So the braking force must be greater than at low velocity.
2 The greater the mass, the greater the braking force needed for a given deceleration.

Stopping distances

30 mph (13 m/s)   30 ft   45 ft   75 ft (22.5 m)

50 mph (22 m/s)   50 ft   125 ft   175 ft (52.5 m)

70 mph (31 m/s)   70 ft   245 ft   315 ft (96 m)
    Thinking distance   Braking distance

Figure 2 Stopping distances

Driving tests always ask about stopping distances. This is the shortest distance a vehicle can safely stop in, and is in two parts:

• **The thinking distance:** the distance travelled by the vehicle in the time it takes the driver to react (i.e. during the driver's reaction time).
• **The braking distance:** the distance travelled by the vehicle during the time the braking force acts.

The stopping distance = the thinking distance + the braking distance.

Figure 2 shows the stopping distance for a vehicle on a dry flat road travelling at different speeds. Check for yourself that the stopping distance at 31 m/s (70 miles per hour) is 96 m.

b) What are the thinking distance, the braking distance and the stopping distance at 13 m/s (30 mph)?

Factors affecting stopping distances

1 **Tiredness, alcohol and drugs** all increase reaction times. So they increase the thinking distance (because thinking distance = speed × reaction time). Therefore, the stopping distance is greater.
2 **The faster a vehicle is travelling**, the further it travels before it stops. This is because the thinking distance and the braking distance both increase with increased speed.
3 **In adverse road conditions**, for example on wet or icy roads, drivers have to brake with less force to avoid skidding. Stopping distances are therefore greater in poor road conditions.
4 **Poorly maintained vehicles**, for example with worn brakes or tyres, take longer to stop because the brakes and tyres are less effective.

c) Why are stopping distances greater in poor visibility?

Figure 3 Stopping distances are further than you might think!

PRACTICAL

Reaction times

Use an electronic stopwatch to test your own reaction time under different conditions in an investigation. Ask a friend to start the stopwatch when you are looking at it with your finger on the stop button. The read-out from the watch will give your reaction time.

• How can you make your data as reliable as possible?
• What conclusions can you draw?

SUMMARY QUESTIONS

1 Each of the following factors affects the thinking distance or the braking distance of a vehicle. Which of these two distances is affected in each case below?
   a) The road surface condition affects the ...... distance.
   b) The tiredness of a driver increases his or her ...... distance.
   c) Poorly maintained brakes affects the ...... distance.
2 a) Use the chart in Figure 2 to work out, in metres, the increase in i) the thinking distance, ii) the braking distance, iii) the stopping distance from 13 m/s (30 mph) to 22 m/s (50 mph). (1 foot = 0.30 m.)
   b) A driver has a reaction time of 0.8 s. Calculate her thinking distance at a speed of i) 15 m/s, ii) 30 m/s.

KEY POINTS

1 The thinking distance is the distance travelled by the vehicle in the time it takes the driver to react.
2 The braking distance is the distance the vehicle travels under the braking force.
3 The stopping distance = the thinking distance + the braking distance.

138   139

SUMMARY ANSWERS

1 a) Braking.   b) Thinking.   c) Braking.

2 a) i) 6 m   ii) 24 m   iii) 30 m

   b) i) 12 m   ii) 24 m

Answers to in-text questions

a) The car speeds up.

b) 9 m, 13.5 m, 22.5 m.

c) The reaction time of the driver is longer because the road ahead is more difficult to see.

KEY POINTS

Can the students make a list of the factors that affect stopping distances and describe the effect of each factor?

P2 2.5   Falling objects

LEARNING OBJECTIVES

Students should learn:

- That the mass of an object is a measure of the material in the object while its weight is the force acting on that object due to its being in a gravitational field.
- The mass of the object is a constant value while the weight depends on the strength of the gravitational field it is in.
- That when an object falls through a fluid, it accelerates until the gravitational force is balanced by frictional forces and this velocity is called the terminal velocity.

LEARNING OUTCOMES

Most students should be able to:

- Explain the difference between mass and weight.
- Calculate the weight of an object of a given mass.
- Describe the forces acting on an object falling through a fluid like air or water, and how these forces affect the acceleration of the object.
- Describe how the velocity of an object released from rest in a fluid changes as it falls.
- Explain why an object reaches a terminal velocity and describe some of the factors that determine this velocity.

Some students should also be able to:

- Explain the motion of an object released from rest falling through a fluid including how the acceleration decreases and becomes zero at terminal velocity.

Teaching suggestions

- **Special needs.** Allow the students to use an experiment template with clear instructions and a results table during the practical task.
- **Learning styles**
  Kinaesthetic: Performing parachute experiments.
  Visual: Obtaining accurate measurements.
  Auditory: Explaining the cause of friction.
  Interpersonal: Collaborating with others in practical work.
  Intrapersonal: Reviewing and evaluating results.

SPECIFICATION LINK-UP   Unit: Physics 2.12.2

Candidates should know and understand:

- *The faster a body moves through a fluid the greater the frictional force that acts on it.*
- *A body falling through a fluid will initially accelerate due to the force of gravity. Eventually the resultant force on the body will be zero and it will fall at its terminal velocity.*

Students should use their skills, knowledge and understanding of 'How Science Works':

- *to calculate the weight of a body using:*

$$\text{weight} = \text{mass} \times \text{gravitational field strength}$$
$$\text{(newton, N)} \quad \text{(kilogram, kg)} \quad \text{(newton/kilogram, N/kg)}$$

- *to draw and interpret velocity–time graphs for bodies that reach terminal velocity, including a consideration of the forces acting on the body.*

Lesson structure

STARTER

Air resistance – What causes air or water resistance? The students need to use their understanding of particles and forces to give a description. (5–10 minutes)

Fluid facts – Give the students cards with information about the physical properties and the explanations in terms of particle behaviour for solids, liquids and gases and ask them to match them up. (5 minutes)

Nobody expects the . . . – key word. See if the students have remembered it from the last topic. How are their reactions now? (2 minutes)

MAIN

- Video clips of falling objects are ideal for this topic, in particular clips of parachutists. (Search for video clips of parachutes at video.google.com.)
- Weight and mass are commonly confused. Let the students handle a 1 kg mass and emphasise that the '1 kg' is the material in the block and this will not change just because you take it to the Moon.
- Weigh the mass and explain that the weight is the force that is pulling it towards the centre of the Earth. If there were less gravity then this force would be less.
- There are a couple of phrases used to describe 'the strength of gravity' and these are sometimes interchanged. Try to stick to 'gravitational field strength' and explain that there is a 'field' around the Earth where its gravity affects other objects. The students should accept this field idea after discussing the effect of a magnetic field on magnetic material close by.
- It may have been a while since the students have used the term 'fluid'; remind them that all liquids and gases are fluid so all motion we see on the Earth is motion through fluids.
- Air resistance is easy to show by throwing various sized bits of paper around, some scrunched some not.
- It is very common for students to believe that when the parachute is opened the sky diver 'shoots upwards'. This is an illusion caused by the fact that the cameraman has not opened her parachute and so continues to fall while the skydiver that has opened his parachute slows rapidly. You can compare this to two cars driving side by side when one suddenly brakes.
- When discussing terminal velocity, point out that this depends on the shape, or aerodynamics, of the object falling. A skydiver can adjust his shape and change speeds. Also point out that with the parachute open, there is still a terminal velocity but this is much less than the one without the parachute opened.
- Use Simulation P2 2.5 provided on the GCSE Physics CD ROM.

PLENARIES

Falling forces – The students should draw a comic strip with stick figures showing the forces at various stages of a parachute jump. (10 minutes)

Charity jump poster – Students can draw a poster encouraging people to jump out of an aeroplane; the poster must explain the science of falling though air. (15–20 minutes)

ACTIVITY & EXTENSION

Falling with style – Skydivers are able to change speed during their flight by altering their body position. The students could put together a brief presentation showing the divers doing this. They could also look at how birds alter their profile while diving for fish.

Practical support

Investigating the motion of a parachutist

This investigation can be trickier than it sounds, mainly because a parachute needs a couple of metres to unfurl and have a significant effect.

Equipment and materials required

For each group: small mass (20 g), string or cotton, scissors, approximately 15 cm by 15 cm square of cloth.

Details

Give the students a few minutes to make a parachute. The higher the parachutes are dropped from, the more effective they are so find somewhere with sufficient height. It is just possible to notice the effect if you drop objects when standing on the desk, but great care must be taken. (This relates to 'How Science Works': designing investigations.)

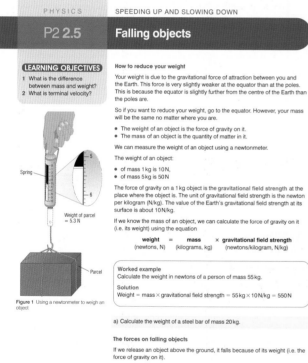

PHYSICS   SPEEDING UP AND SLOWING DOWN

P2 2.5   Falling objects

LEARNING OBJECTIVES

1 What is the difference between mass and weight?
2 What is terminal velocity?

How to reduce your weight

Your weight is due to the gravitational force of attraction between you and the Earth. This force is very slightly weaker at the equator than at the poles. This is because the equator is slightly further from the centre of the Earth than the poles are.

So if you want to reduce your weight, go to the equator. However, your mass will be the same no matter where you are.

● The weight of an object is the force of gravity on it.
● The mass of an object is the quantity of matter in it.

We can measure the weight of an object using a newtonmeter.

The weight of an object:
● of mass 1 kg is 10 N,
● of mass 5 kg is 50 N

The force of gravity on a 1 kg object is the gravitational field strength at the place where the object is. The unit of gravitational field strength is the newton per kilogram (N/kg). The value of the Earth's gravitational field strength at its surface is about 10 N/kg.

If we know the mass of an object, we can calculate the force of gravity on it (i.e. its weight) using the equation

$$\text{weight} = \text{mass} \times \text{gravitational field strength}$$
$$\text{(newtons, N)} \quad \text{(kilograms, kg)} \quad \text{(newtons/kilogram, N/kg)}$$

Worked example
Calculate the weight in newtons of a person of mass 55 kg.

Solution
Weight = mass × gravitational field strength = 55 kg × 10 N/kg = 550 N

a) Calculate the weight of a steel bar of mass 20 kg.

The forces on falling objects

If we release an object above the ground, it falls because of its weight (i.e. the force of gravity on it).

If the object falls freely, no other forces act on it. So the resultant force on it is its weight. It accelerates downwards at a constant acceleration of 10 m/s², called the acceleration due to gravity. For example, if we release a 1 kg object above the ground,

● the force of gravity on it is 10 N, and
● its acceleration (= force/mass = 10 N/1 kg) = 10 m/s².

Figure 1 Using a newtonmeter to weigh an object

Spring

Weight of parcel = 5.3 N

Parcel

Additional physics

a) Object in air accelerates at 10 m/s²

Weight of object

b) Drag force — Object in liquid falls at constant velocity

Weight of object

c) velocity-time graph

Object in air

Terminal velocity in liquid

Object in liquid

Figure 2 Falling objects. a) Falling in air, b) falling in a liquid, c) velocity–time graph for a) and b).

If the object falls in a fluid, the fluid drags on the object. The drag force increases with speed. At any instant, the resultant force on the object is its weight minus the drag force on it. When an object moves through the air (i.e. the fluid is air) the drag force is called air resistance.

● The acceleration of the object decreases as it falls. This is because the drag force increases as it speeds up. So the resultant force on it decreases.
● The object reaches a constant velocity when the drag force on it is equal and opposite to its weight. We call this velocity its terminal velocity. The resultant force is then zero, so its acceleration is zero.

b) Why does an object released in water eventually reach a constant velocity?

FOUL FACTS

If a parachute **fails** to open, the parachutist could reach a terminal velocity of more than 60 m/s (about 140 miles per hour). The drag force is then equal to his or her weight. The force of the impact on the ground would be equal to **many** times the weight, resulting in almost certain death.

SUMMARY QUESTIONS

1 Complete a) to c) using the words below:

equal to   greater than   less than

When an object is released in a fluid:

a) the drag force on it is ...... its weight before it reaches its terminal velocity.
b) its acceleration is ...... zero after it reaches its terminal velocity.
c) the resultant force on it is initially ...... its weight.

2 A parachutist of mass 70 kg supported by a parachute of mass 20 kg reaches a constant speed.

a) Explain why the parachutist reaches a constant speed.
b) Calculate:
   i) the total weight of the parachutist and the parachute,
   ii) the size and direction of the force of air resistance on the parachute when the parachutist falls at constant speed.

PRACTICAL

Investigating the motion of a parachutist

Release an object with and without a parachute.

Make suitable measurements to compare the two situations.

● Why does the object fall at constant speed when the parachute is open?
● Evaluate the reliability of the data you collected. How could you improve the quality of your data?

Drag force

Parachutist falling at constant speed

Weight

Figure 3 Using a parachute

KEY POINTS

1 The weight of an object is the force of gravity on it.
2 An object falling freely accelerates at about 10 m/s².
3 An object falling in a fluid reaches a terminal velocity.

140

141

SUMMARY ANSWERS

1 a) Less than.   b) Equal to.   c) Equal to.

2 a) As the parachutist falls, the drag force increases so the resultant force decreases. The resultant force is zero when the drag force becomes equal and opposite to the weight of the parachutist and the parachute. The speed is then constant.

b) i) 900 N   ii) 900 N upwards

Answers to in-text questions

a) 200 N

b) The drag force on it increases (as its velocity increases) until it is equal and opposite to its weight. The resultant force on it is then zero and its acceleration is zero.

KEY POINTS

Can the students interpret a graph showing the speed of a falling object in terms of the forces acting on the object?

P2 2.6 Speed limits

PHYSICS SPEEDING UP AND SLOWING DOWN

P2 2.6 Speed limits

SPECIFICATION LINK-UP

Unit: Physics 2.12.2

This spread can be used to revisit the following statements covered in this chapter:

- *The factors that affect the stopping distance of a vehicle.*

Candidates should be able, when provided with additional information:

- *To draw and interpret velocity–time graphs for bodies that reach terminal velocity, including a consideration of the forces acting on the body.*

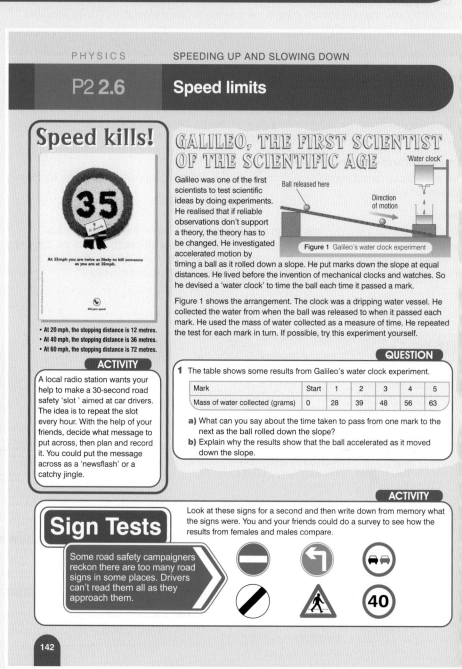

Speed kills!

35

At 35mph you are twice as likely to kill someone as you are at 30mph.

- At 20 mph, the stopping distance is 12 metres.
- At 40 mph, the stopping distance is 36 metres.
- At 60 mph, the stopping distance is 72 metres.

ACTIVITY

A local radio station wants your help to make a 30-second road safety 'slot' aimed at car drivers. The idea is to repeat the slot every hour. With the help of your friends, decide what message to put across, then plan and record it. You could put the message across as a 'newsflash' or a catchy jingle.

GALILEO, THE FIRST SCIENTIST OF THE SCIENTIFIC AGE

Galileo was one of the first scientists to test scientific ideas by doing experiments. He realised that if reliable observations don't support a theory, the theory has to be changed. He investigated accelerated motion by timing a ball as it rolled down a slope. He put marks down the slope at equal distances. He lived before the invention of mechanical clocks and watches. So he devised a 'water clock' to time the ball each time it passed a mark.

Figure 1 Galileo's water clock experiment

Figure 1 shows the arrangement. The clock was a dripping water vessel. He collected the water from when the ball was released to when it passed each mark. He used the mass of water collected as a measure of time. He repeated the test for each mark in turn. If possible, try this experiment yourself.

QUESTION

1 The table shows some results from Galileo's water clock experiment.

Mark	Start	1	2	3	4	5
Mass of water collected (grams)	0	28	39	48	56	63

a) What can you say about the time taken to pass from one mark to the next as the ball rolled down the slope?

b) Explain why the results show that the ball accelerated as it moved down the slope.

ACTIVITY

Sign Tests

Look at these signs for a second and then write down from memory what the signs were. You and your friends could do a survey to see how the results from females and males compare.

Some road safety campaigners reckon there are too many road signs in some places. Drivers can't read them all as they approach them.

40

142

Teaching suggestions

Activities

- **Speed kills!** –You could record this 30-second slot on tape or video. You may also consider uploading it to your school intranet. Media studies students may also have the opportunity to put in a bit of extra work and add a real jingle to the tape.

- **Galileo** – Making a water clock is fiddly but certainly possible; any container with a hole at the bottom should do. Ideally the volume of water in the clock should stay constant, so it has to be continually topped up and allowed to overflow from the top while a constant flow of water is emitted by a hole at the bottom. You should be able to find some basic designs. Ask if the students can come up with any alternative methods of measuring time. One good one is to use a simple pendulum as the oscillations always have the same period as long as it isn't swung too high. The students could verify this.

- **Sign tests** – You could also use a slideshow of the symbols drivers are supposed to be able to recognise and see how many of them the students can identify. An automatic slideshow of 20 or so can be set up with a timing sequence so that each sign is only on screen for a second. Search the web's pictures for 'road signs'. You could also show the PhotoPLUS P2 2.6 'Speed limits' from the GCSE Physics CD ROM here.

- **Anti-skid surfaces** – Any letter should contain the scientific arguments about how the material works and economical arguments about how it will save money in the long run. You might also want to discuss other traffic calming measures such as speed bumps.

- **Safer roads** – There are a large range of drugs tests that are available but these take some time to produce results so are unsuitable for on the spot fines. Testing for alertness could be possible; you could link back to the reaction time tests earlier in the chapter. Many drugs suggest that you do not operate heavy machinery (including cars) while using them, including some stronger cough medicines. It is certainly possible to design a car that would not allow the same driver to drive it for more than a few hours without a break. Ask the students if they think that this is a good idea.

QUESTION

2 Athletes are tested routinely to make sure they do not use drugs that boost performance.
   a) Why are these tests important?
   b) Why do athletes need to be careful about what they eat and drink in the days before a race?
   c) Find out how scientific instruments help to fight the battle against drugs in sport.
   d) Predict what the men's 100 m record will be in 2050.

SPEED RECORDS

In athletics, the 100 m race is a dramatic event. Electronic timers are used to time it and cameras are used to record the finish in case there is a 'dead heat'. The world record for the time has become shorter and shorter over successive years.

● **Jesse Owens**	1936	10.2 s
● **Jim Hines**	1968	9.95 s
● **Maurice Green**	1999	9.79 s
● **Tim Montgomery**	2002	9.78 s
● **Assafa Powell**	2005	9.77 s

Anti-skid surfaces

Have you noticed that road surfaces near road junctions and traffic lights are often different from normal road surfaces?

- The surface is rougher than normal. This gives increased friction between the surface and a vehicle tyre. So it reduces the chance of skidding when a driver brakes.
- The surface is lighter in colour so it is marked out clearly from a normal road surface.

Skidding happens when the brakes are applied too harshly. The wheels lock and the tyres slide on the road as a result. Increased friction between the tyres and the road allows more force to be applied without skidding happening. So the stopping distance is reduced.

ACTIVITY

Discuss the following issues with your friends:

- Should drivers involved in accidents also be tested for tiredness and drugs?
- Would tiredness tests be reliable? Would drivers on medical drugs be caught unfairly?
- Should drivers be pulled over for 'on the spot' tests?

ACTIVITY

Campaigners in the village of Greystoke want the council to resurface the main road at the traffic lights in the village. A child was killed crossing the road at the traffic lights earlier in the year. The council estimates it would cost £45 000. They say they can't afford it. Campaigners have found some more data to support their case.

- There are about 50 000 road accidents each year in the UK.
- The cost of road accidents is over £3000 million per year.
- Anti-skid surfaces have cut accidents by about 5%.

a) Estimate how much each road accident costs.
b) Imagine you are one of the campaigners. Write a letter to your local newspaper to counter the council's response that they can't afford it.

143

ANSWERS TO QUESTIONS

1 a) The time interval is getting smaller.

   b) If the marks are equally spaced and the time it takes to move between them is shorter, then the ball must be getting faster; it is accelerating.

2 a) To make sure the athletes do not take drugs that boost performance.

   b) Some food and some drinks might contain traces of banned substances.

   c) Research.

   d) Somewhere between 9.77 and 9.70 s.

Extension or homework

Is there a limit to human speed? – Using the data presented for the 100 m for men and researching into the same record for women, ask the students to produce a maximum speed limit for humans over 100 m. They could also look at longer distances?

Getting the hump – Where are there speed humps in the local area? Has the speed of the traffic really decreased because of them or have they driven the traffic onto other roads? The students can look at a map of the local area and mark on the areas that have traffic calming measures.

Gifted and talented

These students could try to find out how much a human life is worth. Risk assessors look into various safety measures and decide if the cost is worth the benefits. Billions of pounds are spent on safety features for roads and railways each year, but many billions more could be spent to reduce the risks further but aren't. It should be possible for the students to find out information about this idea and to see if all industries put the same value on a single life.

Learning styles

Kinaesthetic: Making timepieces.

Visual: Watching video reports.

Auditory: Narrating a radio clip.

Interpersonal: Debating the effectiveness of road safety measures.

Intrapersonal: Writing a report/letter about road junction improvements.

ICT link-up

With digital cameras and basic editing software, the students could make quite an impressive 30-second road safety film. They could even incorporate clips downloaded from the Internet of cars braking.

Teaching assistant

Your teaching assistant can be very helpful in the recording of discussions or helping to generate ideas in group work.

SUMMARY ANSWERS

1 a) i) In the opposite direction to.

   ii) In the same direction as.

b) i) Away from the door.

   ii) Away from the door.

2 a) i) 1.6 N/kg

   ii) 1000 N

b) i) 8 m/s², 640 N

   ii) −0.4 m/s², 28 000 N

3 a) The acceleration of X is constant and equal to 10 m/s².

b) The object accelerates at first. The drag force on it increases with speed so the resultant force on it and its acceleration decreases. When the drag force is equal to the weight of the object, the resultant force is zero. The acceleration is then zero so the velocity is constant.

Summary teaching suggestions

- Most of these questions check the students' ability to perform important calculations and should yield clear ideas of where the students need more practice.

- Check the answers to question 2 carefully, as they will probably reveal that some students are still struggling to get to grips with mass, gravity and weight.

SUMMARY QUESTIONS

1 A student is pushing a box across a rough floor. Friction acts between the box and the floor.

a) Complete the sentences below using words from the list.

> **in the same direction as**
> **in the opposite direction to**

   i) The force of friction of the box on the floor is ...... the force of friction of the floor on the box.

   ii) The force of the student on the box is ...... the force of friction of the box on the floor.

b) The student is pushing the box towards a door. Which direction, towards the door or away from the door, is

   i) the force of the box on the student?

   ii) the force of friction of the student on the floor?

2 a) The weight of an object of mass 100 kg on the Moon is 160 N.

   i) Calculate the gravitational field strength on the Moon.

   ii) Calculate the weight of the object on the Earth's surface.

   The gravitational field strength near the Earth's surface is 10 N/kg.

b) Calculate the acceleration and the resultant force in each of the following situations.

   i) A sprinter of mass 80 kg accelerates from rest to a speed of 9.6 m/s in 1.2 s.

   ii) A train of mass 70 000 kg decelerates from a velocity of 16 m/s to a standstill in 40 s without change of direction.

3 The figure shows the velocity–time graphs for a metal object X dropped in air and a similar object Y dropped in a tank of water.

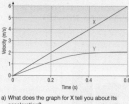

a) What does the graph for X tell you about its acceleration?

b) In terms of the forces acting on Y, explain why it reached a constant velocity.

EXAM-STYLE QUESTIONS

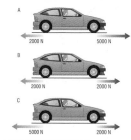

A car travels on a straight, level road. The diagrams show the car at three stages, **A**, **B** and **C** of its journey. The arrows show the forward and backward forces acting on the car.

(a) What is happening to the car at:

   (i) Stage A?

   (ii) Stage B?

   (iii) Stage C?

(b) The driver of the car sees some traffic lights ahead change to red. He applies the brakes. Between seeing the lights change and applying the brakes, there is a time delay called the reaction time.

   (i) Suggest two things that would increase the reaction time of the driver.

   (ii) Suggest two things that would increase the braking distance of the car.

(c) The manufacturer of the car makes the same model but with three different engine sizes. The designers wanted to test which model had the highest top speed. They used light gates (sensors) and data loggers to take their measurements. Why didn't they use stopwatches to collect their data?

EXAM-STYLE ANSWERS

1 a) i) Accelerating   *(1 mark)*

   ii) Travelling at a steady speed   *(1 mark)*

   iii) Decelerating   *(1 mark)*

b) i) Tiredness/taking drugs/drinking alcohol – any two

                                                  (2 marks)

   ii) Wet road surface/poor road surface/bald tyres – any two

                                                  (2 marks)

c) The electronic equipment is more sensitive

   or

   The data collected will be more accurate with the electronic equipment

   or

   It is difficult to get accurate readings using a stopwatch when a car is going so fast   *(1 mark)*

2 a) Weight = mass × gravitational field strength   *(1 mark)*

b) Air resistance/friction   *(1 mark)*

c) Stays the same   *(1 mark)*

d) i) accelerating downwards   *(2 marks)*

   ii) moving at steady speed   *(1 mark)*

3 a) Accelerating downwards   *(1 mark)*

b) i) 55 m/s   *(1 mark)*

   ii) The drag (air resistance) force on her increases   *(1 mark)*
   as her velocity increases   *(1 mark)*
   when it is equal to her weight she travels at a constant (terminal) velocity   *(1 mark)*

c) Velocity is a continuous variable   *(1 mark)*
   Time is also a continuous variable   *(1 mark)*

2 The diagram shows a sky-diver. Two forces, **X** and **Y** act on the sky-diver.

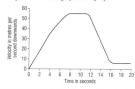

Force **Y** is the weight of the sky-diver.

(a) Write down the equation which links weight, gravitational field strength and mass. (1)

(b) What causes force **X**? (1)

(c) As the sky-diver falls, the size of force **X** increases. What happens to the size of force **Y**? (1)

(d) Describe the motion of the sky-diver when:

(i) force **X** is smaller than force **Y**.

(ii) force **X** is equal to force **Y**. (3)

3 The graph shows how the velocity of a parachutist changes with time during a parachute jump.

(a) Describe the motion of the parachutist during the first 4 seconds of the jump. (1)

(b) (i) What is the terminal velocity of the parachutist before her parachute opens? (1)

(ii) Explain in terms of the forces acting on the parachutist why she reaches terminal velocity. (3)

(c) Explain why the data shown above can be presented as a line graph. (2)

Weighty problems

Weight is something we are all familiar with and take very much for granted. You now understand that it is the force of gravity acting on a mass. In the past this realisation had a big impact on science. Sir Isaac Newton attempted to explain why the Earth didn't fall apart as it spun on its own axis. Many people thought the Earth can't be spinning because it would fall apart if it was. Newton worked out that the force of gravity was easily strong enough to stop the Earth falling apart. Newton suggested a way the Earth's spinning motion could be tested: dropping an object from the top of a very tall tower.

The commonly accepted theory was that the object would fall to Earth behind the tower. Newton said that as the top of the tower was travelling much faster than the surface of the Earth, it would fall in front of the tower. Unfortunately there was not a tower tall enough to test the prediction!

Newton even worked out that gravity would eventually take the object to the centre of the Earth if it were able to go through the Earth. Robert Hooke pointed out an error in Newton's thinking and suggested it would follow an ellipse around the centre of the Earth.

Newton worked on this idea and many years later Edmund Halley used Newton's calculations to work out when a comet would return to be seen from the Earth. Halley died aged 85, some 16 years before his prediction about the comet was proved to be correct.

Use this passage to help you to answer these questions.

a) The observation that the Earth did not fall apart as it rotated produced which hypothesis from Newton? (1)

b) What was the prediction that was made from this hypothesis? (1)

c) What was the unscientific expectation for the object falling from the tower? (1)

d) What was the technology that was missing to test this prediction? (1)

Theories are there to be tested. Newton's theories about motion needed to be tested.

e) What was Halley's prediction that had been based on Newton's theories? (1)

f) Did Halley's prediction support Newton's theory? How do you know? (1)

145

HOW SCIENCE WORKS ANSWERS

a) That the force of gravity was much stronger than the forces that might make it fall apart.

b) That an object falling from a high tower would hit the ground in front of the tower.

c) That the object would fall behind the tower.

d) A very tall tower was missing in the testing.

e) That the comet would reappear at a certain date.

f) Yes, the comet reappeared at the time that Halley predicted from Newton's calculations.

How science works teaching suggestions

• **Literacy guidance**
  • Key terms that should be clearly understood: observation, prediction, hypothesis, theory.
  • Question e) expects a longer answer, where students can practise their literacy skills.

• **Higher- and lower-level answers.** Question e) is a higher-level question and the answers provided above are also at this level. Questions c) and d) are lower level and the answers provided are also lower level.

• **Gifted and talented.** Able students could spend some time discussing e) and perhaps studying the relationship between Hooke and Newton. Able students should appreciate that developments in understanding of space have often used predictions for the occurrence of features that have not been discovered. Their discovery then supports the theory.

• **How and when to use these questions.** When wishing to develop the links between hypothesis, prediction, testing and theory.
  The questions could be used for whole class discussion or for homework with a very able group.

• **Special needs.** Considerable support will be needed to access this topic with less-able students

• **ICT link-up.** Students could carry out research on the Internet into the relationship between Hooke and Newton.

Exam teaching suggestions

• Students should be clear that the term 'steady speed' means a constant speed.

• In everyday language 'mass' and 'weight' are used to mean the same thing. Students must be very clear that in physics they have different meanings, and that weight is a force and always acts vertically downwards.

• A common misconception is that for an object to keep moving at a steady speed there must be a resultant force acting on it. Emphasise to students that a resultant force always causes an acceleration. For an object moving at a steady speed the resultant force must be zero.

• Remind students that frictional forces are always in a direction that opposes motion.

• In questions about 'changes', such as changing forces, students must state whether quantities increase or decrease in order to gain all the marks.

P2 3.1

Energy and work

Students should learn that:

- The term 'work' means the amount of energy transferred to a body.

- When a force is used to move an object, work is done against friction and this is transferred as thermal energy.

LEARNING OUTCOMES

Most students should be able to:

- State that the 'work done' is the amount of energy transferred.

- Calculate the work done when a force moves an object through a distance.

Some students should also be able to:

- Perform calculations including the rearrangement of the work done equation.

Teaching suggestions

- **Gifted and talented.** These students could look into the more formal definition of work done. This is 'that the work done is equal to the force required multiplied by the distance travelled **in the direction** of the force'. This can lead to analysis of an object moving up slopes, where the direction travelled and direction of the force are not the same.

- **Learning styles**

  Kinaesthetic: Carrying out practical tasks.

  Visual: Displaying and presenting results of the activity.

  Auditory: Discussing the effect of friction on movement.

  Interpersonal: Discussing and evaluating the experiments.

  Intrapersonal: Reflecting on the limitation of results.

- **Homework.** The frictional forces on rapidly moving objects are very high. The SR-71 'Blackbird' spy plane used to leak quite a bit of fuel when on the ground, but when it was at full speed it became hotter and the metal expanded and sealed up the gaps. Ask: 'What colour was the plane and why?'

SPECIFICATION LINK-UP   Unit: Physics 2.12.3

- *When a force causes a body to move through a distance, energy is transferred and work is done.*
- *Work done = energy transferred*
- *The amount of work done, force and distance are related by the equation:*

  work done = force applied $\times$ distance moved in direction of force
  (joule, J)   (newton, N)   (metre, m)
- *Work done against frictional forces is mainly transformed into heat.*

Lesson structure

STARTER

Hard at work – Give the students a list of activities and ask them to put them in order of the amount of energy transferred. (5 minutes)

Energy transfer – The students should draw energy transfer diagrams for a range of machines and identify useful energy output. (5–10 minutes)

Energy recap – Ask the students to draw a mind map or concept map showing what they remember about energy and energy transfer. (10 minutes)

MAIN

- The term 'work done' has a very particular meaning in physics and the students will have to accept that it does not mean the same as its everyday usage.

- Two main types of work can be done: work done against a force (as covered in this topic) and work done heating. The examples when people are holding up a heavy object but are doing no mechanical work, should be discussed in terms of energy being transferred to heat by the muscles.

- The calculation is relatively straightforward, but check that the students are confident with it and that they remember to use the correct units.

- In the main practical activity, the students should quickly realise the limitations of the experiments; it is easy to measure the amount of useful work done but very difficult to even estimate how much energy is being wasted.

- They might like to think about ways in which the energy wasted as heat could be measured using their understanding of how the body removes excess heat energy. They should eventually reach, or be lead to, the conclusion that the experiment would have to be carried out in an enclosed room where all of the energy radiated away or carried by evaporating sweat could be accounted for.

- Students could be reminded of the importance of maintaining the correct body temperature and of the ways the body manages this, even when larger amounts of heat are being produced by the muscles.

- The heating effect due to friction should be demonstrated in some way, even if it is simple hand rubbing. You may be able to find footage of Formula One cars braking, where the brake disks literally glow red hot.

- This can lead to a discussion about how frictional forces can be reduced, and how thermal energy can be removed; touching on earlier work.

PLENARIES

Work or not? – Give the students a set of statements about activities and ask them to put them into two piles: 'work is done' and 'no work done'. (5 minutes)

Demonstrating friction – The students design their own demonstration to show that doing work against friction has a heating effect. (10 minutes)

Human efficiency – Ask the students to outline how they would perform an experiment to measure the energy output of a human being over a period of one day, so that they could estimate the efficiency of the human. (10–15 minutes)

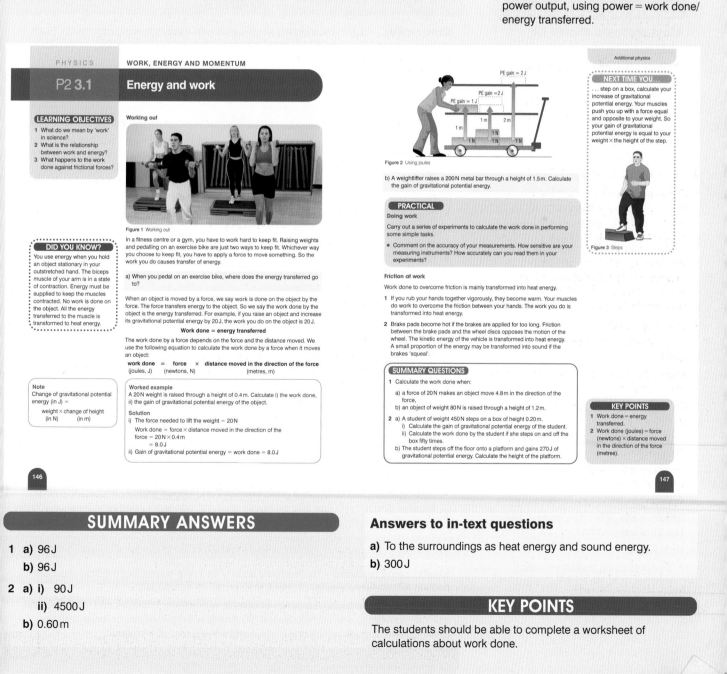

ACTIVITY & EXTENSION IDEAS

Work done against friction

To show that the work done against frictional force causes heating you can use a bicycle.

Equipment and materials required

A bicycle that will stand upside down, gloves.

Details

Turn the bike upside down and get the wheel spinning by turning the pedal by hand. Don't go too fast because you now need to stop the wheel by slowing it down with the palm of your gloved hand against the tyre. Once you know the right speed to cause a noticeable heating effect but no hand damage, you can get a volunteer to have a go. As an alternative you could lift the rear wheel and drive it very quickly before applying the brakes gently. Repeat this until the smell of burning rubber is obvious.

Practical support

Work done during tasks

Any tasks preformed should be relatively simple and non-strenuous. Make sure that the students have no medical conditions that could be triggered by the activities.

Equipment and materials needed

This depends on the exact activity but typically a bench, lots of 1 kg masses, a range of newtonmeters and stopwatches.

Details

- There are many suitable tasks such as standing on and off benches, lifting a set of objects onto shelves or dragging objects or such like. The students will need to know the weight of the objects moved (newtonmeters or bathroom scales) and the heights lifted to (metre rules or tape measures).

- You might like to link back to power, getting the students to measure the time it takes to do the task and sort out the power output, using power = work done/ energy transferred.

PHYSICS   WORK, ENERGY AND MOMENTUM

P2 3.1   Energy and work

LEARNING OBJECTIVES

1 What do we mean by 'work' in science?
2 What is the relationship between work and energy?
3 What happens to the work done against frictional forces?

Working out

Figure 1 Working out

In a fitness centre or a gym, you have to work hard to keep fit. Raising weights and pedalling on an exercise bike are just two ways to keep fit. Whichever way you choose to keep fit, you have to apply a force to move something. So the work you do causes transfer of energy.

a) When you pedal on an exercise bike, where does the energy transferred go to?

When an object is moved by a force, we say work is done on the object by the force. The force transfers energy to the object. So we say the work done on the object is the energy transferred. For example, if you raise an object and increase its gravitational potential energy by 20 J, the work you do on the object is 20 J.

Work done = energy transferred

The work done by a force depends on the force and the distance moved. We use the following equation to calculate the work done by a force when it moves an object:

work done = force × distance moved in the direction of the force
(joules, J)   (newtons, N)   (metres, m)

DID YOU KNOW?

You use energy when you hold an object stationary in your outstretched hand. The biceps muscle of your arm is in a state of contraction. Energy must be supplied to keep the muscles contracted. No work is done on the object. All the energy transferred to the muscle is transformed to heat energy.

Note

Change of gravitational potential energy (in J) =

weight × change of height
(in N)   (in m)

Worked example

A 20 N weight is raised through a height of 0.4 m. Calculate i) the work done, ii) the gain of gravitational potential energy of the object.

Solution

i) The force needed to lift the weight = 20 N

Work done = force × distance moved in the direction of the force
= 20 N × 0.4 m
= 8.0 J

ii) Gain of gravitational potential energy = work done = 8.0 J

PE gain = 2 J
PE gain = 2 J
PE gain = 1 J

1 m   1 m   2 m

1 N   1 N   1 N

Figure 2 Using joules

b) A weightlifter raises a 200 N metal bar through a height of 1.5 m. Calculate the gain of gravitational potential energy.

PRACTICAL

Doing work

Carry out a series of experiments to calculate the work done in performing some simple tasks.

- Comment on the accuracy of your measurements. How sensitive are your measuring instruments? How accurately can you read them in your experiments?

Friction at work

Work done to overcome friction is mainly transformed into heat energy.

1 If you rub your hands together vigorously, they become warm. Your muscles do work to overcome the friction between your hands. The work you do is transformed into heat energy.

2 Brake pads become hot if the brakes are applied for too long. Friction between the brake pads and the wheel discs opposes the motion of the wheel. The kinetic energy of the vehicle is transformed into heat energy. A small proportion of the energy may be transformed into sound if the brakes 'squeal'.

SUMMARY QUESTIONS

1 Calculate the work done when:
   a) a force of 20 N makes an object move 4.8 m in the direction of the force,
   b) an object of weight 80 N is raised through a height of 1.2 m.

2 a) A student of weight 450 N steps on a box of height 0.20 m.
   i) Calculate the gain of gravitational potential energy of the student.
   ii) Calculate the work done by the student if she steps on and off the box fifty times.
   b) The student steps off the floor onto a platform and gains 270 J of gravitational potential energy. Calculate the height of the platform.

NEXT TIME YOU...

... step on a box, calculate your increase of gravitational potential energy. Your muscles push you up with a force equal and opposite to your weight. So your gain of gravitational potential energy is equal to your weight × the height of the step.

Figure 3 Steps

KEY POINTS

1 Work done = energy transferred.
2 Work done (joules) = force (newtons) × distance moved in the direction of the force (metres).

146   147

SUMMARY ANSWERS

1 a) 96 J
   b) 96 J

2 a) i) 90 J
      ii) 4500 J
   b) 0.60 m

Answers to in-text questions

a) To the surroundings as heat energy and sound energy.
b) 300 J

KEY POINTS

The students should be able to complete a worksheet of calculations about work done.

P2 3.2   Kinetic energy

LEARNING OBJECTIVES

Students should learn:

- That kinetic energy is the energy a moving object has.
- That the kinetic energy of an object increases when the object is travelling faster or is more massive.
- That elastic potential energy is energy stored in an object when work is done to change the shape of the object.
- How to calculate the kinetic energy of a moving object. [**HT** only]

LEARNING OUTCOMES

Most students should be able to:

- Explain how the kinetic energy of an object depends on the speed and mass of the object.
- Describe situations where elastic potential energy is stored.

Some students should also be able to:

- Perform calculations using the kinetic energy equation including those that involve rearrangement of the equation. [**HT** only]

Teaching suggestions

- **Gifted and talented.** Students talented in design could build their own elastic powered vehicles and hold a competition on whose can go furthest. The vehicles should all have identical elastic bands and could be cars, boats or aeroplanes. The results can lead to a discussion about which mode of transport is the most efficient.

- **Learning styles**

  Kinaesthetic: Building models.

  Visual: Making detailed observations of moving objects.

  Auditory: Defining key words and units.

  Interpersonal: Reporting and discussing results of experiments.

- **Homework**
  - Students could build their elastic vehicles at home for a future lesson.
  - They could find out the record distance/flight times for these toys.

SPECIFICATION LINK-UP   Unit: Physics 2.12.3

- *For an object that is able to recover its original shape, elastic potential is the energy stored in an object when work is done on the object to change its shape.*
- *The kinetic energy of a body depends on its mass and its speed.*
- *Calculate the kinetic energy of a body using the equation:*

$$\text{kinetic energy} = \tfrac{1}{2} \times \quad \text{mass} \quad \times \quad \text{speed}^2$$
$$\text{(joule, J)} \qquad \text{(kilogram, kg)} \quad \text{((metre/second)}^2, \text{(m/s)}^2) \quad \textbf{[HT only]}$$

Students should use their skills, knowledge and understanding of 'How Science Works':

- *to discuss the transformation of kinetic energy to other forms of energy in particular situations.*

Lesson structure

STARTER

Kinetic cards – Give the students a set of cards with various moving objects on. Each card shows the mass and the velocity; the students have to put them into order with least kinetic energy to most. (5 minutes)

Mass and velocity – Using mini-whiteboards, the students must give accurate definitions of mass and velocity. Ask: 'What are the units of each?' (5 minutes)

MAIN

- The students should remember that moving objects have energy and this is called 'kinetic energy'. Some will still be using the term 'movement energy', but it is time to leave this behind and get them to use the correct term.
- The 'investigating kinetic energy' practical task works well with light gates. If you don't have them then the modified version is a reasonable alternative.
- There are a few sources of error in the results and this would be a good opportunity to look into the nature of taking measurements ('How Science Works') and how repeating readings can improve the quality of the data.
- You could have a set of results in a spreadsheet table so that you can show the relationship graphically, or let the students enter data as they go along. (This relates to 'How Science Works': relationships between variables.)
- Clearly many students will not come up with the relationship themselves, although most will see that the relationship is not a simple linear one. It is more important to show that the data fits a pattern that we already know.
- Some of the students will have a problem with the '½' in the kinetic energy equation and ask you: 'half of what?' This is tricky to explain without going into the derivation, so tell the students that they will find out if they go on to study A level Physics.
- The kinetic energy equation is the most difficult one that the higher attaining students need to rearrange, and you should lead them through this carefully.
- The elastic potential ideas are a bit simpler, but the students will need to be able to give a reasonable definition like the one in their textbook.
- It is important that the students realise that it is not only elastic bands that are elastic. Show them some springs and sponge, or even a football, and explain how energy is stored in these when they are distorted.
- Making elastic band toys is a good endpoint and shows another important energy transfer. The models can also be tested applying concepts from 'How Science Works' in another lesson.

PLENARIES

Kinetic cards revisited – Try the same activity as in the starter, but the students now have to calculate the energy to check their order. (5–10 minutes)

Higher/lower – Go through a series of objects with different masses and velocities and ask the students to say (or calculate) if the kinetic energy is higher or lower than the previous one. Include a trick one that's exactly the same. (5 minutes)

Practical support

Investigating kinetic energy

This experiment can be demonstrated with a ball and motion sensor or with a dynamics trolley and light gates.

Equipment and materials required (Ball)

A ramp (or drainpipe), tennis ball, velocity or distance sensor, balance to measure mass of object.

Details

If you don't have a velocity sensor then the software may be able to convert the distance measurements into speed measurements. Some velocity sensors have two parts; one of which needs to be mounted on the moving object. Clearly a ball won't do so a trolley can be used.

Equipment and materials required (Trolley)

Long ramp, dynamics trolley, card of known length, light gate, balance to measure mass of object.

Details

Mount the card on the trolley so that it interrupts the light gate when it passes through. Position the trolley at various measured heights on the track so that it rolls down the track and its speed is measured at the bottom. The ramp works well at an angle of around 30°.

Alternative equipment

It is possible to measure the speed of the object by letting it pass through a measured distance and timing it with a stopwatch. For this you will need to ensure that the object isn't travelling very fast, so shallow launch angles will be needed. To improve the results, the students will have to repeat each roll several times; this can lead to a discussion about the accuracy of the measurements and the value of repeat readings.

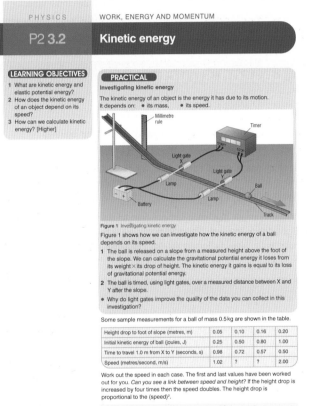

P2 3.2 Kinetic energy

LEARNING OBJECTIVES

1 What are kinetic energy and elastic potential energy?
2 How does the kinetic energy of an object depend on its speed?
3 How can we calculate kinetic energy? [Higher]

PRACTICAL

Investigating kinetic energy

The kinetic energy of an object is the energy it has due to its motion. It depends on: • its mass, • its speed.

Figure 1 shows how we can investigate how the kinetic energy of a ball depends on its speed.

1 The ball is released on a slope from a measured height above the foot of the slope. We can calculate the gravitational potential energy it loses from its weight × its drop of height. The kinetic energy it gains is equal to its loss of gravitational potential energy.

2 The ball is timed, using light gates, over a measured distance between X and Y after the slope.

• Why do light gates improve the quality of the data you can collect in this investigation?

Some sample measurements for a ball of mass 0.5 kg are shown in the table.

Height drop to foot of slope (metres, m)	0.05	0.10	0.16	0.20
Initial kinetic energy of ball (joules, J)	0.25	0.50	0.80	1.00
Time to travel 1.0 m from X to Y (seconds, s)	0.98	0.72	0.57	0.50
Speed (metres/second, m/s)	1.02	?	?	2.00

Work out the speed in each case. The first and last values have been worked out for you. *Can you see a link between speed and height?* If the height drop is increased by four times then the speed doubles. The height drop is proportional to the (speed)².

a) Check the other measurements to see if they fit this rule.

Figure 1 Investigating kinetic energy

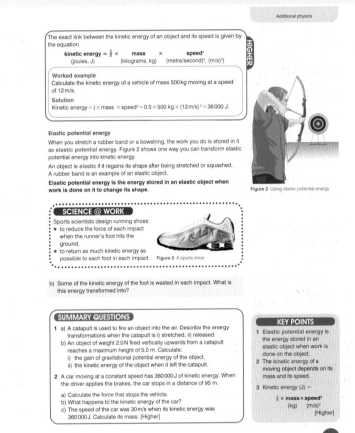

The exact link between the kinetic energy of an object and its speed is given by the equation

$$\text{kinetic energy} = \tfrac{1}{2} \times \text{mass} \times \text{speed}^2$$
$$\text{(joules, J)} \quad \text{(kilograms, kg)} \quad \text{(metre/second)}^2, \text{(m/s)}^2)$$

Worked example

Calculate the kinetic energy of a vehicle of mass 500 kg moving at a speed of 12 m/s.

Solution

Kinetic energy $= \tfrac{1}{2} \times \text{mass} \times \text{speed}^2 = 0.5 \times 500 \text{ kg} \times (12 \text{ m/s})^2 = 36\,000$ J.

Elastic potential energy

When you stretch a rubber band or a bowstring, the work you do is stored in it as elastic potential energy. Figure 2 shows one way you can transform elastic potential energy into kinetic energy.

An object is elastic if it regains its shape after being stretched or squashed. A rubber band is an example of an elastic object.

Elastic potential energy is the energy stored in an elastic object when work is done on it to change its shape.

Figure 2 Using elastic potential energy

SCIENCE @ WORK

Sports scientists design running shoes:
• to reduce the force of each impact when the runner's foot hits the ground,
• to return as much kinetic energy as possible to each foot in each impact.

Figure 3 A sports shoe

b) Some of the kinetic energy of the foot is wasted in each impact. What is this energy transformed into?

SUMMARY QUESTIONS

1 a) A catapult is used to fire an object into the air. Describe the energy transformations when the catapult is i) stretched, ii) released.
 b) An object of weight 2.0 N fired vertically upwards from a catapult reaches a maximum height of 5.0 m. Calculate:
  i) the gain of gravitational potential energy of the object,
  ii) the kinetic energy of the object when it left the catapult.

2 A car moving at a constant speed has 360 000 J of kinetic energy. When the driver applies the brakes, the car stops in a distance of 95 m.
 a) Calculate the force that stops the vehicle.
 b) What happens to the kinetic energy of the car?
 c) The speed of the car was 30 m/s when its kinetic energy was 360 000 J. Calculate its mass. [Higher]

KEY POINTS

1 Elastic potential energy is the energy stored in an elastic object when work is done on the object.
2 The kinetic energy of a moving object depends on its mass and its speed.
3 Kinetic energy (J) =
 $\tfrac{1}{2} \times \text{mass} \times \text{speed}^2$
 (kg)   (m/s)²
 [Higher]

SUMMARY ANSWERS

1 a) i) Chemical energy from the loader is transferred into elastic potential energy of the catapult and some is wasted as heat energy.
  ii) Elastic potential energy in the catapult is transformed into kinetic energy of the object and the rubber band and heat energy (plus a little sound energy).

 b) i) 10 J ii) 10 J

2 a) 3800 N
 b) Friction due to the brakes transforms it from kinetic energy of the car to heat energy in the brakes.
 c) 800 kg.

Answers to in-text questions

a) 1.38 m/s gives 0.5 J of kinetic energy, 1.75 m/s gives 0.8 J of kinetic energy.

b) Heat energy transferred to the surroundings, the foot and the shoe; also sound energy.

KEY POINTS

The students should be able to calculate the kinetic energy of a moving object.

P2 3.3 Momentum

Teaching suggestions

- **Special needs.** As before, a layout template for calculations will help a great deal.
- **Gifted and talented.** Who came up with the ideas about forces and momentum? What is inertia? The students can look up and explain Newton's laws of motion. Ask: 'Why is conservation of momentum considered a very important part of physics?'
- **Learning styles**
  Kinaesthetic: Playing a game of real or virtual snooker.
  Visual: Observing collisions between objects.
  Auditory: Listening to the concept of momentum.
  Interpersonal: Discussing and evaluating the collision demonstrations.
  Intrapersonal: Making deductions about momentum being conserved from experimental evidence.
- **ICT link-up.** Detailed models are available to simulate these collisions. These can be used as a demonstration for individual student use. Snooker or pool games can also be used. See examples at www.fable.co.uk or www.sunflowerlearning.com.

SPECIFICATION LINK-UP   Unit: Physics 2.12.4

- *Momentum has both magnitude and direction.*
- *Momentum, mass and velocity are related by the equation:*

$$\text{momentum} = \text{mass} \times \text{velocity}$$
(kilogram metre/second, kg m/s)   (kilogram, m)   (metre/second, m/s)

- *When a force acts on a body that is moving, or able to move, a change in momentum occurs.*
- *Momentum is conserved in any collision/explosion provided no external forces act on the colliding/exploding bodies.*

Students should use their skills, knowledge and understanding of 'How Science Works':

- *to use the conservation of momentum (in one dimension) to calculate the mass, velocity or momentum of a body involved in a collision or explosion.*

Lesson structure

STARTER

Trying to stop – The students should explain why it takes an oil tanker several kilometres to stop, but a bicycle can stop in only a few metres. (5–10 minutes)

Stopping power – Give the students a set of cards with various sports balls on them. Ask the students to put them in order of difficulty to stop, and then explain what properties make the balls more difficult. (5–10 minutes)

Who is toughest? – The students must design a simple test to determine who is the most difficult person in a rugby team to stop. The test must be a fair one and produce measurable results. (This relates to 'How Science Works': designing a fair test.) (10 minutes)

MAIN

- It is best to begin with a discussion about trying to stop something moving or start something off. Trains are a good example of something with a large mass that can travel quickly. The students will know how long it takes a train to get up to speed and how long it takes it to stop, even in an emergency.
- The demonstration will take a little time to explain, but should give good results. Any discrepancies should be accounted for using the idea that external forces (frictional) have changed the momentum.
- Conservation of momentum is a fundamental concept in physics; just as important as conservation of energy.
- You could talk about the famous jumping 'everybody in China jumping at the same time' idea. It is a scientific myth that this would cause an earthquake or even change the orbit of the Earth. This would actually have no real effect on the Earth at all.
- The shunting affect can be demonstrated by a Newton's Cradle. This can be improvised from a set of ping-pong balls on wire, or similar, if a real one is not available.
- The calculation is a multi-stage one and these often confuse students. Make sure they have plenty of practice calculating the momentum of objects before they try to work out velocities after collisions.
- To extend students, you can look at collisions where both of the trolleys are moving before the collision or collisions where the trolleys 'bounce off' and end up travelling in opposite directions.

PLENARIES

The skate escape – Two people are trapped on a **perfectly** friction-free circular surface just out of reach of each other. They are both 10 m from the edge and all that they have to help them escape is a tennis ball. Ask: 'How do they escape?' (10 minutes)

Impossibly super – In several films, super heroes stop cars or trains by standing in front of them and letting them crash into them. The cars stop dead and the costumed hero doesn't move an inch. Ask: 'What's wrong with the science here?' (10 minutes)

Calculation dominoes – Give groups of students a set of domino cards with questions and numerical answers. Let them play dominoes with them. (5–10 minutes)

Practical support

Investigating collisions

This activity can be carried out with dynamics trolleys or a linear air track. Two light gates are required.

Equipment and materials required

Two or three dynamics trolleys or gliders on a linear air track, card of known length, two light gates.

Details

Mount the card on the first trolley so that it passes through a light gate before the collision. The trolleys can be made to stick together using Velcro or a pin and bit of cork. After the collision, they should pass through the second light gate to measure the new velocity. Keep the light gates close to the collision point so that the trolleys do not slow down too much. If the trolleys have the same mass then the velocity should simply half after the collision. If frictional forces are affecting the result, it is possible to tilt the track slightly, so that the frictional force is balanced by a small component of the weight of the trolleys. It is important to try this if a detailed investigation is taking place.

ACTIVITY & EXTENSION IDEAS

Snooker loopy

Real snooker balls or a computer game can help to show the idea of momentum.

Equipment and materials required

Mini snooker game (bigger is better though) or computer snooker game.

Details

Play the game but use it to show that the balls keep on rolling unless there is a force acting on them. A ball that is hit hard has a lot of momentum and is difficult to stop, but if it hits a group of balls the momentum is quickly transferred to them (smash the white into the pack). The car shunting idea can also be demonstrated using the balls, and you could even line them up so that the last one goes in.

Answers to in-text questions

a) 240 kg m/s

b) 0.48 m/s

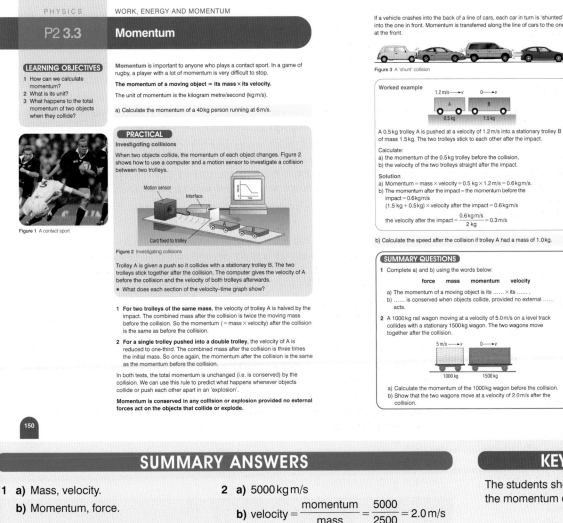

PHYSICS WORK, ENERGY AND MOMENTUM

P2 3.3 Momentum

LEARNING OBJECTIVES

1 How can we calculate momentum?
2 What is its unit?
3 What happens to the total momentum of two objects when they collide?

Momentum is important to anyone who plays a contact sport. In a game of rugby, a player with a lot of momentum is very difficult to stop.

The momentum of a moving object = its mass × its velocity.

The unit of momentum is the kilogram metre/second (kg m/s).

a) Calculate the momentum of a 40 kg person running at 6 m/s.

PRACTICAL

Investigating collisions

When two objects collide, the momentum of each object changes. Figure 2 shows how to use a computer and a motion sensor to investigate a collision between two trolleys.

Figure 1 A contact sport

Figure 2 Investigating collisions

Trolley A is given a push so it collides with a stationary trolley B. The two trolleys stick together after the collision. The computer gives the velocity of A before the collision and the velocity of both trolleys afterwards.

• What does each section of the velocity-time graph show?

1 **For two trolleys of the same mass**, the velocity of trolley A is halved by the impact. The combined mass after the collision is twice the moving mass before the collision. So the momentum (= mass × velocity) after the collision is the same as before the collision.

2 **For a single trolley pushed into a double trolley**, the velocity of A is reduced to one-third. The combined mass after the collision is three times the initial mass. So once again, the momentum after the collision is the same as the momentum before the collision.

In both tests, the total momentum is unchanged (i.e. is conserved) by the collision. We can use this rule to predict what happens whenever objects collide or push each other apart in an 'explosion'.

Momentum is conserved in any collision or explosion provided no external forces act on the objects that collide or explode.

If a vehicle crashes into the back of a line of cars, each car in turn is 'shunted' into the one in front. Momentum is transferred along the line of cars to the one at the front.

Figure 3 A 'shunt' collision

Worked example

A 0.5 kg trolley A is pushed at a velocity of 1.2 m/s into a stationary trolley B of mass 1.5 kg. The two trolleys stick to each other after the impact.

Calculate:
a) the momentum of the 0.5 kg trolley before the collision,
b) the velocity of the two trolleys straight after the impact.

Solution

a) Momentum = mass × velocity = 0.5 kg × 1.2 m/s = 0.6 kg m/s.
b) The momentum after the impact = the momentum before the impact = 0.6 kg m/s
   (1.5 kg + 0.5 kg) × velocity after the impact = 0.6 kg m/s
   the velocity after the impact = $\dfrac{0.6 \text{ kg m/s}}{2 \text{ kg}}$ = 0.3 m/s.

b) Calculate the speed after the collision if trolley A had a mass of 1.0 kg.

GET IT RIGHT!

The unit of momentum is kg m/s (or N s). In calculations always give a unit with your answer. Remember that momentum has a size and direction.

SUMMARY QUESTIONS

1 Complete a) and b) using the words below:

   force   mass   momentum   velocity

   a) The momentum of a moving object is its ...... × its ....
   b) ...... is conserved when objects collide, provided no external ...... acts.

2 A 1000 kg rail wagon moving at a velocity of 5.0 m/s on a level track collides with a stationary 1500 kg wagon. The two wagons move together after the collision.

   a) Calculate the momentum of the 1000 kg wagon before the collision.
   b) Show that the two wagons move at a velocity of 2.0 m/s after the collision.

KEY POINTS

1 Momentum (kg m/s) = mass (kg) × velocity (m/s).
2 Momentum is conserved whenever objects interact, provided no external forces act on them.

SUMMARY ANSWERS

1 a) Mass, velocity.
  b) Momentum, force.

2 a) 5000 kg m/s
  b) velocity = $\dfrac{\text{momentum}}{\text{mass}} = \dfrac{5000}{2500} = 2.0$ m/s

KEY POINTS

The students should be able to calculate the momentum of an object.

P2 3.4   More on collisions and explosions

LEARNING OBJECTIVES

Students should learn that:

- Momentum is a vector quantity and the direction of travel is important in collisions.
- There is no change in momentum in an explosion.

LEARNING OUTCOMES

Students should be able to:

- State that the total momentum before and after an explosion is the same, provided no external forces act.
- Describe how the launching of a bullet causes recoil.

Some students should also be able to:

- Explain that momentum is conserved in all interactions that do not include external forces.
- Apply the conservation of momentum to perform calculations where an explosion occurs causing two objects to recoil from each other.

Teaching suggestions

- **Special needs.** Momentum conservation questions are best posed as a set of diagrams showing the situation before and after the collisions. The students can be led through the calculations with a calculation template until they are more comfortable with the technique.

- **Gifted and talented.**
  - Ask: 'Why doesn't momentum change?' The students could try to link the idea of conservation of momentum to equal and opposite forces. Ask: 'What exactly is a force? What is the scientific definition?'
  - Mathematically skilled students could look at collisions in two dimensions and calculate the resulting velocities.

- **Learning styles**
  Kinaesthetic: Recording results from experiments.
  Visual: Watching demonstration of explosions.
  Auditory: Discussing limitations in the explosion model.
  Interpersonal: Discussing and evaluating the suitability of crash test dummies to model collisions.

SPECIFICATION LINK-UP   Unit: Physics 2.12.4

- *Momentum has both magnitude and direction.*
- *Momentum, mass and velocity are related by the equation:*

  $$\text{momentum} = \text{mass} \times \text{velocity}$$
  (kilogram metre/second, kg m/s)   (kilogram, m)   (metre/second, m/s)

- *When a force acts on a body that is moving, or able to move, a change in momentum occurs.*
- *Momentum is conserved in any collision/explosion provided no external forces act on the colliding/exploding bodies.*

Students should use their skills, knowledge and understanding of 'How Science Works':

- *to use the conservation of momentum (in one dimension) to calculate the mass, velocity or momentum of a body involved in a collision or explosion.*

Lesson structure

STARTER

Explaining explosions – Give the students a set of cards explaining how a chemical explosion causes a projectile to be fired from a cannon. They must sort them into order. (5–10 minutes)

Slow motion – Show a video of a simple explosion frame by frame and ask the students to explain what is happening. (Search for explosion at video.google.com.) (5–10 minutes)

Jumping frogs – Position a few spring-loaded jumping frog toys on the desk and set them off. The students have to explain the energy transfers before they all go off. (5–10 minutes)

MAIN

- Students may only think of explosions as chemical explosions instead of simple spring ones. Talk about an explosion being caused when some kind of stored energy (chemical or elastic) is suddenly transferred into kinetic.

- The explosion experiment usually works well, but you might want to repeat it a couple of times and analyse the mean results. This gives an opportunity for the students to consider the errors inherent in these measurements and why repeat readings are so important. This is an excellent opportunity to explore concepts in 'How Science Works'.

- Show the students some footage of crash test dummies search the web for 'crash test dummy video'.

- A good way of showing the recoil effect of firing a shell from a gun is to show a field gun in operation. These are really quite large and are knocked backwards significantly. When firing a 'twenty-one gun salute', there is little backwards movement because no shell is fired.

- The calculation can be very difficult for many students so lead them through it carefully.

- You can discuss the energy transfers involved with the damping spring and perhaps link this to the suspension on cars.

- The students should be made to realise that the gun has to have much more mass that the projectile, otherwise it would recoil at very high velocities. A modern shell is fired at velocities of up to 1000 m/s and may have a mass of 100 kg.

PLENARIES

Boating – Discuss what happens when somebody steps onto a boat but falls in the water because the boat moves away. Ask the students to explain what happened, perhaps with diagrams. (5 minutes)

Practical support

Investigating a controlled explosion

This demonstration can be used to show that momentum is conserved in explosions.

Equipment and materials required

Four dynamics trolleys, two light gates or velocity sensors or wooden blocks.

Details

- This experiment can be carried out with wooden blocks as shown in the Student Book or with light gates or velocity sensors to measure the speed. If the sensors are used then use interrupter cards as in previous experiments. The momentum of the objects can be calculated using the equation.

- You should make sure that the sensors are positioned close to the explosion point so that not too much energy is lost due to friction. The same kind of experiment can be carried out with a linear air track.

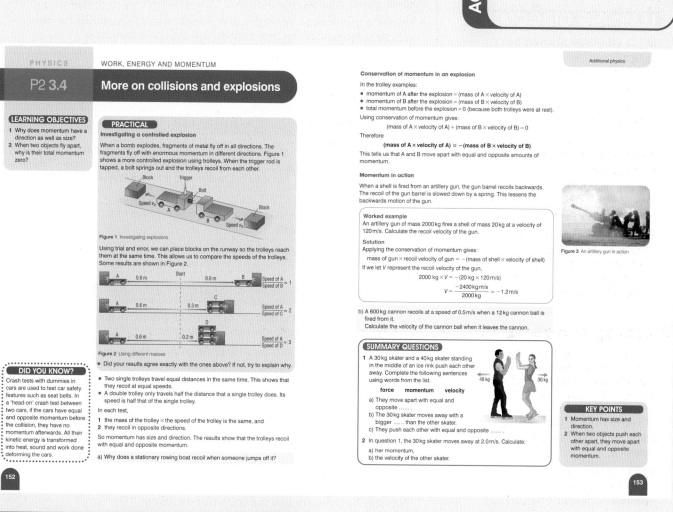

PHYSICS WORK, ENERGY AND MOMENTUM

P2 3.4 More on collisions and explosions

Additional physics

LEARNING OBJECTIVES

1 Why does momentum have a direction as well as size?
2 When two objects fly apart, why is their total momentum zero?

PRACTICAL

Investigating a controlled explosion

When a bomb explodes, fragments of metal fly off in all directions. The fragments fly off with enormous momentum in different directions. Figure 1 shows a more controlled explosion using trolleys. When the trigger rod is tapped, a bolt springs out and the trolleys recoil from each other.

Figure 1 Investigating explosions

Using trial and error, we can place blocks on the runway so the trolleys reach them at the same time. This allows us to compare the speeds of the trolleys. Some results are shown in Figure 2.

Figure 2 Using different masses

- Did your results agree exactly with the ones above? If not, try to explain why.

- Two single trolleys travel equal distances in the same time. This shows that they recoil at equal speeds.
- A double trolley only travels half the distance that a single trolley does. Its speed is half that of the single trolley.

In each test,

1 the mass of the trolley × the speed of the trolley is the same, and
2 they recoil in opposite directions.

So momentum has size and direction. The results show that the trolleys recoil with equal and opposite momentum.

a) Why does a stationary rowing boat recoil when someone jumps off it?

DID YOU KNOW?

Crash tests with dummies in cars are used to test car safety features such as seat belts. In a 'head-on' crash test between two cars, if the cars have equal and opposite momentum before the collision, they have no momentum afterwards. All their kinetic energy is transformed into heat, sound and work done deforming the cars.

Conservation of momentum in an explosion

In the trolley examples:

- momentum of A after the explosion = (mass of A × velocity of A)
- momentum of B after the explosion = (mass of B × velocity of B)
- total momentum before the explosion = 0 (because both trolleys were at rest).

Using conservation of momentum gives:

(mass of A × velocity of A) + (mass of B × velocity of B) = 0

Therefore

(mass of A × velocity of A) = −(mass of B × velocity of B)

This tells us that A and B move apart with equal and opposite amounts of momentum.

Momentum in action

When a shell is fired from an artillery gun, the gun barrel recoils backwards. The recoil of the gun barrel is slowed down by a spring. This lessens the backwards motion of the gun.

Worked example

An artillery gun of mass 2000 kg fires a shell of mass 20 kg at a velocity of 120 m/s. Calculate the recoil velocity of the gun.

Solution

Applying the conservation of momentum gives:

mass of gun × recoil velocity of gun = −(mass of shell × velocity of shell)

If we let V represent the recoil velocity of the gun,

$$2000 \text{ kg} \times V = -(20 \text{ kg} \times 120 \text{ m/s})$$

$$V = \frac{-2400 \text{ kg m/s}}{2000 \text{ kg}} = -1.2 \text{ m/s}$$

b) A 600 kg cannon recoils at a speed of 0.5 m/s when a 12 kg cannon ball is fired from it.
Calculate the velocity of the cannon ball when it leaves the cannon.

Figure 3 An artillery gun in action

SUMMARY QUESTIONS

1 A 30 kg skater and a 40 kg skater standing in the middle of an ice rink push each other away. Complete the following sentences using words from the list.

   force   momentum   velocity

a) They move apart with equal and opposite ....
b) The 30 kg skater moves away with a bigger ...... than the other skater.
c) They push each other with equal and opposite ....

2 In question 1, the 30 kg skater moves away at 2.0 m/s. Calculate:
a) her momentum,
b) the velocity of the other skater.

KEY POINTS

1 Momentum has size and direction.
2 When two objects push each other apart, they move apart with equal and opposite momentum.

152

153

SUMMARY ANSWERS

1 a) Momentum.   b) Velocity.   c) Force.

2 a) 60 kg m/s   b) 1.5 m/s

Answers to in-text questions

a) The boat and the person who jumps off move away with equal and opposite amounts of momentum.

b) 25 m/s

KEY POINTS

The students should calculate the velocity of objects moving apart from an 'explosion'.

P2 3.5 Changing momentum

Students should learn that:

- A resultant force applied to an object will change its momentum.

- The change in momentum can be found by multiplying the force by the time it acts on the object. [**HT** only]

LEARNING OUTCOMES

Most students should be able to:

- State that a resultant force will change the momentum of an object.

- Explain that the longer the force is applied for, and the larger it is, the greater the change in momentum.

Some students should also be able to:

- Calculate the change in momentum of an object from the resultant force and the time it acts. [**HT** only]

- Perform calculations involving the rearrangement of the equation: force = change of momentum/ time taken. [**HT** only]

Teaching suggestions

- **Learning styles**

  Kinaesthetic: Hurling of eggs!

  Visual: Observing different types of impact.

  Auditory: Listening to 'thuds'.

  Interpersonal: Working together on practicals.

  Intrapersonal: Solving problems.

- **Special needs**

  Provide a set of layout templates to guide the students through the calculations until they get in to the habit of laying out their work correctly.

- **Homework**
  - If there is no time in the lesson, the students could construct their egg safety capsule at home for testing next lesson.
  - Additional questions on collisions and calculating the velocity of objects before and after collisions will reinforce the students' skills.

- **Teaching assistant.** A brave teaching assistant can measure out the distances the eggs are thrown in the Olympic style.

SPECIFICATION LINK-UP   Unit: Physics 2.12.4

- *Momentum is conserved in any collision/explosion provided no external forces act on the colliding/exploding bodies.*

- *Force, change in momentum and time taken for the change are related by the equation:*

$$\text{force (newton, N)} = \frac{\text{change in momentum (kilogram metre/second, kg(m/s))}}{\text{time taken for the change (second, s)}} \quad \textbf{[HT only]}$$

Students should use their skills, knowledge and understanding of 'How Science Works':

- *to use the conservation of momentum (in one dimension) to calculate the mass, velocity or momentum of a body involved in a collision or explosion.*

Lesson structure

STARTER

Crumpled cars – Show the students selected photographs of crashed cars (search the web's images at www.google.com) and ask them to describe the damage. They should notice the crumpling effect, but may not realise that this is deliberate design. (5–10 minutes)

Crash flashback – Give the students a momentum problem to solve to refresh the ideas from the last topic. (5 minutes)

'It's not the fall that kills you' – Ask the students to explain what they think this phrase is supposed to mean. Ask: 'What is it that kills you?' (5 minutes)

MAIN

- Changing momentum and calculating the forces involved is quite a tricky concept, and some students will struggle with the mathematics.

- A good starting point is to show a video clip of crash testing (search the web for 'crash testing' video); there are a few available. You should emphasise the large amount of energy that is transferred during the collision and ask the students where they think it is transferred to.

- The 'Investigating impacts' practical clearly shows that the forces involved in impact are reduced by using a material that distorts. These plastic materials absorb some of the energy of the impact. You might like to show what happens if a spring (an elastic material) is used instead.

- The calculations will take a bit of explaining and the students will most likely need to go through the ideas a couple of times. Use plenty of examples including ones involving the trolleys or toys that you have been using.

- Impact times tend to be very short, so you may like to start with longer lasting collisions before moving on to the bullet example.

- After the maths, either demonstrate the egg throwing or let the students have a go at the egg hurling competition (see activity box). This will make the lesson more memorable!

PLENARIES

Bouncy castles – Small children often cry when they fall over, but not on bouncy castles. The students should draw a diagram showing why not. (5 minutes)

Armoured pedestrians – Can pedestrians protect themselves from car impact by wearing soft or hard materials? The students could design a system and, more importantly, point out problems with each other's designs. (10 minutes)

'Owwzatt!' – How should cricketers catch fast moving cricket balls? The students should write out instructions explaining the science behind their ideas. (5–10 minutes)

Practical support

Investigating impacts

The impacts can be investigated on a simple or more detailed level depending on time available.

Equipment and materials required

Dynamics trolley, Plasticine, motion sensor, launch ramp.

Details

- You can compare the two impacts just by observing them or by monitoring the movement with a distance sensor. The trolleys should be launched from the same height on the ramp; firstly onto the brick directly and then with a round blob of Plasticine. With the motion sensor you can then compare the two impacts, and you should be able to show that the second impact took place over a longer time. The first impact should make a nice thud, and this helps you to discuss what happened to the kinetic energy.

- You may like to see if the students can design a crumple zone for the trolley out of paper. Give each student a small amount of sticky tape and a single sheet of A4 paper, and ask them to try to make a crumple zone that they can attach to the front of a trolley to absorb the kinetic energy. The trolley can be rolled from a fixed height on a ramp to make the test fair, and the collisions observed or even measured with a motion sensor. This should give an indication of the effectiveness.

Teaching suggestions – continued

- **Science @ work.** Bullet-proof vests are remarkably complex. It isn't easy making one that is effective against all types of bullets or even knives. The art of designing armour is thousands of years old and its history can be seen as a battle between weapon-smiths and armour designers each trying to outdo each other. Currently weapons designers are a long way ahead, and even the best body armour is of little use against a high powered battlefield rifle. Search online for details of spider silk and bullet-proof vests. Strangely bullet-proof vests are illegal to wear in Australia; perhaps this is something to do with an historical incident?

Answers to in-text questions

a) If a child falls off the swing, the rubber mat reduces the impact force by increasing the impact time when the child hits the ground.

b) The force is bigger.

c) 1800 N

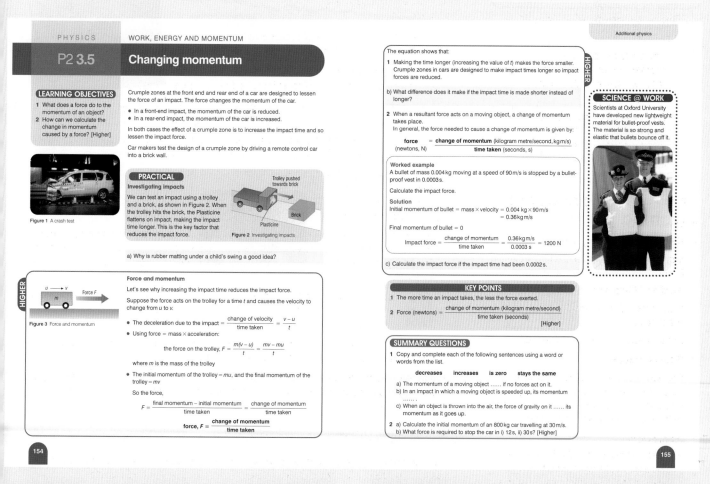

PHYSICS WORK, ENERGY AND MOMENTUM

P2 3.5 Changing momentum

LEARNING OBJECTIVES

1 What does a force do to the momentum of an object?
2 How can we calculate the change in momentum caused by a force? [Higher]

Crumple zones at the front end and rear end of a car are designed to lessen the force of an impact. The force changes the momentum of the car.

- In a front-end impact, the momentum of the car is reduced.
- In a rear-end impact, the momentum of the car is increased.

In both cases the effect of a crumple zone is to increase the impact time and so lessen the impact force.

Car makers test the design of a crumple zone by driving a remote control car into a brick wall.

Figure 1 A crash test

PRACTICAL

Investigating impacts

We can test an impact using a trolley and a brick, as shown in Figure 2. When the trolley hits the brick, the Plasticine flattens on impact, making the impact time longer. This is the key factor that reduces the impact force.

Figure 2 Investigating impacts

a) Why is rubber matting under a child's swing a good idea?

HIGHER

Force and momentum

Let's see why increasing the impact time reduces the impact force.

Suppose the force acts on the trolley for a time t and causes the velocity to change from u to v.

Figure 3 Force and momentum

- The deceleration due to the impact $= \dfrac{\text{change of velocity}}{\text{time taken}} = \dfrac{v - u}{t}$

- Using force = mass × acceleration:

  the force on the trolley, $F = \dfrac{m(v - u)}{t} = \dfrac{mv - mu}{t}$

  where m is the mass of the trolley

- The initial momentum of the trolley $= mu$, and the final momentum of the trolley $= mv$

So the force,

$$F = \dfrac{\text{final momentum} - \text{initial momentum}}{\text{time taken}} = \dfrac{\text{change of momentum}}{\text{time taken}}$$

$$\text{force, } F = \dfrac{\text{change of momentum}}{\text{time taken}}$$

The equation shows that:

1 Making the time longer (increasing the value of t) makes the force smaller. Crumple zones in cars are designed to make impact times longer so impact forces are reduced.

b) What difference does it make if the impact time is made shorter instead of longer?

2 When a resultant force acts on a moving object, a change of momentum takes place.
In general, the force needed to cause a change of momentum is given by:

$$\underset{\text{(newtons, N)}}{\text{force}} = \dfrac{\text{change of momentum (kilogram metre/second, kg m/s)}}{\text{time taken (seconds, s)}}$$

Worked example
A bullet of mass 0.004 kg moving at a speed of 90 m/s is stopped by a bullet-proof vest in 0.0003 s.

Calculate the impact force.

Solution
Initial momentum of bullet = mass × velocity = 0.004 kg × 90 m/s
= 0.36 kg m/s

Final momentum of bullet = 0

$$\text{Impact force} = \dfrac{\text{change of momentum}}{\text{time taken}} = \dfrac{0.36 \, \text{kg m/s}}{0.0003 \, \text{s}} = 1200 \, \text{N}$$

c) Calculate the impact force if the impact time had been 0.0002 s.

SCIENCE @ WORK

Scientists at Oxford University have developed new lightweight material for bullet-proof vests. The material is so strong and elastic that bullets bounce off it.

KEY POINTS

1 The more time an impact takes, the less the force exerted.

2 Force (newtons) $= \dfrac{\text{change of momentum (kilogram metre/second)}}{\text{time taken (seconds)}}$ [Higher]

SUMMARY QUESTIONS

1 Copy and complete each of the following sentences using a word or words from the list.

  decreases   increases   is zero   stays the same

  a) The momentum of a moving object ...... if no forces act on it.
  b) In an impact in which a moving object is speeded up, its momentum ....
  c) When an object is thrown into the air, the force of gravity on it ...... its momentum as it goes up.

2 a) Calculate the initial momentum of an 800 kg car travelling at 30 m/s.
  b) What force is required to stop the car in i) 12 s, ii) 30 s? [Higher]

SUMMARY ANSWERS

1 a) Stays the same.   b) Increases.   c) Decreases.

2 a) 24 000 kg m/s

   b) i) 2000 N   ii) 800 N [HT only]

KEY POINTS

The students should be able to design measures to reduce the forces involved in a range of impacts. These could be on cars or sports equipment, for example in American football.

P2 3.6 Forces for safety

SPECIFICATION LINK-UP
Unit: Physics 2.12.3 and 4

This spread helps students to apply the principles covered in this chapter (as described by the contexts taken from the specification below):

- *When a body speeds up or slows down, its kinetic energy increases or decreases. The forces that cause the change in speed do so by transferring energy to, or from, the body.*

- *The faster a body is moving the more kinetic energy it has. It also has momentum. When working out what happens to bodies as a result of explosions or collisions, it is more useful to think in terms of momentum than in terms of energy.*

Motor News
CLUNK CLICK!

When seat belts were first introduced, some car users claimed that they should not be forced by law to wear them. A very successful campaign was launched to convince car users to 'belt up'. It included the catchy phrase 'Clunk click every trip'. As a result, deaths and injuries in road accidents fell significantly. A seat belt stops its wearer from continuing forwards when the car stops suddenly. Someone without a seat belt would hit the windscreen in a 'short sharp' impact and suffer major injury.

- The time taken to stop someone in a car is longer with a seat belt than without it. So the decelerating force is reduced by wearing a seat belt.
- The seat belt acts across the chest so it spreads the force out. Without the seat belt, the force would act on the head when it hits the windscreen.

ACTIVITY
'Clunk click every trip' is a positive message. Sometimes a negative message has bigger effect. Come up with your own short message to remind parents to check that children in cars must always wear seat belts.

NEWS
Air bags

An airbag in action

A crazy motorist was sent to prison for three years yesterday at Newtown County Court. He drove for twenty miles at top speed down the wrong side of a motorway. He was stopped when he drove into a police car blocking his route. One of the police officers said, 'We braced ourselves for the impact when he didn't stop. The airbags in our car inflated and took the force of the impact.' The bravery of the police officers was commended by the judge.

QUESTION
1   Explain why an inflated air bag in front of a car user reduces the force on a user of a 'head-on' crash.

G-FORCES

We sometimes express the effect of an impact on an object or person as a force-to-weight ratio. We call this the 'g-force'. For example, a g-force of 2g means the force on an object is twice its weight. You would experience a g-force of

- about 3–4g on a fairground ride that whirls you round,
- about 10g in a low-speed car crash,
- more than 50g in a high-speed car crash-force. You would be lucky to survive though!

156

Teaching suggestions

Activities

- **'Clunk click'** – There is always an active campaign for road safety and you should be able to find information from the Royal Society for the Prevention of Accidents web site www.rospa.com. With a search for 'public information film' or 'road safety film', you should be able to find a wide range of films from the 1970s and later, that include road safety measures including some really dated ones. The web site www.thinkseatbelts.com has a road crash simulator and a wide variety of facts about the law and safety; it is well worth a visit.

- **Analysing a road crash** – This is an interesting problem for analysis. The students might like to look at the assumptions made about the crash (the direction of the lorry, that the braking distance chart applies to lorries moving sideways etc.). They could look at impact analysis like this in more detail, including finding out about simulation software.

- **Air bags** – Air bags are quite a cunning device and have to be very rapid in operation to inflate the bag, but allow it to start to deflate before your head hits it too hard. They use the explosive decomposition of sodium azide (NaN_3) into sodium metal and nitrogen gas that inflates the bag in around 50 milliseconds. The head is in contact with the bag for a much longer time than it would be with the dashboard, and so a smaller force is exerted on the head to change its momentum.

- The students might like to consider why you should not mount a child safety seat in a front seat that has an airbag fitted. You should be able to find video clips demonstrating how air bags operate. Download these before the lesson as searches for videos of 'air bags' can give undesired results.

- **g-forces** – The term 'g-force' is very commonly used in relation to aeroplanes. A normal human can withstand around 5g without passing out, while trained pilots in pressured suits can make it up to 9g for a few seconds. Negative, −g, where the blood if forced to the head instead of away from it, is much more difficult to handle. At only −3g so much blood is forced to the head that the capillaries in the eyes burst – nasty.

Analysing a road crash

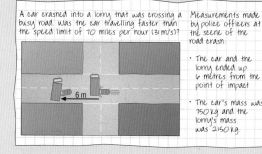

A car crashed into a lorry that was crossing a busy road. Was the car travelling faster than the speed limit of 70 miles per hour (31 m/s)?

Measurements made by police officers at the scene of the road crash:

- The car and the lorry ended up 6 metres from the point of impact
- The car's mass was 750 kg and the lorry's mass was 2150 kg.

QUESTION

2 The speed of a vehicle for a braking distance of 6 m is 9 m/s.
   a) Use this speed to calculate the momentum of the car and the lorry immediately after the impact.
   b) Use conservation of momentum to calculate the velocity of the car immediately before the collision.
   c) Was the car travelling over the speed limit before the crash?

Safety costs

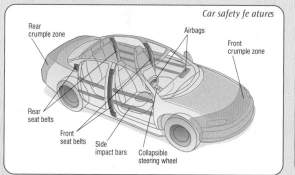

Car safety features

- Rear crumple zone
- Airbags
- Front crumple zone
- Rear seat belts
- Front seat belts
- Side impact bars
- Collapsible steering wheel

Car makers need to sell cars. If their cars are too expensive, people won't buy them. Safety features add to the cost of a new car. Some safety features (e.g. seat belts) are required by law and some (e.g. side impact bars) are optional. The table shows the main safety features in a new car.

Car make and price		
Nippy, £6500	Front seat belts	✔
	Rear seat belts	✔
	Airbags	
	Front crumple zone	✔
	Rear crumple zone	
	Side impact bars	
	Collapsible steering wheel	✔

ACTIVITY

a) With the help of your friends, find out what safety features are in some other new cars. Find out if they are compulsory or optional. List the price (including tax) of each car.
b) Use your information to say if cheaper cars have fewer safety features than more expensive cars.
c) What do you think could be done to make more cars safer?

ACTIVITY

Do you think all cars should have the best safety features money can buy? Or should owners choose these as options? What are the points for and against these views?

Which do you support?

ANSWERS TO QUESTIONS

1 The air bag increases the time taken to stop the person it acts on. This reduces the force of the impact. Also, the force is spread out across the chest by the air bag so its effect is lessened again.

2 a) 26 100 kg m/s
  b) 34.8 m/s
  c) Yes.

157

- **Safety costs** – The costs of cars and optional extras are readily available on manufacturers and dealers web sites, though the students may have to go through some of the pre-ordering stages to get all the information they need. Make sure nobody has a credit card. Adding all of the possible options would make most cars far too expensive, but the students may like to prioritise the features and list which ones should be made mandatory. They could also look into the European Safety feature rating; see www.euroncap.com for a detailed guide.

Extension or homework

The students can find out how pilots are trained and what equipment assists them in resisting high *g*-forces. Ask: 'What physical type of person would make the best fighter pilot?'

Learning styles

Kinaesthetic: Designing safety campaigns.

Visual: Visualising collisions.

Auditory: Reading information aloud.

Interpersonal: Discussing road safety.

Intrapersonal: Deducing the elements involved in a crash investigation.

ICT link-up

The Internet offers up a host of research possibilities for all of these activities. Simulation software also allows the students to look at collisions in more detail and can incorporate impacts at an angle and frictional forces. E.g. look at www.fable.com and www.crocodile-clips.com.

SUMMARY ANSWERS

1 a) i) Equal to.
   ii) Less than.

   b) i) 180 J
      ii) $11\,N \times 20\,m = 220\,Nm = 220\,J$
      iii) Friction between the trolley and the slope causes some of the energy from the student to be transformed to heat energy of the surroundings.

2 a) $\dfrac{700\,kg \times (20\,m/s)^2}{2} = 140\,000\,J$

   b) 1750 N [**HT** only]

3 a) i) 12 kg m/s
      ii) 6 m/s

   b) i) 1.8 J
      ii) 36 J [**HT** only]

4 2000 N [**HT** only]

Summary teaching suggestions

- This chapter has been, by necessity, quite mathematically intensive and several of the questions test the students' skills to deal with the equations.

- The second part of question 1 should show you if the students have a good grasp of work done and understanding that energy is wasted when objects are moved.

- Question 2 links a kinetic energy calculation to acceleration and force calculations; this is a good indicator of thorough understanding.

- Questions 3 and 4 are further calculations and will probably throw-up a wide range of mistakes or weaknesses. Use them to find out the weak spots for revision.

WORK, ENERGY AND MOMENTUM: P2 3.1 – P2 3.6

SUMMARY QUESTIONS

1 a) Copy and complete the following sentences using words from the list.

   equal to   greater than   less than

   When a braking force acts on a vehicle and slows it down,
   i) the work done by the force is …… the energy transferred from the object,
   ii) the kinetic energy after the brakes have been applied is …… the kinetic energy before they were applied.

   b) A student pushes a trolley of weight 150 N up a slope of length 20 m. The slope is 1.2 m high.

   i) Calculate the gravitational potential energy gained by the trolley.
   ii) The student pushed the trolley up the slope with a force of 11 N. Show that the work done by the student was 220 J.
   iii) Give one reason why all the work done by the student was not transferred to the trolley as gravitational potential energy.

2 A 700 kg car moving at 20 m/s is stopped in a distance of 80 m when the brakes are applied.

   a) Show that the kinetic energy of the car at 20 m/s is 140 000 J.
   b) Calculate the braking force on the car. [Higher]

3 A student of mass 40 kg standing at rest on a skateboard of mass 2.0 kg jumps off the skateboard at a speed of 0.30 m/s. Calculate:

   a) i) the momentum of the student,
      ii) the recoil velocity of the skateboard,
   b) the kinetic energy of i) the student, ii) the skateboard, after they move apart. [b] – Higher]

4 A car bumper is designed not to bend in impacts at less than 4 m/s. It was fitted to a car of mass 900 kg and tested by driving the car into a wall at 4 m/s. The time of impact was measured and found to be 1.8 s. Work out the impact force. [Higher]

EXAM-STYLE QUESTIONS

1 The picture shows a catapult.

(a) When a force is applied to the stone, work is done stretching the elastic and the stone moves backwards.

   (i) Write down the equation you could use to calculate the work done.

   (ii) The average force applied to the stone is 20 N. This moves it backwards 0.15 m. Calculate the work done and give its unit.

(b) The work done is stored as energy.

   (i) What type of energy is stored in the stretched elastic?

   (ii) What type of energy does the stone have when is released?

2 (a) The diagram shows three cars, A, B and C, travelling along a straight, level road at 25 m/s.

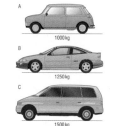

   (i) Explain which vehicle, A, B or C has the greatest momentum.

   (ii) Would you need a more sensitive weighing device to be more certain of your answer to part (i)? Give your reasoning.

EXAM-STYLE ANSWERS

1 a) i) Work done = force × distance moved in direction of the force   *(1 mark)*
   ii) Work done = 20 N × 0.15 m   *(1 mark)*
      work done = 3 J   *(2 marks)*

   b) i) elastic potential energy   *(1 mark)*
      ii) kinetic energy   *(1 mark)*

2 a) i) All travelling at same velocity, so car with greatest mass has greatest momentum.   *(1 mark)*
      Car C has greatest momentum.   *(1 mark)*
      ii) No, as there are large differences in the masses   *(1 mark)*
      so there is no need to read values with a sensitive instrument   *(1 mark)*

   b) All have same mass, so car with greatest velocity has greatest momentum.   *(1 mark)*
      Car F has greatest momentum.   *(1 mark)*

   c) Momentum = mass × velocity   *(1 mark)*
      Momentum = 1500 kg × 25 m/s   *(1 mark)*
      Momentum = 37 500 kg m/s   *(2 marks)*

3 a) *Total* momentum after a collision equals *total* momentum before the collision.   *(2 marks)*
      (momentum before equals momentum after = 1 mark)

   b) Explosions   *(1 mark)*

   c) 0.2 kg × 1.5 m/s + 0 = (0.2 + 0.3) kg × v m/s   *(1 mark)*
      0.3 kg m/s = 0.5 kg × v m/s   *(1 mark)*
      0.6 m/s   *(1 mark)*
      to the right   *(1 mark)*

(b) The diagram shows three identical cars, **D**, **E** and **F**, all of mass 1500 kg, travelling along a straight, level road at different speeds.

Explain which vehicle, **D**, **E** or **F** has the greatest momentum. (2)

(c) Calculate the momentum of car **E**, include the unit with your answer. (4)

A student is doing an investigation of the conservation of momentum with a horizontal air track and two 'gliders'.

(a) Explain what is meant by conservation of momentum. (2)

(b) Apart from collisions, give another type of event in which conservation of momentum applies. (1)

(c) The diagram shows the air track and the two 'gliders', **X** and **Y**.

The mass of **X** is 0.2 kg and its velocity is 1.5 m/s to the right.

The mass of **Y** is 0.3 kg and it is stationary. When 'glider' **X** collides with trolley **Y** they move off together.

Calculate the velocity of the 'gliders' after the collision and give their direction. (4)

Claire was interested in how ancient catapults were used to fire rocks at the enemy. She designed a catapult that was similar to one she found in a history book. She couldn't work out the angle at which to fire the catapult, so she used 'stoppers' to test three different positions. Her catapult looked like this:

As the ball was fired the spoon was pulled by the force of the elastic bands. The spoon hit the wooden support and the ball was fired into the distance. The three positions in which the wooden spoon was stopped are shown in the diagram opposite.

Here are Claire's results:

	Distance travelled (cm)		
	Front	Upright	Back
1st go	110	114	110
2nd go	117	116	112
3rd go	109	121	108
Mean	112	117	110

a) Claire made a prediction that the backward position would make the ball travel the furthest. Do the results support her prediction? Explain your answer. (1)

b) If you had to have a new prediction, what might it be? (1)

c) Do the results show precision? Explain your answer. (1)

d) What is the independent variable in Claire's investigation? (1)

e) Would you describe this as a discrete, categoric or ordered variable? (1)

f) How could it be changed into a continuous variable? (1)

g) What would be the advantage of using a continuous independent variable? (3)

159

HOW SCIENCE WORKS ANSWERS

a) No, there appears to be no real difference between the three sets of data or the upright position makes the ball travel furthest.

b) From these observations it might be that the upright position is able to propel the ball the furthest. If the datum from '2nd go/front' was considered an anomaly then this prediction would be more likely.

c) No, results do not show precision because they have a wide range within each set of results. The results for one actually overlap the other.

d) Position of the release point is the independent variable.

e) Categoric variable.

f) By measuring the angle of the spoon to the upright it could be changed to a continuous variable.

g) Advantage of using continuous independent variables is that you can gain more information from them than categoric variables. A graph could be drawn and a pattern discerned (or not).

How science works teaching suggestions

- **Literacy guidance.** Key terms that should be clearly understood: prediction, precision, independent variable, categoric, continuous variables.

- **Higher- and lower-level answers.** Questions b) and f) are higher-level questions. The answers for these have been provided at this level. Question e) is lower level and the answer provided is also lower level.

- **Gifted and talented.** Able students could suggest how a continuous variable might be used. Also, how the dependent variable might have been measured.

- **How and when to use these questions.** When wishing to develop ideas around detailed experimental design. The questions could be used in small group discussion.

- **Homework.** The data could be presented as a bar chart. Individual plots could be drawn on the same bar to illustrate the difficulty in establishing a clear pattern.

- **Special needs.** A pre-prepared bar chart could aid in an appreciation of the difficulty in establishing patterns with some data.

- **ICT link-up.** Spreadsheet software such as Excel could be used to enter the data and create the bar chart.

Exam teaching suggestions

- Remind students to always show their working in calculations so that they can gain credit even if their final answer is wrong.

- Students do not have to use quantity algebra, but they should be familiar with units and always give a unit for their final answer if this is not given in the answer line on the examination paper.

- Emphasise that work done is the same as energy transferred.

- Emphasise that force, acceleration and momentum have direction.

P2 4.1

Electrical charges

LEARNING OBJECTIVES

Students should learn that:

- When certain insulating materials are rubbed together, they become electrically charged.
- Objects can become charged when electrons are transferred from one to another.
- Similarly charged objects repel each other, while oppositely charged ones attract each other.

LEARNING OUTCOMES

Most students should be able to:

- Describe the process of electrical charging by friction in terms of transfer of electrons.
- State the directions of the forces between charged objects.

Some students should also be able to:

- Work out the type of charge on a charged object from the force on it due to another charged object.

Teaching suggestions

- **Gifted and talented.** Ask: 'Is it actually friction that charges up objects?' Apparently objects of different materials can become charged up just by being left in contact with each other, and rubbing objects together just increases the area of contact. The students can find out about this explanation.

- **Learning styles**

  Kinaesthetic: Charging up objects in practical activities.

  Visual: Imagining the movement of electrons / drawing diagrams to represent forces of attraction/repulsion.

  Auditory: Explaining how objects are becoming charged.

  Interpersonal: Working in pairs to report the results of practical investigations.

  Intrapersonal: Making deductions about the type of charge a material has.

SPECIFICATION LINK-UP   Unit: Physics 2.12.5

- *When certain insulating materials are rubbed against each other they become electrically charged. Negatively charged electrons are rubbed off one material onto the other.*
- *The material that gains electrons becomes negatively charged. The material that loses electrons is left with an equal positive charge.*
- *When two electrically charged bodies are brought together they exert a force on each other.*
- *Two bodies that carry the same type of charge repel. Two bodies that carry different types of charge attract.*

Lesson structure

STARTER

Laws of attraction – Give the students a set of three cards with pictures of bar magnets on them and ask them to arrange them so that they all attract each other or all repel each other. Use real magnets to check the answers. (5 minutes)

Invisible force fields – Give the students two bar magnets and ask them to balance them so that the end of one is floating above the end of the other. Ask: 'Can they balance two magnets above one another?' (5 minutes)

Attractive or repulsive – The students must give definitions of these two words. (5 minutes)

MAIN

- Start by demonstrating the balloon sticking effect; it should be fairly easy to get the balloon to stick to a wall or to your own body. You may also be able to show that two charged balloons repel each other.
- You can discuss the static build up on a TV screen by talking about the amount of dust that builds up on it.
- The use of a Van de Graaff generator is fairly essential. Students tend to get excited and some volunteer to receive a shock. Try some of the demonstrations in 'Practical support'. Make sure that you do not shock any students with any medical problems.
- The students should be familiar with the structure of the atom by now and you should be able to go through this part quickly.
- Emphasis needs to be placed on the idea that it is only the electrons that are free to move. When electrons leave an object it becomes positively charged and when they enter a neutral object it becomes negatively charged.
- Some students struggle with the idea that adding electrons makes something negative. They need to grasp that the electron has a negative charge and so if you have more electrons you have more negative charge.
- To demonstrate the effect that charged objects have on each other, the students can carry out the simple practical activity 'The force between two charged objects' from the students' book. They should have no trouble finding that like charges repel and opposite attract.
- At the end, the students should be able to tell you the simple attraction/repulsion rules.

PLENARIES

Static force – Give the students a set of diagrams with charged objects on them, two or more on each card, and ask them to draw force arrows. Some students can try to draw the direction of the resultant force. (5–10 minutes)

Forever amber – The students should write a newspaper report for the ancient Greek Newspaper νέα, ειδήσεις announcing the discovery and properties of static electricity. It was first discovered using amber or 'electrum' as they called it. (10–15 minutes)

That's magic! – Ask the students to try to design a magic trick based around static electricity. (5–10 minutes)

Practical support

The Van de Graaff generator

This is an impressive and fun piece of equipment that can be used to demonstrate many of the aspects of static electricity. It's not just for giving shocks!

Equipment and materials required

A VDG and accessory kit.

Details

- A VDG is a very temperamental device. Some days it will work very well but on others you will barely get a crackle. Dry days are best, and it is advisable to polish the dome to make it shiny. Keep computer (and mobile phones) away from the VDG

- It is traditional to start by showing the sparks that the VDG can produce. Connect the discharging wand (or discharging dome) to Earth and switch on the generator. Give the dome a couple of minutes to build up charge while you explain what the VDG is doing. Bring the wand close to the dome and with luck you will get reasonably big sparks.

- Hair standing on end can be demonstrated easily, and works best if the student stands on an insulating box. Make sure that the dome is discharged before the student steps off the insulator. If you don't want to use a student, then you may have a hair sample that can be attached to the top of the dome or use a set of polystyrene balls in a container.

- Other demonstrations can include bringing a fluorescent tube close to the dome or demonstrating a current as a flow of charge.

The force between two charged objects

With this simple experiment, the students should be able to find that there are two types of charge and investigate how they affect each other.

Equipment and materials required

For each group: retort stand with boss and clamp, cotton, two perspex rods, two polythene rods and a dry cloth.

Details

The students first need to make a 'hammock' from the cotton to be able to suspend one of the rods from the retort stand; they might find this easier if they use some light card as a base. They then rub one of the rods vigorously with the dry cloth and place it in the hammock. Next they rub one of the other rods and bring it close to the suspended one and note the interaction; the suspended rod should rotate towards or away. They continue this procedure for all of the combinations of rods. If there seems to be little movement, it is probably because the cloth is not dry enough.

SUMMARY ANSWERS

1 a) Gains, to, from.
   b) Loses, from, to.

2 a) Attraction.
   b) Attraction.
   c) Repulsion.

Answers to in-text questions

a) Static electricity builds up on the screen.

b) It loses electrons.

c) The electron is negative. The nucleus is positive. So there is a force of (electrostatic) attraction between them.

KEY POINTS

- Can the students state the laws of attraction/repulsion for charges?
- Can they explain how objects become negatively or positively charged?

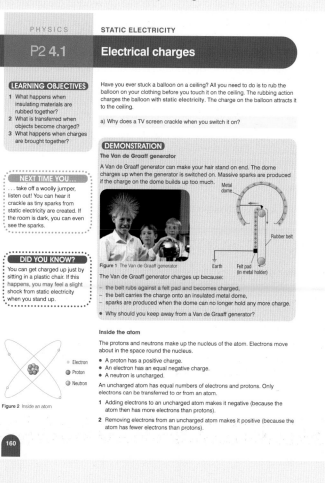

PHYSICS   STATIC ELECTRICITY

P2 4.1   Electrical charges

LEARNING OBJECTIVES

1 What happens when insulating materials are rubbed together?
2 What is transferred when objects become charged?
3 What happens when charges are brought together?

Have you ever stuck a balloon on a ceiling? All you need to do is to rub the balloon on your clothing before you touch it on the ceiling. The rubbing action charges the balloon with static electricity. The charge on the balloon attracts it to the ceiling.

a) Why does a TV screen crackle when you switch it on?

DEMONSTRATION
The Van de Graaff generator

A Van de Graaff generator can make your hair stand on end. The dome charges up when the generator is switched on. Massive sparks are produced if the charge on the dome builds up too much.

Figure 1 The Van de Graaff generator

The Van de Graaff generator charges up because:

– the belt rubs against a felt pad and becomes charged,
– the belt carries the charge onto an insulated metal dome,
– sparks are produced when the dome can no longer hold any more charge.

- Why should you keep away from a Van de Graaff generator?

NEXT TIME YOU...
... take off a woolly jumper, listen out! You can hear it crackle as tiny sparks from static electricity are created. If the room is dark, you can even see the sparks.

DID YOU KNOW?
You can get charged up just by sitting in a plastic chair. If this happens, you may feel a slight shock from static electricity when you stand up.

Inside the atom

The protons and neutrons make up the nucleus of the atom. Electrons move about in the space round the nucleus.

- A proton has a positive charge.
- An electron has an equal negative charge.
- A neutron is uncharged.

An uncharged atom has equal numbers of electrons and protons. Only electrons can be transferred to or from an atom.

1 Adding electrons to an uncharged atom makes it negative (because the atom then has more electrons than protons).

2 Removing electrons from an uncharged atom makes it positive (because the atom has fewer protons than neutrons).

○ Electron
● Proton
○ Neutron

Figure 2 Inside an atom

Charging by friction

Some insulators become charged by rubbing them with a dry cloth.

- Rubbing a polythene rod with a dry cloth transfers electrons to the surface atoms of the rod from the cloth. So the polythene rod becomes negatively charged.
- Rubbing a perspex rod with a dry cloth transfers electrons from the surface atoms of the rod onto the cloth. So the perspex rod becomes positively charged.

b) Glass is charged positively when it is rubbed with a cloth. Does glass gain or lose electrons when it is charged?

PRACTICAL
The force between two charged objects

Two charged objects exert a force on each other. Figure 4 shows how you can investigate this force.

- What happens?

Figure 4 The law of force for charges

Your results in the experiment above should show that:

- two objects with the same type of charge (i.e. like charges) repel each other.
- two objects with opposite types of charge (i.e. unlike charges) attract each other.

Like charges repel. Unlike charges attract.

c) What force keeps the electrons inside an atom?

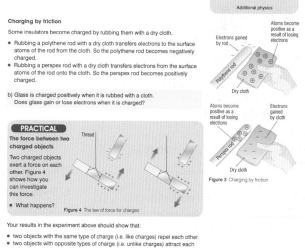

Figure 3 Charging by friction

SUMMARY QUESTIONS

1 Choose words from the list to complete a) and b) below:

   to   from   loses   gains

a) When a polythene rod is charged using a dry cloth, it becomes negative because it ...... electrons that transfer ...... it ...... the cloth.
b) When a perspex rod is charged using a dry cloth, it becomes positive because it ...... electrons that transfer ...... it ...... the cloth.

2 When rubbed with a dry cloth, perspex becomes positively charged. Polythene and ebonite become negatively charged. State whether or not attraction or repulsion takes place when:

a) a perspex rod is held near a polythene rod,
b) a perspex rod is held near an ebonite rod,
c) a polythene rod is held near an ebonite rod.

KEY POINTS

1 Like charges repel; unlike charges attract.
2 Insulating materials that lose electrons when rubbed become positively charged.
3 Insulating materials that gain electrons when rubbed become negatively charged.

Additional physics

160

161

P2 4.2   Charge on the move

LEARNING OBJECTIVES

Students should learn that:

- Conductors cannot become charged when the electrons are free to move to and from earth.
- Charge is carried by electrons moving through conducting materials and this flow of charge is called an electric current.
- A build-up of charge on an isolated body can result in the production of sparks. [**HT** only]

LEARNING OUTCOMES

Most students should be able to:

- Describe the flow of charge in a metal in terms of electron movement.
- Describe how an insulated conductor becomes charged by direct contact with a charged body.
- Explain why metals become discharged when they are connected to the earth.

Some students should also be able to:

- Explain why an earthed metal object cannot be charged.
- Explain loss of charge from a conductor due to a sharp point on the conductor.
- Explain why sparks are produced between an isolated body and an earthed conductor. [**HT** only]

Teaching suggestions

- **Gifted and talented.** Ask: 'Why does chewing metal foil on your fillings really hurt?'

- **Learning styles**
  Kinaesthetic: Using an electroscope.
  Visual: Observing the behaviour of charged objects.
  Auditory: Explaining the behaviour of an electroscope.
  Intrapersonal: Making deductions about the flow of electrons.

- **ICT link-up.** There are several pieces of software that help show that a current in a wire is a flow of electrons. These can really help with the students' visualisation of what is happening.

The students should draw a set of diagrams showing how objects become positively and negatively charged.

SPECIFICATION LINK-UP   Unit: Physics 2.12.5

- *Electrical charges can move easily through some substances, e.g. metals.*
- *The rate of flow of electrical charge is called the current.*
- *A charged body can be discharged by connecting it to earth with a conductor, charge then flows through the conductor.*
- *The greater the charge on an isolated body the greater the potential difference between the body and Earth. If the potential difference becomes high enough, a spark may jump across the gap between the body and any earthed conductor that is brought near it.* [**HT** only]

Lesson structure

STARTER

Energy transfer diagram – The students should draw a complete energy transfer diagram for a torch and an electric motor. (5 minutes)

Twenty questions – The students have twenty 'yes/no' questions to find the secret word 'current'. (5 minutes)

Current – Ask the students to describe what a 'water current' is; try to get them to realise that it is the **flow** of tiny particles of water from one place to another. (5 minutes)

MAIN

- Start by demonstrating a basic torch and discussing with the students:
  - what energy transfers are taking place
  - where the energy is coming from, and
  - where it ends up.

- This leads onto a discussion about what is carrying the energy around the circuit and why we cannot see the electrons doing this.

- Using the gold leaf electroscopes you can demonstrate, or let the class discover, that charge will escape to Earth unless the conductor is insulated.

- You can use a Van de Graaff generator to demonstrate a current is a flow of charge; see the activity box.

- The VDG can also be used to explain the idea of discharging and you should focus on the idea that electrons are moving into or out of charged objects.

- It should be relatively easy to find images or video of lightning strikes (search for 'lightning' at video.google.com); these are always impressive. Explain that the charged clouds are becoming discharged because of the flow of charge from one place to another. A large flow of charge produces a large electric current, so large that the air glows white-hot.

- There is some fairly famous footage showing that cars actually do protect you from lightning strikes. It is worth trying to find a copy of this to show the students as it makes a good end point for discussion. (Search for 'car struck by lightning video'.) The metal frame of the car conducts the current around the occupants and leaves them unharmed.

PLENARIES

Traffic lights – Give the students a set of 'facts' about static electricity and electrical current and ask them to hold up a red card for false, amber for not sure and green for true. (5–10 minutes)

Dangerous sports – The students should discuss which sports are the most dangerous with respect to lightning strikes and why. [They are actually golfing, fishing, camping and hiking.] (5–10 minutes)

'By Thor's mighty hammer!' – There are a lot of legends about the origin of lightning. Ask the students to make up a new one. (5–10 minutes)

ACTIVITY & EXTENSION IDEAS

Demonstrating a current

It is possible to show that an electric current is a flow of charge using a VDG. Higher attaining students should understand the concepts quite well.

Equipment and materials required

VDG, two tall retort stands, polystyrene ball coated in conducting paint and attached to a length of thin cotton, leads, metal plate, crocodile clips and a sensitive galvanometer.

Details

Set up the VDG and a retort stand so that the polystyrene ball rests against the dome and is free to swing on a length of cotton. Place the metal plate nearby so that when the ball swings it can easily reach the plate. Connect the plate through the galvanometer to the Earth connection on the VDG. When the VDG is switched on, the ball should charge up and be repelled by the dome. It will swing towards the metal plate and discharge to Earth, producing a brief current that the galvanometer will register. Test this out first, as it is fiddly to get just right.

Making a gold leaf electroscope

Gold leaf electroscopes have become strangely rare, but you can improvise a basic one or get your students to make a set. You can actually make quite a big one for demonstrations if you have a large conical flask.

Equipment and materials required

A conical flask (250 cm³ or larger), a cork bung to fit, longish nail to go through the cork, flat metal plate, sheet of Dutch metal foil and some sticky tape. You can use real gold if you have it!

Practical support

Charging a conductor

This demonstration requires a gold leaf electroscope. If you don't have one, then a basic one can be made; see activity box.

Equipment and materials required

A gold leaf electroscope, crocodile clips, a lead, cloth and polythene rod.

Details

- To demonstrate that a metal object cannot be charged if it is earthed, set up the gold leaf electroscope and then attach the top plate to a pipe or other earthed object though a lead. Rub the rod vigorously and then bring it near to the top plate, finally touching it. The gold leaf should not move.

- To demonstrate that an insulated metal object can be charged, repeat the same process without the earthing lead. The gold leaf should lift, showing that the top plate becomes charged by induction as the rod approaches. When touching the rod against the plate, it works best if you just touch it with the very corner of the rod and then move it away quickly.

SUMMARY ANSWERS

1 a) The rate of flow of charge.

   b) Electrons that move about freely.

   c) Negatively charged.

2 a) Any charge supplied to it flows to Earth.

   b) Charge leaks off the dome from the tip of the pin into the air. [**HT** only]

FOUL FACTS

Standing near a tree in a thunderstorm is never a good idea. The lightning may hit the tree, but as the wood isn't a good conductor the tree is superheated and explodes sending splinters in all directions. So, if the current doesn't kill you, the flying wood might. There are many ways to avoid being killed, but the best is to get inside a building or metal car. The current will pass through the easiest path and hopefully you will be fine.

Answers to in-text questions

a) The positive end.

b) Electrons transferred to the can pass through it to the ground.

c) It gains electrons.

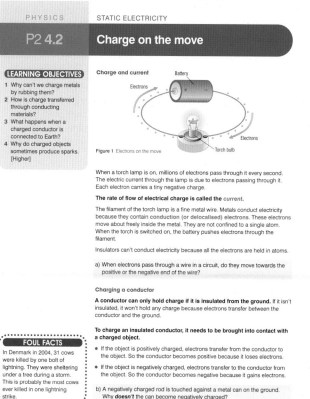

PHYSICS   STATIC ELECTRICITY

P2 4.2   Charge on the move

LEARNING OBJECTIVES

1 Why can't we charge metals by rubbing them?
2 How is charge transferred through conducting materials?
3 What happens when a charged conductor is connected to Earth?
4 Why do charged objects sometimes produce sparks? [Higher]

Charge and current

Figure 1 Electrons on the move

When a torch lamp is on, millions of electrons pass through it every second. The electric current through the lamp is due to electrons passing through it. Each electron carries a tiny negative charge.

The rate of flow of electrical charge is called the *current*.

The filament of the torch lamp is a fine metal wire. Metals conduct electricity because they contain **conduction** (or delocalised) **electrons**. These electrons move about freely inside the metal. They are not confined to a single atom. When the torch is switched on, the battery pushes electrons through the filament.

Insulators can't conduct electricity because all the electrons are held in atoms.

a) When electrons pass through a wire in a circuit, do they move towards the positive or the negative end of the wire?

Charging a conductor

A conductor can only hold charge if it is insulated from the ground. If it isn't insulated, it won't hold any charge because electrons transfer between the conductor and the ground.

To charge an insulated conductor, it needs to be brought into contact with a charged object.

- If the object is positively charged, electrons transfer from the conductor to the object. So the conductor becomes positive because it loses electrons.

- If the object is negatively charged, electrons transfer to the conductor from the object. So the conductor becomes negative because it gains electrons.

b) A negatively charged rod is touched against a metal can on the ground. Why *doesn't* the can become negatively charged?

FOUL FACTS

In Denmark in 2004, 31 cows were killed by one bolt of lightning. They were sheltering under a tree during a storm. This is probably the most cows ever killed in one lightning strike.

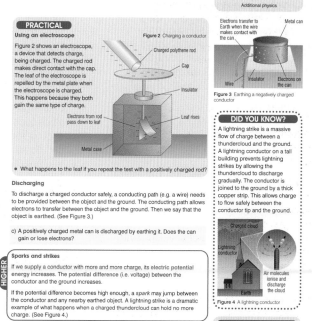

PRACTICAL

Using an electroscope

Figure 2 shows an electroscope, a device that detects charge, being charged. The charged rod makes direct contact with the cap. The leaf of the electroscope is repelled by the metal plate when the electroscope is charged. This happens because they both gain the same type of charge.

Figure 2 Charging a conductor

- What happens to the leaf if you repeat the test with a positively charged rod?

Discharging

To discharge a charged conductor safely, a conducting path (e.g. a wire) needs to be provided between the object and the ground. The conducting path allows electrons to transfer between the object and the ground. Then we say that the object is earthed. (See Figure 3.)

c) A positively charged metal can is discharged by earthing it. Does the can gain or lose electrons?

Figure 3 Earthing a negatively charged conductor

Sparks and strikes

If we supply a conductor with more and more charge, its electric potential energy increases. The potential difference (i.e. voltage) between the conductor and the ground increases.

If the potential difference becomes high enough, a *spark* may jump between the conductor and any nearby earthed object. A lightning strike is a dramatic example of what happens when a charged thundercloud can hold no more charge. (See Figure 4.)

DID YOU KNOW?

A lightning strike is a massive flow of charge between a thundercloud and the ground. A lightning conductor on a tall building prevents lightning strikes by allowing the thundercloud to discharge gradually. The conductor is joined to the ground by a thick copper strip. This allows charge to flow safely between the conductor tip and the ground.

Figure 4 A lightning conductor

SUMMARY QUESTIONS

1 Complete the following sentences:

   a) An electric current is ....
   b) A metal is a conductor because it contains ....
   c) A ...... metal object loses electrons when it is connected to the ground.

2 a) Why can't we charge a metal object if it is earthed?
   b) A drawing pin is fixed to the dome of a Van de Graaff machine with its point in the air. Explain why this stops the dome charging up when the machine is switched on. [Higher]

KEY POINTS

1 Electrical current is the rate of flow of charge.
2 A metal object can only hold charge if it is isolated from the ground.
3 A metal object is earthed by connecting it to the ground.
4 If a metal object gains too much charge, it will produce sparks. [Higher]

P2 4.3

Uses and dangers of static electricity

LEARNING OBJECTIVES

Students should learn:

- How static electricity is used in paint spraying, electrostatic precipitators and photocopiers.
- That static electricity can cause explosions when charge builds up and produces sparks.

LEARNING OUTCOMES

Most students should be able to:

- Describe the role that static electricity plays in paint spraying, smoke precipitation and the photocopier.
- Explain how sparks are caused by the build up of static electricity and why this is dangerous.
- Describe precautions taken to prevent static electricity and to ensure it is discharged safely.

Some students should also be able to:

- Explain safety measures to reduce or remove hazards due to static electricity.

Teaching suggestions

- **Special needs.** It is best to give the students a set of diagrams showing the equipment. They can then add flow charts to the diagrams explaining what is happening in terms of static charge.
- **Learning styles**

  Visual: Observing experiments.

  Auditory: Listening to explanations of explosions.

  Interpersonal: Discussing and evaluating anti-static measures.

  Intrapersonal: Considering the uses of static electricity.

- **ICT link-up.** The original development of the photocopier (from electro-photography through to fully working Xerox machine) is quite a tale of perseverance. The students should find out about this and see some animation of how a photocopier works by searching for 'photocopier history'.
- **Homework.** Several cleaning sprays make the claim that they prevent static build-up. Can the students design a fair experiment to test this claim?

SPECIFICATION LINK-UP   Unit: Physics 2.12.5

- *Electrostatic charges can be useful, for example in photocopiers and smoke precipitators and the basic operation of these devices.*

Students should use their skills, knowledge and understanding of 'How Science Works':

- *to explain why static electricity is dangerous in some situations and how precautions can be taken to ensure that the electrostatic charge is discharged safely.*
- *to explain how static electricity can be useful.*

Lesson structure

STARTER

The wrong carpet – Ask: 'Do some carpets cause more static build up than others?' The students should design a scientific test to find out. (10 minutes)

Shocked – Ask: 'Do you ever get shocked by static electricity?' Have them explain where and why this happens. (5–10 minutes)

It makes your hair stand on end – Static electricity can make your hair stand on end, but what else can? Discuss. (5 minutes)

MAIN

- There are lots of little bits to this lesson because static electricity has a range of uses and dangers.
- Tiny pieces of paper sticking to a charged rod can be used to give the idea of paint droplets being drawn to a charged surface.
- You can show the deflection of a stream of water from a tap by a charged polythene rod to show how charge can be used to direct flow.
- Your ICT department may have an old laser printer. With care (take off the mains lead), this can be dismantled to show the drum, toner cartridge and heating element. Emphasise that the drum contains a material that is not conductive when it is left in the dark, but it is conductive when light is shone onto it. This is what allows the image to be formed.
- The students may be familiar with the ozone smell from these printers. This is caused by the charge ionising oxygen molecules, O_2, and forming ozone, O_3, molecules.
- Demonstrating the dangers of sparks near flammable liquids is worthwhile.
- If you have made a large electroscope you might be able to demonstrate the build up of charge when a powder flows through a pipe. Set a large metal cup onto the electroscope and let cornflower flow down a plastic hosepipe into the cup. You should see some movement of the leaf. This can be saved for the next topic, where it can be studied in more detail.
- You may like to let the students explore discharging with the electroscopes; a fairly brief practical.
- Some students may not believe that things like custard powder can explode. Try the demonstration in the activity box to show their mistake. It makes a memorable end to the lesson!

PLENARIES

Sum it up – The students draw a spider diagram containing information about the uses and dangers of static electricity. They should draw it large enough so that they can add more information next lesson. (10 minutes)

Trouble at mill! – Students to write a police investigation report explaining why the local flourmill blew up last week. (10–15 minutes)

Do you smell gas? – Read out this scenario: 'You come home late at night, open your front door and smell gas! Should you turn on the light to have a look? Pick up the phone to dial for help? Get out your mobile?' The students explain why not. (5–10 minutes)

ACTIVITY & EXTENSION IDEAS

Exploding powder

A very fine powder, like custard powder or cornflower, can explode fairly readily. This demonstration uses a naked flame but sparks can do the same. Test the experiment out before demonstrating it, as it can be difficult to judge the amount of powder required. Use a safety screen and keep your head away from the flying lid.

Equipment and materials required

Metal tin with push-on metal lid (a metal coffee tin works well), candle, small bung with glass pipe through it to blow through, rubber tube and pipette bulb, safety screen, safety glasses.

Details

Drill a hole in the side of the can about half-way up and fit the bung into it. Set up the can with a candle fitted inside to the base so that the flame is about the same height as the hole. Place a small stand between the hole and the candle inside the tin. Set the can up behind a safety screen and place a **small** amount of custard powder onto the stand. Fit a rubber tube to the glass pipe and a pipette bulb on the far end, long enough so that you can be out of the way. Finally light the candle, place the lid on firmly and step back. Press the bulb so that fine powder is blown into the flame. You should get a decent bang.

Practical support

Get rid of the charge

This is simple reinforcement of the discharging ideas from the last topic.

Equipment and materials required

For each group: electroscope, polythene and perspex rods, cloths, metal wires.

Details

The students charge up the electroscopes with the rods and then try to think of ways to discharge them. They should be explaining what is happening to the electrons – are they entering or leaving the electroscope?

PHYSICS · STATIC ELECTRICITY

P2 4.3 Uses and dangers of static electricity

LEARNING OBJECTIVES

1 In what ways is static electricity useful?
2 In what ways is static electricity dangerous?
3 How can we get rid of static electricity where it is dangerous?

Using electrostatics

The electrostatic paint sprayer

Automatic paint sprayers are used to paint metal panels. The spray nozzle is connected to the positive terminal of an electrostatic generator. The negative terminal is connected to the metal panel. The panel attracts paint droplets from the spray, so they spread out to form a fine cloud of paint.

a) Why are the spray nozzle and the panel oppositely charged?

Figure 1 An electrostatic paint sprayer

The electrostatic precipitator

Coal-fired power stations produce vast quantities of ash and dust. Electrostatic precipitators remove this material from the flue gases before they get into the atmosphere.

The particles of ash and dust pass through a grid of wires in the precipitator. Look at Figure 2. The grid wires are negative so the particles become negatively charged when they touch it. The charged particles are attracted onto the positively charged metal plates. The plates are shaken at intervals so the ash and dust that build up on them drop to the floor of the precipitator. They are then removed.

b) What difference would it make if the grid was not charged?

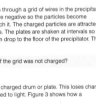

Ash and dust collect on plates

Grid of charged wires

Metal plates charged oppositely to the grid wires

Waste gases carrying ash and dust

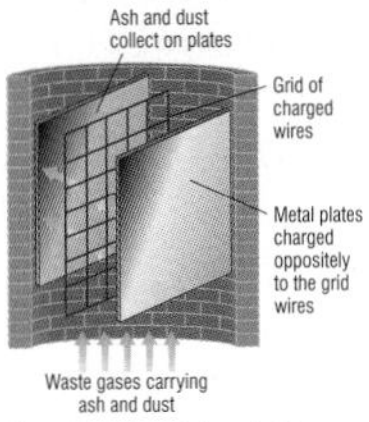

Figure 2 An electrostatic precipitator

The photocopier

The key part of a photocopier is a charged drum or plate. This loses charge from the parts of its surface exposed to light. Figure 3 shows how a photocopier works.

1 Photocopiers with a photoconducting drum – drum positively charged until light falls on it.

Charging wire

2 Light reflected off the paper onto the drum. The areas of black do not reflect so the drum keeps its charge in these areas.

Original document

Lens

3 The black toner sticks to the drum where it is still charged and is pressed onto paper.

Toner

4 The paper is finally heated to stick the toner to it permanently.

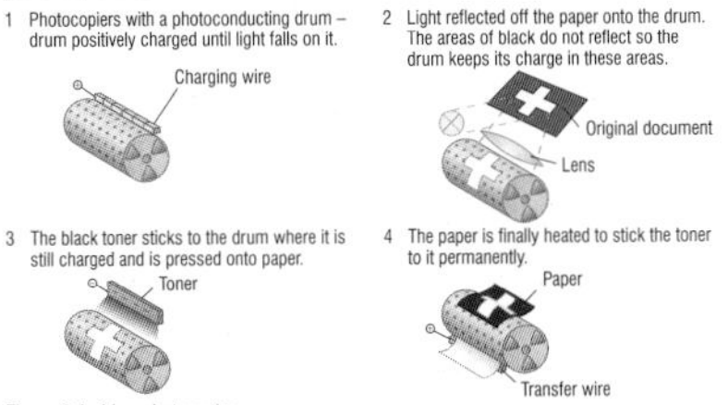

Paper

Transfer wire

Figure 3 Inside a photocopier

c) Why are photocopies sometimes charged when they come out of the photocopier?

Electrostatics hazards

Pipe problems

When a road tanker pumps oil or petrol into a storage tank, the connecting pipe must be earthed. If it isn't, the pipe could become charged. A build-up of charge would cause a spark. This could cause an explosion as the fuel vapour reacts with oxygen in the air.

Static electricity is also generated when grains of powder are pumped through pipes. Friction between the grains and the pipe charges them. An explosion could happen due to a spark igniting the powder.

d) Why is the rubber hose of a petrol pump made of special conducting rubber?

Antistatic floors

In a hospital, doctors use anaesthetic gases during operations. Some of these gases are explosive. If the gas escapes into the air, a tiny spark could make it explode. To eliminate static charge in operating theatres, an antistatic material is used for the floor surface. This material is a poor electrical insulator so it conducts charge to Earth.

e) Why do the doctors and nurses wear antistatic clothes in an operating theatre?

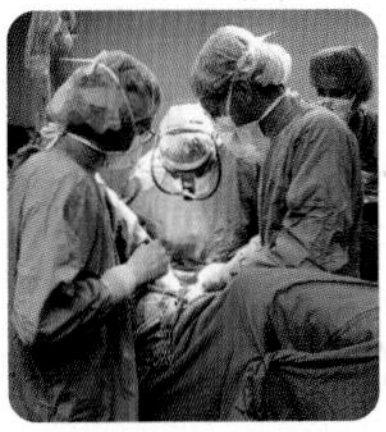

Figure 4 Operating theatres have antistatic floors

PRACTICAL

Getting rid of the charge

Charge up an electroscope.

- How do you discharge it? Explain what happens.

GET IT RIGHT!

Remember that electrostatic charge has its uses as well as its dangers.

SUMMARY QUESTIONS

1 Complete a) and b) using the words below:

   attracted   gain   lose   repelled

a) Positively charged paint droplets from a paint spray are ...... by the spray nozzle. The droplets ...... electrons when they reach the negatively charged metal panel.

b) Dust particles in an electrostatic precipitator touch a positively charged wire. The particles ...... electrons to the wire and are then ...... by a negatively charged metal plate.

2 a) The delivery pipe between the road tanker and the storage tank must be earthed before any petrol is pumped from the tanker. Why is this an important safety measure?

b) Why does an operating theatre in a hospital have antistatic floor covering?

KEY POINTS

1 A spark from a charged object can make powder grains or certain gases explode.

2 To eliminate static electricity, use antistatic materials, and b) earth metal pipes and objects.

SUMMARY ANSWERS

1 a) Repelled, gain.

b) Lose, attracted.

2 a) To conduct any charge on the pipe nozzle to the ground, so it can't cause sparks which would ignite the fuel.

b) To conduct any charge to the ground so it can't cause sparks, which would cause gases used in the theatre to explode.

Answers to in-text questions

a) So that droplets are charged as they leave the spray nozzle and attracted to the panel.

b) Most of the particles would pass straight through it.

c) The powder transfers charge onto the paper from the photocopier drum. The charge stays on the paper sometimes.

d) So that it conducts charge away from the pump nozzle to Earth.

e) So their clothing doesn't become charged and produce sparks.

KEY POINTS

Can the students describe two ways in which sparks can be prevented in industry?

P2 4.4   Static issues

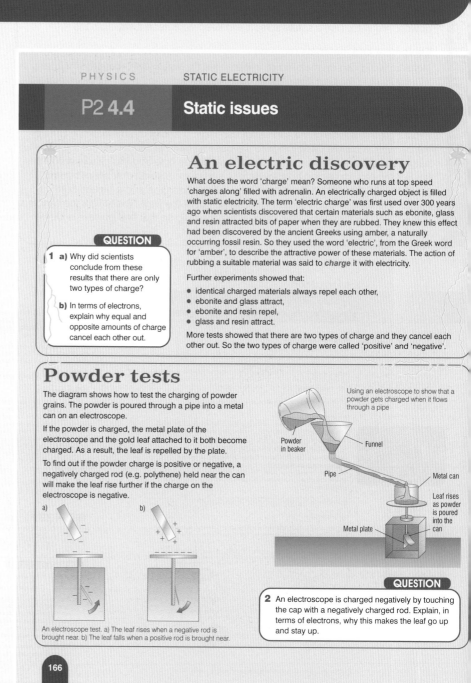

PHYSICS   STATIC ELECTRICITY

P2 4.4   Static issues

An electric discovery

What does the word 'charge' mean? Someone who runs at top speed 'charges along' filled with adrenalin. An electrically charged object is filled with static electricity. The term 'electric charge' was first used over 300 years ago when scientists discovered that certain materials such as ebonite, glass and resin attracted bits of paper when they are rubbed. They knew this effect had been discovered by the ancient Greeks using amber, a naturally occurring fossil resin. So they used the word 'electric', from the Greek word for 'amber', to describe the attractive power of these materials. The action of rubbing a suitable material was said to *charge* it with electricity.

Further experiments showed that:

- identical charged materials always repel each other,
- ebonite and glass attract,
- ebonite and resin repel,
- glass and resin attract.

More tests showed that there are two types of charge and they cancel each other out. So the two types of charge were called 'positive' and 'negative'.

QUESTION

1 a) Why did scientists conclude from these results that there are only two types of charge?

b) In terms of electrons, explain why equal and opposite amounts of charge cancel each other out.

Powder tests

The diagram shows how to test the charging of powder grains. The powder is poured through a pipe into a metal can on an electroscope.

If the powder is charged, the metal plate of the electroscope and the gold leaf attached to it both become charged. As a result, the leaf is repelled by the plate.

To find out if the powder charge is positive or negative, a negatively charged rod (e.g. polythene) held near the can will make the leaf rise further if the charge on the electroscope is negative.

Using an electroscope to show that a powder gets charged when it flows through a pipe

Powder in beaker
Funnel
Pipe
Metal can
Leaf rises as powder is poured into the can
Metal plate

a)   b)

An electroscope test. a) The leaf rises when a negative rod is brought near. b) The leaf falls when a positive rod is brought near.

QUESTION

2 An electroscope is charged negatively by touching the cap with a negatively charged rod. Explain, in terms of electrons, why this makes the leaf go up and stay up.

166

Teaching suggestions

Activities

- **An electric discovery** – The first writings on electrical charge are thought to be those of Thales of Miletus. He is considered, by some, to be the first recorded scientist because of his belief that the world could be explained without reference to gods or supernatural forces. Ask: 'Why are the two types of charge called positive and negative? Scientists could have chosen any words that indicated some kind of 'oppositeness'.'

- **Powder tests** – This test can be carried out using very fine powder, e.g. cornflower powder, and letting it roll along different tubes into a metal cup of a gold leaf electroscope. It can be difficult to get the powder charged up enough to detect without a long tube. The best way to get a long tube is to use a **dry** hosepipe and make the powder go through by rippling it along the length and finally into the can.

- **The ink jet printer** – To demonstrate the spitting action of an ink jet you can use melting point tubes. Dip the tube in ink at one end, so that a tiny drop moves into the tube. Seal the far end with a Plasticine blob or push it into a bit of cork. If you heat the middle of the tube strongly with a Bunsen, the ink should spit out. It won't be a very accurate method and you can't direct the ink. You could show the deflection of flowing water, again to show how charge can be used to change the path of the liquid.
  You can use Animation P2 4.3 'Photocopier' from the GCSE Physics CD ROM at this point.

- **A chip problem** – The vast majority of microprocessors use CMOS technology, as it needs less power to operate and so produces less heat. This means that computer systems are very vulnerable to static electricity until they are earthed in a circuit board. You should be able to find an anti-static wrist strap used by installers and the anti-static bag and foam that the chips are kept in prior to installation. Can the students design an experiment to see how effective the anti-static strap and packaging are?

The ink jet printer

An ink jet printer has an 'ink gun' inside that directs a jet of charged ink droplets at the paper. The ink droplets pass between two metal 'deflecting' plates before reaching the paper.

- By making one plate positive and the other negative, the droplets can be deflected as they pass between the plates. This happens because the droplets are attracted to the oppositely charged plate.
- The plates are made positive and negative by applying a potential difference to them. The potential difference is controlled by signals from the computer. The computer is programmed to make the inkjet print characters and graphics on the paper at high speed.

An ink jet printer

QUESTION

3 What do you think would happen if the ink droplets are too big?

A chip problem

Computer chips can be damaged by static electricity. Most microcomputers contain *CMOS* chips. Tiny amounts of charge on the pins of a CMOS chip can destroy its electrical properties. To prevent chips being damaged by static electricity, manufacturers insert them into antistatic foam sheets before packaging them.

Special tools are available to transfer chips to and from circuits to prevent them becoming charged in the transfer. Touching the chip briefly when a charged object is nearby would cause it to become charged. The figure shows how this can happen.

Microchip damage

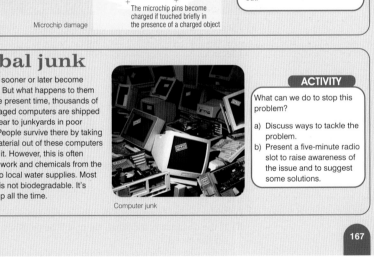

Electrons attracted onto pins

Microchip on an insulated surface

The microchip pins become charged if touched briefly in the presence of a charged object

ACTIVITY

A company that makes computers has found that some of its chips don't work. The supplier says the company must be more careful when the chips are used. Imagine you work in the company. You think the problem is at the supplier. Send an e-mail to the supplier to find out.

Global junk

Computers sooner or later become out of date. But what happens to them then? At the present time, thousands of old or damaged computers are shipped out every year to junkyards in poor countries. People survive there by taking valuable material out of these computers and selling it. However, this is often dangerous work and chemicals from the junk get into local water supplies. Most of the junk is not biodegradable. It's mounting up all the time.

Computer junk

ACTIVITY

What can we do to stop this problem?

a) Discuss ways to tackle the problem.
b) Present a five-minute radio slot to raise awareness of the issue and to suggest some solutions.

167

ANSWERS TO QUESTIONS

1 **a)** All charged objects either attract or repel each other. You only need two types to fit the force rule.

  b) All the extra electrons carrying the negative charge would make up for the deficit of electrons in the positive charge.

2 Electrons transfer to the electroscope so the leaf and the stem both become positively charged. The leaf therefore goes up. The charge stays on the electroscope so the leaf stays up.

3 They would not be deflected by the correct amount.

Special needs

If the students are to research any of the above topics, they should be provided with a template to collect information on. This should include a list of suitable web sites to look at and enough space for the students to make relevant notes. See for example, www.howstuffworks.com.

ICT link-up

Ideally any research templates should be in electronic form so that the students can paste the images into it. A word processor or presentation package can be used to make a file with headings and questions that students can use as a template. With this they can assemble notes and images.

Teaching assistant

The assistant should help with the research to make sure that the students are focused on the tasks and not having any IT difficulties.

Learning styles

Kinaesthetic: Researching into history of electricity.

Auditory: Explaining how static electricity can damage computers.

Interpersonal: Debating ways to reduce computer waste.

Intrapersonal: Writing a report of computer waste/static damage.

- **Global junk** – The ecological damage due to the computer industry is quite large as many resources are used in the manufacture, and some heavy metals are incorporated in the machines. A typical computer accounts for 6000 MJ of energy during its construction, use and disposal. Even though computers are becoming more efficient and using less energy each, more and more people are using them so the cost to the environment increases. Do the students think that computers are benefiting society enough to justify their costs?

Extension or homework

Printer history – Printer technology has evolved rapidly over the last 20 years. Ink jet printers are now so cheap that they are given away free with computers – but it wasn't always this way. The first low-resolution black and white ink jet was released in 1988 and cost £1000. Usable laser printers were developed by Hewlett-Packard and Apple in 1984, again the prices were well above £1000. The students can look into the development of these two static-based devices.

SUMMARY ANSWERS

1 a) i) When she moved on the chair, her clothing rubbed against the chair and charged her.

ii) The charge on her discharged to the door handle as a spark.

b) i) Negatively charged.   **ii)** It would attract it.

2 a) i) From, to.   **ii)** On.

b) i) From, to.   **ii)** To, from.

3 a) Negative.

b) To attract the droplets on to it.

c) Electrons flow along the wires to the spray nozzle, are carried by the charged paint droplets, and return to the voltage supply from the metal panel.

4 a) i) They would go in the same direction onto the paper, so there would be a straight line on the paper as it moves past the jet.

ii) By contact with the grid wires.

b) To stop the fuel becoming charged or charging the fuel nozzle as it flows out of the nozzle. To stop the aircraft fuel tank becoming charged so no sparks are produced.

Summary teaching suggestions

- The students should be able to come up with a complete explanation of charging and discharging and the forces between objects. The answers to questions 1 and 2 should show this clearly.

- The remaining two questions test the applications and dangers of static electricity; again the students should be clearly describing the movement of charge and the attraction and repulsion effects.

STATIC ELECTRICITY: P2 4.1 – P2 4.4

SUMMARY QUESTIONS

1 a) Helen has just had a shock. She got up from a plastic chair to open the door and got an electric shock when she touched the door handle.
   i) How did she become charged?
   ii) Why did she feel a shock when she touched the door handle?
b) An object was charged by rubbing it with a dry cloth. When it was held near a negatively charged rod, it repelled the rod.
   i) State if the object was charged positively or negatively.
   ii) Would the object attract or repel a positively charged rod?

2 Complete the sentences below using words from the list.

   from   on   to

a) A polythene rod is charged negatively by rubbing it with a cloth.
   i) Electrons transfer ...... the cloth ...... the rod.
   ii) The electrons ...... the rod cannot move about freely.
b) A positively charged rod is touched on an insulated metal object.
   i) Electrons transfer ...... the metal object ...... the rod.
   ii) If the metal object is then 'earthed', electrons transfer ...... it ...... the ground.

3 A paint sprayer in a car factory is used to paint a metal panel. The spray nozzle is connected to the negative terminal of a voltage supply unit. The metal panel is connected to the positive terminal of the voltage supply unit.
a) What type of charge is gained by the paint droplets when they leave the spray nozzle?
b) Why is the metal panel made positive?
c) Why is there an electric current along the wires joining the metal panel and the paint spray nozzle to the voltage supply unit?

4 a) i) In an ink jet printer, what difference would it make if the droplets were not charged?
   ii) In an electrostatic precipitator, how are the dust particles charged?
b) When an airplane is being refuelled, explain why a wire is connected between the aircraft and the fuel tanker?

EXAM-STYLE QUESTIONS

1 A plastic rod is rubbed with a dry cloth.

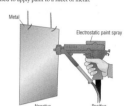

(a) The rod becomes negatively charged. Explain how this happens. **(3)**

(b) What charge is left on the cloth? **(1)**

(c) What happens if the negatively charged rod is brought close to another negatively charged rod. **(1)**

2 The picture shows an electrostatic paint spray being used to apply paint to a sheet of metal.

(a) The paint droplets are given a positive charge as they leave the nozzle. Explain why. **(2)**

(b) The sheet of metal is given a negative charge. Explain why. **(3)**

(c) (i) A painter wanted to find out the best distance between the nozzle of the paint spray and the sheet of metal to be painted. What could the painter use to measure the independent variable in this investigation? **(1)**

(ii) Why would it be a good idea for the painter to carry out some trials before deciding upon the range of the independent variable? **(2)**

EXAM-STYLE ANSWERS

1 a) Electrons are rubbed off the cloth *(1 mark)*
and are transferred onto the rod. *(1 mark)*
Electrons have a negative charge, so rod gains a negative charge. *(1 mark)*

b) Positive *(1 mark)*

c) They repel each other *(1 mark)*

2 a) Drops all have same charge so they repel each other *(1 mark)*
so paint spreads out to give a fine spray. *(1 mark)*

b) Opposite charge to paint spray *(1 mark)*
so paint is attracted to metal *(1 mark)*
and less paint is needed. *(1 mark)*

c) i) Ruler or any instrument that measures distance. *(1 mark)*
ii) If the distance is too small there will be splashing of paint off the metal. *(1 mark)*
If the distance is too great no paint will reach the metal. *(1 mark)*

3 The waste gases and smoke particles pass through the negatively charged metal grid. *(1 mark)*
The smoke particles gain negative charge *(1 mark)*
so they are repelled from the grid. *(1 mark)*
They are attracted to the positively charged collecting plates. *(1 mark)*
The smoke particles stick to the plates. *(1 mark)*
The collecting plates are periodically knocked so the smoke particles fall off and are taken away. *(1 mark)*

4 G E A F B *(4 marks)*
(minus 1 for each letter not in correct order)

HOW SCIENCE WORKS QUESTIONS

The picture shows an electrostatic smoke precipitator. This is used to separate smoke particles from waste gases in a chimney.

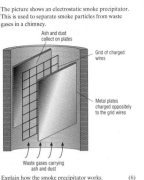

Ash and dust collect on plates

Grid of charged wires

Metal plates charged oppositely to the grid wires

Waste gases carrying ash and dust

Explain how the smoke precipitator works. (6)

A photocopier uses static electricity to make photocopies.

The following sentences describe how the photocopier works.

The sentences are in the wrong order.

A Black ink powder is attracted to the charged parts of the plate.

B The paper is heated so the powder melts and sticks to the paper.

C The copying plate is given a charge.

D This is now a photocopy of the original page.

E Where light hits the plate the charge leaks away, leaving a pattern of the page.

F Black ink powder is transferred onto a piece of paper.

G An image of the page to be copied is projected onto the charged copying plate.

Arrange the sentences in the right order. Start with sentence **C** and finish with sentence **D**.

C ▸ ☐ ▸ ☐ ▸ ☐ ▸ ☐ ▸ D

(4)

Lightning conductors are very important in protecting buildings from lightning strikes. New designs must be thoroughly tested. They must work first time and every time. They have to be tested in a standard way. This method is described in the diagram below.

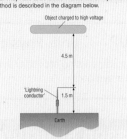

Object charged to high voltage

4.5 m

'Lightning conductor' 1.5 m

Earth

The conditions must be followed strictly. This includes the temperature of the room and the humidity. The charge is built up on the object above the lightning conductor and photographs are taken of the 'lightning' as it forms. This allows accurate measurements to be made of the time taken for the lightning conductor to respond. The measurements are made in microseconds.

a) Explain why it is important that the testing is carried out in exactly the same way each time. (1)

b) To find the correct temperature for these tests, the scientists carried out surveys.
   Suggest when they carried out the surveys. (1)

c) What do you think they were measuring? (1)

d) How many sets of data do you think they collected? (1)

e) What is the sensitivity of the equipment used to time the response of the lightning conductor? (1)

f) Explain why repeat tests on the same lightning conductor might give different results. (1)

g) Should this testing be carried out by the company manufacturing the lightning conductors or by an independent company? Explain your answer. (1)

169

Exam teaching suggestions

- Weaker students often think that for an object to be positively charged it has gained protons. Emphasise that it is only electrons that move during the transfer of charge.

- This section of the specification is very qualitative. To gain full marks in questions such as question 3, students must write their explanations clearly and in a logical sequence.
  Encourage them to plan their answer before putting pen to paper.

- In question 4 students are given the statements that form a description to put in the correct order. They should read through all the statements first, before attempting to order them.

- Students must be able to describe both uses and dangers of static electricity.

HOW SCIENCE WORKS ANSWERS

a) To ensure that the results are valid, i.e. it is a type of control for different people carrying out the testing.

b) When lightning was striking.

c) The air temperature.

d) As many as possible (e.g. a minimum of 50 as there is likely to be a wide range of temperatures.)

e) Microseconds are used to time the response of the lightning conductor.

f) The lightning conductor may have been damaged.

g) It could be done by both. However, a potential buyer would want to be assured of its reliability and therefore an independent company would be better. The testing will probably be monitored by an independent company.

How science works teaching suggestions

- **Literacy guidance**
  - Key terms that should be clearly understood: control, reliability, sensitivity, bias.
  - Question d) expects a longer answer, where students can practise their literacy skills.

- **Higher- and lower-level answers.** Question d) is a higher level question and the answer provided above is also at this level. Question b) is lower level and the answer provided is also lower level.

- **Gifted and talented.** Able students could consider how the speed of the conduction of the charge is measured. It is not as simple as it sounds here. The charge is built up and it is this relationship to the discharge through the lightning conductor that has to be measured.

- **How and when to use these questions.** When wishing to develop idea of controls in developing testing regimes and the potential for bias.
  The questions could be prepared for homework and then used in class in a plenary.

- **Homework.** Prepare questions at home. Consider the testing regime needed for other equipment such as trip switches or transformers.

- **Special needs.** Some students will need a more visual representation of the testing apparatus to appreciate what is happening.

P2 5.1   Electric circuits

LEARNING OBJECTIVES

Students should learn:

- That electrical circuits are drawn using standard symbols.
- The symbols used to represent common circuit components.

LEARNING OUTCOMES

Most students should be able to:

- Recognise and draw the circuit symbols for a cell, a battery, a switch, a lamp, a resistor, a variable resistor, a diode, a fuse, a voltmeter, an ammeter, a thermistor and an LDR.
- Describe the function of each of the above components.

Some students should also be able to:

- Draw circuit diagrams using the above symbols.

Teaching suggestions

- **Special needs.** Some students have particular difficulties with connecting up electronic circuits correctly, because they cannot match the neat circuit diagrams with the jumble of wires they are given. With these students it is best to use fixed boards, like the Locktronic ones. It is a good idea to write the names of the component on them until the students connect the symbol and name correctly.
- **Gifted and talented.** For the circuit building exercise, these students should be asked to look at the currents through the different branches of the circuit and find any relationships. They could even look into the potential differences and see if they can come up with the relationship before you discuss it in future lessons.
- **Learning styles**
  Kinaesthetic: Doing circuit building activities.
  Visual: Recognising symbols.
  Auditory: Listening to explanations of circuit behaviour.
  Interpersonal: Discussing and collaborating on circuit building.
- **Teaching assistant.** Your teaching assistant will be quite busy helping the students assemble the circuits. Make sure that you both describe how to construct the circuit in exactly the same way, so that you do not confuse the students.
- **Homework.** Get the students to memorise the symbols and have a quick test at the beginning of the next lesson.

SPECIFICATION LINK-UP   Unit: Physics 2.12.6

- *To interpret and draw circuit diagrams using standard symbols.*
  (See Student Book page 234 for symbols)

Lesson structure

STARTER

It's symbolic – Show a set of slides/diagrams to the students containing common symbols and ask them to say what they mean. Use road signs, hazard signs, washing symbols, etc. (5–10 minutes)

Describe the circuit – Give the students diagrams of two circuits containing cells, switches and lamps, one series and one parallel, and ask them to describe them both in a paragraph. (5–10 minutes)

Shoddy diagrams – Show the students a set of poorly draw circuit diagrams and ask them to explain how they could be improved or draw corrected circuits. (10 minutes)

MAIN

- Much of this topic will be revision. The students should be familiar with the basic ideas of circuits and circuit symbols from Key Stage 3.
- It is best to use this topic to check the students' circuit building skills, so that you can be sure that they can carry out the investigations later.
- Ask: 'Do symbols have to look like what they represent?' When introducing each symbol, show the students a real device represented by that symbol.
- You could show them that there are several physically different looking devices that match each symbol. For example, there are a range of different ammeters represented by the same symbol.
- Most students cope well with the basic symbols for lamps, switches and batteries. You will probably find that they struggle more with the various resistors.
- Point out the difference between a cell and a battery. Many students still do not understand that a battery is a series of cells. It helps to physically show a 1.5 V cell and then put two or more together to produce a battery. You can point out that the word 'battery' means 'a collection put close together' as in 'battery hens' and a 'battery of guns'.
- The best way to describe resistors is by discussing what is added to the basic resistor symbol:
  - The variable resistor has an arrow through it showing that you can adjust it.
  - The LDR has arrows going towards it representing light.
  - The fuse has a thin line representing the thin wire that runs inside it.
- With the remaining time, you should let the students build a couple of circuits. Those in the 'Circuits tests' activity are fine, or you could challenge higher attaining students further (see 'Gifted and talented').

PLENARIES

Match them up – Show the students a set of pictures/photographs of circuits and a set of circuit diagrams. They have to match them up. (5 minutes)

Symbol domino loop – Give the students a set of cards showing circuit symbols and descriptions of their functions. They have to place these cards in a complete loop, matching the symbol to the function. Can they name them all? (5–10 minutes)

Circuit problems – The students have to spot problems with diagrams of simple circuits, marking errors and suggesting corrections. (5 minutes)

ACTIVITY & EXTENSION IDEAS

Circuit building equipment

There are several schools of thought on which circuit building equipment is best. I have assumed that you are building circuits from separate components and simple leads, so you may have to modify the equipment lists for this chapter to suit your preferences. Using battery packs is not very economic when compared to low voltage power supplies, unless your students are careless and destroy a lot of bulbs.

Circuit building

This is more of a support activity to help students remember how to build basic circuits.

Equipment and materials required

Battery pack (3 V), three torch bulbs (3 V), leads, ammeter.

Details

Ask the students to set up a simple series circuit with two bulbs, and then a parallel one with a bulb on each branch. Can they make a parallel circuit with one bulb on one branch and two on the other? What can they say about the brightness of the bulbs? They should draw circuit diagrams of all these circuits before they construct them.

Practical support

Circuit tests

This is a simple introduction to building circuits allowing the students to refresh their skills.

Equipment and materials required

Cells (1.5 V), torch bulb (1.5 V), leads, diode, variable resistor.

Details

The students set up a simple circuit with the variable resistor and the bulb. They should find that the variable resistor can be used to alter the brightness of the bulb and be told that this is due to the current being changed. The students then include a diode in the circuit. They should then reverse the diode. This will show that the diode only allows the current in one direction.

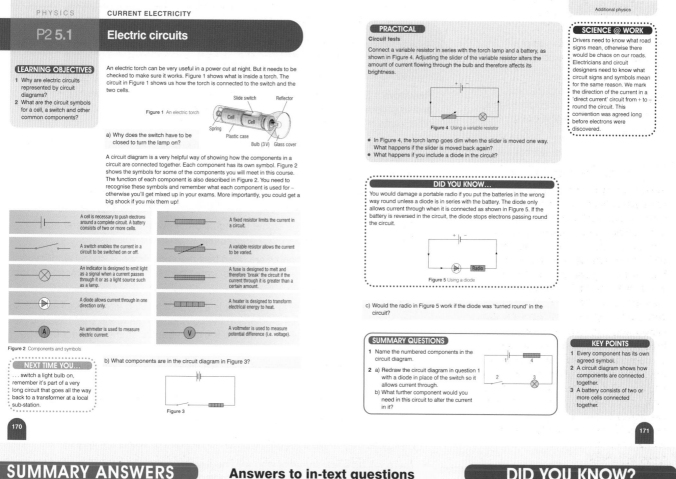

PHYSICS   CURRENT ELECTRICITY

P2 5.1 Electric circuits

LEARNING OBJECTIVES

1 Why are electric circuits represented by circuit diagrams?
2 What are the circuit symbols for a cell, a switch and other common components?

An electric torch can be very useful in a power cut at night. But it needs to be checked to make sure it works. Figure 1 shows what is inside a torch. The circuit in Figure 1 shows us how the torch is connected to the switch and the two cells.

Figure 1 An electric torch

a) Why does the switch have to be closed to turn the lamp on?

A circuit diagram is a very helpful way of showing how the components in a circuit are connected together. Each component has its own symbol. Figure 2 shows the symbols for some of the components you will meet in this course. The function of each component is also described in Figure 2. You need to recognise these symbols and remember what each component is used for – otherwise you'll get mixed up in your exams. More importantly, you could get a big shock if you mix them up!

A cell is necessary to push electrons around a complete circuit. A battery consists of two or more cells.

A switch enables the current in a circuit to be switched on or off.

An indicator is designed to emit light as a signal when a current passes through it or as a light source such as a lamp.

A diode allows current through in one direction only.

An ammeter is used to measure electric current.

A fixed resistor limits the current in a circuit.

A variable resistor allows the current to be varied.

A fuse is designed to melt and therefore 'break' the circuit if the current through it is greater than a certain amount.

A heater is designed to transform electrical energy to heat.

A voltmeter is used to measure potential difference (i.e. voltage).

Figure 2 Components and symbols

NEXT TIME YOU...
... switch a light bulb on, remember it's part of a very long circuit that goes all the way back to a transformer at a local sub-station.

b) What components are in the circuit diagram in Figure 3?

Figure 3

PRACTICAL

Circuit tests

Connect a variable resistor in series with the torch lamp and a battery, as shown in Figure 4. Adjusting the slider of the variable resistor alters the amount of current flowing through the bulb and therefore affects its brightness.

Figure 4 Using a variable resistor

● In Figure 4, the torch lamp goes dim when the slider is moved one way. What happens if the slider is moved back again?
● What happens if you include a diode in the circuit?

DID YOU KNOW...

You would damage a portable radio if you put the batteries in the wrong way round unless a diode is in series with the battery. The diode only allows current through when it is connected as shown in Figure 5. If the battery is reversed in the circuit, the diode stops electrons passing round the circuit.

Figure 5 Using a diode

c) Would the radio in Figure 5 work if the diode was 'turned round' in the circuit?

SUMMARY QUESTIONS

1 Name the numbered components in the circuit diagram.

2 a) Redraw the circuit diagram in question 1 with a diode in place of the switch so it allows current through.
   b) What further component would you need in this circuit to alter the current in it?

SCIENCE @ WORK

Drivers need to know what road signs mean, otherwise there would be chaos on our roads. Electricians and circuit designers need to know what circuit signs and symbols mean for the same reason. We mark the direction of the current in a 'direct current' circuit from + to – round the circuit. This convention was agreed long before electrons were discovered.

KEY POINTS

1 Every component has its own agreed symbol.
2 A circuit diagram shows how components are connected together.
3 A battery consists of two or more cells connected together.

170 / 171

SUMMARY ANSWERS

1 Cell, switch, indicator, fuse.

2 a)

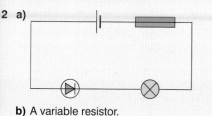

b) A variable resistor.

Answers to in-text questions

a) So current passes through it and through the lamp bulb.

b) Two cells, a switch and a heater.

c) No.

KEY POINTS

The students should be able to identify and draw circuit symbols (matching exercise).

DID YOU KNOW?

Diodes have limitations; if too high a voltage is placed on them in the wrong direction they 'break down' and allow a current to flow. This breakdown voltage is different for different types of diode, but it means that we cannot always rely on a diode to prevent the current flowing the wrong way. It's best to put the batteries in the right-way round.

P2 5.2 Resistance

LEARNING OBJECTIVES

Students should learn:

- How to use an ammeter and voltmeter.
- How to measure the resistance of a component.
- That a wire at a constant temperature obeys Ohm's law.
- That the resistance of a metal wire does not depend on the direction of the current.

LEARNING OUTCOMES

Most students should be able to:

- Measure the resistance of a resistor using an ammeter and voltmeter.
- Calculate the resistance of a device from the current through it and the potential difference across it.
- State Ohm's law for a metal wire.

Some students should also be able to:

- Perform calculations that involve rearrangement of the resistance equation.

Teaching suggestions

- **Special needs.** For resistance calculations, provide the students with a question sheet that has templates for the layout for equations so that they go through the process step by step.
- **Gifted and talented.** The students can find out about resistor coding bands used on simple resistors. Give them one each to take home, and ask them to come back with the resistance and tolerance.
- **Learning styles**
  Kinaesthetic: Building a range of circuits.
  Visual: Obtaining and presenting resistance information.
  Auditory: Explaining the pattern of the results.
  Interpersonal: Discussing and evaluating results.
  Intrapersonal: Making deductions about the behaviour of devices.
- **Homework.** Give the students a set of current–potential difference data for three different diameters of wire of the same length, and ask them to plot the three on the same set of axes. Ask: 'What can you say about the relationship between the diameter and the resistance?'

SPECIFICATION LINK-UP   Unit: Physics 2.12.6

- *Current–potential difference graphs are used to show how the current through a component varies with the potential difference across it.*
- *The current through a resistor (at a constant temperature) is directly proportional to the potential difference across the resistor.*
- *Potential difference, current and resistance are related by the equation:*

$$\text{potential difference} = \text{current} \times \text{resistance}$$
$$\text{(volt, V)} \qquad \text{(ampere, A)} \quad \text{(ohm, } \Omega\text{)}$$

- *The resistance of a component can be found by measuring the current through and potential difference across the component.*

Students should use their skills, knowledge and understanding of 'How Science Works':

- *to apply the principles of basic electrical circuits to practical situations.*

Lesson structure

STARTER

Resistors – Show the students the circuit symbols for all of the different types of resistor and ask them to describe the similarities in the symbols. Ask: 'What do they think the other parts of the symbols mean?' (5 minutes)

Reading the meter – Show the students some pictures of analogue meters and ask them to read off the value shown. Use a variety of different scales for the meters. (5 minutes)

MAIN

- It is very important that the students understand how to use an ammeter and voltmeter, and they have a good opportunity to do that in this lesson.
- Currents through components are often less than one ampere, so the students will have to get used to using 'milliamperes' (most people just use 'milliamps') in a lot of their work.
- A simple analogy explaining resistance is a student moving along a packed corridor with his eyes closed. Other students in the corridor will get in the way, resisting his progress. If all of the other students are moving about a lot, the resistance will be higher – a bit like the wire heating up.
- During the movement, the electrons will lose energy as they collide with the ions in the metal. Link this idea to earlier energy transformation work. It is always important to check that the students do not think that electrons are used up as they move. They just lose (transfer) energy.
- Some computer simulations of electron movement show that the electrons are losing energy as they move through the potential difference. These are very useful.
- There will be a few students who will find it strange that the letter 'I' is used to represent current in equations. It is surprisingly difficult to find out why. The students may be more comfortable just using word equations. The Greek letter omega is chosen to represent ohms, because it sounds the same (as good a reason as any).
- The practical activity in the Student Book is a good way of checking the students' skills in using the meters and using the equation. It will also give opportunities for students to manipulate variables and design a fair test (this relates to 'How Science Works').

PLENARIES

An electron's tale – Students write a paragraph about the journey of an electron around a circuit containing a lamp and resistor. They should write about the energy changes that are going on in the circuit. (10 minutes)

ACTIVITY & EXTENSION IDEAS

Resistance and length of a wire

This traditional experiment works very well and has often been a source of centre-assessed practical work in the past. Most students find the experiment easier if they use high resistivity wire, such as constantan, as this produces resistances that are easy to understand (1 Ω), as opposed to copper wires which have very low resistances and can make the graphs harder to draw for some.

Equipment and materials required

Ammeter, voltmeter, metre ruler, 3 V battery pack (or power supply), leads, switch, two crocodile clips, test wire, heatproof mat.

Details

The students set up the circuit used for the measurement of resistance of a wire, but they connect the crocodile clips to the test wire at measured lengths. This allows them to find out how resistance varies with length. There are many ways to improve the accuracy and precision of this experiment (this relates to 'How Science Works'). The experiment should be carried out on a heatproof mat as short lengths can get hot.

✎ Practical support

Investigating the resistance of a wire

The students can investigate if the resistance of a wire depends on the current flowing through it. Constantan wires works well, as these do not change resistance as much when they heat up. It is also advisable to use battery packs or power packs with lockable voltage outputs, as the wires can heat up and cause burns if high currents are used.

Equipment and materials required

For each group: a power supply or battery pack, connecting leads, switch, crocodile clips, variable resistor, length of wire (30–50 cm), heatproof mat, ammeter and voltmeter.

Details

The students connect up the circuit with the variable resistor and test wire in series. The ammeter is also placed in series and the voltmeter in parallel across the test wire. Some students will struggle to set this up, so check the circuits before they are switched on. Using the variable resistor, the students can control the current through the test wire and measure both the current and the potential difference. In general, they should find that the resistance stays constant unless the wire heats up too much. The experiment shouldn't get too hot if low p.d.s are used but use a heatproof mat anyway.

Teaching suggestions – continued

- **ICT link-up.** If you get different groups to investigate the current–potential difference characteristics of different lengths (or diameters) of wire, then the data can be collected in a spreadsheet. This can be used to calculate the mean resistance of the wire from the data, and then to check for a relationship between the length (or diameter) and the resistance by quickly plotting a graph.

- **Teaching assistant.** As in the previous lesson, the assistant will be best employed in helping the students construct their circuits. They can also help some students with the plotting of graphs.

SUMMARY ANSWERS

1 a)

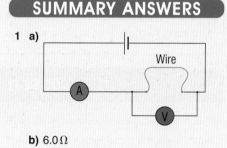

b) 6.0 Ω

2 W: 6.0 Ω; X: 80 V; Y: 2.0 A; Z: 24 Ω

KEY POINTS

The students should plot a graph of the results of their investigations to find the relationship between current and potential difference.

Answers to in-text questions

a) 8.0 Ω

b) 10 Ω

Additional physics

PHYSICS   CURRENT ELECTRICITY

P2 5.2   Resistance

LEARNING OBJECTIVES

1 Where should you put an ammeter and a voltmeter in a circuit?
2 What is resistance and what is its unit?
3 What is Ohm's law?
4 What happens if you reverse the current in a resistor?

Ammeters and voltmeters

Figure 1 Using an ammeter and a voltmeter

Look at the ammeter and the voltmeter in the circuit in Figure 1.

- The ammeter measures the current through the torch lamp. It is connected in series with the lamp so the current through them is the same. The ammeter reading gives the current in amperes (A) (or milliamperes, (mA) for small currents, where 1 mA = 0.001 A).
- The voltmeter measures the potential difference (p.d.) across the torch lamp. It is connected in parallel with the torch lamp so it measures the pd across it. The voltmeter reading gives the p.d. in volts (V).

Electrons passing through a torch lamp have to push their way through lots of vibrating atoms. The atoms resist the passage of electrons through the torch lamp.

We define the resistance of an electrical component as:

$$\text{Resistance (ohms)} = \frac{\text{potential difference (volts)}}{\text{current (amperes)}}$$

The unit of resistance is the *ohm*. The symbol for the ohm is the Greek letter Ω.

We can write the definition above as:

$$R = \frac{V}{I}$$

where V = potential difference (volts)
I = current (amperes)
R = resistance (ohms).

Worked example
The current through a wire is 2.0 A when the potential difference across it is 12 V.

Calculate the resistance of the wire.

Solution

$$R = \frac{12V}{2.0A} = 6.0\,\Omega$$

GET IT RIGHT!
Ammeters are always connected in series and voltmeters are always connected in parallel.

a) The current through a wire is 0.5 A when the current through it is 4.0 V. Calculate the resistance of the wire.

PRACTICAL

Investigating the resistance of a wire

Does the resistance of a wire change when the current through it is changed? Figure 2 shows how we can use a variable resistor to change the current through a wire. Make your own measurements and use them to plot a current–potential difference graph like the one in Figure 2.

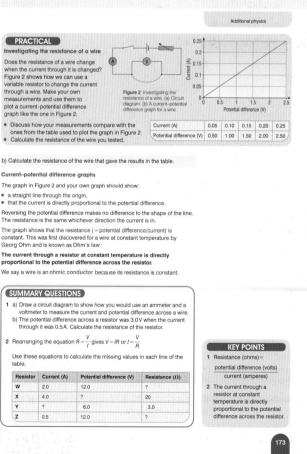

Figure 2 Investigating the resistance of a wire. (a) Circuit diagram. (b) A current–potential difference graph for a wire.

- Discuss how your measurements compare with the ones from the table used to plot the graph in Figure 2.
- Calculate the resistance of the wire you tested.

Current (A)	0.05	0.10	0.15	0.20	0.25
Potential difference (V)	0.50	1.00	1.50	2.00	2.50

b) Calculate the resistance of the wire that gave the results in the table.

Current–potential difference graphs

The graph in Figure 2 and your own graph should show:

- a straight line through the origin,
- that the current is directly proportional to the potential difference.

Reversing the potential difference makes no difference to the shape of the line. The resistance is the same whichever direction the current is in.

The graph shows that the resistance (= potential difference/current) is constant. This was first discovered for a wire at constant temperature by Georg Ohm and is known as Ohm's law:

The current through a resistor at constant temperature is directly proportional to the potential difference across the resistor.

We say a wire is an ohmic conductor because its resistance is constant.

SUMMARY QUESTIONS

1 a) Draw a circuit diagram to show how you would use an ammeter and a voltmeter to measure the current and potential difference across a wire.
   b) The potential difference across a resistor was 3.0 V when the current through it was 0.5 A. Calculate the resistance of the resistor.

2 Rearranging the equation $R = \frac{V}{I}$ gives $V = IR$ or $I = \frac{V}{R}$

Use these equations to calculate the missing values in each line of the table.

Resistor	Current (A)	Potential difference (V)	Resistance (Ω)
W	2.0	12.0	?
X	4.0	?	20
Y	?	6.0	3.0
Z	0.5	12.0	?

KEY POINTS

1 Resistance (ohms) =
$$\frac{\text{potential difference (volts)}}{\text{current (amperes)}}$$

2 The current through a resistor at constant temperature is directly proportional to the potential difference across the resistor.

P2 5.3

More current–potential difference graphs

Teaching suggestions

- **Gifted and talented.** Ask; 'How does a diode work?' This simple semiconductor is quite difficult to explain, but these students can try to find out how they operate.
- **Learning styles**
  Kinaesthetic: More building of circuits.
  Visual: Presenting data graphically.
  Auditory: Discussing patterns in results.
  Interpersonal: Reporting on behaviour of components.
  Intrapersonal: Evaluating investigations.
- **ICT link-up.** Using data logging equipment is a very good way of collecting data for current–potential difference graphs. Once set up, the students just have to adjust the variable resistor, press the space bar to take readings and then repeat until all the data is collected. The graphs can be displayed in seconds.

SPECIFICATION LINK-UP   Unit: Physics 2.12.6

- *Current–potential difference graphs are used to show how the current through a component varies with the potential difference across it.* (See Student Book page 238 for graphs.)
- *The resistance of a filament lamp increases as the temperature of the filament increases.*
- *The current through a diode flows in one direction only. The diode has a very high resistance in the reverse direction.*
- *The resistance of a light-dependent resistor (LDR) decreases as light intensity increases.*
- *The resistance of a thermistor decreases as the temperature increases (i.e. knowledge of negative temperature coefficient thermistor only is required).*
- *The current through a component depends on its resistance. The greater the resistance the smaller the current for a given potential difference across the component.*

Students should use their skills, knowledge and understanding of 'How Science Works':

- *to apply the principles of basic electrical circuits to practical situations.*

Lesson structure

STARTER

Pop! – Set up a circuit with a filament bulb that will have too high a current. Switch it on when the room is silent (so that they can hear the 'tink' sound) and ask the students to explain what happened. (5–10 minutes)

Three switches – Ask: 'You are outside a room with three switches that control three light bulbs inside the room; one switch for each light. How can you work out which switch controls which light if you are only allowed to open the door and go into the room once?' (5 minutes)

MAIN

- Start this topic with a reminder of the practical work from last lesson.
- The initial practical activities can take up a lot of time if the students wish to take plenty of measurements. You may like to let some groups do one of the experiments while the rest do the other, and then get them to share the results.
- The results should show that the filament lamp does not have a straight line on its current–potential difference graph. This is because it is heating up and the resistance is increasing, the greater the current in the wire. (This relates to 'How Science Works': identifying relationships between variables.)
- Link this back to the students' ideas about what happens to a material when it gets hotter. The ions are vibrating more and the electrons are having more collisions with them. This increases the resistance.
- A diode is a more complex device. It behaves in a non-ohmic way. The reasons for its behaviour are beyond Key Stage 4, but you might like to ask the gifted and talented group to look into it.
- Some students will have heard of light emitting diodes and think that all diodes give out light. You could demonstrate one of these in a circuit, showing that it only lights up if it is placed in the circuit the right way. The arrow on the symbol shows the direction of the current.
- As with the initial practical task, you might like to set different groups different tasks for the thermistor and LDR.
- These two devices can be investigated to cover many of the investigative aspects of 'How Science Works'.

PLENARIES

Inside the black box – An electrical component has been placed inside a black box with only the two connections visible. The students should design an experiment to find out what it is. (5 minutes)

Practical support

Investigating different components

The students can investigate how the resistance of a filament lamp and a diode change when the p.d. across them is changed.

Equipment and materials required

For each group: a power supply or battery pack, connecting leads, variable resistor, ammeter, voltmeter, filament lamp, fixed resistor and diode.

Details

The students connect up the circuit with the component under test in series with the variable resistor. The ammeter is also placed in series and the voltmeter is placed in parallel with the test component. Using the variable resistor, the students change the p.d. across the component and record the current and p.d. From the results, the students produce a current–potential difference graph. They should also try the circuit with the current flowing in the opposite direction, to show that this does not affect the lamp but is very important for the diode.

Thermistors and light-dependent resistors (LDRs)

The students can investigate a LDR by finding out how its resistance is related to the distance it is from a bright light. Sensitive thermistors can have a significant change in resistance from just placing them between finger and thumb to warm them up.

Answers to in-text questions

a) i) 5 Ω   **ii)** 10 Ω
b) It decreases.
c) The resistance is constant.
d) The resistance decreases.

DID YOU KNOW?

The longest lasting light bulb has been on for more than 100 years. It's in a fire station in Livermore, USA, and was installed in 1901. It is never off, except in power cuts and when it was moved to the new fire station. You might like to check if it's still going!

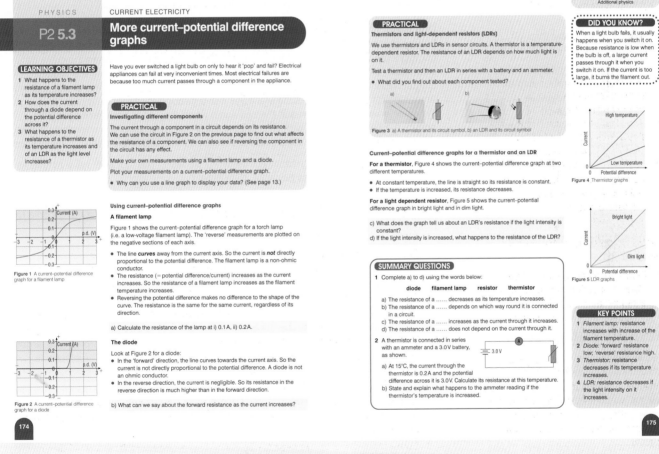

SUMMARY ANSWERS

1 **a)** Thermistor. **b)** Diode. **c)** Filament lamp. **d)** Resistor.

2 **a)** 15 Ω

  b) The ammeter reading increases because the resistance of the thermistor decreases.

KEY POINTS

Get the students to construct a sentence describing how the resistance of a filament lamp, diode, thermistor and light dependent resistor change.

P2 5.4   Series circuits

Students should learn that:

- In a series circuit the same current passes through all components.

- The p.d. of the voltage supply is shared across the components in a series circuit.

- Cells in series add their potentials to give a higher voltage.

- The total resistance in a series circuit is the sum of the component resistances.

LEARNING OUTCOMES

Most students should be able to:

- State that the current through components in series is the same.

- Find the total potential difference across several components in series, given the potential difference across each component.

- Find the total potential difference of a group of cells connected in series.

- Calculate the total resistance in a series circuit.

Some students should also be able to:

- Analyse a simple series circuit to find the current and p.d. across components.

Teaching suggestions

- **Special needs.** Provide the students with a printed set of circuit rules containing the ones from this topic and the next, to help them remember them all.

- **Gifted and talented.** There are a set of rules about the current and potentials in a circuit called Kirchhoff's laws. These are basically an electrical statement of the laws of conservation of energy, and the students should be able to find out what they are.

- **Learning styles**
  Kinaesthetic: Carrying out practical activities with series circuits.
  Visual: Obtaining data from meter readings.
  Auditory: Discussing results.
  Interpersonal: Collaborating on experiments.
  Intrapersonal: Evaluating results, including the accuracy of measuring instruments.

SPECIFICATION LINK-UP   Unit: Physics 2.12.6

- *The potential difference provided by cells connected in series is the sum of the potential difference of each cell (depending on the direction in which they are connected).*

- *For components connected in series:*
  - *The total resistance is the sum of the resistance of each component.*
  - *There is the same current through each component.*
  - *The total potential difference of the supply is shared between the components.*

Students should use their skills, knowledge and understanding of 'How Science Works':

- *to apply the principles of basic electrical circuits to practical situations.*

Lesson structure

STARTER

Duff battery – Ask the students to correct this information: 'A chemical reaction in a battery makes electrons. These move quickly around a circuit and go through the components until there are no electrons left. The battery 'runs out' when there are no chemicals left in it to make electrons from.' [e.g. 'A chemical reaction in the battery provides electrons with energy. These electrons move slowly around the circuit and push other electrons through it. As the electrons move through the components of the circuit they lose energy until they reach the cell again when they have transferred all of the energy they were provided with. The battery 'runs out' when all of the chemicals in it have reacted together and it cannot provide the electrons with any more energy.'] (5 minutes)

Series – Ask: 'What is the meaning of the word 'series'?' The students have to give as many examples of its use as possible. (5 minutes)

One way only – Ask: 'In what situation are we allowed only one way through something?' Let the students think of a few. Ask: 'If there is only one way to go on a tour, do the same number of people come out as go in?' (5 minutes)

MAIN

- When discussing series and parallel circuits, many teachers use the analogy of a central heating system with the water representing the electrons, a pump representing the battery etc. There are limitations with this concept, but it can help lower ability students.

- The students need to be reminded that the current is a flow of electrons. The larger the current, the more electrons are passing a point each second. The electrons cannot be destroyed and they do not escape from the circuit.

- The students tend to understand the current rules quite well, but struggle more with the idea that the potential difference is shared. They should test this out in the practical task.

- Generally, try to move students from using 'voltage' to 'potential difference', as reflected in the specification.

- As noted in the practical, there can be some minor errors produced by the meters so you will have to explain them to the students. This is a useful opportunity to consider 'How Science Works': accuracy/precision/reliability.

- Simulation software can be used to show the measurement of the p.d. across many lamps connected in series. It is also easy to add more cells to show that the total p.d. drop across the components always matches the p.d. of the battery.

- Many students will simply accept that the total resistance of a set of components in series is just the same as the individual resistances without the need for calculations.

- Test their understanding by showing them a set of resistors in series, and asking for the total resistance. Students should have no problems with this.

- You might like to show some more difficult resistors such as $1.5\,\text{M}\Omega$ or $33\,\text{m}\Omega$ to get the students used to them.

Practical support

Investigating potential differences in a series circuit

This experiment helps to verify the rule about potential differences in series circuits.

Equipment and materials required

For each group: a power supply or battery pack (1.5 V), connecting leads, variable resistor, 1.5 V lamp and three voltmeters.

Details

The students connect up a lamp and variable resistor in series. Connect up one voltmeter across the cell (with voltage, V_{tot}), one across the lamp (with voltage, V_1) and one across the variable resistor (with voltage, V_2). When the circuit is switched on the students should find that $V_1 + V_2 = V_{tot}$ when the variable resistor is set to any position. You may find that the voltmeters don't quite show this, and so it is a good time to discuss errors and the limitation of the equipment (this relates to 'How Science Works').

Teaching suggestions – continued

- **ICT link-up.** If at all possible, show a simulation of electron movement through the circuit to show that the electrons pass all the way around the circuit and are not used up. The simulation should also have some way of showing that the electrons are transferring energy as they go.

- **Homework.** Give the students some series circuit diagrams with missing voltages, currents or resistances. Ask them to find the missing values. This should test their knowledge of the current–p.d.–resistance relationship and the total resistance rule.

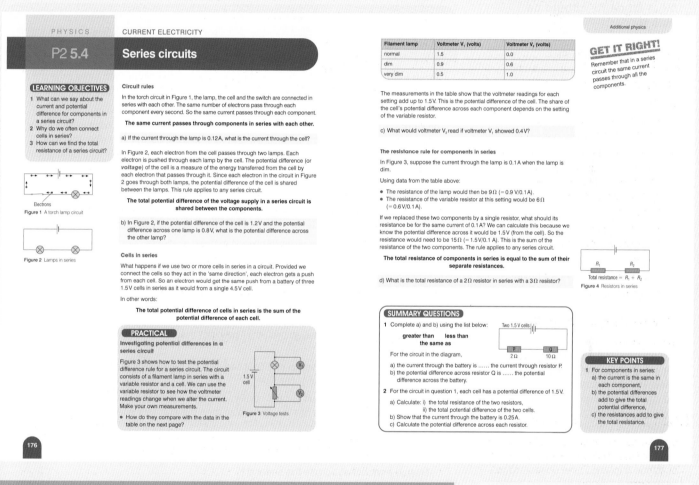

177

PLENARIES

Current loop – Let the students play a looped question game with questions based on electrical circuits; no branches allowed. (5 minutes)

Controlling current – Give the students a set of cards representing cells (1.5 V) and resistors (1 Ω, 2 Ω, 5 Ω etc.) and ask them to put some of them together to produce a current of 1 A, then a current of 0.5 A. (5 minutes)

Circuit rules – The students should start making a list of circuit rules that help them work out the currents, potential differences and resistances in series and parallel circuits. (5–10 minutes)

KEY POINTS

The students should fill in the missing values from a set of circuit diagrams to show that they understand current and potential difference.

Answers to in-text questions

a) 0.12 A

b) 0.4 V

c) 1.1 V

d) 5 Ω

SUMMARY ANSWERS

1 **a)** The same as. **b)** Less than.

2 **a) i)** 12 Ω **ii)** 3.0 V

b) $\dfrac{3\,V}{12\,\Omega} = 0.25\,a$

c) P = 0.5 V, Q = 2.5 V

P2 5.5   Parallel circuits

LEARNING OBJECTIVES

Students should learn:

- That the potential difference across components in parallel is the same.
- That the total current in a parallel circuit is the sum of the currents in the individual branches.

LEARNING OUTCOMES

Most students should be able to:

- Recognise components in parallel with each other.
- Calculate the current in a branch of a parallel circuit, given the total current and the current in the other branches.
- Identify, for resistors of known resistance in parallel, which resistor has the most current passing through it and which has the least.

Some students should also be able to:

- Analyse simple parallel circuits to find the current through branches and the p.d. across components.

Teaching suggestions

- **Special needs.** There are some more tricky circuits here and the students may need a step-by-step guide to assemble them: 'connect the positive end of the battery to the ammeter', etc. You might also think about attaching labels A_1, A_2 to the ammeters to reduce confusion.
- **Learning styles**
  Kinaesthetic: Carrying out practical tests involving parallel circuits.
  Visual: Recording and presenting data.
  Auditory: Explaining the observations.
  Interpersonal: Working in small groups in practical work.
  Intrapersonal: Making deductions about current and p.d. in circuits.
- **ICT link-up.** A range of software is available to simulate circuit construction and measure current and voltages. This can be much easier to use than assembling larger parallel circuits with a number of voltmeters and ammeters.
- **Homework.** Give the students some series and parallel circuits to analyse. They should find the missing currents, potential differences and resistances.
- **Teaching assistant.** The students will have much more difficulty connecting devices up in parallel than they did in series, so your teaching assistant will again have to help out with construction of these circuits.

SPECIFICATION LINK-UP   Unit: Physics 2.12.6

- *For components connected in parallel:*
  - *The potential difference across each component is the same.*
  - *The total current through the whole circuit is the sum of the currents through the separate components.*

Students should use their skills, knowledge and understanding of 'How Science Works':

- *to apply the principles of basic electrical circuits to practical situations.*

Lesson structure

STARTER

Circuit jumble – Show the students a diagram of a parallel circuit with three branches and several components on each branch. The wires and components are jumbled up and the students have to redraw the circuit properly. (5–10 minutes)

The river – Show the students a picture of a river that branches and rejoins. Ask then to explain what happens to the current in the river before, during and after the split. (5–10 minutes)

Parallel – Ask: 'What does the word 'parallel' mean?' The students can give as many uses as possible. (5 minutes)

MAIN

- The initial investigation is straightforward and the students should be able to find the rule easily. A discussion of errors involved in the ammeter readings helps to get across concepts involving single measurements from 'How Science Works'.
- A simulation can be used if there are not enough ammeters, but you should show the results in a real circuit too.
- Spend a bit of time explaining that at the junction of a branch some of the electrons go one way while the rest go the other way, but they all come from and go back to the battery.
- The bypass idea helps some students realise that because there are more paths for the current a larger current can flow.
- The second simple circuit should confirm that the p.d. is the same across both of the resistors. If the resistors are the same size then the currents should also be the same through each branch.
- To stretch higher attaining students, ask them to investigate a circuit that has two resistors on one branch and one on the other. Ask: 'Does the p.d. across the first branch match that across the second?'
- The circuit analysis will show if the students have got a firm grip of the equations. You may have to lead them through the analysis one step at a time. Try a couple more circuits if time permits.

PLENARIES

The light that shines twice as bright lasts half as long – If two lamps are connected to a battery in parallel, they will shine more brightly than if they were connected in series but they will only last half as long. Can the students explain why? (5–10 minutes)

Stair lights – Can the students design a simple circuit that can be used to turn the lights on and off from the top and bottom of a set of stairs. If time permits, they could build one. (10–15 minutes)

Parallel analogies – Can the students come up with any more analogies for a parallel circuit besides the ones from the 'Did you know' box? They should explain them to each other to decide which is best. (5–10 minutes)

Practical support

Investigating parallel circuits

This experiment shows that that the current is divided through parallel branches.

Equipment and materials required

For each group: a power supply or battery pack (1.5 V), connecting leads, variable resistor, two 1.5 V lamps and three ammeters.

Details

The students set up the circuit with two parallel branches, each with an ammeter. The third ammeter is placed in series with the power supply or battery to measure total current, and the variable resistor is used in series with the battery to control the current. The readings from the two ammeters on the branches (A_2 and A_3) should be equal to the total current from the battery (A_1). As in the experiment from the last lesson, there can be inaccuracies in the readings so go through the results with the students and discuss the reasons for these errors (this relates to 'How Science Works').

Potential difference in a parallel circuit

This is another simple circuit used to verify that the potential difference across parallel components is the same.

Equipment and materials required

For each group: a power supply or battery pack (1.5 V), connecting leads, a 2 Ω resistor and a 5 Ω resistor, a variable resistor, and two voltmeters.

Details

The students connect up the circuit as shown and measure the p.d. across the two resistors. This should be the same. To show that this fact does not change, replace one of the resistors with a variable one and alter its resistance.

Answers to in-text questions

a) 0.30 A

b) The 3 Ω resistor.

P2 5.5   Parallel circuits

LEARNING OBJECTIVES

1 What can we say about the current and potential difference for components in a parallel circuit?
2 How can we calculate currents and potential differences in parallel circuits?

DID YOU KNOW?

A bypass is a parallel route. A heart bypass is another route for the flow of blood. A road bypass is a road that passes a town centre instead of going through it. For components in parallel, charge flows separately through each component. The total flow of charge is the sum of the flow through each component.

PRACTICAL

Investigating parallel circuits

Figure 1 shows how you can investigate the current through two lamps in parallel with each other. You can use ammeters in series with the lamps and the cell to measure the current through the lamp.

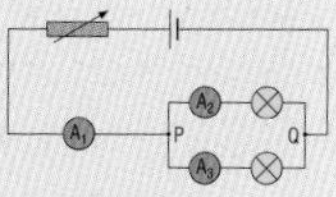

Set up your own circuit and collect your data.

Figure 1 At a junction

- How do your measurements compare with the ones in the table for different settings of the variable resistor shown below?
- Discuss if your own measurements show the same pattern.

Look at the sample data below:

Ammeter A₁ (A)	Ammeter A₂ (A)	Ammeter A₃ (A)
0.50	0.30	0.20
0.30	0.20	0.10
0.18	0.12	0.06

In each case, the reading of ammeter A_1 is equal to the sum of the readings of ammeters A_2 and A_3.

This shows that the current from the cell is equal to sum of the currents through the two lamps. This rule applies wherever components are in parallel.

a) If ammeter A_1 reads 0.40 A and A_3 reads 0.1 A, what would A_2 read?

The total current through the whole circuit is the sum of the currents through the separate components.

Potential difference in a parallel circuit

Figure 2 shows two resistors X and Y in parallel with each other. A voltmeter is connected across each resistor. The voltmeter across resistor X shows the same reading as the voltmeter across resistor Y. This is because each electron from the cell either passes through X or through Y. So it delivers the same amount of energy from the cell, whichever resistor it goes through. In other words:

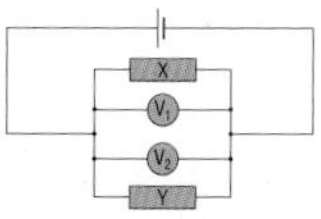

Figure 2 Components in parallel

For components in parallel, the potential difference across each component is the same.

Calculations on parallel circuits

Components in parallel have the same potential difference across them. The current through each component depends on the resistance of the component.

- The bigger the resistance of the component, the smaller the current through it. The resistor which has the largest resistance passes the smallest current.
- We can calculate the current using the equation:

$$\text{current (amperes)} = \frac{\text{potential difference (volts)}}{\text{resistance (ohms)}}$$

b) A 3 Ω resistor and a 6 Ω resistor are connected in parallel in a circuit. Which resistor passes the most current?

Worked example

The circuit diagram shows three resistors $R_1 = 1\,\Omega$, $R_2 = 2\,\Omega$ and $R_3 = 6\,\Omega$ connected in parallel to a 6 V battery.

Calculate:

i) the current through each resistor,
ii) the current through the battery.

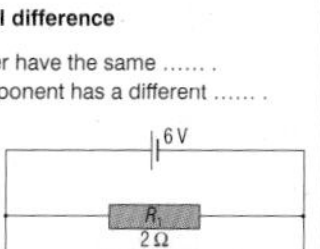

Solution

i) $I_1 = \dfrac{V_1}{R_1} = \dfrac{6}{1} = 6\,\text{A}$

$I_2 = \dfrac{V_2}{R_2} = \dfrac{6}{2} = 3\,\text{A}$

$I_3 = \dfrac{V_3}{R_3} = \dfrac{6}{6} = 1\,\text{A}$

ii) The total current from the battery $= I_1 + I_2 + I_3 = 6\,\text{A} + 3\,\text{A} + 1\,\text{A} = 10\,\text{A}$

SUMMARY QUESTIONS

1 Choose words from the list to complete a) and b):

   current   potential difference

   a) Components in parallel with each other have the same ....
   b) For components in parallel, each component has a different ....

2 The circuit diagram shows three resistors $R_1 = 2\,\Omega$, $R_2 = 3\,\Omega$ and $R_3 = 6\,\Omega$ connected to each other in parallel and to a 6 V battery.

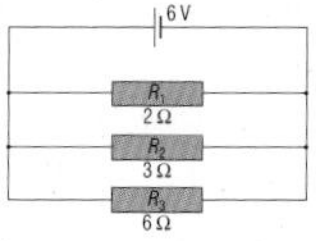

   Calculate:

   a) the current through each resistor,
   b) the current through the battery.

KEY POINTS

1 For components in parallel,
   a) the potential difference is the same across each component,
   b) the total current is the sum of the currents through each component,
   c) the bigger the resistance of a component, the smaller its current is.

SUMMARY ANSWERS

1 **a)** Potential difference. **b)** Current.

2 **a)** R_1: 3 A; R_2: 2 A; R_3: 1 A

   b) 6 A

KEY POINTS

Can the students find the current through the branches of a parallel circuit when given the resistances and battery voltage? Give the students some parallel circuits to analyse. They should be able to fill in missing values.

P2 5.6 Circuits in control

SPECIFICATION LINK-UP

Unit: Physics 2.12.6

This spread can be used to revisit:

Students should use their skills, knowledge and understanding of 'How Science Works':

- to apply the principles of basic electrical circuits to practical situations.

Teaching suggestions

Activities

- **A magic eye** – The magic eye circuit is not too difficult to build, so show one to the students. In reality these circuits often have transistors or relays to switch on the second circuit containing the motor or fan, but for the students' designs this is not necessary.

- **The development of microelectronics** The computing power available on a microchip has followed a pattern first described by Gordon E Moore (founder of Intel) in 1965. He suggested that the available computing power on a microchip would double every year. This hasn't quite happened; it seems to have doubled every two years from 1965 to the current day. A high power computer chip has close to one billion transistors on it (although many of these are from on chip memory); though, according to Moore's law, this information will be out of date by the time you read it!

- Connecting 'control chips' to human brains is the topic of many stories, generally about how this would be a bad idea. There are alternative views presented in a few stories and the students should be encouraged to look into both sides of the issue. Imagine being able to instantly remember anything or reach out to a billion people at once and ask them a question. Imagine being able to upload knowledge directly into your brain without having to go to lessons. This leads us to . . .

- **No more school!** – It has always been assumed that using computers helps learning, but does it? There is very little research and what there is seems to show that this assumption is wrong. Ask: 'Do students with computers learn more just because they are wealthier?' In the poem or discussion, the students not only need to consider if the learning

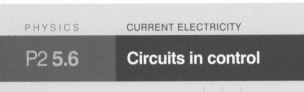

PHYSICS   CURRENT ELECTRICITY

P2 5.6 Circuits in control

A magic eye

When you go shopping, doors often open automatically in front of you. An automatic door has a sensor that detects anyone who approaches it. Children think there's a magic eye. But Figure 1 shows you it's no more than an electric circuit.

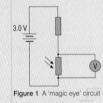

3.0 V

Figure 1 A 'magic eye' circuit

The 'light beam' sensor in Figure 1 is a light-dependent resistor (LDR) in series with a resistor and a battery. A voltmeter is connected across the LDR to show what happens when the LDR is covered. If you make and test this circuit, you should find the voltmeter reading goes up when the LDR is covered. This can be used to switch an electric motor or an alarm circuit on.

ACTIVITIES

a) Use your knowledge of electric circuits to discuss why the voltmeter reading in Figure 1 goes up when you cover the LDR?

b) Design a circuit using a thermistor instead of an LDR to switch an electric fan on if the room gets too hot.

The development of microelectronics

- The first amplifier, the electronic valve, was invented in the 1920s.
- The first electronic switch, the transistor, was invented in the 1940s.
- The microchip was invented in the 1970s.
- The World Wide Web was invented in the 1990s.

The latest computers contain microchips which each contain millions of tiny electronic switches. We measure the capacity of a chip in *bytes*, where a byte is a sequence of bits of data (0's and 1's).

ACTIVITY

Imagine a microchip that could be inserted into the human brain to control your actions and thoughts. Would this be good or bad? Discuss with your friends why it could be good and why it might be bad.

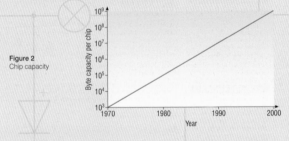

Figure 2 Chip capacity

Figure 2 shows the growth in the capacity of chips since the first one was invented. As chip capacity has increased, electronic devices have become smaller and smaller, as well as more and more sophisticated. They have also become cheaper and cheaper. If cars had changed in the same way, everyone in the world could have a car for less than £1 that would travel 10 000 kilometres on a litre of petrol.

experience will be as good but also the lack of social interactions. Ask: 'Would we end up as a society of people who never go out of the house? Would teachers be forced to become comedians in the amusement camps?' You could try out some jokes to see how you would get on.

- **Robots in charge** – When using the word 'robot', students often just think of the human-shaped robots in films and TV. Show them the wide range of real machines, very few of which are humanoid.

- There are many films, TV shows and books with robots in them to discuss, and there is no space to list them here; but at some point, one of the students may bring up the three laws of robotics: a set of rules that are meant to protect humans from their machines. These were formulated by Isaac Asimov and are:

  – A robot may not harm a human being, or, through inaction, allow a human being to come to harm.

  – A robot must obey the orders given to it by human beings, except where such orders would conflict with the First Law.

  – A robot must protect its own existence, as long as such protection does not conflict with the First or Second Law.

News Flash

No more school!

The Government today announced that children will not have to go to school for lessons any more. Instead, each child will sit in front of a home computer every day. Children who do not go on-line for their lessons will be sent to 'boot camps' to learn. The schools will reopen as amusement arcades with entertainers instead of teachers.

ACTIVITY

Do you think this government policy is a good or a bad idea?

Either: Write a poem about it

or hold a discussion about the issue.

ANSWERS TO QUESTIONS

1 A daytime fire alarm.

2 A greenhouse alarm if the sunlight is too strong or the temperature is too high.

Robots in charge

ACTIVITY

Science fiction writers often write far-fetched stories about robots.

a) Robots are only automated machines programmed to do certain tasks. So why does the word 'robot' catch everyone's attention?

b) Use a science-fiction story to discuss the boundary between science fiction and science.

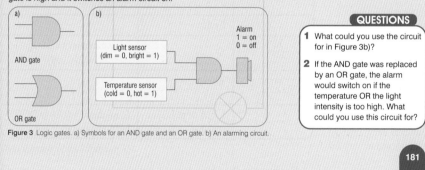

Robots took over the world in the last century – but only in a play by the Czech writer, Karel Čapek. He used the word 'robot' for machine 'slaves'. Real robots were not invented until many years later. Now we use robotic machines for:

- *routine jobs, such as on assembly lines in factories,*
- *dangerous jobs, such as bomb disposal,*
- *space exploration, such as the two Rover robots which landed on Mars in 2004.*

without seeing the real world at all. Let the students design a complete personal isolation system that cuts them off from the outside, when they want to live in the unreal world.

Learning styles

Kinaesthetic: Researching into the development of microelectronics.

Visual: Imagining future technology.

Auditory: Reading short science fiction stories out loud.

Interpersonal: Debating robotic technology.

Intrapersonal: Writing a poem about new school policy.

Gifted and talented

Those talented in literature or language could write their own robot-based short story, perhaps in collaboration with the English department.

Electronic logic

We use logic circuits in lots of electronic devices, including computers. A logic circuit has an output that depends on the inputs. Figure 3 shows the symbols for two simple logic circuits, an AND gate and an OR gate. Figure 3 shows an AND gate with a temperature sensor and a light sensor connected to its inputs. If the temperature AND the light intensity are too high, the output of the AND gate is high and it switches an alarm circuit on.

a)

AND gate

OR gate

b)

Light sensor
(dim = 0, bright = 1)

Temperature sensor
(cold = 0, hot = 1)

Alarm
1 = on
0 = off

Figure 3 Logic gates. a) Symbols for an AND gate and an OR gate. b) An alarming circuit.

QUESTIONS

1 What could you use the circuit for in Figure 3b)?

2 If the AND gate was replaced by an OR gate, the alarm would switch on if the temperature OR the light intensity is too high. What could you use this circuit for?

Special needs

For the 'No more school!' discussion, provide the students with some scripts for each role. Print them out double-spaced, or give them in electronic form, so that the students can modify them easily.

Homework

The students will have to read the science fiction stories at home and report on them in the next lesson.

- Can the students find any problems with these laws? For example, I could tell my neighbour's robot to self destruct just for fun. Asimov wrote a number of stories about getting around these rules and the eventual consequences of them.

- **Electronic logic** – Logic circuits can be very complex and the students can come up with a range of designs. Ask: 'Can you design an alarm that only goes off when these conditions are met: There is a loud sound at night, or the back door is opened and the alarm switch is on.'
  - You could introduce the NOT gate that converts a high signal to a low one and vice versa.

Extension or homework

- **Rise of the robots** – Ask the students to read a short science fiction story with robots in it, and write a review of the science. Ask: 'Are the things in the story possible?'

- **Living in your own world** – Ask: 'Are people becoming more isolated from each other even when they are crowded together?' Passengers on trains often listen to music through a personal stereo while reading a book and avoiding all contact with other people, except through text messaging. Soon we will be able to project video onto the inside of glasses or directly into the eye with tiny lasers; we could be walking around

ICT link-up

- Show some clips from films featuring robots. How realistic do the students feel they are?

- Robotic toy dogs (and other pets) are available. They show some of the features of possible future technology.

SUMMARY ANSWERS

1 a)

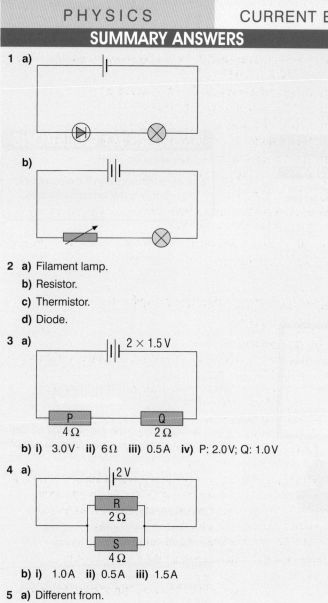

b)

2 a) Filament lamp.

b) Resistor.

c) Thermistor.

d) Diode.

3 a) $2 \times 1.5\,V$

P $4\,\Omega$ Q $2\,\Omega$

b) i) 3.0 V   **ii)** 6 Ω   **iii)** 0.5 A   **iv)** P: 2.0 V; Q: 1.0 V

4 a) 2 V

R $2\,\Omega$

S $4\,\Omega$

b) i) 1.0 A   **ii)** 0.5 A   **iii)** 1.5 A

5 a) Different from.

b) The same as.

Summary teaching suggestions

- When the students answer these questions they should be drawing accurate circuit diagrams. They should not be leaving gaps of any kind or using the wrong symbols.

- The students should easily be able to match up the devices with their description; if not, then play the domino game mentioned in the plenary in lesson 5.1 again.

- Questions 3 and 4 should be used to compare series and parallel circuits. Higher attaining students should be getting quite competent at circuit analysis by now.

SUMMARY QUESTIONS

1 Sketch a circuit diagram to show:
   a) a torch bulb, a cell and a diode connected in series so that the torch bulb is on,
   b) a variable resistor, two cells in series and a torch bulb whose brightness can be varied by adjusting the variable resistor.

2 Match each component in the list to each statement a) to d) that describes it.

   diode   **filament lamp**   **resistor**   **thermistor**

   a) Its resistance increases if the current through it increases.
   b) The current through it is proportional to the potential difference across it.
   c) Its resistance decreases if its temperature is increased.
   d) Its resistance depends on which way round it is connected in a circuit.

3 a) Sketch a circuit diagram to show two resistors P and Q connected in series to a battery of two cells in series with each other.
   b) In the circuit in a), resistor P has a resistance of 4 Ω, resistor Q has a resistance of 2 Ω and each cell has a potential difference of 1.5 V. Calculate
      i) the total potential difference of the two cells,
      ii) the total resistance of the two resistors,
      iii) the current in the circuit,
      iv) the potential difference across each resistor.

4 a) Sketch a circuit diagram to show two resistors R and S in parallel with each other connected to a single cell.
   b) In the circuit in a), resistor R has a resistance of 2 Ω, resistor S has a resistance of 4 Ω and the cell has a potential difference of 2 V. Calculate
      i) the current through resistor R,
      ii) the current through resistor S,
      iii) the current through the cell, in the circuit.

5 Complete the following sentences using words from the list below:

   different from   **equal to**   **the same as**

   a) For two components X and Y in series, the potential difference across X is …… the potential difference across Y.
   b) For two components X and Y in parallel, the potential difference across X is …… the potential difference across Y.

EXAM-STYLE QUESTIONS

1 In a circuit diagram, symbols are used to represent different components.

   Complete the table below. The first line has been done for you.

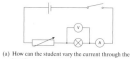

Symbol	Component	What the component does
—Ⓐ—	ammeter	Measures the current in a circuit
—Ⓥ—	voltmeter	a)
—||—	b)	Supplies energy to a circuit
c)	diode	d)
e)	f)	Varies resistance as the temperature varies
g)	g)	h)

2 A student sets up a circuit to investigate how the potential difference across a filament lamp varies with the current through it.

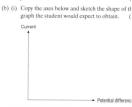

   (a) How can the student vary the current through the lamp?

   (b) (i) Copy the axes below and sketch the shape of the graph the student would expect to obtain.

   Current

   → Potential difference

      (ii) Explain the shape of the graph you have drawn.

      (iii) What do we call the line drawn through points on a graph plotted from experimental data which smooths out variations in measurements?

EXAM-STYLE ANSWERS

1

Symbol	Component	What the component does
		Measure the potential difference across a component
	Cell	
⊕▷		Allows current flow in one direction only
▱	Thermistor	
	Light dependent resistor	Resistance varies with light intensity

(1 mark for each correct cell)

2 a) By changing the setting on the variable resistor.   *(1 mark)*

   b) i) curve drawn   *(1 mark)*
      shape correct   *(1 mark)*
    ii) as more current flows the lamp gets hotter   *(1 mark)*
      so its resistance increases.   *(1 mark)*
    iii) A line of best fit.   *(1 mark)*

3 a) 9 Ω   *(1 mark)*

   b) $\text{Current} = \dfrac{\text{potential difference}}{\text{resistance}}$ *(1 mark)*

    $\text{current} = \dfrac{4.5}{9}$ *(1 mark)*

    $\text{Current} = 0.5\,A$ *(1 mark)*

   c) Potential difference = current × resistance
    Potential difference = 0.5 × 4   *(1 mark)*
    Potential difference = 2 V   *(1 mark)*

HOW SCIENCE WORKS QUESTIONS

The diagram shows an electric circuit.

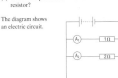

4.5 V

(a) Calculate the total resistance in the circuit. (1)

(b) What is the current through the 4 Ω resistor? (3)

(c) What is the potential difference across the 4 Ω resistor? (2)

The diagram shows an electric circuit.

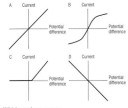

The reading on ammeter A_1 is 6 A and on A_3 is 2 A.

(a) (i) What is the reading on ammeter A_2? (4)

(ii) What is the reading on ammeter A_4? (1)

(b) The graphs **A**, **B**, **C** and **D** show how the current through a component varies with the potential difference across it.

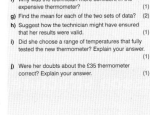

Which graph represents

(i) a resistor at constant temperature?

(ii) a diode? (2)

(c) Why can't the data in part (b) be presented as bar charts? (2)

The laboratory has just bought a new digital thermometer. It uses a thermistor to measure the temperature. It costs £35 because it is accurate and sensitive. The chief technician is very anxious to know if the thermometer works properly. She read all of the data that came with it. It claims that the thermometer will be accurate to ±0.3°C over a range of −50°C to 150°C and it will read to 0.1°C.

a) What is the range over which this instrument should work accurately? (1)

b) What might happen if you used the instrument to read temperatures below −50°C? (1)

c) What is the sensitivity of the thermometer? (1)

d) What is meant by 'the thermometer will be accurate to ±0.3°C'? (1)

The chief technician wanted to check the claims made by the company selling the thermometer. She decided to test its accuracy for herself. She set up some water baths at different temperatures. She used a £400 thermometer that measured to 0.01°C. A company specialising in testing thermometers had independently calibrated this instrument. She compared the readings given by the two thermometers. These are her results.

Thermistor	Temperature of water bath (°C)		
£400	20.15	26.78	65.43
£35	19.9	26.6	65.6

e) Why did the technician doubt the claims made by the company selling the thermometer? (1)

f) Why was the technician more confident in the expensive thermometer? (1)

g) Find the mean for each of the two sets of data? (2)

h) Suggest how the technician might have ensured that her results were valid. (1)

i) Did she choose a range of temperatures that fully tested the new thermometer? Explain your answer. (1)

j) Were her doubts about the £35 thermometer correct? Explain your answer. (1)

183

HOW SCIENCE WORKS ANSWERS

a) The range over which this instrument should work accurately is −50°C to 150°C.

b) It might work, but it would not be accurate.

c) 0.1°C is the sensitivity of the thermometer.

d) It cannot be relied on to be giving a more accurate temperature than 0.3°C above or below that recorded.

e) The company could be biased.

f) It had been independently calibrated.

g) 37.45°C and 37.4°C.

h) e.g. checked the temperature of the water with the two thermometers at the same time.

i) No. The new thermometer had a range of −50°C to +150°C.

j) No, because all are within the ±0.3°C.

How science works teaching suggestions

- **Literacy guidance**
  - Key terms that should be understood: accuracy, sensitivity, calibrated, bias, range.
  - Question d) expects a longer answer, where students can practise their literacy skills.

- **Higher- and lower-level answers.** Questions d) and g) are higher-level questions. The answers for these have been provided at this level. Question a) is lower level and the answer provided is also lower level.

- **Gifted and talented.** Able students could be asked to provide a protocol for testing these thermometers over the full range.

- **How and when to use these questions.** When wishing to develop ideas around accuracy and sensitivity. The questions could be used for homework.

- **Homework.** Questions could be done for homework.

- **Special needs.** The questions could be adapted for thermometers in the lab and they could be checked for accuracy.

- **ICT link-up.** Researching of the many different thermometers and how their accuracy and range are related to their task.

---

4 a) i) p.d. across 2 Ω resistor is same as p.d across 1 Ω resistor because they are in parallel. *(1 mark)*

p.d. across 1 Ω resistor = current × resistance

p.d. = 6 A × 1 Ω *(1 mark)*

p.d. = 6 V

Current in 2 Ω resistor = $\dfrac{6\,V}{2\,\Omega}$ *(1 mark)*

Current = 3 A *(1 mark)*

ii) Reading on A_4 = 6 A + 3 A + 2 A = 11 A *(1 mark)*

b) i) Graph A *(1 mark)*

ii) Graph C *(1 mark)*

c) The independent variable has to be categoric/ordered/not continuous for a bar chart. *(1 mark)*

The independent variable in this case – potential difference – is a continuous variable. *(1 mark)*

Exam teaching suggestions

- Students must know all the circuit symbols given in the specification.

- Students should practise drawing circuits carefully with a ruler. It helps many pupils to have components in front of them and connect up circuits that they draw.

- Emphasise that ammeters go in series and voltmeters go in parallel.

- Students should be clear about the differences between series and parallel circuits. They should practise doing calculations on both types of circuit. Emphasise that in parallel circuits the potential difference is the same across each of the parallel components in the circuit.

P2 6.1 Alternating current

Teaching suggestions

- **Gifted and talented.** Ask: 'Why is our mains electricity frequency 50 Hz? What is the physical reason for this and is it the same in all countries? How was this frequency and voltage decided on and why?'

- **Learning styles**

  Kinaesthetic: Operating the CRO.

  Visual: Observing a.c. wave traces.

  Auditory: Listening to descriptions of mains electricity.

  Intrapersonal: Interpreting the information from a CRO trace.

- **ICT link-up.** There are computer-based oscilloscopes that can display traces. These are very useful for demonstrations, because the display can be projected so that everybody can see at once. (Search the web for 'oscilloscope' simulation.) It's still worth showing the students an old-fashioned one too.

Lesson structure

STARTER

Mains facts – Ask the students a set of true/false questions about mains electricity to see what they already know. (5–10 minutes)

Wave forms – Show the students a wave diagram (e.g. picture from Student Book on the GCSE Physics CD ROM) and ask them to discuss it. (5 minutes)

Electricity dominoes – The students connect question/answer dominoes on basic electrical terms like current, potential difference, cell etc. (5 minutes)

MAIN

- Many of the students will have been wondering what the other two outputs on a power supply are for. Show them that a bulb will light up from a d.c. source and also from the a.c. source.

- The d.c. outputs are colour coded for positive and negative, but the a.c. ones aren't: ask the students why they think this is.

- In a d.c. circuit the electrons eventually make it around the complete circuit. In an a.c circuit they just oscillate back and forth a few centimetres. Describe this to the students pointing out that the electrons are still transferring energy.

- Make sure that the students know that mains is 230 V a.c. at 50 Hz. This is frequently asked for in examination papers. Don't use these high voltages in demonstrations.

- Higher-tier students really need to be aware that the neutral wire oscillates slightly around the Earth potential.

- Some students may know that fluorescent lamps in some buildings flicker or buzz. Let them hear a 50 Hz signal using a signal generator and loudspeaker, and they will probably recognise the noise.

- The oscilloscope is a complex device, but the students only need to know about the time base and the Y-gain. (See 'Practical support'.)

- Higher-tier students will need to be able to take measurements from CRO traces. Make sure that they are only using the controls that they need. You can explain what some of the other buttons do, but make sure that the students know that they only have to be able to read the traces.

- If you have a computer-based oscilloscope, it is much better to use this for demonstrations rather than a small CRO. Connect it up to a signal generator or a.c. power supply to show the traces. The whole class should be able to see it at once if you use a data projector too.

Practical support

The oscilloscope

Oscilloscopes can be fiddly to use and are expensive, but they are essential to understanding alternating current. If not enough equipment is available, let the students use what there is, one group at a time.

Equipment and materials required

Per group: cathode ray oscilloscope, low voltage a.c. source, battery and leads.

Details

The greatest problem the students will have with this experiment is setting the time base and volts per centimetre (Y-gain) dials on the CRO. If these are incorrectly set, then the students will not get a useful trace. To make things easier for them, put small blobs of paint on the scale around the dials showing the correct setting to show a 2 V, 50 Hz trace clearly. This will be a common function, so don't worry too much about defacing the scopes. If you want to show what would happen to the trace if the frequency of p.d. is changed, you can set up a signal generator instead of the a.c. source.

DID YOU KNOW?

A rapid car battery recharge can produce currents of over 100 A for short periods. At 12 V this means that it is transferring 1200 J each second. For comparison, a normal AA battery operates at 1.5 V and produces a current of only 100 mA, so transfers 0.15 J each second.

Answers to in-text questions

a) The bulb would flicker continuously.

b) 325 V

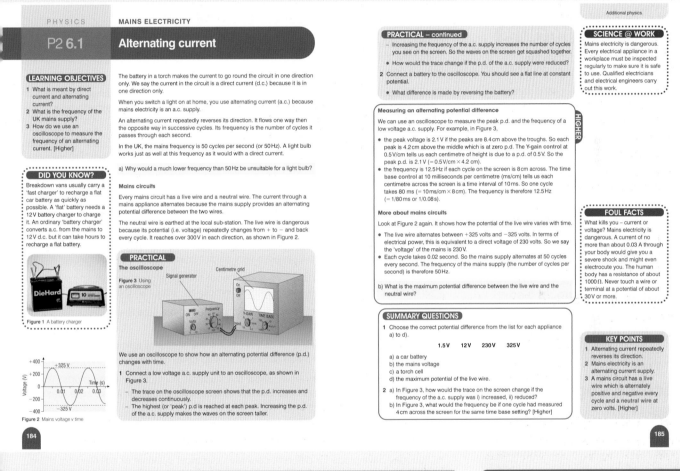

PHYSICS   MAINS ELECTRICITY

P2 6.1   Alternating current

LEARNING OBJECTIVES

1 What is meant by direct current and alternating current?
2 What is the frequency of the UK mains supply?
3 How do we use an oscilloscope to measure the frequency of an alternating current? [Higher]

DID YOU KNOW?

Breakdown vans usually carry a 'fast charger' to recharge a flat car battery as quickly as possible. A 'flat' battery needs a 12 V battery charger to charge it. An ordinary 'battery charger' converts a.c. from the mains to 12 V d.c. but it can take hours to recharge a flat battery.

Figure 1 A battery charger

Figure 2 Mains voltage v time

The battery in a torch makes the current to go round the circuit in one direction only. We say the current in the circuit is a direct current (d.c.) because it is in one direction only.

When you switch a light on at home, you use alternating current (a.c.) because mains electricity is an a.c. supply.

An alternating current repeatedly reverses its direction. It flows one way then the opposite way in successive cycles. Its frequency is the number of cycles it passes through each second.

In the UK, the mains frequency is 50 cycles per second (or 50 Hz). A light bulb works just as well at this frequency as it would with a direct current.

a) Why would a much lower frequency than 50 Hz be unsuitable for a light bulb?

Mains circuits

Every mains circuit has a live wire and a neutral wire. The current through a mains appliance alternates because the mains supply provides an alternating potential difference between the two wires.

The neutral wire is earthed at the local sub-station. The live wire is dangerous because its potential (i.e. voltage) repeatedly changes from + to − and back every cycle. It reaches over 300 V in each direction, as shown in Figure 2.

PRACTICAL

The oscilloscope

Figure 3 Using an oscilloscope

We use an oscilloscope to show how an alternating potential difference (p.d.) changes with time.

1 Connect a low voltage a.c. supply unit to an oscilloscope, as shown in Figure 3.

 – The trace on the oscilloscope screen shows that the p.d. increases and decreases continuously.

 – The highest (or 'peak') p.d is reached at each peak. Increasing the p.d. of the a.c. supply makes the waves on the screen taller.

PRACTICAL – continued

 – Increasing the frequency of the a.c. supply increases the number of cycles you see on the screen. So the waves on the screen get squashed together.

 • How would the trace change if the p.d. of the a.c. supply were reduced?

2 Connect a battery to the oscilloscope. You should see a flat line at constant potential.

 • What difference is made by reversing the battery?

Measuring an alternating potential difference

We can use an oscilloscope to measure the peak p.d. and the frequency of a low voltage a.c. supply. For example, in Figure 3,

 • the peak voltage is 2.1 V if the peaks are 8.4 cm above the troughs. So each peak is 4.2 cm above the middle which is at zero p.d. The Y-gain control at 0.5 V/cm tells us each centimetre of height is due to a p.d. of 0.5 V. So the peak p.d. is 2.1 V (= 0.5 V/cm × 4.2 cm).

 • the frequency is 12.5 Hz if each cycle on the screen is 8 cm across. The time base control at 10 milliseconds per centimetre (ms/cm) tells us each centimetre across the screen is a time interval of 10 ms. So one cycle takes 80 ms (= 10 ms/cm × 8 cm). The frequency is therefore 12.5 Hz (= 1/80 ms or 1/0.08 s).

More about mains circuits

Look at Figure 2 again. It shows how the potential of the live wire varies with time.

 • The live wire alternates between +325 volts and −325 volts. In terms of electrical power, this is equivalent to a direct voltage of 230 volts. So we say the 'voltage' of the mains is 230 V.

 • Each cycle takes 0.02 second. So the mains supply alternates at 50 cycles every second. The frequency of the mains supply (the number of cycles per second) is therefore 50 Hz.

b) What is the maximum potential difference between the live wire and the neutral wire?

SUMMARY QUESTIONS

1 Choose the correct potential difference from the list for each appliance a) to d).

    1.5 V   12 V   230 V   325 V

 a) a car battery
 b) the mains voltage
 c) a torch cell
 d) the maximum potential of the live wire.

2 a) In Figure 3, how would the trace on the screen change if the frequency of the a.c. supply was i) increased, ii) reduced?
 b) In Figure 3, what would the frequency be if one cycle had measured 4 cm across the screen for the same time base setting? [Higher]

SCIENCE @ WORK

Mains electricity is dangerous. Every electrical appliance in a workplace must be inspected regularly to make sure it is safe to use. Qualified electricians and electrical engineers carry out this work.

FOUL FACTS

What kills you – current or voltage? Mains electricity is dangerous. A current of no more than about 0.03 A through your body would give you a severe shock and might even electrocute you. The human body has a resistance of about 1000 Ω. Never touch a wire or terminal at a potential of about 30 V or more.

KEY POINTS

1 Alternating current repeatedly reverses its direction.
2 Mains electricity is an alternating current supply.
3 A mains circuit has a live wire which is alternately positive and negative every cycle and a neutral wire at zero volts. [Higher]

184

185

PLENARIES

a.c./d.c? – Give the students a set of electrical devices and ask them to stack them in two piles: a.c. operation and d.c. operation. Ask: 'What about devices like laptops that have transformers and rectifiers to convert?' (5 minutes)

Traces – Show the students a series of oscilloscope traces and ask them to say if the peak p.d. is higher or lower, and the frequency higher or lower, than the previous one. (5 minutes)

Making connections – Ask the students to complete the sentence 'Electrical energy is a very convenient form of energy because . . .' including these words 'energy', 'transfer' and 'current'. (5 minutes)

SUMMARY ANSWERS

1 a) 12 V   b) 230 V
  c) 1.5 V   d) 325 V

2 a) The number of cycles on the screen would:
   i) Increase.   ii) Decrease.
  b) 25 Hz [HT only]

KEY POINTS

The students should be asked to draw traces showing the difference between a.c. and d.c.

P2 6.2   Cables and plugs

LEARNING OBJECTIVES

Students should learn:

- That mains plugs and sockets are made from robust insulating materials.
- The names and colours of the wires in a three-pin plug.
- The structure of an electrical and a three-pin plug.
- About the function of the live wire, the neutral wire and the earth wire.

LEARNING OUTCOMES

Most students should be able to:

- Describe the design and function of a three-pin mains plug, including the choice of materials and the colours of the wires.
- Recognise errors in the wiring of a three-pin plug.
- Explain why it is necessary to connect some devices to the earth via the earth wire.
- Explain, in terms of safety, why the fuse in the plug of an appliance and the switch of an appliance are on the live side of the appliance.

Some students should also be able to:

- Explain the choice of materials used for the mains parts of a three-pin main plug.

Teaching suggestions

- **Special needs.** Provide the students with a large diagram of plug wiring. They should then label the parts, colour the wires and describe the materials uses for each part.
- **Gifted and talented.** Get the students to write a 'How to wire a plug' guide as found in some DIY stores. The guide should contain idiot-proof step by step instructions of what equipment you need and what you should do.
- **Learning styles**
  Kinaesthetic: Wiring or handling mains plugs.
  Visual: Making observations about faults.
  Auditory: Explaining the dangers of faulty wiring.
  Interpersonal: Discussing and evaluating the materials used in plugs and cables.
  Intrapersonal: Appreciating the dangers associated with high voltage electricity.
- **Homework**
  Safety in the home: The students should make a safety poster to be sent to every house in the country encouraging electrical safety.

SPECIFICATION LINK-UP   Unit: Physics 2.12.7

- *Most electrical appliances are connected to the mains using cable and a three-pin plug.*
- *The structure of electrical cable.*
- *The structure of a three-pin plug.*
- *Correct wiring of a three-pin plug.*

Lesson structure

STARTER

Mystery object – Put a mains plug in a bag and ask one student to describe it to the rest of the class, but only using shape and texture. This can be made more difficult by using a continental plug. (5 minutes)

Material sorting – Give each group of students a bag containing a range of materials and ask them to sort the materials in any way they wish. They must explain how they sorted them to other groups. (10 minutes)

Colour coding – Ask: 'How many different types of thing are colour coded?' The students should make a list of things that are organised by putting colours on them. (10 minutes)

MAIN

- If you have a metal electric heater then use it to introduce the idea of earthing a device.
- Discuss the materials used in a plug and cable by actually showing them. If you have very old devices you might like to show how these have improved over the years. The students need to be able to explain why each material has been chosen.
- The colour coding is usually well understood, but some students will know that black and red wires are used in mains circuits in houses – this can lead to some confusion.
- If you choose to let the students wire plugs, then make sure that there is no chance of the plugs being plugged in.
- The activity can take quite a bit of time, but some students turn out to be exceptionally good. Get these students to help other groups when they are finished.
- Afterwards, or as an alternative, show the students some badly wired plugs. This works best if the plugs are real, but use diagrams if necessary. Make sure these can't be plugged in by using a plug wiring board.
- Some of the faults should be hard to spot. One commonly missed mistake is the cable grip gripping the wires instead of the larger cable.
- You may have plugs for different countries electrical systems or adapters for them. Showing them to students will emphasise that each country has its own designs for plugs.
- A tip for wiring a plug is: When looking down onto a plug as it is being wired the **BR**own wire connects to the **B**ottom **R**ight, the **BL**ue wire connects to the **B**ottom **L**eft. The other wire goes to the other pin!

PLENARIES

Plug poetry – Ask the students to write a plug-wiring rhyme of their own. (5 minutes)

Materials summary – The students should make a table listing the parts of a plug and cable, the materials used and the reasons for those choices. (5–10 minutes)

Wonky wiring – Show the students incorrectly wired plugs and ask them to describe the problems. (5–10 minutes)

Additional physics

ACTIVITY & EXTENSION IDEAS

Wiring a three-pin plug

- Wiring a three-pin plug is a handy skill, and most students enjoy the challenge, but you must be very conscious of the safety concerns. Most appliances come with a pre-fitted moulded plug anyway, so it is becoming less common to have to wire your own.
- **Safety:** Most importantly turn off the mains electricity to the laboratory and never allow the students to plug in their plugs. Even if they are wired correctly, the exposed end of the cable will be live. You should check that no sockets remain live when the main electricity supply is turned off. There are usually some wall sockets that are not connected to the lab circuit breakers. You can also put bolts/screws through the Earth pin to prevent them being plugged in.

Equipment and materials required

For each student: a plug, wire strippers, suitable screwdriver, and 50 cm length of three-core mains cable.

Details

There are many different designs of plugs, some are easier to wire than others. The students will need to be shown how to strip the cable and then the wires without cutting into the core. They will also need help with deciding how much of the metal to expose and how long the wires should be, as most plugs require the Earth wire to be longer than the other two. Make sure that the mains cables are at least 30 cm long, otherwise the students will end up pulling out the wires when they try to strip them. You also need to make sure that all of the bits go back in the right plug, otherwise next time there will be bits missing.

Plug wiring board

If you have concerns about the safety of plug wiring in your laboratory, then you can pass around a plug board for the students to see faulty wiring.

Equipment and materials required

A plank of wood with six incorrectly wired plugs mounted on it.

Details

All that is involved is mounting six plugs onto a board with the pins sticking through it so that they cannot be plugged in. Drill or chisel out the board, stick the cases down and wire up the six plugs in incorrect ways so that the students can try to explain what has been done wrong. You might like to glue the pins into the wood to make sure that they don't fall out. Here are some examples of problems: wires stripped all the way back to the cable grip so that they short, live and neutral wire swapped, wires not tightened at the pins, fuse replaced with metal pin or similar, cable gripping wires not cable, cracked case (glue it down then whack it with a screwdriver). If you have a bigger board then add others.

Answers to in-text questions

a) So each one can be switched on or off without affecting the others.

b) Brass is harder than copper or zinc.

c) The live wire could be exposed where the cable is worn away or damaged.

P2 6.2   Cables and plugs

LEARNING OBJECTIVES

1 What is the casing of a mains plug made from and why?
2 What colour are the live, neutral and earth wires?
3 Which wire is connected to the longest pin in a three-pin plug?

FOUL FACTS

Mains electricity is dangerous. Mains wiring must by law be done by properly qualified electricians.

When you plug in a heater with a metal case into a wall socket, you 'earth' the metal case automatically. This stops the metal case becoming 'live' if the live wire breaks and touches it. If the case did become 'live' and you touched it, you would be electrocuted.

Plugs, sockets and cables

The outer casings of plugs, sockets and cables of all mains circuits and appliances are made of hard-wearing electrical insulators. That's because plugs, sockets and cables contain 'live' wires.

Sockets are made of stiff plastic materials with the wires inside. Figure 1 shows part of a wall socket circuit. It has an 'earth' wire as well as a live wire and a neutral wire.

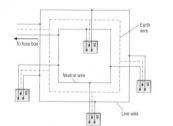

Figure 1 A 'wall socket' circuit

- The 'earth wire' of this circuit is connected to the ground at your home.
- The longest pin of a three-pin plug is designed to make contact with the 'earth wire' of a wall socket circuit. So when you plug an appliance with a metal case to a wall socket, the case is automatically earthed.

a) Why are sockets wired in parallel with each other?

Plugs have cases made of stiff plastic materials. The live pin, the neutral pin and the earth pin, stick out through the plug case. Figure 2 shows inside a three-pin plug.

- The pins are made of brass because brass is a good conductor and does not rust or oxidise. Copper isn't as hard as brass even though it conducts better.
- The case material is an electrical insulator. The inside of the case is shaped so the wires and the pins cannot touch each other when the plug is sealed.

- The plug contains a fuse between the live pin and the live wire. The fuse melts and cuts the live wire off if too much current passes through it.

b) Why is brass, an alloy of copper and zinc, better than copper or zinc for the pins of a three-pin plug?

Cables used for mains appliances (and for mains circuits) consist of two or three insulated copper wires surrounded by an outer layer of rubber or flexible plastic material.

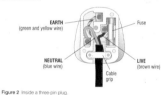

Figure 2 Inside a three-pin plug.

- The brown wire is connected to the live pin.
- The blue wire is connected to the neutral pin.
- The green-yellow wire (of a three-core cable) is connected to the earth pin. A two-core cable does not have an earth wire.

- Copper is used for the wires because it is a good electrical conductor.
- Plastic is a good electrical insulator and therefore prevents anyone touching the cable from receiving an electric shock.
- Two-core cables are used for appliances which have plastic cases (e.g. hairdryers, radios).

Figure 3 Mains cable

c) Why are cables that are worn away or damaged dangerous?

SUMMARY QUESTIONS

1 Choose words from the list to complete the sentences a) to e):

    earth   live   neutral   series   parallel

a) The ...... wire in a mains plug is blue.
b) If too much current passes through the fuse, it blows and cuts the ...... wire off.
c) Appliances plugged into the same mains circuit are in ...... with each other.
d) The metal frame of an appliance is connected to the ...... wire of a mains circuit when it is plugged in.
e) The fuse in a plug is in ...... with the live wire.

2 a) Match the list of parts 1–4 in a three-pin plug with the list of materials A–D.

    1 cable insulation   2 case   3 pin   4 wire
    A brass   B copper   C rubber   D stiff plastic

b) Explain your choice of material for each part in a).

KEY POINTS

1 Cables consist of two or three insulated copper wires surrounded by an outer layer of flexible plastic material.
2 Sockets and plugs are made of stiff plastic materials which enclose the electrical connections.
3 In a three-pin plug or a three-core cable, the live wire is brown, the neutral wire is blue, the earth wire is yellow/green. The earth wire is used to earth the metal case of a mains appliance.

SUMMARY ANSWERS

1 a) Neutral. b) Live. c) Parallel. d) Earth. e) Series.

2 a) 1C; 2D; 3A; 4B

   b) 1 rubber is flexible and is an insulator.
      2 stiff plastic is an insulator, it doesn't wear and it can't be squashed.
      3 brass is a good conductor and doesn't deteriorate.
      4 copper is an excellent conductor and copper wires bend easily.

KEY POINTS

The students should be able to draw up a table showing how the parts of a mains plug are connected and the correct materials.

P2 6.3 Fuses

LEARNING OBJECTIVES

Students should learn:

- That fuses and circuit breakers are devices that cut off electrical circuits when too large a current flows.
- About the advantages of using circuit breakers to cut off circuits instead of fuses.
- How to choose the correct rating of fuse for a device.
- That double insulated devices have a shell made of insulating materials and so do not need to be earthed.

LEARNING OUTCOMES

Most students should be able to:

- Explain how and why a fuse cuts off an electrical circuit.
- Explain why the fuse in the plug of an appliance protects the appliance.
- List the advantages of a circuit breaker over a fuse.
- Explain why it is important that devices are earthed or are double insulated.

Some students should also be able to:

- Explain why earthing the metal case of an appliance protects the user.

Teaching suggestions

- **Special needs.** For the 'Electromagnets' starter, give the students a set of cards to put in order.
- **Learning styles**
  Visual: Observing the melting of fuses and switching off of current by circuit breakers.
  Auditory: Listening to explanations of how fuses work.
  Interpersonal: Discussing the hazards of mains electricity.
  Intrapersonal: Appreciating the importance of earthing and fuses.
- **ICT link-up.** The students could find out about the numbers of fires and deaths caused by faulty wiring each year using the Internet.
- **Homework.** This is a good opportunity to get the students to make a poster about mains electricity and safety. The poster should be targeted at reducing deaths and injury from shocks and house fires.

SPECIFICATION LINK-UP   Unit: Physics 2.12.7

- If an electrical fault causes too great a current, the circuit should be switched off by a fuse or a circuit breaker.
- When the current in a fuse wire exceeds the rating of the fuse it will melt, breaking the circuit.
- Appliances with metal cases are usually earthed.
- The Earth wire and fuse together protect the appliance and the user.

Students should use their skills, knowledge and understanding of 'How Science Works':

- to recognise dangerous practice in the use of mains electricity.

Lesson structure

STARTER

Heating effect – Ask: 'Why do wires get hot when a current passes through them?' The students should explain. (5 minutes)

Electromagnets – Demonstrate an electromagnetic switch or relay and get the students to draw a flow chart of what is happening. (10 minutes)

MAIN

- Fuses are a bit dull without demonstrations, so try to fit in a few of the ones in the activity box.
- If you are showing a fuse melting, use one with a glass casing so that the students can see the wire becoming hot and then melt. This will disappoint some students that think a fuse actually explodes in some way.
- You can show the students the differences between fuses, by showing them the fuse wire that is found in them. Connect up some 1 A, 3 A and 5 A fuse wire together in series with an ammeter and variable resistor, and pass an increasing current through it to show that the 1 A fuse wire melts first. Hopefully this will be when a current of 1 A passes through it, but just how accurately is fuse wire manufactured? This would give a good opportunity to discuss aspects of 'How Science Works' on making measurements.
- Many students will think that the fuse is a device that protects the user of a device. It is important to point out that the fuse really prevents a device from catching fire through overheating. Emphasise that it only takes a small current to kill and a 3.5 A device with a 5 A fuse in it can provide a current of 1.5 A without troubling the fuse.
- Earthing confuses some, but just point out that the basic idea is to give an easy path for the current to take if there is a fault. Usually if the device is earthed, then a large current would flow if the live wire touched the case and the fuse should melt and cut off the device. This is the common reason why a device keeps melting fuses and so, if the students see this happen, they should realise that the live wire is loose.
- Even if the fuse does not melt (usually because of putting 13 A fuses in everything), the Earth wire provides a low resistance path for the current and the user would not be electrocuted by touching the case.
- You can demonstrate the use of circuit breakers as outlined in the activity box. The students should realise the advantages fairly quickly. If you want to go into extra detail, then you can show a large model circuit breaker and refer back to the work on electromagnets from earlier in the course.

PLENARIES

Dump your fuses – The students can produce an outline of an advertisement from a company that manufactures circuit breakers that is trying to convince householders to swap their fuse boxes for breaker boxes. (10–15 minutes)

Mains safety – The students produce a catchphrase or slogan to encourage people to use mains electricity safely. (5–10 minutes)

Demonstrating circuit breakers

Most power supplies come with a built in circuit breaker so it is simple to demonstrate one.

Equipment and materials required

Low voltage power supply with circuit breaker and a lead.

Details

- Connect up the power supply so that the positive and negative d.c. outputs are shorted by the lead. Turn up the voltage to maximum and then switch on the supply. It will hum for a few seconds and the lead will get warm before the breaker cuts the current off.

- Your laboratory should also have a main circuit breaker with a test switch that will cut off the supply to the benches and you can demonstrate this. Don't make the mistake of testing it if your computer or projector is plugged into the circuit.

Electrical fires

With this you can demonstrate what could happen if no fuse was present.

Equipment and materials required

Power supply, two crocodile clips, heat resistant mat, safety screen and 20 cm length of thin constantan or nichrome wire, variable resistor, safety glasses.

Details

Simply connect the wire up behind the screen and pass a current through it. Turn the current up slowly using the variable resistor so that the students can see that the wire starts to glow red-hot and then white-hot before melting. If you wish you can place some paper on the wire and show it catching fire. Try exactly the same with a 1 A fuse in the circuit and the fuse should melt safely first and cut off the circuit. If you want to show that even low voltages can cause a fire, then try using wire wool and a 1.5 V cell.

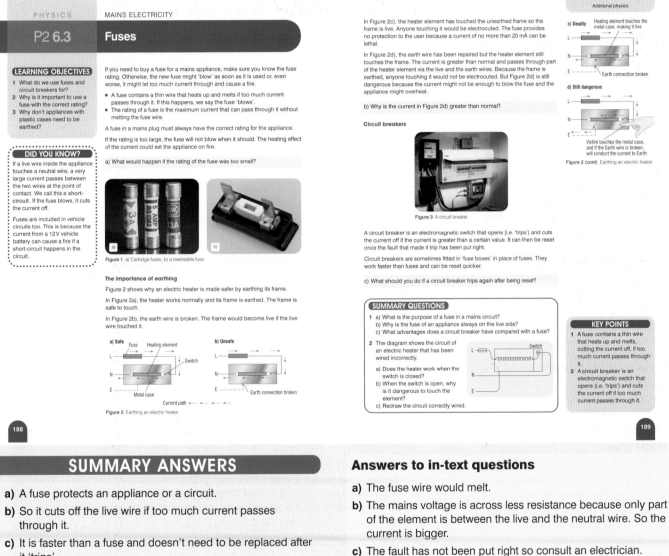

Additional physics

PHYSICS   MAINS ELECTRICITY

P2 6.3   Fuses

LEARNING OBJECTIVES

1 What do we use fuses and circuit breakers for?
2 Why is it important to use a fuse with the correct rating?
3 Why don't appliances with plastic cases need to be earthed?

If you need to buy a fuse for a mains appliance, make sure you know the fuse rating. Otherwise, the new fuse might 'blow' as soon as it is used or, even worse, it might let too much current through and cause a fire.

- A fuse contains a thin wire that heats up and melts if too much current passes through it. If this happens, we say the fuse 'blows'.
- The rating of a fuse is the maximum current that can pass through it without melting the fuse wire.

A fuse in a mains plug must always have the correct rating for the appliance.

If the rating is too large, the fuse will not blow when it should. The heating effect of the current could set the appliance on fire.

a) What would happen if the rating of the fuse was too small?

DID YOU KNOW?

If a live wire inside the appliance touches a neutral wire, a very large current passes between the two wires at the point of contact. We call this a short-circuit. If the fuse blows, it cuts the current off.

Fuses are included in vehicle circuits too. This is because the current from a 12 V vehicle battery can cause a fire if a short-circuit happens in the circuit.

Figure 1 a) Cartridge fuses, b) a rewireable fuse

The importance of earthing

Figure 2 shows why an electric heater is made safer by earthing its frame.

In Figure 2a), the heater works normally and its frame is earthed. The frame is safe to touch.

In Figure 2b), the earth wire is broken. The frame would become live if the live wire touched it.

Figure 2 Earthing an electric heater

In Figure 2c), the heater element has touched the unearthed frame so the frame is live. Anyone touching it would be electrocuted. The fuse provides no protection to the user because a current of no more than 20 mA can be lethal.

In Figure 2d), the earth wire has been repaired but the heater element still touches the frame. The current is greater than normal and passes through part of the heater element via the live and the earth wires. Because the frame is earthed, anyone touching it would not be electrocuted. But Figure 2d) is still dangerous because the current might not be enough to blow the fuse and the appliance might overheat.

b) Why is the current in Figure 2d) greater than normal?

Circuit breakers

Figure 3 A circuit breaker

A circuit breaker is an electromagnetic switch that opens (i.e. 'trips') and cuts the current off if the current is greater than a certain value. It can then be reset once the fault that made it trip has been put right.

Circuit breakers are sometimes fitted in 'fuse boxes' in place of fuses. They work faster than fuses and can be reset quicker.

c) What should you do if a circuit breaker trips again after being reset?

SUMMARY QUESTIONS

1 a) What is the purpose of a fuse in a mains circuit?
b) Why is the fuse of an appliance always on the live side?
c) What advantages does a circuit breaker have compared with a fuse?

2 The diagram shows the circuit of an electric heater that has been wired incorrectly.
a) Does the heater work when the switch is closed?
b) When the switch is open, why is it dangerous to touch the element?
c) Redraw the circuit correctly wired.

c) **Deadly** Heating element touches the metal case, making it live

Earth connection broken

d) **Still dangerous**

Victim touches the metal case, and if the Earth wire is broken, will conduct the current to Earth

Figure 2 (cont) Earthing an electric heater

KEY POINTS

1 A fuse contains a thin wire that heats up and melts, cutting the current off, if too much current passes through it.

2 A circuit breaker is an electromagnetic switch that opens (i.e. 'trips') and cuts the current off if too much current passes through it.

SUMMARY ANSWERS

1 a) A fuse protects an appliance or a circuit.

b) So it cuts off the live wire if too much current passes through it.

c) It is faster than a fuse and doesn't need to be replaced after it 'trips'.

2 a) Yes.   b) The element is live.

c)

L — Switch

N

E

Answers to in-text questions

a) The fuse wire would melt.

b) The mains voltage is across less resistance because only part of the element is between the live and the neutral wire. So the current is bigger.

c) The fault has not been put right so consult an electrician.

KEY POINTS

The students should make a comparison of how fuses and circuit breakers operate.

P2 6.4

Electrical power and potential difference

LEARNING OBJECTIVES

Students should learn:

- That the power of an electrical device is the rate at which it transfers energy.
- How to calculate the electrical power of a device using the current and potential difference.

LEARNING OUTCOMES

Most students should be able to:

- State that the power of a device is the amount of energy it transfers each second.
- Calculate the power of an electrical device from the current and the potential difference.

Some students should also be able to:

- Perform calculations involving the rearrangement of the electrical power equation.

Teaching suggestions

- **Special needs.** The calculations here can be very confusing to some students, and they should be provided with a template to encourage them to lay them out correctly; this is especially important in the rearrangement of the equations.
- **Gifted and talented.** Can the students produce a comparison between electrical potential difference and gravitational potential difference? This is a trick task, but one that can cement understanding of what a potential difference represents.
- **Learning styles**

  Visual: Making observations about the energy-use of lamps.

  Auditory: Explaining how energy is transferred in electrical circuits.

  Intrapersonal: Making deductions about the relationship between power current and potential difference.

- **Homework.** Give the students a worksheet with questions based on the electrical power equation and choice of fuses.

SPECIFICATION LINK-UP   Unit: Physics 2.12.8

- *Electric current is the rate of flow of charge.*
- *When an electrical charge flows through a resistor, electrical energy is transformed into heat energy.*
- *The rate at which energy is transformed in a device is called the power.*

$$\frac{power}{(watt, W)} = \frac{energy\ transformed\ (joule,\ J)}{time\ (second,\ s)}$$

- *Power, potential difference and current are related by the equation:*

$$\underset{(watt,\ W)}{power} = \underset{(ampere,\ A)}{current} \times \underset{(volt,\ V)}{potential\ difference}$$

Students should use their skills, knowledge and understanding of 'How Science Works':

- *to calculate the current through an appliance from its power and the potential difference of the supply, and from this determine the size of fuse needed.*

Lesson structure

STARTER

Power – Can the students give a scientific definition of the word power? Can they remember any equations? You could even set them a mechanical power question. (5 minutes)

Electrical units – The students match up electrical quantities, with their definitions, abbreviations and units. (5–10 minutes)

Key words – Students quickly scan the double page spread and write out all of the key words. (5–10 minutes)

MAIN

- Start with a brief recap about power; the students should remember how to calculate the power of a mechanical device.
- Point out that if energy is being transferred by a device, then some form of work must be being done so there is a power output. With electricity there is no force or distance moved, so there must be another way of finding the power output.
- The next section involves a derivation of an equation; higher attaining groups should be fine with this, but lower ability students will probably struggle to grasp this section fully.
- Take some time to go through what each of the phrases means and to come up with the final equation; some students will find this difficult. The definition of potential difference as 'electrical energy per unit charge' is one that many students will find particularly hard to understand.
- In the end, most students will happily accept that the power is the current times the potential difference even if they don't thoroughly understand why. For most this is fine, but it may be worth persisting with those you want to move on to the higher level.
- The calculations are not difficult but the students should have quite a bit of practice. Get them to work out the power of several devices before moving on to rearrangement.
- Sometimes examiners ask the students to work out the power of a mains device without giving the voltage. They expect them to remember that mains is 230 V so make sure that they do.
- Show the students real fuses to point out that they are all the same size, so it is easy to use the wrong one without thinking. They might like to see the 30 A fuses used for cookers. Ask: 'Why are these physically larger?'
- When choosing a fuse, always choose one that is slightly higher than the operating current otherwise it will melt during normal operation. For example, if the device needs exactly 3 A, then a 5 A fuse should be used.

ACTIVITY & EXTENSION IDEAS

Enlightenment

This is a simple way to show that the higher the power rating of a device the more energy it transfers.

Equipment and materials required

Three identical lamps except that one has a 40 W bulb, the others have 60 W and 100 W. As with all mains devices these should have passed safety tests.

Details

Just plug all of the lamps in and turn them on. The students should easily see the difference in brightness and relate this to the amount of energy being transferred. Explain that all are operating at 230 V; the students should then calculate the current in each lamp. [0.17 A, 0.26 A, 0.43 A] Ask: 'What fuse should each of the lamps have?'

Answers to in-text questions

a) About 1 W

b) 1150 W

c) The normal current through the lamp is much less than 13 A. A 13 A fuse may not blow if there is a fault in the lamp.

SUMMARY ANSWERS

1 a) Power, current.

   b) Potential difference, current.

2 a) i) 36 W   ii) 460 W

   b) i) 3 A   ii) 5 A

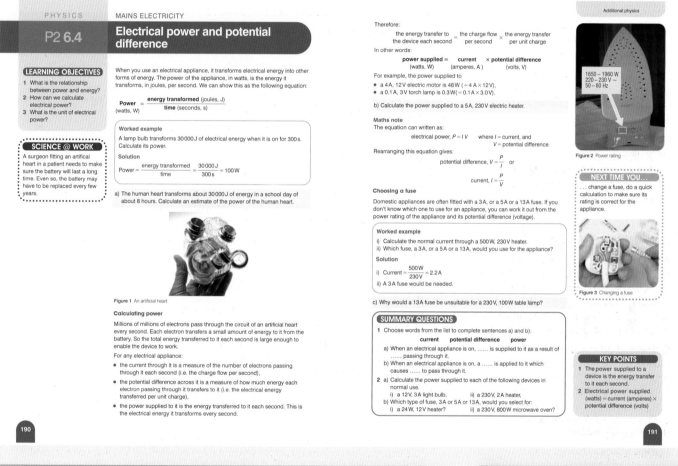

PHYSICS   MAINS ELECTRICITY

P2 6.4 Electrical power and potential difference

LEARNING OBJECTIVES

1 What is the relationship between power and energy?
2 How can we calculate electrical power?
3 What is the unit of electrical power?

SCIENCE @ WORK

A surgeon fitting an artificial heart in a patient needs to make sure the battery will last a long time. Even so, the battery may have to be replaced every few years.

When you use an electrical appliance, it transforms electrical energy into other forms of energy. The power of the appliance, in watts, is the energy it transforms, in joules, per second. We can show this as the following equation:

$$\text{Power (watts, W)} = \frac{\text{energy transformed (joules, J)}}{\text{time (seconds, s)}}$$

Worked example

A lamp bulb transforms 30 000 J of electrical energy when it is on for 300 s. Calculate its power.

Solution

$$\text{Power} = \frac{\text{energy transformed}}{\text{time}} = \frac{30\,000\,J}{300\,s} = 100\,W$$

a) The human heart transforms about 30 000 J of energy in a school day of about 8 hours. Calculate an estimate of the power of the human heart.

Figure 1 An artificial heart

Calculating power

Millions of millions of electrons pass through the circuit of an artificial heart every second. Each electron transfers a small amount of energy to it from the battery. So the total energy transferred to it each second is large enough to enable the device to work.

For any electrical appliance:

• the current through it is a measure of the number of electrons passing through it each second (i.e. the charge flow per second),
• the potential difference across it is a measure of how much energy each electron passing through it transfers to it (i.e. the electrical energy transferred per unit charge),
• the power supplied to it is the energy transferred to it each second. This is the electrical energy it transforms every second.

Therefore:

the energy transfer to the device each second = the charge flow per second × the energy transfer per unit charge

In other words:

power supplied = current × potential difference
(watts, W)   (amperes, A)   (volts, V)

For example, the power supplied to

• a 4 A, 12 V electric motor is 48 W (= 4 A × 12 V),
• a 0.1 A, 3 V torch lamp is 0.3 W (= 0.1 A × 3.0 V).

b) Calculate the power supplied to a 5 A, 230 V electric heater.

Maths note

The equation can written as:

electrical power, $P = IV$ where I = current, and V = potential difference

Rearranging this equation gives:

$$\text{potential difference, } V = \frac{P}{I} \quad \text{or}$$

$$\text{current, } I = \frac{P}{V}$$

Choosing a fuse

Domestic appliances are often fitted with a 3 A, or a 5 A or a 13 A fuse. If you don't know which one to use for an appliance, you can work it out from the power rating of the appliance and its potential difference (voltage).

Worked example

i) Calculate the normal current through a 500 W, 230 V heater.
ii) Which fuse, a 3 A, or a 5 A or a 13 A, would you use for the appliance?

Solution

i) $\text{Current} = \dfrac{500\,W}{230\,V} = 2.2\,A$

ii) A 3 A fuse would be needed.

c) Why would a 13 A fuse be unsuitable for a 230 V, 100 W table lamp?

SUMMARY QUESTIONS

1 Choose words from the list to complete sentences a) and b):

   current   potential difference   power

   a) When an electrical appliance is on, …… is supplied to it as a result of …… passing through it.
   b) When an electrical appliance is on, a …… is applied to it which causes …… to pass through it.

2 a) Calculate the power supplied to each of the following devices in normal use.
      i) a 12 V, 3 A light bulb,   ii) a 230 V, 2 A heater,
   b) Which type of fuse, 3 A or 5 A or 13 A, would you select for:
      i) a 24 W, 12 V heater?   ii) a 230 V, 800 W microwave oven?

Additional physics

1650 – 1960 W
220 – 230 V ~
50 – 60 Hz

Figure 2 Power rating

NEXT TIME YOU…

… change a fuse, do a quick calculation to make sure its rating is correct for the appliance.

Figure 3 Changing a fuse

KEY POINTS

1 The power supplied to a device is the energy transfer to it each second.
2 Electrical power supplied (watts) = current (amperes) × potential difference (volts)

PLENARIES

Match the fuse – The students need to match the fuse with an electrical device after being told the power rating. Use 3 A, 5 A, 13 A and 30 A fuses. (5–10 minutes)

Electrical error – 'I'm sick of all my stuff fusing; I'm going to put a 13 amp fuse in all of my things so that they'll all keep working.' Ask: ' Is this a good plan or not?' Discuss. (5 minutes)

Motor question – Get the students to calculate how high an electric motor operating at 230 V and 2 A can lift a 100 N weight in 10 seconds. (5 minutes)

SCIENCE @ WORK

The batteries used in artificial hearts and pacemakers contain explosive materials (as do the pacemakers themselves). If a body is cremated and the pacemaker hasn't been removed, then the pacemaker will explode in the incinerator and cause quite a bit of damage and a really loud bang. This does not help the grieving relatives.

KEY POINTS

Get the students to match up fuses with devices by using the power equation. What size fuses would be needed for the same devices in the USA with a mains voltage of 110 V?

P2 6.5 Electrical energy and charge

LEARNING OBJECTIVES

Students should learn:

- That an electric current is a flow of charge; in metal wires this charge is carried by electrons.
- That the unit of charge is the coulomb where one ampere represents a flow of charge of one coulomb per second.
- That charge transferred is current × time.
- That potential difference is energy transferred per unit charge.
- That a resistor transfers electrical energy into thermal energy.

LEARNING OUTCOMES

Most students should be able to:

- State that an electrical current is a flow of charge.
- Calculate the charge transferred by a current in a specified time.
- Calculate the energy transferred using the p.d. and the charge transferred.

Some students should also be able to:

- Perform calculations involving rearrangement of the charge = current × time equation and the potential difference = energy transferred per unit charge equation.

Teaching suggestions

- **Special needs.** Use calculation templates to help the students through the equations and to make sure that they are laying out their calculations clearly.
- **Gifted and talented.** Ask: 'How many electrons are passing each second at a point, if there is a current of 1 A and each electron carries a charge of 1.6×10^{-19} C?' [The students should be able to figure out that 1 C of charge passes each second, so the number of electrons is given by $1 \text{ C}/1.6 \times 10^{-19}$ C which is 6.25×10^{18} electrons. This shows just how small the charge on a single electron is.] These numbers are impossible for a calculator to handle without using scientific notation, so it's a good opportunity to improve these skills.

SPECIFICATION LINK-UP   Unit: Physics 2.12.8

- *Electric current is the rate of flow of charge.*
- *Energy transformed, potential difference and charge are related by the equation:*

$$\text{energy transformed} = \text{potential difference} \times \text{charge}$$
$$\text{(joule, J)} \qquad \text{(volt, V)} \qquad \text{(coulomb, C)} \qquad \textbf{[HT only]}$$

- *The amount of electrical charge that flows is related to current and time by the equation:*

$$\text{charge} = \text{current} \times \text{time}$$
$$\text{(coulomb, C)} \quad \text{(ampere, A)} \quad \text{(second, s)} \qquad \textbf{[HT only]}$$

Lesson structure

STARTER

Stuck for words? – Pair up the students and give one of them cards with electrical words including charge, current etc. Ask them to mime the words to the other students. (5 minutes)

Electrical transformation – How many electrical devices can the students draw energy transfer diagrams for? (10 minutes)

Charge! – How many meanings of the word 'charge' can the students come up with? (5 minutes)

MAIN

- This is another fairly mathematically intense topic with two important equations; keep the emphasis on the electrons carrying charge from place to place and so carrying energy. The spread is only needed for students taking the Higher Tier exam.
- The first equation comes from the definition of current and charge. The size of the electric current is just how much charge passes each second (just as the size of a water current is how many litres of water pass each second). Use water flowing down a tube into a big measuring cylinder if you want a visual illustration.
- It is probably best to avoid using the symbols for current '*I*' and charge '*Q*' in equations, as these lead to more confusion. If the students are confident enough, they can use $Q = It$ to save a bit of writing, but don't let it confuse them.
- The derivation of the energy-transferred equation will again be confusing for some. For these students just concentrate on the end equation.
- Using the equation is fairly straightforward – the most difficult part is remembering it.
- Check that the students are using the correct units. With so many equations it's easy for them to pick the wrong one. A reference wall display is very handy.
- There may be situations on higher level examination papers where the students are expected to combine the equations, so give these students some examples, e.g. 'How much energy is transferred when a current of 2 A passes through a potential difference of 4 V for 1 minute'?
- The last section deals with energy transfer. You should go through the description of the energy being provided to the electrons, then carried by them and transferred to the lamp and resistor, carefully. The students should be picturing electrons as energy carriers by now, and then thinking of a coulomb as the charge carried by a big bunch of electrons.
- Try more examples of this, making sure that the students are picking up the idea that **each** coulomb of charge (bunch of electrons) is getting the same number of joules as the battery provides volts.
- It's actually the changes in the electric field that the charge produces that transfers the energy, but the students need not worry about this.

PLENARIES

Electrical spelling – Hold a spelling competition about electrical words using mini-whiteboards. If a student gets a word wrong, they get knocked out. The last one in wins 'coulomb eliminates a fair few'. (5 minutes)

Map it out – The students should produce a summary or mind map of the information about mains electricity and electrical energy calculations. (15 minutes)

Electric crossword – The students have finished this look into current and mains electricity, so let them have a go at a crossword with answers based on this chapter. (10 minutes)

Teaching suggestions – continued

- **Learning styles**

  Visual: Imagining the movement of electrons in a wire carrying charge and energy.

  Auditory: Listening to detailed explanations of charge and energy.

  Interpersonal: Working in pairs, discussing answers to problems.

  Intrapersonal: Working individually to answer calaculations.

- **Homework.** Use this opportunity to give the students some additional calculations to check their understanding and ability.

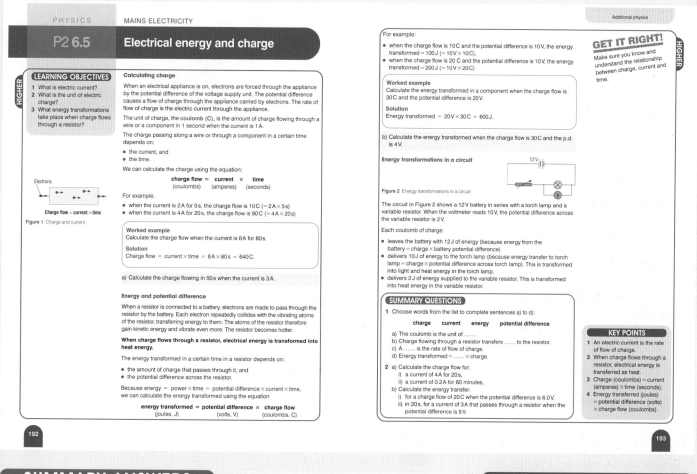

PHYSICS   MAINS ELECTRICITY

P2 6.5 Electrical energy and charge

HIGHER

LEARNING OBJECTIVES

1 What is electric current?
2 What is the unit of electric charge?
3 What energy transformations take place when charge flows through a resistor?

Calculating charge

When an electrical appliance is on, electrons are forced through the appliance by the potential difference of the voltage supply unit. The potential difference causes a flow of charge through the appliance carried by electrons. The rate of flow of charge is the electric current through the appliance.

The unit of charge, the **coulomb (C)**, is the amount of charge flowing through a wire or a component in 1 second when the current is 1 A.

The charge passing along a wire or through a component in a certain time depends on:

- the current, and
- the time.

We can calculate the charge using the equation:

charge flow = current × time
(coulombs)   (amperes)   (seconds)

For example:

- when the current is 2 A for 5 s, the charge flow is 10 C (= 2 A × 5 s)
- when the current is 4 A for 20 s, the charge flow is 80 C (= 4 A × 20 s)

Worked example
Calculate the charge flow when the current is 8 A for 80 s.

Solution
Charge flow = current × time = 8 A × 80 s = 640 C.

a) Calculate the charge flowing in 50 s when the current is 3 A.

Energy and potential difference

When a resistor is connected to a battery, electrons are made to pass through the resistor by the battery. Each electron repeatedly collides with the vibrating atoms of the resistor, transferring energy to them. The atoms of the resistor therefore gain kinetic energy and vibrate even more. The resistor becomes hotter.

When charge flows through a resistor, electrical energy is transformed into heat energy.

The energy transformed in a certain time in a resistor depends on:

- the amount of charge that passes through it, and
- the potential difference across the resistor.

Because energy = power × time = potential difference × current × time, we can calculate the energy transformed using the equation

energy transformed = potential difference × charge flow
(joules, J)   (volts, V)   (coulombs, C)

Electrons

Charge flow = current × time
Figure 1 Charge and current

For example:

- when the charge flow is 10 C and the potential difference is 10 V, the energy transformed = 100 J (= 10 V × 10 C),
- when the charge flow is 20 C and the potential difference is 10 V, the energy transformed = 200 J (= 10 V × 20 C)

Worked example
Calculate the energy transformed in a component when the charge flow is 30 C and the potential difference is 20 V.

Solution
Energy transformed = 20 V × 30 C = 600 J.

b) Calculate the energy transformed when the charge flow is 30 C and the p.d. is 4 V.

Energy transformations in a circuit

Figure 2 Energy transformations in a circuit

The circuit in Figure 2 shows a 12 V battery in series with a torch lamp and a variable resistor. When the voltmeter reads 10 V, the potential difference across the variable resistor is 2 V.

Each coulomb of charge:

- leaves the battery with 12 J of energy (because energy from the battery = charge × battery potential difference)
- delivers 10 J of energy to the torch lamp (because energy transfer to torch lamp = charge × potential difference across torch lamp). This is transformed into light and heat energy in the torch lamp.
- delivers 2 J of energy supplied to the variable resistor. This is transformed into heat energy in the variable resistor.

SUMMARY QUESTIONS

1 Choose words from the list to complete sentences a) to d):

charge   current   energy   potential difference

a) The coulomb is the unit of ....
b) Charge flowing through a resistor transfers ...... to the resistor.
c) A ...... is the rate of flow of charge.
d) Energy transformed = ... × charge.

2 a) Calculate the charge flow for:
   i) a current of 4 A for 20 s,
   ii) a current of 0.2 A for 60 minutes,
   b) Calculate the energy transfer:
   i) for a charge flow of 20 C when the potential difference is 6.0 V,
   ii) in 20 s, for a current of 3 A that passes through a resistor when the potential difference is 5 V.

GET IT RIGHT!
Make sure you know and understand the relationship between charge, current and time.

KEY POINTS

1 An electric current is the rate of flow of charge.
2 When charge flows through a resistor, electrical energy is transferred as heat.
3 Charge (coulombs) = current (amperes) × time (seconds).
4 Energy transferred (joules) = potential difference (volts) × charge flow (coulombs).

192

193

SUMMARY ANSWERS

1 a) Charge.
  b) Energy.
  c) Current.
  d) Potential difference. [**HT** only]

2 a) i) 80 C
     ii) 720 C
  b) i) 120 J
     ii) 300 J [**HT** only]

Answers to in-text questions

a) 150 C
b) 120 J

KEY POINTS

The students should be able to answer a range of questions using the two equations so a worksheet based task is appropriate.

SPECIFICATION LINK-UP
Unit: Physics 2.12.7

Students should use their skills, knowledge and understanding of 'How Science Works':

- *to recognise errors in the wiring of a three-pin plug.*
- *to recognise dangerous practice in the use of mains electricity.*

Teaching suggestions

Activities

- **Spot the hazards!** – In addition to spotting the hazards in the stately manor, you can get the students to perform a safety check of the laboratory or any other classrooms they visit during the school day. Ask: 'How safe is your school and what can be done about it?' This would also be a good time to explain why it is not wise to poke pencils into the bench sockets or try to unscrew the covers with coins.

- **Circuit breakers for safety** – A four-star skull rating may be suitable for the table if the students can't think of any.

- A common TV murder technique is to throw a live hairdryer into a bathtub of water. Would a RCCB prevent this? If so, why aren't all fuses replaced with this technology?

- **Cutting out the cowboys** – It took a great deal of time for the government to come to the decision to regulate electrical work in the home in the same way as they regulated work on gas pipes. All work on the ring main should now be performed or checked by a qualified electrician. This has made quite a few home DIYers unhappy. Do the students think that it is unfair that they cannot wire their own house? What would happen if there were a fire after they had sold the house?

- **Electrical jargon** – 'There was serious trouble in a physics lesson today; two students were charged.'

ACTIVITY

Spot the hazards!

Imagine you are a safety inspector who has been asked to check the electrics in Shockem Hall. How many electrical faults and hazards can you find just by looking around the main hall?

Circuit breakers for safety

A special 'RCCB' socket should be used for outdoor appliances such as lawnmowers. These sockets each contain a residual current circuit breaker instead of a fuse. This type of circuit breaker switches the current off if the live current and the neutral current differ by more than 30 mA. This can happen, for example, if the insulation of the live wire becomes worn and current 'leaks' from the live wire to 'earth'.

A residual current circuit breaker

QUESTIONS

1 What other appliances would you use an RCCB for besides a lawn mower?

List them in the table like the one below.

Appliance	Hazard	Rating
Lawnmower	The blades might cut the cable	
Electric drill		

2 Design a hazard rating icon like a star rating but use something different to stars. A '4-star hazard' doesn't sound right.

194

- **Holiday time** – You should be able to find a range of adapters for different purposes to show the students. Spanish mains supply is at 220 V and 50 Hz, so most devices are compatible (but kettles take a bit longer to boil apparently and you ask the students why this is). The sockets only have holes for two pins and simple adapters can be used. Many sockets also have an Earth connection at the edge.

Extension or homework

- **Sparky.** Some of the students may be interested in becoming an electrician or an electrical engineer. They should find out about what qualification and training they will need for this career.

- **Special needs.** You could provide the students with separate cards with the appliance and hazard information for the circuit breakers activity. They can match them up and add the danger rating.

- **Gifted and talented.** The students are familiar with the colour coding or wires in electrical devices; they could try to find out about the wiring used in mains circuits. They should research this and the nature of ring mains.

Cutting out the cowboys

The UK government has passed a law to stop unqualified people doing electrical work. This is because many accidents have happened due to shoddy electrical work, not just by unqualified 'cowboy' electricians but also by householders in their own homes. If you want to be an electrician, you have to train for several years as an apprentice and study for exams. When you qualify, you can register as an approved electrician.

ACTIVITY

The new law is intended to reduce accidents due to unsafe electrical work. But what other effects will it have? It might make rewiring jobs by qualified electricians too expensive and create more work for the cowboys.

Discuss whether this new law is a good law and if there are other ways of regulating electrical work.

ACTIVITY

a) What do these expressions mean? See if you and your friends can add more electrical examples.

b) Use the jargon in a discussion with your friends about something that happened in your favourite TV soap. Award one point each time jargon is used and see who wins.

c) Is jargon unsafe? Can it be misunderstood? Think of a situation where jargon is dangerous.

Electrical jargon

People often complain about jargon – the words that experts use. But sometimes, we use jargon without realising it, especially electrical jargon because we all use electricity. Sometimes, we even use it in our everyday conversations.

Here are some examples:

'Don't blow a fuse.'

'She's a sparky character.'

'Can't you short-circuit the usual procedure?'

Holiday time!

ACTIVITY

Find out what type of adaptor you would need if you go on holiday to Spain.

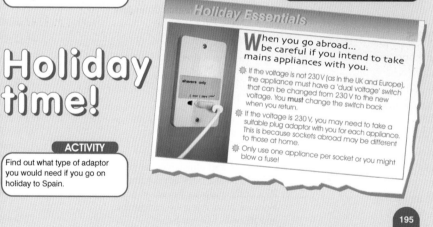

Holiday Essentials

When you go abroad... be careful if you intend to take mains appliances with you.

* If the voltage is not 230 V (as in the UK and Europe), the appliance must have a 'dual voltage' switch that can be changed from 230 V to the new voltage. You **must** change the switch back when you return.

* If the voltage is 230 V, you may need to take a suitable plug adaptor with you for each appliance. This is because sockets abroad may be different to those at home.

* Only use one appliance per socket or you might blow a fuse!

195

Learning styles

Kinaesthetic: Researching into alternative electrical mains systems.

Visual: Observing safety hazards.

Auditory: Reading information aloud.

Interpersonal: Discussing different mains systems.

Intrapersonal: Writing a report on house fires.

Teaching assistants

During any research task, the assistant should be making sure that the students are using the appropriate web sites.

ICT link-up

There are plenty of opportunities here for ICT based research; as usual a list of suitable web sites should be provided along with a template of some kind if possible.

ANSWERS TO QUESTIONS

1 Examples: an electric drill, a hedge trimmer, a power washer, outdoor lights, an electric water pump.

2 Own hazard rating icon.

SUMMARY ANSWERS

1 a) i) The neutral wire.
   ii) The live wire.
   b) i) The waves on the screen would be taller.
   ii) There would be more waves on the screen.

2 a) Live, neutral.
   b) i) Neutral.
   ii) Live.
   iii) Earth.

3 a) i) Parallel.
   ii) Series, live.
   b) i) A fuse has a wire that melts if too much current passes through it. A circuit breaker has a switch that is pulled open if too much current passes through it.
   ii) A circuit breaker is faster. Also a circuit breaker does not need to need to be replaced, but a fuse does.

4 a) i) 10.8 A
   ii) 13 A
   b) 920 W

5 1200 C [HT only]

6 a)

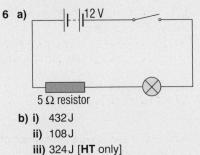

5 Ω resistor

   b) i) 432 J
   ii) 108 J
   iii) 324 J [HT only]

Summary teaching suggestions

- Make sure that the students can interpret an oscilloscope trace with question 1; a few extra traces should help.

- Wiring plug questions are quite common and you need to make sure that the students know the positions and colours of the wires and the role of fuses using the next two questions.

- Question 4 checks the students' calculations skills; they should cope well with these and you might want to stretch higher attaining students with a few more taxing questions if they find these too easily.

- The last question should stretch all of the students; be on the lookout for the students tackling the question in clear logical steps.

MAINS ELECTRICITY: P2 6.1 – P2 6.6

SUMMARY QUESTIONS

1 a) In a mains circuit, which wire:
   i) is earthed at the local sub-station;
   ii) alternates in potential?
   b) An oscilloscope is used to display the potential difference of an alternating voltage supply unit. How would the trace change if:
   i) the p.d. is increased,
   ii) the frequency is increased?

2 Complete a) and b) using words below:
   earth   live   neutral
   a) When a mains appliance is switched on, current passes through it via the ...... wire and the ...... wire.
   b) In a mains circuit:
   i) the ...... wire is blue,
   ii) the ...... wire is brown,
   iii) the ...... wire is green yellow.

3 a) Complete the sentences:
   i) Wall sockets are connected in ...... with each other.
   ii) A fuse in a mains plug is in ...... with the appliance and cuts off the ...... wire if too much current passes through the appliance.
   b) i) What is the main difference between a fuse and a circuit breaker?
   ii) Give two reasons why a circuit breaker is safer than a fuse.

4 a) i) Calculate the current in a 230 V, 2.5 kW electric kettle.
   ii) Which fuse, 3 A or 5 A or 13 A, would you fit in the kettle plug?
   b) Calculate the power supplied to a 230 V electric toaster when the current through it is 4.0 A.

5 Calculate the charge flow through a resistor when the current is 6 A for 200 s.   [Higher]

6 A 5 Ω resistor is in series with a lamp, a switch and a 12 V battery.
   a) Draw the circuit diagram.
   b) When the switch is closed for 60 seconds, a direct current of 0.6 A passes through the resistor. Calculate:
   i) the energy supplied by the battery,
   ii) the energy transformed in the resistor,
   iii) the energy transformed in the lamp.   [Higher]

EXAM-STYLE QUESTIONS

1 An electric heater is connected to a 230 V mains supply. The current flowing through the heater is 12 A.
   (a) What is the power of the heater?   (2)
   (b) The heater is switched on for 30 minutes. Calculate how much charge flows through the heater during this time and give the unit.   (4)

2 The diagram shows a three-pin plug.

   (a) State the colour of each wire.
   Live .... Neutral .... Earth ....   (3)
   (b) State and explain which parts of the plug are made out of . . .
   (i) plastic   (ii) brass   (4)

3 Explain:
   (a) why appliances with metal cases need to be earthed, but appliances with plastic cases do not.   (4)
   (b) which wire in a circuit should contain the fuse.   (2)
   (c) why the rating of the fuse in an appliance should be slightly higher than the normal working current through the appliance.   (2)

4 Cells and the electrical mains are both sources of electrical energy. Describe the currents and potential differences from each of these types of supply.   (7)

5 Most domestic appliances are connected to the 230 V mains supply with a 3-pin plug containing a fuse. 3A, 5A and 13A fuses are available.
   (a) A food mixer has a normal current of 2 A. What is the power of the mixer?   (2)
   (b) What fuse should be used in the plug for a 2.8 kW kettle?   (4)

EXAM-STYLE ANSWERS

1 a) Power = current × potential difference
       Power = 12 A × 230 V   (1 mark)
       Power = 2760 W   (1 mark)

   b) Charge = current × time   (1 mark)
       Time = 30 × 60 s   (1 mark)
       Charge = 12 A × 1800 s   (1 mark)
       Charge = 21 600 coulombs   (1 mark)

2 a) Live – brown   (1 mark)
       Neutral – blue   (1 mark)
       Earth – green/yellow   (1 mark)

   b) i) Cable grip and plug cover are plastic   (1 mark)
          because plastic does not conduct.   (1 mark)
      ii) Pins of the plug are brass   (1 mark)
          Because brass is a good conductor
          and the pins will not bend.   (1 mark)

3 a) If the live wire touches the metal case of an appliance   (1 mark)
       the case will become live   (1 mark)
       current will flow through anyone who touches the case   (1 mark)
       if the case is plastic it does not conduct.   (1 mark)

   b) The live wire   (1 mark)
       or current could still flow if the fuse blows.   (1 mark)

   c) Fuse value needs to be higher or it would melt during normal use.   (1 mark)
       Should only be slightly higher or it will take too long to melt.   (1 mark)

4 Cells provide direct current.   (1 mark)
   Direct current always passes in the same direction.   (1 mark)
   Mains supplies alternating current.   (1 mark)
   Alternating current is constantly changing direction.   (1 mark)
   Frequency of the mains supply is 50 Hz.   (1 mark)
   Potential difference from a cell is approximately 1.5 V.   (1 mark)
   Potential difference from the mains is about 230 V.   (1 mark)

(c) (i) A 9 kW shower is wired directly to the mains. It has a separate fuse in the household fuse box. Explain why? (3)

(ii) The fuse for the shower keeps melting. The householder replaces it with a nail. Why is this dangerous? (2)

6 The pictures show situations in which electricity is not being used safely.

a)

b)

c)

For each picture (a), (b) and (c), explain how electricity is not being used safely. (6)

7 An oscilloscope can be used to measure the potential difference of different electrical supplies.

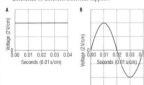

A

B

The diagrams show the traces produced on a centimetre grid by two different supplies.

(a) What is the potential difference of supply A? (3)

(b) (i) What type of supply is supply B? (1)

(ii) What is the peak potential difference of supply B? (1)

(iii) What is the frequency of supply B? (3)

[Higher]

HOW SCIENCE WORKS QUESTIONS

'There I was watching Rovers beat United, when it blew a fuse. No, it wasn't the United manager, it was the box. I reckon it was down to the United fans switching off their tellies when we scored that second goal. It must have been some sort of surge. Anyway, I fixed it before the end of the game. I put a bit of wire into where the fuse had burned and the telly worked perfectly. Unfortunately the house burned down! Anyway Rovers won and that's the important thing . . .'

a) Would you say that putting a piece of wire to replace a fuse was based on good science? Explain your answer. (1)

b) Do you think there was a link between Rovers scoring a second goal and the television fuse blowing? Was it causal, due to association or due to chance? Explain your answer. (1)

The fire brigade did a thorough investigation into the cause of the fire. They recovered a reel of the wire used in place of the 3A fuse that should have been used. Their scientists at the Fire Service laboratory found that six equal lengths of this wire fused at currents of 6.5 A, 6.1 A, 6.2 A, 5.8 A, 6.0 A and 6.1 A. They also discovered a fault in the television that had caused it to overheat. This had caused the curtains to catch fire and burn the house down.

c) i) Calculate the mean value of the measurements above. (1)

ii) Comment of the precision of the results. (1)

iii) Why did they test equal lengths? (1)

d) Is it likely that there was a causal link between the 'repair' of the fuse and the house burning down? Explain your answer. (1)

e) Why can you trust this investigation? (1)

197

Exam teaching suggestions

- Students must be familiar with S.I. units. They need to remember to convert time into seconds for most calculations.

- The best way for students to learn about wiring a plug is to actually do it. Most enjoy this activity. If possible show students some incorrectly wired plugs and get them to 'spot the mistakes'.

- Questions 3 and 4 require students to 'explain' and 'describe'. You should remind students that these words mean they must give detail in their answers in order to gain all the available marks. Expect weaker students to score around half marks for each question.

HOW SCIENCE WORKS ANSWERS

a) No! It is based on a whim!!

b) No, there was no relationship between Rovers scoring a second goal and the television fuse blowing. It would not have blown the fuse. The result of the subsequent experiment was that the house burned down, so it clearly wasn't!

c) i) 6.1 A

ii) Not very precise as the current ranged from 5.8 A to 6.5 A.

iii) Different lengths would heat up by different amounts and would fuse at different currents.

d) Yes. The only difference between the television before and after the 'repair' of the fuse was the bit of wire.

e) It would have been carried out in a scientific way, i.e. the tests would have been valid and reliable and reported without bias.

How science works teaching suggestions

- **Literacy guidance.** Key terms that should be understood: causal links, good and poor science based on a whim.

- **Higher- and lower-level answers.** Question d) is a higher-level question and the answer provided above is also at this level. Question a) is lower level and the answer provided is also lower level.

- **Gifted and talented.** Able students could learn about how such forensic investigations can detect the source of a fire after a house has burned down.

- **How and when to use these questions.** When wishing to develop ideas around good and poor science. The questions could be done for homework or in small group discussions.

- **Special needs.** Identify to these students where a fuse is and how dangerous it is to tamper with fuses, once they have blown. Remind these students that all electrical work needs to be carried out by a qualified electrician and show how most modern appliances have non-changeable fuses.

---

5 a) $P = IV$, $P = 2A \times 230V$ *(1 mark)*
  $P = 460W$ *(1 mark)*

b) 2.8 kW = 2800 W   *(1 mark)*
  $I = P/V$
  $I = 2800W/230V$ *(1 mark)*
  $I = 12.2A$ *(1 mark)*
  Hence use 13 A fuse   *(1 mark)*

c) i) $I = 9000W/230V$ *(1 mark)*
    $I = 39A$ *(1 mark)*
    Current too large to be safe in a plug   *(1 mark)*
  ii) Nail will allow very large currents to flow   *(1 mark)*
    This will cause heating and possibly a fire   *(1 mark)*

6 a) Too many appliances plugged into one socket will cause too much current   *(1 mark)*
  which may overheat/be a fire risk   *(1 mark)*

b) plastic insulation on wire is broken   *(1 mark)*
  risk of electric shock to anyone touching wire   *(1 mark)*

c) toaster is switched on   *(1 mark)*
  knife could conduct giving an electric shock   *(1 mark)*

7 a) line is at 2 cm   *(1 mark)*
  peak p.d. = 2 cm × 2 V/cm   *(1 mark)*
  peak p.d. = 4 V   *(1 mark)*

b) i) a.c. supply   *(1 mark)*
  ii) peak p.d. is 4 V   *(1 mark)*
  iii) one cycle is 4 cm
    Time period = 4 cm × 0.01 s/cm   *(1 mark)*
    Time period = 0.04 s
    Frequency = 1/time = 1/0.04   *(1 mark)*
    Frequency = 25 Hz   *(1 mark)*

197

P2 7.1

Nuclear reactions

LEARNING OBJECTIVES

Students should learn that:

- When a nucleus emits an alpha particle, its mass number is reduced by 4 and its proton number by 2.

- When a nucleus decays by beta emission, its mass number stays the same but its proton number increases by 1.

- Background radiation is present everywhere due to cosmic rays and decay of unstable isotopes in rocks.

LEARNING OUTCOMES

Most students should be able to:

- State the relative charge and mass of the constituents of an atom.

- State how many protons and neutrons are in a nucleus, given its mass number and its atomic number.

- Describe the origins of background radiation.

Some students should also be able to:

- Describe what happens to an isotope when it undergoes alpha or beta decay.

Teaching suggestions

- **Special needs.** It is probably best to provide the students with a list of the terms and symbols used in this topic, along with diagrams representing the basic decays for them to label.

- **Gifted and talented.** Alchemists dreamed for thousands of years that lead could be transformed into gold. With nuclear physics this can now actually be achieved. The students should find out who has done this and why the market has not been flooded with this artificial gold.

- **Learning styles**

  Kinaesthetic: Modelling the changes during nuclear decay.

  Visual: Imagining the structure of an atom.

  Auditory: Explaining how a nucleus changes during nuclear decay.

  Intrapersonal: Making deductions about the nature of the nucleus.

SPECIFICATION LINK-UP   Unit: Physics 2.12.9

- *The relative masses and relative electric charges of protons, neutrons and electrons.*
- *In an atom the number of electrons is equal to the number of protons in the nucleus. The atom has no net electrical charge.*
- *Atoms may lose or gain electrons to form charged particles called 'ions'.*
- *All atoms of a particular element have the same number of protons.*
- *Atoms of different elements have different numbers of protons.*
- *Atoms of the same element that have different numbers of neutrons are called isotopes.*
- *The total number of protons in an atom is called its atomic number.*
- *The total number of protons and neutrons in an atom is called its mass number.*

Lesson structure

STARTER

Fact or fiction – The students use red, amber and green cards to decide if a series of statements about radioactivity are false, they don't know, or true. (5–10 minutes)

Nuclear action – The students should produce a mind map showing what they remember about radioactivity and nuclear power. (15 minutes)

Radiation danger – Can the students remember why radioactivity is so dangerous? They should explain the damage it can do to humans. (5–10 minutes)

MAIN

- There is quite a lot of information in this topic and students are likely to become confused if they move too quickly through it. The main source of confusion is often with the large number of scientific terms.

- Start with a reminder of the structure of an atom, but do not dwell on it too long because this will be the fifth or sixth time they have been through it.

- The terms 'proton number' and 'atomic number' are often interchanged.

- Similarly you may find references to 'nucleon number' instead of 'mass number' in some textbooks.

- Watch out for students getting confused about finding the number of neutrons. Some think that there is always the same number of neutrons as protons.

- Some students find it very difficult to write out the superscript and subscripts on the isotopes in the correct positions. Try to encourage them to be precise.

- You may find animations of nuclear decays helpful, as the students can see the alpha or beta particle leave the nucleus and how it is changed by the process. (See Simulation P2 7.1 'Nuclear reaction' on the GCSE Physics CD ROM.)

- Somebody might ask where the electron comes from in beta decay. They may think that a neutron is an electron and a proton stuck together, and it just splits.

- Gamma ray emission is really just the dumping of excess energy by the nucleus after another form of decay leaves it with a bit too much energy. As there are no particles emitted there is no change to the nucleus.

- The background radiation section is a basic recap of information the students should have studied before. It should be pointed out that almost all of our exposure is from natural sources.

- **ICT link-up.** Use Simulation P2 7.1 'Nuclear reaction' from the GCSE Physics CD ROM to show the changes in the nucleus during decays. This helps the students imagine what is going on a lot better.

- **Homework.** Give the students some additional questions on the constituents of different isotopes, and ask them to determine what new isotopes are formed following certain decays. You might like to stretch some students by giving them some decay sequences. The students will need a periodic table.

PLENARIES

Definitions – The students must give accurate definitions of the terms: 'ion, mass number, atomic number, isotope, alpha particle, beta particle and gamma ray.' (10 minutes)

Name that isotope – Provide the students with a table describing different isotopes with gaps in and ask them to complete the table. They may need a periodic table to help. (5–10 minutes)

Say it with words – Give the students a couple of nuclear decay equations and ask them to describe what the equations show in words. (5–10 minutes)

ACTIVITY & EXTENSION IDEAS

Nuclear reminders – It's worthwhile reminding students of the nature and properties of the three radiations. Have a look back to the demonstrations in P1.

PHYSICS   NUCLEAR PHYSICS

P2 7.1   Nuclear reactions

LEARNING OBJECTIVES

1 How does the nucleus of an atom change when it emits an alpha particle or a beta particle?
2 How can we represent a nuclear reaction?
3 Where does background radiation come from?

The atom has a nucleus composed of protons and neutrons surrounded by electrons. In a nuclear reaction, neutrons and protons crash into each other and get rearranged. At speeds approaching the cosmic speed limit, the speed of light, they can even annihilate each other or create new particles.

The table gives the relative masses and the relative electric charges of a proton, a neutron and an electron.

	Relative mass	Relative charge
proton	1	+1
neutron	1	0
electron	0.0005	−1

An uncharged atom has equal numbers of protons and electrons. A charged atom, an ion, has unequal numbers of protons and electrons.

The atoms of the same element each have the same number of protons. The number of protons in a nucleus is denoted by **Z**. It is called the **atomic number** (or proton number).

Isotopes are atoms of the same element with different numbers of neutrons.

The number of protons and neutrons in a nucleus is called its mass number, denoted by **A**.

An isotope of an element X, which has Z protons and A protons and neutrons, is represented by the symbol $^A_Z X$. For example, the uranium isotope $^{238}_{92}U$ contains 92 protons and 146 neutrons (= 238 − 92) in each nucleus. So its relative mass is 238 and its relative charge is 92.

a) How many protons and how many neutrons are in the nucleus of the uranium isotope $^{235}_{92}U$?

Radioactive decay

An unstable nucleus becomes more stable by emitting an α (alpha) or a β (beta) particle or by emitting γ (gamma) radiation.

α emission

- An α particle consists of two protons and two neutrons. Its relative mass is 4 and its relative charge is 2. So we can represent it by the symbol $^4_2\alpha$.
- When an unstable nucleus emits an α particle, its atomic number goes down by 2 and its mass number goes down by 4.

For example, the thorium isotope $^{228}_{90}Th$ decays by emitting an α particle. So it forms the radium isotope $^{224}_{88}Ra$.

b) How many protons and how many neutrons are in $^{228}_{90}Th$ and $^{224}_{88}Ra$?

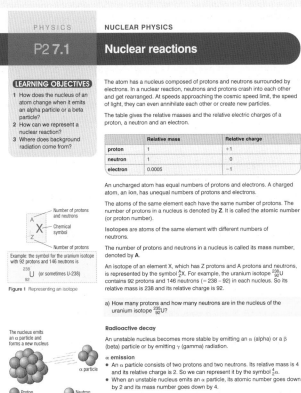

Number of protons and neutrons
$^A_Z X$ ← Chemical symbol
Number of protons

Example: the symbol for the uranium isotope with 92 protons and 146 neutrons is
$^{238}_{92}U$ (or sometimes U-238)

Figure 1 Representing an isotope

The nucleus emits an α particle and forms a new nucleus

α particle

○ Proton   ● Neutron

$^{228}_{90}Th \longrightarrow {}^{224}_{88}Ra + {}^4_2\alpha$

Figure 2 α emission

β emission

- A β particle is an electron created and emitted by a nucleus which has too many neutrons compared with protons. A neutron in its nucleus changes into a proton and a β particle. This is instantly emitted at high speed by the nucleus.
- The relative mass of a β particle is effectively zero and its relative charge is −1. So we can represent a β particle by the symbol $^0_{-1}\beta$.
- When an unstable nucleus emits a β particle, its atomic number goes up by 1 but its mass number stays the same (because the neutron changes into a proton).

For example, the potassium isotope $^{40}_{19}K$ decays by emitting a β particle. So it forms a nucleus of the calcium isotope $^{40}_{20}Ca$.

c) How many protons and how many neutrons are in $^{40}_{19}K$ and $^{40}_{20}Ca$?

γ emission

γ radiation is emitted by some unstable nuclei after an α particle or a β particle has been emitted. γ radiation is uncharged and has no mass. So it does not change the number of protons or the number of neutrons in a nucleus.

The origins of background radiation

Background radiation is ionising radiation from space (cosmic rays), from devices such as X-ray tubes and from radioactive isotopes in the environment. Some of these isotopes are present because of nuclear weapons testing and nuclear power stations. But most of it is from substances in the Earth. For example, radon gas is radioactive and is a product of the decay of uranium in rocks found in certain areas.

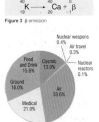

A neutron in the nucleus changes into a proton

A β particle is created in the nucleus and instantly emitted

$^{40}_{19}K \longrightarrow {}^{40}_{20}Ca + {}^0_{-1}\beta$

Figure 3 β emission

Figure 4 The origins of background radioactivity

Nuclear weapons 0.4%
Air travel 0.3%
Food and Drink 15.6%
Cosmic 13.0%
Nuclear reactors 0.1%
Ground 16.0%
Air 33.6%
Medical 21.0%

		Change in the nucleus	Particle emitted
1	α decay	Nucleus loses 2 protons and 2 neutrons	2 protons and 2 neutrons emitted as an α particle
2	β decay	A neutron in the nucleus changes into a proton	An electron is created in the nucleus and instantly emitted

KEY POINTS

SUMMARY QUESTIONS

1 How many protons and how many neutrons are there in the nucleus of each of the following isotopes?
a) $^{12}_6C$
b) $^{60}_{27}Co$
c) $^{235}_{92}U$

2 A substance contains the radioactive isotope $^{238}_{92}U$, which emits alpha radiation. The product nucleus X emits beta radiation and forms a nucleus Y. How many protons and how many neutrons are present in:
a) a nucleus of $^{238}_{92}U$,
b) a nucleus of X,
c) a nucleus of Y?

198   199

SUMMARY ANSWERS

1 a) 6 p + 6 n
  b) 27 p + 33 n
  c) 92 p + 143 n

2 a) 92 p + 146 n
  b) 90 p + 144 n
  c) 91 p + 143 n

Answers to in-text questions

a) 92 p, 143 n

b) $^{228}_{90}Th = 90 p + 138 n$; $^{224}_{88}Ra = 88 p + 136 n$

c) $^{40}_{19}K = 19 p + 21 n$; $^{40}_{20}Ca = 20 p + 20 n$

KEY POINTS

The students should complete decay equations showing alpha, beta and gamma decay. This could be in the form of a card game.

P2 7.2

The discovery of the nucleus

Students should learn:
- That the alpha-scattering experiments carried out by Rutherford and his research team led Rutherford to deduce the nuclear model of the atom. [**HT** only]
- About such experiments, the results they produced and why these results led Rutherford to deduce the nuclear model of the atom. [**HT** only]
- That the nuclear model of the atom was accepted because it explained alpha scattering much better than the previous models could. [**HT** only]
- That the 'plum pudding' model of the atom was replaced by the nuclear model. [**HT** only]

Most students should be able to:
- Describe the Rutherford scattering experiment and the evidence it produced. [**HT** only]
- Explain how this evidence leads to the nuclear model of the atom. [**HT** only]
- Describe the 'plum pudding' model and explain why this model proved to be inadequate. [**HT** only]

Some students should also be able to:
- Draw and explain the paths of alpha particles scattered by a nucleus. [**HT** only]

Teaching suggestions

- **Special needs.** Provide a diagram of the experiment so that the students can add the conclusions to the evidence presented.
- **Gifted and talented.** Ask: 'How was the neutron discovered?' Because it has no electrical charge, it is much more difficult to detect than the electron or proton. The students should find out who discovered it and how.
- **Learning styles**
  Kinaesthetic: Modelling scattering experiment.
  Visual: Imagining the behaviour of alpha particles in the scattering experiment.
  Auditory: Explaining how the conclusions match the evidence.
  Interpersonal: Discussing and evaluating the experiment.
  Intrapersonal: Appreciating the techniques and difficulties involved.

SPECIFICATION LINK-UP   Unit: Physics 2.12.9

Students should use their skills, knowledge and understanding of 'How Science Works':

- *to explain how the Rutherford and Marsden scattering experiment led to the plum pudding model of the atom being replaced by the nuclear model. [**HT** only]*

Lesson structure

STARTER

Believe it or not? – What does it take to change the students' minds about something? How much evidence would be needed to convince them that NASA have really sent men to the Moon? (5–10 minutes)

What's in the tin? – Peel the label off a tin of sponge pudding (spotted dick is best). Show the unmarked tin to the students and ask then to describe ways they could find out about what's inside without opening it. (5–10 minutes)

Who's the boss? – Give the students a set of cards with academic job titles and ask them to rank them in order of seniority. Use 'dean, professor, lecturer, fellow, research assistant, postgraduate and undergraduate'. (5 minutes)

MAIN

- This topic is all about a famous experiment and it should be built up as such. Through hard work and brilliant ideas, our idea of 'what an atom is' was developed.
- You might want to establish the context; electrons (cathode rays) had not long been discovered and Rutherford had discovered that one element could change into another when it emitted an 'alpha particle'.
- The actual experiment took weeks in a very dark laboratory where Geiger or Marsden had to count tiny flashes of light through a microscope. Each flash was one alpha particle hitting the fluorescent screen.
- If you have electron tubes, you can show a little bit of what this would be like (see activity box).
- The most important result of the experiment was the few particles that bounced back. These showed that there was something massive at the centre of the atom.
- One possible analogy would be to spread a large sheet of paper out vertically and behind it fix a small metal disc held firmly by a stand. If you threw darts at it, most would go straight through but one in a thousand may hit the metal disc and bounce back.
- It will be impossibly difficult for the students to imagine the size of an atom and then the relative size of the nucleus. You might like to point out that 99.99% of the chair they are sitting on is just empty space; then again so is 99.99% of their bodies!
- The problem with plum puddings is that nobody eats them any more, so many students don't understand what you are on about. Try illustrating with a real plum (or spotted dick) pudding. They are cheap and you can always eat it afterwards.

PLENARIES

It's not like a solar system – Some people think of an atom as being a bit like a solar system. The students should make a list of similarities but, more importantly, the differences. (5–10 minutes)

New improved recipe! – The term 'plum pudding' is out of date. Can the students come up with another material/object/whatever that would be a bit more modern? (5 minutes)

I don't believe it – Can the students write a letter to an unconvinced scientist that wants to hold on to the plum pudding model? (10–15 minutes)

ACTIVITY & EXTENSION IDEAS

A scattering experiment

It is possible to model the scattering experiment of Rutherford using a hidden cone and marbles. The marbles are rolled at the cone and scatter in directions similar to those in the original experiment. You should find a kit available in a good science equipment catalogue. This is really only suitable for small groups though. More useful animations can be found at various web sites on the Internet.

Electron tubes

These are generally only used at A-level, but you could use them here with higher attaining groups.

Details

Use the manual for the tube to set it up. It will require an extremely high-tension power supply and some proper connecting leads. These shouldn't be able to provide a dangerous current but take care with any high voltages. With the tube you should be able to show the phosphorescence effect of a charged particle and some magnetic deflection if you wish.

Teaching suggestions – continued

- **Homework.** Whatever happened to Ernest Marsden? Hans Geiger will always be famous for the co-invention of the Geiger-Muller tube, but what did Marsden do? The students can compare the fates of these two nuclear physicists for homework.
- **ICT link-up.** Use Animation P2 7.2 'Nucleus' to help students understand the nature of the nucleus.

Practical support

Lucky strike

This practical really needs no additional explanation. A more advanced version is outlined in the activity box.

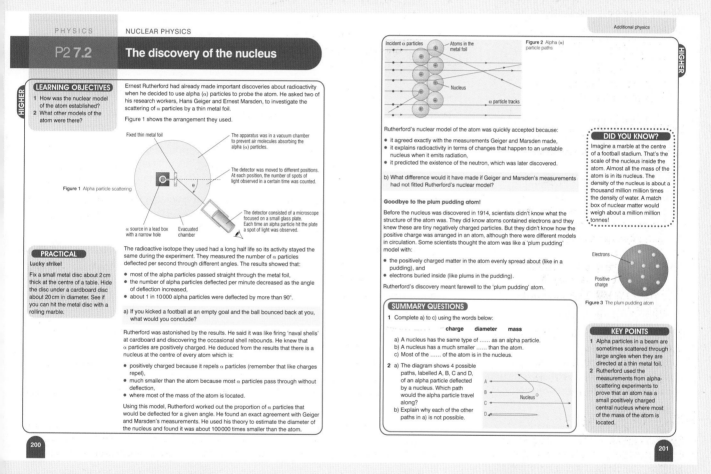

SUMMARY ANSWERS

1 a) Charge.
  b) Diameter.
  c) Mass. [**HT** only]

2 a) Path B.
  b) A is wrong because it is attracted by the nucleus; C is wrong because it is unaffected by the nucleus; D is wrong because it is repelled by the nucleus through too great an angle. [**HT** only]

Answers to in-text questions

a) It had hit something much heavier.
b) Rutherford's model would have been incorrect.

DID YOU KNOW?

There are objects made up of purely nuclear material. A neutron star is made up of neutrons packed together as tightly as the protons and neutrons in a nucleus.

KEY POINTS

The students should link the observations of Rutherford to the conclusions he made about atomic structure.

P2 7.3   Nuclear fission

Students should learn:

- That uranium and plutonium isotopes are used in nuclear fission reactors as fuel.
- That nuclear fission is the splitting of large nuclei into small ones; a process that releases energy.
- How a fission reactor operates.

Most students should be able to:

- List the isotopes used as fuel in nuclear fission reactors.
- Describe what happens in a fission event.
- Sketch a labelled diagram to show how a chain reaction may occur.

Some students should also be able to:

- Explain how a chain reaction in a nuclear reactor can take place.

Teaching suggestions

- **Special needs.** Give the students a large diagram of the reactor, so that they can label the parts and write their notes around it.
- **Gifted and talented.** The students can find out about the choice of materials used for the moderator, control rods and coolant in different types of reactor.
- **Learning styles**

  Visual: Drawing and labelling the components of the power station.

  Auditory: Discussing the safety of fission.

  Interpersonal: Discussing and evaluating the safety features of the power station.

  Intrapersonal: Appreciating the rapid build up in a chain reaction.
- **Homework.** The emergency shutting down of a reactor is called 'scramming'. Where does this term come from. There are a couple of possibilities.
- **ICT link-up.** Animations and simulations showing chain reactions are available in commercial software. There are also some simple animations available freely on the Internet. Search for 'chain reaction simulation'.

SPECIFICATION LINK-UP   Unit: Physics 2.12.10

- *There are two fissionable substances in common use in nuclear reactors, uranium-235 and plutonium-239.*
- *Nuclear fission is the splitting of an atomic nucleus.*
- *For fission to occur the uranium-235 or plutonium-239 nucleus must first absorb a neutron.*
- *The nucleus undergoing fission splits into two smaller nuclei, and 2 or 3 neutrons and energy is released.*
- *The neutrons may go on to start a chain reaction.*

Students should use their skills, knowledge and understanding of 'How Science Works':

- *to sketch a labelled diagram to illustrate how a chain reaction may occur.*

Lesson structure

STARTER

Protection from radiation – Can the students describe the penetrating powers of the three radiations and explain how we can be protected from them? (5–10 minutes)

Lucky lady – A woman bets £1 on roulette and wins, doubling her money. Then she bets the winnings and wins again. She keeps doing this until she has won 20 times in a row. Ask: 'How much has she won?' [£1,048,575] (10 minutes)

Power station basics – The students should draw a quick diagram showing how a fossil fuel power station operates. (10 minutes)

MAIN

- You can show an example of a chain reaction with dominoes. Set them up so that one knocks over two more, and these two knock over four, etc. After only a few steps, you could have hundreds and then thousands falling.
- In a nuclear chain reaction, the released neutrons are important.
- In a nuclear reactor core, it is important to keep the reaction critical. If it becomes 'super critical', the reactor will heat up but not like a nuclear explosion. More likely the reaction becomes 'sub-critical' and slows down.
- Good moderators slow down the fast neutrons without absorbing them. If the moderator absorbs too many neutrons, then the chain reaction cannot continue. In some reactors, graphite is used instead of water.
- The control rods have to be good at absorbing neutrons. When they are inserted the number of available neutrons is decreased, and the reaction becomes sub-critical, cooling the core down. Cadmium and boron are common materials for this job.
- In an emergency, the rods are dropped completely into the core, rapidly reducing the reaction to almost zero. The reactor still produces some heat through natural (non-induced) decay of the radioactive materials. This means that it still has to be cooled or it will meltdown.
- The coolant may be water or some more exotic material such as liquid sodium. It has to be able to rapidly carry thermal energy from the core, but in doing this it becomes radioactive.
- The core itself is very heavily shielded and only a few gamma rays can escape.

Flow – The students should draw a flow chart and energy transfer diagram showing what happens in a nuclear fission reactor. (10 minutes)

The China syndrome – If a nuclear core melts down, it gets so hot that it can melt the rock beneath it and start sinking into the Earth. If an American reactor melts down, ask 'What's to stop it melting all the way through to China?' (5–10 minutes)

Let's split – The word 'fission' means 'to break into parts'. How many other words can the students think of that mean roughly the same thing? How many words can they think of that mean the opposite? (5 minutes)

The 'critical mass' of pure U-235 is 50 kg. The first nuclear weapon had 60 kg in three pieces and most of the material did not undergo fission. A more efficient design has a 'neutron reflector' material around it that will go supercritical and explode with only 15 kg of material.

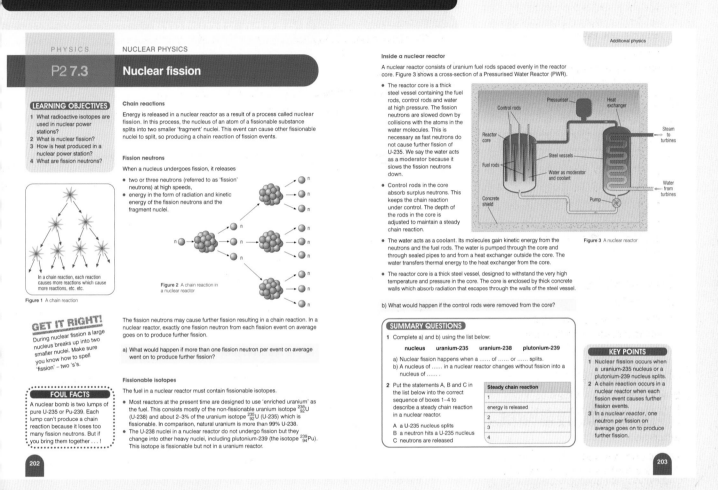

Answers to in-text questions

a) The chain reaction would go out of control and the reactor would explode.

b) The chain reaction would go out of control and the reactor would explode.

1 a) Nucleus, uranium-235, plutonium-239.

   b) Uranium-238, plutonium-239.

2 1A, 2C, 3B, 4A.

The students should be able to draw a chain reaction diagram.

P2 7.4

Nuclear fusion

Students should learn that:

- The Sun releases energy due to nuclear fusion of hydrogen isotopes in its core.

- Nuclear fusion is the joining of two small nuclei and this process releases energy.

- Nuclear fusion reactors are difficult to build mainly due to the difficulty of reaching sufficiently high temperatures and pressures.

Most students should be able to:

- Describe the nuclear fusion process happening in the Sun.

- Outline how experimental nuclear fusion reactors work on Earth.

Some students should also be able to:

- Describe some of the problems associated with nuclear fusion reactors.

Teaching suggestions

- **Gifted and talented**

  - Ask: 'What's so special about iron?' The students can find out more detail about nuclear energy release by researching binding energy. It is this energy that is released by fusion and fission processes when the nucleons rearrange. If they go on to look at stars and supernovae they will discover the importance of iron in these explosions.

  - Alternatively, students could find out about the claims made by Pons and Fleischmann in the late 1980s regarding 'cold fusion'.

- **Learning styles**

  Visual: Following the sequence of a nuclear fusion diagram.

  Auditory: Discussing advantages of fusion over fission.

  Interpersonal: Debating the possibility of fusion power.

  Intrapersonal: Evaluating the difficulties of making progress with the research.

- **Homework.** The poster comparing the two types of nuclear power could be a homework task, as could research into the latest developments.

SPECIFICATION LINK-UP   Unit: Physics 2.12.10

- *Nuclear fusion is the joining of two atomic nuclei to form a larger one.*
- *Nuclear fusion is the process by which energy is released in stars.*

Lesson structure

STARTER

Star One – Ask: 'Where does the Sun get its energy?' The students brainstorm their ideas and then discuss possible problems with them. (5–10 minutes)

A Sun myth – The Sun has a lot of mythology based on it. What stories do the students know? (5–10 minutes)

Solar fact or solar fiction? – Give the students a set of statements about the Sun and ask them to separate fact from fiction. (5–10 minutes)

MAIN

- Students may confuse the words 'fission' and 'fusion' in general conversation, but should be able to remember the difference when writing answers.

- The reactions in the Sun are hugely powerful. Its power output is around 4×10^{26} watts. The students might like to imagine how many light bulbs' worth that represents.

- The students might want to know what you mean by 'the antimatter counterpart of the electron'. This is a topic for A-level study really, so just say that it is exactly the same size as an electron but all of its other properties are opposite.

- If you like, you can act out the reaction process in the Sun with marbles or with molecular modelling kits. The balls should be close together though. Alternatively, show the Animation P2 7.4 'Nuclear fusion' from the GCSE Physics CD ROM.

- The overall process shown is four protons (hydrogen nuclei) converting into one helium nucleus, and so the Sun is generally said to be converting hydrogen into helium. This means that the percentages of hydrogen and helium are slowly changing.

- The reactions also produce a lot of positrons and neutrinos.

- The main difficulty to overcome is the fact that the protons strongly repel each other. In the Sun, the gravitational forces are strong enough to keep the very high temperature protons close enough together so that they will collide and fuse. It is this process that is proving very difficult to replicate on Earth.

- Some of the students will have heard the term 'plasma' before and when you tell them that it is at a temperature of several thousand degrees, they will assume it has a lot of thermal energy and will be very dangerous. The plasma is actually of very low density and so hasn't got that much thermal energy.

- When discussing the promising future of fusion-produced energy, remind the students that we have been working on the project for a long time and it has proven very difficult to achieve. There is a lot of work yet to be done and opportunities for great scientists to make a difference.

- Fusion-reactor research continues with the construction of the latest testing facility in France. This International Thermonuclear Experimental Reactor (Iter) may actually be able to sustain a reaction long enough for it to be useful. It will cost over 10 billion euros though.

- There are possible hazards associated with a fusion reactor: free neutrons are produced and could be absorbed by the materials in the reactor. This would produce dangerous radioactive isotopes. However, there would be much less radiation released than in the nuclear fission reaction.

- **ICT link-up.** The latest state of nuclear fusion research is available online. The students should be able to find news articles about the new and previous research centres. (Search for 'nuclear fusion breakthrough'.)

PLENARIES

Bring it together – The word 'fusion' means 'to combine together'. How many examples of fusion can the students think of, and how many words that mean the same thing? (5 minutes)

A bright future – A company claims to have developed a working nuclear fusion plant and wants to build one in the local area. Do the students object or rejoice? They should have a quick discussion and vote. (5 minutes)

Compare and contrast – The students should make a poster, comparing and contrasting the processes of nuclear fission and nuclear fusion. (20 minutes)

PHYSICS | NUCLEAR PHYSICS

P2 7.4 Nuclear fusion

LEARNING OBJECTIVES

1 Where does the Sun's energy come from?
2 What happens during nuclear fusion?
3 Why is it difficult to make a nuclear fusion reactor?

Imagine if we could get energy from water. Stars release energy as a result of fusing small nuclei like hydrogen to form larger nuclei. Water contains lots of hydrogen atoms. A glass of water could provide the same amount of energy as a tanker full of petrol – if we could make a fusion reactor here on the Earth.

Fusion reactions

Two small nuclei release energy when they are fused together to form a single larger nucleus. The process releases energy only if the relative mass of the product nucleus is no more than about 55 (about the same as an iron nucleus). Energy must be supplied to create bigger nuclei.

Figure 1 A fusion reaction

The Sun is mostly 75% hydrogen and about 25% helium. The core is so hot that it consists of a 'plasma' of bare nuclei with no electrons. These nuclei move about and fuse together when they collide. When they fuse, they release energy. Figure 2 shows how protons fuse together to form a $^4_2$He nucleus. Energy is released at each stage.

Figure 2 Fusion reactions in the Sun

○ Proton
● Neutron

FOUL FACTS

A hydrogen bomb is a uranium bomb surrounded by the hydrogen isotope, $^2_1$H. When the uranium bomb explodes, it makes the surrounding hydrogen fuse and release even more energy. A single hydrogen bomb would completely destroy London!

- When two protons (i.e. hydrogen nuclei) fuse, they form a 'heavy hydrogen' nucleus, $^2_1$H. A positron, the antimatter counterpart of the electron, is created and emitted at the same time.
- Two more protons collide separately with two $^2_1$H nuclei and turn them into heavier nuclei.
- The two heavier nuclei collide to form the helium nucleus $^4_2$He.
- The energy released at each stage is carried away as kinetic energy of the product nucleus and other particles emitted.

a) Look at Figure 2 and work out what is formed when a proton collides with a $^2_1$H nucleus.

Fusion reactors

There are enormous technical difficulties with fusion. The 'plasma' of light nuclei must be heated to very high temperatures before the nuclei will fuse. This is because two nuclei approaching each other will repel each other due to their positive charge. If the nuclei are moving fast enough, they can overcome the force of repulsion and fuse together.

In a fusion reactor:

- the plasma is heated by passing a very large electric current through it,
- the plasma is contained by a magnetic field so it doesn't touch the reactor walls. If it did, it would go cold and fusion would stop.

Figure 3 An experimental fusion reactor

Scientists have been working on these problems since the 1950s. A successful fusion reactor would release more energy than it uses to heat the plasma. At the present time, scientists working on experimental fusion reactors are able to do this by fusing 'heavy hydrogen' nuclei to form helium nuclei – but only for a few minutes!

b) Why is a fusion reactor unlikely to explode?

A promising future

Practical fusion reactors could meet all our energy needs.

- The fuel for fusion reactors is readily available as 'heavy hydrogen' and is present in sea water.
- The reaction product, helium, is a non-radioactive inert gas so is harmless.
- The energy released could be used to generate electricity.

SUMMARY QUESTIONS

1 Complete a) and b) using the words below:

larger   small   stable

a) When two ...... nuclei moving at high speed collide, they form a ...... nucleus.
b) Energy is released in nuclear fusion if the product nucleus is not as ...... as an iron nucleus.

2 a) Why does the plasma of light nuclei in a fusion reactor need to be very hot?
b) Why would a fusion reactor that needs more energy than it produces not be much use?

KEY POINTS

1 Nuclear fusion occurs when two nuclei are forced close enough together so they form a single larger nucleus.
2 Energy is released when two light nuclei are fused together.
3 A fusion reactor needs to be at a very high temperature before nuclear fusion can take place.

204 | 205

SUMMARY ANSWERS

1 a) Small, larger.
   b) Stable.

2 a) So the nuclei have enough kinetic energy to overcome the force of repulsion between them and fuse.

   b) The energy output would be less than the energy input so it would not produce any energy overall.

Answers to in-text questions

a) $^3_2$He nucleus.

b) If it goes out of control, the plasma would touch the walls and go cold.

KEY POINTS

Can the students outline the nuclear fusion processes in the Sun and the problems we have copying them on Earth?

P2 7.5   Nuclear energy issues

Teaching suggestions

Activities

The Manhattan project

The use of nuclear bombs on Japan at the end of World War II is obviously a contentious matter. Issues to discuss include:

- The lack of warning or demonstration to Japan – the first bomb was dropped on Hiroshima without any form of warning. This was to prevent the remaining Japanese forces from trying to intercept the mission. After this bombing leaflets were dropped on Japanese cities to say that more bombs would come if there were no surrender. Three days later the warning was fulfilled at Nagasaki.

- The two nuclear weapons used in the bombings were of very different designs. On Hiroshima the 'little boy' uranium bomb was dropped, while three days later the 'fat man' plutonium bomb was dropped. Ask: 'Was the second bomb dropped to test this different technology?'

- Ask: 'Were the Americans demonstrating their technology to the Russians to warn them about future gains in Europe?'

- Ask: 'How many civilians in Japanese-controlled China and prisoner camps were dying every month? How many were saved by a quick end to the war?'

- Ask: 'What did the scientists that made the bombs think about their use? What did they do after the war?'

PHYSICS   NUCLEAR PHYSICS

P2 7.5   Nuclear energy issues

The Manhattan project

In the Second World War, scientists in Britain and America were recruited to work in Arizona on the Manhattan project, the project to build the first atomic bomb. They knew they would be in deadly competition with scientists in Nazi Germany. They also knew that if they lost the race, the war would be lost.

By 1945, the first atomic bomb was ready to be used. Nazi Germany had already surrendered. The allied forces were still involved in bitter fighting against Japan in the Far East. Their leaders knew the planned invasion of Japan would claim the lives of many allied troops. An atomic bomb was dropped on the Japanese city of Hiroshima to force Japan to surrender. The explosion killed 140 000 people. The Japanese government did not give in until after a second atomic bomb was dropped on the Japanese city of Nagasaki a week later.

ACTIVITY

Discuss these questions as a small group:

a) Most people think the British and American governments were right to build an atomic bomb. But do you think scientists should continue to work on deadly weapons?

b) Many people think the power of the atomic bomb should have been demonstrated to Japan by dropping it on an uninhabited island. What do you think?

Cold fusion

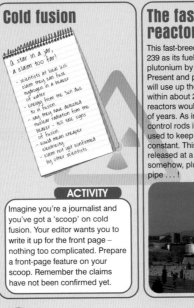

ACTIVITY

Imagine you're a journalist and you've got a 'scoop' on cold fusion. Your editor wants you to write it up for the front page – nothing too complicated. Prepare a front-page feature on your scoop. Remember the claims have not been confirmed yet.

The fast-breeder reactor

This fast-breeder reactor uses plutonium-239 as its fuel. It can 'breed' its own plutonium by fusion from uranium-238. Present and planned uranium reactors will use up the world's supply of uranium within about 200 years. Fast-breeder reactors would extend that to thousands of years. As in the uranium reactor, control rods in the reactor core are used to keep the rate of fission events constant. This ensures energy is released at a constant rate. ***But*** if somehow, plutonium got stuck in a pipe . . . !

ACTIVITY

a) Finish the sentence at the end of the paragraph.

b) The UK government built and tested an experimental fast-breeder reactor on the coast of Northern Scotland at Dounreay. It has now been closed. So why are many people still worried about it? Imagine you are one of them. Write a letter to your local newspaper about your concerns.

Nuclear reprocessing – a hot problem!

The students may have debated this issue before, but they could look at the reprocessing techniques in more detail. Ask: 'What happens to the chemicals used in the reprocessing? If they become radioactive where are they stored?'

The fast-breeder reactor

- You could use this activity to discuss the fail-safe designs of nuclear reactors. Ask: 'What is the likelihood of the control rods not working? The reactor was cooled by liquid sodium metal; what would happen if this leaked?'

- All of the reactors at Dounreay have now been shut down, except for some experimental nuclear submarine reactors. The process of decommissioning has begun and the government hopes to have the site back to 'green field' status by 2047!

Nuclear reprocessing – a hot problem!

Used fuel rods contain uranium-238 and plutonium-239. After removal from a reactor, a used fuel rod is left to cool in a large tank of water for up to a year. Then the fuel in it is removed and the uranium and plutonium content is taken out chemically. This process is called reprocessing. The rest of the fuel is stored in sealed containers at secure sites. Reprocessed uranium and plutonium can be used in fast-breeder reactors to generate electricity. Plutonium can also be used to make nuclear bombs.

The UKs THORP reprocessing plant in Cumbria reprocesses waste from other countries as well as from the UK. Lots of scientists are employed there. It generates income but it also generates lots of controversy. Many people think it should be closed.

ACTIVITY

Should we reprocess nuclear waste for other countries? Should we reprocess our own nuclear waste or just store it? Discuss the issue as a group. Send an e-mail to your MP to tell him/her what you think.

Atom smashers

Here's something you don't need to know for your GCSE exam – yet! We now know that neutrons and protons are made of smaller particles called **quarks**. Physicists use big machines (like the one in the picture) called accelerators to make charged particles travel extremely fast. They discovered that a beam of fast-moving electrons is scattered by three small particles inside each neutron and proton. They worked out that

- a proton is made of two 'up' quarks and a 'down' quark,
- a neutron is made of two 'down' quarks and an 'up' quark.

You'll learn more about the quark family at AS level!

ACTIVITY

What conclusions can you make about the charge of an 'up' quark and the charge of a 'down' quark?

New improved nuclear reactors

Most of the world's nuclear reactors presently in use will need to be replaced in the next 20 years. They were built to last for no more than about 30 to 40 years. We all want electricity and we want it without burning fossil fuel. Reactor companies have been developing new improved 'third-generation' nuclear reactors to replace existing nuclear reactors when they are taken out of use.

These new types of reactors have:

- a standard design to cut down capital costs and construction time,
- a longer operating life – typically 60 years,
- improved safety features,
- much less effect on the environment.

Some of the new reactors are designed with 'passive' safety features, where natural processes (for example, convection of outside air through cooling panels along the reactor walls) are used to prevent accidents. Such features are additional to 'active' safety controls, such as the use of control rods and safety valves. Some scientists claim these 'new' features are about giving nuclear power a more 'positive image'.

ACTIVITY

New reactors are being built in many countries. Should new reactors be built in the UK? Discuss the benefits and the drawbacks of such a programme.

207

Atom smashers

The quark forms part of the standard model in particle physics. The charges of the quarks are $+\frac{2}{3}e$ for an 'up' quark and $-\frac{1}{3}e$ for a 'down' quark (where e is the charge of a proton). If you put the right combinations together you should find a neutron ends up with zero charge, while a proton ends up with $+1e$ charge. For more fun, the students can find out about leptons and mesons: the other fundamental particles.

New improved nuclear reactors

- Public opposition to new nuclear reactors is still very strong. The students are better informed than most about the technology, so what do they think? No matter how many safety features are employed, the damage caused by a single reactor melting down can be so devastating that student fears can never be soothed.

- However, the long-term damage from a coal power station could be just as great, but because the damage is caused over a period of 50 or more years it is not easily noticed.

Gifted and talented

Antimatter – Scientists have recently manufactured a few atoms of anti-hydrogen. Ask them to find out what this is and how it was made. Can they find out anything else about antimatter?

Learning styles

Kinaesthetic: Researching into the history of nuclear weapons.

Visual: Obtaining more information on particle physics.

Auditory: Discussing the use of nuclear weapons.

Interpersonal: Discussing the operation and evolution of fast-breeder reactors.

Intrapersonal: Writing a report on cold fusion or reprocessing.

ICT link-up

To find out more about particle physics visit the web site of 'The Particle Adventure'. There are several copies of the site online, so you should find it easily.

SUMMARY ANSWERS

1 a) i) 6 p + 8 n

   ii) 90 p + 138 n

  b) i) 7 p + 7 n

   ii) $^{14}_{7}$N

  c) i) 88 p + 136 n

   ii) $^{224}_{88}$Ra

2 a) i) Stays the same.

   ii) Decreases.

  iii) Increases.

  b) i) The reactor would overheat and the materials in it might melt. In the meltdown the reactor pressure might be high enough to cause an explosion releasing radioactive material into the atmosphere.

   ii) The excess neutrons would be absorbed and the reaction would slow down releasing less energy.

3 a) i) The process where two small nuclei fuse together to form a single larger nucleus.

   ii) Because they are both positively charged.

  iii) To overcome the force of repulsion between them due to their charge.

  b) The plasma needs to be very hot. The plasma is difficult to control.

4 a) i) Fusion.

   ii) Fission.

  iii) Fission.

  b) The fuel is readily available. The products of fusion are not radioactive.

Summary teaching suggestions

- Question 1 checks the understanding of isotopes, nuclear change and nuclear nomenclature. Watch out for the students putting the mass and proton numbers in the wrong place.

- The last three questions are about reactors. There may still be some students confusing fission and fusion. Get them to do a table comparing the two techniques.

NUCLEAR PHYSICS: P2 7.1 – P2 7.5

SUMMARY QUESTIONS

1 a) How many protons and how many neutrons are in a nucleus of each of the following isotopes?
i) $^{14}_{6}$C,   ii) $^{228}_{90}$Th

b) $^{14}_{6}$C emits a β particle and becomes an isotope of nitrogen (N).
  i) How many protons and how many neutrons are in this nitrogen isotope?
  ii) Write down the symbol for this isotope.

c) $^{228}_{90}$Th emits an α particle and becomes an isotope of radium (Ra).
  i) How many protons and how many neutrons are in this isotope of radium?
  ii) Write down the symbol for this isotope.

2 a) Complete the sentences using words from the list.

   decreases   increases   stays the same

When energy is released at a steady rate in a nuclear reactor,
  i) the number of fission events each second in the core ....
  ii) the amount of uranium-235 in the core ....
  iii) the number of radioactive isotopes in the fuel rods ....

b) Explain what would happen in a nuclear reactor if:
  i) the coolant fluid leaked out of the core,
  ii) the control rods were pushed further into the reactor core.

3 a) i) What do we mean by nuclear fusion?
  ii) Why do two nuclei repel each other when they get close?
  iii) Why do they need to collide at high speed in order to fuse together?

b) Give two reasons why nuclear fusion is difficult to achieve in a reactor.

4 a) Complete the sentences using words from the list.

   fission   fusion

  i) In a ...... reactor, two small nuclei join together and release energy.
  ii) In a ...... reactor, a large nucleus splits and releases energy.
  iii) The fuel in a ...... reactor contains uranium-235.

b) State two advantages that nuclear fusion reactors would have in comparison with nuclear fission reactors.

EXAM-STYLE QUESTIONS

1 The diagram shows two isotopes of the element carbon.

   • Proton
   ○ Neutron
   × Electron

(a) What are isotopes of an element? *(2)*

(b) (i) What is the atomic number of carbon?
  (ii) What are the mass numbers of the two isotopes of carbon shown in the diagram? *(3)*

(c) Which of the particles •, ○ and ×, shown in the diagram:
  (i) has a negative charge?
  (ii) has no charge?
  (iii) has the smallest mass? *(3)*

2 In a nuclear reactor, energy is produced by the process of nuclear fission.

Describe as fully as you can the process of nuclear fission.

The answer has been started for you. Copy and complete:

Atoms of uranium-235 are bombarded by neutrons. .... *(6)*

3 Nuclear fusion is the process by which energy is released in stars.
Describe as fully as you can the process of nuclear fusion. *(4)*

EXAM-STYLE ANSWERS

1 a) Atoms of an element with same numbers of protons *(1 mark)*
   but different numbers of neutrons. *(1 mark)*

  b) i) 6 *(1 mark)*
   ii) 12 and 14 *(2 marks)*

  c) i) electron *(1 mark)*
   ii) neutron *(1 mark)*
   iii) electron *(1 mark)*

2 A uranium-235 nucleus absorbs a neutron. *(1 mark)*
  The nucleus splits into two smaller nuclei *(1 mark)*
  and two or three neutrons *(1 mark)*
  and energy is released. *(1 mark)*
  The neutrons may go on to hit other nuclei *(1 mark)*
  and start a chain reaction. *(1 mark)*

3 The nuclei *(1 mark)*
  of lighter elements join together *(1 mark)*
  they form heavier elements *(1 mark)*
  the process releases energy. *(1 mark)*

4 a) $^{226}_{88}$Ra → $^{222}_{86}$Rn + $^{4}_{2}$α
  1 mark for each correct number *(4 marks)*

  b) $^{14}_{6}$C → $^{14}_{7}$N + $^{0}_{-1}$β
  1 mark for each correct number *(4 marks)*

  c) neutron becomes a proton and an electron *(1 mark)*
  proton stays in the nucleus *(1 mark)*
  electron is emitted as a beta particle *(1 mark)*

5 a) e.g. food and drink, medical sources, nuclear accidents, cosmic rays *(2 marks)*

  b) make measurements in different rooms *(1 mark)*
  measure at different times of day *(1 mark)*
  repeat all measurements and find an average *(2 marks)*

  c) i) categoric variable *(1 mark)*
   ii) bar chart *(1 mark)*

4 (a) Radon is formed when radium-226 decays by the emission of an alpha particle.

Copy and complete the nuclear equation below.

$$^{226}_{88}\text{Ra} \longrightarrow \text{.......} \, \text{Rn} + \text{.......} \, \alpha$$ (4)

(b) Nitrogen is formed when carbon-14 decays by the emission of a beta particle.

Copy and complete the nuclear equation below.

$$^{14}_{6}\text{C} \longrightarrow \text{.......} \, \text{N} + \text{.......} \, \beta$$ (4)

(c) What changes take place in the carbon-14 nucleus when it decays by emitting a beta particle? (3)

5 Background radiation is with us all the time and comes from many different sources, such as radon gas.

(a) Name two other sources of background radiation. (2)

(b) Some scientists are measuring the amount of radon gas inside a house. The gas is released into the air from rocks in the ground. Suggest what the scientists could do to make their measurements as reliable as possible. (4)

(c) The table gives some values for the dose of background radiation from the ground in different parts of the UK.

Area of UK	Dose in millisieverts per year
South west	0.35
South east	0.20
Midlands	0.25
North west	0.30
North east	0.23

(i) What type of variable is the 'Area of UK'? (1)

(ii) What would be the best way to represent this data on a bar chart or line graph? (1)

HOW SCIENCE WORKS QUESTIONS

Iodine-125 is a radioactive isotope used by doctors as a gamma emitter for measuring bone density in humans. It can also be used in the treatment of prostate cancer.

It is important to know how the activity of iodine-125 changes with time. The following measurements were taken in two identical tests of iodine-125.

Time (days)	0	50	100	150	200	250
Sample A (counts/min)	100	56	31	17	10	6
Sample B (counts/min)	100	55	31	18	9	5

a) Are the differences in activity between the two samples due to random or systematic error? Explain your answer. (1)

b) The tests were carried on for several years and the results stayed more or less constant after a couple of years. This was said to be due to the ever-present background radiation.
Explain why the background radiation introduces a systematic error into the measurements. (1)

c) What are the environmental issues involved in using this isotope? (1)

PRESS RELEASE

Fifteen-year studies of prostate cancer patients using iodine-125 have been completed. The Medical Director from a US company confirmed that results show only 4% of patients had died from the prostate cancer. A British consultant urologist said that after 5 years, 93% of patients were disease-free.

d) Suggest two questions you might want to ask the scientists who gave this press release. (2)

HOW SCIENCE WORKS ANSWERS

a) The differences are due to random error. The differences show no pattern and radioactive decay is a random process.

b) The background radiation levels stay more or less constant in these time scales and so will affect each reading equally.

c) Environmental issues are that it must be used sensibly and stored safely to ensure as little as possible gets into the environment.

d) e.g. What did the people die from?
How many people were in the survey?
Do all prostate cancer patients get this treatment?
Was there a control group?
How many would have died anyway?

How science works teaching suggestions

- **Literacy guidance.** Key terms that should be understood: random error, systematic error, mean.

- **Gifted and talented.** Able students could explore the ways in which gamma radiation can be measured and suggest some units for the table.

- **How and when to use these questions.** When wishing to develop ideas around systematic and random error and the ways in which science can lead to technological development and environmental issues.

  The questions could be used in small discussion groups.

- **Homework.** The questions could be used for homework with more able students.

- **Special needs.** These students will need to be aware of the advantages and problems associated with using radioisotopes.

- **ICT link-up.** Students could use the Internet to research how gamma radiation can be detected. Search the web for 'detecting gamma radiation'.

Exam teaching suggestions

- In examinations students often confuse fission and fusion.

- In question 2 students might like to illustrate their answer with a diagram. They can get credit for this but the diagram needs to be clear, labelled and include several fissions, large and small nuclei and neutrons.

- There are many sources of background radiation. Students will gain credit for any sensible answer.

- Students should practise balancing nuclear equations for both alpha and beta decays.

P2 | Examination-Style Questions

Examiner's comments

If used as a test, allow about 30 minutes for students to complete these questions.

Many students will be able to explain the shape of the graph but find it difficult to sketch the graph themselves.

When calculating K.E. students commonly forget to square the speed term. They should be sure to show their working.

Answers to Questions

1 (a) Total momentum before = total momentum after
(1 mark)

$0 = 2\,kg \times v\,m/s + 0.0005\,kg \times 100\,m/s$ *(1 mark)*

$0 = 2v\,kg\,m/s + 0.05\,kg\,m/s$

$v = -0.05/2\,m/s$

$v = -0.025\,m/s$ *(sign not essential for the mark)*
(1 mark)

(b) Change in momentum = force × time taken for the change. *(1 mark)*

If the force is applied for a longer time the gain in momentum is greater *(1 mark)*

so the velocity of the ball is greater. *(1 mark)*
[HT only]

2 (a) There is a drag force acting upwards on the ball.
(1 mark)

The drag force increases as the speed increases.
(1 mark)

Eventually drag force is equal to the weight (resultant force = zero). *(1 mark)*

(b) e.g. Eye at level of the ball.
Take time as lower surface of the ball passes the mark each time.
Repeat the test. *(2 marks)*

(c) Straight line, showing initial acceleration. *(1 mark)*
Line curves. *(1 mark)*
Horizontal line to show terminal velocity. *(1 mark)*

3 (a) Negative electrons *(1 mark)*
stuck into a lump of positive matter. *(1 mark)*

(b) First explanation: Most of the atom is empty space. *(1 mark)*
Second explanation: The nucleus has a positive charge *(1 mark)*
and a large mass. *(1 mark)*
[HT only]

continues opposite ❯

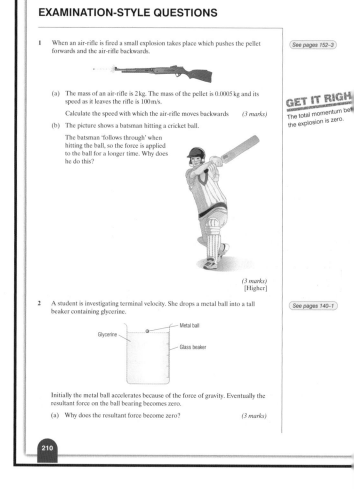

EXAMINATION-STYLE QUESTIONS

1   When an air-rifle is fired a small explosion takes place which pushes the pellet forwards and the air-rifle backwards.   *See pages 152–3*

(a)   The mass of an air-rifle is 2 kg. The mass of the pellet is 0.0005 kg and its speed as it leaves the rifle is 100 m/s.

Calculate the speed with which the air-rifle moves backwards   *(3 marks)*

(b)   The picture shows a batsman hitting a cricket ball.

The batsman 'follows through' when hitting the ball, so the force is applied to the ball for a longer time. Why does he do this?

(3 marks)
[Higher]

GET IT RIGH
The total momentum be
the explosion is zero.

2   A student is investigating terminal velocity. She drops a metal ball into a tall beaker containing glycerine.   *See pages 140–1*

Glycerine —
Metal ball
Glass beaker

Initially the metal ball accelerates because of the force of gravity. Eventually the resultant force on the ball bearing becomes zero.

(a)   Why does the resultant force become zero?   *(3 marks)*

210

GET IT RIGHT!

Students should understand that the total momentum before the explosion is zero.

The student watches the ball slowly moving through the glycerine. As it does, she times how long it takes to get to each mark on the beaker.

(b) Describe what precautions she should take to make her results as accurate as possible. *(2 marks)*

(c) Copy the axes below and sketch the line you would expect on the graph of speed of ball against time. *(3 marks)*

At one time scientists believed in a 'plum pudding' model of the atom.

See pages 200–1

(a) What is meant by the 'plum pudding' model of the atom? *(2 marks)*

(b) Rutherford and Marsden carried out an experiment that led to this model being replaced by the nuclear model.

They fired alpha particles at thin gold foil. Some of the observations from their experiment are given below.
For each observation write down the matching explanation.
One has been done for you.

Observation	Explanation
Most of the particles go straight through the gold foil without being deflected.	
Some particles are deflected through small angles.	The nucleus is charged.
A few alpha particles are deflected back through angles greater than 90°.	

(3 marks)
[Higher]

GET IT RIGHT!

There are three marks here, so try to make three points.

In a fitness centre people use machines containing pulleys to move 'weights'.

See pages 146–9

(a) Some of the 'weights' are marked '5 kg'.

This is incorrect physics. Explain why. *(2 marks)*

(b) Calculate the work done on a 30 N weight when one of the machines raises it 2 m. Give a unit with your answer. *(4 marks)*

(c) A running machine displays the speed a person would be travelling if they were running on the road.

Calculate the kinetic energy of a person of mass 70 kg running at a speed of 5 m/s. Give a unit with your answer. *(4 marks)*
[Higher]

GET IT RIGHT!

Remember to square the speed when calculating kinetic energy.

> *continues from previous page*

4 (a) 5 kg is a mass. *(1 mark)*
Weight is measured in newtons. *(1 mark)*

(b) Work done = force × distance moved in the
direction of the force *(1 mark)*
Work done = 30 N × 2 m *(1 mark)*
Work done = 60 *(1 mark)*
Units of Nm or joules *(1 mark)*

(c) kinetic energy = $\frac{1}{2}$ × mass × velocity^2 *(1 mark)*
kinetic energy = $\frac{1}{2}$ × 70 kg × (5 m/s)^2 *(1 mark)*
kinetic energy = 875 J *(2 marks)*
[HT only]

Key Stage 3 curriculum links

The following link to 'What you already know':

- Forces can cause objects to turn about a pivot.

- The principle of moments and its application to situations involving one pivot.

- Light travels in a straight line at a finite speed in a uniform medium.

- Non-luminous objects are seen because light scattered from them enters the eye.

- Light is reflected at plane surfaces.

- How light is refracted at the boundary between two different materials.

- White light can be dispersed to give a range of colours.

- The effect of colour filters on white light and how coloured objects appear in white light and in other colours of light.

- Light can travel through a vacuum but sound cannot, and light travels much faster than sound.

- The relationship between the loudness of a sound and the amplitude of the vibration causing it.

- The relationship between the pitch of a sound and the frequency of the vibration causing it.

- About the movements of planets around the Sun and to relate these to gravitational forces.

- About the use of artificial satellites and probes to observe the Earth and to explore the Solar System.

QCA Scheme of work
8K Light
9I Energy and electricity
9J Gravity and space
9L Pressure and moments

Link with Units P1 and P2

The following link to units in the specification that should have been studied earlier.

From Unit P1 the students should have studied:

- That many devices take in input energy in one form and transform (change) it to output energy in another form. They never transform all of the input energy to the output form we want or transfer (move) it all to the place we want. We need to know how efficient devices are so that we can choose between them and try to improve them.

- Electromagnetic radiations are disturbances in an electric field. They travel as waves and move energy from one place to another. They can all travel through a vacuum and do so at the same speed. The waves cover a continuous range of wavelengths called the electromagnetic spectrum. The uses and hazards of the radiations in different parts of the electromagnetic spectrum depend on their wavelength and frequency.

- Radioactive substances emit radiation from the nuclei of their atoms all the time. These nuclear radiations can be very useful but may also be very dangerous. It is important to understand the properties of different types of nuclear radiation.

- Current evidence suggests that the universe is expanding and that matter and space expanded violently and rapidly from a very small initial point, i.e. the universe began with a 'Big Bang'.

From Unit P2 the students should have studied:

- Even when things are moving in a straight line, describing their movement is not easy. They can move with different speeds and can also change their speed and/or direction (accelerate). Graphs can help us to describe the movement of the body. These may be distance–time graphs or velocity–time graphs.

- To change the speed of a body an unbalanced force must act on it.

- The size of the current in a circuit depends on how hard the supply tries to push charge through the circuit and how hard the circuit resists having charge pushed through it.

- Mains electricity is useful but can be very dangerous. It is important to know how to use it safely.

- Electrical appliances transform energy. The power of an electrical appliance is the rate at which it transforms energy. Most appliances have their power and the potential difference of the supply they need printed on them. From this we calculate their current and the fuse they need.

- Nuclear fission is the splitting of atomic nuclei and is used in nuclear reactors as a source of heat energy that can be transformed to electrical energy. Nuclear fusion is the joining together of atomic nuclei and is the process by which energy is released in stars.

PHYSICS

P3 | Further physics

What you already know

Here is a quick reminder of previous work that you will find useful in this unit

Forces
- The gravitational pull between any two objects depends on their masses and the distance between them.
- The weight of an object is the force of gravity on the object.
- When an object is at rest or moving at constant velocity, the forces acting on it are balanced.

Light and sound
- We see objects which are not light sources because they reflect or scatter light.
- Refraction occurs when a light ray changes its direction as it passes from one transparent substance to another.
- Light travels faster than sound. Light travels through a vacuum. Sound cannot travel through a vacuum.

Magnetism
- Permanent magnets are made of steel because steel does not lose its magnetism easily.
- An electromagnet is a coil of insulated wire wrapped round an iron core. When an electric current passes through the coil, the core is magnetised. The core loses its magnetism when the current is switched off.

Space
- The Earth orbits the Sun and the Moon orbits the Earth.
- The Sun and the stars emit light. Planets and satellites are seen by reflected light from the Sun.

Figure 1 Light travels faster than sound

RECAP QUESTIONS

1 Which of the forces A–D listed below act on each of the following objects:

    A air resistance   B force of gravity
    C friction   D magnetic attraction

a) A falling ball in air
b) A paper clip lifted by a magnet
c) A cyclist stopping.

2 a) In a thunderstorm, why is there a delay between a lightning flash and hearing the thunder from the flash?
b) Why do we not hear noise from the Sun?

3 a) Why is a permanent magnet made from steel not iron?

b) Why is the core of an electromagnet made from iron not steel?

4 A Moon B A communications satellite
  C Jupiter D Sun

a) List the objects A–D in order of increasing distance from the Earth.

b) List the objects A–D in order of increasing mass.

c) Which of the objects A–D orbit the Earth?

d) Which one of the objects A–D causes a solar eclipse?

SPECIFICATION LINK-UP

Unit: Physics 3

This section of the course covers the complete specification for Unit P3:

How do forces have a turning effect?

Even if the forces acting on a body are balanced in the sense that they do not cause the body to change speed, they can still make the body turn.

What keeps bodies moving in a circle?

A body remains stationary, or keeps moving at the same speed in a straight line, unless an unbalanced force acts upon it. If a body moves in a circular path there must be an unbalanced force acting upon it all the time.

What provides the centripetal force for planets and satellites?

The planets, like the Earth, orbit the Sun. Artificial satellites, which are used for communications and monitoring, orbit the Earth. Gravitational force provides the centripetal force that allows all of these bodies to orbit.

What do mirrors and lenses do to light?

Mirrors and lenses can be used to form images in optical devices such as cameras and magnifying glasses. The most commonly used mirrors and lenses have surfaces with a uniform curvature and these are the only ones that need to be considered. All objects and images will be located vertically on the principal axis.

What is sound?

Sounds are mechanical vibrations that can be detected by the human ear. This means they are in the frequency range 20–20 000 Hz.

What is ultrasound and how can it be used?

Just as there is electromagnetic radiation with frequencies we cannot see, there are 'sound' waves with frequencies we cannot hear. These ultrasound waves have several important uses.

How can electricity be used to make things move?

Electric currents produce magnetic fields. Forces produced in magnetic fields can be used to make things move. This is called 'the motor effect' and is how devices, such as the electric motor and circuit breakers, create movement.

How do generators work?

If an electrical conductor 'cuts' through magnetic field lines, an electrical potential difference is induced across the ends of the conductor. This is called the 'generator effect' and is used in generators to produce electricity.

How do transformers work?

Transformers are used to step-up (increase) or step-down (decrease) a.c. potential differences.

What is the life history of stars?

Astronomers believe that gravitational forces are responsible for the formation of galaxies of stars, and for stars like the Sun having a long stable period.

Making connections

Artificial joints

People who suffer from damaged hip joints can now have replacement joints fitted. A replacement hip joint must be carefully designed to fit the patient. The hip joint is a ball-and-socket joint. The replacement material is carefully chosen to be strong and won't wear away. It needs to last so the patient doesn't need another replacement for many years. When it is first fitted, the patient has to be very careful – one false turn can force the ball out of the socket! You'll learn more about the turning effect of a force in this unit.

Brain waves

Brain scanners can now be used to locate your thoughts. The MRI scanner was invented by the American chemist, Paul Lauterbur, and the British physicist, Sir Peter Mansfield. For their invention, they were jointly awarded the 2003 Nobel Prize for medicine. MRI stands for Magnetic Resonance Imaging. Magnetic fields are used to scan the brain and make hydrogen atoms in brain tissue emit tiny radio signals. The radio signals are detected and used to produce a visual image of the brain. The images show that seeing or hearing or thinking about different things makes different parts of the brain active. You will find out more about scanners and magnetic fields in this unit.

The endoscope

Doctors use endoscopes to see directly inside the body. For example, an endoscope inserted into the oesophagus can be used to see inside the stomach if a stomach ulcer is suspected. An endoscope consists of two bundles of optical fibres, one to shine light into the body and the other to see what's inside. A tiny lens over the second bundle is used to form an image on the ends of the fibres in the bundle. The image can then be seen at the other end of the fibre bundle. You will find out more about lenses in this unit.

Images from space

The main component of the Hubble Space Telescope (HST) is a 4.2 metre wide concave mirror. It can gather and focus light from galaxies of stars billions of light years away. Because the HST orbits the Earth high above the atmosphere, light reaching it isn't affected by the atmosphere. So HST images are clearer than images from telescopes on the ground. You will find out more about concave mirrors and stars in this unit.

ACTIVITY

Medical scanners and large telescopes use electric motors to turn heavy objects. Such objects need to be turned so they point in precise directions. Use a low-voltage electric motor to turn an object and see how well you can control the object's position.

Chapters in this unit

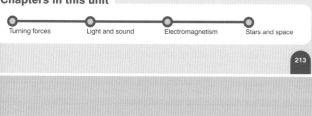

Turning forces — Light and sound — Electromagnetism — Stars and space

---

Teaching suggestions

- **Making connections** – Refer to PhotoPLUS P3 Unit opener. You can expand further on the devices and developments mentioned with images easily found on the Internet. Search www.images.google.com for endoscopes, brain scanner and so on. Find video at video.google.com and explanations at www.howstuffworks.com. The students could be set a homework task to research one of the developments in more detail, for example for 'Artificial joints' let the students find out about the materials used in the manufacture of these joints. Firstly they should discuss the condition inside the body, this should lead then to the understanding that the material must be very hardwearing but also chemically uncreative.

RECAP ANSWERS

1 **a)** A, B **b)** B, D **c)** A, B, C

2 **a)** Light travels faster than sound, so the light from the flash reaches you before you hear the sound from the flash.

  b) Sound cannot travel through space because space is a vacuum.

3 **a)** Steel retains its magnetism and iron doesn't.

  b) An iron core loses its magnetism when the current is switched off whereas steel doesn't.

4 **a)** B, A, D, C **b)** B, A, C, D **c)** A and B **d)** A

⭕ Chapters in this unit

- ⭕ **Turning forces**
- ⭕ **Light and sound**
- ⭕ **Electromagnetism**
- ⭕ **Stars and space**

P3 1.1

Moments

LEARNING OBJECTIVES

Students should learn:

- That a moment is the turning effect of a force about a pivot.
- That the size of a moment is measured in newton metres (Nm).
- How to calculate the moment using the correct equation.

LEARNING OUTCOMES

Most students should be able to:

- Calculate the moment of a force including use of correct units.
- Draw a diagram showing the moment of a force.
- Describe the turning effect of a force on a force diagram.

Some students should also be able to:

- Perform calculations including rearrangement of the moment equation.
- Explain simple observations about the turning effect of a force.

Teaching suggestions

- **Special needs.** It is best to have a set of diagrams for the students to mark the forces and moments on. These should have calculation templates below the diagram to help the students develop a clear layout.

- **Gifted and talented.** These students can look into situations where the force and seesaw are at angles other than 90°. This may involve a bit of geometry to calculate the perpendicular distances of the forces. (Situations like this arise in A-level physics studies quite often, but should not appear on the GCSE exams.)

- **Learning styles**

  Kinaesthetic: Carrying out practical activities investigating moments.

  Visual: Using diagrams to visualise the action of forces.

  Auditory: Discussing the action of tools.

  Interpersonal: Reporting the outcome and conclusion of an experiment and getting feedback from other groups.

  Intrapersonal: Making deductions about the evidence produced by the experiment.

- **Homework.** The students can label the load, effort and pivot for a range of diagrams and calculate the turning moment for a range of situations.

SPECIFICATION LINK-UP   Unit: Physics 3.13.1

- *The turning effect of a force is called the moment.*
- *The size of the moment is given by the equation:*

$$\underset{\text{(newton metre, Nm)}}{\text{moment}} = \underset{\text{(newton, N)}}{\text{force}} \times \underset{\text{(metre, m)}}{\text{perpendicular distance from the line of action of the force to the axis of rotation}}$$

Lesson structure

STARTER

Right tool for the job – Give the students two worksheets, showing tools like a crowbar, screwdriver, spanner, etc. and some jobs that they are used for, such as opening a box, paint tin, bolt. Ask them to match them up. Then ask the students to explain how they work. (10 minutes)

Nut – Show the students an over-tightened nut, impossible to undo with fingers alone, and ask them to explain how it can be undone. Use a spanner to undo it easily. (5 minutes)

Force facts – Get the students to draw a mind map to show their prior knowledge about forces. (5–10 minutes)

MAIN

- The students will have studied levers and moments during Key Stage 3, but here they will be looking at more advanced situations; in particular the idea that the force and perpendicular distance are important. Refer to electronic resource P3 1.1 'Balancing moments' on the GCSE Physics CD ROM.

- You should demonstrate the turning effect of a force in a variety of ways, including the use of tools, opening doors, etc.

- When discussing different tools, it helps a lot to show them in action. At each stage describe where the forces are acting and where the pivot is.

- One simple demonstration of the increased moment when the distance is increased is to hold out a retort stand by the pole at arms' length, this becomes more difficult the further away the stand is held.

- You could also show pictures or a video of a strongman competition, where the contestants hold things like car batteries at arms' length and discuss why this is so difficult.

- The students need to use the correct terms for load, effort and pivot, so get them to draw or label a few diagrams. Check that they are getting the directions of the forces and moment correct.

- Watch out for a few students confused about clockwise and anticlockwise and try to convince the students that talking about rotation to the right/left or up/down is not a good description.

- The investigation is straightforward, and all of the students should reach a sensible conclusion easily.

- Consider the accuracy of the measurements made and the reliability of the data collected (this relates to: 'How Science Works').

- It is important to stress at this point that it is the perpendicular distance that is important. In most situations the students come across, the force will be at right angles to the lever so this will be easy, but you might like to stretch the higher-attaining students with some tilted seesaws.

- The calculations are not too difficult at this stage but you will have some students giving the unit as newtons per metre instead of newton metres.

- Ideally avoid calculations involving centimetres; get the students to convert all distances to metres and they will have an easier time.

PLENARIES

Incomprehensible instructions – Ask the students to draw diagrams showing how to assemble a flat-pack cabinet without any words. You will have to provide the basic diagrams but remove some of the information. (10–15 minutes)

The claw – Can the students design a grabbing device that can be used to grab an object that is around a corner? (5–10 minutes)

Pivot – Ask the students to list as many devices that use a simple pivot as possible. (5 minutes)

Practical support

Investigating the turning effect of a force

The turning effect can be measured through a range of methods but this one avoids the need for a pivot that the ruler will slide off.

Equipment and materials required

For each group: Retort stand with two clamp arms, 50 or 30 cm ruler with hole drilled towards one end, newtonmeter (10 W), 10 g mass holder with 4 × 10 g masses, some cotton.

Details

The newtonmeter should be attached halfway along the ruler and the arm of the clamp should fit through the hole in the ruler. The weights are then suspended near the end of the ruler and can be slid back and forth.

The students will need to be reminded to measure the distances from the pivot, not from the end of the ruler.

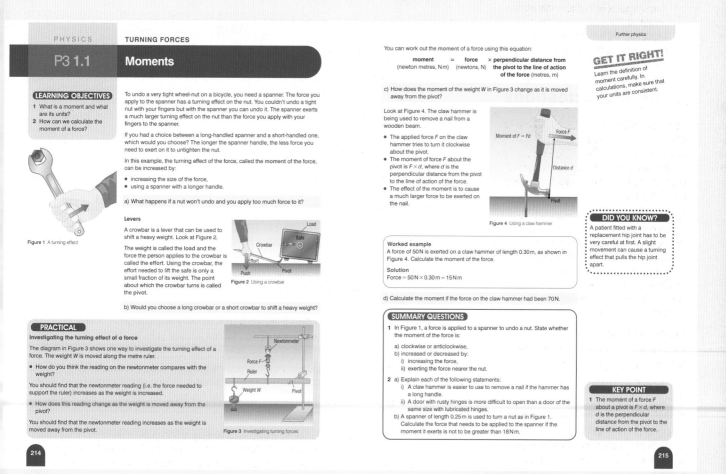

PHYSICS

P3 1.1 — Moments

TURNING FORCES

LEARNING OBJECTIVES

1 What is a moment and what are its units?
2 How can we calculate the moment of a force?

To undo a very tight wheel-nut on a bicycle, you need a spanner. The force you apply to the spanner has a turning effect on the nut. You couldn't undo a tight nut with your fingers but with the spanner you can undo it. The spanner exerts a much larger turning effect on the nut than the force you apply with your fingers to the spanner.

If you had a choice between a long-handled spanner and a short-handled one, which would you choose? The longer the spanner handle, the less force you need to exert on it to untighten the nut.

In this example, the turning effect of the force, called the moment of the force, can be increased by:

- increasing the size of the force,
- using a spanner with a longer handle.

a) What happens if a nut won't undo and you apply too much force to it?

Figure 1 A turning effect

Levers

A crowbar is a lever that can be used to shift a heavy weight. Look at Figure 2.

The weight is called the load and the force the person applies to the crowbar is called the effort. Using the crowbar, the effort needed to lift the safe is only a small fraction of its weight. The point about which the crowbar turns is called the pivot.

Figure 2 Using a crowbar

b) Would you choose a long crowbar or a short crowbar to shift a heavy weight?

PRACTICAL

Investigating the turning effect of a force

The diagram in Figure 3 shows one way to investigate the turning effect of a force. The weight W is moved along the metre ruler.

- How do you think the reading on the newtonmeter compares with the weight?

You should find that the newtonmeter reading (i.e. the force needed to support the ruler) increases as the weight is increased.

- How does this reading change as the weight is moved away from the pivot?

You should find that the newtonmeter reading increases as the weight is moved away from the pivot.

Figure 3 Investigating turning forces

You can work out the moment of a force using this equation:

$$\text{moment} = \text{force} \times \text{perpendicular distance from}$$
$$\text{(newton metres, Nm)} \quad \text{(newtons, N)} \quad \text{the pivot to the line of action}$$
$$\text{of the force (metres, m)}$$

c) How does the moment of the weight W in Figure 3 change as it is moved away from the pivot?

Look at Figure 4. The claw hammer is being used to remove a nail from a wooden beam.

- The applied force F on the claw hammer tries to turn it clockwise about the pivot.
- The moment of force F about the pivot is F × d, where d is the perpendicular distance from the pivot to the line of action of the force.
- The effect of the moment is to cause a much larger force to be exerted on the nail.

Figure 4 Using a claw hammer

Worked example

A force of 50 N is exerted on a claw hammer of length 0.30 m, as shown in Figure 4. Calculate the moment of the force.

Solution

Force = 50 N × 0.30 m = 15 Nm

d) Calculate the moment if the force on the claw hammer had been 70 N.

SUMMARY QUESTIONS

1 In Figure 1, a force is applied to a spanner to undo a nut. State whether the moment of the force is:

a) clockwise or anticlockwise,
b) increased or decreased by:
   i) increasing the force,
   ii) exerting the force nearer the nut.

2 a) Explain each of the following statements:
   i) A claw hammer is easier to use to remove a nail if the hammer has a long handle.
   ii) A door with rusty hinges is more difficult to open than a door of the same size with lubricated hinges.

b) A spanner of length 0.25 m is used to turn a nut as in Figure 1. Calculate the force that needs to be applied to the spanner if the moment it exerts is not to be greater than 18 Nm.

GET IT RIGHT!

Learn the definition of moment carefully. In calculations, make sure that your units are consistent.

DID YOU KNOW?

A patient fitted with a replacement hip joint has to be very careful at first. A slight movement can cause a turning effect that pulls the hip joint apart.

KEY POINT

1 The moment of a force F about a pivot is F × d, where d is the perpendicular distance from the pivot to the line of action of the force.

214 | 215

Answers to in-text questions

a) Either the spanner bends or it deforms the nut.

b) A long one.

c) The moment increases.

d) 21 Nm

P3 1.2

Centre of mass

LEARNING OBJECTIVES

Students should learn:

- That the centre of mass of a body is the point at which the mass may be considered to be concentrated.
- That the centre of mass of a sheet of material can be found by a simple suspension experiment.

LEARNING OUTCOMES

Most students should be able to:

- Find the centre of mass of a sheet of uniform thickness using a suspension experiment.
- Find the centre of mass of a symmetrical object.

Some students should also be able to:

- Explain why a freely-suspended object comes to rest with its centre of mass directly below the point of suspension.

Teaching suggestions

- **Gifted and talented.** Ask these students: 'How could you find the centre of mass of an irregular 3D object?'

- **Learning styles**

    Kinaesthetic: Carrying out centre of mass tests.

    Visual: Making shape models.

    Auditory: Explaining how the centre of mass can be found.

    Interpersonal: Collaborating during the experiments.

    Intrapersonal: Considering the force acting on objects.

- **ICT link-up.** Refer to PhotoPLUS P3 1.2 'Centre of mass' on the GCSE Physics CD ROM. You could use a simulation package that shows how forces affect objects when the line of the force acts through the centre of mass and when it doesn't. This could involve collisions where the impact is offline causing the objects to rotate. (See www.fable.co.uk)

SPECIFICATION LINK-UP   Unit: Physics 3.13.1

- *The centre of mass of a body is that point at which the mass of the body may be thought to be concentrated.*
- *If suspended, a body will come to rest with its centre of mass directly below the point of suspension.*
- *The centre of mass of a symmetrical body is along the axis of symmetry.*

Students should use their skills, knowledge and understanding of 'How Science Works':

- *to describe how to find the centre of mass of a thin sheet of a material.*

Lesson structure

STARTER

Force diagrams – Ask the students to label the forces on a car moving at a steady speed along a horizontal road. Discuss why the students have drawn the weight where they have. (5–10 minutes)

Fearful symmetry – Give the students a set of shapes and ask them to draw on the lines of symmetry. (5– 10 minutes)

Mental gymnastics – Show the students a really complex balancing act, such as ten people balanced on a motorcycle and ask them to explain why they do not fall off. (5 minutes)

MAIN

- Most of the students are actually familiar with the idea of a centre of mass. They have been drawing force arrows that act through the centre of objects for some time.

- They will not be aware that they have been assuming that the mass seems to be concentrated at this point, however, so discuss this idea. Let them imagine drawing force arrows for every atom in a boat, and realise its easier to find the 'average' position where the weight acts.

- Rulers and other uniform objects will balance easily and the students will understand that the centre of mass is in the middle. The students should also realise that the centre of mass of a non-uniform object will be closer to the 'big end'.

- With higher-attaining students, you may wish to discuss the concept of equilibrium more fully. They should be made aware that two conditions must be met: the moments must be balanced and so must the horizontal and vertical forces.

- There can be some situations where the centre of mass is actually outside the physical body of an object. Students can find this quite strange, because a force cannot be applied at this point to suspend the object. Point out that this point will always be directly below a suspension point when the object hangs freely.

- Show the students, or allow them to find, the position of the centre of mass of symmetrical objects by drawing the lines of symmetry and lifting the object at this point.

- The centre of mass experiment is quite simple and the students should have a go at it. They should start with simple geometric shapes to confirm that the centre of mass is where they expect and then move on to irregular shapes. An accurate technique should involve three suspensions and three lines crossing at the same point. Ask: 'What do you do if they don't? How might that happen?' (This relates to: 'How Science Works': reliability)

PLENARIES

Where is the centre? – Show the students another set of shapes and ask them to figure out where the centre of mass may be by looking at the symmetry. (5–10 minutes)

Topple – The students make a table listing objects designed to topple over and some designed to be stable. (5–10 minutes)

Practical support

Suspended equilibrium

This demonstration should show the students that the objects will come to rest with their centre of mass directly below the point of suspension.

Equipment and materials required

Long stand, string and a range of objects.

Details

Simply suspend the objects from the stand using string. They should come to rest with the centre of mass directly below the suspension point. You can suspend the same object from several different points to show roughly where the centre of mass is. Try to use a range of objects to show that the centre of mass can actually be outside the physical object.

Safety: Protect furniture and the floor from falling objects.

A centre of mass test

This is a good practical that is accessible to all of the students.

Equipment and materials required

Retort stands, bosses and clamps, string and pendulum bobs (plumb lines), corks, long pins, card and scissors.

Details

The students should cut out a range of shapes from the cards: rectangles, triangles and irregular. The cork is held in the clamp so that the pins can be pushed through the card into it. Wrap the plumb line around the pin and push it through a point near the edge of the card into the cork. The shape should hang freely. Now the students should gently press the line against the card (squeezing from both sides) and mark a point near the bottom of the shape. They then remove the card and draw a line from the mark to the pinhole. Repeat this process twice more; the centre of mass should be where all three lines cross. The students may find some shapes where the centre of mass is actually outside the shape, e.g. a circle with the central region cut out.

Answers to in-text questions

a) If the ruler is uniform, the centre of mass is at the centre.

b) It is along the line of symmetry 33 mm above the centre.

P3 1.2   Centre of mass

LEARNING OBJECTIVES

1. What is the centre of mass of a body?
2. How can we find the centre of mass of a thin sheet of a material?

The design of racing cars has changed a lot since the first models. But one thing that has not changed is the need to keep the car near the ground. The weight of the car must be as low as possible. Otherwise the car would overturn when cornering at high speeds.

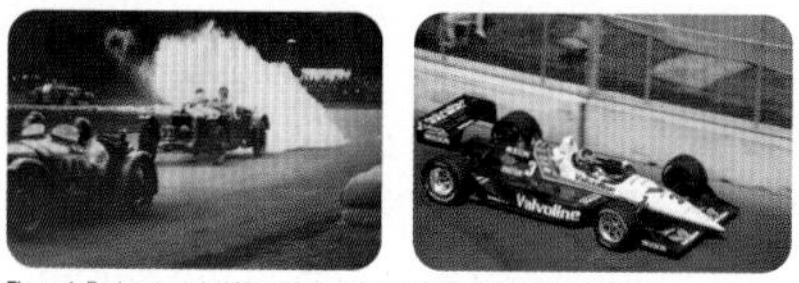

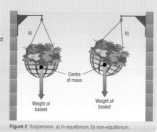

Figure 1 Racing cars: a) 1920s racing car design, b) modern racing car design

We can think of the weight of an object as if it acts at a single point. This point is called the centre of mass (or the centre of gravity) of the object.

The centre of mass of an object is the point where its mass may be thought to be concentrated.

a) Balance a ruler on the tip of your finger. The point of balance is at the centre of mass of the ruler. How far is the centre of mass from the middle of the ruler?

PRACTICAL

Suspended equilibrium

If you suspend an object and then release it, it will come to rest with its centre of mass directly below the point of suspension, as shown in Figure 2a). The object is then in equilibrium. Its weight does not exert a turning effect on the object because its centre of mass is directly below the point of suspension.

If the object is turned from this position and then released, it will swing back to its equilibrium position. This is because its weight has a turning effect that returns the object to equilibrium, as shown in Figure 2b).

Figure 2 Suspension. a) In equilibrium, b) non-equilibrium.

The centre of mass of a symmetrical object

For a symmetrical object, its centre of mass is along the axis of symmetry. You can see this in Figure 3.

If the object has more than one axis of symmetry, its centre of mass is where the axes of symmetry meet.

- A rectangle has two axes of symmetry, as shown Figure 3a). The centre of mass is where the axes meet.
- The equilateral triangle in Figure 3b) has three axes of symmetry, each bisecting one of the angles of the triangle. The three axes meet at the same point, which is the centre of mass of the triangle.

PRACTICAL

A centre of mass test

Figure 4 shows how to find the centre of mass of a flat card. The card is at rest, freely suspended from a pin.

Its centre of mass is directly below the pin. A 'plumbline' can be used to draw a vertical line on the card from the pin downwards.

The procedure is repeated with the card suspended from a second point to give another similar line. The centre of mass of the card is where the two lines meet.

Test your results to see if you can balance the card at this point on the end of a pencil.

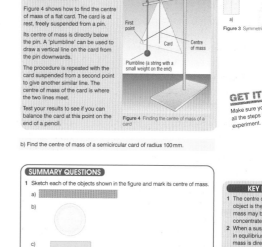

Figure 4 Finding the centre of mass of a card

b) Find the centre of mass of a semicircular card of radius 100 mm.

Figure 3 Symmetrical objects

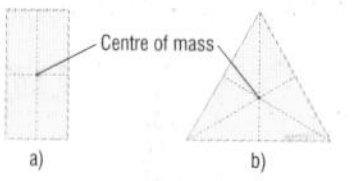

GET IT RIGHT!

Make sure you can describe all the steps in the above experiment.

SUMMARY QUESTIONS

1. Sketch each of the objects shown in the figure and mark its centre of mass.
   a)
   b)
   c)

2. Explain why a child on a swing comes to rest directly below the top of the swing.

KEY POINTS

1. The centre of mass of an object is the point where its mass may be thought to be concentrated.
2. When a suspended object is in equilibrium, its centre of mass is directly beneath the point of suspension.
3. The centre of mass of a symmetrical object is along the axis of symmetry.

SUMMARY ANSWERS

1. **a)** and **c)** At the point where the diagonals meet. **b)** At its centre.

2. The weight of the child has a turning effect about the top of the swing when the child's centre of mass is not directly below the top. The turning effect makes the child return to the middle.

KEY POINTS

Can the students write a sequence of steps to find the centre of mass of a piece of card (uniform lamina)?

P3 1.3 Moments in balance

Teaching suggestions

- **Gifted and talented.** If the moments are balanced this does not mean that the object is not rotating; it means that the rate of rotation (angular velocity) is not changing. This is a similar situation to balanced forces on a moving object and you may like to discuss this with the higher attaining students.

- **Learning styles**
  Kinaesthetic: Carrying out practical activities on moments.
  Visual: Displaying moment information as diagrams.
  Auditory: Hearing and repeating the principle of moments.
  Interpersonal: Discussing and evaluating experimental technique.
  Intrapersonal: Making deductions about the position of the centre of mass.

- **Teaching assistant.** Some of the students will need additional support in getting the beam to balance, so the teaching assistant can work with these groups.

SPECIFICATION LINK-UP   Unit: Physics 3.13.1

- *If a body is not turning, the total clockwise moment must be exactly balanced by the total anticlockwise moment about any axis.* [HT only]

Students should use their skills, knowledge and understanding of 'How Science Works':

- *to calculate the size of a force, or its distance from an axis of rotation, acting on a body that is balanced.* [HT only]

Lesson structure

STARTER

Which way? – Show the students several seesaws with a variety of people on and ask them to find out which way they would start rotating. End with one that is balanced. (5–10 minutes)

Elephant vs mouse – An elephant has a mass of 2000 kg and a mouse a mass of only 10 g. If they want to balance on a seesaw and the elephant is 0.5 m from the pivot, how far away should the mouse sit? [100 km!] (5 minutes)

MAIN

- Having a large seesaw would be particularly useful during this topic. The larger the seesaw the easier it tends to be to balance.

- The terms 'pivot' and 'fulcrum' are generally interchangeable so the students can use either, although 'pivot' is favoured in exam questions.

- Take the initial explanation of the balanced seesaw slowly so that the students get the idea that it is possible to balance large masses with smaller ones. If you have a good-sized seesaw then show what is going on using it.

- The principle of moments is very important and the students should be able to state it clearly for any questions.

- You may be able to find a grocer's balance or a newton balance to demonstrate how the principle of moments can be used to find the weight of objects.

- The first practical should be quite short. Encourage the students to take great care to get the best results. Keep the equipment out and use it again for the second practical.

- Consider aspects of taking measurements from 'How Science Works' in both practicals.

- The calculation should be reasonably straightforward. Give the students plenty of practice at calculating missing values in equilibrium situations; they will need to be able to find these. Check for clear layout again and that the students are still using the correct units.

- The second practical is very similar to the first and again the students will need to take several measurements to get a reasonable result.

- The summary questions should allow the student to show their skills with the calculations.

PLENARIES

Clever quote – Archimedes is said to have said 'Give me a lever long enough and a fulcrum on which to place it, and I shall move the world.' The students should explain what they think this means. (5 minutes)

In balance – Ask: 'How can a 10 kg, a 5 kg and a 1 kg mass be balanced on a metre rule?' How many combinations can the students come up with in 5 minutes? Putting them all directly above the pivot counts as one. (5–10 minutes)

Odd one out – Show the students a set of diagrams of three balanced seesaws and one unbalanced one. Can they find the odd one out? (5 minutes)

Practical support

Measuring an unknown weight

This can be a quick demonstration or a challenge for the groups to be as accurate as possible.

Equipment and materials required

For each group: beam, pivot (wooden triangular block), ruler, known mass (100 g) and unknown mass. A suitable top-pan balance should be available.

Details

The students set up the apparatus as shown in Figure 2 in the students' book. They must attempt to balance the masses and measure the distances so that they can find the unknown mass. The greatest problem will be getting a stable balance with the ruler, so the students will have to take great care and get as close as possible. To get a more precise reading, the students should repeat the measurements at least three times using different distances and find the mean value. At the end of the experiment, the students can use the top-pan balance to check their results.

Measuring the weight of a beam

This experiment works best with large beams but make sure that they are uniform.

Equipment and materials required

For each group: beam, pivot (wooden triangular block), ruler, an appropriate mass (about half the mass of the ruler).

Details

The students have to balance the ruler, by placing the pivot and then balancing the beam by adjusting the position of the mass. This is much more difficult than it seems, so the students should be given a bit of time to do it. Ideally the students should repeat the experiment several times with the pivot in different positions. This allows you to discuss the reasons to perform repeat experiments (this relates to: 'How Science Works').

Answers to in-text questions

a) Her moment about the pivot must equal the moment of the boy about the pivot. The moment is her weight × the distance from the pivot. Because she is heavier, she needs to be nearer the pivot than the boy to give an equal moment to the boy's moment.

b) 2.5 N

c) 1.2 N

d) The effort acts further from the pivot than the load does. So a smaller effort gives an equal and opposite moment to a larger load.

Teaching suggestions continued

- **ICT link-up.** If the students are having difficulty balancing the rulers, it may be best to use a simulation of the experiment. This will give exact results and allows the students to look into situations where there are several forces causing turning effects at once, but it doesn't have the tactile feel of the real equipment. See Animation P3 1.3 'Seesaw moments'.

- **Homework.** There is plenty of scope for the students to analyse more equilibrium and non-equilibrium questions concerning moments.

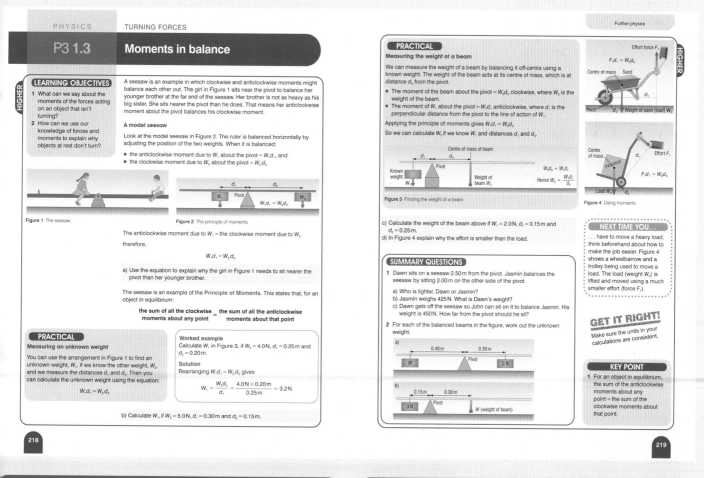

PHYSICS TURNING FORCES

P3 1.3 **Moments in balance**

LEARNING OBJECTIVES

1 What can we say about the moments of the forces acting on an object that isn't turning?
2 How can we use our knowledge of forces and moments to explain why objects at rest don't turn?

A seesaw is an example in which clockwise and anticlockwise moments might balance each other out. The girl in Figure 1 sits near the pivot to balance her younger brother at the far end of the seesaw. Her brother is not as heavy as his big sister. She sits nearer the pivot than he does. That means her anticlockwise moment about the pivot balances his clockwise moment.

A model seesaw

Look at the model seesaw in Figure 2. The ruler is balanced horizontally by adjusting the position of the two weights. When it is balanced:

- the anticlockwise moment due to W_1 about the pivot = $W_1 d_1$, and
- the clockwise moment due to W_2 about the pivot = $W_2 d_2$

Figure 1 The seesaw

Figure 2 The principle of moments

$$W_1 d_1 = W_2 d_2$$

The anticlockwise moment due to W_1 = the clockwise moment due to W_2

therefore,

$$W_1 d_1 = W_2 d_2$$

a) Use the equation to explain why the girl in Figure 1 needs to sit nearer the pivot than her younger brother.

The seesaw is an example of the Principle of Moments. This states that, for an object in equilibrium:

the sum of all the clockwise moments about any point = the sum of all the anticlockwise moments about that point

PRACTICAL

Measuring an unknown weight

You can use the arrangement in Figure 1 to find an unknown weight, W_1, if we know the other weight, W_2, and we measure the distances d_1 and d_2. Then you can calculate the unknown weight using the equation:

$$W_1 d_1 = W_2 d_2$$

b) Calculate W_1, if W_2 = 5.0 N, d_1 = 0.30 m and d_2 = 0.15 m.

Worked example

Calculate W_1, in Figure 3, if W_2 = 4.0 N, d_1 = 0.25 m and d_2 = 0.20 m.

Solution

Rearranging $W_1 d_1 = W_2 d_2$ gives

$$W_1 = \frac{W_2 d_2}{d_1} = \frac{4.0 N \times 0.20 m}{0.25 m} = 3.2 N$$

PRACTICAL

Measuring the weight of a beam

We can measure the weight of a beam by balancing it off-centre using a known weight. The weight of the beam acts at its centre of mass, which is at distance d_0 from the pivot.

- The moment of the beam about the pivot = $W_0 d_0$ clockwise, where W_0 is the weight of the beam.
- The moment of W_1 about the pivot = $W_1 d_1$ anticlockwise, where d_1 is the perpendicular distance from the pivot to the line of action of W_1.

Applying the principle of moments gives $W_1 d_1 = W_0 d_0$

So we can calculate W_0 if we know W_1 and distances d_1 and d_0.

Figure 3 Finding the weight of a beam

$$W_0 d_0 = W_1 d_1$$

$$\text{Hence } W_0 = \frac{W_1 d_1}{d_0}$$

c) Calculate the weight of the beam above if W_1 = 2.0 N, d_1 = 0.15 m and d_0 = 0.25 m.

d) In Figure 4 explain why the effort is smaller than the load.

SUMMARY QUESTIONS

1 Dawn sits on a seesaw 2.50 m from the pivot. Jasmin balances the seesaw by sitting 2.00 m on the other side of the pivot.

a) Who is lighter, Dawn or Jasmin?
b) Jasmin weighs 425 N. What is Dawn's weight?
c) Dawn gets off the seesaw so John can sit on it to balance Jasmin. His weight is 450 N. How far from the pivot should he sit?

2 For each of the balanced beams in the figure, work out the unknown weight.

a)

b)

Figure 4 Using moments

NEXT TIME YOU...

... have to move a heavy load, think beforehand about how to make the job easier. Figure 4 shows a wheelbarrow and a trolley being used to move a load. The load (weight W_0) is lifted and moved using a much smaller effort (force F_1).

GET IT RIGHT!

Make sure the units in your calculations are consistent.

KEY POINT

1 For an object in equilibrium, the sum of the anticlockwise moments about any point = the sum of the clockwise moments about that point.

218

219

SUMMARY ANSWERS

1 **a)** Jasmin. **b)** 340 N **c)** 1.89 m

2 **a)** 1.5 N **b)** 1.5 N

KEY POINTS

The students should be able to state the equilibrium conditions for moments. Present it on a seesaw for visual impact.

P3 1.4   Stability

LEARNING OBJECTIVES

Students should learn:

- That the stability of an object depends on a range of factors but principally on:
  - the relationship between the centre of mass of the object. [**HT** only]
  - the line of action of the weight of the object. [**HT** only]
  - the shape of the base of the object. [**HT** only]

LEARNING OUTCOMES

Most students should be able to:

- Describe how the shape of an object affects the stability of the object. [**HT** only]
- Interpret and draw diagrams showing the stability of objects. [**HT** only]

Some students should also be able to:

- Explain design features that make objects more stable. [**HT** only]

Teaching suggestions

- **Gifted and talented.** An interesting thing to look at is why spinning tops are stable when they are spinning but clearly not when they are stationary. See if the students can come up with any ideas as to why this is.

- **Learning styles**

  Kinaesthetic: Modelling tipping objects.

  Visual: Making observations about the tipping point of objects.

  Auditory: Explaining the behaviour of stable and unstable objects.

  Interpersonal: Evaluating experiments together as a group.

  Intrapersonal: Writing a report on improving stability.

- **Teaching assistant.** A teaching assistant can help some groups increase the angle of the ramp by very small increments to get the most accurate data in the toppling investigation.

- **ICT link-up.** Use Animation P3 1.4 'Stability' from GCSE Physics CD ROM.

- **Homework.** The students could improve the design of a range of household objects to improve their stability.

SPECIFICATION LINK-UP   Unit: Physics 3.13.1

- *Recognise the factors that affect the stability of a body.* [**HT** only]
- *If the line of action of the weight of a body lies outside the base of the body there will be a resultant moment and the body will tend to topple.* [**HT** only]

Students should use their skills, knowledge and understanding of 'How Science Works':

- *to analyse the stability of bodies by considering their tendency to topple.* [**HT** only]

Lesson structure

STARTER

A balancing act – Ask the students to balance their pens (or other objects) on their fingers; find out who can do it for the longest. (5 minutes)

One leg – Get one of the students to stand on one leg. The other students then describe how the student tried to keep their balance. (5 minutes)

Odd jobs – How many jobs can the students think of that require a good sense of balance? Discuss or make a list. (5 minutes)

MAIN

- You can start this topic with the introductory practical. Try the brick resting on different sides. The practical can be extended in several ways. See 'Practical support'.

- You should be able to find a range of objects to test around the laboratory: retort stands, conical flasks, lamps, etc.

- For the objects you can use the suspension technique from lesson 1.2 to find the location of the centre of mass and then talk about whether it is high or low on the object.

- Take each of the example situations in turn. If you have models you can use these on an adjustable ramp to show when they topple. You can also discuss how realistic the models are.

- Test the bus by finding its topple angle before and after adding Plasticine to the top deck, to simulate the weight of passengers. In reality very few buses will travel on roads that are so severely tilted, but what about strong gusts of wind?

- Additional situations you can look at include racing cars. These have very low centres of mass, but if they are moving quickly the large forces involved can flip them over dramatically.

- Show some videos of sumo wrestling and ask the students why it is so difficult to throw each other over. Search for 'sumo' at www.video.google.com.

- Investigating the factors that affect stability offers good opportunities to cover the skills and concepts involved in designing fair tests (this relates to: 'How Science Works').

PLENARIES

Jenga – If you have it, then this block building game is a challenging plenary. Similar games can be made by your technology department. (15 minutes)

Don't look down – The students have to produce an advice booklet for amateur tightrope walkers using their knowledge of moments and stability. (10–15 minutes)

High chair – The students should design a high chair that is more stable than a standard design. (5–10 minutes)

Practical support

Tilting and toppling tests

This can be a simple experiment or a more advanced investigation; see the extension below.

Equipment and materials required

Standard building brick, protractor, bench protector (e.g. carpet).

Details

Allow the students to tilt the brick when it is resting on various sides, they can use the protractor to measure the tipping angle. They should find that the angle is greatest when the centre of mass is lowest on the brick.

The tipping point – extension

This is a more detailed version of the basic brick experiment. It requires adjustable ramps that can be raised and the angle measured; these can be improvised if necessary. You can use this technique to find the tipping point of other objects mentioned in the text, such as model buses, pins or high chairs. Use Plasticine to simulate adding passengers to the top or bottom decks.

Equipment and materials required

For each group: adjustable ramp, protractor, rectangular block.

Details

The students should find the angle that the block tips by raising the ramps' angle until the block tips over. This should be when the centre of mass lies just beyond the base of the block. The students may be able to check this if their geometry is up to it. Repeating the experiment with the block lying on different sides should give the same result for the position of the centre of mass. If you find that the blocks start to slide down the ramp you might have to cover it with a rubber mat or similar.

Answers to in-text questions

a) Its weight acts through the point of contact so it has no turning effect.

b) People open an upper drawer that produces a turning force that topples the filing cabinet.

c) So its centre of mass is as low as possible, which makes it more stable.

d) Less stable.

e) To provide a wider base if the child loses balance.

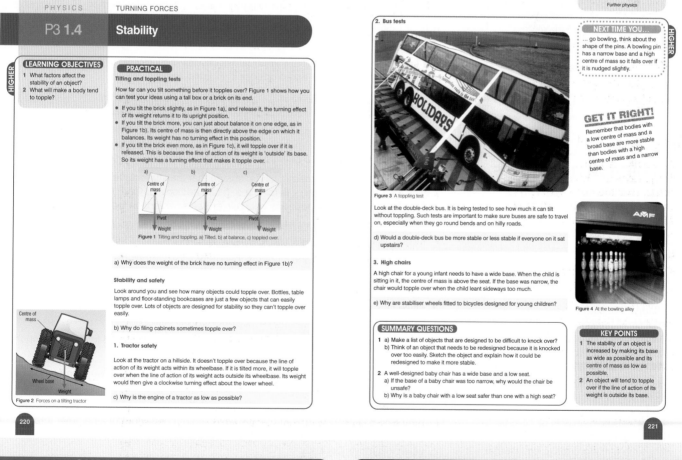

PHYSICS   TURNING FORCES

Further physics

P3 1.4   Stability

LEARNING OBJECTIVES
1 What factors affect the stability of an object?
2 What will make a body tend to topple?

PRACTICAL

Tilting and toppling tests

How far can you tilt something before it topples over? Figure 1 shows how you can test your ideas using a tall box or a brick on its end.

• If you tilt the brick slightly, as in Figure 1a), and release it, the turning effect of its weight returns it to its upright position.
• If you tilt the brick more, you can just about balance it on one edge, as in Figure 1b). Its centre of mass is then directly above the edge on which it balances. Its weight has no turning effect in this position.
• If you tilt the brick even more, as in Figure 1c), it will topple over if it is released. This is because the line of action of its weight is 'outside' its base. So its weight has a turning effect that makes it topple over.

a)   b)   c)
Centre of mass   Centre of mass   Centre of mass
Pivot   Pivot   Pivot
Weight   Weight   Weight

Figure 1 Tilting and toppling. a) Tilted, b) at balance, c) toppled over.

a) Why does the weight of the brick have no turning effect in Figure 1b)?

Stability and safety

Look around you and see how many objects could topple over. Bottles, table lamps and floor-standing bookcases are just a few objects that can easily topple over. Lots of objects are designed for stability so they can't topple over easily.

b) Why do filing cabinets sometimes topple over?

1. Tractor safety

Look at the tractor on a hillside. It doesn't topple over because the line of action of its weight acts within its wheelbase. If it is tilted more, it will topple over when the line of action of its weight acts outside its wheelbase. Its weight would then give a clockwise turning effect about the lower wheel.

c) Why is the engine of a tractor as low as possible?

Centre of mass
Wheel base
Weight
Figure 2 Forces on a tilting tractor

220

2. Bus tests

NEXT TIME YOU...
... go bowling, think about the shape of the pins. A bowling pin has a narrow base and a high centre of mass so it falls over if it is nudged slightly.

HOLIDAYS

Figure 3 A toppling test

Look at the double-deck bus. It is being tested to see how much it can tilt without toppling. Such tests are important to make sure buses are safe to travel on, especially when they go round bends and on hilly roads.

d) Would a double-deck bus be more stable or less stable if everyone on it sat upstairs?

3. High chairs

A high chair for a young infant needs to have a wide base. When the child is sitting in it, the centre of mass is above the seat. If the base was narrow, the chair would topple over when the child leant sideways too much.

e) Why are stabiliser wheels fitted to bicycles designed for young children?

GET IT RIGHT!

Remember that bodies with a low centre of mass and a broad base are more stable than bodies with a high centre of mass and a narrow base.

Figure 4 At the bowling alley

SUMMARY QUESTIONS

1 a) Make a list of objects that are designed to be difficult to knock over?
   b) Think of an object that needs to be redesigned because it is knocked over too easily. Sketch the object and explain how it could be redesigned to make it more stable.

2 A well-designed baby chair has a wide base and a low seat.
   a) If the base of a baby chair was too narrow, why would the chair be unsafe?
   b) Why is a baby chair with a low seat safer than one with a high seat?

KEY POINTS

1 The stability of an object is increased by making its base as wide as possible and its centre of mass as low as possible.

2 An object will tend to topple over if the line of action of its weight is outside its base.

221

SUMMARY ANSWERS

1 a) A table, a low-loader vehicle, a traffic cone, etc.

   b) A supermarket trolley, a tall electric kettle, etc.   [HT only]

2 a) The chair would topple over if the baby in the chair leans too far sideways.

   b) The lower the centre of mass, the harder it is to topple it over.   [HT only]

KEY POINTS

Can the students give an explanation of why one object is more difficult to knock over than another? They should use diagrams to explain their ideas.

P3 1.5   Circular motion

LEARNING OBJECTIVES

Students should learn:

- That an accelerating object can be undergoing a change in direction without the speed of the object changing
- That a centripetal force is a force acting towards the centre of a circle, i.e. perpendicular to the direction of motion of the object.

LEARNING OUTCOMES

Students should be able to:

- State that the force required for an object to move in a circle is a centripetal force.
- Draw a diagram showing the force necessary to make an object undergo circular motion.

Most students should be able to:

- Draw a diagram showing the force necessary to make an object undergo circular motion.

Some students should also be able to:

- Identify the forces that provide the centripetal force on an object in a given situation.

Teaching suggestions

- **Gifted and talented.** Ask: 'Why do velodromes (cycle tracks) have banked tracks? How does this help the cyclists?'
- **Learning styles**
  Kinaesthetic: Swinging objects and trying to lasso things.
  Visual: Imagining the forces acting on objects.
  Auditory: Discussing misconceptions about circular motion.
  Interpersonal: Discussing and evaluating the motion of objects.
  Intrapersonal: Making deductions about the forces acting on objects undergoing circular motion.
- **Teaching assistant.** If you choose to let the students spin objects or try to lasso them, your teaching assistant can work with some of the groups to ensure that they are throwing the rope correctly.
- **ICT link-up.** Refer to PhotoPLUS P3 1.5 'Circular motion' and Animation P3 1.7 'Planet and Satellite Orbits' on the GCSE Physics CD ROM. A computer simulation package will allow a more precise investigation of the factors that affect the forces involved in circular motion. This will allow the students to

SPECIFICATION LINK-UP   Unit: Physics 3.13.2

- *When a body moves in a circle it continuously accelerates towards the centre of the circle. This acceleration changes the direction of motion of the body, not its speed.*
- *The resultant force causing this acceleration is called the centripetal force.*
- *The direction of the centripetal force is always towards the centre of the circle.*
- *The centripetal force needed to make a body perform circular motion increases as:*
  - *the mass of the body increases*
  - *the speed of the body increases*
  - *the radius of the circle decreases.*

Students should use their skills, knowledge and understanding of 'How Science Works':

- *to identify which force(s) provide(s) the centripetal force in a given situation.*
- *to interpret data on bodies moving in circular paths.*

Lesson structure

STARTER

Roundabout – Show the students a video clip of somebody on a roundabout. Then ask them to draw a force diagram explaining the forces acting on the person. (5–10 minutes)

True or false – Give the students a range of explanations for what is happening in circular motion and get them to decide if they are true or false. (5–10 minutes)

You spin me right round – How important is circular motion? Get every student to give one example of a machine that produces it. (10 minutes)

MAIN

- If possible start with some video clips to illustrate circular motion. There are lots of potential things to show, including fairground rides, planetary motion and sports. This will show the importance of this type of motion.
- In the testing circular motion activity, ensure that the students realise that the object flies off in a tangent when it is released. It can be hard for them to see this, but you can demonstrate what happens yourself, or use slow motion video clips.
- Show some footage from a hammer throwing competition. If this can be shown in slow motion, point out the release of the hammer and the direction it travels when released.
- You will need to remind the students that unbalanced forces cause acceleration and that acceleration can mean a change in the direction of an object without a change in speed.
- Make sure that you convince the students that it is an inward (centripetal) force that causes circular motion; this can be surprisingly difficult.
- Try to explain what would happen if there was a resultant outward force acting on the object.
- The factors that affect the force required are reasonably obvious, but can be quite difficult to demonstrate, apart from the effect of mass.
- If the students spin the objects around faster, they may be able to feel that they are providing a larger inward force. Again watching the behaviour of a hammer thrower will show that it takes a great deal of effort to keep the hammer moving in a circle when it is moving quickly.
- The lasso activity (see 'Practical support') is great fun, and with a bit of practice you can show off your skills.

find qualitative results when the speed, radius and masses are varied in turn (this relates to: 'How Science Works': designing fair tests). (See www.fable.co.uk)

- **Homework.** The students could find as many items that use 'centrifugal' forces as possible and explain why they are scientifically incorrect.

PLENARIES

Washing machines – Can the students correctly explain how a washing machine removes water from the washing during the spin cycle? (10 minutes)

Wrong again – The students should write a correct version of this explanation: 'An object will go around in a circle when the centrifugal force pushes it outwards. The object will speed up because the force makes it accelerate.' (5–10 minutes)

Prove it – The students should use their scientific knowledge to prove that a centripetal force is needed to make an object move in a circle. (5 minutes)

Practical support

Testing circular motion

Equipment and materials required

String, bungs with a hole through.

Details

- **Safety:** This is a simple demonstration, but be careful that the bungs don't hit anybody!
- You may prefer to do this as a demonstration with some classes; otherwise the students can experience the circular moment for themselves. They will feel a force in the string pulling outwards and this is where the notion of 'centrifugal force' comes from. Point out that the force on the **bung** is inwards and it is this force that makes the bung travel in a circle. If you add more bungs, there should be a greater force required to keep them moving in a circle.

ACTIVITY & EXTENSION IDEAS

Lasso – extension

This experiment is a great way of showing that an object flies off at a tangent when the centripetal force is removed. It is best carried out outdoors but works inside too.

Equipment and materials required

Lasso, thin rope will do, model steer (this can be anything really).

Details

Show the students how to lasso a steer; the technique involves releasing the rope when it is to your side; not in front of you. With a bit of practice it gets quite easy to throw the rope in the right direction, but not to actually hit the target. Allow the students to have a go, making sure that they understand that the rope will move in a tangent to the circle when it is released.

PHYSICS TURNING FORCES

P3 1.5 Circular motion

Further physics

LEARNING OBJECTIVES

1 How can a body moving at a steady speed be accelerating?
2 What is the direction of a centripetal force?

Fairground rides whirl you round in circles and make your head spin. But you don't need to go to a fairground to see objects moving in circles.

- A vehicle on a roundabout or moving round a corner travels in a circle.
- A satellite moving across the sky moves on a circular orbit round the Earth.
- An athlete throwing a 'hammer' or a discus spins round in a circle before releasing the hammer.

PRACTICAL

Testing circular motion

An object whirled round on the end of a string moves in a circle, as shown in Figure 2. The pull force on the object from the string changes the object's direction of motion.

Figure 1 A hammer thrower

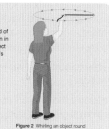

Figure 2 Whirling an object round

For an object moving in a circle at constant speed, at any instant:

- the object's velocity is directed along a tangent to the circle,
- its velocity changes direction as it moves round,
- the change of velocity is towards the centre of the circle.

The object therefore accelerates continuously towards the centre of the circle.

So the force on the object acts towards the centre of the circle.

a) In Figure 2, which direction would the object move if the string suddenly snapped at the position shown?

Centripetal force

Any object moving in a circle must be acted on by a resultant force that acts towards the centre of the circle. We say the resultant force is a **centripetal** force because it *always* acts towards the centre of the circle.

- The centripetal force on a vehicle moving round a roundabout is due to friction between the tyres and the road.
- The centripetal force on an aircraft circling round is due to the combined effect of its weight and the lift force on it. The centripetal force is the resultant of these two forces.

Figure 3 Circling round

b) What causes the centripetal force on a satellite moving in a circular orbit round the Earth?

Centripetal force factors

How much force is needed to keep an object moving in a circle?

You could find out using a radio-controlled model car.

- If it goes too fast, it will skid off in a straight line. The centripetal force needed increases if the speed is increased.
- If the circle is too small, it will skid off. So the centripetal force needed increases if the radius of the circle is decreased.

c) Why is the speed for no skidding much less on an icy roundabout?

How does the force depend on the mass of the object?

If you whirl a rubber bung round on the end of a thread, you can feel the pull force. If you tie another rubber bung on, you will find the pull force (for the same speed and radius) has increased. This shows that the greater the mass of the object, the greater the centripetal force is.

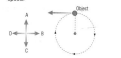

Figure 4 Centripetal force factors

GET IT RIGHT!

- For a body to move in a circle, there must always be a resultant force acting on the body towards the centre of the circle.
- Centripetal force is not a force in its own right; it is always provided by another force such as a gravitational force or an electric force.

SUMMARY QUESTIONS

1 The figure shows an object moving clockwise in a circle at constant speed.

Complete the sentences using directions A, B, C or D as shown in the figure.

a) When the object is at the position shown, its velocity is in direction ...... and the force on it is in direction ....

b) When the object has moved round by 90° from the position shown in the diagram, its velocity is in direction ...... and the force on it is in direction ....

2 In each of the following situations, a single force acts as the centripetal force. Match each situation with the force, a) to d), that causes the circular motion.

electrostatic force   friction   gravity   pull (tension)

a) A car travelling round a bend.
b) A stone being whirled round on the end of a string.
c) A planet moving round the Sun.
d) An electron orbiting the nucleus of an atom.

KEY POINT

1 For an object moving in a circle at constant speed,
- the object accelerates continuously towards the centre of the circle,
- the centripetal force needed increases, i) as the mass or the speed of the object increases, ii) as the radius of the circle decreases.

222

223

SUMMARY ANSWERS

1 a) D, C.
  b) C, B.

2 a) Friction.
  b) Pull (tension).
  c) Gravity.
  d) Electrostatic force.

Answers to in-text questions

a) It would fly off at a tangent.

b) The force of gravity due to the Earth on it.

c) There is much less friction so the centripetal force is less and the car must go slower.

KEY POINTS

The students should be able to draw diagrams showing the direction of the force on objects travelling in a circle and explain what affects the magnitude of them.

P3 1.6   Gravitational attraction

Teaching suggestions

- **Gifted and talented.** You might like to look into the equation for gravitational attraction as described by Newton: $F = Gm_1m_2/r^2$ and what this means. The students should be aware that the attraction falls off with the square of the distance, so that doubling the distance reduces the force by a factor of four. Can they calculate the mass of the Earth using their weight when given G and the radius of the Earth?
- **Learning styles**

  Kinaesthetic: Researching into the discovery of gravitation.

  Visual: Imagining the gravitational forces on probes and other objects.

  Auditory: Discussing Newton's discovery of the universality of gravitation.

  Interpersonal: Discussing and evaluation Newton's work as a group.

  Intrapersonal: Understanding and reflecting on the difficulties of developing a scientific theory.
- **ICT link-up.** Refer to Animation P3 1.6 'Gravity'. Students could design a spreadsheet to calculate gravitational field strengths from data provided. (See the exploring gravity activity in 'Activity and extension ideas'.)
- **Homework.** Practise calculations involving gravitational field strengths.

Lesson structure

STARTER

Mass and weight – Can the students remember and explain the difference between these two ideas? (5 minutes)

Moon myth – The students need to come up with a mythical explanation of why the Moon travels around the Earth. (5–10 minutes)

MAIN

- Newton's realisation was that gravitational forces are the cause of our weight and the cause of the orbits of the planets. He did have to go through a lot of data and ideas produced by earlier scientists, such as Johannes Kepler, leading to his famous quote 'If I have seen further, it is by standing on the shoulders of giants.'
- The students should be able to come up with the idea that larger objects will produce a larger gravitational attraction.
- It is more difficult to understand that the attraction diminishes with distance, but discussing that the force from distant objects, like the Sun, acting on the students is very small should help.
- Make sure that the students understand that the attraction diminishes by a factor of four when the separation doubles. Check that they know how strong the attraction would be if the separation was four times as great.
- As before, the students may be used to the phrase 'strength of gravity' as opposed to 'gravitational field strength'. This isn't that important as long as they can recognise the phrase in questions.
- You could discuss the surface gravitational field strength of various planets. This is not always as obvious as the students might think, because of the effect of the distance from the centre of mass of the planet. Jupiter has a mass of 317 times that of Earth's, but its surface gravitational field strength is only 2.3 times that of Earth due to its large radius.
- The calculations are simple, but let some students have a go at rearranging the equation.
- As a final point, you might like to explain to the students that gravitational fields do not stop; they just become weaker and weaker the further away that you are from the object. We are being pulled by every star in the galaxy, but this pull is so small compared to the pull of the Earth that we do not notice it.

PLENARIES

Freefall – Show the students the behaviour of objects in freefall in the space shuttle or international space station and ask them to explain the behaviour. (10 minutes)

Drawn together – Can the students place a set of cards with the masses and separation of objects into order of the gravitational force between them? (5–10 minutes)

ACTIVITY & EXTENSION

Exploring gravity – The students could investigate the relationships between gravitational attraction, the masses and the separation of objects, in more depth, using a spreadsheet. Set up a spreadsheet that calculates the magnitude of gravitational attraction using the masses and separation of objects. The students can then alter these values and see how the size of the attraction changes. You may wish to get the students to plot graphs of how the force changes with distance for a range of masses, so that they can appreciate the shape. To simplify the numbers involved, you might not want to use the true value for the universal gravitation constant G. Instead use a value of 1 for this, and explain to the students that you have simplified the equation.

Practical support

Weight

Details

Some students are worried about their weight, and so you should not push them into weighing themselves. You may like to discuss the relationship between older systems of measurement such as pounds and ounces, and why many scales are marked in kilograms when they should be showing newtons.

SCIENCE @ WORK

The regions where the surface gravity on the Earth is weakest are above the deepest oceans. This is because the density of the water is much less than that of rock, so there is a bit less mass below you to pull you down. If you want to lose weight, then go on a cruise but remember that your mass won't change.

P3 1.6   Gravitational attraction

LEARNING OBJECTIVES

1 What is the force of gravity?
2 What factors affect the gravitational attraction between two objects?

What goes up must come down – unless it can overcome the force of gravity acting on it.

The Earth exerts a force of gravity on us all. In fact, any two objects exert a force of gravitational attraction on each other. The force depends on the mass of each object. The Earth is a massive object so its force of gravitational attraction on each of us keeps us on the ground.

a) What keeps the Earth moving in a circle round the Sun?

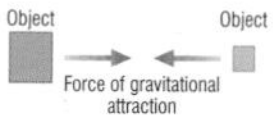

Newton's rules on gravity

Sir Isaac Newton devised the theory of gravity over 300 years ago. He used his theory to explain why the planets orbit the Sun and why the Moon orbits the Earth. He said that the force of gravity between two objects:

- is an attractive force,
- is bigger the greater the mass of each object is,
- is smaller the greater the distance between the two objects is.

He used his theory to make many successful predictions, such as the return of comets.

b) Why is the force of gravitational attraction between two objects in front of you too small to notice?

Object   Object

Force of gravitational attraction

Figure 1 Gravitational attraction

GET IT RIGHT!

Remember that gravitational forces are always attractive.

On a space journey

When a space probe moves away from the Earth towards the Moon, the force of gravity on it:

- due to the Earth decreases as it moves away from the Earth,
- due to the Moon increases as it moves towards the Moon.

c) Why would it be easier to launch a space probe from the Moon than from the Earth?

Gravitational field strength

The gravitational field strength of the Earth at its surface is 10 newtons per kilogram (N/kg).

So the force of gravity on a 50 kg person on the Earth is 500 N (= 50 kg × 10 N/kg). (Look back to page 140 if necessary.)

The gravitational field strength of the Moon at its surface is 1.6 N/kg. So the force of gravity on a 50 kg person on the Moon would be 80 N (= 50 kg × 1.6 N/kg).

DID YOU KNOW...

Gravity keeps us on the Earth without flattening us. But if a black hole came near, nothing could escape from it if it came too near. Its gravitational field would drag objects in so it would become bigger and drag even more objects in. Bursts of gamma radiation from distant galaxies might be the last sign of a star sucked in by a black hole.

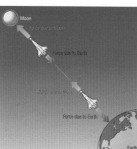

Moon
Force due to Moon

Force due to Earth

Force due to Earth

Earth

Figure 2 The forces on a space probe

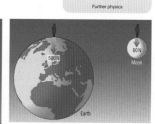

500N

80 N

Moon

Earth

Figure 3 Gravitational field strength

PRACTICAL

Newtons to kilograms

Use weighing scales marked in newtons to weigh yourself and then work out your mass in kilograms.

Why is an object heavier on the Earth than on the Moon? The reason is that the Earth's mass is much greater so it exerts a greater force on an object on its surface than the Moon does.

d) A space probe is midway between the Earth and the Moon. Which is bigger, the force of gravity on it due to the Earth or the force of gravity due to the Moon?

SCIENCE @ WORK

The force of gravity on an object on the Earth's surface can be affected by what is underneath it. Dense rocks in the Earth would cause a tiny increase in the force of gravity on an object at the surface. By measuring the surface gravity, geophysicists can detect dense substances in the Earth.

SUMMARY QUESTIONS

1 Complete the sentences below using words from the list.

     decreases   increases   stays the same

a) When a comet approaches the Sun, the force of gravity on it ....
b) When a satellite orbits the Earth at a constant height, the size of the force of gravity ....
c) When a rocket leaves the Earth, the force of gravity on it ....

2 a) Explain why an astronaut can walk more easily on the Moon than on the Earth.
b) Explain why you could throw an object higher on the Moon than on the Earth.

KEY POINT

1 The force of gravity between two objects
- is an attractive force,
- is bigger the greater the mass of each object is,
- is smaller the greater the distance between the two objects is.

SUMMARY ANSWERS

1 a) Increases.
   b) Stays the same.
   c) Decreases.

2 a) The force of gravity is less on the Moon so it is easier for the astronaut to move up and down.

   b) The force of gravity is less on the Moon so the ball can go higher for the same change of gravitational potential energy.

Answers to in-text questions

a) The force of gravity on it due to the Sun.

b) Their mass is too small.

c) The force of gravity on the Moon is less, so less energy would be needed to escape from the Moon.

d) The force of gravity due to the Earth.

KEY POINTS

The students should be able to describe how factors affect the gravitational forces between two objects. This could be shown as a cartoon strip.

P3 1.7 Planetary orbits

LEARNING OBJECTIVES

Students should learn:

- That gravitational forces cause planets to orbit the Sun and moons to orbit planets.
- About the relationship between the time taken for a planet to orbit the Sun and the distance the planet is from the Sun.

LEARNING OUTCOMES

Most students should be able to:

- State that an object must move at a particular speed in order to stay in a circular orbit at a fixed distance.
- Describe the relationships between the distance from the Sun and a planet's speed and orbital period.

Some students should also be able to:

- Explain and use the relationships between the distance from the Sun and a planet's speed and orbital period.

Teaching suggestions

- **Gifted and talented.** The students can look into the ways distances are measured by astronomers. Ask: 'What is an AU exactly and what is a light year and parsec? Why are these distances used instead on the 'normal' ones?'

- **Learning styles**

  Kinaesthetic: Modelling the motion of planets.

  Visual: Observing models of the Solar System.

  Auditory: Discussing the relationship between radius of orbit and orbital period.

  Intrapersonal: Making deductions based on the relationships.

- **ICT link-up.** There are several orbital simulations available on the Internet that can be used to show the behaviour of planets. Some of these simulate the motion of two objects and others show the motion and forces of the whole Solar System. (See www.solarsystem.org.uk/planet10)

  Use Animation P3 1.7 'Orbits' from the GCSE Physics CD ROM.

- **Homework.** The students should explore the orbits of comets comparing them to the orbits of the planets. They should discuss the size of the force acting on the comet and the speed.

SPECIFICATION LINK-UP   Unit: Physics 3.13.3

- *The orbit of any planet is an ellipse (slightly squashed circle) with the Sun at one focus.*
- *Gravitational force provides the centripetal force that allows planets and satellites to maintain their circular orbits.*
- *The further away an orbiting body is the longer it takes to make a complete orbit.*
- *To stay in orbit at a particular distance, smaller bodies, including planets and satellites, must move at a particular speed around larger bodies.*

Students should use their skills, knowledge and understanding of 'How Science Works':

- *to interpret data on planets and satellites moving in orbits that approximate to circular paths.*

Lesson structure

STARTER

Match them up – Give the students a set of cards with the planets' names on them and descriptions of where the names come from (e.g. 'Mars' and 'the Roman god of war') and ask them to match them up. (5–10 minutes)

Naming planets – The students should make up their own mnemonic to help remember the order of planets instead of the standard 'My Very Easy Method Just Speeds Up Naming Planets'. (10 minutes)

Planet facts – Test the students' knowledge of the planets by asking them true/false questions. (5–10 minutes)

MAIN

- Start the topic with some form of quick recap about the planets and their orbits.

- The students should have no difficulty remembering that the orbits are ellipses, but show them the shapes all the same.

- If at all possible, use a simulator to show the motion of the planets around the Sun. This is really the only way to show that the planets are moving faster the closer they are to the Sun.

- You may have an orrery. These don't impress the students much, but they do get the ideas across.

- The simplification that a smaller object orbits a larger one is fine for most students. Some may ask about what happens to similarly sized objects. See 'Activity and extension ideas' for points to discuss.

- Take some time reminding the students that objects move in circles when the force is directed toward the centre and link this to the diagrams of planetary motion.

- You could discuss the planets speeding up and slowing down and so moving in ellipses if the students are curious.

- The AU is an interesting unit merely used for convenience. It makes the distances easier to understand and you can illustrate this by showing the distances in metres. One AU is 149 598 000 000 m; tricky to plot on a graph.

- A graph of the orbital period against the radius of orbit could show a clear relationship, so it is best to get the students to plot this or even investigate the relationship in a spreadsheet. (This relates to: 'How Science Works': relationships between variables.)

- Discussion of asteroids can make an interesting conclusion to the lesson. Talk about the asteroid belt, but many students will be much more interested in stray asteroids.

Advanced orbits – Two objects that are gravitationally linked orbit the centre of mass of them both. This is a point between the centres of the two objects. For the Earth–Sun system, the Sun is so much larger than the Earth that the point is close to the centre of the Sun, and the Sun doesn't seem to be performing much of an orbit. The students could look at the complexities of this motion through simulations. Free software is available online; try a search for 'gravity simulation' and you should find a few good simulations.

Spot the planet – Show the students two photographs of the same part of the night sky with a planet in it, taken a few days apart. They should be able to see that the planet has moved with respect to the background of stars. The same can be done for an asteroid; use the web site from 'Did You Know'? to find suitable images.

DID YOU KNOW?

Is anyone worried about asteroid impacts? In 2029 the asteroid '2004 MN4' will come inside the orbits of geostationary communications satellites; that's too close for comfort. You can find out more about asteroids that will pass close to the Earth from www.neo.jpl.nasa.gov, the web site of the Near Earth Object research.

Answers to in-text questions

a) There would probably be a bigger variation of temperature each year. The tides would be more variable.

b) Its orbit is about 5 times bigger and it takes about 12 times longer, so it must travel slower than the Earth.

PHYSICS   TURNING FORCES

P3 1.7 Planetary orbits

LEARNING OBJECTIVES

1 What provides the centripetal force that keeps planets and satellites moving in their orbits?

2 How does the time for a planet to orbit the Sun depend on its distance from the Sun?

The Moon orbits the Earth in a circular orbit. The Earth orbits the Sun in an orbit that is almost circular. In general, the planets orbit the Sun in elliptical orbits which are slightly squashed circles. In each case, an object orbits a much bigger object. The centripetal force on the orbiting object is due to the force of gravitational attraction between it and the larger object.

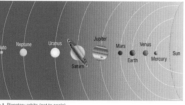

Figure 1 Planetary orbits (not to scale)

a) If the Earth's orbit were more elliptical, how would we be affected?

Look at the diagram in Figure 2. It shows the force of gravity acting on a planet in a circular (or almost circular) orbit round the Sun. The force of gravity on the planet due to the Sun acts towards the centre of the Sun. The planet's direction of motion is changed by this force so it continues to circle the Sun.

Figure 2 A circular orbit

To stay in orbit at a particular distance, a planet must move at a particular speed around the Sun.

- If its speed is too low, it will spiral into the Sun.
- If its speed is too high, it will fly off its orbit and move away from the Sun.

The further a planet is from the Sun, the less its speed is as its moves round the Sun.

This is because the force of gravity is weaker further from the Sun. So the speed of the planet needs to be less than if it were closer to the Sun. Otherwise, the planet would fly off its orbit and move away from the Sun.

DID YOU KNOW?

The word 'planet' is the Greek word for 'wanderer'. Astronomers in ancient Greece called them 'wandering stars'. This is because we see the other planets move gradually through the constellations as they move round the Sun on their orbits.

The further a planet is from the Sun, the longer it takes to make a complete orbit.

This is because the distance round the orbit, i.e. the circumference, is greater and the planet moves slower. So the time for each complete orbit (= circumference ÷ speed) is longer.

b) The table shows the average radius of orbit for some of the planets and the time for each complete orbit. How does this show that the speed of Jupiter is less than the speed of the Earth?

Planet	Radius of orbit (AU)	Time for each orbit (years)
Mercury	0.39	0.24
Venus	0.72	0.61
Earth	1.00	1.00
Mars	1.52	1.88
Jupiter	5.20	11.9
Saturn	9.53	29.5

1 astronomical unit (AU) = mean distance from the Sun to the Earth

DID YOU KNOW?

Many asteroids orbit the Sun in elliptical orbits between Mars and Jupiter. Sometimes they collide and get thrown into orbits that cross the Earth's orbit. An asteroid impact with the Earth about 65 million years ago is thought to have finished off the dinosaurs. Figure 3 shows an object in an elliptical orbit around the Sun.

SUMMARY QUESTIONS

1 Choose the correct word from the list below to complete each of the sentences a) to d).

    Earth   planet   satellite   Sun

a) The Moon is a natural ...... in orbit round the ....

b) A communications satellite stays in its orbit because of the force of gravity between it and the ....

c) The further a ...... is from the Earth, the slower its speed is and the longer it takes to orbit the ....

d) The orbit of a ...... is almost circular with the ...... near the centre of the orbit.

2 a) Use the information in the table above to deduce which of the three planets, Venus, Earth or Jupiter, travels

    i) slowest,

    ii) fastest on its orbit.

b) The Earth moves in its orbit at a speed of about 30 km/s. Use the information in the table to estimate the speed of Mercury in its orbit.

GET IT RIGHT!

Gravitational attraction provides the centripetal force that keeps planets in their orbits around the Sun.

Figure 3 An elliptical orbit
1. The orbit is defined by the two 'foci' F_1 and F_2, (such that the sum of the distances OF_1 and OF_2 is constant).
2. The Sun is at one focus of the ellipse.

KEY POINTS

1 To stay in orbit at a particular distance, a small body must move at a particular speed around a larger body.

2 The larger an orbit is, the longer the orbiting body takes to go round the orbit.

PLENARIES

Planet X – Imagine that a new planet has been discovered at a distance of 6 AU from the Sun. Ask: 'What would the properties of the planet be and what would you call it?' (10 minutes)

Flat Earth – Imagine that some people believe that the Earth is flat. Let the students write a pamphlet trying to convince these people that the Earth is a sphere. (10–15 minutes)

Planetary model – The students could produce a scale model of the Solar System from Plasticine. (15–20 minutes)

SUMMARY ANSWERS

1 a) Satellite, Sun.

  b) Earth.

  c) Satellite, Earth.

  d) Planet, Sun.

2 a) i) Jupiter. ii) Venus.

  b) 49 km/s

KEY POINTS

Can the students interpret a graph of the relationship between the orbital period of the planet and the distance from the Sun? They could state the relationship on a diagram between the Sun and one of the planets.

P3 1.8   Satellites

Teaching suggestions

- **Gifted and talented.** A more efficient system to get into space would be to use a space elevator. This enormous construction (over 72 000 km tall) could lift objects directly into orbit. The students could find out about this possibility for the far future.
- **Learning styles**
  Kinaesthetic: Researching into the development of satellites.
  Visual: Examining and interpreting satellite imagery.
  Auditory: Explaining the advantages and disadvantages of different types of orbit.
  Interpersonal: Discussing how satellites can be lifted to their orbits.
  Intrapersonal: Writing a report on a particular satellite.
- **ICT link-up.** One impressive satellite resource is 'Google Maps'. The web page is www.maps.google.com, and it allows you to view road maps and overlay satellite imagery. The resolution is quite impressive for some areas, but less so for others. From the page you should be able to find famous places, such as the Pentagon and Buckingham Palace. There may even be images of your locality or even your school. These images are used in the Google Earth software which makes navigation easier. See Animation P3 1.7 'Orbits' on the GCSE Physics CD ROM.

SPECIFICATION LINK-UP   Unit: Physics 3.13.3

- *The further away an orbiting body is the longer it takes to make a complete orbit.*
- *To stay in orbit at a particular distance, smaller bodies, including planets and satellites, must move at a particular speed around larger bodies.*
- *Communications satellites are usually put into a geostationary orbit above the equator.*
- *Monitoring satellites are usually put into a low polar orbit.*

Students should use their skills, knowledge and understanding of 'How Science Works':

- *to interpret data on planets and satellites moving in orbits that approximate to circular paths.*

Lesson structure

STARTER

Timeline – Can the students match important events in space exploration to a set of dates? (5–10 minutes)

Powering satellites – Can the students explain how orbiting satellites are powered? What about probes sent to the distant reaches of the Solar System? (10 minutes)

I spy – Show the students a video clip from a film showing a spy satellite in use. Ask them to discuss if they think it was realistic and what they think the true capabilities are. (5–10 minutes)

MAIN

- Use a lot of images of satellites to illustrate this lesson, if you have a GPS receiver then use it to introduce the lesson.
- The explanation of launching the satellite mountain should be linked with the real way of launching satellites; the rocket.
- You can give the impression of the movement of geostationary satellites using a globe. Stick a model satellite on a stick and attach it above the Equator so that it revolves with the globe.
- To show that it appears in the same position in the sky, use another stick to show the angle from your home town to the satellite; this stays constant.
- In reality the geostationary satellite would be six times the radius of the Earth distant. This can be illustrated with a really long stick or just discussed.
- Another important type of orbit to point out is the polar orbit. This has a short orbital period and the satellite passes over the poles. Many satellites are placed in these orbits, including weather and spy satellites.
- There are many other possible orbits, but the lower limit is about 120 km up otherwise the atmosphere would slow the satellite down. The important point is that the lower the orbit the faster the satellite has to travel to stay in that orbit.
- The students should be able to come up with a range of uses of the satellites on their own.
- The students should be given the opportunity to look at some images taken by satellites. There are plenty of weather and land survey images available. (See ' ICT link-up' for some details.)

- **Homework.** The students could produce a fact sheet about a particular satellite using information they find from books and the Internet.

ACTIVITY & EXTENSION IDEAS

Adverts in space – There have been suggestions of placing very large advertisements in orbit around the Earth. These would be foil sheets unfurled after launch that will be several hundred square kilometres in area, so that you could read them from the ground. What do the students think of this? You could let them design one if there is time.

The satellite business – The students could research the costs of launching satellites and which countries have the capability. They might want to look at the success rates of launches and the environmental impact. Recently private companies have started offering services with very mixed success rates. The students can research the spaceX project (www.spacex.com) or try to find similar projects.

DID YOU KNOW?

There are a couple of very small objects that are 'gravitationally linked' to the Earth but you can't really call them moons. An asteroid with the less than impressive name '3753 Cruithne' is in a very convoluted orbit around the Earth and the object 'J002E3' may be a piece of space junk or a recently captured small asteroid.

Answers to in-text questions

a) It can give the location and the height above sea level.

b) 12

c) They would be slowed by drag from the atmosphere and would fall back to Earth.

PHYSICS   TURNING FORCES

P3 1.8   Satellites

LEARNING OBJECTIVES

1 What is the period of an orbit?
2 What is a geostationary orbit?

If you go to a remote area or go sailing at sea, take a GPS receiver with you. Then you will know exactly where you are. Global positioning satellites (GPS) send out signals that are used by a receiver to pinpoint its position. A GPS receiver fitted to a car tells a driver exactly where the car is and which direction it is going in.

a) Why is a GPS receiver useful to a mountaineer?

Satellite orbits

Every satellite orbiting the Earth was launched into its orbit from the ground or from a space vehicle. Imagine launching a satellite into orbit from the top of a very tall mountain. Look at Figure 2.

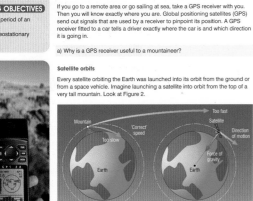

Figure 2 Launching a satellite

Figure 1 A hand-held GPS receiver

- If the satellite's speed is too low, it will fall to the ground.
- If its initial speed is too great, it will fly off into space.
- At the 'correct' speed, it orbits the Earth.

For two satellites in orbits at different heights, the satellite in the higher orbit moves at a slower speed and travels further on each complete orbit. So the satellite in the higher orbit takes longer than the other satellite to complete each orbit.

The period of a satellite is the time it takes to make one complete orbit.

b) A satellite has a period of 2 hours. How many complete orbits would it make in 24 hours?

Using satellites

We use satellites for communications and for monitoring.

- Communications satellites are usually in an orbit at a particular height above the equator so they have a period of 24 hours. They orbit the Earth in the same direction as the Earth's spin. So they stay above the same place on the Earth's surface as they go round the Earth. We describe such orbits as **geostationary**.

Geostationary orbits are about 36 000 kilometres above the Earth. The force of gravity there keeps a satellite moving in a circular orbit with a period of 24 hours.

Figure 3 A satellite in orbit

- Monitoring satellites are fitted with TV cameras pointing to the Earth. We use them for many purposes, including weather forecasting, military and police surveillance and for environmental monitoring. They are in much lower orbits than geostationary satellites. This is so we can see as much detail on the Earth as possible. They orbit the Earth once every two or three hours. Their orbits usually take them over the Earth's poles so they can scan the whole Earth every day.

c) Why is it not possible to put satellites into really low orbits?

SUMMARY QUESTIONS

1 Complete the sentences below using words from the list.

equator   high   low   poles

a) A geostationary satellite is in a ...... orbit that is directly above the Earth's ....
b) A monitoring satellite is in a ...... orbit that is directly above the Earth's ....

2 GPS satellites orbit the Earth about once every 12 hours.

a) Does a GPS satellite orbit the Earth above or below i) a geostationary satellite, ii) a weather satellite that has a period of 2 hours?
b) Why are GPS satellites easier to launch than geostationary satellites?

GET IT RIGHT!

All geostationary satellites orbit above the equator.

KEY POINTS

1 A satellite in a geostationary orbit has a period of 24 hours and stays at the same position directly above the Earth's equator.
2 Geostationary orbits are usually used for communication satellites.
3 Monitoring satellites are usually in low polar orbits.

PLENARIES

Triumph of the soviets! – It's 1957 again, so can the comrades design a celebratory poster to mark the glorious launch of the Sputnik 1! (15 minutes)

Time delay – Can the students act out a discussion about satellite communications but incorporate the four-second time delay that would happen if they were on opposite sides of the globe? (5 minutes)

It's wrong to wish on space hardware – Ask: 'How could you tell the difference between a low orbiting satellite and a star using only your eyes? Would it be possible to see a geostationary satellite? Why not?' (5 minutes)

SUMMARY ANSWERS

1 a) High, equator.
  b) Low, poles.

2 a) i) Below. ii) Above.

  b) Less energy is needed because the orbit is nearer the ground than a geostationary orbit is.

KEY POINTS

The students need to be able to compare geostationary and other satellites. They could construct a table to show advantages and disadvantages.

P3 1.9

Turning issues

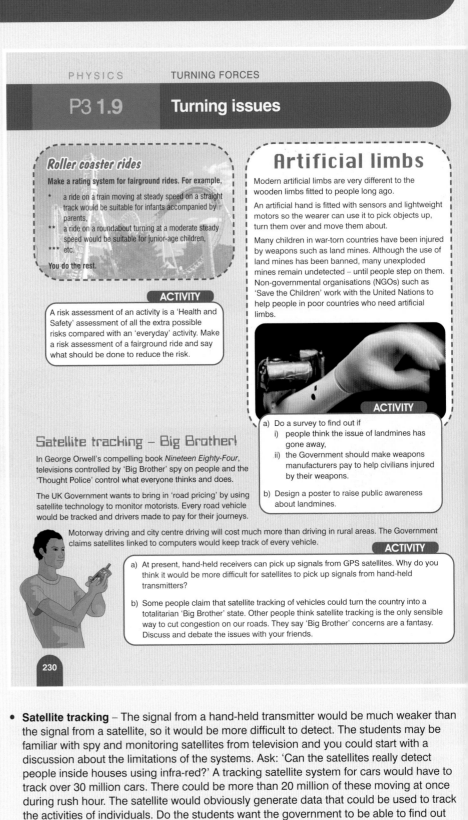

PHYSICS   TURNING FORCES

P3 1.9   Turning issues

Roller coaster rides

Make a rating system for fairground rides. For example,

* a ride on a train moving at steady speed on a straight track would be suitable for infants accompanied by parents,

** a ride on a roundabout turning at a moderate steady speed would be suitable for junior-age children,

*** etc.

You do the rest.

ACTIVITY

A risk assessment of an activity is a 'Health and Safety' assessment of all the extra possible risks compared with an 'everyday' activity. Make a risk assessment of a fairground ride and say what should be done to reduce the risk.

Satellite tracking – Big Brother!

In George Orwell's compelling book *Nineteen Eighty-Four*, televisions controlled by 'Big Brother' spy on people and the 'Thought Police' control what everyone thinks and does.

The UK Government wants to bring in 'road pricing' by using satellite technology to monitor motorists. Every road vehicle would be tracked and drivers made to pay for their journeys.

Motorway driving and city centre driving will cost much more than driving in rural areas. The Government claims satellites linked to computers would keep track of every vehicle.

ACTIVITY

a) At present, hand-held receivers can pick up signals from GPS satellites. Why do you think it would be more difficult for satellites to pick up signals from hand-held transmitters?

b) Some people claim that satellite tracking of vehicles could turn the country into a totalitarian 'Big Brother' state. Other people think satellite tracking is the only sensible way to cut congestion on our roads. They say 'Big Brother' concerns are a fantasy. Discuss and debate the issues with your friends.

Artificial limbs

Modern artificial limbs are very different to the wooden limbs fitted to people long ago.

An artificial hand is fitted with sensors and lightweight motors so the wearer can use it to pick objects up, turn them over and move them about.

Many children in war-torn countries have been injured by weapons such as land mines. Although the use of land mines has been banned, many unexploded mines remain undetected – until people step on them. Non-governmental organisations (NGOs) such as 'Save the Children' work with the United Nations to help people in poor countries who need artificial limbs.

ACTIVITY

a) Do a survey to find out if
  i) people think the issue of landmines has gone away,
  ii) the Government should make weapons manufacturers pay to help civilians injured by their weapons.

b) Design a poster to raise public awareness about landmines.

230

Teaching suggestions

Activities

- **Roller coaster rides** – There are a couple of roller coaster simulators available. These would be very impressive to use when discussing the rides. You might like to show the students a real risk assessment form that has to be filled in when arranging a school visit. Make sure that the students are assessing the needs of a wide range of people, e.g. is the ride suitable for pregnant people, people with various medical conditions or disabilities?

- **Artificial limbs** – There are still countries that manufacture and use land mines, including some of the major nations. They call them 'area denial munitions' instead of land mines, because it sounds friendlier. The agreement that many countries signed up to is called the 'Ottawa Treaty'; the students can look this up to find out which counties have ratified the treaty.

- **Satellite tracking** – The signal from a hand-held transmitter would be much weaker than the signal from a satellite, so it would be more difficult to detect. The students may be familiar with spy and monitoring satellites from television and you could start with a discussion about the limitations of the systems. Ask: 'Can the satellites really detect people inside houses using infra-red?' A tracking satellite system for cars would have to track over 30 million cars. There could be more than 20 million of these moving at once during rush hour. The satellite would obviously generate data that could be used to track the activities of individuals. Do the students want the government to be able to find out where they are at all times?

- **A lucky miss** – The likelihood of being killed by falling space junk is currently very small. Somewhere between two and four hundred pieces fall to the ground every year, but there are no records of anybody being killed by one. The biggest problem with space junk is that it can collide with other satellites. The total number of obsolete man-made objects in orbit is approximately 13 000 and this grows every year. Even a tiny particle moving at 10 000 km/h can damage an orbiting satellite or even kill an astronaut. A 0.2 mm fleck of white paint once put a crater in the space shuttle's front window during a collision. Anything larger than 1 mm would have punched a hole through the glass. Find the 'Centre for orbital and re-entry debris studies' for more details.

A LUCKY MISS!

(Artist's impression!)

Did the junk come from a communications satellite?

Fred Green is the luckiest person in the country. A piece of space junk dropped out of the sky and hit the ground next to him. It destroyed his favourite rose bush. A few moments earlier, he had been cutting some roses from the bush!

With more and more satellites in space, there's going to be more and more junk whirling round the Earth – used rockets, redundant satellites, solar panels that snap off. Some space junk will re-enter the atmosphere and burn up. Some of it will crash to the ground. It is not likely to go away. But should we just ignore it as more and more junk accumulates in orbits above the Earth?

ACTIVITY

Imagine we're in the 25th century and a space refuse collection service has been set up. Write a job advert for a space refuse collector, highlighting all the perks. Turn the drawbacks like cosmic radiation into 'benefits'.

Paying for space

Lots of money is spent on space exploration and space technology. Most of the money is from taxes. People have different views about paying for space.

It's good for our image.

We can track down criminals quicker.

We all benefit from space exploration and technology.

I think the money would be better spent on other things such as health.

ACTIVITY

a) With the help of your friends, list the direct benefits you get from space exploration and space technology.

b) The next big step into space will probably be to send astronauts to Mars. Would you like to go on this epic journey? Discuss your views in a small group.

231

Extension or homework

- **A dog's life** – The initial soviet satellite programme was designed to test a range of equipment to prepare for a manned flight. During the programme, the Soviets decided to launch various animals into orbit on craft that were not designed to return. The first of these was Laika, a dog launched inside Sputnik 2. The students could write an article commemorating these animals or prepare for a debate about the use of animals in scientific research.

- **Great milestones in space exploration** – The students could develop a timeline of the major developments in space exploration from the development of the ballistic rocket in WWII through to the planned completion of the international space station. This could easily fill a whole wall, if different groups work on different aspects of the project.

Special needs

Provide templates for the research projects with a few pre-chosen web sites, so that the students do not find the more complex sites. For the role play you could provide some scripts to help out.

Gifted and talented

Ask: 'How does the GPS system work? In most places the accuracy is to within two metres, but how can satellites be used to find out position on the Earth to this precision? What is the European system that is being developed to do the same job and why is it being developed?'

Learning styles

Kinaesthetic: Researching into the costs of space exploration.

Visual: Presenting information in a poster about land mines.

Auditory: Discussing the risks of fairground rides.

Interpersonal: Debating the appropriateness of satellite tracking of cars.

Intrapersonal: Writing a report on the preparation needed to reach Mars.

ICT link-up

Much of the information about space exploration can be found on the Internet, especially images. (See www.nasa.gov)

- **Paying for space** – The discussion about space exploration should really be about the use of resources, as the money is basically recycled through the economy anyway. Ask: 'Are the resources renewable or is space exploration causing irreparable environmental damage?' If the students find out about the materials used as fuels and in the construction of the rockets, they can debate the impact. This is useful for considering how decisions affecting science are made (this relates to: 'How Science Works'). The Mars project is still in the early planning stage; the students should find out about the massive range of obstacles that are in the way.

SUMMARY ANSWERS

1 **a)** It would be less stable as it would be easier to disturb.

   b) i) 0.012 N m

2 0.06 N   [**HT** only]

3 **a)** Equal to.

   b) Greater than.

   c) Less than.

   d) Equal to.

4 **a) i)** 24 hours, eastwards.

   ii) Circular and directly over the Equator.

   b) It would be too high to see clouds in detail.

Summary teaching suggestions

- For question 1, the diagram should be clearly labelled; make sure that the force is drawn in the right direction and the students can see which way the object will rotate due to this. If the students struggle, then provide them with some photocopies of a few similar situations to label.

- With question 2, the students should be imagining where the centre of mass is and what happens when part of an object is removed. They need to be linking low centre of mass with increased stability. The last part involves the calculation and a bit of rearrangement. If you have time, you could make a similar item out of card and cotton and demonstrate the effect of cutting off the Sun.

- Question 3 would work well as an interactive question where the students can see an animation and then drag and drop the answers to the correct place. The animation should show the speeds of the motion of the objects, and use red arrows to show the size of the forces involved and possibly green to show the velocity.

- In question 4, make sure that the students not only know the period of orbit but also that the satellite *must* be above the Equator to be geostationary. There are geosynchronous satellites that orbit every 24 hours, but these are not above the Equator. You can remind the students that geostationary satellites are 36 000 km from the Earth's surface and this is too distant to get high-resolution images.

TURNING FORCES: P3 1.1 – P3 1.9

SUMMARY QUESTIONS

1 The figure shows a toy suspended from a ceiling.

a) How would the stability of the toy be affected if the Sun was removed from it?

b) The star on the toy has a weight of 0.04 N and is a distance of 0.30 m from the point P where the thread is attached to the toy.
Calculate the moment of the star about P.

2 The crescent moon attached to the toy in question 1 is at a distance of 0.20 m from P. Calculate the weight of the crescent.   [Higher]

3 A space station and a small satellite are in the same orbit above the Earth.
Copy and complete the following sentences using words from the list.

> **greater than   less than   equal to**

a) The speed of the space station is ...... the speed of the satellite.

b) The centripetal force needed by the space station is ...... the centripetal force needed by the satellite.

c) The force of gravity on the satellite is ...... the force of gravity on the space station.

d) The time taken for the satellite to orbit the Earth once is ...... the time taken by the space station to orbit the Earth once.

4 **a) i)** What is the period and direction of motion of a geostationary satellite?
   ii) Describe the orbit of a geostationary satellite.
   b) Explain why a geostationary satellite would be no use for weather forecasting.

232

EXAM-STYLE QUESTIONS

1 (a) What is meant by the *centre of mass* of an object?   (1)

(b) The drawing shows a thin sheet of card. There are holes in the card at **A** and **B**.

Describe how you would find the centre of mass of the sheet of card.
Include a diagram with your answer.   (6)

2 The diagram shows a painter standing on a plank. The plank rests on two supports.

The weight of the painter is 700 N. He is standing 2 m from support **A**.

(a) Calculate the moment of his weight about support **A**.   (4)

(b) The painter moves along the plank away from support **A**.
State and explain what happens to the moment of his weight about support **A**.   (2)

3 A teacher is talking to her class about circular motion. She demonstrates with a bung fastened to a piece of rubber tubing that she swings around in a horizontal circle.

EXAM-STYLE ANSWERS

1 **a)** The point where the mass of the object can be thought to be concentrated.   *(1 mark)*

   b) • Diagram showing card suspended from a pin through a hole.   *(1 mark)*
   • Plumb line suspended from the pin.   *(1 mark)*
   • Card allowed to come to rest.   *(1 mark)*
   • Position of string marked.   *(1 mark)*
   • Procedure repeated with pin in second hole.   *(1 mark)*
   • Centre of mass where lines cross.   *(1 mark)*

2 **a)** Moment = force × perpendicular distance from the line of action of the force to the axis of rotation.   *(1 mark)*
   Moment = 700 N × 2 m.   *(1 mark)*
   Moment = 1400 N m.   *(1 mark)*
   Clockwise.   *(1 mark)*

   b) As he moves away the perpendicular distance increases   *(1 mark)*
   so the moment increases.   *(1 mark)*

3 **a) i)** A.   *(1 mark)*
   ii) B.   *(1 mark)*

   b) i) Centripetal force decreases.   *(1 mark)*
   ii) Centripetal force decreases.   *(1 mark)*
   iii) Centripetal force increases.   *(1 mark)*

   c) i) Control variables.   *(1 mark)*
   ii) Independent variable.   *(1 mark)*

4 **a) i)** Gravitational force.   *(1 mark)*
   ii) Satellite is continuously changing direction   *(1 mark)*
   so continuously changing velocity   *(1 mark)*
   so accelerating.

   b) i) Satellite stays over same point on Earth.   *(1 mark)*
   ii) Orbit has time period of 24 hours.   *(1 mark)*
   iii) Communications satellite.   *(1 mark)*

The diagram below shows an overhead view of the bung.

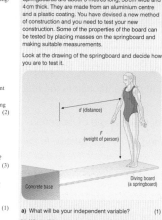

(a) (i) In which direction, **A**, **B**, **C** or **D**, does the centripetal force act?

(ii) The teacher lets go of the tubing at the instant shown in the diagram.
In which direction, **A**, **B**, **C** or **D**, does the bung move? (2)

(b) What will happen to the centripetal force if the teacher:
(i) uses a bung with a smaller mass?
(ii) swings the bung more slowly?
(iii) swings the bung on a shorter piece of tubing? (3)

(c) In each case in part (b) she keeps all the other variables constant, apart from the variable under investigation.
(i) What do we call the variables that are kept constant in an investigation? (1)
(ii) What is the general name for the 'variable under investigation'? (1)

There are many satellites orbiting the Earth in circular paths.

(a) (i) What force provides the centripetal force that allows satellites to maintain their circular orbits? (1)
(ii) A satellite moving at a steady speed in a circular orbit is continuously accelerating.
Explain why. (2)

(b) Some satellites are in *geostationary orbits*.
(i) What is meant by a *geostationary orbit*? (1)
(ii) What is the time period of a geostationary orbit? (1)
(iii) What type of satellite is usually put into a geostationary orbit? (1)

HOW SCIENCE WORKS

Springboards are about 5 metres long, 50 cm wide and 4 cm thick. They are made from an aluminium centre and a plastic coating. You have devised a new method of construction and you need to test your new construction. Some of the properties of the board can be tested by placing masses on the springboard and making suitable measurements.

Look at the drawing of the springboard and decide how you are to test it.

d (distance)

F (weight of person)

Concrete base

Diving board (a springboard)

a) What will be your independent variable? (1)

b) What will be your dependent variable? (1)

c) Suggest a suitable range for your independent variable. (1)

d) Suggest a suitable number of interval measurements for the independent variable. (1)

e) What sensitivity would you require for measuring your dependent variable? (1)

f) State two control variables you should use. (2)

g) Draw a table for your results. (3)

233

HOW SCIENCE WORKS ANSWERS

a) Could be either the force or the moment arm.

b) The distance the tip of the board moves down. This should be a measurable variable – 'degree of bend' is difficult to measure.

c) A range based on a reasonable expectation of the mass of the diver or where the diver will take off.

d) At least five interval measurements.

e) Probably millimetres. Could be discussed.

f) Depends on the chosen independent variable. Also, e.g., position on board with respect to the width.

g) E.g.

Mass (kg)	50	60	70	80	90
Drop (mm)					
Drop (mm)					
Drop (mm)					

How science works teaching suggestions

- **Literacy guidance.** Key terms that should be understood: independent and dependent variable, range interval measurements, control, sensitivity.

- **Higher- and lower-level answers.** Question b) is a higher-level question and the answer provided above is also at this level. Question d) is lower-level and the answer provided is also lower-level.

- **Gifted and talented.** Able students could calculate the moment of the forces. They could also begin to appreciate the difference between putting masses on the board and the jumping of a diver from the board. They might discuss how the results of this simple experiment relate to real issues of how a springboard is used.

- **How and when to use these questions.** When wishing to develop experimental design.
The questions could be prepared for homework and discussed in class.

- **Special needs.** The students could watch a video of diving in slow motion if easily available, to appreciate where the divers take off and the degree of bending.

Exam teaching suggestions

- The experiment to find the centre of mass of a lamina appears regularly on examination papers. Students should carry out the experiment for themselves with both regular and irregular lamina.

- Question 2 requires students to calculate a moment having been given a weight. Many students forget that if they are given as mass in a question they must first calculate the corresponding weight before they can find the moment.

- The concept of centripetal force is a difficult one for many students. They often think that in the demonstration described in question 3 the bung would fly outwards from the circle rather than at a tangent to the circle. It is useful to demonstrate to them what happens.

- It should be emphasised that centripetal force does not exist in its own right but is always provided by another force. In situations where bodies are performing circular motions students need to identify the force that provides centripetal force.

P3 2.1

Reflection

LEARNING OBJECTIVES

Students should learn:

- The angle of incidence is the angle between the normal and the incident ray of light, while the angle of reflection is the angle between the reflected ray and the normal.
- That the angle of incidence and the angle of reflection are equal for plane mirrors.

LEARNING OUTCOMES

Most students should be able to:

- Draw a diagram showing reflection by a plane mirror which shows the angle of incidence, reflection and the normal.
- Explain that the image in a mirror is virtual; it cannot be projected.

Some students should also be able to:

- Draw a diagram to show the formation of the image of a point object in a plane mirror.

Teaching suggestions

- **Special needs.** Use printed worksheets that the students can mount the mirror on. These can also have the angles of incidence that should be used added to them.
- **Gifted and talented.** There are two laws of reflection. The students should find out what the other law is and explain what it means.
- **Learning styles**

  Kinaesthetic: Carrying out practical activities and manipulating lenses.

  Visual: Observing ray paths and tabulating practical results.

  Auditory: Discussing the properties of images.

  Interpersonal: Evaluating the experiments.

- **Teaching assistant.** Any assistants can help groups who have forgotten how to use the ray boxes.
- **Science @ work.** The students can try to write a message backwards without the help of a mirror. Check the results.

SPECIFICATION LINK-UP   Unit: Physics 3.13.4

- *The normal is a construction-line perpendicular to the reflecting/refracting surface at the point of incidence.*
- *The angle of incidence is equal to the angle of reflection.*
- *The nature of an image is defined by its size relative to the object, whether it is upright or inverted relative to the object and whether it is real or virtual.*
- *The nature of the image produced by a plane mirror.*

Students should use their skills, knowledge and understanding of 'How Science Works':

- *to construct ray diagrams to show the formation of images by plane, convex and concave mirrors.*

Lesson structure

STARTER

Ray diagram – Ask the students to draw a ray diagram showing how they can see a non-luminous object, such as the writing in their books. (5–10 minutes)

Light knowledge – The students need to list the properties of light and any other facts that they know about it. (5–10 minutes)

Virtually real – Ask: 'What does the word 'virtual' mean?' The students should give several examples of its use. What about the word 'real'? (5–10 minutes)

MAIN

- This topic should be fairly familiar with the students at first, but they will not really have looked into different shaped mirrors or real and virtual images. See P3 2.1 'Reflection' on the GCSE Physics CD ROM.
- The students need to be aware of the difference between diffuse reflection, where no image is formed and normal reflection. The difference is obvious when showing them a mirror and a sheet of paper.
- When discussing the position of the image in the mirror, use the image distance activity in 'Activity and extension ideas'.
- Some students will have trouble remembering the difference between convex and concave mirrors. The con*cave* mirror has *'caved in'wards*.
- The normal is a very important part of ray diagrams and the students must be drawing it on all such diagrams. All angles are measured from the normal, so make sure that the students are not measuring them from the surface of the mirror to the incident or reflected ray.
- Many students remember the law of reflection, but the experiment allows them to become familiar with the equipment that they may not have used for several years. Check that they are forming and directing the rays correctly and that they are drawing a normal to aim the rays at.
- Discuss the accuracy of measurements and errors involved in the experiment (this relates to: 'How Science Works').
- One minor point that crops up with drawing mirrors is that the hatching should be drawn on the back of the mirror. The students should also know that, for normal plane glass mirrors, the reflective surface is on the back surface and rays should be drawn to this.
- Getting across the ideas of real and virtual images can be tricky; a real image is formed when the light rays really pass a point but a virtual image is formed when the light rays seem to have come from a point; they never actually met at the point.
- If you have time available, the construction of periscopes is good for some groups, a bit easy for higher-attaining students though, as it will probably have been done in Key Stage 3. You can check the understanding of the laws of reflection by asking the students to draw a diagram of how a periscope works.

Practical support

Investigating the reflection of light

The students may have carried out similar experiments during Key Stage 3, but it is worthwhile to get them used to the equipment again. The experiment is best carried out in a darkened lab, but full blackout is not required.

Equipment and materials required

Power supply, ray box, single slit, ray box stops, plane mirror, ruler, protractor and a sheet of A3 paper.

Details

The students set up the ray box so that it produces a single ray. The mirror is fixed to the back of the paper using a holder or Blu-Tack, so that the ray can be reflected by it. Then the students shine rays at the centre of the mirror from a range of angles and measure the angles of incidence and reflection. This is best done by marking the path of each ray at two points with a cross and then joining these with a ruler. The lines should be drawn to the back of the mirror where reflection takes place. You might find that the experiment works best if the mirror is tilted downwards very slightly.

PLENARIES

Mirror maze – Ask the students to add mirrors to a simple maze diagram so that a light ray can pass through it to the centre. (5–10 minutes)

Pepper's ghost – Show the students this simple illusion and ask them to come up with an explanation of how it works. (5 minutes)

Light taboo – Split the students in groups and give them some cards with key words on (mirror, ray, reflect, normal, etc.) and a list of words they can't use in describing the key word. How many can the group get in the time limit? (5–10 minutes)

DID YOU KNOW?

One of the first movies to shock people was the moving image of a train towards the camera. The film *Arrival of a Train*, by the Lumiere brothers, is just a 50 second clip of a train arriving at a station. You should be able to find a copy of this clip by searching for 'trainarrival.mov' on the Internet. Somehow it's not as frightening as it used to be. There are plenty of other early clips around to show how cinema has developed.

PHYSICS — LIGHT AND SOUND

P3 2.1 Reflection

LEARNING OBJECTIVES

1 What is an angle of incidence?
2 What can we say about the reflection of a light ray at a plane mirror?

If you have visited a 'Hall of Mirrors' at a funfair, you will know that the shape of a mirror affects what you see. If you see:

- a tall, thin image of yourself, you are looking in a convex mirror, which is one that bends out,
- a short, broad image of yourself, you are looking into a concave mirror, which is a mirror that bends in.

If you want to see a normal image of yourself, look in a plane (i.e. flat) mirror. You see an exact 'mirror' image of yourself.

An image seen in a mirror is due to reflection of light by the mirror. Figure 1b) shows how an image of a point object is formed by a plane mirror. The diagram shows the path of two light rays from the object that reflect off the mirror. The image and the object in Figure 1 are equal distances from the mirror.

Figure 1 a) Mirror images

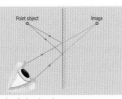

b) Image formation by a plane mirror

a) If you stand 0.5 m in front of a plane mirror, your image is 0.5 m behind the mirror.
What is the distance between you and your image?

PRACTICAL

Investigating the reflection of light

We can use a ray box and a plane mirror to investigate reflection, as shown in Figure 2.

- What did you find out?
- Comment on the reliability of your investigation. (See pages 5, 9 and 15.)

Figure 2 The law of reflection

Look at Figure 2.
The perpendicular line to the mirror is called the normal.
The angle of incidence is the angle between the incident ray and the normal.
The angle of reflection is the angle between the reflected ray and the normal.
Measurements show that for any light ray reflected by a mirror:

angle of incidence = angle of reflection

b) If the angle of reflection of a light ray from a plane mirror is 20°, what is:
  i) the angle of incidence,
  ii) the angle between the incident ray and the reflected ray?

Real and virtual images

The image in Figure 1 is a **virtual** image. When you look at a mirror image, the light rays that reflect off the mirror into your eye appear to come from the image. A virtual image can't be projected onto a screen like the movie images that you see at a cinema. An image like this is described as a **real image** because it is formed by focusing light rays onto a screen.

c) When you use a face mirror, is your image real or virtual?

SCIENCE @ WORK

Ambulances and police cars often carry a 'mirror image' sign at the front. This is so a driver in a vehicle in front looking into the rear-view mirror can read the sign.

Figure 4 A mirror sign on an ambulance

SUMMARY QUESTIONS

1 Two plane mirrors are placed perpendicular to each other. Draw a ray diagram to show the path of a light ray at an angle of incidence of 60° that reflects off both mirrors.

2 A point object O is placed in front of a plane mirror, as shown:

Object O

Mirror

a) Copy and complete the path of the two rays from O after they have reflected off the mirror.
b) i) Use the reflected rays to locate the image of O.
  ii) Show that the image and the object are equidistant from the mirror.

DID YOU KNOW?

The first 'movie' films terrified people. The sight of a horse galloping towards them often made people dive under their seats.

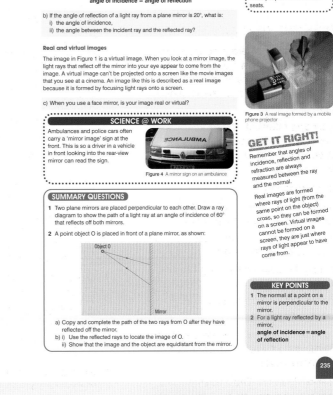

Figure 3 A real image formed by a mobile phone projector

GET IT RIGHT!

Remember that angles of incidence, reflection and refraction are always measured between the ray and the normal.

Real images are formed where rays of light (from the same point on the object) cross, so they can be formed on a screen. Virtual images cannot be formed on a screen, they are just where rays of light appear to have come from.

KEY POINTS

1 The normal at a point on a mirror is perpendicular to the mirror.
2 For a light ray reflected by a mirror,
angle of incidence = angle of reflection

234 / 235

SUMMARY ANSWERS

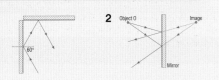

1

2 Object O — Image — Mirror

Answers to in-text questions

a) 1.0 m
b) i) 20° **ii)** 40°
c) Virtual.

KEY POINTS

The students should draw and label a diagram showing reflection by a plane mirror and use the Law of Reflection to mark the angles.

P3 2.2 Curved mirrors

LEARNING OBJECTIVES

Students should learn:

- That a concave mirror can produce a magnified or diminished image, which is always virtual but may be inverted or erect.
- That a convex mirror produces a virtual image that is diminished.

LEARNING OUTCOMES

Most students should be able to:

- Draw diagrams showing the positions of images by concave and convex mirrors.
- Describe the properties of images formed by concave and convex mirrors.

Some students should also be able to:

- Draw diagrams showing the formation and nature of the image of an object at different distances from a concave mirror.
- Calculate the magnification produced by a convex or concave mirror.

Teaching suggestions

- **Special needs.** Provide the students with partially complete ray diagrams for the mirrors so that they can add the rays more easily.
- **Gifted and talented.** The students can find out how to find the position of the images produced by a converging lens using the lens formula. This is $1/f = 1/u + 1/v$ where f is the focal length of the lens, u is the distance from the object to the lens and v is the distance from the lens to the image. This can be taxing for students who have difficulty in adding and subtracting fractions, but it does yield precise positions. It can also yield negative values for the position; can the students explain what this means?
- **Learning styles**

  Kinaesthetic: Carrying out experiments with lenses.

  Visual: Obtaining experimental data on the location and size of images.

  Interpersonal: Discussing and collaborating during experiments.

  Intrapersonal: Evaluating the outcomes of the experiments.

SPECIFICATION LINK-UP   Unit: Physics 3.13.4

- *The nature of an image is defined by its size relative to the object, whether it is upright or inverted relative to the object and whether it is real or virtual.*
- *The nature of the image produced by a convex mirror.*
- *The nature of the image produced by a concave mirror for an object placed at different distances from the mirror.*

Students should use their skills, knowledge and understanding of 'How Science Works':

- *to construct ray diagrams to show the formation of images by plane, convex and concave mirrors.*
- *to calculate the magnification produced by a lens or mirror using the formula:*

$$\text{magnification} = \frac{\text{image height}}{\text{object height}}$$

Lesson structure

STARTER

Distorted – Find some pictures of distorted images in curved mirrors and ask the students to say what the original object was. There is software that can do this, so you can distort images of some member of staff – great fun! (5 minutes)

Solar cooker – Can the students draw a diagram of a solar cooker/solar oven and explain how it works? Ask: 'What shape is it?' (5–10 minutes)

MAIN

- Let the students handle some concave mirrors so that they can appreciate the initial points from the textbook. Use this time to check that they understand that the images can be real or virtual.
- With some students you will want to use the term 'inverted' for an upside down image and possibly 'erect' for an image the right way up.
- The diagram of the image formation is very important. The students need to be able to understand the ray path and the idea of a focal point. Get them to draw a couple of diagrams for themselves, showing the important construction rays.
- The students should be able to see the image for a distant object by looking into the mirror and seeing distant objects behind them. By adjusting the mirror's position, they should be able to see a clearly focussed image of something out of the window.
- The idea of magnification is fairly simple and a few practice calculations should give the students the idea. You might like to ask the students why magnification is important and what types of devices magnify images.
- Try a calculation for a diminished image just to make sure that the students understand that the magnification can be less than 1.
- The investigation is quite a hard one and will take some time for the students to get right. The main difficulty is getting an image without blocking the light from the object and the students will have to adjust the apparatus until they can do this.
- This presents a good opportunity to cover many investigative aspects of 'How Science Works', e.g. relationships between variables.
- Finally let the students look into a convex mirror. They might be familiar with these from security mirrors in shops.

PLENARIES

Comparing mirrors – Get the students to summarise their knowledge of the behaviour of convex and concave mirrors in a table. (10 minutes)

Shaving mirror – Ask: 'What shape should the shaving mirror be and why?' (10 minutes)

Practical support

Investigating the concave mirror

The experiment can be carried out with an optical bench or with a metre rule. Use mirrors that are just curved in one dimension; these can be tilted easily.

Equipment and materials required

For each group: concave mirror (focal length ~20 cm), 2 × metre ruler, illuminated object, and graph paper to act as a screen.

Details

* The students need to measure the size of the object at the start of the experiment. A simple object could be a piece of card with a 1 cm square hole cut into it. To check that it is in focus, stick a thin wire across it diagonally.

* Position the mirror at the end of the metre ruler tilted so that the image will be to the side of the mirror. This will allow the screen to be moved without getting in the way of the rays from the object. Shine a bright light through the object and move the screen until the image is clear. It should be simple to use the graph paper to measure the image size. The object can be moved through a range of distances and so the relationship between focal length, distance and magnification can be explored.

Teaching suggestions continued

* **Homework.** The students can find out how many different objects have mirrors and whether these are concave or convex.

* **ICT link-up.** Use Simulation P3 2.2 'Concave mirrors' from the GCSE Physics CD ROM.

PHYSICS   LIGHT AND SOUND

P3 2.2   Curved mirrors

LEARNING OBJECTIVES

1 Why is a distorted image seen in a curved mirror?
2 What do we mean by magnification?
3 What can we use concave and convex mirrors for?

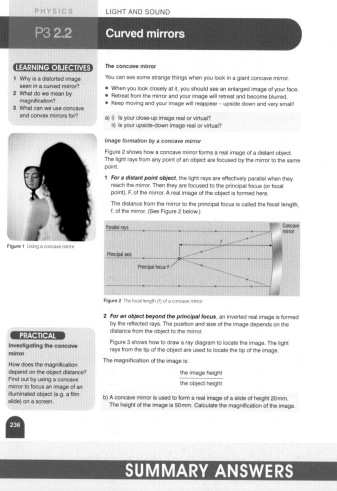
Figure 1 Using a concave mirror

The concave mirror

You can see some strange things when you look in a giant concave mirror.

* When you look closely at it, you should see an enlarged image of your face.
* Retreat from the mirror and your image will retreat and become blurred.
* Keep moving and your image will reappear – upside down and very small!

a) i) Is your close-up image real or virtual?
   ii) Is your upside-down image real or virtual?

Image formation by a concave mirror

Figure 2 shows how a concave mirror forms a real image of a distant object. The light rays from any point of an object are focused by the mirror to the same point.

1 **For a distant point object**, the light rays are effectively parallel when they reach the mirror. Then they are focused to the principal focus (or focal point), F, of the mirror. A real image of the object is formed here.

The distance from the mirror to the principal focus is called the **focal length**, f, of the mirror. (See Figure 2 below.)

Figure 2 The focal length (f) of a concave mirror

PRACTICAL

Investigating the concave mirror

How does the magnification depend on the object distance? Find out by using a concave mirror to focus an image of an illuminated object (e.g. a film slide) on a screen.

2 **For an object beyond the principal focus**, an inverted real image is formed by the reflected rays. The position and size of the image depends on the distance from the object to the mirror.

Figure 3 shows how to draw a ray diagram to locate the image. The light rays from the tip of the object are used to locate the tip of the image.

The magnification of the image is:

$$\frac{\text{the image height}}{\text{the object height}}$$

b) A concave mirror is used to form a real image of a slide of height 20 mm. The height of the image is 50 mm. Calculate the magnification of the image.

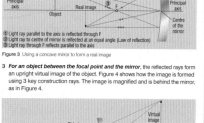
① Light ray parallel to the axis is reflected through F
② Light ray to centre of mirror is reflected at an equal angle (Law of reflection)
③ Light ray through F reflects parallel to the axis
Figure 3 Using a concave mirror to form a real image

3 **For an object between the focal point and the mirror**, the reflected rays form an upright virtual image of the object. Figure 4 shows how the image is formed using 3 key construction rays. The image is magnified and is behind the mirror, as in Figure 4.

Observer sees an enlarged upright image
Figure 4 Using a concave mirror to form a virtual image

c) Describe the image you see when you look at yourself in a concave mirror?

The convex mirror

We use convex mirrors as rear-view mirrors in cars. The driver has a much wider field of view than with a plane mirror. Figure 5a) shows why. The image of an object viewed in a convex mirror is virtual and smaller than the object as shown in Figure 5b).

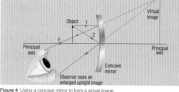
Figure 5 A rear-view mirror

SCIENCE @ WORK

Dentists use small concave mirrors to see different parts of your teeth. This saves them having to do handstands or turning you upside down to get a good view of your molars!

SUMMARY QUESTIONS

1 Complete the following sentences using words from the list:

   behind   in front   inverted   real   upright   virtual

  a) The image formed by a concave mirror of a distant tree is …… and ……. The location of the image is …… of the mirror.
  b) The image formed by a convex mirror of a distant tree is …… and ……. The location of the image is …… the mirror.

2 a) An object is placed midway between a concave mirror and its principal focus. Draw a ray diagram to show the formation by the concave mirror of the image of this object.
  b) Describe the image and calculate its magnification.

KEY POINTS

1 The principal focus of a concave mirror is the point where parallel rays are focused to by the mirror.
2 A concave mirror forms:
  • a real image if the object is beyond the principal focus of the mirror,
  • a virtual image if the object is between the mirror and the principal focus.
3 A convex mirror always forms a virtual image of an object.

236   237

SUMMARY ANSWERS

1 a) Real, inverted, in front.
  b) Virtual, upright, behind.

2 a)

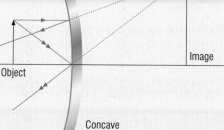
F   Object   Image
Concave mirror

  b) The image is virtual, upright and twice as large as the object.

Answers to in-text questions

a) i) Virtual. ii) Real.
b) 2.5
c) Upright, magnified, virtual.

KEY POINTS

The students should complete some ray diagrams finding the position of the image produced by concave and convex mirrors.

P3 2.3 Refraction

LEARNING OBJECTIVES

Students should learn:

- That refraction is the changing of direction of a wave at an interface between different materials.
- That refraction occurs because light changes speed when it moves from one medium to another.
- That a prism disperses white light into a spectrum because each frequency is refracted by a different amount.

LEARNING OUTCOMES

Most students should be able to:

- Draw diagrams showing how light is refracted when entering and leaving a transparent substance.
- Describe how the speed of light changes when light passes into or out of a transparent substance.

Some students should also be able to:

- Draw a range of diagrams showing how light is refracted when entering and leaving a glass block or prism.
- Draw a diagram showing the dispersion of light by a prism and explain the process that causes this effect.

Teaching suggestions

- **Special needs.** As with the reflection experiments, you may want to use worksheets that have the position of the glass block and incident rays marked on to save some time.
- **Gifted and talented.** The speed that light travels in a material and how much refraction takes place at its surface are determined by something called the 'refractive index' of the material. Can the students find out why diamond separates out light into different colours so well?
- **Learning styles**
  Kinaesthetic: Carrying out refraction activity.
  Visual: Observing refraction of light rays.
  Auditory: Explaining the behaviour of light rays.
  Interpersonal: Reporting the outcomes of the experiment to other groups.
  Intrapersonal: Interpreting the evidence of refraction experiments.
- **Homework.** Ask: 'What was Newton's work on light? How did he explain what light was and how it behaved?'
- **ICT link-up.** Use P3 2.3 'Refraction' from the GCSE Physics CD ROM.

SPECIFICATION LINK-UP Unit: Physics 3.13.4

- *The normal is a construction-line perpendicular to the reflecting/refracting surface at the point of incidence.*
- *Refraction at an interface.*
- *Refraction by a prism.*

Lesson structure

STARTER

See through – Students should give definition of the three words: 'transparent', 'opaque', and 'translucent'. (5–10 minutes)

Broken pencil – Place a pencil in a beaker of water. Can the students come up with an explanation of why the pencil looks broken? (5 minutes)

Light speed – The Moon is 380 000 km away and light travels at 3×10^8 m/s, so how long would it take to send a signal there and back? [2.5 seconds]. (5 minutes)

MAIN

- Make sure that when the students are using the term 'bending' when talking about refraction, they are not thinking that the light is 'following a curved path'. Most of the refraction here is a clear and sudden change of direction.
- During the initial investigation, watch out for the students marking out and then drawing the rays correctly. They should notice that the ray leaves the block in the same direction as it entered.
- The students may also notice some total internal reflection and you might like to remind them of the uses of this phenomenon.
- If possible, demonstrate the changing of wave speed with a ripple tank or use a simulation. You can't beat seeing the waves speeding up and slowing down.
- The reason for the change in speed is difficult to explain, but most students just accept it.
- There are several analogies about why the change in speed causes a change in direction; a column of soldiers marching from a road into mud, a four-wheel drive vehicle doing the same. Use whichever one the students are comfortable with.
- Refraction from a prism can be shown as a demonstration, or you might like the class to have a go. You can get an excellent spectrum using your data projector as a white light source.
- Getting a good recombination of a spectrum into white light is difficult, but it is worth trying so that you can tell the story of Newton.
- NB. Did you know that Newton is credited with inventing the cat-flap – developed to stop the cat interrupting his optics experiments!

PLENARIES

The magic penny – Place a penny at the bottom of an opaque cup so that you just about can't see it. Pour water into the cup and it reappears. The students should explain why, using a diagram. (5–10 minutes)

Fish – Show a diagram of a fish near the edge of a canal and a fisherman sitting on the bank. There is no straight line of sight because of the edge of the bank, but they can see each other. How? (5 minutes)

Reflect or refract – Make a big diagram for the wall to show the difference between these words, so that nobody gets it wrong again. (5–10 minutes)

Practical support

Investigating refraction

The students may have performed a similar experiment during Key Stage 3, but here the emphasis should be placed on taking measurements from the normal.

Equipment and materials required

For each group: Power supply, ray box, single slit, ray box stops, rectangular glass block, ruler, protractor and a sheet of A3 paper.

Details

The glass block should be placed in the centre of the A3 sheet of paper. It's a good idea to draw around it in case it gets knocked. The students can shine rays into the block from a range of angles aiming for a fixed point on the front surface. They should draw small crosses to mark the path and then measure the angles of incidence and refraction. The angles must be measured from the normal. Gifted students may want to know the actual relationship, which is Snell's law that states that the sine of the angle of incidence divided by the sine of the angle of refraction is a constant for a particular material. Some students could look at Perspex blocks.

Investigating refraction by a prism

This can be run as a simple demonstration or you can let the students have a quick go.

Equipment and materials required

For each group: Power supply, ray box, single slit, ray box stops, prism.

Details

Simply shine the ray through the prism and rotate the prism until a spectrum is produced. Newton was able to recombine the dispersed rays back into a ray of white light with a second prism, but this takes a great deal of skill.

Refraction of water waves

Equipment and materials required

Ripple tank with wave generator, thin glass block.

Details

Set up the ripple tank with enough water in it to cover the glass block. It should be strongly illuminated from below so that the shadow of waves can be seen on the ceiling (or the board if you have a mirror). Show the students the behaviour of simple waves and then place the glass block in to show that wave speed changes above the block. Rotating the block will show that the wave direction is different when the block is at an angle. This show the waves are being refracted.

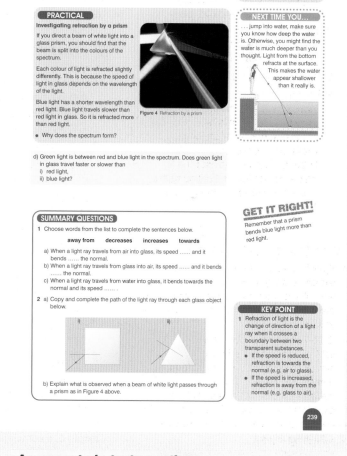

SUMMARY ANSWERS

1 **a)** Decreases, towards.

b) Increases, away from.

c) Decreases.

2 **a) i)**   **ii)**

b) White light consists of all the colours of the spectrum. The beam is split into these colours because each colour is refracted slightly differently, owing to their different speeds in glass.

Answers to in-text questions

a) Yes.

b) The top part moves faster than the lower part of the wave so the wave topples over at the top.

c) The same.

d) i) Slower.   **ii)** Faster.

KEY POINTS

The students should be able to describe the process of refraction and the speed changes that take place. They could express the key points in a short poem or rap.

P3 2.4   Lenses

LEARNING OBJECTIVES

Students should learn:

- That a converging lens is a lens that refracts parallel light rays together so that they are brought together at a focal point.
- That a converging lens can be used in a magnifying glass.
- That a diverging lens refracts parallel light rays apart so that they seem to have come from a focal point.
- That diverging lenses can be used in spectacles to correct short-sightedness.

LEARNING OUTCOMES

Most students should be able to:

- Draw a diagram showing the ray paths for converging and diverging lenses.
- Describe the images formed by converging and diverging lenses.

Some students should also be able to:

- Calculate the magnification of the image formed by a lens

Teaching suggestions

- **Special needs.** Provide a framework for writing up the experiment, including a results table to fill in.
- **Gifted and talented.** Ask: 'What is a strong lens?' There is a system that measures the power of a lens in a unit called a 'dioptre' (D) and the students can find out about the relationship between the focal length and the power. Ask: 'What is the difference between a lens of power +5 D and one of power −5 D?'
- **Learning styles**

  Kinaesthetic: Carrying out practical activities.

  Visual: Observing image formation from lenses.

  Auditory: Discussing results.

  Interpersonal: Collaborating on experiments.

  Intrapersonal: Evaluating results.

SPECIFICATION LINK-UP   Unit: Physics 3.13.4

- *The nature of the image produced by a diverging lens.*
- *The nature of the image produced by a converging lens for an object placed at different distances from the lens.*

Students should use their skills, knowledge and understanding of 'How Science Works':

- *to construct ray diagrams to show the formation of images by diverging lenses and converging lenses.*

Lesson structure

STARTER

Sorted – Give the student a pile of different lenses. Ask them to sort them out and see if they find the converging and diverging lenses and then sort them into order of power. (5–10 minutes)

Anagrams – Can the students solve the anagrams for the key words? 'nels, grencginov, catnofreri, ggdniiver, asgsl' [lens, converging, refraction, diverging, glass]. (5 minutes)

MAIN

- It is best to avoid the terms 'concave' and 'convex' when describing lenses. These can be misleading when there are two refracting surfaces to a lens. The terms 'converging' and 'diverging' are more appropriate to describe the overall function of the lens.
- It is not always necessary to draw the shapes of the lenses on diagrams. A simple vertical line marked converging or diverging is perfectly suitable and much easier to draw.
- Even though the refraction takes place at the front and back surface of a lens, only one refraction should be drawn, i.e. the overall refraction at the centre of the lens.
- Using the experiment, the students should be able to find out about the two situations described in the textbook. They may also find out about what happens when the object is placed at the focal length of the lens.
- Make sure that the students are becoming comfortable with drawing ray diagrams and are able to use them to find the position and properties of the image. They will have more practice of this during the next topic.
- With a higher attaining group, you should consider the expanded version of the converging lens experiment; it can require a great deal of skill.
- Let the students use a real magnifying glass to check its properties. They should also see the physical differences between a powerful and weak converging lens.

PLENARIES

Finding the focal length – Can the students design a simple experiment to find the focal length of a converging lens? What about a diverging lens? (5–10 minutes)

Spot the lens – Show the students a range of ray diagrams of optical instruments (eye, microscope, telescope, camera, projector, etc.) and ask them to spot the lenses. Can they say what type each lens is? (5–10 minutes)

Practical support

Investigating the converging lens

This experiment works best with an optical bench of some kind but a ruler can be used if necessary.

Equipment and materials required

For each group: a 10 cm converging lens, metre ruler, illuminated object, screen.

Details

As before, use an object of measured size such as a hole in a card with wires to help focusing. A screen of card with graph paper can be used to focus the image on and measure its dimensions. The object is placed at one end of the ruler and is lit from behind. The lens is placed at a measured distance from the object and then the screen is moved until the image is in focus. The procedure is repeated by moving either the lens or object to change the distance between them. In this way, the students can see the effect of the object distance and the focal length of the lens on the magnification.

Magnification of a converging lens – extension

By expanding the converging lens experiment, the students can find the relationship between the image distance, magnification and focal length of the lens in detail. This is a challenging experiment, but one that yields excellent results.

Equipment and materials required

For each group: a 10 cm converging lens, metre rule, illuminated object, screen.

Details

The students will have to find the magnification of the image for a range of image distances for a particular lens. This relationship should be given by $m = (v/f)-1$, where m is the magnification, f the focal length of the lens and v the image distance. Plotting a graph of magnification (y-axis) against image distance (x-axis) should produce a straight line with $1/f$ as the gradient.

ACTIVITY & EXTENSION

- **Magnification of a converging lens** – see 'Practical support'.

SCIENCE @ WORK

The lens in the human eye is not the only refracting surface. In fact the lens is less optically powerful than the cornea, but the lens can change shape and this changes its power. By adjusting the shape of the lens we can focus at a wide range of distances, unlike a glass lens that has a fixed focal length.

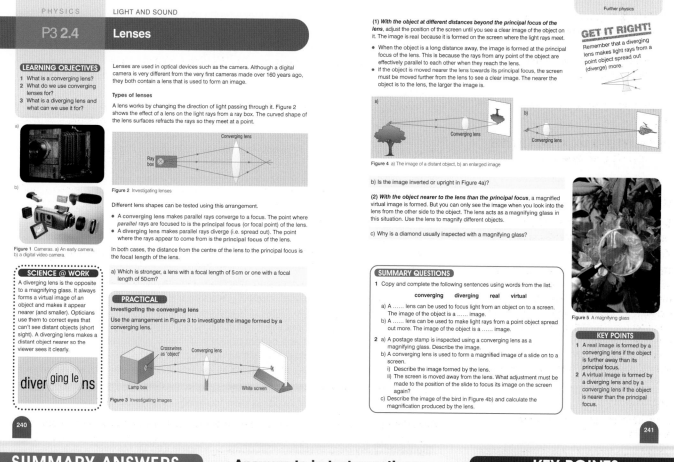

PHYSICS — LIGHT AND SOUND

P3 2.4 — Lenses

LEARNING OBJECTIVES

1 What is a converging lens?
2 What do we use converging lenses for?
3 What is a diverging lens and what can we use it for?

Lenses are used in optical devices such as the camera. Although a digital camera is very different from the very first cameras made over 160 years ago, they both contain a lens that is used to form an image.

Types of lenses

A lens works by changing the direction of light passing through it. Figure 2 shows the effect of a lens on the light rays from a ray box. The curved shape of the lens surfaces refracts the rays so they meet at a point.

Figure 2 Investigating lenses

Different lens shapes can be tested using this arrangement.

- A converging lens makes parallel rays converge to a focus. The point where *parallel* rays are focused to is the principal focus (or focal point) of the lens.
- A diverging lens makes parallel rays diverge (i.e. spread out). The point where the rays appear to come from is the principal focus of the lens.

In both cases, the distance from the centre of the lens to the principal focus is the focal length of the lens.

a) Which is stronger, a lens with a focal length of 5 cm or one with a focal length of 50 cm?

Figure 1 Cameras. a) An early camera, b) a digital video camera.

SCIENCE @ WORK

A diverging lens is the opposite to a magnifying glass. It always forms a virtual image of an object and makes it appear nearer (and smaller). Opticians use them to correct eyes that can't see distant objects (short sight). A diverging lens makes a distant object nearer so the viewer sees it clearly.

diverging lens

PRACTICAL

Investigating the converging lens

Use the arrangement in Figure 3 to investigate the image formed by a converging lens.

Figure 3 Investigating images

(1) **With the object at different distances beyond the principal focus of the lens**, adjust the position of the screen until you see a clear image of the object on it. The image is real because it is formed on the screen where the light rays meet.

- When the object is a long distance away, the image is formed at the principal focus of the lens. This is because the rays from any point of the object are effectively parallel to each other when they reach the lens.
- If the object is moved nearer the lens towards its principal focus, the screen must be moved further from the lens to see a clear image. The nearer the object is to the lens, the larger the image is.

Figure 4 a) The image of a distant object, b) an enlarged image

b) Is the image inverted or upright in Figure 4a)?

(2) **With the object nearer to the lens than the principal focus**, a magnified virtual image is formed. But you can only see the image when you look into the lens from the other side to the object. The lens acts as a magnifying glass in this situation. Use the lens to magnify different objects.

c) Why is a diamond usually inspected with a magnifying glass?

GET IT RIGHT!

Remember that a diverging lens makes light rays from a point object spread out (diverge) more.

SUMMARY QUESTIONS

1 Copy and complete the following sentences using words from the list.

converging   diverging   real   virtual

a) A ...... lens can be used to focus light from an object on to a screen. The image of the object is a ...... image.
b) A ...... lens can be used to make light rays from a point object spread out more. The image of the object is a ...... image.

2 a) A postage stamp is inspected using a converging lens as a magnifying glass. Describe the image.
b) A converging lens is used to form a magnified image of a slide on to a screen.
   i) Describe the image formed by the lens.
   ii) The screen is moved away from the lens. What adjustment must be made to the position of the slide to focus its image on the screen again?
c) Describe the image of the bird in Figure 4b) and calculate the magnification produced by the lens.

Figure 5 A magnifying glass

KEY POINTS

1 A real image is formed by a converging lens if the object is further away than its principal focus.
2 A virtual image is formed by a diverging lens and by a converging lens if the object is nearer than the principal focus.

240 / 241

SUMMARY ANSWERS

1 a) Converging, real.
   b) Diverging, virtual.

2 a) Upright, enlarged and virtual.
   b) i) Inverted, magnified and real.
      ii) The slide must be moved towards the screen.
   c) The image is real, inverted and enlarged. Magnification = 3.

Answers to in-text questions

a) A 5 cm focal length lens.
b) Inverted.
c) To make it appear much larger so any flaws can be seen.

KEY POINTS

The students need to be able to explain the difference between a real and virtual image. They could mix the words up in each definition they come up with, and swap with their partner to sort out the correct definitions from the jumbled words.

P3 2.5 Using lenses

LEARNING OBJECTIVES

Students should learn:

- That a converging lens is used in a magnifying glass and camera.
- That a camera forms a real, inverted and diminished image focussed on the film.
- That a magnifying glass forms a virtual, erect and magnified image.

LEARNING OUTCOMES

Most students should be able to:

- Draw a ray diagram showing the operation of a camera.
- Describe the image formed when a convex lens is used as a camera or as a magnifying glass.

Some students should also be able to:

- Draw a ray diagram to show how a convex lens is used as a magnifying glass.

Teaching suggestions

- **Special needs.** Construction of ray diagrams is difficult. Provide the students with partially completed diagrams with one or two of the construction rays already drawn.
- **Gifted and talented.** Lenses are often used in combinations. The students could find out about the different devices that use these combinations, such as microscopes and telescopes.
- **Learning styles**

  Kinaesthetic: Manipulating lenses to generate images.

  Visual: Following sequences when drawing ray diagrams.

  Auditory: Listening to descriptions of how optical devices work.
- **ICT link-up.** You can use software to quickly assemble combinations of lenses. This is a good way to demonstrate the effects to the whole class using a projector.
  See www.crocodileclips.com.
- **Teaching assistant.** The teaching assistant can show the internal workings of a camera to groups in turn.

SPECIFICATION LINK-UP   Unit: Physics 3.13.4

- *The use of a converging lens in a camera to produce an image of an object on a detecting device (e.g. film).*

Students should use their skills, knowledge and understanding of 'How Science Works':

- *to construct ray diagrams to show the formation of images by diverging lenses and converging lenses*
- *to explain the use of a converging lens as a magnifying glass and in a camera*
- *to calculate the magnification produced by a lens or mirror using the formula:*

$$\text{magnification} = \text{image height/object height}$$

Lesson structure

STARTER

Lens list – The students list all the devices that they can think of that contain lenses. (5 minutes)

Key word hunt – Students to find all of the key words in the topic and put them in reverse order. (5–10 minutes)

Mystery objects – Show close up photographs of a range of mystery objects and see who can get the most right. (5 minutes)

MAIN

- During this topic the students will really need to master their ray diagrams to understand how the images are formed.
- Drawing these ray diagrams for lenses takes time to get right. The students will need to draw a few diagrams before they get the hang of it. They should remember and use the ideas from the previous lesson.
- Go through the stages of drawing a scale ray diagram step by step. You might want to give the students an ordered checklist like the one 'Activity and extension ideas'.
- You will find some students drawing diagrams to an inappropriate scale and finding that their image is off the page; they will get better with practice.
- In reality drawing any two of the three rays will show the position of the image, but drawing the third is always a good check to see if the other two are right.
- If you have an old SLR camera you can take it apart to show how it operates. In particular, you should show how the lens is moved further away from the film to bring the image into focus on it.
- You can demonstrate the focusing effect of a camera using an optical bench and a screen as film (see 'Practical support'). You can also use this to show that a virtual image is formed when the object is too close to the lens.
- If you have a digital camera with auto focus, you should be able to show the lens movement by pointing it at a distant object and then a very close one. Hopefully the lens will move in and out with a reassuring 'shzzzzzt'.
- You can show a diverging lens, but the students will not be able to form a real image with it. The students could come up with a modified checklist for drawing the ray diagram themselves.

PLENARIES

'Elementary my dear Watson' – Students to imagine that Mr Maxwell's apartment seems to have caught fire during a particularly sunny day. Ask: 'What could the round glass paperweight found on his window ledge have to do with it?' (5–10 minutes)

Optical crossword – The students can learn the key words from light and optics by answering questions and filling in a crossword. (10 minutes)

Eagle eyes – Using a conventional projector (the resolution on a digital one is not good enough) show an eye test and see how many lines down some volunteers can go. (5 minutes)

Drawing converging lens ray diagrams

This is the best order to draw the diagrams:

- Use a pencil and ruler. No pens.
- Draw the optical axis, a horizontal line across the page.
- Draw the lens as a big vertical line, not a lens shape.
- Draw on the object as a vertical arrow.
- Draw the first construction ray from the top of the object to the lens parallel to the optical axis. At the lens it refracts through to the focal point and keeps going.
- Draw the second construction ray from the top of the object straight through the centre of the lens. It does not refract and it keeps on going, even after it meets the first ray.
- Draw the third ray from the top of the object through the *nearest* focal point and up to the lens. The ray refracts so that it is parallel to the optical axis.
- The image is formed between the point where the three lines cross and the optical axis, so draw it on.

Answers to in-text questions

a) i)

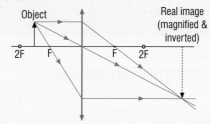

Object — Real image (magnified & inverted) — 2F, F, F, 2F

ii) A projector.

b) Towards the object.

c) To inspect objects in detail.

d) The image is always smaller than the object.

DID YOU KNOW?

There are plenty of broken digital cameras about. Extract the CCD and the students can look at the pixel array using a magnifying glass, 'killing two birds with one stone'.

Practical support

Operation of a camera

Use the same equipment as the last lesson to show how the lens has to be moved in a camera to get a focussed image.

Equipment and materials required

For each group: a converging lens (~10 cm), metre ruler, illuminated object, screen.

Details

Set the screen in a fixed position at the end of the ruler or optical bench. Position the lens 10 cm in front of it, then place an illuminated object somewhere along the bench. By moving the lens the image can be brought into focus on the screen. If the object is at a different position, then you will have to move the lens to bring it into focus again. If the object is placed within the focal length of the lens, then you should not be able to get a real image.

P3 2.5 — Using lenses

LEARNING OBJECTIVES

1 What type of lens is used in a camera and in a magnifying glass?
2 What type of image is formed in a camera and in a magnifying glass?

The position and nature of the image formed by a lens depends on:

- the focal length of the lens, and
- the distance from the object to the lens.

If we know the focal length and the object distance, we can find the position and nature of the image by drawing a ray diagram.

Formation of a real image by a converging lens

The object must be beyond the principal focus, F, of the lens, as shown in Figure 1. The image is formed on the other side of the lens to the object.

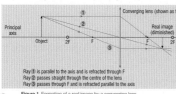

Ray ① is parallel to the axis and is refracted through F
Ray ② passes straight through the centre of the lens
Ray ③ passes through F and is refracted parallel to the axis

Figure 1 Formation of a real image by a converging lens

GET IT RIGHT!

Make sure your ray diagrams are neat and that you put arrows on the rays.

DID YOU KNOW?

Each pixel in a digital camera is a tiny light sensor that produces a voltage when light is directed at it. The voltage depends on the light intensity. Different pixels are used for red, green and blue light. The picture can be seen on a small screen attached to the camera. When a picture is taken, the voltage of every pixel is recorded. The picture can later be recreated on the screen or downloaded to a computer.

The diagram shows that:

- three key 'construction' rays from a single point of the object are used to locate the image,
- the image is real, inverted and smaller than the object.

Notice that:

1 **ray 1** is refracted through F, the principal focus of the lens, because it is parallel to the lens axis before the lens,

2 **ray 2** passes through the lens at its centre without change of direction; this is because the lens surfaces are parallel to each other at the axis,

3 **ray 3** passes through F, the principal focus of the lens, before the lens so it is refracted by the lens parallel to the axis.

The image is smaller than the object because the object distance is greater than twice the focal length (f) of the lens. This is how a **camera** is used.

a) i) Draw a ray diagram to show that a real, inverted and magnified image is produced if the object is between f and 2f from the lens.
ii) What optical device projects a magnified image on to a screen?

The camera

In a camera, a converging lens is used to produce a real image of an object on a film (or on an array of 'pixels' in the case of a digital camera). The position of the lens is adjusted to focus the image on the film, according to how far away the object is.

- For a distant object, the distance from the lens to the film must be equal to the focal length of the lens.
- The nearer an object is to the lens, the greater the distance from the lens to the film.

b) If an object moves closer to the camera, does the lens of a camera need to be moved towards or away from the object?

Formation of a virtual image by a converging lens

The object must be between the lens and its principal focus, as shown in Figure 3. The image is formed on the same side of the lens as the object.

The diagram shows that the image is virtual, upright and larger than the object.

The image can only be seen by looking at it through the lens. This is how a magnifying glass works.

c) Why did Sherlock Holmes always carry a magnifying glass?

Formation of a virtual image by a diverging lens

The image formed by a diverging lens is always virtual, upright and smaller than the object. Figure 4 shows why.

d) Why is a diverging lens no use as a magnifying glass?

SUMMARY QUESTIONS

1 a) Copy and complete the ray diagram to show how a converging lens in a camera forms an image of an object.

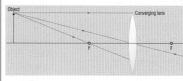

Object — Converging lens — F, F

b) State whether the image is i) real or virtual, ii) magnified or diminished, iii) upright or inverted.

2 a) Draw a ray diagram to show how a converging lens is used as a magnifying glass.
b) State whether the image is i) real or virtual, ii) magnified or diminished, iii) upright or inverted.

GET IT RIGHT!

Make sure you know the basic design for a camera.

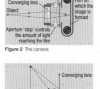

Figure 2 The camera

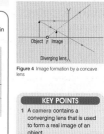

Figure 3 Formation of a virtual image by a converging lens

Figure 4 Image formation by a concave lens

KEY POINTS

1 A camera contains a converging lens that is used to form a real image of an object.
2 A magnifying glass is a converging lens that is used to form a virtual image of an object.

SUMMARY ANSWERS

1 a)

Object — Converging lens — F, F

b) i) Real. **ii)** Diminished. **iii)** Inverted.

2 a)

Converging lens — Image — F, Object, F

b) i) Virtual. **ii)** Magnified. **iii)** Upright.

KEY POINTS

The students need to be able to draw ray diagrams for a camera and magnifying glass. They could draw these on either side of a revision card.

P3 2.6   Sound

LEARNING OBJECTIVES

Students should learn:

- That the human ear can detect a range of frequencies from 20 Hz to 20 000 Hz.
- That sound is a mechanical wave that requires a medium to travel through and so cannot pass through empty space.
- About the difference between a sound wave and a light wave.

LEARNING OUTCOMES

Most students should be able to:

- State the range of hearing for a typical human.
- Describe the properties of a sound wave, including its longitudinal nature.
- Describe the behaviour of a sound wave, including reflection and refraction.

Some students should also be able to:

- Explain why mechanical vibrations produce sound waves.

Teaching suggestions

- **Special needs.**
  - The students may need extra assistance with the oscilloscopes.
  - Squared paper help a lot with sketching waveforms.
- **Gifted and talented.** Ask: 'Is there any relationship between the physical size of an animal's ear and the range of frequencies it can detect?' The students will need to find information from textbooks or, more likely, the Internet.
- **Learning styles**
  Kinaesthetic: Carrying out experiments.
  Visual: Observing oscilloscope traces.
  Auditory: Listening to sounds of varying frequency.
  Intrapersonal: Appreciating the wave motion of sound.
- **Homework.** The students could look into how the ear operates and why the range of frequencies we hear is limited.
- **ICT link-up.** Yet again, there are some fine simulations of the behaviour of sound waves showing particle behaviour. These are very handy when discussing what is happening to these invisible particles.
  See www.sunflowerlearning.com.

SPECIFICATION LINK-UP   Unit: Physics 3.13.5

- *Sound is caused by mechanical vibrations and travels as a wave.*
- *Sounds in the range 20–20 000 Hz can be detected by the human ear.*
- *Sound cannot travel through a vacuum.*
- *The pitch of a note increases as the frequency increases.*
- *The loudness of a note increases as the amplitude of the wave increases.*
- *Sound waves can be reflected and refracted.*

Students should use their skills, knowledge and understanding of 'How Science Works':

- *to compare the amplitudes and frequencies of sounds from diagrams of oscilloscope traces.*

Lesson structure

STARTER

Good vibrations – How do different instruments produce sound waves? The students should describe what is going on for five different ways of producing a sound. (5–10 minutes)

Sound facts – Give the students a set of 'facts' about sound and let them use traffic light cards to indicate if they agree (green), don't know (amber) or disagree (red). (5–10 minutes)

Sound storm – The students should draw a spider diagram/mind map to show their prior understanding of sound. (5 minutes)

MAIN

- The contents of this lesson are mostly revision for the students, so you can spend a bit of time clearing up any misconceptions.
- The initial practical/demonstration should remind the students of the basics of sound, and allow you to describe the operation of a signal generator and loudspeaker in more detail.
- If possible, use a bell jar to show that particles are required for sound waves to travel.
- Remind the students of the nature of mechanical longitudinal waves using a slinky. They will have to be able to describe what is happening to the particles in air.
- Students should know that sound can be reflected and this is simply called an 'echo'. Go through this again when you use the slinky.
- The behaviour of particles in air is actually more complex than the students might think. The particles actually *are* moving around from place to place quite rapidly but in a random way. A sound wave is a vibration super-imposed on top of this random motion. Some simulations will show this, but others will show the particles vibrating around fixed positions for simplicity. You can discuss the limitations of the models.
- It can be worth discussing sound absorbing materials and the lengths sound recording studios will go to prevent reflections.
- You can investigate the reflection of sound waves in more detail using 'Reflecting sound waves' from 'Practical support', if you feel it is appropriate.
- Refraction of sound is very hard to show, but the students should be aware that things like distant traffic sounds are louder at night.
- In the next lesson the students will need some musical instruments, so ask them to bring some in.

- **Teaching assistant.** If you only have limited equipment, your teaching assistant can look after the groups operating the oscilloscopes while you move on with other tasks.

Practical support

Investigating sound waves

This makes a better demonstration than a student practical, but if you have lots of equipment it can be useful to get the students used to it for the next topic.

Equipment and materials required
Signal generator and loudspeaker.

Details
At the start of the investigation, you will need to show the students how to operate the signal generator and how it should be connected to the loudspeaker. Some generators have several outputs, so make sure that the students are using the right one if they are having a go. To see the vibrations of the loudspeaker clearly, they can drop some discs from a hole punch onto it – these will bounce around. To test the hearing limits of the students, it is better to get them to raise their hands at the start and put them down when they can no longer hear the noise. Some students can still hear the high frequency sounds when you secretly turn the power off, truly amazing!

Investigating longitudinal waves

Equipment and materials required
A slinky and some sticky tape.

Details
To demonstrate longitudinal waves, stretch the spring out slightly and then move one end of the slinky in and out while keeping the other end still. The emphasis should be on the vibrations of the particles without them actually progressing. Sticking a bit of paper on a point on the spring can show this more effectively.

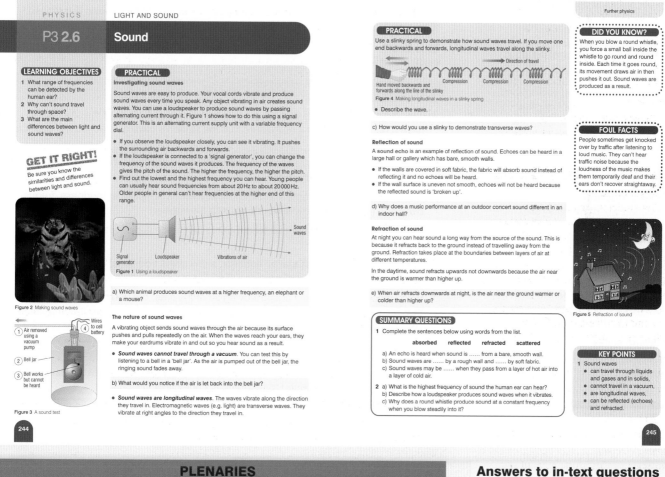

Figure 2 Making sound waves

Figure 3 A sound test

Figure 1 Using a loudspeaker

Figure 4 Making longitudinal waves in a slinky spring

Figure 5 Refraction of sound

PLENARIES

Oscilloscope guide – Can the students write their own guide to using an oscilloscope so that they can always find the trace? (5–10 minutes)

Let's hear it then – The students need to design a simple experiment that will show that sound travels faster in solid materials than it does in air. (5–10 minutes)

Speed of sound – Can the students come up with a method for measuring the speed of sound in air? What about water or even a solid like iron? (10 minutes)

Answers to in-text questions

a) A mouse.

b) The sound becomes audible again.

c) Wave one end from side to side.

d) There are no reflections, so each note dies away more quickly outdoors.

e) Colder.

P3 2.7

Musical sounds

Students should learn:

- That the pitch of a sound increases as the frequency increases.
- That the loudness of the sound increases as the amplitude increases.
- That the quality of a sound depends on the instrument that produces it.

Most students should be able to:

- Describe the properties of a sound wave in terms of frequency and amplitude.
- Describe the differences between a pure note and one produced by a musical instrument.

Some students should also be able to:

- Explain how sound is produced by different types of musical instruments and compare the sound they produce.

Teaching suggestions

- **Gifted and talented.** Ask: 'What happened when two notes are played together?' The students should look at the waveform generated when two tuning forks are used at the same time. The effect can be generated by putting two loudspeakers playing at slightly different frequencies next to each other too. This beat phenomenon is very important in music.

- **Learning styles**

  Kinaesthetic: Carrying out practical activities.

  Visual: Making observations about the behaviour of musical instruments.

  Auditory: Listening to a range of instruments.

  Interpersonal: Reporting on the relationship between the sound of an instrument and the waveform it produces.

- **ICT link-up.** If you haven't a range of instruments to show, then you could use a synthesiser or software like GarageBand (for Macintosh) to produce the sounds, or ask the music or ICT department if they can supply some synthesiser software. Use Animation P3 2.7 'Musical sounds' from the GCSE Physics CD ROM.

SPECIFICATION LINK-UP   Unit: Physics 3.13.5

- *The pitch of a note increases as the frequency increases.*
- *The loudness of a note increases as the amplitude of the wave increases.*
- *The quality of a note depends upon the waveform.*

Students should use their skills, knowledge and understanding of 'How Science Works':

- *to compare the amplitudes and frequencies of sounds from diagrams of oscilloscope traces.*

Lesson structure

STARTER

The intro round – Using a personal music player (through headphones on low volume), a student listens to the introductions of some songs and has to reproduce them using only their vocal skills. (5–10 minutes)

It's music to my ears – Play some short extracts of music, from classical to punk and ask the students to list the instruments they can hear. Ask: 'Which music is the best?' (5 minutes)

Tone deaf? – Play the students some pure notes and see if they can identify the notes. (5–10 minutes)

MAIN

- The investigation is quite extensive and it may be difficult for all of the students to have a go. At the end of it make sure that the students have all reached the correct conclusions.

- If you want the students to sketch out some of the waveforms, then give them some squared paper to help them out.

- Make sure that the students are using the key words (amplitude, loudness, frequency, pitch and period) correctly when describing the waves.

- You will need to make sure that the students can relate period and frequency correctly.

- After consolidating the students' findings, show some additional musical instruments to show how complex waveforms can quickly become.

- Voice recognition systems are improving all of the time, but you may want to show the limitations of the current technology. The operating system of your computer, or some of your applications, will probably have voice recognition built in so give it a try and see how it does. Try to confuse it with sentences like: 'Which witches wear our weather predicting watches?'

- Resonance is an important phenomena; showing the structure of instruments will show how they are designed to resonate at certain key frequencies.

- You should be able to use a signal generator and loudspeaker to make an acoustic guitar resonate. Play about with the frequency until the guitar starts humming.

PLENARIES

Compare traces – The students must compare three oscilloscope traces in terms of frequency, amplitude and quality of the note. (5–10 minutes)

Perfect pitch – Which of the students can produce the purest note according to the oscilloscope? Try whistling compared to singing. (5–10 minutes)

Name that tune – Can the students identify songs from their introductions? Play 10 five-second clips and see who gets the most. (5–10 minutes)

Practical support

Investigating different sounds

You may well not have enough equipment to let the students carry this out as a full class practical, but it is worth considering letting them use it in small groups one at a time so that they can appreciate the techniques involved.

Equipment and materials required

For each group: signal generator, loudspeaker, microphone, oscilloscope, and some musical instruments.

Details

The main problems you may have are the background noise in the classroom and lack of experience with the oscilloscope. A teaching assistant or helpful technician may help with the latter, but the background noise will always distort the waveforms from instruments in a class practical; you may want to show what the waves should look like with a demonstration at the end of the practical. Most signal generators have two outputs, so you can connect one to the loudspeaker and one to the CRO. This removes the background noise completely. Make sure that you mark the cm/s dial so that the students know which one to adjust. They should not need to alter any other settings to display the wave. Musically inclined students should be able to use a range of instruments and compare the waveform with the pure wave of the tuning forks.

Answers to in-text questions

a) An ambulance, a police vehicle, a fire engine, an ice cream van.

b) The waves are not as tall.

c) The waves would be smaller in height and stretched out more.

ACTIVITY & EXTENSION IDEAS

- **Analysing sounds with computers** – The students could look into the waveforms involved in speech using standard computer systems. There is specialist software for speech analysis available, but you will probably find that the software that comes with the operating system is good enough to show basic patterns. The software can also be used to manipulate the voice: speeding it up and slowing it down and manipulating the pitch.
- **Resonance** – If you have a resonance box with strings mounted on to it, you can show the effect of changing the tension in the string or changing its length. If not, then one of your guitar-owning students can help out.
- **Scientific instruments** – Why not make some pan pipes with test tubes? Just fill a set up with differing amounts of water and give them a play.

PHYSICS   LIGHT AND SOUND

P3 2.7 Musical sounds

LEARNING OBJECTIVES

1 What happens to the pitch of a note as the frequency decreases?
2 What happens to the loudness of a note as the amplitude increases?
3 Why do notes from different musical instruments have different waveforms?

What type of music do you like? Whatever your taste in music is, when you listen to it you usually hear sounds that are produced by instruments designed for the purpose. Even your voice is produced by a biological organ that has the job of producing sound.

- Musical notes are easy to listen to because they are rhythmic. The sound waves change smoothly and the wave pattern repeats itself regularly.
- Noise consists of sound waves that vary randomly in frequency without any pattern.

a) Name four different vehicles that produce sound through a loudspeaker or a siren?

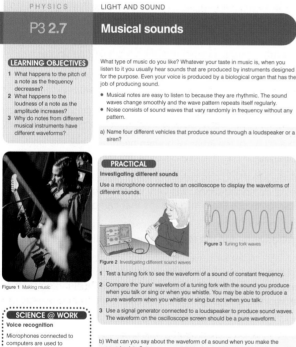

Figure 1 Making music

SCIENCE @ WORK

Voice recognition

Microphones connected to computers are used to recognise individual voices. The computer is programmed to measure and recognise the frequencies in a voice waveform. However, it sometimes fails to recognise a voice if the speaker has a cold.

PRACTICAL

Investigating different sounds

Use a microphone connected to an oscilloscope to display the waveforms of different sounds.

Figure 2 Investigating different sound waves

Figure 3 Tuning fork waves

1 Test a tuning fork to see the waveform of a sound of constant frequency.

2 Compare the 'pure' waveform of a tuning fork with the sound you produce when you talk or sing or when you whistle. You may be able to produce a pure waveform when you whistle or sing but not when you talk.

3 Use a signal generator connected to a loudspeaker to produce sound waves. The waveform on the oscilloscope screen should be a pure waveform.

b) What can you say about the waveform of a sound when you make the sound quieter?

Your investigations should show you that:

- **increasing the loudness of a sound** makes the waves on the screen taller. This is because the **amplitude** of the sound waves (the maximum disturbance) is bigger the louder the sound is,
- **increasing the frequency of a sound** (the number of waves per second) increases its **pitch**. This makes more waves appear on the screen.

Figure 4 shows the waveforms for different sounds from the loudspeaker:

A) Loud and high-pitched

B) Loud and low-pitched

C) Quiet and high-pitched (higher pitch than A)

Figure 4 Investigating sounds

c) How would the waveform change if the loudness and the pitch are both reduced?

Musical instruments

When you play a musical instrument, you create sound waves by making the instrument and the air inside it vibrate. Each new cycle of vibrations makes the vibrations stronger at certain frequencies. We say the instrument resonates at these frequencies. Because the instrument and the air inside it vibrate strongly at these frequencies when it is played, we hear characteristic notes of sound from the instrument.

- A wind instrument such as a flute is designed so that the air inside resonates when it is played. You can make the air in an empty bottle resonate by blowing across the top gently.
- A string instrument such as a guitar produces sound when the strings vibrate. The vibrating strings make the surfaces of the instrument vibrate and produce sound waves in the air.
- A percussion instrument such as a drum vibrates and produces sound waves when it is struck.

SUMMARY QUESTIONS

1 A microphone and an oscilloscope are used to investigate sound from a loudspeaker connected to a signal generator. What change would you expect to see on the oscilloscope screen if the sound is
   a) made louder at the same frequency,
   b) made lower in frequency at the same loudness?

2 a) How does the note produced by a guitar string change if the string is
      i) shortened, ii) tightened?
   b) Compare the sound produced by a violin with the sound produced by a drum.

NEXT TIME YOU...
... play a musical instrument, think about how it produces sound.

GET IT RIGHT!
Be sure you know the meaning of the terms frequency and amplitude

PRACTICAL

4 Test a musical instrument. Playing a flute produces a waveform that changes smoothly, as in Figure 5. However, unlike a tuning fork or signal generator waveform, the waveform is a mixture of frequencies rather than a single frequency.

Figure 5 Flute wave pattern

KEY POINTS

1 The loudness of a note depends on the amplitude of the sound waves.
2 The pitch of a note depends on the frequency of the sound waves.

SUMMARY ANSWERS

1 a) The waves would be taller but would have the same spacing.

  b) The waves would be more stretched out but would have the same height.

2 a) i) The note has a higher pitch (frequency).
     ii) The note has a higher pitch (frequency).

  b) The sound of a violin (played correctly) lasts as long as the violin bow is in contact with a string. The sound of a drum dies away after the drum skin has been struck. A drum note is less rhythmical than a violin note.

KEY POINTS

The students need to be able to give definitions of the key words and to be able to describe a trace on an oscilloscope. Definitions could be presented on a wavy line.

P3 2.8   Ultrasound

Students should learn:

- That ultrasound is sound with a frequency above 20 000 Hz and cannot be heard by humans.
- That ultrasonic waves can be used to clean materials and to detect flaws in their construction.
- That ultrasonic waves are reflected by the different layers of tissue and fluid in a body and so can be used to make measurements or produce images of internal organs.

Most students should be able to:

- Compare ultrasound to audible sound waves.
- Describe a range of uses of ultrasound, including cleaning and detecting cracks.

Some students should also be able to:

- Explain how ultrasound can be used for medical scanning and the advantages of ultrasound over X-ray techniques.
- Work out the distance between interfaces from diagrams of oscilloscope traces.

Teaching suggestions

- **Special needs.** Students can be given a cloze activity to summarise the uses of ultrasound.
- **Gifted and talented.** There is plenty more to find out about ultrasound scans. The students could look into the different types of scans that are used (A and B scans) and how the current three-dimensional imaging is progressing.
- **Learning styles**
  Kinaesthetic: Testing ultrasound practical task.
  Visual: Obtaining information about the behaviour of ultrasound.
  Auditory: Explaining the difference between ultrasound and audible sound.
  Interpersonal: Discussing the uses of ultrasound.
  Intrapersonal: Making deductions about the behaviour of ultrasound.
- **Homework.** Ask: 'What is sound with a frequency lower than 10 Hz called? Can any animals hear it and does it have any uses?'

SPECIFICATION LINK-UP   Unit: Physics 3.13.6

- *Electronic systems can be used to produce ultrasound waves that have a frequency higher than the upper limit of hearing for humans.*
- *Ultrasound waves are partially reflected when they meet a boundary between two different media. The time taken for the reflections to reach a detector is a measure of how far away such a boundary is.*
- *Ultrasound waves can be used in industry for cleaning and quality control.*
- *Ultrasound waves can be used in medicine for pre-natal scanning.*

Students should use their skills, knowledge and understanding of 'How Science Works':

- *to compare the amplitudes and frequencies of ultrasounds from diagrams of oscilloscope traces.*
- *to determine the distance between interfaces in various media from diagrams of oscilloscope traces.* **[HT only]**

Lesson structure

STARTER

Bats! – Ask: 'How do scientists know that bats can hear sounds at a frequency above 20 000 Hz?' Student could design an experiment to prove it. (5–10 minutes)

Speed calculation – Make sure that the students can calculate the speed of an object. Give them a question when a runner runs to a point and back again. (5 minutes)

Mystery scans – Show the students some ultrasound scans of things other than a foetus, and see if they can identify the organs involved. (5–10 minutes)

MAIN

- The lesson can start with a recap of the limits of human hearing to get the students reacquainted with the apparatus.
- Apparatus limitations will decide if you can carry out the ultrasound experiments as a class practical or as a set of demonstrations. It is very worthwhile to let the students do it themselves, if you can organise them into groups that can get on with it while others look into the uses of ultrasound.
- The uses are fairly straightforward, and the students should easily manage to go through them.
- If you would like to liven up the lesson, look at ultrasonic cleaning; try to find some images from the ultrasonic cleaning of teeth (search for 'ultrasonic cleaning teeth'). The pictures you find will impress and disgust the students more than those for cleaning jewellery.
- You probably won't be able to generate ultrasonic reflection from cracks, but the students need to know how to interpret the traces from this technique. In particular they need to see that each boundary will cause a reflection and that the distance the sound wave has travelled is twice the distance to the crack.
- Given speed of sound in the material, the students will have to calculate the distance to the reflecting surface.
- When discussing ultrasonic scanners, the students need to know that certain tissues reflect different amounts of the signal and this is how they can be told apart. The bone reflects best and this shows up as white on the diagrams.
- There are plenty of images, including animated ones, available for this discussion but try to find some images other than the traditional baby scans, e.g. kidney and heart scans, to show that that there is more than one use for the technique.
- The students may have to be reminded what ionisation is and why it is harmful.

Practical support

Testing ultrasound

This experiment shows the properties of ultrasound well, and can be carried out as a demonstration or a full class practical if equipment is available.

Equipment and materials required

For each group: oscilloscope, signal generator, two microphones, loudspeaker and a range of thin materials such as an aluminium plate, plywood, rubber sheets etc.

Details

The first part of the experiment is simply a matter of using the scales on the oscilloscope well. Some may be confused due to the high frequency. To carry out the absorption tests, the students simply put the different materials over the microphone making sure that there aren't any obvious gaps. Reflection can be tested by arranging a material at 45° between the loudspeaker and microphone; there should be a clear reflection from solid surfaces. Partial reflection and partial transmission can be shown by placing a microphone behind the 45° reflector, to measure transmitted amplitude and another in front of it to measure the reflected amplitude.

Teaching suggestions – continued

- **ICT link-up.** The students can use the Internet to find out about the frequency ranges that different species can detect. They could also look into how the species can generate such high frequency noises. Use Animation P3 2.8 'Ultrasonic scanner' from the GCSE Physics CD ROM.

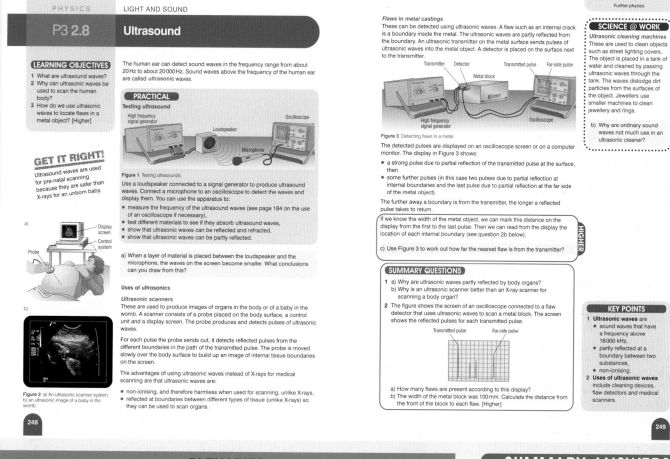

PHYSICS   LIGHT AND SOUND

P3 2.8   Ultrasound

LEARNING OBJECTIVES

1 What are ultrasound waves?
2 Why can ultrasonic waves be used to scan the human body?
3 How do we use ultrasonic waves to locate flaws in a metal object? [Higher]

The human ear can detect sound waves in the frequency range from about 20 Hz to about 20 000 Hz. Sound waves above the frequency of the human ear are called ultrasonic waves.

GET IT RIGHT!

Ultrasound waves are used for pre-natal scanning because they are safer than X-rays for an unborn baby.

PRACTICAL

Testing ultrasound

Figure 1 Testing ultrasounds

Use a loudspeaker connected to a signal generator to produce ultrasound waves. Connect a microphone to an oscilloscope to detect the waves and display them. You can use the apparatus to:

- measure the frequency of the ultrasonic waves (see page 184 on the use of an oscilloscope if necessary),
- test different materials to see if they absorb ultrasound waves,
- show that ultrasonic waves can be reflected and refracted,
- show that ultrasonic waves can be partly reflected.

a) When a layer of material is placed between the loudspeaker and the microphone, the waves on the screen become smaller. What conclusions can you draw from this?

Uses of ultrasonics

Ultrasonic scanners

These are used to produce images of organs in the body or of a baby in the womb. A scanner consists of a probe placed on the body surface, a control unit and a display screen. The probe produces and detects pulses of ultrasonic waves.

For each pulse the probe sends out, it detects reflected pulses from the different boundaries in the path of the transmitted pulse. The probe is moved slowly over the body surface to build up an image of internal tissue boundaries on the screen.

The advantages of using ultrasonic waves instead of X-rays for medical scanning are that ultrasonic waves are:

- non-ionising, and therefore harmless when used for scanning, unlike X-rays,
- reflected at boundaries between different types of tissue (unlike X-rays) so they can be used to scan organs.

Figure 2 a) An ultrasonic scanner system, b) an ultrasonic image of a baby in the womb

248

Flaws in metal castings

These can be detected using ultrasonic waves. A flaw such as an internal crack is a boundary inside the metal. The ultrasonic waves are partly reflected from the boundary. An ultrasonic transmitter on the metal surface sends pulses of ultrasonic waves into the metal object. A detector is placed on the surface next to the transmitter.

Figure 3 Detecting flaws in a metal

The detected pulses are displayed on an oscilloscope screen or on a computer monitor. The display in Figure 3 shows:

- a strong pulse due to partial reflection of the transmitted pulse at the surface, then
- some further pulses (in this case two pulses due to partial reflection at internal boundaries and the last pulse due to partial reflection at the far side of the metal object).

The further away a boundary is from the transmitter, the longer a reflected pulse takes to return.

If we know the width of the metal object, we can mark this distance on the display from the first to the last pulse. Then we can read from the display the location of each internal boundary (see question 2b below).

c) Use Figure 3 to work out how far the nearest flaw is from the transmitter?

SUMMARY QUESTIONS

1 a) Why are ultrasonic waves partly reflected by body organs?
  b) Why is an ultrasonic scanner better than an X-ray scanner for scanning a body organ?

2 The figure shows the screen of an oscilloscope connected to a flaw detector that uses ultrasonic waves to scan a metal block. The screen shows the reflected pulses for each transmitted pulse.

Transmitted pulse   Far-side pulse

a) How many flaws are present according to this display?
b) The width of the metal block was 100 mm. Calculate the distance from the front of the block to each flaw. [Higher]

SCIENCE @ WORK

Ultrasonic cleaning machines

These are used to clean objects such as street lighting covers. The object is placed in a tank of water and cleaned by passing ultrasonic waves through the tank. The waves dislodge dirt particles from the surfaces of the object. Jewellers use smaller machines to clean jewellery and rings.

b) Why are ordinary sound waves not much use in an ultrasonic cleaner?

KEY POINTS

1 **Ultrasonic waves** are
  - sound waves that have a frequency above 18 000 kHz,
  - partly reflected at a boundary between two substances,
  - non-ionising.

2 **Uses of ultrasonic waves** include cleaning devices, flaw detectors and medical scanners.

249

PLENARIES

The pressure's on – Show the students some footage of a submarine being hunted by a destroyer in WWII, then ask the students to draw a diagram to explain how SONAR works. (5–10 minutes)

Comparing light and sound – The students should make a detailed comparison of light and sound waves. (5–10 minutes)

Optical learning – Students could make a revision checklist about light and sound. (10 minutes)

Answers to in-text questions

a) The material absorbs some of the ultrasonic sound from the loudspeaker.

b) They do not vibrate fast enough.

c) 30 mm from the transmitter.

KEY POINTS

Can the students state the properties of ultrasound and the advantages its use has over X-rays in some situations. This could be presented as a series of bullet points on a revision card.

SUMMARY ANSWERS

1 a) The organs have a different density to the surrounding tissue. So ultrasound is reflected at the tissue/organ boundaries.

  b) Ultrasound is not ionising radiation whereas X-rays are. Ionising radiation is harmful to living tissue. Ultrasound is reflected at the boundaries between different types of tissue, whereas X-rays are not.

2 a) Two.
  b) 32–34 mm and 50 mm.   **[HT only]**

PHYSICS   LIGHT AND SOUND

P3 2.9   Light and sound issues

SPECIFICATION LINK-UP

Unit: Physics 3.13.5

This spread can be used to revisit the following substantive content covered in this chapter:

- *Sound is caused by mechanical vibrations and travels as a wave.*
- *Sounds in the range 20–20 000 Hz can be detected by the human ear.*
- *Sound cannot travel through a vacuum.*
- *The pitch of a note increases as the frequency increases.*
- *The loudness of a note increases as the amplitude of the wave increases.*
- *Sound waves can be reflected and refracted.*

Teaching suggestions

Activities

- **Noisy machines** – Most of the British law concerning nuisance noise in an area is actually in the form of local bylaws. The students should visit the local council's web site to see what their policies are and what can be done about disturbances. There is also the Noise Act of 1996. This is a bit technical, but the general ideas are clearly presented and it can be used to introduce the students to the complexities of legislation.

- **Sound absorbers** – Getting the sound just right in concert halls has always been a major problem. The students can look into some of the most recent constructions to see how this has been accomplished. The University of Salford's acoustic department's web site has a lot of information about this topic, including details of physics and computer models. Search their web site at www.acoustics.salford.ac.uk to find out about these. One of the most highly regarded hall recently constructed is the Walt Disney Concert Hall in Los Angeles, about which you can find information from www.musiccentre.org.

- **Lasers** – Many students will think of lasers as high-energy cutting beams that are incredibly dangerous. If you have a low powered laser then it is worth showing, so that the students realise that most laser beams are only harmful to the eyes. You can link the ideas discussed here back to the topic of

Noisy machines

Jack is very upset because the garage next door have put a car wash right next to his house. It's very noisy and it's on most of the time from 9am to 9pm. His doctor can only offer him tranquillisers to calm him down.

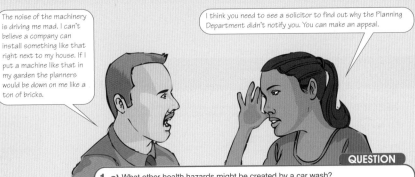

> The noise of the machinery is driving me mad. I can't believe a company can install something like that right next to my house. If I put a machine like that in my garden the planners would be down on me like a ton of bricks.

> I think you need to see a solicitor to find out why the Planning Department didn't notify you. You can make an appeal.

QUESTION

1 a) What other health hazards might be created by a car wash?

b) Discuss what else Jack can do about this problem. Could his councillor do more?

c) Find out what the law is about noisy machinery near houses and write a letter to Jack to advise him what he could do.

Sound absorbers

Music in a concert hall sounds different when the hall is full of people compared with when it is empty. People absorb sound as well as creating it. The designers of a concert hall need to make sure sound does not reflect from side to side in the hall. Soft materials are used to line the walls to stop echoes. However, the sound is deadened if too much material is used.

QUESTION

2 In a test of different absorber materials, a microphone and a loudspeaker were put in a large box at fixed positions. Different materials in turn were used to pad the box. The table shows some measurements using the loudspeaker to produce sound.

Material	Wave height (mm)	
	without material	with material
soft wallpaper	40	25
cushion fabric	40	10
plaster board	40	35
wood panel	40	45

a) Why does the sound need to be the same loudness and frequency each time a test is carried out?

b) What conclusions can you draw from these measurements?

250

analogue and digital communication from the earlier units. The students might like to find out about the history of optical data storage looking at CD, laserdisc, DVD, HD-DVD and blue-ray DVD.

- **Optoelectronics** – The right to privacy is a difficult issue even in schools. Many of the students will have phone cameras that they use every day without thinking of the privacy of the other students in the school. The students can discuss this along with the celebrity debate. If the students are going to look at the factors that would influence them to buy a phone, have a few of the free brochures from the various phone companies that the students can choose from. You could also get the students to work out the cost of buying or renting and using the phone for a full year.

- **Digital radio** – When discussing the pricing difference, have a catalogue of products available. The price difference is actually rapidly decreasing, and within a decade it is likely that the analogue systems will be much more expensive than the digital versions. Compare a cassette tape player with a CD player, and the future becomes obvious. Computers, on the other hand, will always cost more for more powerful versions and the digital divide may still put poorer people at a disadvantage in education and leisure.

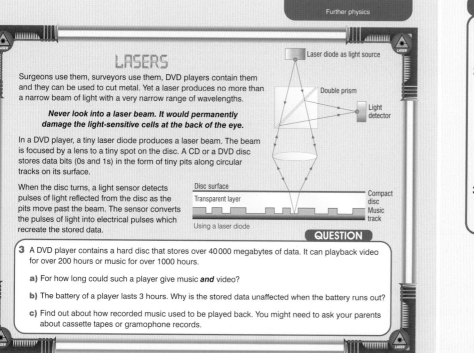

LASERS

Surgeons use them, surveyors use them, DVD players contain them and they can be used to cut metal. Yet a laser produces no more than a narrow beam of light with a very narrow range of wavelengths.

Never look into a laser beam. It would permanently damage the light-sensitive cells at the back of the eye.

In a DVD player, a tiny laser diode produces a laser beam. The beam is focused by a lens to a tiny spot on the disc. A CD or a DVD disc stores data bits (0s and 1s) in the form of tiny pits along circular tracks on its surface.

When the disc turns, a light sensor detects pulses of light reflected from the disc as the pits move past the beam. The sensor converts the pulses of light into electrical pulses which recreate the stored data.

Laser diode as light source

Double prism

Light detector

Disc surface

Transparent layer

Compact disc
Music track

Using a laser diode

QUESTION

3 A DVD player contains a hard disc that stores over 40 000 megabytes of data. It can playback video for over 200 hours or music for over 1000 hours.

a) For how long could such a player give music ***and*** video?

b) The battery of a player lasts 3 hours. Why is the stored data unaffected when the battery runs out?

c) Find out about how recorded music used to be played back. You might need to ask your parents about cassette tapes or gramophone records.

Optoelectronics

Digital cameras have revolutionised photography – no films, no developing, instant transmission and enlargement, repeat pictures, etc., etc. Photography companies have had to adapt or close down. Newspapers and magazines can get pictures from anywhere in the world in an instant.

ACTIVITY

a) Famous people often complain when 'unauthorised' photographs of them appear in newspapers and magazines. Discuss whether or not famous people should have a greater right to privacy than everyone else.

b) The digital camera is an example of an optoelectronic device. A videophone is another example. Cost, weight and portability are important factors in developing and marketing a new device.

Imagine you are going out to buy a digital camera (or a videophone). Discuss which of the factors above or any other factors would be most important to you in choosing which make is best.

251

ANSWERS TO QUESTIONS

1 a) Air pollution due to dust particles, microbes in the air if hose equipment is not clean.

2 a) To make sure the test is a fair comparison of the different materials.

   b) Cushion fabric is the best absorber, soft wallpaper is next and plaster board is next. Wood panel reflects sound waves more than plaster board does.

3 a) About 166 hours.

   b) The data is permanently stored on the disc.

Extension or homework

● **Big telescopes** – Astronomical telescopes have to have very large mirrors or lenses. The students can find out some of the details of the largest telescopes and how they work.

● **Good absorbers** – A simple experiment into the quality of sound absorbers can be carried out using a sound sensor and some insulating materials. Place the sensor inside a tube that is lagged with the various materials, and position a sound source of fixed volume at a fixed distance from the tube. Compare the reading on the sound sensor for each of the materials.

Special needs

If the students are going to research any of the issues then provide them with a list of suitable web sites.

Gifted and talented

These students could look into drawing ray diagrams for reflecting and refracting telescopes. Ask: 'How do these enlarge images and what are the advantages of a reflecting telescope over a refracting one?' There is also plenty of background in the development of telescopes that they can look into.

Learning styles

Kinaesthetic: Researching into the history of digital storage.

Visual: Making a poster about noise reduction or landmine use.

Auditory: Explaining how sound quality can be improved in auditoria.

Interpersonal: Reporting on the development of digital TV and radio.

Intrapersonal: Evaluating the usefulness of a mobile phone.

SUMMARY ANSWERS

1 a) They are the same.

b)

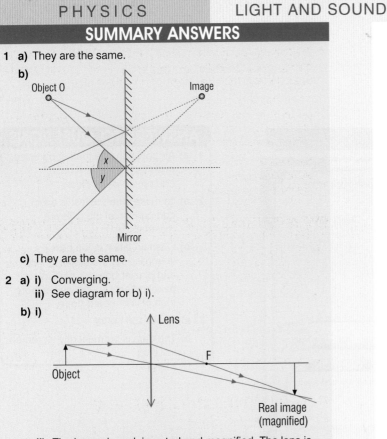

c) They are the same.

2 a) i) Converging.
ii) See diagram for b) i).

b) i)

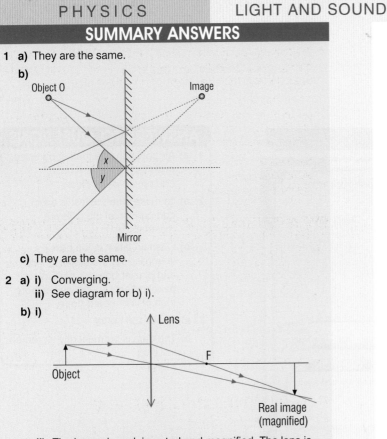

Real image (magnified)

ii) The image is real, inverted and magnified. The lens is being used as a projector lens.

3 a) The sound waves spread out as they travel away from the loudspeaker, so the amplitude becomes smaller and the sound becomes fainter.

b) i) The frequency of the sound waves increases.
ii) The amplitude of the sound waves increases.

4 a) 0.75 mm
b) They could not be detected because they would be absorbed by the tissue.

Summary teaching suggestions

Use the questions to check the details of the students' knowledge. You can do this after the appropriate topic, as homework or as a mini-test at the end of the chapter.

- Question 1 is straightforward and the students should be stating the law of reflection pretty much word for word. The completion of the ray diagrams is more taxing and it is really important that the students are actually using a ruler to draw the diagrams. If they have forgotten the image distance, then remind them using the technique from the first lesson.

- Question 2 would work well on an interactive whiteboard, where a student completes the diagram and then another drags the words to the correct place.

- With question 3, you should be looking for the students talking about the dissipation in energy or at least the spreading out of the energy. They should be giving a complete explanation of the changes in the waveforms, but try to get them to draw the changes in the waveform too. This will make sure that they recognise the differences shown in any diagrams on the examination. If there are any difficulties, then use a card sort game where the students put waves in order of amplitude/loudness and then with the same cards they put the waves in order of frequency/pitch.

SUMMARY QUESTIONS

1 The figure shows an incomplete ray diagram of image formation by a plane mirror.

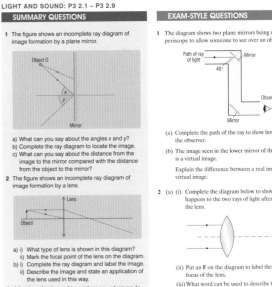

a) What can you say about the angles x and y?
b) Complete the ray diagram to locate the image.
c) What can you say about the distance from the image to the mirror compared with the distance from the object to the mirror?

2 The figure shows an incomplete ray diagram of image formation by a lens.

a) i) What type of lens is shown in this diagram?
   ii) Mark the focal point of the lens on the diagram.
b) i) Complete the ray diagram and label the image.
   ii) Describe the image and state an application of the lens used in this way.

3 A loudspeaker is used to produce sound waves. In terms of the amplitude or frequency of the sound waves,
a) explain why the sound is fainter further away from the loudspeaker,
b) explain what happens to the sound waves if i) the pitch of the sound increases, ii) the sound becomes louder.

4 Ultrasonic waves used for medical scanners have a frequency of 2000 kHz.
a) Calculate the wavelength of these ultrasonic waves in human tissue. (The speed of ultrasound in human tissue is 1500 m/s.)
b) Ultrasonic waves of this frequency in human tissue are not absorbed much. Why is it important in a medical scanner that they are not absorbed?

EXAM-STYLE QUESTIONS

1 The diagram shows two plane mirrors being used in a periscope to allow someone to see over an obstacle.

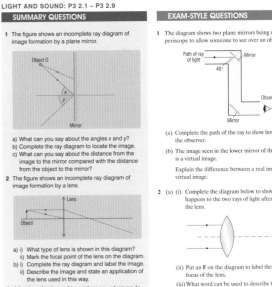

(a) Complete the path of the ray to show how it reaches the observer. (2)

(b) The image seen in the lower mirror of the periscope is a virtual image.
Explain the difference between a real image and a virtual image. (4)

2 (a) (i) Complete the diagram below to show what happens to the two rays of light after they enter the lens. (2)

(ii) Put an F on the diagram to label the principal focus of the lens. (1)
(iii) What word can be used to describe this type of lens? (1)

(b) (i) Complete the diagram below to show what happens to the two rays of light after they enter the lens. (2)

(ii) Put an F on the diagram to label the principal focus of the lens.
(iii) What word can be used to describe this type of lens?

EXAM-STYLE ANSWERS

1 a) Completed periscope diagram. *(2 marks)*

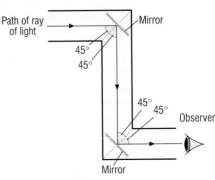

b) Real image: rays actually pass through the image *(1 mark)* so it can be formed on a screen. *(1 mark)*
Virtual image: rays just appear to pass through the image. *(1 mark)*
Image cannot be formed on a screen. *(1 mark)*

2 a) i) Completed ray diagram

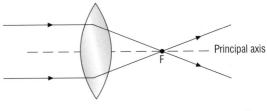

(2 marks)
ii) F correctly labelled. *(1 mark)*
iii) Converging/convex. *(1 mark)*

Further physics

3 This question is about sound. Sound travels as a wave.

(a) Explain why sound waves cannot travel through a vacuum. (2)

(b) What happens to the sound you hear when . . .

(i) the frequency of the sound wave decreases?

(ii) the amplitude of the sound wave increases? (4)

4 An *ultrasound* scan can be used to produce a picture of an unborn baby.

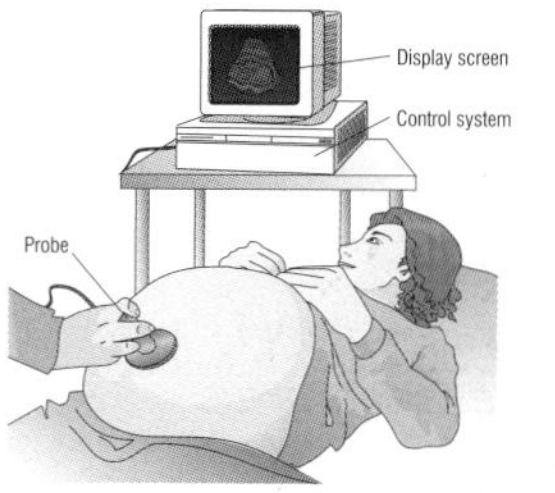
Display screen
Control system
Probe

(a) What is *ultrasound*? (1)

(b) Explain how ultrasound can be used to produce a picture of an unborn baby. (3)

(c) Why are ultrasound waves used for this rather than X-rays? (2)

HOW SCIENCE WORKS

Jenny carried out an investigation into the refractive index of a piece of glass. The refractive index is a measure of how much light is refracted as it enters a transparent substance from air. The refractive index can be calculated by using the following equipment.

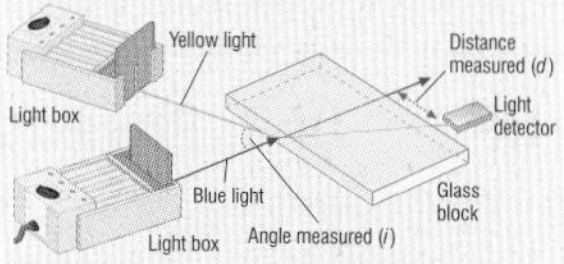
Yellow light
Distance measured (d)
Light box
Light detector
Blue light
Glass block
Light box
Angle measured (i)

The blue light beam passes straight through the block. The narrow beam of yellow light is aimed at the point where the blue light enters. Angle *i* is measured. The light detector is used to measure exactly where the yellow light leaves the glass block and the distance from the blue to the yellow beam is measured, *d*. From these two measurements and the width of the block the refractive index can be calculated.

a) What was the advantage of using a light detector rather than her eye? (1)

b) What sensitivity would you suggest for the ruler measuring the distance *d*? (1)

c) Jenny did the measurement five times at different angles.
They should all produce the same refractive index, because the same block of glass is being used.
Here are Jenny's results.

Angle of yellow to blue light, (i)	40°	42°	44°	46°	48°
Calculated refractive index	1.492	1.548	1.523	1.497	1.543

What was the range of the dependent variable? (1)

d) What was the mean of the dependent variable? (1)

e) Use the table below to decide which type of glass Jenny was using. (1)

Type of glass	Refractive index
Heaviest flint glass	1.89
Heavy flint glass	1.65
Light flint glass	1.575
Crown glass	1.52
Zinc crown glass	1.517

253

b) i) Completed ray diagram

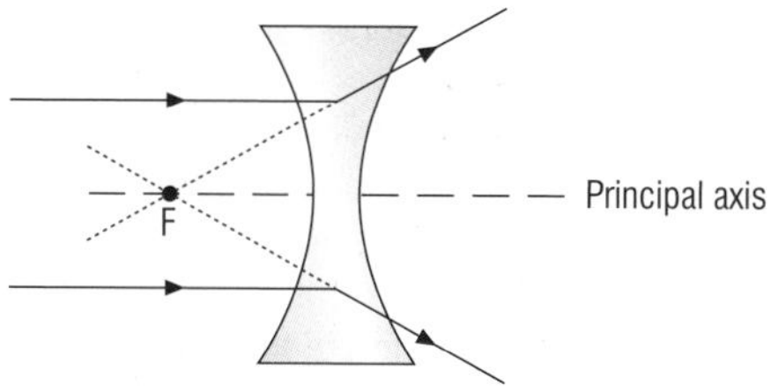
F
Principal axis

(2 marks)

ii) F correctly labelled. *(1 mark)*

iii) Diverging/concave. *(1 mark)*

3 a) Sound caused by vibration of particles, e.g. air particles. *(1 mark)*

No particles in a vacuum, so no sound,. *(1 mark)*

b) i) pitch *(1 mark)*
of sound is lower. *(1 mark)*

ii) volume *(1 mark)*
of sound louder. *(1 mark)*

4 a) Sound waves with a frequency greater than 20 000 Hz. *(1 mark)*

b) Ultrasound reflects from boundaries between different tissues. *(1 mark)*

Computer uses time taken to receive reflection *(1 mark)*
to calculate distance to the tissue boundary. *(1 mark)*

c) X-rays are ionising radiation. *(1 mark)*
They may harm the baby.
Ultrasound does not harm the baby. *(1 mark)*

Exam teaching suggestions

- Students will benefit from lots of practice at drawing ray diagrams so they become familiar with using construction rays. They must produce neat, clear diagrams drawn with a ruler.
- There are many opportunities here for students to perform practical work to reinforce their understanding. They could also identify lenses and mirrors in common devices such as microscopes, telescopes and cameras.
- Students will gain extra marks in question 3 for using the correct terms – pitch and volume – rather than simply stating that sounds are lower or louder.

HOW SCIENCE WORKS ANSWERS

a) Either greater accuracy or precision. Worth discussing the difference here and how using this instrument would increase both precision and accuracy.

b) Millimetres.

c) The range of the dependent variable was 1.492 to 1.548.

d) The mean of the dependent variable was 1.5206; reasonably 1.52.

e) Jenny was using Crown glass.

How science works teaching suggestions

- **Literacy guidance**
  - Key terms that should be understood: accuracy, precision, dependent independent variable.
  - Question a) expects a longer answer, where students can practise their literacy skills.
- **Higher- and lower-level answers.** Question a) is a higher-level question and the answers provided above is also at this level. Question e) is lower level and the answer provided is also lower level.
- **How and when to use these questions.** When wishing to develop ideas of sensitivity, precision and accuracy as well as using data to identify a substance.
  The questions could be used in small discussion groups.
- **Homework.** The questions could be set as a homework exercise.
- **Special needs.** Students could be taken through the classic pin/refraction experiment to show the effect of light passing through water.

P3 3.1 The motor effect

LEARNING OBJECTIVES

Students should learn:

- That the force on a current carrying conductor in a magnetic field can be increased by increasing the current or magnetic field strength.
- The direction of the force can be reversed by reversing the current.
- How this force can be used to make objects move.

LEARNING OUTCOMES

Most students should be able to:

- Describe the effect of increasing the current or magnetic field strength on a current carrying wire.
- Describe how an electric motor and loudspeaker work

Some students should also be able to:

- Describe and explain the effect of making changes to the design or operation of an electric motor.

Teaching suggestions

- **Special needs.** For students who have difficulty manipulating small objects, you will need to provide some scaled-up motors that are partially pre-assembled.
- **Gifted and talented.** There are devices called linear motors that can be used to move objects without the rotation associated with normal motors. The students could find out about the invention of these devices and the uses they have been put to.
- **Learning styles**
  Kinaesthetic: Constructing an electric motor.
  Visual: Watching a video/animation of the motor effect.
  Auditory: Explaining the effect of changing variables in the motor.
  Interpersonal: Collaborating on motor construction.
  Intrapersonal: Understanding and reflection of the effect of a magnetic field on a current carrying wire.
- **Homework**
  - The students should find out about the first electric motor as developed by Michael Faraday; can they find a diagram and explain how it works?
  - A simpler homework would be to find as many devices that use an electric motor as possible.
- **ICT link-up.** Use Simulation P3 3.1 'Electric Motor' from the GCSE Physics CD ROM.

SPECIFICATION LINK-UP   Unit: Physics 3.13.7

- *When a conductor carrying an electric current is placed in a magnetic field, it may experience a force.*
- *The size of the force can be increased by:*
  - *increasing the strength of the magnetic field*
  - *increasing the size of the current.*
- *The conductor will not experience a force if it is parallel to the magnetic field.*
- *The direction of the force is reversed if either the direction of the current or the direction of the magnetic field is reversed.*

Students should use their skills, knowledge and understanding of 'How Science Works':

- *to explain how the motor effect is used in simple devices.*

Lesson structure

STARTER

Magnetic fields – The students should draw the shape of a magnetic field around a bar magnet and explain how they can find this shape. (10 minutes)

Electricity and magnetism recap – Use true/false/don't know cards and a set of electricity questions to establish the students' prior knowledge. (5–10 minutes)

Twenty questions – Let the students ask you up to twenty questions with yes/no answers to find out this lesson's topic. (5 minutes)

MAIN

- Before the first experiment, make sure that the students are aware of what magnetic field lines are and where they would be in the arrangement you are going to use. The experiment itself yields obvious results.
- When discussing the size of the force, most students intuitively realise that if you make the current 'stronger' or the magnet 'stronger' then the effect will be 'stronger' too.
- You can use diagrams to explain what is meant by perpendicular or parallel to the magnetic field lines.
- The trickiest part of the motor to explain is the action of the split-ring commutator, but the students should get a better grasp of this when they construct their own motors. If they don't get them right, the coil will just oscillate in place.
- Show the students a carbon brush to show how they work. If you have an old one, you can show how the brushes wear out.
- Construction of electrical motors from kits can take up a great deal of time in the lesson. If you want to complete the task more quickly, then give the students pre-wound cores for their motors.
- A real motor, as used in a drill, will have several separate coils. Using their understanding of the motor effect, the students should be able to explain why this is necessary.
- Use a very large loudspeaker to show its action. If you can, strip away all of the paper including the central part to expose the magnet and the coil.
- You may be able to use a direct current to levitate the magnet, showing the students that there is no vibration and hence no sound.

PLENARIES

True/false – Check understanding of the key concepts with a set of true/false questions about the key concepts covered in this topic. (5–10 minutes)

Loudspeaker links – Show the students an electrical waveform that is to be fed into a loudspeaker. Ask them to describe the motion of the magnet in the speaker, including when it will be moving up or down and when its movement will be fastest. (5–10 minutes)

Space boots – In space, astronauts are weightless but need some way of walking around the outer surface of a space station. Can the students design a system to do this? (10 minutes)

Practical support

Investigating the motor effect

The motor effect is easy to demonstrate or to let the students find out about.

Equipment and materials required

Battery, length of wire (stiff wire works best), variable resistor, leads, two magnets mounted on U frame (or a U-shaped magnet).

Details

The students place the wire between the two magnets and pass a small current through it. The variable resistor allows them to control the current to see if increasing it has the expected effect. Make sure that the students see the effect of reversing the current and changing the angle between the magnets and the wire. It can be hard to get the wire to run in the same direction as the field lines, but a piece of stiff wire can be bent into shape.

Make and test an electric motor

The success of making these motors depends on the exact kits you have and the patience of the students.

Equipment and materials required

Motor building kits, low voltage power supply or battery packs.

Details

To get a decent effect, the students should wrap the coil wire about ten times around the spool. It is important to get the length of the wire right; they should wrap it then take it off again before cutting it to the correct length and stripping the ends. The wire is then held in place with a small rubber hoop. It is worth checking that the students haven't wrapped so much wire that the spool won't turn. The brushes are the hardest bit to get right; the students will need detailed worksheets for this. If they don't work first time, then take them off and pull the wire completely straight again; this is much easier than trying to fiddle with them when they are mounted.

Fleming's left-hand rule

This isn't necessary for the specification, but can help solidify some students' understanding of the motor effect. To find the direction of the force acting on a current carrying wire the students can use Fleming's left-hand rule. They hold out their **left** hand with the thumb and first two fingers perpendicular to each other. Point the **f**irst finger in the direction of the magnetic **f**ield (from north to south), point the se**c**ond finger in the direction of the **c**urrent. The thu**m**b will point in the direction of the **m**ovement.

Answers to in-text questions

a) No change, the actions cancel each other out.

b) The material must conduct electricity.

c) A direct current will not produce a changing magnetic field.

P3 3.1 — The motor effect

LEARNING OBJECTIVES

1 When a current-carrying conductor in a magnetic field experiences a force, how can we make the force bigger?
2 When a current-carrying conductor in a magnetic field experiences a force, how can we reverse the direction of the force?
3 How do we use the motor effect to make objects move?

FOUL FACTS

An electric drill contains an electric motor. Dentists use electric drills to drill teeth. What do surgeons use electric drills for? Ugh!

PRACTICAL

Investigating the motor effect

When a current is passed along a wire in a magnetic field, a force may be exerted on the wire. This effect is known as the **motor effect**. Figure 1 shows how you can investigate it.

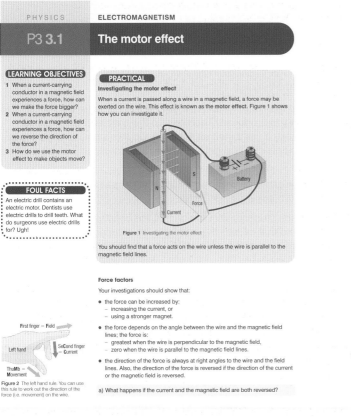

Figure 1 Investigating the motor effect

You should find that a force acts on the wire unless the wire is parallel to the magnetic field lines.

Force factors

Your investigations should show that:

● the force can be increased by:
  – increasing the current, or
  – using a stronger magnet.

● the force depends on the angle between the wire and the magnetic field lines; the force is:
  – greatest when the wire is perpendicular to the magnetic field,
  – zero when the wire is parallel to the magnetic field lines.

● the direction of the force is always at right angles to the wire and the field lines. Also, the direction of the force is reversed if the direction of the current or the magnetic field is reversed.

a) What happens if the current and the magnetic field are both reversed?

First finger = Field
Left hand
SeCond finger = Current
ThuMb = Movement

Figure 2 The left hand rule. You can use this rule to work out the direction of the force (i.e. movement) on the wire.

The electric motor

An electric motor is designed to use the motor effect. We can control the speed of an electric motor by changing the current. Also, we can reverse its turning direction by reversing the current.

The simple motor shown in Figure 3 consists of a rectangular coil of insulated wire (the armature coil) that is forced to rotate. The coil is connected via two metal or graphite 'brushes' to the battery. The brushes press onto a metal 'split-ring' commutator fixed to the coil.

When a current is passed through the coil, the coil spins because:

● a force acts on each side of the coil due to the motor effect,
● the force on one side is in the opposite direction to the force on the other side.

The split-ring commutator reverses the current round the coil every half turn of the coil. Because the sides swap over each half-turn, the coil is pushed in the same direction every half-turn.

b) Why are the brushes made of metal or graphite?

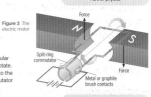

Figure 3 The electric motor

The loudspeaker

A loudspeaker is designed to make a diaphragm attached to a coil vibrate when alternating current passes through the coil.

● When a current passes through the coil, a force due to the motor effect makes the coil move.
● Each time the current changes its direction, the force reverses its direction. So the coil is repeatedly forced backwards and forwards. This motion makes the diaphragm vibrate so sound waves are created.

c) Why does a loudspeaker not produce sound when direct current is passed through it?

PRACTICAL

Make and test an electric motor

Make and test a simple electric motor like the one in Figure 3.

DID YOU KNOW?

Graphite is a form of carbon which conducts electricity and is very slippy. It therefore causes very little friction when it is in contact with the rotating commutator.

Figure 4 A loudspeaker

SUMMARY QUESTIONS

1 Choose words from the list to complete each of the sentences.

   coil   current   force   magnet

   a) When a ...... passes through the ...... of an electric motor, a ...... acts on each side of the ....
   b) The ...... along each side is in opposite directions so the ...... is in opposite directions and the ...... turns.

2 a) Explain why a simple electric motor connected to a battery reverses if the battery connections are reversed.
   b) Discuss whether or not an electric motor would run faster if the coil was wound on i) a plastic block, ii) an iron block instead of a wooden block.

KEY POINT

1 In the motor effect, the force:
● is increased if the current or the strength of the magnetic field is increased,
● is at right angles to the direction of the magnetic field and to the wire,
● is reversed if the direction of the current or the magnetic field is reversed.

SUMMARY ANSWERS

1 a) Current, coil, force, coil
  b) Current, force, coil

2 a) The direction of the current is reversed and so the force on the coil is in the opposite direction.

  b) An iron block would have eddy currents which would oppose the movement and slow the motor.
  i) Faster because the coil is lighter.
  ii) Faster because the field is much stronger due to the presence of iron.

KEY POINTS

The students should be able to draw a diagram showing the effect of a magnetic field on a current carrying wire including the direction of the force.

P3 3.2 Electromagnetic induction

Students should learn:

- That moving a wire through a magnetic field so that it cuts magnetic field lines will induce a p.d. along the length of the wire.
- That moving the wire faster or increasing the field strength will increase the p.d.
- About the function of the slip rings and brushes in an a.c. generator.

Most students should be able to:

- Describe how a current can be induced in a moving wire and how to increase the size of the p.d. driving the current.

Some students should also be able to:

- Describe and explain how the p.d. from a generator or dynamo changes if the rate of cutting of the magnetic field lines increases.
- Explain how an a.c. generator produces alternating current including the function of the slip rings and brushes. [**HT** only]

Teaching suggestions

- **Special needs.** Provide diagrams of the wire-moving experiment and the simple generator for the students to annotate.

- **Gifted and talented**
  - Ask: 'How can an alternating current generator be made to produce direct current?' The students should find out about the modifications to the design that are necessary.
  - Ask: 'How can the Earth's magnetic fields be used to generate electricity in space?' Recent experiments by NASA have tried to generate a current and the students could look into these.

- **Learning styles**

  Kinaesthetic: Carrying out practical tasks on the generator.

  Visual: Predicting the effect of changing the design of a generator on the output voltage.

  Auditory: Explaining why a p.d. is induced in a moving wire.

  Interpersonal: Discussing and evaluating the outcomes of the generator investigation.

  Intrapersonal: Making deductions about the cause of an induced p.d.

SPECIFICATION LINK-UP   Unit: Physics 3.13.8

- *If an electrical conductor 'cuts' through magnetic field lines an electrical potential difference is induced across the ends of the conductor.*
- *If a magnet is moved into a coil of wire, an electrical potential difference is induced across the ends of the coil.*
- *If the wire is part of a complete circuit, a current is induced in the wire.*
- *If the direction of motion, or the polarity of the magnet, is reversed the direction of the induced potential difference and the induced current is reversed.*
- *The generator effect also occurs if the magnetic field is stationary and the coil is moved.*
- *The size of the induced potential difference increases when:*
  - *the speed of the movement increases*
  - *the strength of the magnetic field increases*
  - *the number of turns on the coil increases*
  - *the area of the coil is greater.*

Students should use their skills, knowledge and understanding of 'How Science Works':

- *to explain, from a diagram, how an a.c. generator works, including the purpose of the slip rings and brushes. [**HT** only]*

Lesson structure

STARTER

Making electricity – The students should outline what they know about how electricity is produced by whatever means they like. (10 minutes)

Generating ideas – Pair up the students and ask the pairs to come up with an explanation of how electricity is produced. Then pair up the pairs and ask them to compare their ideas and make a combined explanation. Do this a couple more times until you have only two explanations and get the whole class to discuss which the best is. (10–15 minutes)

MAIN

- From the first practical, the students should come to the conclusion that it is a wire moving in a magnetic field that causes the current to be induced. They should also reach the conclusion that the current is larger when the wire is moved more quickly.

- If possible the students should be talking about the dynamo effect inducing a potential difference and this causes a current if a circuit exists.

- A simple hand dynamo can be used to light up a bulb. If this is spun faster then the bulb should shine brighter but the bulb goes out when it stops, showing one of the problems with bicycle dynamos.

- Connecting the hand dynamo up to an oscilloscope will allow you to show that the peak voltage increases when the dynamo is spun faster as well as the frequency.

- Show an animation of a coil rotating to explain the waveform produced by a dynamo. (See 'ICT link-up').

- Demonstrate moving a magnet into and out of a coil to show the effect. If you have two coils, one with more turns than the other, you should also show that the current depends on the number of turns.

- You can find large diagrams and animations of very large power station generators to give the students a better impression of their structure.

PLENARIES

Energy considerations – A generator produces electricity, but energy cannot be created or destroyed. The students should describe where the energy is coming from and draw an energy transfer diagram. This should include wasted energy. (5–10 minutes)

Dynamic dynamo danger – Can the students come up with a *mechanical* way of keeping a bicycle light lit when the cycle is stopped for short periods? No batteries allowed. (10–15 minutes)

It's a wind-up – A wind-up radio is one device that uses induction to produce electricity on the go. Can the students think of any of their devices that could use wind-up power? Do they think that their devices could catch on? (5–10 minutes)

Teaching suggestions continued

- **Homework.** The students should explain how kinetic energy is used in a variety of ways to turn a generator. They should describe a variety of turbines.

- **ICT link-up.** A search for 'generator animation' on the Internet will yield a free animation showing the rotation of a coil cutting a magnetic field and inducing a potential. Use Simulation P3 3.2 'Electromagnetic Induction' from the GCSE Physics CD ROM.

Practical support

Investigating a simple generator

This practical works best with a really strong magnet and a spot galvanometer. Make sure that the magnet doesn't get too close to the galvanometer otherwise the coil can be damaged.

Equipment and materials required

Strong U-shaped magnet, stiff wire, leads, sensitive ammeter or galvanometer.

Details

The students simply move the wire up and down through the magnet, cutting the magnetic field lines. The ammeter should register a small current in one direction when the wire is moving down and a small current in the opposite direction when it is moving up. The size of the current should increase if the wire is moved more quickly. Make sure that the students see that there is no current when the wire is not moving even when it is within the magnetic field.

Answers to in-text questions

a) i) The current increases
   ii) The direction of the current reverses.
   iii) No current is produced.

b) The wires leading to the coil would get twisted up. No brushes are needed.

c) i) There is no current.
   ii) A p.d. is produced in the opposite direction.

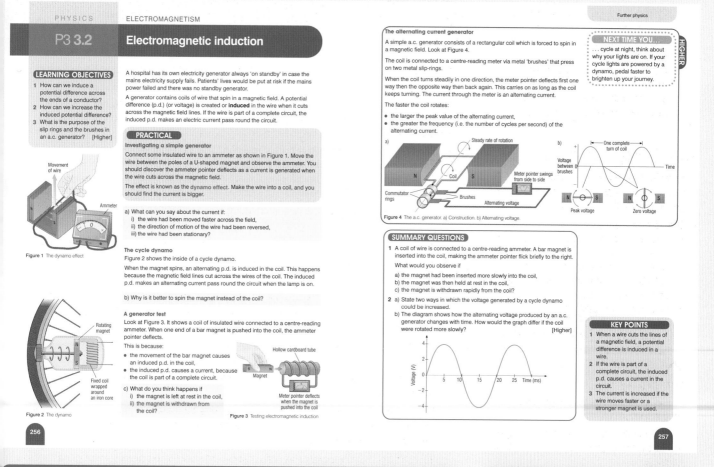

Figure 1 The dynamo effect
Figure 2 The dynamo
Figure 3 Testing electromagnetic induction
Figure 4 The a.c. generator. a) Construction. b) Alternating voltage.

SUMMARY ANSWERS

1 a) The pointer would move to the right but not as far.

   b) The pointer returns to zero.

   c) The pointer would move rapidly to the left.

2 a) Spin the coil faster, use more loops of coil, use stronger magnets.

   b) The peak voltage would be lower and the period would be longer. [**HT** only]

KEY POINTS

The students should be able to give a complete description of how a current is produced in a generator. They could present this as a sequencing question for fellow students to answer.

257

P3 3.3 Transformers

LEARNING OBJECTIVES

Students should learn:

- That transformers require alternating current because they rely on changing magnetic fields.
- That the core of a transformer is a laminated iron block.

LEARNING OUTCOMES

Most students should be able to:

- Describe, in detail, the operation of a transformer in terms of changing magnetic fields.
- Describe the basic structure of a transformer.

Some students should also be able to:

- Explain the features of a transformer that make it more efficient.

Teaching suggestions

- **Special needs.** A sequence of diagrams showing how the field in a transformer core changes should be provided.
- **Gifted and talented.** Discuss the energy losses in transformers by eddy currents and other heating effects.
- **Learning styles**

  Kinaesthetic: Making a transformer.

  Visual: Imagining the changes in the magnetic fields in a transformer core.

  Auditory: Discussing real transformers.

  Interpersonal: Collaborating in the construction of transformers.

  Intrapersonal: Evaluating the materials used for transformers.

SPECIFICATION LINK-UP   Unit: Physics 3.13.9

- *The basic structure of the transformer.*
- *An alternating current in the primary coil produces a changing magnetic field in the iron core and hence in the secondary coil. This induces an alternating potential difference across the ends of the secondary coil.*
- *In a step-up transformer the potential difference across the secondary coil is greater than the potential difference across the primary coil.*
- *In a step-down transformer the potential difference across the secondary coil is less than the potential difference across the primary coil.*
- *The uses of step-up and step-down transformers in the National Grid.*

Students should use their skills, knowledge and understanding of 'How Science Works':

- *To determine which type of transformer should be used for a particular application.*

Lesson structure

STARTER

Transformers! – Without letting the students use their textbooks, ask them to draw and label all of the parts of a transformer. (10 minutes)

Jeopardy – Give the students a set of answers like 'an iron core', 'the primary coil', etc. and ask them to make a set of questions to go with them. (10 minutes)

Safety first – The students complete this sentence scientifically 'If a carbon fishing rod touches a very high voltage cable . . . '. (5 minutes)

MAIN

- The students will have come across transformers in an earlier unit, but in this topic they need to get a real understanding of the electromagnetic effects that make the device work.
- The first part of the lesson is purely revision. The students should remember that transformers are used to change voltages for a.c. and that the National Grid uses step-up and step-down transformers. Can the students remember the reasons that these transformers are needed?
- Take time to go through the operation of the transformer step by step. Perhaps the students could draw a flow chart of the operation. Use Animation P3 3.3 'Transformers' from the GCSE Physics CD ROM.
- When they are making their transformers, check that they understand the operation correctly. They should be able to describe what each of the coils is doing and the changes in the magnetic fields.
- By connecting a dual trace oscilloscope to the input and output coils of a transformer, you can show the relationship between the waveforms clearly.
- Understanding that changing fields are needed will let the students explain why direct current cannot be transformed in this way.
- Show the students a range of real transformers, if possible, to show that some coils can have thousands of turns on them.
- You could also discuss the physical limitation on making coils. The more turns the larger the coils have to be. This can be reduced by making thinner wires, but then the current may become too high for them to cope with. Insulation also becomes a problem and more electrical insulation prevents thermal energy escaping and so the coils can overheat.
- With the higher-attaining students, you may wish to describe the formation of eddy currents in solid metal blocks. It is these that reduce the efficiency of the device by heating the metal. Laminating the core reduces these currents.

Practical support

Make a model transformer
A transformer is relatively simple to build given enough wire. Make sure that the students cannot produce voltages higher than about 5 V though.

Equipment and materials required
Transformer core (laminated if possible), insulated wire, low-voltage a.c. power supply, 1.5 V torch lamp, 1.5 V cell and a.c. ammeter (optional).

Details
- If possible use a power supply that can be locked at 1 V, so that the students cannot produce high output voltages with the transformer. The students should wrap about 10 loops of wire for the input coil and a maximum of about 15 for the output coil. This will produce a step-up transformer, but only up to the required 1.5 V for the bulb.
- You can also use this opportunity to test if different materials could be used as a transformer core, if you do not want to set the task as a plenary. Use an ammeter to measure the size of the induced current for different materials. (This relates to: 'How Science Works': fair testing.)

PLENARIES

Combinations – Give the students a circuit with a set of four transformers in a row. Give them the input voltage and the number of turns on each transformer and ask them to work out the final output voltage. (5–10 minutes)

Transformer tests – The students design a controlled experiment to test which material is best for a transformer core. They need to include some way of measuring the current induced in the secondary coil. (This relates to: 'How Science Works': fair testing.) (15 minutes)

Answers to in-text questions

a) The magnetic field in the core would be much weaker because the core is not a magnetic material.

b) The lamp would be brighter.

c) The lamp would not light up with direct current in the primary coil.

d) Iron is easier to magnetise and demagnetise as the alternating current increases and decreases each half cycle.

PHYSICS   ELECTROMAGNETISM

P3 3.3   Transformers

LEARNING OBJECTIVES
1 Why do transformers only work with a.c.?
2 What is the core of a transformer made from?

A typical power station generator produces an alternating potential difference of about 25 000 volts. Mains electricity to homes and offices is at 230 volts.

When you plug a heater into the mains, electricity reaches you from a power station via a network of cables called the National Grid. The alternating p.d. of the cables (the grid voltage) is typically 132 000 volts.

A transformer is used at each stage to change the alternating p.d. We also use transformers in low-voltage supply units to step the mains p.d. down from 230 V.

How a transformer works
A transformer has two coils of insulated wire, both wound round the same iron core, as shown in Figure 1. When alternating current passes through the primary coil, an alternating p.d. is induced in the secondary coil.

This happens because:
- alternating current passing through the primary coil produces an alternating magnetic field,
- the lines of the alternating magnetic field pass through the secondary coil and induce an alternating p.d. in it.

If a lamp is connected across the secondary coil, the induced p.d. causes a current in the secondary circuit. So the lamp lights up. Electrical energy is therefore transferred from the primary to the secondary coil. This happens even though they are not electrically connected in the same circuit.

a) Why would the lamp not light up as brightly if the iron core was replaced with a wooden core?
b) What happens if you wrap more turns on the secondary coil?
c) What happens if you use a 1.5 V cell instead of the 1 volt a.c. supply unit?

Iron core
Primary coil   Secondary coil
a.c. generator   Lamp bulb
Figure 1 Transformer action

Transformers in action
Transformers only work with alternating current. With a direct current, there is no changing magnetic field so the secondary voltage is zero.

The core of the transformer 'guides' the field lines in a loop through the coils. But the field must be changing to induce a p.d. in the secondary coil.

Figure 3 shows a practical transformer.

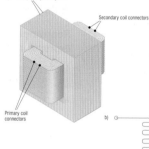
a) Iron plates glued together
Secondary coil connectors
Primary coil connectors
b)
Figure 3 Transformers in circuits. a) A practical transformer. b) Circuit symbol.

The primary and secondary coils are both wound round the same part of the core. The core is layered (laminated) to cut out induced currents in the iron layers. If it wasn't laminated, the efficiency of the transformer would be greatly reduced.

d) Why is the core made of iron not steel?

NEXT TIME YOU...
... use a mobile phone charger, remember it contains:
- a small transformer that steps the mains voltage down,
- diodes that convert the alternating p.d. from the transformer to a direct p.d.

GET IT RIGHT!
Make sure you can explain how a transformer works.

PRACTICAL
Make a model transformer
Wrap a coil of insulated wire round the iron core of a model transformer as the primary coil. Connect the coil to a 1 volt a.c. supply unit and connect a second length of insulated wire to a 1.5 V torch lamp. When you wrap the second wire round the iron core, the lamp should light up.

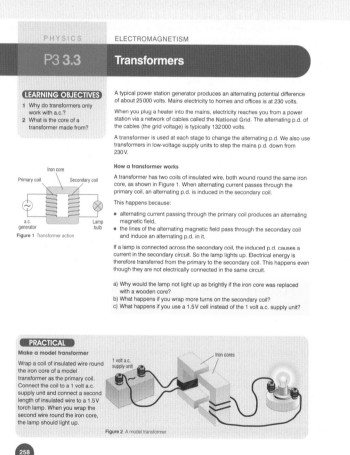
1 volt a.c. supply unit
Iron cores
Figure 2 A model transformer

SUMMARY QUESTIONS
1 Copy and complete the following sentences about a transformer using words from the list.

   current   magnetic field   p.d.   primary   secondary

   In a transformer, an alternating ...... is passed through the ...... coil. This coil creates an alternating ...... which passes through the ...... coil. As a result, an alternating ...... is induced in the ...... coil.

2 a) Why does a transformer not work with direct current?
   b) Why is it important that the coil wires of a transformer are insulated?
   c) Why is the core of a transformer made of iron?

KEY POINTS
1 A transformer consists of a primary coil and a secondary coil wrapped on the same iron core.
2 Transformers only work using alternating current.

258   259

SUMMARY ANSWERS

1 Current, primary, magnetic field, secondary, p.d., secondary.

2 a) Direct current in the primary coil would not produce an alternating magnetic field, so no p.d. would be induced in the secondary coil.

   b) The current would short-circuit across the wires instead of passing through them. This would cause the coil to overheat if it did not cause a fuse to blow.

   c) Iron is a magnetic material, so it makes the magnetic field much stronger. It is easily magnetised and demagnetised when the current alternates.

KEY POINTS
Can the students give a complete description of the way the transformer is working? They could present this as an annotated diagram or flow chart.

P3 3.4

Transformers and the National Grid

Students should learn:

- That a step-up transformer increases the potential difference while a step-down transformer decreases it.
- How to calculate the change in potential difference produced by a transformer. [**HT** only]
- That the National Grid uses transformers to save electrical energy.

LEARNING OUTCOMES

- Use the transformer equation to explain how the turns ratio determines its use as a step-up or step-down transformer.
- Explain why it is more efficient to transfer electrical energy at high voltages.

Some students should also be able to:

- Use and rearrange the transformer equation. [**HT** only]

Teaching suggestions

- **Special needs.** Provide worksheets to help with the calculations. These should show each of the stages required to reach the answer.
- **Gifted and talented.** The students should look into the relationship between the number of turns on a transformer and the input and output currents. Ask: 'What does a step-down transformer do to the current?' They will need to use the relationship $P = IV$ to understand this.
- **Learning styles**

  Kinaesthetic: Carrying out a practical task in investigation.

  Visual: Interpreting a diagram of the National Grid.

  Interpersonal: Understanding the need for transformers in the Grid.

  Intrapersonal: Evaluating transformer efficiency experiment.

- **Homework.** The students should perform additional calculations using the transformer equation to makes sure that they thoroughly understand it.
- **ICT link-up.** Use Animation P3 3.4 and also PhotoPLUS P3 3.5 'More power' from the GCSE Physics CD ROM.

SPECIFICATION LINK-UP   Unit: Physics 3.13.9

- The potential difference (p.d.) across the primary and secondary coils of a transformer are related by the equation:

$$\frac{p.d.\ across\ primary}{p.d.\ across\ secondary} = \frac{number\ of\ turns\ on\ primary}{number\ of\ turns\ on\ secondary} \quad \text{[HT only]}$$

- In a step-up transformer the potential difference across the secondary coil is greater than the potential difference across the primary coil.
- In a step-down transformer the potential difference across the secondary coil is less than the potential difference across the primary coil.
- The uses of step-up and step-down transformers in the National Grid.

Students should use their skills, knowledge and understanding of 'How Science Works':

- to determine which type of transformer should be used for a particular application.

Lesson structure

STARTER

The big connective – Get the students to finish the paragraph 'The National Grid is very useful . . . '. (5–10 minutes)

The National Grid game – The students could play a round of the National Grid game as described in the extension to lesson 3.5. (10–15 minutes)

Rearranging – Challenge the students to rearrange the transformer equation to arrive at expressions for the four different values on their own. (5–10 minutes)

MAIN

- This topic again partly revises previous material, but many students struggle with the transformer equation and it is worth going through this again in depth.
- The students will need plenty of practice with the transformer equation, particularly with the rearrangement of it. This is one of the situations where the students will find using the symbols easier than writing out the full equation.
- The transformer efficiency material is new. Somebody might point out that no device is 100% efficient, but just explain that you are using this number to make the calculations easier and everybody will be happy.
- The students should understand that if the device is 100% efficient, then the power output is the same as the power input; but remind them of this anyway.
- You will also have to remind the students of the relationship: power = current × potential difference from earlier electrical work.
- By discussing the relationship $P = IV$, the students should understand that to provide a higher power you could increase the current or potential difference. This then leads on to the problem with a larger current: excessive heating and energy loss.
- The final calculations are difficult for many, because they involve several stages. Separating out these stages clearly will help.

ACTIVITY & EXTENSION IDEAS

Investigating transformer efficiency
The students can verify if the transformer is efficient by measuring the power in and out of a transformer arrangement.

Equipment and materials required
For each group; transformer (this could be made by the students as in the last topic), two a.c. ammeters, two a.c. voltmeters, low-voltage a.c. power supply, 3V lamp.

Details and fix
- Set p.d. and fix the power supply so that it will produce a p.d. that will give a suitable output p.d. from the transformer to light the lamp. Arrange the transformer so that an ammeter and voltmeter measure the input current and input p.d. and the second ammeter and voltmeter to measure the output characteristics. The students can then measure the input power using $P = IV$ and also the output power. From this they can calculate the efficiency.

- To extend the investigation, the students can find out if the efficiency is increased by increasing the number of turns on each coil (while maintaining the same ratio), or if a laminated iron core really has an effect.

Answers to in-text questions
a) 60 turns.

b) i) 6A **ii)** 0.26A

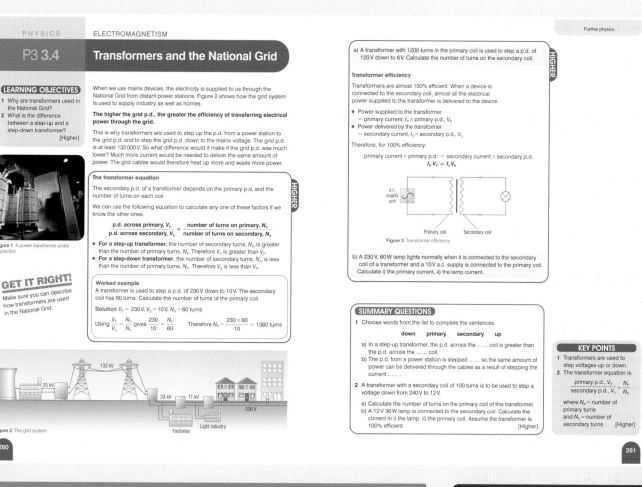

PHYSICS ELECTROMAGNETISM

P3 3.4 Transformers and the National Grid

LEARNING OBJECTIVES
1 Why are transformers used in the National Grid?
2 What is the difference between a step-up and a step-down transformer?
[Higher]

Figure 1 A power transformer under inspection

GET IT RIGHT!
Make sure you can describe how transformers are used in the National Grid.

When we use mains devices, the electricity is supplied to us through the National Grid from distant power stations. Figure 2 shows how the grid system is used to supply industry as well as homes.

The higher the grid p.d., the greater the efficiency of transferring electrical power through the grid.

This is why transformers are used to step up the p.d. from a power station to the grid p.d. and to step the grid p.d. down to the mains voltage. The grid p.d. is at least 132 000 V. So what difference would it make if the grid p.d. was much lower? Much more current would be needed to deliver the same amount of power. The grid cables would therefore heat up more and waste more power.

The transformer equation

The secondary p.d. of a transformer depends on the primary p.d. and the number of turns on each coil.

We can use the following equation to calculate any one of these factors if we know the other ones.

$$\frac{\text{p.d. across primary, } V_P}{\text{p.d. across secondary, } V_S} = \frac{\text{number of turns on primary, } N_P}{\text{number of turns on secondary, } N_S}$$

- For a step-up transformer, the number of secondary turns, N_S, is greater than the number of primary turns, N_P. Therefore V_S is greater than V_P.
- For a step-down transformer, the number of secondary turns, N_S, is less than the number of primary turns, N_P. Therefore V_S is less than V_P.

Worked example
A transformer is used to step a p.d. of 230V down to 10V. The secondary coil has 60 turns. Calculate the number of turns of the primary coil.

Solution $V_P = 230\text{V}$, $V_S = 10\text{V}$, $N_S = 60$ turns

Using $\frac{V_P}{V_S} = \frac{N_P}{N_S}$ gives $\frac{230}{10} = \frac{N_P}{60}$ Therefore $N_P = \frac{230 \times 60}{10} = 1380$ turns

Figure 2 The grid system

132 kV
25 kV
33 kV 11 kV
230 V
Factories Light industry

260

---

a) A transformer with 1200 turns in the primary coil is used to step a p.d. of 120V down to 6V. Calculate the number of turns on the secondary coil.

Transformer efficiency

Transformers are almost 100% efficient. When a device is connected to the secondary coil, almost all the electrical power supplied to the transformer is delivered to the device.

- Power supplied to the transformer
  = primary current, $I_P \times$ primary p.d., V_P
- Power delivered by the transformer
  = secondary current, $I_S \times$ secondary p.d., V_S

Therefore, for 100% efficiency:

primary current × primary p.d. = secondary current × secondary p.d.

$$I_P V_P = I_S V_S$$

a.c. supply unit

Primary coil Secondary coil

Figure 3 Transformer efficiency

b) A 230V, 60W lamp lights normally when it is connected to the secondary coil of a transformer and a 10V a.c. supply is connected to the primary coil. Calculate i) the primary current, ii) the lamp current.

SUMMARY QUESTIONS

1 Choose words from the list to complete the sentences.

down primary secondary up

a) In a step-up transformer, the p.d. across the ...... coil is greater than the p.d. across the ...... coil.
b) The p.d. from a power station is stepped ...... so the same amount of power can be delivered through the cables as a result of stepping the current ....

2 A transformer with a secondary coil of 100 turns is to be used to step a voltage down from 240V to 12V.

a) Calculate the number of turns on the primary coil of this transformer.
b) A 12V 36W lamp is connected to the secondary coil. Calculate the current in i) the lamp, ii) the primary coil. Assume the transformer is 100% efficient. [Higher]

KEY POINTS
1 Transformers are used to step voltages up or down.
2 The transformer equation is:
$$\frac{\text{primary p.d., } V_P}{\text{secondary p.d., } V_S} = \frac{N_P}{N_S}$$
where N_P = number of primary turns and N_S = number of secondary turns [Higher]

261

PLENARIES

Transformer matching – Can the students match up the transformers with the changes in voltage? (5–10 minutes)

Power to the people – An electrical engineer wants to change the mains voltage in his village to 460V a.c. to save energy. Ask: 'What transformer would be needed and why wouldn't this be a sensible proposal?' (5–10 minutes)

UK to USA – An electrical engineer wants to change an a.c. voltage of 230V (UK mains) to one of 120V (US mains). Students could make an instruction booklet explaining exactly how to do this, including equipment needed and diagrams. (10–15 minutes)

Word search – Give the students a word search with all of the key words from this chapter. Make it more difficult by not giving them a word list. They have to find the words by checking through the chapter again. (10–15 minutes)

KEY POINTS

The students must be able to use the transformer equation to answer a range of questions. Working in pairs, they should write a question for their partner plus a model answer they can use to mark it. Then they try each other's question.

SUMMARY ANSWERS

1 **a) i)** Secondary, primary.

  b) Up, down.

2 **a)** 2000 turns.

  b) i) 3A **ii)** 0.15A [**HT** only]

P3 3.5 More power to you

Teaching suggestions

Activities

- **A revolutionary discovery** – There is a lot to learn about Faraday's work and the students can look into this. They could also look at the 'Royal Institution Christmas Lectures' leading to an important discussion about the public's perception of science. How do the students view the study of science now as they are nearing the end of the course? Do they think that they are informed enough to make sensible decisions during their lives?

- **Alternating or direct current?** – For this activity, you might like to provide some data on the cost per unit of a variety of energy resources so that the students can make a fair comparison. The students can find this data for themselves, but they should be aware that different web sites quote different values. For more depth, the students could look into the profits of the electricity generation companies and the National Grid Company. Ask: 'Should this money be going to funding new research into alternative energy?' Using the information gathered, the students could make a presentation and come to a conclusion about who should pay for what.

PHYSICS   ELECTROMAGNETISM

P3 3.5   More power to you

Before 1926	District power stations supply a.c. or d.c. electricity	Most power stations burn coal
1926	Grid system set up	All power stations generate 240 V.* 50 Hz a.c.
1948	Grid system and power companies nationalised	Big new power stations built including oil-fired and nuclear power stations
1990	Grid system and power companies privatised (except nuclear power)	New gas-fired power stations built
Now	Power companies such as National Grid operate internationally	Wind farms being established

(*changed to 230 V in 1994)

A revolutionary discoverer

I was born in 1791 and when I left school, I started an apprenticeship binding books. I was so fascinated by Sir Humphry Davy's books on science that I wrote to him at the Royal Institution in London to ask him for a job. He must have been very impressed by my enthusiasm because he took me on and trained me in science. Many years later, I followed in his footsteps and became the Director of the Royal Institution. I made lots of important scientific discoveries including how to generate electricity. Who am I?

Are you M . . . . . ?

Alternating or direct current?

Before the National Grid was set up in 1926, electricity for each district was from a local power station. Some power stations generated alternating current and others generated direct current.

As explained on page 184, the potential of a mains live wire alternates between +325 V and −325 V. A direct potential of 230 V would deliver the same power so we say the UK mains supply is 230 V. Before d.c. power stations were converted to supply a.c.,

- some people said d.c. was safer because a live wire reaches a much higher potential with a.c. than with d.c.,
- some people said the power stations could be further away if a.c. was used instead of d.c.

ACTIVITY

Imagine you are a local newspaper reporter in 1926. You live in a d.c. town. Your editor has asked you to write a short piece (no more than 100 words) on why a.c. is better than d.c. Remember that:

- people in the rural areas don't have electricity because it's too expensive, and
- people with electricity might need to rewire their houses because alternating voltages are higher than direct voltages.

Grid changes

New gas-fired power stations built after 1990 generate cheaper electricity than other power stations. Most oil-fired and many coal-fired power stations were closed because they were uncompetitive. North Sea gas is running out. We now need new electricity sources to reduce greenhouse gases.

ACTIVITY

Who should pay for new electricity sources, the electricity consumer or the taxpayer? Discuss the issue in your group.

262

- **Superconducting motors** – The main difficulty with superconducting materials is that they only operate at very low temperatures, most at only tens of degrees kelvin. Scientists are constantly trying to increase this operating temperature by developing new compounds. The most important landmark achieved is a superconductor that will operate at 97 K (−176°C). This is above the temperate of liquid nitrogen, which is a much cheaper coolant than previously required. This breakthrough, in 1987, led to the development of many devices that rely on very strong magnetic fields, including MRI machines.

- You might be able to find a video clip of a magnet hovering above a superconducting fluid; the Meissner effect.

- **PUPS!** – Some real organisations that the students may want to find out about are: revolt (www.revolt.co.uk), a UK based web site; Power Line Health Facts (www.powerlinefacts.com) a US based organisation; the National Grid (www.nationalgrid.com/uk), the UK's electrical distribution system, and their web site that counters some claims (www.emf.info). The students can use the information available from these web sites to create a range of posters, booklets or presentations.

- Use PhotoPLUS P3 3.5 'More power' from the GCSE Physics CD ROM.

Superconducting motors

A superconducting wire has no resistance. In theory, a very large current can pass through it without heating the wire. A superconducting motor would be much lighter and more efficient than an ordinary motor.

It would need:

- a rotating coil made of superconducting wires, and
- a magnetic field produced by a fixed superconducting coil.

Lighter and more efficient electric motors in cars would cut fuel usage and reduce greenhouse gases. Research scientists working on superconducting materials know their work could have a gigantic pay-off!

Further physics

An experimental superconducting motor

QUESTION

1 Why would superconducting motors be
a) lighter, b) more efficient?

The Daily

All the News...
All the Showbiz...
All the Info...
All the Time!

GOSS

P.U.P.S

People Under Powerlines become Pretty Upset Protesters!

PROTEST!

EXCLUSIVE REPORT!!!

People living under overhead power lines in the Hillside district marched to the Town Hall yesterday.

They want the power lines re-routed. They claim that the radiation from the power lines is a health risk.

A spokesperson said the council has agreed to a public meeting to listen to their concerns.

NEW THEORIES IN LEUKAEMIA:–
MELATONIN/MAGNETIC FIELD LINK?

Studies of illnesses in communities show there may be an increased risk of childhood leukaemia associated with exposure to 50 Hz alternating magnetic fields. The increased risk seems to be present where magnetic fields are stronger than about 0.5% of the Earth's magnetic field.

One hypothesis is that it may be due to the disruption in the night-time production of melatonin in the pineal gland at the back of the eye. Melatonin in the body is thought to sweep up the bits of damaged cells that cause cancer.

(source: *SciWorld News*, May 2005)

QUESTION

2 a) List some other causes of cancer in humans.
b) What does 'increased risk' mean?
c) The abstract puts forward the 'melatonin theory' as a hypothesis. What is a hypothesis? (See page 6.)

ACTIVITY

a) Rewrite the news report to give it a scientific flavour using the abstract – but keep it to less than 100 words.
b) If you're going to protest in a group, give yourself a better name than PUPS! Come up with something better and design a campaign poster.

263

ANSWERS TO QUESTIONS

1 a) They would not need heavy iron magnets.

b) There would be no power wasted in the wires, as the wires would have no resistance.

2 a) Ionising radiation, carcinogenic (cancer-causing) substances.

b) People are at risk due to other causes. There is an extra risk for those exposed to these magnetic fields.

c) A hypothesis is put forward as an 'unproven' theory to be tested by scientific experiments. If lots of experiments are carried out and they all support the hypothesis, it gains scientific credibility and is accepted as a theory. But at any stage, it could be overthrown by any conflicting scientific evidence.

Extension or homework

Any of the research based activities can be set as a homework task, in particular the PUPS task can produce a lot of information which the students will have to evaluate and this can take some time.

- **National Grid Game** – Using a National Grid map (one is available via the web site www.nationalgrid.com/uk/faqs/index) the students could design an electricity-based quiz, where the player has to move from one power station to another by answering questions. Each player could start at a random location and have to make their own way, one connection at a time, back to the point closest to their home town. Keep any games designed to use as a starter or plenary in future years.

Special needs

The information available on power lines can be quite technical. If possible make a digested form of this information highlighting the key findings for the students to use.

Gifted and talented

Some of the tasks here are very open-ended and allow the students to express their skills in a variety of ways. Designing the National Grid game would be a good challenge for a group of students.

Learning styles

Kinaesthetic: Researching into a range of issues and topics.

Visual: Presenting cost data for electricity generation.

Auditory: Discussing benefits and evidence.

Interpersonal: Reporting on the costs of electricity generation.

Intrapersonal: Considering the evidence on the effects of power lines on human health.

SUMMARY ANSWERS

1 a) Current, force.

  b) Current, lines, field.

2 a) Down.

  b) It is zero.

  c) The forces on the sides make the coil turn.

3 a) i) Step-up, ii) step-down.

  b) Direct current through the primary coil does not produce an alternating magnetic field. No p.d. is induced in the secondary coil, as the magnetic field through it does not change.

4 A high Grid p.d. means that less current is needed to deliver the same amount of power. Less current means less heating in the grid cables and so less wasted power.

5 a) 12V

  b) 0.5A

  c) 5A [**HT** only]

Summary teaching suggestions

- **Lower and higher level answers**
  - Both questions 1 and 3 are basic completion questions and make good whiteboard interactivities if you wish. Accompany both with the appropriate diagrams and get the students to label up the parts of the motor and transformer too.
  - Question 2 is a fairly visual one. If you have taught Fleming's left-hand rule then you should be seeing some of the kinaesthetic learners using this technique. If not, then remind them of it. Higher-attaining students should say more than 'the coil rotates'. They should link back to their knowledge of moments and be explaining that the forces cause a moment and this produces rotation.
  - Question 5 is a calculation question. Some students will need help in remembering the two relevant equations. Higher-attaining students should be looking to justify their explanations for part b) by using the equations, perhaps with some example calculations of their own.

- **When to use the questions?** – The questions can be used as a quick recap at the end of the chapter or as plenary/extension/homework questions during it.

SUMMARY QUESTIONS

1 Complete the following sentences using words from the list.

    field   force   lines   current

a) A vertical wire is placed in a horizontal magnetic field. When a ...... is passed through the wire, a ...... acts on the wire.

b) A force acts on a wire in a magnetic field when a ...... passes along the wire and the wire is not parallel to the ...... of the ....

2 The figure shows a rectangular coil of wire in a magnetic field. When a direct current passes clockwise round the coil, an upward force acts on side X of the coil.

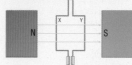

a) What is the direction of the force on side Y of the coil?

b) What can you say about the force on each side of the coil parallel to the magnetic field lines?

c) What is the effect of the forces on the coil?

3 a) Complete the sentences using words from the list.

    step-down   step-up

i) A transformer that changes an alternating p.d. from 12V to 120V is a ...... transformer.

ii) A ...... transformer has more turns on the primary coil than on the secondary coil.

b) Explain why a transformer does not work on direct current.

4 Explain why power is transmitted through the National Grid at a high p.d. rather than a low p.d.

5 A transformer has 50 turns in its primary coil and 500 turns in its secondary coil. It is to be used to light a 120V, 60W lamp connected to the secondary coil.

a) Calculate the primary p.d.,

b) Calculate the current in the lamp,

c) Calculate the current in the primary coil. [Higher]

EXAM-STYLE QUESTIONS

1 The diagram shows a simple electric motor.

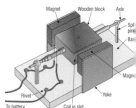

Explain why the motor turns when a current is passed through the coil.

2 The diagram shows a simple generator.

Explain why there is an alternating current in the lamp when the coil is turned. Include in your answer why the brushes and slip rings are needed.
[Higher]

3 An oscilloscope is connected to an a.c. generator. The trace produced on the oscilloscope is shown below.

The controls of the oscilloscope are not altered.

EXAM-STYLE ANSWERS

1 The coil is inside the magnetic field produced by the magnets. *(1 mark)*

  When a current flows through the coil it experiences a force due to the magnetic field. *(1 mark)*

  There is a downward force on one side of the coil. *(1 mark)*

  And an upward force on the other side of the coil *(1 mark)*

  so the coil turns around the axle. *(1 mark)*

  When the coil is vertical the brushes are not in contact and the current stops. *(1 mark)*

  The coil keeps moving past the vertical until brushes make contact *(1 mark)*

  so current in the coil is reversed *(1 mark)*

  so the coil continues to turn in the same direction. *(1 mark)*
  [**HT** only]

2 The rotating coil cuts through the magnetic field. *(1 mark)*

  A potential difference is induced across the ends of the coil. *(1 mark)*

  There is a complete circuit so current flows through the lamp. *(1 mark)*

  As coil turns, the direction of the current reverses every half turn so the current is a.c.. *(1 mark)*

  The slip rings rotate with the coil *(1 mark)*

  and the brushes connect the slip rings to the circuit *(1 mark)*

  otherwise the wires would tangle. *(1 mark)*
  [**HT** only]

3 a) i) Completed grid – shape and number of waves same as original, amplitude doubled
    - Sine wave shape. *(1 mark)*
    - Number of waves the same. *(1 mark)*
    - Amplitude doubled. *(1 mark)*

   ii) So the effect of doubling the number of turns on the coil could be observed. *(1 mark)*

  b) Completed grid – number of waves and amplitude of original sine wave both doubled
    - Sine wave shape. *(1 mark)*
    - Number of waves doubled. *(1 mark)*
    - Amplitude doubled. *(1 mark)*

HOW SCIENCE WORKS

Darren had been studying electromagnetism and learned how a potential difference could be induced by the movement of a magnet through a coil. He thought that he would find out how the speed of a magnet falling through a coil would change the p.d. produced.

The equipment was set up as below. He decided to vary the speed of the magnet by adjusting the height the magnet was dropped from.

Darren predicted that there would be a directly proportional relationship between the height the magnet was dropped from and the voltage induced.

Magnet

Voltmeter

The first attempt proved impossible. The voltmeter fluttered a little as the magnet passed, but a reading could not be taken.

a) Why was this preliminary test a failure? (1)
Darren put an oscilloscope in place of the voltmeter.

b) These were his results.

Height (cm)	5	15	25	35	45	50
Voltage (V)	0.06	0.15	0.21	0.24	0.26	0.27

Draw a graph of these results. (3)

c) Was Darren's prediction correct? (1)

d) What was the sensitivity of the oscilloscope? (1)

e) Was the oscilloscope sensitive enough for the range of the independent variable? (1)

f) How could Darren improve the accuracy of his results? (1)

g) How might Darren demonstrate the reliability of his results? (1)

h) What technological development might come from this idea? (1)

265

On a grid like the one shown above draw what the trace would look like if:

(a) (i) the number of turns on the coil is doubled while the speed of rotation and the magnetic field are kept constant. (3)
   (ii) Why are the speed of rotation and the magnetic field kept constant in (a) part i)?

(b) the speed of rotation is doubled while the number of turns on the coil and the magnetic field are kept constant. (3)

4 The diagram shows a transformer.

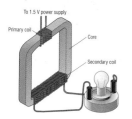

To 1.5 V power supply

Primary coil

Core

Secondary coil

(a) Explain how an alternating current in the primary coil produces an alternating current through the lamp. (4)

(b) The potential difference across the primary coil is 1.5 V. There are 6 turns on the primary coil and 24 turns on the secondary coil.

Calculate the potential difference across the lamp. (4)
[Higher]

---

4 a) Current produces a magnetic field in the iron core. *(1 mark)*
Alternating current, so a changing magnetic field. *(1 mark)*
Inducing and alternating p.d. across the secondary coil.
(1 mark)
So an alternating current flows through the lamp. *(1 mark)*

b) $\dfrac{V_p}{V_s} = \dfrac{N_p}{N_s}$ *(1 mark)*

$V_s = \dfrac{V_p N_s}{N_p}$ *(1 mark)*

$V_s = \dfrac{1.5\,V \times 24}{6}$ *(1 mark)*

$V_s = 6\,V$ [**HT** only] *(1 mark)*

Exam teaching suggestions

- Most students enjoy constructing their own motor from one of the many kits available and this is useful to reinforce their understanding of how a motor works.

- Both question 1 and question 2 require an extended prose answer. Students should practise producing these, putting their ideas in a sensible order and using scientific terms correctly.

- Question 3 requires students to sketch oscilloscope traces for a generator under different conditions. This is considerably more difficult than recognising which variables have changed from an oscilloscope trace and will be challenging for less-able students.

- In question 4 students must use the transformer formula. In examination questions many candidates make mistakes when rearranging this formula. Students should check that their answer makes sense – e.g. if they are dealing with a step-up transformer is their calculated secondary voltage larger than the primary voltage?

HOW SCIENCE WORKS ANSWERS

a) The voltmeter was not sensitive enough. It also would not give a read-out of the voltage, so it would be impossible to get an accurate result even if it was sensitive enough.

b) Height on the X axis, voltage on the Y axis. Axes fully labelled and plots correctly plotted, note inconsistent X axis data.

c) In part. The voltage increased as the height increased, but it was not directly proportional.

d) 0.01 V.

e) Not at the greater heights.

f) Improve the sensitivity of the oscilloscope. Repeat his results.

g) By checking it against other data/other similar research/get someone else to repeat his work or calculate theoretical relationships.

h) Open for good ideas! E.g. measuring the speed of an object moving through a tube?

How science works teaching suggestions

- **Literacy guidance**
  - Key terms that should be understood: prediction, sensitivity, reliability, accuracy graph drawing conclusions; technological developments.
  - The questions expecting a longer answer, where students can practise their literacy skills: a), g) and h)

- **Higher- and lower-level answers.** Questions c) and h) are higher-level questions. The answers for these have been provided at this level. Question a) is lower-level and the answers provided are lower-level.

- **Gifted and talented.** Able students could work out the relationship of the height to the voltage. They could consider the controls necessary.

- **How and when to use these questions.** When wishing to develop graph drawing skills and data analysis.
  The questions could be discussed in groups.

- **Homework.** The questions could be given for homework.

- **Special needs.** The experimental set up should be demonstrated to the students.

- **ICT link-up.** Able students could consider how data logging could be used for the voltage and for a direct recording of the speed of the falling magnet.

P3 4.1 Galaxies

SPECIFICATION LINK-UP   Unit: Physics 3.13.10

LEARNING OBJECTIVES

Students should learn:

- That a galaxy is a collection of millions or billions of stars bound together by gravitational attraction.
- That stars are formed by the action of gravitational forces of gas clouds.

LEARNING OUTCOMES

Most students should be able to:

- Describe the structure of a galaxy.
- Describe how the Universe changed after the Big Bang and how gravitational forces brought matter together to form structures like galaxies and stars.

Some students should also be able to:

- Explain why stars stay in a galaxy and why there are vast spaces between galaxies.

NEXT TIME YOU . . .

Look out at the Universe remember that most of it is missing. Astronomers can measure the mass of galaxies but the number of stars in them is not enough to account for all of it. There are a few theories about where this mass is, including brown dwarf stars and superheavy particles. Some students might like to find out more about this missing mass.

SPECIFICATION LINK-UP   Unit: Physics 3.13.10

- *Our Sun is one of the many billions of stars in the Milky Way galaxy.*
- *The Universe is made up of billions of galaxies.*

Lesson structure

STARTER

Galaxies – Show the students some images of galaxies and ask them to describe their shapes. How do they think that these were formed? (10 minutes)

From the beginning – The students draw a simple comic strip showing what they know about the beginning of the Universe. (10 minutes)

Brainstorm – In groups, the students connect up all of their ideas and knowledge about stars and the origin of the Universe. (10–15 minutes)

MAIN

- This is a bit of a 'story' topic where you have to convey a sense of wonder at the scale of the Universe and its age.
- Computer animations of the interaction of galaxies will be very helpful with this topic, so try to find a few.
- Hopefully the students will remember the lesson on the Big Bang. Get them to give their own descriptions of this, mentioning the creation of space, matter, energy and time.
- They should also know that the Universe expanded rapidly and is still expanding, so discuss the evidence we have for this: background radiation and red shift.
- It can be hard to get across the sheer scale of the Universe, the number of stars in each galaxy and the number of galaxies. The words 'billions of billions' tend to wash over the students. Try to get across the sheer size as best you can.
- The Dark Age of the Universe just means that no visible light was produced. Get the students to connect this with the lack of stars.
- Make sure that the students understand the reasons why matter did not come together in large quantities before the formation of neutral atoms, i.e. repulsion by the protons.
- The lumpiness of the Universe is a direct result of early fluctuations in the structure. You might want to show them the famous COBE picture of the early unevenness in the Universe. It was this tiny amount of variation that leads to the structures we see today.
- At the end, it is important to remind the students of the processes that are releasing energy in the stars. They will cover this in a bit more depth in lesson 4.3.

PLENARIES

Galactic poetry – Let the students write a poem about galaxies, gravity and the origin of the Universe. (10–15 minutes)

Sizes and distances – Can the students put a set of cards in order of how large the objects are and then arrange them in order of how far away from us they are? (5–10 minutes)

Putting it together – The students can cut and paste the stages of galactic evolution into the correct order. (10 minutes)

Teaching suggestions

- **Gifted and talented.** These students can look into the different types of galaxy that have been formed and the explanation for their shapes. They could even look at the more exotic structures such as 'active galaxies'.

- **Learning styles**

  Kinaesthetic: Doing the cut and paste activity.

  Visual: Studying the shape of galaxies.

  Auditory: Listening to the descriptions of the origin of the Universe and galaxies.

  Interpersonal: Discussing and evaluating the evidence for the Big Bang and galaxy formation.

  Intrapersonal: Considering the evidence for the Big Bang model.

- **Homework.** The students should find out about a galaxy other than our own. Ask: 'What is its name, how big is it, how far way and where in the sky can it be found?' A picture is compulsory.

- **ICT link-up.** Use the Internet to search for animations of galaxy formation and you should come up with some impressive computer generated imagery. You should also find with some free-to-use PowerPoint® presentations.

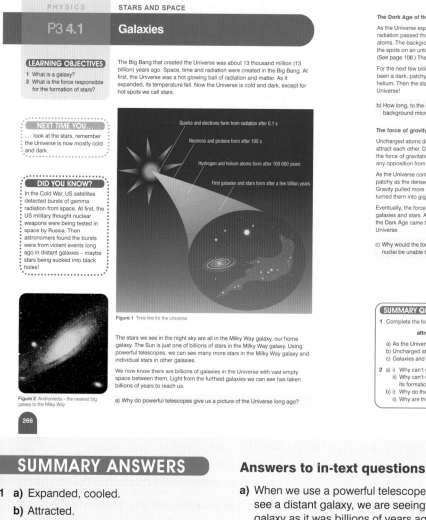

PHYSICS   STARS AND SPACE

P3 4.1   Galaxies

LEARNING OBJECTIVES

1 What is a galaxy?
2 What is the force responsible for the formation of stars?

The Big Bang that created the Universe was about 13 thousand million (13 billion) years ago. Space, time and radiation were created in the Big Bang. At first, the Universe was a hot glowing ball of radiation and matter. As it expanded, its temperature fell. Now the Universe is cold and dark, except for hot spots we call stars.

NEXT TIME YOU...

... look at the stars, remember the Universe is now mostly cold and dark.

DID YOU KNOW?

In the Cold War, US satellites detected bursts of gamma radiation from space. At first, the US military thought nuclear weapons were being tested in space by Russia. Then astronomers found the bursts were from violent events long ago in distant galaxies – maybe stars being sucked into black holes!

Quarks and electrons form from radiation after 0.1 s

Neutrons and protons form after 100 s

Hydrogen and helium atoms form after 100 000 years

First galaxies and stars form after a few billion years

Figure 1 Time line for the Universe

The stars we see in the night sky are all in the Milky Way galaxy, our home galaxy. The Sun is just one of billions of stars in the Milky Way galaxy. Using powerful telescopes, we can see many more stars in the Milky Way galaxy and individual stars in other galaxies.

We now know there are billions of galaxies in the Universe with vast empty space between them. Light from the furthest galaxies we can see has taken billions of years to reach us.

a) Why do powerful telescopes give us a picture of the Universe long ago?

Figure 2 Andromeda – the nearest big galaxy to the Milky Way

The Dark Age of the Universe

As the Universe expanded, it became transparent as radiation passed through the empty space between its atoms. The background microwave radiation that causes the spots on an untuned TV was released at this stage. (See page 108.) The Dark Age of the Universe had begun!

For the next few billion years, the Universe would have been a dark, patchy, expanding cloud of hydrogen and helium. Then the stars and galaxies formed and lit up the Universe!

b) How long, to the nearest billion years, has background microwave radiation been travelling for?

The force of gravity takes over

Uncharged atoms don't repel each other. But they can attract each other. During the Dark Age of the Universe, the force of gravitational attraction was at work without any opposition from repulsive forces.

As the Universe continued to expand, it become more patchy as the denser parts attracted nearby matter. Gravity pulled more matter into the denser parts and turned them into gigantic clumps.

Eventually, the force of gravity turned the clumps into galaxies and stars. A few billion years after the Big Bang, the Dark Age came to an end as the stars lit up the Universe.

c) Why would the force of gravity between two helium nuclei be unable to pull the nuclei together?

Figure 3 Arno Allan Penzias and Robert Woodrow Wilson standing on the radio antenna which unexpectedly discovered the Universe's microwave background radiation

Figure 4 The force of gravity takes over

Further physics

SUMMARY QUESTIONS

1 Complete the following sentences using words from the list.

    attracted   cooled   expanded   formed

   a) As the Universe ......, it ....
   b) Uncharged atoms ...... each other.
   c) Galaxies and stars ...... from uncharged atoms.

2 a) i) Why can't we take a photo of the Milky Way galaxy from outside?
      ii) Why can't we take photos of a distant galaxy at different stages in its formation?
   b) i) Why do the stars in a galaxy not drift away from each other?
      ii) Why are there vast spaces between the galaxies?

KEY POINTS

1 As the Universe expanded, it cooled and uncharged atoms formed.
2 The force of gravity pulled matter into galaxies and stars.

266   267

SUMMARY ANSWERS

1 a) Expanded, cooled.

  b) Attracted.

  c) Formed.

2 a) i) We could not send a probe far enough.

    ii) Galaxies take millions of years to form; we couldn't wait that long.

  b) i) Gravitational forces hold the stars together.

    ii) The Universe has expanded leaving these vast spaces.

Answers to in-text questions

a) When we use a powerful telescope to see a distant galaxy, we are seeing the galaxy as it was billions of years ago because the light from it has taken billions of years to reach us.

b) About 13 billion years.

c) They are both positively charged, so they repel each other. The force of repulsion is much greater than the force of gravity between them.

KEY POINTS

Can the students describe the early stages of the Universe and how the changes in temperature/energy led to the formation of galaxies? They could present this as a sequencing exercise for another class to attempt.

P3 4.2   The life history of a star

LEARNING OBJECTIVES

Students should learn:

- That the Sun is a typical small star and how it developed into its current 'main sequence' state.
- That the Sun will continue to develop, passing through a red giant and white dwarf stage before reaching the end of its energy-producing life.
- That bigger stars can explode in a supernova and produce exotic objects like neutron stars or black holes.

LEARNING OUTCOMES

Most students should be able to:

- Describe the stages in the complete life cycle of a typical star such as the Sun.
- Outline the stages that larger stars can go through in producing neutron stars and black holes.

Some students should also be able to:

- Describe what a black hole is and what its main property is.

Teaching suggestions

- **Special needs.** Give the students a set of diagrams to cut out and paste in order. They should add information to these during the lesson.
- **Gifted and talented.** The life cycle of a star can be described through a diagram know as the 'Hertzsprung–Russell' diagram. The students should find out what this is and how the life of the Sun would be represented on it.
- **Learning styles**

  Kinaesthetic: Sorting and/or cutting pasting cards.
  Visual: Looking at pictures and animations of the life cycle of stars.
  Auditory: Explaining the processes that are causing the changes in stars.
  Intrapersonal: Appreciating the large timescales involves in stellar evolution.

- **Homework.** The students could write a story, or draw a comic strip, about an ageless observer that watches the life of our Solar System from beginning to end.
- **ICT link-up.** Search the Internet for 'life cycle of stars' or 'life cycle of stars video'. These are much better at showing the processes than diagrams, so try to use one.

SPECIFICATION LINK-UP   Unit: Physics 3.13.10

- *Stars form when enough dust and gas from space is pulled together by gravitational attraction. Smaller masses may also form and be attracted by a larger mass to become planets.*
- *Gravitational forces balance radiation pressure to make a star stable.*
- *A star goes through a life cycle (limited to the life cycle of stars of similar size to the Sun and stars much larger than the Sun).*

Students should use their skills, knowledge and understanding of 'How Science Works':

- *to explain how stars are able to maintain their energy output for millions of years.*

Lesson structure

STARTER

The celestial sphere – Show the students some photographs of the night sky pointing out a large range of stars. Ask the student to find a pattern in the stars and come up with a legend of how it got there. (10 minutes)

The seven ages of man – Can the students come up with a list of words used to describe the stages of human development and ageing? [Shakespeare had infant, whining schoolboy, lover, soldier, justice, old age and finally a second childhood (senility), but these are hardly scientific.] (5–10 minutes)

MAIN

- The constituents that form to make a star are mostly hydrogen gas.
- During the collapse, the material heats up by frictional processes and begins to radiate infra-red radiation so astronomers are hoping to detect this to confirm the formation process. This is very difficult because the protostar would have a lot of gas and dust still surrounding it (a Bok Globule).
- Stars are formed in groups as the different parts of the original nebula collapse. One of these is in the heart of the Orion Nebula; you could show pictures of stellar nurseries.
- It is worth quickly going through the basic fusion process, if the students are unfamiliar with it at this point.
- Use the term 'equilibrium' when describing the two processes involved in maintaining the star, so that the students link this ideas across all of the work on forces.
- With students wishing to move on to further physics courses, you might want to talk about the main sequence here; see 'Gifted and talented'.
- The description of the change into a red giant should be accompanied by an animation. You should be able to find one showing the expansion of our Sun swallowing up Mercury and Venus.
- The white dwarf phase produces an object of massive density. Beware: the students may still be thinking that the object is 'gas' so it is light.
- You can do a comparison of the radii, surface temperatures and density of the Sun, a red giant and a white dwarf.
- The last phase of the life cycle of stars interests the students, so make it dramatic. The students may have heard of it before, but show them some pictures of the objects.
- The students should be left with the idea that the processes involved take millions of years and that our Sun has plenty of life left in it yet.

PLENARIES

Sequence sort – Give the students a set of cards describing the *processes* that are happening in the life cycle of stars (but not the name of the stages) and ask them to sort them into order. (10 minutes)

SDRAWKCAB – The students should draw a flow chart of the life cycle of a star, but make it backwards. (5 minutes)

Stellar research

- Give the students a stellar object each to research (or pair them up), to make a wall display about the life cycle of stars. They will need access to the Internet and various drawing tools.

- The students should find examples and details about a range of objects associated with the life cycle of stars. Some suitable objects to find out about are: our Sun (sol), stellar nurseries, protostars, giant molecular clouds, neutron stars, black holes, pulsars, white dwarfs, brown dwarfs, red giants, blue giants and planetary nebulae.

- Observing the birth of a star: the students could find out about the infra-red techniques used to 'see' the birth of stars through the dust clouds that surround them.

DID YOU KNOW?

Before nuclear fusion was discovered and recognised as the process that releases energy in the Sun, scientists had worked out the age of the Sun to be a maximum of 10 million years because they thought it was burning and releasing energy from chemical reactions.

PHYSICS   STARS AND SPACE

P3 4.2   The life history of a star

DID YOU KNOW?
The Sun will turn into a red giant bigger than the orbit of Mercury. By then, the human race will probably have long passed into history. But will intelligent life still exist?

LEARNING OBJECTIVES

1 What will eventually happen to the Sun?
2 What evidence is there for black holes?

The birth of a star

Stars form out of clouds of dust and gas.

- The particles in the clouds gather together under their own gravity. The clouds merge and become more and more concentrated to form a protostar, the name for a star to be.
- As a 'protostar' becomes denser, it gets hotter. If it becomes hot enough, the nuclei of hydrogen atoms and other light elements fuse together. Energy is released in the process so the core gets hotter and brighter and starts to shine. A star is born!

a) Where does the energy to heat a protostar come from?

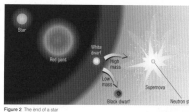
Figure 2 The end of a star

Shining stars

Stars like the Sun radiate energy because of hydrogen fusion in the core. This is the main stage in the life of a star. It can continue for billions of years until the star runs out of hydrogen nuclei to fuse together.

- Energy released in the core keeps the core hot so the process of fusion continues. Radiation flows out steadily from the core in all directions.
- The force of gravity that makes a star contract is balanced by the outward pressure of radiation from its core. These forces stay in balance until most of the hydrogen nuclei in the core have been fused together.

b) Why doesn't the Sun collapse under its own gravity?

Figure 1 Star birth

The end of a star

When a star runs out of hydrogen nuclei to fuse together, it will swell out.

- As it swells, it cools down and turns red. It becomes a **red giant**. At this stage, helium and other light elements in its core fuse to form heavier elements.
- When there are no more light elements in its core, fusion stops. No more radiation is released and the star collapses on itself. As it collapses, it heats up and turns from red to yellow to white. It becomes a **white dwarf**, a hot, dense white star much smaller in diameter than it was. Stars like the Sun then fade out and go cold.

Bigger stars end their life much more dramatically. Their collapse continues past the 'white dwarf' stage then suddenly reverses in a cataclysmic explosion known as a **supernova**. Such an event can outshine an entire galaxy for several weeks.

DID YOU KNOW?
The Sun is about 5000 million years old and will probably continue to shine for another 5000 million years.

c) What force causes a red giant to collapse?

What remains after a supernova occurs?

The explosion compresses the core of the star into a **neutron star**, an extremely dense object composed only of neutrons. If the neutron star is massive enough, it becomes a **black hole**. Its gravitational field would then be so strong that nothing could escape from it, not even light or any other form of electromagnetic radiation.

d) What force causes matter to be dragged into a black hole?

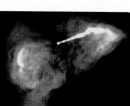
Figure 3 M87 is a galaxy that spins so fast at its centre that it is thought to contain a black hole with a billion times more mass than the Sun

SUMMARY QUESTIONS

1 a) The list below shows some of the stages in the life of a star. Put the stages in the correct sequence.

   A main stage   B protostar   C red giant   D white dwarf

   b) i) Which stage in the above list is the Sun at now?
      ii) What will happen to the Sun after it has gone through the above stages?

2 a) Complete the sentences using words from the list.

   collapse   expand   explode

   i) The Sun will eventually ...... then ....
   ii) A white dwarf with a large enough mass will ...... then ....
   b) i) What is the main condition needed for a neutron star to form a black hole?
      ii) Why is it not possible for light to escape from a black hole?

KEY POINTS
1 Low mass star:

   protostar → main stage → red giant → white dwarf → black dwarf

2 High mass star, after the white dwarf stage:

   white dwarf → supernova → neutron star → black hole if sufficient mass

---

SUMMARY ANSWERS

1 a) B, A, C, D.

   b) i) A

      ii) It will fade out and go cold.

2 a) i) Expand, collapse.

      ii) Explode, collapse.

   b) i) The neutron star must have sufficient mass.

      ii) The gravitational field is so strong that nothing can escape from it.

Answers to in-text questions

a) The potential energy of gas and dust decreases when it gathers and is transformed into heat energy.

b) The outward pressure of radiation from its core stops it collapsing.

c) Gravity.

d) Gravity.

KEY POINTS

Get the students to draw a comic strip showing the complete life cycle of small and large stars.

P3 4.3   How the chemical elements formed

LEARNING OBJECTIVES

Students should learn:

- That elements as heavy as iron are formed in nuclear fusion processes in stars. [**HT** only]
- That heavier elements are formed in supernova explosions. [**HT** only]
- That the material produced in stars can be spread out in explosions and can end up in new solar systems. [**HT** only]

LEARNING OUTCOMES

Most students should be able to:

- State that elements as heavy as iron are formed by nuclear fusion processes. [**HT** only]
- Describe a supernova event and how such events can lead to the formation of new stars. [**HT** only]

Some students should also be able to:

- Explain why the Earth contains elements heavier than iron as well as lighter elements. [**HT** only]

Teaching suggestions

- **Gifted and talented.** There are smaller explosions involving stars called 'simple novas'. Can the students find an explanation of what causes these?

- **Learning styles**

  Kinaesthetic: Researching into Mars exploration.

  Visual: Solving the mystery message.

  Auditory: Discussing the chances of discovering intelligent life.

  Intrapersonal: Writing a report on the likelihood of life on Mars.

- **Homework.** The end of the world is inevitable; one day, in billions of years time, we will have to abandon the Earth and move on. The students could design a monument to be left behind on the dead planet, marking the birthplace of the Human Race.

- **ICT link-up.** Use an astronomy CD or Internet searches to help students find out about exploration of the Solar System and Mars, in particular. Search the Internet for 'exploration solar system Mars' and see www.nasa.com.

SPECIFICATION LINK-UP   Unit: Physics 3.13.10

- *Fusion processes in stars produce all naturally occurring elements. These elements may be distributed throughout the Universe by the explosion of a star (supernova) at the end of its life. [**HT** only]*

Students should use their skills, knowledge and understanding of 'How Science Works':

- *to explain why the early Universe contained only hydrogen but now contains a large variety of different elements. [**HT** only]*

Lesson structure

STARTER

Nuclear processes – Get the students to draw a spider diagram showing their knowledge of nuclear fusion and fission. (10 minutes)

Star stuff – 'We are all made of stars.' What do the students think this means; is it a scientific statement? You could play the song of the same title while the students think about their answers. (5 minutes)

Building blocks – How many separate elements can the students name? You could play the famous periodic table element song. Ask: 'What is the meaning of the word 'element'?' (5–10 minutes)

MAIN

- Start by again reminding the students about nuclear fusion processes, but expand on these ideas leading to the manufacture of heavier nuclei such as carbon.

- Some of the students should remember that there is a limit to this process: iron nuclei. This is because it takes more energy to produce heavier nuclei than would be given out.

- Ask the students where they think that the extra energy required comes from; they could come up with the idea that the supernova explosion provides it.

- This can lead on to a discussion of the energy output from a supernova, which is something like 10^{46} joules. The power output of the Sun is 10^{28} watts, so it would take about 32 billion years to release this amount of energy. Hopefully this will give the students some impression of the scale of the explosion.

- Some of the students may know that, in addition to the original quantity of lead when the Earth formed, some lead has been formed from the nuclear decay of heavier elements.

- The last part of the spread picks up the idea of extra-terrestrial life. Some students will have strong opinions about this as they will have been exposed to a lot of 'facts' from various sources.

- It is worth getting the latest details on the search for life on Mars to have a discussion with the students. (See 'Activity and extension ideas.')

- In addition, you can discuss the techniques needed to spot planets in other solar systems. This is a rapidly developing field with none known until 1989. Detection of planets around the size of the Earth is the next big step in this project.

PLENARIES

My life as a proton – The students should imagine that they are a proton in a hydrogen molecule in a giant gas cloud. Ask: 'How do they get from here to a proton in a uranium atom inside a nuclear reactor over the course of ten billion years?' (10–15 minutes)

Star jewellery – Students could make an advert for a piece of finely crafted 'star stuff'; made in the heart of a supernova and costing a mere £20 000. It's only made of copper though! (10 minutes)

Don't panic! – Students to imagine that a large object has entered the Solar System and it appears to be slowing down. In a year it will reach our home world and enter orbit. Students could prepare a poster to alert the public without causing global panic. (15–20 minutes)

Mars

Mars is the most studied planet in the Solar System besides the Earth. It has huge mythological and scientific importance. If evidence of life can be found so close to us, it would mean that the likelihood of life outside the Solar System would be very high. The students can look in detail about the history of Mars and its exploration. Highlights include the 'canals' and volcanoes on Mars, the Viking and Pathfinder probes and the proposed manned exploration later in the twenty-first century. They can look into some of the less scientific ideas too, including the invasion from *War of The Worlds* and the many faces and pyramids that 'prove' that there is life.

Hidden message

To show how difficult it is to find a message in random background noise, try this task.

Details

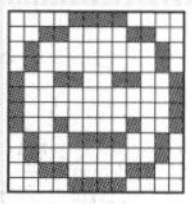

Create a 12 by 12 table in a word processor and fill in the cells with the symbols ':' and 'X' so that they create a shape; a smiley face works well. Get the word processor to convert the table into text and delete any line breaks, to end up with a long sequence of ':'s and 'X's. Without telling the students about the size of the grid, see if they can find out what the symbol is. A smaller starting grid will make this easier.

DID YOU KNOW?

You can find a before/after picture of Sanduleak (SN1987A) easily on the Internet. You should also find images of the object taken by the Hubble Space Telescope several years later, showing the material thrown off by the explosion in a set of rings. The reason for the ring formation is still under investigation.

P3 4.3   How the chemical elements formed

LEARNING OBJECTIVES

1 How were the heavy elements formed?
2 Why does the Earth contain heavy elements?

Figure 1 The Crab Nebula

DID YOU KNOW?

The Crab Nebula is the remnants of a supernova explosion that was observed in the 11th century. In 1987, a star in the southern hemisphere exploded and became the biggest supernova to be seen for four centuries. Astronomers realised that it was *Sanduleak II*, a star in the Andromeda galaxy millions of light years from Earth.

FOUL FACTS

If a star near the Sun exploded, the Earth would probably be blasted out of its orbit. We would see the explosion before the shock wave hits us.

The birthplace of the chemical elements

* **Light elements are formed as a result of fusion in stars.**

Stars like the Sun fuse hydrogen nuclei (i.e. protons) into helium and similar small nuclei, including carbon. When it becomes a red giant, it fuses helium and the other small nuclei into larger nuclei.

Nuclei larger than iron cannot be formed by this process because too much energy is needed.

* **Heavy elements are formed when a massive star collapses then explodes as a supernova.**

The enormous force of the collapse fuses small nuclei into nuclei larger than iron. The explosion scatters the star into space.

The debris from a supernova contains all the known elements from the lightest to the heaviest. Eventually, new stars form as gravity pulls the debris together.

Planets form from debris surrounding a new star. As a result, such planets will be composed of all the known elements too.

a) Lead is much heavier than iron. How did the lead we use form?

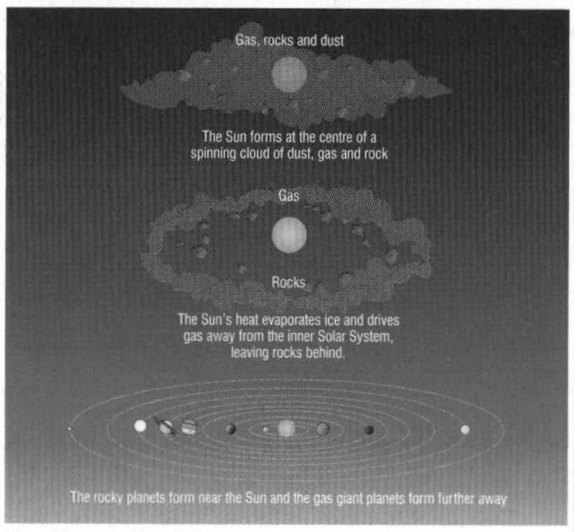

Gas, rocks and dust

The Sun forms at the centre of a spinning cloud of dust, gas and rock

Gas

Rocks

The Sun's heat evaporates ice and drives gas away from the inner Solar System, leaving rocks behind.

The rocky planets form near the Sun and the gas giant planets form further away

Figure 2 Formation of the Solar System

Planet Earth

The heaviest known natural element is uranium. It has a half life of 4500 million years. The presence of uranium in the Earth is evidence that the Solar System must have formed from the remnants of a supernova.

b) Plutonium 239 has a half life of about 24 000 years. So why is it not found naturally like uranium?

Is there or has there been life on other planets, either in our own Solar System or around other stars? Astronomers can see Earth-like planets in orbit round other stars. We know that molecules of carbon-based chemicals are present in space. Life on Earth probably developed from chemicals reacting in lightning storms.

So are we looking for any scientific evidence about life elsewhere?

* **Space probes sent to Mars** have tested the atmosphere, rocks and soil on Mars looking for any microbes or any chemicals that might indicate life was once present on Mars.
* **The search for extra-terrestrial intelligence,** known as SETI, has gone on for more than 40 years using radio telescopes. Signals from space would indicate the existence of living beings with technologies at least as advanced as our own. No signals have been detected – yet!

c) Why is carbon an important element?

Figure 3 Life on Mars?

DID YOU KNOW?

Elements such as plutonium are heavier than uranium. Scientists can make these elements by bombarding heavy elements like uranium with high-speed neutrons. They would have been present in the debris which formed the Solar System. Elements heavier than uranium formed then have long since decayed.

SUMMARY QUESTIONS

1 Match each statement below with an element in the list.

helium   hydrogen   iron   uranium

a) Helium nuclei are formed when nuclei of this element are fused.
b) This element is formed in a supernova explosion.
c) Stars form nuclei of these two elements (and others not listed) by fusing smaller nuclei.
d) The early Universe mostly consisted of this element.

2 Choose the correct words from the list to complete each of the sentences a) to c).

galaxy   planets   stars   supernova

a) Fusion inside ...... creates light elements. Fusion in a ...... creates heavy elements.
b) A ...... scatters the elements throughout a ....
c) ...... and planets formed from the debris of a ...... contain all the known elements.

NEXT TIME YOU...

... are told by someone that aliens are here from space, remember there's no scientific evidence so far for life beyond the Earth.

KEY POINTS

1 Elements as heavy as iron are formed inside stars as a result of nuclear fusion.
2 Elements heavier than iron are formed in supernovas.

SUMMARY ANSWERS

1 a) Hydrogen.
 b) Uranium.
 c) Helium, iron.
 d) Hydrogen. [**HT** only]

2 a) Stars, supernova.
 b) Supernova, galaxy.
 c) Stars, supernova. [**HT** only]

Answers to in-text questions

a) In a supernova explosion.

b) Its half life is very short compared with the age of the Sun. Any plutonium formed when the Sun formed would have decayed long ago.

c) Carbon atoms are in all the molecules that make up living objects.

KEY POINTS

The students should be able to outline the manufacture of elements in stars and know that elements heavier than iron are only produced in supernovae explosions. They could present this as one in a set of revision cards made from the key points in this chapter.

P3 4.4   Universal issues

PHYSICS   STARS AND SPACE

P3 4.4   Universal issues

SPECIFICATION LINK-UP

Unit: Physics 3.13.10

This spread can be used to revisit the following substantive content covered in this chapter:

- *Stars form when enough dust and gas from space is pulled together by gravitational attraction. Smaller masses may also form and be attracted by a larger mass to become planets.*

- *Gravitational forces balance radiation pressure to make a star stable.*

- *A star goes through a life cycle (limited to the life cycle of stars of similar size to the Sun and stars much larger than the Sun).*

- *Fusion processes in stars produce all naturally occurring elements. These elements may be distributed throughout the Universe by the explosion of a star (supernova) at the end of its life. [HT only]*

Students should use their skills, knowledge and understanding of 'How Science Works':

- *To explain how stars are able to maintain their energy output for millions of years.*

- *To explain why the early Universe contained only hydrogen but now contains a large variety of different elements. [HT only]*

Teaching suggestions

Activities

- **Sail to the stars** – The Voyager space probes each carry a golden record with messages and information about the Earth. The students could find out what the record contains and how it is that aliens are supposed to be able to decode it, as they won't speak any Earthly language. To find more details search the Internet for 'Voyager message'. Can the students design a more up-to-date alternative to this record and what music would they send? Using a PC, the students could actually burn a disc containing a message, some images and music.

- Solar sails are still in their early experimental stage, but some test vehicles have been launched. The students can find out about the results of these experiments.

Light years

The light year is the distance travelled by light in 1 year. The nearest star to the Sun is about 3 light years away. The most distant galaxies are about 10 thousand million light years away. Light takes about

- 5 minutes to reach us from the Sun,
- 6 hours to reach us from Pluto, the most remote planet,
- 3 years from Proxima Centauri, the nearest star beyond the Sun,
- 100 000 years to cross the Milky Way galaxy,
- 2 million years to reach us from Andromeda, the nearest large galaxy beyond the Milky Way,
- 10 000 million years from the most distant galaxy.

QUESTION

Imagine the Sun scaled down to the size of a football. The Earth would be the size of a grain of rice about 30 metres away. Estimate how far it would be to:

a) Pluto,   **b)** the nearest star,   **c)** the furthest galaxies.

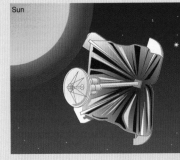

Sail to the stars

The Sun gives out a steady stream of radiation in all directions. Some scientists reckon the pressure of solar radiation could be used to carry a spaceship to the stars. The spaceship would need to have gigantic sails to catch enough solar radiation.

The force of the radiation would accelerate the spaceship almost to the speed of light. It could reach the nearest star within a few years and it could send back video pictures. The spaceship could carry a message from all the people on the Earth.

ACTIVITY

What message would you want to be carried on the spaceship? Turn your message into a poster.

272

- **Space costs** – The cost of the Apollo programme that led to the American landing on the Moon was $25 billion in 1968. Including all of the prior programmes to get this far, the total cost was about $100 billion; in today's terms this would be approaching half a trillion dollars! The students should be able to find out the current costs associated with the International Space Station and the projected costs of the proposed future Mars mission. Ask: 'How do these costs compare with the costs of other projects? Are they justified?'

- **Worm holes** – Test the students' understanding of the grandfather paradox. If they went back in time to a point before their grandfather had produced their father and killed him, what would happen? If an advanced civilisation did invent a time machine, how could they prevent this kind of problem happening? Perhaps the students should make a set of rules about what they could and could not do on a journey to the past.

- **The 'big picture'** – There is clearly a lot to discuss and debate here. Much information about the 'Intelligent Design' theory is available online, but most scientists view the concept as a 'pseudo-religious' one that is not in any way testable and therefore not scientific. Ask: 'What are the requirements of a scientific theory? What are the physical requirements for life to start spontaneously, and where and when do scientists think that these conditions were met on the Earth?'

Space costs

Space missions take years to plan and cost enormous sums of money. Many people argue that the money could be spent better on improving life here on Earth – ending extreme poverty in poor countries, providing better health care and housing, solving the problem of greenhouse gases, etc., etc. Others argue that scientific progress in the past has given us prosperity and living standards beyond the dreams of previous generations.

You must be joking, Columbus!

ACTIVITY

a) Imagine you are Christopher Columbus and you need to convince wealthy people to fund your project to find a sea route west to China. They think you'll drop off the edge of the world and never be seen again. Write a speech to convince them.

b) Fast-forward to the 21st century and turn your speech into an argument for a space project.

All that pollution!

Worm holes

Gravity bends light. That's what Einstein predicted in 1915. He worked out how much a ray of light would bend if it skimmed the Sun. Astronomers discovered he was right when they observed the solar eclipse of 1919. Einstein's light-bending theory also predicted black holes.

Science fiction stories often stretch Einstein's ideas to 'worm holes', 'teleportation', 'warp speeds', 'time travel', etc., etc. Step into a teleporter and you go through a wormhole to anywhere in space and time. As if!

ACTIVITY

a) Write a short news report on what you saw when you 'visited' a famous historical event.

b) Science fiction is no more scientific than 'reading your stars'. What do you think?

The 'big picture'

For many centuries, the Church held the view that the Earth is at the centre of the Universe. Galileo used his observations of stars and planets to challenge this view. Now we accept that the Earth is an insignificant planet orbiting one of the countless stars in one of countless galaxies in the Universe. But why did intelligent life develop on the Earth?

- Was it the Goldilocks theory – not too hot, not too cold, just right for life?
- Was it Intelligent Design – intelligent life needs an intelligent designer?

ACTIVITY

What do you think? Find out what other people think and debate the issue in your group.

273

Extension or homework

- **The songs of distant Earth** – Let the students manufacture the disc described in the 'Sail to the stars' activity. If you have a digital video camera, you could let the students record a message each onto the disc. Make sure that they have different things to say, otherwise the aliens will quickly grow bored!

- **The hundred-light-year-diary** – What if it were possible to send short messages to the past? If a worm hole has opened up that will allow the students to send one text message a day five years into the past; would they use it? If messages from their thirty-year-old 'future selves' started to appear giving them advice, would they follow that advice? See the short story: *The Hundred-Light-Year-Diary*, Greg Egan, for some consequences.

Special needs

For the 'big picture' debate, you might want to provide some pre-written roles, such as a priest, atheist, scientist, old woman, etc. The students could edit these for their debate.

Gifted and talented

During the discussion for the 'big picture', higher attaining students may like to look up the 'Anthropic Principle'. This discusses why the Universe is the way it is and if it is inevitable that intelligent life will evolve.

Learning styles

Kinaesthetic: Researching and role-play.

Visual: Imagining the possibilities and consequences of time travel.

Auditory: Listening and discussing.

Interpersonal: Debates on a range of issues.

Intrapersonal: Reflecting on the origin and nature of intelligent life.

ICT link-up

See 'The songs of distant Earth' extension.

SUMMARY ANSWERS

1 a) Planet.

   b) Galaxy.

   c) Stars.

   d) Stars, galaxy.

2 a) Gravity.

   b) The core doesn't become hot enough to fuse hydrogen nuclei.

   c) The outward pressure of radiation from its core.

   d) Fusion.

3 a) A, C, B, D, E.

   b) i) It will fade out.

      ii) It will explode as a supernova, leaving a neutron star at its core. If the mass of the neutron star is large enough, it will be a black hole.

4 a) i) A large star that explodes.

      ii) A star that becomes a supernova suddenly becomes much brighter then it fades. A star like the Sun has a constant brightness.

   b) i) A massive object which nothing can escape from.

      ii) They would be pulled in by the force of gravity and then disappear.

5 a) i) Helium.

      ii) Helium.

   b) i) Lead, uranium.

      ii) Heavy elements can only have formed in a supernova. The presence of heavy elements in the Earth tell us the Solar System formed from the debris of a supernova.

[**HT** only]

Summary teaching suggestions

- Question 1 is a relatively simple one to test the students' basics knowledge of the structure of the Universe. This can be converted to a drag-and-drop activity on an interactive whiteboard. Here it could be expanded to cover questions about the Big Bang by adding a few more sentences.

- Question 2 looks at some of the more difficult aspects and will show if the students can apply their knowledge.

- Question 3 can be converted into a card sort game, but add additional information to the cards to show the processes that are happening during that stage. For example, for the 'present stage' card add 'nuclear fusion in the core is releasing energy and the pressure of the radiation balances the gravity of the star'. For the second part of the question the students can write out their own cards for the missing stages.

- Question 4 is about more exotic objects. If the students seem to struggle, then show them the pictures of the objects again. Few students will have trouble remembering a black hole swallows up other matter, but make sure that they are saying that this is because of the very strong gravitational pull. They must mention that this is so strong that even light cannot escape.

- Question 5 is relatively simple, as the students just have to remember that light elements are produced in stars, while very heavy ones are made in supernovae explosions.

STARS AND SPACE: P3 4.1 – P3 4.4

SUMMARY QUESTIONS

1 Complete each sentence below using words from the list.

   galaxy   planet   stars

   a) A ...... isn't big enough to be a star.

   b) The Sun is inside a ....

   c) ...... became hot after they formed from matter pulled together by the force of gravity.

   d) The force of gravity keeps ...... together inside a ....

2 a) What force pulls dust and gas in space?

   b) Why do large planets like Jupiter not produce their own light?

   c) What stops the Sun collapsing under its own weight?

   d) What is the name for the type of reaction that releases energy in the core of the Sun?

3 a) The stages in the development of a star like the Sun are listed below. Put the stages in the correct sequence.

A dust and gas	B present stage
C protostar	D red giant
E white dwarf	

   b) After the white dwarf stage,
      i) what will happen to the Sun,
      ii) what will happen to a star that has much more mass than the Sun?

4 a) i) What is a supernova?
      ii) How could we tell the difference between a supernova and a distant star like the Sun at present?

   b) i) What is a black hole?
      ii) What would happen to stars and planets near a black hole?

5 a) i) Which element as well as hydrogen formed in the early Universe?
      ii) Which of the two elements is formed from the other one in a star?

   b) i) Which two of the elements listed below is not formed in a star that gives out radiation at a steady rate?

      carbon   iron   lead   uranium

      ii) How do we know that the Sun formed from the debris of a supernova?

      [Higher]

274

EXAM-STYLE QUESTIONS

1 Stars go through a life cycle. Some stars eventually become *black holes*.

   (a) What type of star may eventually become a *black hole*? (2)

   (b) Describe what is meant by a *black hole*. (2)

2 The sentences below describe the life cycle of a star such as the Sun.

   A The star contracts to form a white dwarf.

   B The star is in a stable state.

   C The star expands to form a red giant.

   D Gravitational forces pull dust and gas together and the star is formed.

   (a) Put the sentences in the correct order. (3)

   ☐ → ☐ → ☐ → ☐

   (b) At which stage in its life is the Sun, **A, B, C** or **D**? (1)

   (c) What balances the gravitational forces to make a star stable? (2)

3 Describe as fully as you can what is meant by:

   (a) the Milky Way (3)

   (b) a neutron star (2)

   (c) a supernova. (2)

4 (a) Explain how a star generates energy. (3)

   (b) The early universe contained only hydrogen but now contains many heavier elements. The inner planets of the solar system contain atoms of these heavier elements.

      (i) Where did these atoms come from?
      (ii) What does this tell us about the age of the solar system? (3)

      [Higher]

EXAM-STYLE ANSWERS

1 a) Stars **much** larger than the Sun. *(2 marks)*

   b) Matter that has a very strong gravitational field *(1 mark)*
      so not even electromagnetic radiation can escape. *(1 mark)*

2 a) D B C A *(3 marks)*
      (−1 for each letter not in correct order)

   b) B *(1 mark)*

   c) Radiation pressure *(1 mark)*
      acting outwards. *(1 mark)*

3 a) A galaxy *(1 mark)*
      containing millions of stars *(1 mark)*
      including the Sun. *(1 mark)*

   b) An extremely dense star *(1 mark)*
      composed only of neutrons. *(1 mark)*

   c) An enormous explosion *(1 mark)*
      when a massive star has collapsed past the white dwarf stage. *(1 mark)*

4 a) By the process of nuclear fusion *(1 mark)*
      light nuclei fuse to form heavier nuclei *(1 mark)*
      releasing energy. *(1 mark)*

   b) i) The heavier elements come from fusion processes *(1 mark)*
         distributed by supernovae explosions. *(1 mark)*
      ii) Solar system was formed from past supernovae so is relatively young. *(1 mark)*

      [**HT** only]

HOW SCIENCE WORKS

The Earth at the centre of the Universe?

A Chinese myth (600 BC) tells how the Earth was created by Phan Ku. He carved the mountains and the rivers and then created the Moon and the stars. Other cultures have their own myths of the relationship between the Earth and other 'heavenly' bodies in the sky. The word 'myth' comes from the Greek word for 'story'. Anaxagoras (fifth-century BC) claimed that the Moon and the Sun were merely rocks and not gods. This was frowned upon by the Greek authorities who exiled him from Athens. Observations clearly showed that the Moon, the Sun and the stars moved across the sky and re-appeared the next day. Therefore the Earth must be at the centre of the Universe. It was a matter of making the detailed observations and calculations fit this model. Philolaus was the first person recorded to have suggested that the Earth moved around the Sun. The Greeks concluded that this hypothesis was wrong, because if it were true, there would be a constant wind. Ptolemy (second-century AD) worked hard to support the Earth-centred theory with mathematical calculations of great complexity. Copernicus in the sixteenth century countered Ptolemy's view of the Universe by using data about the size of the Moon. Copernicus believed that

- the Earth and the planets orbited the Sun,
- the Moon orbited the Earth,
- the movement of the stars was due to the Earth rotating.

Bruno went further and suggested that the stars could have planets and these could have life on them. The Church burnt him to death in 1600 because of his religious beliefs. The Copernican view of the Universe suffered a set-back because it had been supported by Bruno. However, the Copernican model was eventually accepted – largely as a result of Galileo's astronomical observations and his long struggle with the Church to gain acceptance of the Copernican model.

Use this passage to illustrate examples of the following scientific ideas:

a) myths   (1)
b) observation   (1)
c) data   (1)
d) hypothesis   (1)
e) a theory that has been disproved   (1)
f) a theory that remains to be disproved   (1)
g) political influence on science.   (1)

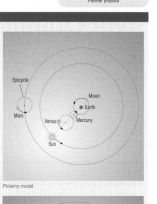

Ptolemy model

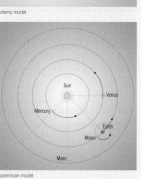

Copernican model

275

HOW SCIENCE WORKS ANSWERS

a) Myths: how the Earth was created by Phan Ku, but of course there are many more that could be discussed here.

b) Observations: that the Sun, moon, planets and stars move across the sky.

c) The data concerning the size of the moon. Ptolomy's Earth-centred model required the moon to speed up and slow down and hence therefore appear to change its size as seen from Earth. The moon, when measured, did not show these changes in apparent size.

d) Example of hypothesis: Anaxagoras hypothesised that the Sun and the moon were made of rocks.

e) Ptolomy's Earth-centred theory of the universe.

f) Copernicus' theory of the universe because it is supported by much evidence, but theories are not completely proven in all instances and therefore always open to being disproved. This is more obviously shown by Bruno. Planets are being discovered around stars, but there is no evidence of life outside of the Earth.

g) Anaxagoras and Bruno were examples of political influences on science.

How science works teaching suggestions

- **Literacy guidance**
  - Key terms that should be understood: myths, observation, hypothesis, theory, political influence.
  - The questions expecting a longer answer, where students can practise their literacy skills: c) and f).

- **Higher- and lower-level answers.** Questions c) and f) are higher-level questions. The answers for these have been provided at this level. Questions a) and b) are lower level and the answers provided are lower level.

- **Gifted and talented.** Able students could research the definitions of a theory and a model. The difference between the two is not always clear. Perhaps, the best way to differentiate is that a model puts together ideas into a common framework. A theory does the same but is capable of being used to generate hypotheses, predictions and therefore being tested.

- **How and when to use these questions.** When wishing to illustrate the development of scientific methods in the earlier days of science.
  The questions will need small group discussion with help, or whole class discussion.

- **Homework.** Students could prepare their thoughts for homework.

Exam teaching suggestions

- There is no practical element to the topics in this chapter. However, students can investigate the topics using the many computer simulations available.

- In question 1 there is no credit for an answer that refers to a black hole in terms of an empty void.

- Students should be familiar with appropriate terms such as red giant and white dwarf. In examinations weaker candidates often get these confused.

- Question 2 requires students to order the statements. All students should be able to complete this correctly. Higher attaining students should be able to write their own version of the life cycle in extended prose.

P3   Examination-Style Questions

Answers to Questions

1. (a) Moment = force × perpendicular distance from the line of action of the force to the axis of rotation. *(1 mark)*
   Moment = 600 N × 1.5 m *(1 mark)*
   Moment = 900 N m *(1 mark)*
   Clockwise *(1 mark)*

   (b) If see-saw is balanced
   total clockwise moment = total anticlockwise moment. *(1 mark)*
   450 N × perpendicular distance = 900 N m *(1 mark)*
   Perpendicular distance = 900 N m/450 N *(1 mark)*
   Perpendicular distance = 2 m *(1 mark)*

2. (a)

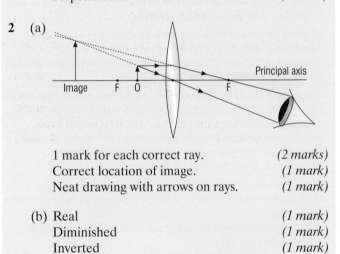

   1 mark for each correct ray. *(2 marks)*
   Correct location of image. *(1 mark)*
   Neat drawing with arrows on rays. *(1 mark)*

   (b) Real *(1 mark)*
   Diminished *(1 mark)*
   Inverted *(1 mark)*

   continues opposite ❯

EXAMINATION-STYLE QUESTIONS

1. The drawing shows Aimie and Charlie sitting on a see-saw.

   (*See pages 218–19*)

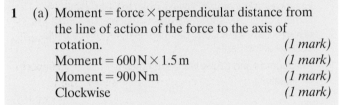

   (a) Aimie weighs 600 N and sits 1.5 m from the middle of the see-saw.
   Calculate the moment of Aimie's weight about the middle of the see-saw. *(4 marks)*

   (b) Charlie weighs 450 N.
   How far from the middle of the see-saw must Charlie sit for the see-saw to balance horizontally? *(4 marks)*
   [Higher]

   GET IT RIGHT!
   Remember to state whether the moment is clockwise or anticlockwise.

2. The diagram shows a converging lens being used as a magnifying glass. The size and position of an object at **O** is shown. The points marked **F** are the principal foci of the lens.

   (*See pages 242–3*)

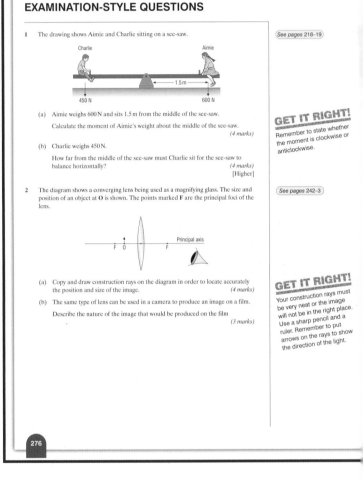

   (a) Copy and draw construction rays on the diagram in order to locate accurately the position and size of the image. *(4 marks)*

   (b) The same type of lens can be used in a camera to produce an image on a film.
   Describe the nature of the image that would be produced on the film. *(3 marks)*

   GET IT RIGHT!
   Your construction rays must be very neat or the image will not be in the right place. Use a sharp pencil and a ruler. Remember to put arrows on the rays to show the direction of the light.

GET IT RIGHT!

Students should remember to state whether the moment is clockwise or anticlockwise.

Students need to realise that the law of moments applies.

Students must state what will **increase** the p.d. Credit would not be given for 'change the strength of the field', or 'change the number of turns'.

BUMP UP THE GRADE

Students should appreciate the importance of neat, accurate ray diagrams, or they will not be able to locate the image.

Students do not need to know the formula for centripetal force but they should appreciate the factors that vary it.

The diagram shows a simple a.c. generator.

(See pages 256–7)

The coil is turned as shown in the diagram.

(a) State two ways of reversing the direction (polarity) of the induced potential difference. *(2 marks)*

(b) State three ways of increasing the size of the induced potential difference. *(3 marks)*
[Higher]

GET IT RIGHT!

Read the question carefully, be sure that you state what will **increase** the p.d.

The Earth orbits the Sun because there is an attractive force between them which provides a centripetal force.

(See pages 222–8)

(a) What is the name of this attractive force? *(1 mark)*

(b) What would happen to the size of this force if:
  (i) the mass of the Earth were greater?
  (ii) the distance between the Sun and the Earth were greater? *(2 marks)*

(c) What would happen to the time taken for one orbit if the distance between the Sun and the Earth were greater? *(1 mark)*

(d) How are the stars and the planets formed? *(3 marks)*

(See pages 268–9)

❯ *continues from previous page*

3 (a) Reversing the direction of the magnetic field. *(1 mark)*

Reversing the direction of rotation. *(1 mark)*

(b) Increasing the speed of rotation. *(1 mark)*
Increasing the strength of the magnetic field. *(1 mark)*

Increasing the number of turns on the coil. *(1 mark)*
[**HT** only]

4 (a) Gravitational force. *(1 mark)*

(b) (i) The force would be greater. *(1 mark)*
(ii) The force would be smaller. *(1 mark)*

(c) The time taken would be greater. *(1 mark)*

(d) Stars formed from dust and gas *(1 mark)* pulled together by gravitational attraction. *(1 mark)*

Smaller masses form and are attracted to orbit stars – these are planets. *(1 mark)*

Notes

Notes

Notes

Notes

Notes

Notes

Notes